SOCIAL ACCOUNTING:
THEORY, ISSUES, AND CASES

Melville Series
on
Management, Accounting, and Information Systems

Consulting Editor   *John W. Buckley*

SOCIAL ACCOUNTING: THEORY, ISSUES, AND CASES

by

LEE J. SEIDLER

Graduate School of Business Administration
New York University

LYNN L. SEIDLER

MELVILLE PUBLISHING COMPANY

Los Angeles, California

Copyright © 1975, by John Wiley & Sons, Inc.
Published by **Melville Publishing Company,**
a Division of John Wiley & Sons, Inc.

Library of Congress Cataloging in Publication Data:

Seidler, Lee J.   comp.
   Social accounting: theory, issues, and cases.
   (Melville series on management, accounting, and
information systems)
   Includes bibliographical references.
   1. Evaluation research (Social action programs)—
United States—Addresses, essays, lectures.   2. Cost
effectiveness—Addresses, essays, lectures.
3. Accounting—Addresses, essays, lectures.   I. Title.

H61.S45   1975   300   74-12116

ISBN 0-471-77488-X

Dr. Stockmann: Something must be done in the matter—and that quickly.

Peter: You say, amongst other things, that what we offer visitors in our Baths is a permanent supply of poison.

Dr. Stockmann: Well, can you describe it any other way, Peter? Just think—water that is poisonous, whether you drink it or bathe in it! . . .

Peter: And your reasoning leads you to this conclusion, that we must build a sewer to draw off the alleged impurities . . .

Dr. Stockmann: Yes. Do you see any other way out of it?

Peter: . . . Have you taken the trouble to consider what your proposed alterations would cost? According to the information I obtained, the expenses would probably mount up to fifteen or twenty thousand pounds.

Henrik Ibsen,
An Enemy of the People

Preface

In the late 1960's American society became increasingly concerned with a series of issues related to questions about the performance of social and economic institutions, the efficiency of government, and the quality of life in general. Why this wave of concern arose at that particular time is no more explicable than any other similar historical phenomenon. It was probably due to a combination of disillusionment with the failures of the programs of the oversold "War on Poverty," combined with an increased tendency to question the established order of society, itself engendered by the activism of the opponents of the very questionable Indochina War. Perhaps the ennui generated by a decade of sustained prosperity and an excess of materialism contributed to the tide.

Regardless of the reasons, this questioning, along with the not unrelated increased concern with the deterioration of the environment, produced a surge of interest in "social accounting" and "social accountability." How could government expenditures be allocated more efficiently? How could social programs be operated more effectively? How could free economic enterprises be made to take greater responsibility for the indirect consequences of their activities? How can pollution be controlled at a reasonable cost?

Economists, systems analysts, activist lawyers, ecologists, and others answered the call. The non-accounting world has often shown a proclivity to adopt accounting terminology—if not accountants—and concepts such as "Corporate Accountability" and "Social Audit" joined the typical editorial use (and misuse) of "debit" and "credit." That the vague concept of a social audit in no way represented an audit, or that there was no definition of to whom corporations would be accountable has troubled no one save a few pedantic accountants.

Accountants tended to stand on the sidelines during the first rush to the social accounting fountain. Virtually all of the useful work in social accounting performed during the 1960's was done by economists. For example, all of the cases in the Brookings Institution study, *Measuring Benefits of Government Expenditures* (1965), and virtually all the 57 papers in the Joint Economic Committee's *The Analysis and Evaluation of Public Expenditures* (1969) were written by economists; none were authored by accountants.

Only a very few accountants, such as David Linowes, had the temerity to suggest that accountants ought to also do this work. The exhortations of the few were ignored at first, but gradually the message registered. Suddenly, in the 1970's, social accounting, *by accountants,* became fashionable. Articles in accounting journals proliferated, more corporations issued still misnamed social audits, CPA firms accepted consulting engagements related to social problems, and schools offered courses wholly or partly oriented towards social accounting.

Unfortunately, or possibly fortunately, the bull market in social accounting started to grow before anyone had clearly determined what the term meant. Accountants, accustomed to a methodology that has changed little since it was first published in 1494, tend to be disconcerted by such a lack of specification. Thus, the first literature in the field by accountants has tended to define terms. There has been a flood of articles with such titles as "What is social accounting?" or "Who is a social accountant?" Precious little in the way of cases or technical discussions has appeared.

This book is an attempt, albeit modest, to move accountants a bit further into social accounting. Ralph Estes' *Accounting and Society* (Melville Publishing Company, 1972) is, in several respects, the predecessor of this volume. Designed for accounting students in comparatively elementary courses, Estes' articles illustrate the potential impact of accountants in the social dimension. *Accounting and Society* is intended to interest students and accountants in social accounting. The idea for this volume was developed when this writer acted as a prepublication reviewer of Estes' work. I suggested that if Estes' book did succeed, a second volume ought to discuss "How to do it." Thus, the present work.

WHAT IS SOCIAL ACCOUNTING?

Despite the less than charitable view expressed above towards those who are excessively concerned with a definition of this embryonic field, the editor now suggests his own concept of the subject. This delimitation is presented as an explanation of a working bias, to explain the selection of the terms in the book, rather than some immutable notion of what social accounting should or should not be.

As a general guide, social accounting is the modification and application, by accountants, of the skills, techniques and discipline of conventional (managerial and financial) accounting, to the analysis and solution of problems of a social nature. This concept views social accounting as essentially an extension of the principles, practices, and particularly the *skills,* of conventional accounting and accountants. It does not see social accounting as a totally new group of theories and techniques, unrelated to what is considered generally to comprise the body of knowledge used by, or reasonably available, to present accountants.

This rather conventional delimitation of social accounting requires that what is called social accounting should be capable of being done by accountants. This is not to suggest that efforts to improve the efficiency of social institutions and social decision making should be made only by accountants. Economists, scientists, mathematicians, systems analysts, sociologists, and others will continue to have a major, probably dominant, role in the improvement of social systems analysis and evaluation. Accountants, however, possess talents and a body of knowledge which, with appropriate modification, seem to have potential for considerable contribution in a social dimension. "Appropriate modification" may well involve basic and significant modification of the existing body of knowledge. It may also involve some utilization or appropriation, by accountants, of techniques from economics, finance, mathematics, behavioral sciences, and other disciplines.

This leads to what is *not* included in this definition of social accounting—and hence what is not discussed in this volume.

National income accounting is another area that utilizes accounting terminology extensively. However, virtually all the development of national income accounting has been done by economists; persons styling themselves as accountants have played almost no role. In recent years, there have been some calls for accountants to improve the statistics used in national accounts, and to assist in the development of a set of "social accounts." The accounting department of the University of Illinois has offered a course in this area, but there is little other evidence to suggest any change in the historical non-participation of accountants. On this basis, national income accounting has been excluded from this volume.

Human resource accounting has become a fashionable part of accounting. There is some debate whether accounting for human resources is a new dimension of accounting, with a claim to being included in social accounting, or whether it merely represents an improvement in inadequate conventional accounting for intangible assets. I see no need to resolve that debate here, except insofar as space in this volume is concerned. Certainly, the measurement of, and attribution of values to, human lives will be a required aspect of social accounting calculations. Therefore discussions of the methodology have been included. However, more general discussions of accounting for human resources—while possibly relevant—have been excluded due to space considerations.

My earlier definition of social accounting would tend to exclude materials that are totally based on mathematical applications in a social dimension. For the most part, I have held to that line. However, the dividing line between quantitative analysis and accounting has been growing increasingly vague. As such, I have included a few illustrations of mathematical applications that might be marginal to current accounting, but which may well appear conventional in a few years.

It should be emphasized that this "definition" of social accounting should in no way be taken to imply that it is a body separate from the total body of accounting knowledge. To the contrary, it is integral and, as I noted in an article not included in this volume,* conventional accounting must accord increasing attention to social considerations in the determination of accounting principles.

USE OF THIS BOOK

This volume is for those who have already seen the light. It is intended to provide more advanced materials—issues, problems, and cases—for accountants, students, researchers, and others who are already interested in social accounting.

Academically, it can be used as the primary source of materials in a social accounting course such as that offered at New York University. Alternatively, it can serve to provide supplemental readings and cases in other accounting courses in which the instructor wishes to inject a social dimension.

The social accounting course at New York University† lists as a prerequisite only the intensive, fundamentals course required of all Masters of Business Administration candidates. That course is the usual, compressed overview of accounting offered in most Masters of Business Administration programs. The

---

*Lee J. Seidler, "Accountant: Accountant for Thyself," *The Journal of Accountancy* (June 1973), p. 38.

†The outline of the social accounting course at New York University may be found in *Accounting Trends VIII, Innovating Accounting and Information Systems Course Outlines,* by Thomas J. Burns (McGraw-Hill, 1973).

undergraduate equivalent would vary; in some cases a rigorous elementary course would suffice, while in others the addition of intermediate accounting might be more appropriate.

I have, on several occasions, suspended the accounting prerequisite for students, usually from other schools in the University, who wished to take the social accounting course. The results have not been entirely satisfactory. Such students are often highly motivated and add considerably to class discussions. However, they tend to be deficient in the technical skills necessary to complete the research project. This lack of skills has sometimes been remedied by teaming these students with others who are more competent in accounting.

In general, then, these materials are considered most suitable for students who have had some introduction to accounting.

SOURCES OF READINGS

As noted above, there currently exists the paradoxical situation that accountants have yet to produce a significant application-oriented literature in the area I have delimited as social accounting. However, such inconsistencies rarely slow true zealots, and I have not allowed that shortage to interfere with the preparation of this volume.

A large part of the readings included herein have been used in the Socio-economic Accounting course I teach at New York University. They have been gathered over a considerable period of time, from many sources.

In selecting the materials, attention has been given to providing an indication of the scope and variety of sources that may be utilized in the development of social accounting principles and practices. Social accounting will, of necessity, draw on literature far removed from accounting. Thus, the book includes Carl Cohen's essentially political view of the logic for charitable organization tax exemptions, and the Nobel Prize winning physicist Heisenberg's analysis of the politico-economics of building and locating large particle accelerators.

As noted in the first article in the book, a social concept of income must be derived in some societal consensus as to what is "good" and what is "bad." Clearly, no one volume could purport to present more than a fraction of the materials that would be relevant to the development of such an income theory. I have attempted, however, to provide at least an inkling of certain major trends in American social and economic history, such as excerpts from significant documents, landmark cases, and legislation. These are intended only as guides to further study, and obviously are not as a comprehensive treatment of the subject.

GOVERNMENT STUDIES FOR FURTHER RESEARCH

The various federal and state environmental laws, along with the generally increasing concern for the environment and the efficiency of government programs have created a virtual flood of Government-developed literature on these subjects. An attempt has been made to include a sample of this literature in this volume. Indeed, in many cases government publications constitute the best materials available. For example, the three volume study, *The Analysis and Evaluation of Public Expenditures: The PPB System*, prepared in 1969 by the Joint Economic Committee of the Congress, remains the most comprehensive and thoughtful analysis of public expenditure decision making yet published. Several of the papers in this volume have been selected from this collection.

For those interested in further inquiry, technical discussions, or research in the various topics dealt with in this volume, the body of government publications constitutes a gold mine of materials. This information has been produced so rapidly in recent years that it is difficult for one person to keep current even in a bibliographical sense, and virtually impossible to procure and read more than a minor portion of the new material. For example, the initial output from the Northeast Corridor Transportation Project alone (on which the Dienemann-Lago paper in this book is based) is a group of volumes more than two feet thick.

The usual government publications bibliographical sources will provide some assistance in finding these materials. However, the quantity and diversity is such as to often preclude obtaining copies of all "interesting" publications. Somewhat more selective views of the output of government agencies can often be obtained through direct correspondence with the agencies, accompanied by careful specification of the researcher's interests. Correspondence with legislators (or their assistants) who are interested in particular aspects of the subject will often pinpoint particularly relevant materials.

However, for the professional practitioner, teacher, or doctoral student with a serious interest in this subject, a trip to Washington, with considerable time in the Library of Congress and visits to the appropriate regulatory agencies is virtually indispensable. Several days of study at the "fountain" of most of the output will pay great dividends in subsequent research. Since the cost of most government publications is low (and many are free if obtained through the originating agencies), the researcher will often be relieved of the tediousness of extensive photocopying.

Significant publications—and concerned researchers—will also often be found at the state, and sometimes, at the local government level.

It is difficult to overemphasize the dimensions of the body of materials that awaits researchers in these areas. Perhaps the next major piece of socioeconomic legislation should include a provision for codification of all previous studies.

INCLUSION OF STUDENT RESEARCH PAPERS

This book of readings is somewhat unusual in that some of the papers are the previously unpublished works of Masters of Business Administration candidates at the Graduate School of Business Administration, New York University. Several reasons suggested the use of these papers. There are few good examples of practical applications of social accounting, particularly performed by accountants. Many of the available studies are too long and detailed for inclusion in this book. Unfortunately too, most of the projects performed by accounting firms in this area appear to be of a proprietary nature, and are not available for reproduction.

Equally important, these student studies can serve as examples to both instructors and students of the type of project that it is reasonable to expect from well-qualified graduate students, working within the framework of the research requirement for a two credit, one semester course in social accounting.

As is common in a small (about fifteen students), research-oriented graduate course, considerable class time was devoted to discussion of the projects, before and during preparation. At the end of the semester, the students were encouraged to present their work as "papers" delivered to the group. The vast majority chose to do so. The delivery of the "papers" occasioned considerable comment and often, suggestions for revisions. Unfortunately, unless the student pursues the same subject for his master's thesis, as a few have done, the revisions have rarely been completed. The papers included herein have not been revised; they reflect only minor editorial modifications and some abridgement. However, a brief note follows some of the papers, summarizing the most significant criticisms.

In the social accounting class at New York University, an assortment of papers from prior years is made available to the students. Not only do they serve as examples, but most usefully, as a basis for further research in the topic. For obvious reasons, the New York City rapid transit situation has been explored by four groups of students so far.

In some fairness, it might be noted that the Masters of Business Administration candidates at New York University are not necessarily representative of all Masters of Business Administration students. About three-quarters are fully employed, typically in career positions, often in middle management capacities. Dzaluk, for example, was the Mayor of Portchester, New York, the town in which the methadone clinic he studied was located. On the other hand, Arfania (abortion study) is a "typical" Masters of Business Administration day student.

The last and most pleasant step in the preparation of any book is the writing of the acknowledgements. I am especially grateful to the authors who kindly gave consent for their work to be reproduced here.

Many of the readings required for the first offering of my social accounting course are included here. John Liapakis, a research assistant at the Graduate School of Business Administration, was of great assistance in assembling these materials. Professor Michael Schiff, then chairman of the accounting area, gave considerable encouragement to my starting the course. Shlomo Gertzulin, also a research assistant at the Graduate School of Business Administration, searched both in New York and Washington to find materials. Professor Akira Ishikawa, one of my colleagues, made many helpful suggestions.

I wish to also thank John Crain, Vice President of Melville Publishing Company, for his enthusiasm and continued support.

New York, New York   *Lee J. Seidler*

Contents

III

THE POLITICS OF SOCIAL ACCOUNTING

IV

CORPORATE SOCIAL ACCOUNTING AND REPORTING

V

ENVIRONMENTAL ACCOUNTING   240

VI

ACCOUNTING FOR HUMAN LIVES AND RESOURCES   317

VII

PROBLEMS IN THE DEVELOPMENT OF AN ACCOUNTANT'S CONCEPT OF SOCIAL INCOME

VIII

CASES IN SOCIAL ACCOUNTING

I

INTRODUCTION: THE NATURE OF SOCIAL ACCOUNTING

Dollar Values in the Social Income Statement

Lee J. Seidler

This article, by the editor of this volume, makes a case for the preparation of socially oriented financial statements and other accounting analysis, in dollar terms. It suggests the difficulties that would be involved in quantification, but concludes that accountants do possess the requisite skills for the task.

However, in some contradiction to the conclusions of the article, the author admits that in the past there has been little evidence of broad interest by accountants in this subject.

Are the profits of a corporation fairly measured if no expense is shown for the air or water pollution it causes? Are the limited and finite funds available better spent on job training for disadvantaged minority groups or on high school drop-out prevention programs? Should we build more superhighways or improve mass transit systems?

Such questions suggest the necessity for new methods of accounting to support better policy decisions. Conventional accounting techniques, based largely on the existence of reasonably established and verifiable market prices are of little use when large portions of both inputs and outputs lie outside the normal price system. Thus, the repeated calls for improvements in measurement techniques and quite logically, for the development of some forms of social accounting.

SOURCE: From *World*, Spring 1973, Peat, Marwick, Mitchell & Co.

The keynote speaker at the 1969 annual meeting of the American Accounting Association called upon accountants to assist in the development of socially based income concepts.[1] Both the AICPA and the AAA established committees on Socioeconomic Accounting. The Journal of Accountancy has featured articles on the social aspects of accounting, as have *The Accounting Review* and other publications.[2] The AICPA has published a volume, *Social Measurement.*

From all this activity it might appear that accountants are making significant progress in the development of principles and practices applicable to social measurement. A closer look suggests a less optimistic view. The article, papers, and the book are either exhortations to action, calls to accountants to assume their "social responsibility," or discourses on the difficulties of performing social accounting, but they are pitifully short on examples of actual technique. The evidence of significant progress is at best, limited.

Does this mean that no progress is being made in the measurement and evaluation of social inputs and outputs? Fortunately for American society, if not for the accounting profession, some advances are being made in the development of techniques of social accounting, but not by accountants.

In 1965, The Brookings Institution published *Measuring Benefits of Government Investments,* a collection of case studies involving the measurement of costs and benefits of nine separate socially oriented projects.[3] Not one accountant, academic or professional, can be found among the writers of the cases. In 1969, the Joint Economic Committee published a three volume collection, *The Analysis and Evaluation of Public Expenditures,* composed of papers by a total of 57 authors.[4] The work is concerned with the theory and practice of social accounting. Not one of the authors is an accountant; virtually all of the academic contributions are the work of economists.

More exhaustive examples may be cited, but the general points are clear: (1) there is considerable interest, at private and public levels, in performing social measurements and, (2) accountants are making little tangible progress in the area.

Even with the logical difficulties inherent in determining causes for *inaction,* we can postulate several possible explanations for the present lack of accounting contributions. A simple explanation, perhaps more associative than causal, is that accountants have not in the past shown any significant interest in applying their skills to areas outside normal enterprise accounting. Quite possibly that limited interest is due to the lack of a link between the apparently concrete aspects of conventional enterprise accounting and the amorphous, elusive ideas inherent in accounting for social costs and benefits.

One possibility of establishing such linkage, and thus of providing a central focus for accounting efforts in the social dimension would be the establishment of at least a tentative accounting concept of social profit. Clearly, a major part of the development of financial accounting theory and practice has centered around efforts to improve income determination. The purpose of this article is to offer a similar central focus in social accounting, with the goal of finally increasing the *active* interest of accountants in the subject.

The concepts and the underlying assumptions which follow are highly tentative: they are proposed only as a starting point for future development.

The short-lived Socioeconomic Accounting Committee of the American Accounting Association spent the better part of its one year existence (1969-1970) attempting to construct a clear and valid definition of social accounting. One rather promising effort suggested that no new definition was actually necessary: all accounting is for socioeconomic purposes. It was suggested that the definition of accounting itself should be essentially that: *Accounting is the art and/or science of measurement and, interpretation of activities and phenomena which are essentially of a social and economic nature.*

Such a definition would exclude a primary concern with the measurement of purely physical phenomena, such as hardness, color, time or distance, although related measurements might enter into accounting calculations. Similarly, accounting is not concerned, at a primary level, with measurements of such human, but non-economic activities as individual attitudes, although again, such measurements might enter into accounting calculations.

Clearly, the operations of business enterprises would constitute relevant phenomena under this definition, whether considered in terms of the enterprise as a whole (conventional financial accounting) or in its constituent parts (conventional managerial accounting).

Thus, so called conventional "accounting" appears as a subset in this rather more encompassing definition of accounting. National income accounting would also obviously fall under such a definition. Here, we encounter a difficulty, since virtually all those who perform this type of macro-accounting style themselves as economists or statisticians. National income accounting, thus far, has been almost exclusively concerned with simple economic or financial measurements with almost no attention paid to social or qualitative aspects of inputs and outputs.

Current conventional accounting focuses around two entities, the business enterprise (financial and managerial accounting) and the nation state (national income accounting) "Social accounting" as used in this article, deals with an area, which constitutes somewhat of a middle ground between these two.

In social accounting, measurements would be made from the point of view of society, or some subset of society; such as a particular government body or a given group in the population. In enterprise accounting the entity is the focus of measurement. However, in social accounting the undertaking is not necessarily a specific business enterprise, as in conventional accounting. The definition of the entity is flexible; it will vary with the circumstances and with the definition of "society." It may be a company, an area or a project, such as a government experiment in job training.

Another distinction in this form of social accounting lies in the terms of measurement. Rather than concern with the changes in the economic resources of a group of shareholders, social accounting measures the change in the "general welfare" resulting from the activity being measured.

Some examples of this social accounting would include the so-called, but misnamed "social audit" of a business corporation. In such a context the business entity remains the focus of the accounting, but the inputs and outputs are defined as consumption of and additions to society's resources, rather than only those resources that the firm pays for or receives in money. Therefore, pollution caused by the firm is an additional cost; socially desirable outputs would be revenues.

Another use for social accounting would be to measure the effectiveness of certain programs undertaken by government bodies. The social costs of a program, principally taxes, would be compared with the social revenues, the improvement in the general welfare, which it generates. The clear definition of the effects to be measured obviously constitute one of the principal problems of the field.

Sarte, in *Existentialism,* postulates that man is condemned to continuous decision-making. This process of decision-making is unavoidable; it is the essence of existence.

Consider the accountant in this context. His work is to produce measurements, estimates, and usually financial statements. If he does not produce these results, if he tells his client that the theoretical complexities of the situation preclude a judgment, his very reason for existence ceases. Like Sartre's man, the accountant is thus condemned to make decision. He must produce annual financial statements, even though it is clear to him (and his critics) that there are theoretical deficiencies in his methodology.

How does the accountant exist under such an imperative? He does so, as George O. May noted, by establishing conventions. Where theoretical limitations preclude "truth" in an answer which *must* be given, the accountant developes some (hopefully logical) arbitrary compromise. To the extent that he convinces other accountants and users to accept such simplifying compromises, they become accounting conventions.

The accountant is not so naive as to believe that productive assets actually lose their revenue producing potential in exactly equal fractions of their original cost each year, or in accordance with any other arbitrary curve of decay. He recognizes that he is incapable of attributing the joint cost of equipment in any theoretically defensible way to the revenues of the periods in which the asset is used. But, he *must* produce an income figure at the end of the year. Therefore, he adopts the simplifying convention of straight-line depreciation or of some other usage curve. The accountant knows that it is not a "correct" portrayal of the circumstances; (hopefully) the user also understands. They have agreed on a convention permitting the accountant to produce a result, which although not perfectly correct, appears to provide information that users have found to be worth its cost.

It is quite fashionable for economists and mathematicians to criticize the way in which accounting calculations are performed. The adherence to original cost, overhead allocations, depreciation methods, etc. are all apt targets which have allowed members of these other honored disciplines (and numerous accountants) to demonstrate their intellectual superiority over mere bookkeepers at scores of academic meetings and in the endless pages of academic journals.

It takes no great skill to demonstrate the theoretical errors of most accepted accounting conventions; it requires considerably more ability to offer alternative conventions which will better satisfy the totality of the needs of those who must use financial statements.

Similarly, it is not possible to make theoretically defensible calculations of a social nature with our presently available information and limited perceptions of human behavior and motivations. However, given our environment and the problems now facing us, a more rational basis for the allocation of scarce funds is imperative.

The device which will allow such calculations will be the development of social accounting conventions, i.e. agreed upon compromises and simplifying assumptions which will allow practicing accountants to make reasonably useful social calculations.

An example of the type of issues or problems which might lend themselves to a social accounting approach may provide a better focus.

Consider a project now being attempted at New York University. This institution, like many other private universities, suffers from a large operating deficit and resulting financial difficulties.

When we speak of the "deficit," the context is that of conventional accounting. The revenues of the University come principally from tuition, research and (nominal) state aid. The major cost categories are instruction, research, libraries, student-aid and overhead. (There are also substantial costs and revenues associated with real estate, hospital operations, and similar activities which are ignored, for simplicity, in this discussion.)

Conventional matching of these costs and revenues under enterprise accounting principles shows the University in a deficit.

The University might also be viewed in a social accounting context: what does its operation cost society, and what benefits does it produce for society? In this light, we might reverse the normal income statement of the University. The amounts shown as revenues to the University actually represent "costs" to society; the payments which society gives the University for its services. The University's costs represent the services it has performed, such as research and teaching; "benefits" to society. The two income statements might appear as shown in Figure 1.

Conventional income statement	Social income statement
Revenues:	Revenues:
Tuition paid to University	Value of instruction to Society
Research grants*	Value of research to Society
State aid	
Less Costs:	Less Costs:
Instructional	Tuition paid to University
Research costs*	Cost of research
Student aid	State aid
Overheads	Other—Lost Production, etc.
Result:	Result:
(Deficit)	Profit

*Research is shown as the same figure in both parts of the conventional statement, at the amount received and expended.

Figure 1

The preparation of the social income statement will essentially be a process of attributing values to the various captions. Consider the revenues.

From a social view, the educational outputs of the University consist of citizens, presumably better educated when they leave the University than when they arrived, and therefore of greater value to society.

The attribution of value to this output, however, involves a number of problems. There are reasonably good figures to indicate that the incomes of graduates exceed those of non-graduates. One could therefore compute the present value of the net increment supposedly due to education. Of course, there is the rather fundamental question of whether it is the education that caused some or all of the difference in incomes, e.g., that changed the people, or is the result to some extent merely associative.

We then face issues of attribution of the net income increment to the various parties benefiting from it. "Social" benefits would seem to imply benefits to society as a whole; but a large part of the increment in income due to education is internalized by the student himself. For him, education to a great extent is a market transaction. Society will benefit, however, from increased tax collections from increased earnings (net of decreased tax collections while the student was in school). Society will also benefit from the assumed increased social and intellectual productivity of the graduate.

Then there is the question of which society will benefit. Is "society" to be regarded as New York City? In that case, in or out migration of graduates will have some effects. If "society" is the United States, NYU's high proportion of foreign students may also have some very substantial effects.[5]

The research output would also have to be valued in social terms. Some amount of work has been done in this respect, particularly under National Science Foundation sponsorship, to estimate the rate of return from investments in various categories of research.[6] The valuation of the research output would include such items as increased productivity due to research, lives saved, health improved, etc. In NYU's case, about two-thirds of the research is biomedical, where payoffs can be reasonably estimated. The assigning of specific values to other categories of research; historical or even that in accounting, might be rather more difficult.

On the cost side, the accounting appears less difficult. Payments for tuition, research and state-aid are denominated in cash. Nevertheless, some problems remain. Payments for research and state-aid comes from governments or government funded agencies; they are a direct cost to society. Tuition payments, however, come from individuals, who personally pay for and personally receive and internalize the benefits of education. This, of course, is the same question which was raised in connection with outputs. It will be discussed below in the context of the "matching concept."

There would appear to be several uses for calculations of this nature. Immediately, and assuming that the social income statement shows a substantial "profit," as contrasted with the conventional statement, such a calculation should have value as a fund raising device. In the broader sense, estimates of the relative social productivity of the institution should be of considerable value as questions of state support to cover deficits become critical.

In conventional enterprise accounting the determination of the amount to be labelled "net income" has been the central focus of virtually continuous debate. The contentious issues, however, have really not involved the nature of profit; virtually all of the controversy has been over the timing of the recognition of profits. Ultimately all elements of gain or loss, recurring or non-recurring, those recognized at point of sale, or through accretion, will find their way to the equity section of the balance sheet, to show as an increase in the wealth of the firm.

Unfortunately, this would not be the case in accounting in a social vein. Conventional enterprise accounting measures money flows (present, past, or future) in and out of the enterprise. Resource flows which do not have a money cost to the firm (or yield a revenue) are ignored, although ignoring them may actually result in the recording of a profit. For example, a factory which manages to dispose of an effluent by dumping it in the local river will show no expense for this disposal. Another enterprise, located inland, which must pay for the disposal of its waste will show a lower profit. Thus, the factory which is "appropriating" a public resource, the river, will show a higher profit for doing so. This may be logical from a financial accounting view, but it seems socially counterproductive.

In social accounting, profit must be determined in relation to some concept of social gain. There is no neat market system, or clearly defined money flows to determine social revenues and costs. While some of those committed with excessive zeal to the causes of ecology and anti-pollution would appear to have an absolute set of values as to what is good and bad, it takes little imagination to suggest that precisely what is socially desirable and what may not be could be the subject of some debate.

At the broadest level, there are issues as to "what is good for people." Ideas of individual freedom may clash with concepts of national commitment and discipline; concepts of the sanctity of private property with desires to improve the distribution of wealth, etc.

At a more operational level, there may be conflicts between two apparently desirable and relatively uncontroversial social actions. Recently, the New York City Council considered legislation which would require that supermarket meats be completely packaged in transparent materials. This would permit the purchaser to see the underside of the meat which is normally concealed by the usual opaque paper tray. Only a butcher intent on defrauding the consumer (or a paper manufacturer) could oppose the suggestion; it clearly seemed socially desirable.

At the same time, anti-pollution groups were attempting to reduce the use of plastic packaging materials, on the quite correct grounds that they were not biodegradable and hence, when discarded, remained to blight the landscape. Similarly, if burned in the City's incinerators, plastic produces far more toxic fumes than paper.

Obviously, the two apparently desirable proposals are in conflict with each other. The situation also demonstrates that even quite desirable social programs have negative social aspects. This is in contrast (or possibly in addition to (negative economic aspects, e.g., damage to paper or plastic producers. And, if the economic costs to the respective manufacturers result in reduced employment, we continue on to a new level of social costs.

Recall the early example of social accounting, evaluating New York University in a social context. Assume that a study indicates that the present value of the total future earnings of a New York high school graduate, starting from a point four years after high school graduation, is $200,000. Assume that the present value of the total future earnings of a comparably endowed, but NYU educated student at the same date is $150,000. Assume that the degree cost the NYU graduate $20,000 (including earnings foregone). Thus, the profit to the student, inherent in the education, is $30,000. Like all profits, it will eventually be taxed, let us say, at $5000. Therefore, the net gain to the student is $250,000.

Clearly, the $5000 to be paid in taxes is a second order social benefit, assuming that the "state" is considered society. The treatment of the $25,000 of benefits to the student is less clear. These benefits are appropriated or internalized by the graduate. From the graduate's (or his family's) point of view, the education is very much a market transaction. Tuition has been paid to purchase the benefits which will flow from education. There seems to be little difference between this transaction and any other market purchase of services other than that the activity is carried out by a socially desirable institution. Is it then logical to consider the additional earnings of the graduate, a private gain, as a "social" gain?

Let us consider a slightly different example. A national park, such as Yellowstone, would seem to be a prototype "social institution," and its use would logically be considered socially beneficial. However, the park is used by individuals, who like the NYU graduate, internalize the benefits.*

If we exclude the benefits that are appropriated by individuals from being denoted as social benefits, then we encounter a rather paradoxical result. The more the park is used by individuals, the greater will be its cost, but the lower will be its social benefit. This does not seem entirely logical. Yet, the only difference between the park and the University, both social institutions, is that in the latter case the benefits are directly received in an aesthetic sense, while those from the University include a large element of hard cash.

American history may provide direction for a solution to this issue. The fundamental idea of the social contract which sharply influences the thinking of those who framed the constitution is that government acts to improve the condition of individuals, not of "society." The history of federal legislation suggests, even more strongly, that the trend of American social legislation has been that of collective (government) action to affect the circumstances of individuals. To the extent that the chosen individuals receive the intended benefits, the legislation *is* performing its function. Thus, it would seem appropriate not to exclude those social benefits which are appropriated by individuals, *if they are the intended recipients of the particular social program.*

This last conclusion points up a required preliminary step in making social accounting determinations; the social purpose (or purposes) of the entity under examination must be postulated as a preliminary to any social calculation. Effects which correspond to the purpose or logically flow from it, should be considered social benefits; effects which tend to thwart the purpose of the project should be considered as costs.

This last point suggests a possible format for social evaluation of profit seeking corporations, as contrasted with the model of the non-profit organization offered earlier.

There would be general agreement that the production of a drug company manufacturing antibiotics would be socially desirable. By contrast, the production of illicit narcotics, stimulants, depressants, or other drugs leading to addiction would be considered socially undesirable. Ineffective, but harmless patent medicines might lie socially somewhere between these two extremes. We need add only

---

*It should not be particularly difficult to price up the value of the direct benefits, using some form of analysis based on the cost of alternative available recreational facilities.

a few other examples to indicate that any attempts to directly evaluate the social desirability of the production of various products would certainly be bogged down in a mass of contradictory value judgments.

Therefore, why not, as suggested to me by Professor David Solomons, adopt the convention that all production, as long as it can be freely sold in the market, is socially desirable. Instead of evaluating the social merits of the production, measure the favorable or negative social effects that flow from the production process. This analysis would suggest an alternate form of social income statement, for profit seeking enterprises, as noted in Figure 2.

The caption "Socially desirable outputs not sold" would include such benefits as job training, health improvement of workers and the deliberate employment of disadvantaged minorities. Socially undesirable effects not paid for could include air and water pollution generated by the company, health problems caused by use of its products, etc. The resulting net social profit or loss figure would be capable of manipulation comparable to that performed on conventional financial data.

There has been no indication in this paper thus far that the measurements in social accounting are contemplated in any unit other than money. Obviously, we are not condemned to postulate social accounting in monetary terms; social inputs and outputs could be measured in ergs, dynes, utils, or perhaps most appropraitely, "plaisirs." Whatever unit happens to strike the fancy of the particular author could be adopted. We are breaking new ground and there is no necessity to be tied to hoary and perhaps materialistic accounting traditions. Indeed, among the students in my social accounting course there is invariably a feeling that expressing social measurements in terms of dollars is, in some sense, obscene.

Of course, such ideas are not new. In the period following the revolution, the Russians theorized that measurements in money terms were vestiges of the old system. Attempts were made to develop systems of value measurement in terms of "socialist utility." They were not successful, however, and the communist planners reluctantly returned to money terms.

It is difficult to see why any measurement unit, other than money, should have any particular attraction, except for semantic or aesthetic connotations. Money is merely a common denominator; the same would hold for any other postulated unit of welfare, pleasure or satisfaction. Money has the advantage, however, that reasonably realistic values for many inputs and outputs have already been stipulated by the "market." Any other system would require substantially greater effort to apply values to a wide variety of costs and benefits.

There is an obviously difficult problem in attributing values to some of the high subjective phenomena that would be encountered in any social accounting system. These difficulties have led to the suggestion that absolute numerical values, whether expressed in dollars or any other unit, might not be necessary. At this stage, and probably for the foreseeable future, many of the elements which will be required in social accounting determinations do not appear to be suscep-

---

Social income statement of a profit seeking organization

Value added by production of the enterprise

+ Socially desirable outputs not sold

− Socially undesirable effects not paid for

= Net social profit (or loss)

Figure 2

tible to specification in cardinal numerical terms. It may be possible, however, to quantify some of these factors, such as satisfaction, on some ordinal scale, such as a ranking system. While there seems to be general agreement that the ultimate goal of a social accounting system ought to be to make monetary or at least unitary determinations, perhaps a useful intermediate step would be to utilize rather more simple, but usable ordinal systems.

It is difficult to argue with such contentions, particularly since they appear to promise some acceleration in the ability of the accountant to measure social phenomena. Nevertheless, all such alternative number systems suffer from one rather compromising flaw; they are typically comprehensible only to those who invent or at least constantly work with them. Bidding systems for the game of bridge are an excellent analogy.

Certain professionals, such as doctors and lawyers, enjoy one significant advantage over accountants; they are required to communicate the technical details and nuances of their profession only to other initiated members. Outsiders, clients and patients, tend to demand results rather than comprehension. Thus, lawyers and doctors are quite free to develop elaborate jargons which are comprehensible only to the practitioners of the art. Aside from providing a pleasant sense of camaraderie such specialized languages have the additional desired effect of excluding lay practitioners of the art.

But social accounting results, like the outputs of the conventional accounting process, must be communicated to the uninitiated—to the non-accountant. Indeed, the best use which can be made for social accounting calculations would be their adoption by politicians, whose ranks include few accountants. Money measurements are the most common language of most people; they would be most useful in social accounting.

As in any new area, and social accounting is no exception, there are evangelists and skeptics. Those less enthused about the possibilities of social accounting generally raise certain objections, which might be considered at this point.

The most common objection is that it is not possible to make valid social accounting calculations; there are too many areas involved.

In response, consider the problem of measuring the net income of a complex corporation, such as a major oil company—for the first time. It would take but a few moments to list the problems—joint product costs, depreciation, valuation of mineral reserves—which make it impossible to determine income for any one year on a theoretically justifiable basis.

Of course, accountants do determine the income of such complex businesses every year, and they have been doing so for some time. Such determinations involve a process of compromise with theory and the evolution of a set of agreed upon simplifying conventions. As noted earlier, accountants are virtually "condemned" to make annual income determinations and they do so, albeit sometimes with a good deal of inaccuracy. Certainly, the complexities of social measurements do not appear much more foreboding than those of an international oil company; practice should yield some reasonably accepted results.

Nevertheless, one must admit that there are some rather awesome problems associated with making many social accounting determinations. For example, how are we to attribute a value to increases in human self esteem and dignity associated with job training or educational programs. Behavioral psychologists freely admit that they have made little progress in quantifying or even determining attitude changes.[7]

Once again, the writer retreats to conventional financial accounting. In that mundane discipline, there are analogous situations. Consider, for example, the valuation of "proven" mineral reserves. It is obvious that proven reserves have a real and significant value, rarely bearing any relation whatsoever to the historical cost of finding them. Nevertheless, accountants have strongly resisted suggestions that they attempt "discovery value" accounting. Instead, conventional accounting resorts to recording the arbitrary and absolutely illogical, historical cost.*

With the equally elusive "goodwill" of a going firm, accountants do not even attempt to put an arbitrary, unrelated figure on the balance sheet, unless zero can be considered to be an arbitrary value. No attempt is made to account for such values.

Thus, the conventional accounting often avoids those areas where it is not practicable to tread. While other instances of this "discretion" such as the failure to recognize the effects of inflation, have produced a great deal of criticism of conventional accounting, it has by no means been rendered useless.

While the above should not be taken to excuse the sloth of our professional accounting rule making bodies, it does suggest that it will not be necessary to solve all the problems of social accounting before practice can be undertaken. There will be flaws theoretically and practically in social accounting determinations. Such flaws will constitute a valid criticism only if they result in answers which are less valid than no answers at all, or if practicing social accountants fail to modify their techniques as knowledge increases.

---

*The practice followed by most major companies, expensing unsuccessful exploratory costs, produces a balance sheet valuation for reserves which is totally unrelated to reality. So-called "full costing" which also avoids any attempts at valuation is, at least, closer to discovery value, in absolute terms.

REFERENCES

1.   Mancur L. Olson, "Measurement Problems in the Social Accounts," (unpublished)

2.   See, for example, D. F., Linowes, "Socio-Economic Accounting," (*J. of A.,* November 1968); R. G. King, "Cost-Effectiveness Analysis: Implications for Accountants," (*J. of A.,* March 1970); Bruns and Snyder, "Management Information for Community Action" (Management Services, July-August, 1969); Sybil Mobley, "The Challenges of Socio-Economic Accounting," (*Accounting Review,* October, 1970).

3.   Robert Dorfman, ed., *Measuring Benefits of Government Investments,* (Washington, The Brookings Institution, 1965).

4.   The Analysis and Evaluation of Government Expenditures (3 vols.) papers presented to the JEC of the U. S. Congress, 1969.

5.   These questions are discussed in greater detail in Hansen and Weisbrod, Benefits, Costs and Finance of Public Higher Education, Chicago; Markham, 1969.

6.   National Science Foundation, *A Review of the Relationship between Research and Development and Economic Growth,* February, 1971. In particular, see Zvi Griliches, "A Memorandum on Research and Growth."

7.   See, for example, P. Zimbardo and E. Ebbesen, *Influencing Attitudes and Changing Behavior Massachusetts,* Addison-Wesley, 1970 p. 25. The authors note that attitudes which have been measured experimentally," . . . are rarely socially significant ones . . ."

Measuring the Quality of Life

Robert K. Elliott

In contrast with the preceding article, Elliott downgrades the necessity to provide dollar values in social accounting calculations. Accountants are already involved in the social dimension, he argues, and are preceding in advance of the development of the "principles" of social accounting, that might permit dollar quantification.

Elliott is somewhat less optimistic than Seidler about the ability of accountants to produce results that will clearly, or objectively, distinguish between widely differing social alternatives.

This, and the preceding article, were presented together at several meetings. The published versions reflect the interaction resulting from these presentations.

Social accounting is a concept in search of a workable method. Clearly, it is an idea whose time has come. Not so clear are the objectives and limitations of social accounting and the standards and methods needed for its performance. Academic accountants are now involved in an energetic drive to develop such principles.

This intellectual search, however, is painfully slow. In the meantime, various decision makers are demanding information on social effects, and the practicing accounting profession is simply plunging into social accounting. Although the reports developed could be more elegant if solidly based on a neat set of principles, they nevertheless have the important advantages of timeliness and relevance.

In taking this pragmatic approach, the profession has been putting social accounting to work in such projects as analyzing nonfinancial data for grant receiving organizations, input/output factors in community welfare programs, cost/benefit measures for pollution control, urban renewal, crime, mass transit and traffic problems. The General Accounting Office (the Federal watchdog agency responsible directly to the Congress) has been active in the field for a decade, measuring benefits—not just costs—of various Federal programs. The experience gained in these endeavors is helping to form the necessary definitions and guidelines and is helping to alert business leaders to the importance of social measurement. The purpose of this article is to disclose some of the implementation problems facing the social accounting practitioner and to explain how and why the accountant fits into social accounting. But before considering these subjects, it is desirable to establish the need for social accounting and to provide at least a provisional definition of it.

Robert K. Elliott is a partner with the accounting firm of Peat, Marwick, Mitchell & Co.

SOURCE: From *World,* Spring 1973, Peat, Marwick, Mitchell & Co.

Social accounting is necessary because there is a tremendous need for information to solve the problems of unbridled growth of population and of per capita consumption that already are placing severe strains on the environment and exhausting the world's natural resources. Although new power sources, alternate raw materials, and efficient recycling may help, it is nevertheless obvious that there is a physical limit to growth potential. Computer simulations using a number of alternate assumptions have indicated that unless economic growth is halted, there will be an economic and ecological crash within 50 to 100 years. Some have disputed the assumptions and the model used, but there is widespread agreement on the existence of a severe problem. And that is only part of our social concern. It also includes the problems of racial and religious equality, urban blight, the breakdown in the transportation system, unemployment, welfare, old age support, health, and education. As if these were not problems of sufficiently staggering magnitude, technology continues to introduce brand new areas of trouble. For example, as more and more jobs are automated, huge masses will be unemployed, or the work will spread around so that most people will be underemployed.

In order to solve these immense social problems we must operate with a reasonable degree of efficiency, and this can only be done in the presence of vast quantities of useful information. That information will be the product of social accounting. The fact is that social progress will be hindered until there are adequate measures of progress toward social goals.

Social accounting can be defined as the reporting of accountability for *all* resources used by a corporation (or, for that matter, any entity). Typically, corporations have reported on the use of financial resources to the suppliers of those resources—owners and creditors. In a social accounting, the corporation reports on its use of human and natural resources to the suppliers of those resources, who are—in the broadest sense—the general public. The concerns giving rise to the pressures for social accounting and the most relevant terms in which to report this accountability, all boil down to one concept—"quality of life." Social accounting is simply concerned with the corporation's impact on quality of life.

In actual application, this vague abstraction must be made operational. In practice, the social accountant must analyze the various "constituencies" of the corporation—that is, those groups that have a distinct and identifiable interest in corporate activity—and then analyze just how the corporation affects their quality of life. For a manufacturing concern, the constituencies and impacts to be measured might be as follows:

Constituencies	Impacts to be measured
Employees	Product performance
Dealers	Economic performance
Customers	Development of human resources
Suppliers	Use of environment

Constituencies	Impacts to be measured
Communities	Community welfare
Public	Government relations
Government	
Creditors	
Owners	

As an example of this form of analysis, we could consider the effect of a manufacturing plant on the community in which it is located. General Motors has a vehicle assembly plant in Wilmington, Delaware. This plant consumes space, air, utilities, and has various other effects upon the community. A citizen of Wilmington (as a citizen, that is assuming he is not an employee, customer, investor, etc.) has little immediate interest in the overall social performance of General Motors; he is mainly interested in the company's performance in Wilmington. Specifically, he would like to know such things as the long-term viability of the Wilmington operation; stability of employment levels; local taxes paid; contributions to local charities; labor relations; hiring, promotion, and pay practices; air, water, and noise pollution; power and water consumption; plant appearance; traffic flow; impact on local politics; and general corporate citizenship. A report on these matters to the community of Wilmington would constitute one element in the overall social accounting of General Motors.

Such a report would not only be useful to members of the community in assessing corporate performance, but would also help management establish goals by assuring that a more complete consideration is given to total business needs and public expectations. Also the preparation of such a report would help management to think through the total consequences of their actions, thus resulting in better decisions.

Recently, a number of corporations have devoted part of their annual reports to stockholders to the area of social responsibility. It is clear, however, that these corporate reports, while salutary, are *not* social accounting. The reason is that they are still essentially oriented to financial accounting. After all, a corporation must be somewhat socially responsible just to survive. In effect, these companies are telling their stockholders that they are not behaving in an antisocial way that might endanger their fiscal health—a result that could ensue if they were boycotted for discriminatory hiring, or closed down for excessive pollution. Even if these possibilities are not imminent, the company may still reap long-term financial benefits by improving its public image, thus enhancing, for example, sales and personnel recruitment.

It comes down to this: real social accounting must report to the suppliers of resources—and stockholders are not the suppliers of human and natural resources to the corporation.

Perhaps the most difficult and important decisions to be made about social accounting are practical ones: what is to be measured and what is the unit of measurement? There is a tendency to measure costs instead of benefits. For example, many persons are quite concerned over the staggering costs of welfare programs in New York. Few measure the programs in terms of the benefits they bring, whether they are to rehabilitate people and put them to work or simply to support lives that otherwise would be lost. Cost gives no indication of these benefits. But, in social terms, most reasonable people would agree that even if human beings are simply prevented from starving, that is a useful, measurable benefit.

It is not, however, a benefit that can be measured in dollars. We cannot say a human life prevented from starving is worth $50,000. We can say that for x billion dollars spent we supported y number of lives. That is a useful type of cost/benefit measure, even though not expressed completely in dollars.

The conclusion that quality of life cannot be reduced to dollar measures also has support in other professions, as illustrated in the following quote from a well known political scientist:

"In short, national economic accounting has promoted a 'new Philistinism'—an approach to life based on the principle of using monetary units as the common denominator of all that is important in human life. The 'new Philistinism' shows up in different forms:

The cost-benefit analysis who recognize no benefits (or disbenefits) that cannot be expressed in dollars and cents.

The econometricians still operating on the ludicrous premise that there is, or should be, a 'single-valued objective welfare function' by which one could judge alternative courses of action.

The pathetic effort in the United States to debate policies for the 'Great Society' and the 'quality of life' on the basis of concepts developed decades ago to fight depression and provide minimum material sustenance for the population."

This bias can be overcome only by persistent efforts to develop broader models that include many more variables than those thus far used by economists.

Measuring in terms of costs has great appeal to accountants precisely because such measurements are expressed in dollars and already appear in the regular books of account of the disbursing organization. These are terms that accountants are accustomed to dealing with. Unfortunately, costs are much more relevant to the disbursing organization than to the social constituency which is the intended user of the information. Furthermore, costs tend to become merged over the years and are difficult to identify and allocate, and often cannot be separated from economic costs. For example, providing a pension plan for retiring employees is socially beneficial. It gives them security in their old age. But, it is also an economic cost because in order to attract employees at all, the company must be competitive in its employee benefit plan.

Costs are rather poor measures of effectiveness anyway. For example, one could present simply the cost of providing hospital service. The uninformed user of this information might deduce that a hospital that is spending more to provide service is providing greater social benefit than one that is spending less, since costs are the only measurement at hand. The social benefit from hospitals is improved health. Therefore, the benefit measure should be cast in terms of health, not costs.

Instead of costs, social accounting must measure social impacts, whether they be social benefits or social detriments. Which, of course, again raises several problems. Should the social accountant measure only the side effects of corporate action, or should he measure all the effects, including the mainstream effects? With an automobile manufacturer, for example, the side effects include the pollution created by producing automobiles and by operating them after they are manufactured, as well as traffic injuries and fatalities. Long-range side effects—the result of putting millions of cars on the roads—include increasing urbanization. The mainstream effect is the automobiles themselves, which are a desired means of personal transportation. Some economists and social accountants maintain that mainstream effects are best measured in the marketplace. If, they say, the market is willing to spend $3,000 for an automobile, that is an excellent indication of its social utility.

But, that is simply not true, because individual decisions are usually short term. When one person buys a car, he is merely looking for personal transportation. Multiply that decision by the millions who purchase cars and not only is there an increase in personal transportation, but the side effects of mounting urbanization and pollution. So to say that the market should value mainstream effects is not adequate because the aggregate effects are much greater than the sum of the individual decisions. Probably most persons would agree that the market does a poor job of measuring the social utility of, say, Saturday night specials or heroin.

In addition, if social accountants measure only side effects, there is a serious problem of distorting decisions, because often the side effects will be mainly negative. If the social reporting does not also measure the mainstream effects, which are often positive, a lopsided picture will emerge. Ideally, therefore, the social accountant would measure all social effects.

Obviously, there are limits to what can be measured. Often the ripples going out from mainstream effects are endless. What, for example, is the ultimate social impact of the economic decision to import slaves three centuries ago? We will never know. So, the task of the social accountant will be to measure as far out from the mainstream effects as he can; in effect, as far as the measurement techniques will allow. Presumably, as these techniques improve, the radius of useful measurement will expand.

The next question concerns the unit of measure to be used. In financial areas, it is easy to get agreement on the unit of measure because commercial organizations are formed to maximize the return of dollars. The dollar is therefore an obvious unit of measure. In social areas, however, the quantity to be maximized is quality of life. Some day it may be possible to develop a quality of life measurement unit; but, for now, this is not a realistic possibility. Therefore, what the social accountant must do is break down quality of life into constituent elements and use surrogate measures. For example, one does not have much quality of life if his personal safety is threatened, so a surrogate measure might be the crime rate. Pollution diminishes quality of life; therefore a surrogate measure would be pollution rates. An adequate income is necessary for quality of life, so a surrogate measure would be the level and distribution of personal income.

The difficulty with using surrogate measures is that since they are not expressed in common measurement units, it is difficult to make rational choices based on them. Should the Federal government, for example, allocate marginal resources to cancer research or to raising the reading ability of ghetto children? If the benefits are expressed in different units the choice is not obvious. Those who would express everything in dollars might say cancer has a benefit of $1 billion and reading has a benefit of $2 billion; therefore, reading wins. Most likely, though, the public would simply reject those dollar measures as being quite arbitrary, and revert to qualitative measures. The existence of objective information, even though indifferent units, should improve the decision process from the way it functions today. No matter what improvements are made in social accounting, however, the choice between cancer research and reading ability will probably always remain a difficult societal decision.

For the accounting profession, the major question concerns the extent to which accountants should become involved in social measurement. Other professions—sociology, economics, ecology—would seem to have primary competence in social accounting. What expertise can the accountant bring? The answer to this question is two-fold: first, the accountant can design social information systems, and second, he can attest to reported information.

In the design area, accountants are experienced designers and operators of large-scale information systems and, in fact, are uniquely qualified to assemble and validate quantitative information. There is really no reason the accounting profession cannot broaden this expertise from the financial area into social accounting.

In addition to designing these information systems, the accountant can attest to their reliability. The public accountant's reputation for independence and integrity qualifies him for this task. After all, if information is developed and is not in some way validated, its limited creditibility will diminish its usefulness for decision-making.

In any case, as pointed out above, accountants have already become involved in the field.

There are plenty of accountants who believe that we should put our financial house in order before reaching out to embrace new, and perhaps more difficult, problems. Unfortunately, financial accounting is such a complex subject that we shall probably never reach ultimate solutions to financial problems. The danger is that we may commit the resources of the profession to a perpetual quest for truth in an area of declining (and perhaps disappearing) relevance, while failing to make any useful progress on a crucial problem of increasing relevance.

Interestingly, the authoritative literature of accounting gives implicit support to the extension of the scope of accounting practice into social measurement. For example, this passage adopted in 1939 seems prophetic when placed in a social accounting context, rather than the more familiar financial accounting context:

"The committee regards corporation accounting as one phase of the working of the corporate organization of business, which in turn it views as a machinery created by the people in the belief that, broadly speaking, it will serve a useful purpose. The test of the corporate system and of the special phase of it represented by corporate accounting ultimately lies in the results which are produced. These results must be judged from the standpoint of society as a whole—not from that of any one group of interested parties.

The uses to which the corporate system is put and the controls to which it is subject change from time to time, and all parts of the machinery must be adapted to meet such changes as they occur."[2]

Although there are no theoretical reasons that CPAs cannot become involved with social accounting, there are some very practical constraints which would hamper the profession at this point. They fall into three classes: the level of skill within the profession, entrance requirements to the profession, and the problem of legal liability.

First, certain skills essential for social accounting are underrepresented in the profession today. These include economics, engineering, mathematics, law, sociology, and behavioral science, among others.

Second, in terms of entrance requirements, the profession persists in the "myth of the generalist." It recommends a single formal education program as preparation for becoming a CPA, and administers a single, general qualifying examination. Once a person clears these formal hurdles, he is deemed to be competent in any of the many facets of accounting. In fact, the profession forbids formal designated specializations. As a result of this series of formal hurdles for admission to the profession and the lack of recognition for special expertise, many types of persons urgently needed in the profession are effectively screened out. They do not desire, or are not able, to meet these mechanistic requirements (of little or no relevance to their intended field of specialization) and could achieve no professional recognition if they did gain admittance.

The third practical problem is that of legal liability. The present potentially ruinous levels of liability have already made the CPA sufficiently defensive that he is hesitant to accept new responsibilities. In an uncharted area such as social accounting, the legal threat is unknown and, hence, foreboding.

Our social problems will not go away. To hold them in check, let alone to ameliorate them, we will require vastly greater amounts of objective social information. Accountants can, and should, be involved in creating this information. But to become effectively involved, accountants must take some positive actions.

Academic accountants must:

* attract into accounting promising candidates outside the traditional mold, that is, conceptual, verbal, socially oriented persons,
* broaden the accounting curriculum to include newly required skills,
* establish links with other professions to assure an interchange of relevant information,
* establish research programs in social accounting, and
* develop courses to update current practitioners on social accounting.

Public and corporate accountants must:

* change their self-image from communicators of *financial information* to communicators of *decision-making* information,
* become acquainted with social accounting,
* hire and welcome into the profession those who will be able to cope with the ambiguous social data,
* become acquainted with effectiveness measures used in other professions,
* support academic accountants in this area,
* experiment with social accounting,
* install effectiveness measures instead of just cost measures in their own spheres of influence, and
* begin to look beyond financial statements and operations to their impact on all corporate constituencies.

If the profession implements these recommendations and begins to move vigorously toward the goals of social accounting, then it could find itself in a leadership position in this vital and fascinating area with its inherent opportunities to provide a highly useful and laudable service to society.

REFERENCES

1.   Bertram M. Gross, "The State of the Nation: Social Systems Accounting," in *Social Indicators,* edited by Raymond A. Bauer, Cambridge; The M. I. T. Press 1966, pp. 167-168.

2.   Accounting Research Bulletin No. 1, American Institute of Certified Public Accountants, 1939, incorporated into Accounting Research Bulletin No. 43, which is still in effect today.

II
DEVELOPING AN ACCOUNTANT'S CONCEPT OF SOCIAL INCOME

On the Facility, Felicity, and Morality of Measuring Social Change

C. West Churchman

The following article has been placed here to suggest a simple, but vital point: a concept of social profit must have a philosophical basis.

As was noted earlier in this volume, any "social profit" must be one deemed profitable by the society within which the calculation is made. When accounting evaluations are made of profit-seeking enterprises, there appears to be a fairly universal consensus as to the notion of profit. Even in the Communist countries, the definition of accounting profit is not significantly different from that found in the bastions of capitalism.

However, what is deemed socially desirable, that is, socially profitable, varies considerably as one travels throughout the world. The relative values of lives and property; of individual freedom versus loyalty to the state; of survival versus the available food supply; of individual pursuit of wealth versus the value of income equality differ with prevailing social and economic systems, religious and ethical philosophy, and even with latitude and longitude.

Social accounting, as described herein, is relevant primarily to the United States. Following Churchman's article is a series of documents that the editor deems to be significant in American social-economic history. The selected documents have been assembled in an attempt to suggest some of the major currents in American history that may be drawn upon by social accountants as they attempt to determine socially acceptable concepts of social profits.

It is impossible to make anything resembling a fair attempt at this task within the confines of one section of one book. Moreover, no accounting professor has a claim to any extraordinary comprehension of the major trends of American history as they might reflect upon the development of a concept of social profit. Such a determination, as Churchman suggests, will be the result of a long process of study and debate, with ultimate agreement improbable, if not impossible.

However, despite the magnitude of this task, a start must be made, if for no other reason than to provide a basis for criticism and further progress. This group of documents seems to provide a reflection of the trend of American social-economic values. They attempt to define the relationship between the government and the governed, and to suggest the views of the writers of the Constitution of the United States toward the sanctity of personal safety and property and the limits of government action. Several of these documents reflect significant legal decisions that have stood the test of time; others present the themes of major pieces of legistlation.

It is hoped that the documents will provide the reader with at least a start toward determining a workable concept of social profit.

In a recent unpublished paper entitled "Questions of Metric," Stafford Beer cites some letters to the *London Times* addressed to a question of social change. The issue concerned the seven hundred years old Norman Church of St. Michael of Stewkley, which stands square in the middle of a possible runway of a possible Third London Airport—not by design surely. A cost benefit analysis had been made by a commission for each alternative site of the proposed airport. In the instance of St. Michael's Church, the commission had used the extant fire insurance policy on the church as the base. This method of analysis caused considerable anger among antiquarians throughout the United Kingdom. A Mr. Osborn suggested instead that one should take the initial investment, say 100 pounds in 1182, and discount it at 10 per cent per annum to 1982; the approximate result is a one followed by 33 zeros—a mere decillion pounds. As Beer points out, if you adopt either cost-benefit strategy, you automatically decide the issue. If you use the fire insurance approach, the church is virtually an irrelevant consideration in the decision of where to build the airport; whereas if you use the discount approach, the church is all that matters: it is inconceivable that one should build the runway there.

What I found most significant about this story of measuring proposed social change was the ease with which both the commission and Mr. Osborn were able to assign numbers. The facility is clearly a product of the history of enterprising accountants and economists, people who have spent their lives assigning numbers to social changes. So facile has the process become that so long as there is a hint of reasonableness, the numbers themselves carry the conviction of their accuracy. And both the commission and Mr. Osborn seem to have a plausible viewpoint. The commission might argue as follows: evidently, people do value St. Michael of Stewkley, in the sense that they are willing to pay a price for its value in the event that it is destroyed. This value is clearly represented by the amount of fire insurance they are willing to subscribe to, because the only reward for paying the

---

C. West Churchman is Professor of Business Administration and Research Philosopher at the University of California, Berkeley.

SOURCE: From *The Accounting Review,* No. 1 (January, 1971), pp. 30-35, Copyright by the American Accounting Association, 1971.

premium is the expectation of a return provided the church is destroyed. Mr. Osborn, on the other hand, might argue that an investment was made in the year 1182, which could instead have been deposited in the yet-to-be Bank of England. Cashing in on the investment in 1982 would be like "cashing in" on the church to build a runway in 1982; assuming rational decision making, the total imputed value of the investment cannot be greater than the current value of the church.

My main point is that the facility of assigning numbers means that only a modicum of plausibility is needed to convince people that the numbers represent reality. In both of the cases cited, just a little more thinking would have ruined the case. All one has to do is apply Immanuel Kant's moral law, which, paraphased, says that if a particular principle is used to measure social change for policy making, then this principle should be universally applied. The principle, of course, may contain reasoned exceptions and stipulations, but once it is enunciated, it ought to be applicable to all instances, or else it is basically unfair, i.e., immoral. Now the commission's principle seems to read as follows: whenever there is a positive value (benefit) to destroying an object X, then the cost of destruction is to be computed by using the extant fire or life insurance as a base. The commission's policy, if universalized, would neatly solve the population problem. There is surely a value in not having all the people which the demographers predict will be here in the year 2000 if nothing is done to prevent it. So—merely calculate the benefit of eliminating X and compare it with X's life insurance. The result is that only the best will survive—the Kennedys and the Onassises. Mr. Osborn's principle, on the other hand, is very nice for old criminals and professors: the investment in their birth for hospitals, nurses and doctors discounted to age 70 would make the decision to execute or retire unthinkable.

The two examples, then, are silly. So why mention them? Why, just to challenge any number assigners to come up with a better method, based on a principle which will pass Kant's test. More to the point, the examples clearly show how number assignment is based on very strong value and reality assumptions.

Suppose for the moment that we look at the reality aspect of measuring social change. We'd surely like to say that a measurement should reflect what really occurs. But what does this stipulation mean? We could make its meaning clear if somehow or other we could get outside the measuring system and what it is trying to measure. If we could do this, then we'd say to ourselves, "There's reality R in its box, and when R changes it sends a message or impulse to the measuring system M in its box. Since we're outside all this, and can observe it accurately, let's see if the numbers generated by M accurately correspond to the changes in R." We'd certainly have to fuss over the criteria of accurate correspondence, but that would be a technical matter we could hand over to some of the brilliant minds who like to fuss with these matters.

But of course this way of describing reality doesn't work at all, as any auditor knows. It isn't sufficient to stipulate that a good audit has occurred if a second party testifies that the auditor's numbers correspond to reality, because the second party may belong to the auditor's firm, or a competitor's firm, or the broad class of the inexperienced. To make any sense at all of this way of defining reality, we have to set down the stipulations of the competent, disinterested observer,[1] which as experienced auditors know, is no easy task. To accomplish the task we need a fairly elaborate theory of competence and honesty. So here is the same theme again: to know that we are measuring real change we need to have a strong theoretical base.

But suppose now that we do succeed in finding a satisfactory basis for assessing competence and honesty. Would we then want to say that M is measuring real social change if a sufficiently large class of competent, disinterested observers agree that it is? *Why* should agreement imply that reality is being measured? Here I'd like to introduce a pragmatic principle at least as old as William James. If I tell you that the last book on the top shelf of my study's bookshelf is red, and I present affidavits of color competent observers which certify my account, have I described reality to you? No, said James, because the description makes no difference whatsoever in your behavior relative to your practical goals. To be real for you is to make a difference for you. If I'd said that the red book is that set of dull platitudes of Chairman Mao, then some of you might report me, or admire me more, or whatever, and then reality comes into being.

Suppose we go back to Stewkley where the British Division of the Cleveland Wrecking Company is about to smash a priceless glass window of St. Michael's. We want to measure this social change. "There goes 3000 pounds," says the commission, and could hardly care less. "There goes a decillion pounds," says Mr. Osborn, and could hardly care more. But what has really happened? If we employed the method suggested earlier, we would bring in our disinterested observer to decide which number accurately maps reality. He would say things like "20 windows were broken, each 700 years old," or, "it took two weeks to haul St. Michael's away at an expense of 1472 pounds and a sixpence."

Such a disinterested observer, in fact, would be very like many experts who today are measuring social change. Consider, for example, the issue of population. Here beyond a doubt is social change. In Paul and Ann Ehrlich's *Population Resources Environment,*[2] we are told that the doubling rate of the world's population around 1970 is about 30 to 35 years, in 1930 was 45 years, in 1850, 200 years. The book contains a number of other numbers: food production, pollution production, and so on. All of these numbers say something about social change, but you will note that they are all very much like the disinterested observer of the smashing of St. Michael's. No doubt in both cases the reports may be a bit shocking, and in this sense they "make a difference." But the difference may have no pragmatic import whatsoever. The Ehrlichs have much to say about the number of people who will starve if things go on as at present. This is much like telling us that the round ball will break St. Michael's window unless its basic policy of motion is changed. Another disinterested observer, also using numbers, could tell us how many people felt sad and for how long when learned about St. Michael's or the starving children of Biafra.

It is really astonishing how many crisis numbers are being thrown at the public these days. They all describe what programmers call the rate of activity in a certain sector of society. Since often the rate of activity-pollution or poverty or information-spread yields uneasy or horrible feelings, people and politicians are apt to conclude that something must be done to lessen the rate, or even to make it negative. But even if the disinterested observer is telling us about real impending disaster provided in activity continues to increase, it by no means follows that he is telling us about real social change in a pragmatic sense. The reality question is, "So what?" Only when we can measure in such a way that we know what to do about the result, only then will we measure social change.

The point I am trying to make is that the amount of change in some property of society or its environment by itself does not "measure" social change. What is needed besides is the basis of decision making which shows how the amount of change makes a difference. A good illustration is the so-called "protein gap," which very much interests the nutritionists these days. We are told,[3] for example, that a pregnant woman who lacks a sufficient amount of protein in her diet may well give birth to a deformed baby. We are also told that the amount of protein (note, again, the amount theme) in certain areas of the world is seriously deficient. What can be called the Fallacy of Filling the Gap immediately infers that we should produce and distribute more protein. Perhaps we should, but the protein gap by itself does not imply any such action. Besides a knowledge of the gap, we need to assume that the crisis warrants certain expenditures, that policies of making more protein will not introduce concomitant gaps and inequities in other areas, e.g., by changing the ecology of fish life. It so happens that protein is used as calories in calorie deficient diets, so that filling the protein gap by no means solves the nutritional problem. And so on.

Of course a profession may adopt a separatist philosophy to avoid the tremendous responsibility of measuring real social change in a pragmatic sense. The profession of accounting may say the same thing that many demographers say: "Look, we can't tell you what to do about the activity rate, but we can tell you what the rate is. We're like the speedometers on automobiles which measure changes in the car's velocity. The driver must decide what to do about a reading of eighty miles per hour." But the analogy doesn't work, for a very obvious reason: it's perfectly clear to both driver and auto designer that velocity is a critical aspect of the driving experience, and the method of correcting for too much or too little is also obvious. Given that we ought to drive automobiles if we want to, the speedometer is a great help and accurately measures social change. But the critical question is still there: ought we to drive automobiles? The speedometer is silent on this point. Given that we ought to reduce population by forcing every lady to take the pill, then the expert can or soon will tell us how to do the job.

But the demographer is silent on the question whether we should so force pill taking.

The fallacy of the separatist philosophy is the one I mentioned earlier: once you begin to emphasize some aspect of real change by putting numbers on it, you may divert attention from the real issue. Consequently, I can't help but feel that the professions which try to place numbers on social change have the responsibility to go the entire way—to understand why the numbers make a difference and why the difference they make is the right difference.

For example, I believe the accounting profession should become deeply involved in helping society to measure the most critical aspects of social change—of pollution, population, information, whatever. But to do so, I think the profession will have to change some important traditional attitudes. It is to these social changes of the profession that I'd like to address the concluding remarks.[4]

In recent years, we have heard a great deal about how accounting and economics need to be enlarged to include "social indicators" or "social accounting." But I don't think the need is for more numbers, at all. The need is for the basis of justifying the numbers—the model or world view which tells us what difference the numbers make.

Decision-oriented accounting is quite different from accounting's traditional role in the private sector. Often the service which accounting has given is essentially comparisons: the accounts tell us how this period's costs, inventories, turnover, profit, etc., compare with last period's. Comparative accounting is much like the rate-of-change of an activity mentioned earlier. It is useful if we know that the comparison makes a real difference in decision making, useless otherwise. Hence one basic change of attitude is towards finding a model for decision making. Of course, what I am saying is that the professions of operations research and accounting need to form a long-overdue alliance. But I think both professions will have to give up one cherished attitude—namely, the assurance of the expert. The "model" to which I referred is by no means easy to create, nor can any of us feel assured that a candidate model represents social reality. No longer can we call upon the disinterested, competent observer to settle our issues. There is no "outside" which can observe the "inside" trying to depict reality.

Returning to Stewkley once more, both the commission and Mr. Osborn had a model; there is no competent, disinterested observer to tell us which is right, if either. But is this so? Why not say as before that if a sufficiently large group of sufficiently competent experts agree, or—via the Delphi technique[5]—converge on agreement, then the model can be taken as representing reality? The answer, of course, is that to assume that a convergence of agreement of experts represents reality is to presuppose a fairly elaborate theory of the relationship between reality and expert knowledge, as well as a theory about how expert opinion is to be ascertained. Also assumed is our old friend the value judgment. Experts may tell us that in so-and-so many years we can expect brain-to-computer linkages and genetic engineering. This is like telling us that the population will double, the protein source will shrink, the air will be dangerously polluted. To repeat, what is left out of the expert's opinions is all we really need to know: what to do about it if they accurately portray a real trend.

No, if we are to serve society by measuring social change, I think we'll have to do so in an entirely different mode from the traditional one of being the separate, disinterested, and objective observers. These stipulations seem clear (to me):

1. We are not the only or even the basic methodology of assessing social change. There are other equally forceful methods: aesthetic, religious and political are three good examples.

2. We are not objective in the old-fashioned sense of "being apart," and "non-biased." Our bias is based on our conception (world view) of how socially reality works and what "makes a difference."

3. (My own bias.) In Beer's paper mentioned earlier, which has a very similar theme to this one but a radically different approach, Beer argues for a "meta" measuring system, one that measures the "eudomonia," or "prosperity," which is flowing through the social system. Beer approaches the problem in this manner because he likes to see the world as a flow, with feedbacks and other cybernetic devices. My bias is to look for the fiber of the system, the structure that ought to hold it together. This approach amounts to saying that we require an explicit moral base for measuring social change. Far more important than "agreement of experts" is the moral prescription which says that our measure should be based on a policy of moral universality—everyone to count as an end—and not a means only—a deep analysis of how people are affected by the difference the measure will make.

For example, Mr. Osborn was nearer to being right than the commission, but for the wrong reasoning. The point is not whether to discount from the past—but whether to discount into the future. I can see no moral justification in our saying that the numerical reward (joy, aesthetic pleasure, inspiration) of some future viewer of St. Michael's must be discounted back to present value, much as a future insurance premium would be—though I have some feeling-deficient friends who say just this: "The hell with the values of a generation as yet unborn, or at least 10% the hell per annum." So if we paint our world view with the Third London Airport as a temporary value for, say, thirty years of use and then no value thereafter, but St. Michael's will always bring joy to some thousands or so, then the cost number to be assigned to smashing the church is very large, because no future joy is to be discounted to present value on moral grounds.

Now there is no authority for my moral law, and many may disagree with it. Indeed, many should disagree with it, because the essence of moral discourse should be debate, not agreement. Anyone like myself who takes part in measuring social change must on the one hand declare and argue for his moral position, but should never on pain of displaying hubris, assume that he is the authority. So I declare and argue for the position that every social policy needs not only a cost-benefit number, but that the basic theory of assigning such a number should be revealed and assessed for its moral implications—i.e., whether if generalized it would imply a world where people are treated as ends rather than means only.

4. As number assigners we must be stubborn but not necessarily humorless. We will insist that the value of a life can be numbered and compared, no matter what our enemies say. So the population scarers may horrify us, but let us number the cost of a human starved to death. Of course, we can't be all that deadly serious about it, either. We should take on a lesson from Kenneth Boulding, who suggests that each citizen be assigned 22 deciles of a child, which he can sell on the open market place. This way the population will remain stable, assuming no bootlegging operations occur. You see, once we give up the silly notion that numbers have the final answers, we can really enjoy ourselves now and then.

5. I hope the accounting profession will join other professional associations in looking at today's problems of society and suggesting some ways of assigning numbers to social change that make a difference—with all the humility, humor and purposefulness possible.

NOTES

1.   "Independent" in CPA language.
2.   San Francisco: W. H. Freeman and Co., 1970.
3.   See International Action to Avert the Protein Crisis New York; (United Nations 1968).
4.   To be sure, some changes have already been suggested.
5.   Olaf Helmer, *Social Technology* (New York: Basic Books, 1966).

Toward a Concept of Social Value

J. M. Clark

This essay, originally drafted more than sixty years ago, suggests a concept of social profit that is as valid today as the day it was written. Indeed, readers will note that Clark could have predicted one of the difficulties of the 1972 democratic candidate for the presidency. In January, 1972, George McGovern made a proposal in a speech in Ames, Iowa to limit inheritances to $500.000. Because that figure approximated the value of a good family farm in Iowa, the suggestion was greeted with somewhat less than complete enthusiasm. The reader will note that Clark indicates that the inheritance privilege is valued not only by the rich, but by "the mass of smaller property owners."

Of somewhat broader significance, Clark provides a clear, crisp argument that social measurements must be concerned with the costs or values to society—not merely to individuals—of the externalities borne or appropriated by individuals. In particular, he makes the point that virtually every measure or law calling for so-called social reform involves a departure from valuations placed by the free market. The cost or benefits of these social reform measures might be measured by these departures.

While Clark was, of course, speaking to his economist contemporaries, the arguments are entirely appropriate for today's social accountants. As the authors of so many of the papers in this volume indicate, the economists have heeded Clark's admonitions. Perhaps it is now time for the accountants to do so.

The search for standards of social value in the economic realm is a baffling task, yet far from an unprofitable one. We shall presumably never discover a definite yardstick of social value comparable to the dollar yardstick of exchange values; but we may find standards by which those of the market may be revised, or in some instances replaced. An economist should be prepared to face such a search, with all its difficulties, if he accepts three basic propositions.

One is that the problem of the collective efficiency of private enterprise involves quantities and qualities, of which actual market prices are not the only measure, and, I would add, some of which command no market price at all under present conditions,[1] although with changes in law and custom they might perhaps come to command one. Another is that measures of value which may be less exact than those of the market are also much more fundamental. And a third is that our most fundamental concepts would be independent of institutions of competitive exchange; they should be such as would hold even in a socialistic state.

This independent basis is necessary if there is to be any common meeting-ground for debate between socialists, radicals, and conservatives. It is necessary

---

SOURCE: J. M. Clark, *A Preface to Social Economics,* New York, 1936.

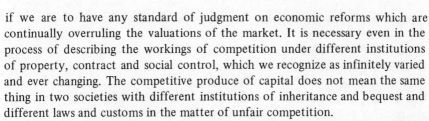

if we are to have any standard of judgment on economic reforms which are continually overruling the valuations of the market. It is necessary even in the process of describing the workings of competition under different institutions of property, contract and social control, which we recognize as infinitely varied and ever changing. The competitive produce of capital does not mean the same thing in two societies with different institutions of inheritance and bequest and different laws and customs in the matter of unfair competition.

Or, let us take the statement that the rental value of land tends to equal the excess of the (competitive valuation of the) goods and services produced upon it above the (competitive) expenses of production. This becomes quite indefinite the moment we realize that the net produce in question may or may not include robbing the neighbors of their light and air, obstructing the streets, fouling streams, increasing or destroying the beauty of the landscape or the business character of the neighborhood, admitting tenants whose very presence destroys the value of other real estate in the adjoining blocks, etc., etc.[2] There are many different kinds of competitive products of land as there are regulations governing these matters, and merely to describe the differences, without passing any sort of judgment on them, we must use terms that go behind the competitive value of the exchangeable product.

The world is full of unpaid costs and unappropriated services.[3] In proportion as we rise above bare material necessities we reach intangible utilities that are harder and harder to appropriate, such as knowledge and personal privacy. The age of material power is the age when these higher and more elusive utilities come increasingly into the focus of social attention. The age of the railroad and the interlocking credit system is an age when business transactions have more far-reaching effects than ever before, and more than can ever be bought and sold directly. The age of researches in bacteriology and environmental determinism is an age when innumerable effects, always in existence, are being discovered and valued as never before. The age of democracy is an age when everyone can exercise to the full the two great social impulses: the impulse to be like one's fellows and the impulse to be different, to be distinguished. But these emulative and especially these insidious utilities are in a peculiar way the ones in which one man's gain is another's loss: they eat each other up, and the resultant is a social utility far different from the sum of its individually appropriate parts.

To illustrate, patents and copyrights are enforced, sometimes very imperfectly, and books are bought and sold, but can we imagine Darwin attempting to collect toll from all who used the ideas and proofs contained in "The Origin of Species"? Or even a weather bureau supporting itself by selling its reports? A photographer once sold a woman's picture to be used in advertising a toilet preparation. The woman objected, but in this case the court asked, not whether she had suffered, but merely whether the negative was the property of the photographer. This led to the passage of a state statute protecting this right, and progressive courts in other states might now rule differently.[4] Thus the scope of appropriable rights changes, by legistlation or judicial evolution and the meaning of a system of free exchange changes with it.

Early railroads were estimated to have increased the value of neighboring lands by an amount five times their own cost. How much the western roads subtracted from land values in New England and New York will probably never be known with enough exactness to enable us to compare the gain and the loss. In the panic of 1873 the more conservative banks of New York City were called on to contribute from their funds to relieve the less provident banks from the consequences of their lack of caution. For the soundest bank must suspend if the others do. A few city banks had made profits by bidding for the deposits of country bankers and then, when called on for cash, fell back for support on those who had strengthened themselves by refraining from this extra-hazardous class of business. It was only natural that, in later panics, support was less freely given. It is hardly a blessing to the morale of a system of wholly independent banks to know that the careful ones must bear a part of the cost of others' carelessness, and that careless banks can often benefit by the preparedness of their neighbors, on the ground that all are "in the same boat" and that the soundest institution will suffer if others suspend, and will suffer more seriously if failures of others shake public confidence.

Careful sanitation, even more than sound banking, renders services to the general public which cannot well be appropriated and bought or sold in private bargains, and the result is the socializing of preventive medicine, just as the prevention of epidemics in banking is socialized, and for a similar reason. The stableman who has just screened his premises might, to be sure, try to collect compensation. One can almost see him going around selling safety from fly-borne contagions, so much to one man for one dollar, half as much to another for fifty cents and none to the man who will not buy. Or if we look at the matter in light, and consider the danger of spreading disease as one of the costs of the livery business, what law of free exchange would force the manager of the stable to pay either the expense of reasonable precautions or full compensation for the consequences of neglect?

Again, how shall we compare, socially, the products of two factories one of which is built with an eye to such beauty as circumstances permit and operated so as to give the workers an opportunity for gorwth, while the other furnishes an environment of unrelieved ugliness and a large percentage of "dead-end jobs?"

Part of the value of things that are sold today consists in taking away value from things that were sold last December. The utility of some women's gowns is being constantly attacked from two sides. To those whose clothes must be a mark of distinction and the latest thing, their value is gone as soon as they are imitated by too many people, or people not of the right sort, or as soon as fashion makes its next move. The fraternities at a certain college are satisfied to be housed in frame dwellings until one or two build handsome edifices of brick and stone. The others must then follow suit or be handicapped in the competition for the most eligible neophytes. Until Smith bought a Pierce Arrow, Jones and Brown were happy with their Fords. What is the net social utility of a new gown, a new house, a new automobile?

The legal doctrine of *damnum absque injuria* covers a multitude of such unpaid costs, and the unearned increment is a great catch-all of unappropriated services. Viewed as a study of individual utilities and not of organic social values,[5] a theory of inappropriables is merely a tracing of such products and costs as law and custom do not yet recognize and a revealing of responsibilities which have not yet been brought home effectively in markets or in courts. Thus the net economic value of a given service may be considered to include (1) potentially exchangeable by-products in the way of service or damage, valued at the price they would presumably command in exchange; (2) unmarketables measured by a standard derived from market price.

We may go farther than this, if we are studying such fundamental values as might prevail in a Socialist state as well as in our own. We may value things by others standards than that of competitive exchange, especially if those other standards are already effective in society or may reasonably be expected to become so. Thus the old "rich-man-poor-man complication" may emerge from the thought-tight compartment in which it has been more or less successfully interned, and demand a place in the sun, for there is ample proof that society does not wholly acquiesce in the idea that the desires of rich and poor should all have economic weight in proportion to the respective purchasing powers of these classes as they stand under the present distribution of incomes.

Here we have a truly organic social valuation. The theory of social value does not stop with the theory of inappropriables, which is merely an unusually complete summing up of individual values, utilities and costs, though this of itself is highly important to society as an organism. The ultimate question is: what is the value to society of these utilities consumed by individuals, or the cost to society of these costs which individuals bear?

Does the enjoyment of an inherited estate by the heir have a social value adequately measured by its present selling price? Certainly not if a Lloyd George succeeds in making another estimate effective.

Society weighs men by different standards, varying all the way from the humanitarian standard of equality to that of the most extreme apostles of the superman. Does anyone really accept the scale of the competitive market? We shall have found such a man, when we have found one who honestly approves of existing conditions of poverty: not one who is resigned to them as an inevitable evil, but one who would not lessen them if he could. So long as this does not represent the prevailing sentiment, so long it will be impossible to say that market value measures "social value" in the sense of "value to society." Where society does not even acquiesce in these evils, market values are "social" only in the sense of occurring in an organic social situation, through processes of an organic social character. The prevailing standards are mostly much nearer the humanitarian, and this fact is ever coming to the surface where men are deliberately following a common policy, or wherever some emergency breaks through the superstructure of convention and throws us back upon first principles and elemental needs.

A ticket to the Yale-Harvard game may be cheap enough to be sold for $2 and too valuable to be bought for $10, and the principle of this paradox applies to public land under the homestead act and land-rushes in Oklahoma, to bread in Germany, to train accommodations sold to war refugees by a relief committee, to the administration of justice (though all too imperfectly), and to public education. An allied principle governs poor-relief, minimum wage laws, etc., etc.

When some necessary article sells for a high price in the market, the result is that those who need it most cannot get it, and there are some things so very valuable that this exclusion of the poor cannot be allowed. Mention has been made of the American Homestead Acts, under which a price is demanded for the land, often a very high price, though not in money, and a price which the poor can pay readily while the rich cannot afford it. Where the price is chiefly personal trouble and sacrifice, the work of occupying and improving the land, it is quite effective in preserving the land for those who need it most. The rich may hire dummies and so evade the price, but they will not pay it, for it calls for too high a sacrifice of what they already enjoy, a sacrifice which their desire is not great enough to outweigh.

It is a commonplace of economic writers that our free land while it lasted saved us from many economic ills against which we must now be on our guard. Would it be equally commonplace to say that an economic system which weighs men's wants according to their financial purchasing power under the competitive regime has been saved from some of its worst consequences by having as a safety-valve a frontier where that standard has been overruled in favor of equality between man and man? It is, of course, not a matter of chance that the commodity sold in this unbusinesslike way is no finished product but raw land, the mere opportunity to produce.

Equality of opportunity, then, is what "free land" secures, and this is very far from being the same thing as equality of reward. Therefore it may be claimed that we shall never sell potatoes on the same equalitarian plan, or that if we do, we shall no longer be following the rule of equal opportunity, but shall be undertaking to nullify differences in reward.

This objection would have had more force, some years ago, than at present when governments are beginning to act on the assumption that the opportunity to be productive includes such food, clothes, shelter, and even amusement, as are necessary to maintain physical and mental health and efficiency. We are continually enlarging our conception of what is necessary to an efficient life, at the same time that we have come to emphasize more and more the effect of environment in determining the character and powers of men. It is easy to carry this latter principle to unwholesome extremes; indeed one of the gravest questions now confronting us is how to draw the line between the use and abuse of this most potent charge of intellectual dynamite. At any rate, it is conceivable that in a world wholly committed to the philosophy of determinism, "Equality of opportunity" might come to mean nothing short of equal environments for all. As this is impossible so long as homes and family life survive, it is little more than a bogey to conjure with. We are concerned here only with a tendency of thought which is having a very definite effect on men's attitude toward the present distribution of incomes.

Enough instances could be easily cited to show the all-pervading economic influence of standards of value contrary to those of the free market. Now unless economics can take and use such standards in advance of their becoming effective in the market place, it misses by so much its chances to contribute scientifically to economic reform. As a matter of fact, economists do use these standards constantly in their practical thinking on matters of public policy. Every time an economist supports an ordinance limiting the height of buildings or a bill for industrial insurance he is applying the theory of unpaid costs. When he votes for subsidizing a pioneer railroad he is paying for inappropriable services. When he urges a minimum wage law he is recording a social estimate of the value of a certain standard of living for the poor; an estimate different from that which the forces of free exchange could make effective. Every measure of economic reform on which he expresses an opinion represents an estimate of a social value of one sort or another, different from that of the market. And every debate with opponents of the present order, and every passage in a text book which discusses the justification of private property,[7] assumes standards of judgment, vague or inexact perhaps, yet standards of a truly economic sort, by which the valuations of the market, as products of the present order, are to be criticized and upheld or condemned.

But of all this working philosophy, scarcely a breath penetrates to the rarified atmosphere of technical discussions of the theory of value and distribution. Here the economist holds aloof from the implications of his own thought and actions. He either accepts the market value of a product as measuring the social value produced, or he gives up the idea of social value and treats prices and products as purely individualistic things, measuring comparative and not absolute utilities. On this latter basis we may conclude that unless the utility of a pair of shoes to any individual is greater than any other utility which he must sacrifice to get the shoes, he will not buy them. And by carrying the argument a trifle farther we may gain, as a basis for judging the worth of our institutions, the doctrine that they afford John Doe an opportunity to do as well by himself as he is, under those institutions, able to do.

He does this by rendering other people services whose utility to them is at least as great as the estimated utility to them of anything they were willing to go without in order to buy John Doe's services. Either party to an exchange may be in an economy of keen pleasure or in a "pain economy" of the most hopeless sort. If, under institutions less humane than ours, a man were to sell himself into slavery, through pressure of sheer present starvation, such a theory might comment that even in his case gain was in excess of cost, since the utility of food to a starving man is infinite! Or if a laborer is forced to enter a health-destroying trade to keep his family out of the poorhouse, why, the keeping of one's family out of the poorhouse has extremely high utility, and the balance of marginal utilities and marginal costs remains intact. If these be the limits of economic science, then it simply does not lay hold on the deepest economic issues of our time. Economists may deal with these issues in a practical way, but the theory of value and distribution will remain insulated.

However, if we can develop a concept of economic value and valuation with reference to society as a whole, independent of market valuations and capable of scientific application to concrete cases, we shall have an intellectual instrument that will pierce the insulation and establish a connection with the ideas that are making things happen.

It is a substantial gain to regard a price as the resultant of conflicts of many kinds of values, positive and negative, individual and social.[8] But if economics merely accepts and records the outcome as representing the effective social importance of that particular commodity, there is still something lacking. Many a commodity commands a price merely because its negative social value is less than the costs involved in suppressing its use utterly.

Whiskey has at once positive and negative social value and motivates prohibitionists to much expenditure of time, effort and money. Yet this negative "power in motivation" has no effect on the price until it actually prevails in a prohibition law. And then—the price goes higher and not lower,[9] and the outlawed trade becomes more profitable financially than ever before.

The idea of a strong positive value to a minority, in marginal equilibrium with a weak negative value to a majority,[10] does not seem adequately to represent the case. Certainly the price does not express any such equilibrium, but only one side of it. Exchange value will remain positive till the negative social value accumulates such overwhelming momentum as to stamp out the trade entirely. What balances the majority's disapproval is not the desire of the minority, but the whole cost of making the majority will effective. There is no marginal equality of effort between policemen and the customers of an illicit drinking-place. Moreover other values than that of temperance itself may be affected in the attempt to stamp out illicit sales.

The positive value of freedom may deter us from prohibiting the sale of many quack remedies, or outlawing many questionable business practices, which predominant social judgment and sentiment oppose.[11] Or if society were willing to make a sacrifice of freedom in one case, the question of consistency might arise. The negative value of class-legislation has prevented many weaker values from reaching effective expression. The social value of the constitution, or rather, of the traditional interpretation of the bill of rights, has played a decisive part in determining many market prices. Here we have what may be called organic social values playing a part in the field of commerce.

Such values are, of course, all-pervading. Let us take again the case of the distribution of public lands to homesteaders. The value of the land to individuals is one thing, and that of itself has a value to society in that it has weight in determining social choices. But the value to society of a general condition of widely distributed landholding is more than the direct utility which the individuals buy with their quarter-sections, and more than the increase in the values of other property which result from the pioneer settlements. It comes to the settlers, but it benefits others as well, in many intangible ways which lead us to speak of it as an organic social value. (Always remembering that there is no such thing apart from the individuals of which society is composed.)

When men strive for mere superiority over one another, the net sum of all their strivings may be nil, if we look merely at the individual gains and losses in the prestige for which they are contending. Is there no social value here at all? Yes, there is, but it is not the kind of value which individuals are so busy pursuing. It is rather the general social value that goes with free opportunity to pursue one's desires and impulses and to be responsible for one's destiny. These have very high social value, although other competing values have for some time been gaining as the cult of individualism has weakened. In the eye of society, the absurdities of fashion and the rivalries of hostesses are not so much value in themselves as almost negligible by-products of freedom, which is itself so valuable that it is hardly worth asking whether these particular results are plus or minus.

Again, inheritance is maintained for many reasons, first among which comes the fact that property owners and potential property owners want it. This includes the man who regards an income of a quarter of a million as genteel poverty, although as this class provokes most of the hostility that is felt nowadays toward inheritance, we can hardly say that their enjoyment of their ancestral fortunes is a net addition to the social value of the institution. More important are the mass of smaller property owners and potential property owners who also want to be able to hand on their property to their families. The institution is also upheld as a stimulus to the saving of capital, but most of all perhaps it is borne along by the inertia of immemorial custom.

All of these facts represent, and very properly, strong social values, but not the same social value as that of the millionaire's enjoyment of his fifth country estate, which may be a positive source of weakness. And for that very reason it is entirely out of place to assume that everything which heirs buy with their money has social value proportionate to the price paid. Any system of private inheritance means a certain sacrifice of the ideal of equal opportunity, and this sacrifice is a social cost. If some heirs are vicious spendthrifts, the damage they do is a further cost incurred in attaining a definite social end.

What is the conclusion to which these somewhat obvious illustrations point? Simply this: that if we consider the social value of everything to be represented by its normal exchange value or price, we are really ascribing to a commodity as that commodity's social value the whole resultant of those broader forces and values to which it may stand in the relationship of an insignificant or unwelcome by-product, or even in that of a cost of production.[12] It is the freedom which has social value and not the nostrums or the products of sharp practices which may shelter under its wing. Freedom may be an end in itself like any other utility which affects economic values, and it may also take effect in increasing the output of goods in general. Neither fact can elevate its incidental abuses, recognized as such, to the rank of social utilities or values. The net social value of the latter is negative, not positive,[13] and men in touch with live issues will not long be satisfied with any theory bearing the name of social value which does not embody this principle so unmistakably that he who runs may read.

It is so simple! The marvel is that such an obvious statement of fact could be considered to constitute an economic heresy in any school of thought. The distinction may make little difference in static theory, which ignores institutional changes and rules out as dynamic or abnormal most of the sources of abuse, though it would at least reveal some very significant and unexpected assumptions which have lain implicit in the static hypothesis. But into the dynamic study of the actual world the static hypothesis must not be carried. Here abuses are normal and institutions are active forces campaigning against them, with constant changes of plan and shifts of fortune. Wasteful advertising is waste, not social product, though we may not know how to get rid of it without sacrificing more than we should gain. The wasteful consumption of inherited wealth is a social cost incurred in producing whatever values are attached to the institution of inheritance. If static doctrine is to be adapted to deal with dynamic facts, it is at this point, in the concept of value itself, that the modification must begin.

One further result may be noted. If things may have exchange value when their social value is a minus quantity, how shall we say of things which have positive social value that the exchange value, actual or normal, gives a correct measure of their relative social importance? The simplest exchange is not free from these complex relationships which we have been discussing. Each one is a unit in a great social joint product. Thus the theory of social value is anti-marginal in the sense that the part—say the single commodity—takes its price from the value of the whole rather than the whole getting its price from the utility of the marginal part. In a similar way railway rates cannot be fixed by the marginal cost of separate services without running the whole road into bankruptcy.

These, then, are some of the elements which must count in a theory of social value. The theory of inappropriables, the conscious social weighting of men and their desires on different scales from that of free exchange, the insistence that institutional valuations and commodity valuations be distinguished and not both attributed to single commodities, and the readiness on occasion to reverse the marginal method of analysis; all have their place in the interpretation. Such studies can be vitally useful, even if they never reach the exactness of a yardstick.

Indeed, some will probably say that this discussion has been carried into fields which lie outside the realm of economics altogether. If this criticism rests on an unshakable conviction that economics is limited to the subject of exchange values, there is little more to be said, save that exchange value described in terms of itself is meaningless. Our traditional description runs in terms of psychological premises, and therefore goes beyond the boundaries of the world of exchange values; but no one has objected on the score of transgressing the bounds of economics. One might explain this on the ground that this school of economics did not go far into psychology—not far enough, in fact, to secure an adequate and sound equipment of psychological assumptions. But was that a virtue? This paper aims to study, not exchange values in a vacuum, but their relation to human motives and desires, and the reader may judge if the purpose has been maintained. In the course of the study, enough has been said to show many matters truly economic which cannot be contained in the pigeon-hole of exchange value. It is highly probable that the study of economics would still have a separate existence even in a socialistic state.

What, then, are the proper boundaries of economic science? Unless they have been finally and authoritatively established in some writing which has escaped my notice, I feel free to contend that it is less important to keep inside any traditional limits than to follow our natural questionings wherever they may lead, and to whatever work we are specially fitted for and find undone.

In doing this we should accept the authoritative results of other specialists in the field of psychology, sociology and ethics. We should certainly not ignore their work where it touches our problems, and the last thing we should do is to set up premises of our own in these matters which are at war with the generally accepted conclusions of those best fitted to know. It would be a strangely futile state of things in which the proper premises of two sciences should contradict each other, and a still more futile state in which economists might not either justify or criticize the economic system without being accused of going outside the field about which they are supposed to know.

Economics can certainly not follow a policy of Jeffersonian nonintercourse toward other fields of knowledge. The ultimate problems in which humanity is interested are not those of social value in the sense of "value in society" as registered by market standards. Men are interested in the values of things to society, and they rightly demand that economics should contribute to the solution of these problems. Our studies of exchange values are destined to be judged by this broader criterion, and we might as well prepare them with this in mind. To do this it is not enough to study the causes of exchange values, seeing personal utilities as the results of social suggestion and market values as conditioned by social habits and laws. We must study results as well as causes if we are to find what function values perform in the life of society, for this function does not stop with the fixing of a market price. Moreover we cannot be satisfied to take institutions for granted as if they were complete ends in themselves independent of the transactions of the market in which they take effect. If we cannot understand the social value of goods sold under a franchise without reference to the Dartmouth College Case, neither can we understand the social value of the Bill of Rights without reference to its effect on two-cent fare laws. A legal economic institution existing somewhere without reference to individual economic acts is something disembodied, unthinkable.

This view of institutions as independent and inscrutable entities may spring from overworking of the analogy between social organization and biological organisms, under which human institutions are regarded as the outgrowth of quasi-biological laws, inscrutable to the economist and independent of the desires that clash in the market. To use this premise is to enter the realm of sociology, only the doctrine selected happens to be discredited among sociologists.

So far as laws are the embodiment of custom we need only ask "How did the custom grow?" Out of separate acts, mostly acts of free choice, gradually hardening into a habit, and becoming recognized by law. The habit is the decisive thing, for without it the law quickly becomes a dead letter. This means that an institution, to continue, must rest on masses of individual acts and choices. It is not independent of them. Such habits represent the fact that the cost, effort and risk of deciding each choice on its separate merits is too great for humanity to bear. These habits may start as mere calf-paths of the social mind, and may later become ludicrously or dangerously wasteful. But we cannot discover that fact if we take the calf-path for granted, or study it merely as an example of the social value of a line of least resistance to each successive traveller. We must study it in the light of economy of effort for all the traffic of the city street which may, if the city be Boston and the legends be true, have been built on the track of the calf's meanderings.

Or, to use another figure, if we explain why it does not pay a locomotive engineer to run his engine off the rails in the search for a more economical route, that is good so far as it goes, but it is hardly more than the beginning of wisdom in railroad economics. While the engineer is running on the old route, the managers are studying whether the saving from a tunnel or a cut-off will apply to a large enough volume of traffic to be worth its cost to the road. There are few calf-paths on the route of a well managed railway. The greatest use of the data of social science should be in eliminating the calf-paths of social habits, by methods as like those used in calculating the best route for a railway as the more elusive nature of the probem will permit.

The outcome of this process will be laws: laws which, instead of embodying past customs seek to modify them and improve on them. Such laws are conscious means to calculated ends and their value lies wholly in their expected results. We have, then, considered two kinds of legal values, those which embody custom and those which do not, and we find that neither can be understood apart from the multitude of concrete cases on which they take effect.

When the study of economics brings us face to face with these broader values of institutions, one simple inquiry can always be made. We want to know, first and foremost, what society is giving in exchange for what it gets; what price is paid for the fulfillment of any one of its impulses, whether this be the impulse to personal display, the impulse to law and order, or any other.

This inquiry is in itself a mere question of fact with no doctrines of social ethics attached to it, but it cannot fail to have an effect on social policies and judgments. Teach a man the psychological facts of impulsive or ideo-motor action and he is never again quite so completely at the mercy of a chance stimulus. Teach a state that its citizens have a persistent myopia which warps them regularly in a given direction and brings disaster on many, as when workmen underestimate industrial risks—teach a state this, and it sets to work studying antidotes or remedies. And if the state itself, *via* its representative organs or its citizens acting collectively, have any such myopias, the first thing is to exhibit them for what they are.

Peoples do have such myopias, beyond a doubt. Their valuations are not wholly rational, are not always justified by their results, and show distinct leanings now in one direction and now in another.

The epithets "conservative," "radical" and "progressive" apply to whole states and whole areas as well as to individuals, and states change their mood somewhat in these respects from time to time, a state may be so hidebound that it seems to set almost infinite value on traditional institutions as such, although the phrase "setting a value" implies too much of rational choice to be fittingly applied to the mere social "moment of inertia" which is at work in such cases. When a society awakes to the fact that it is setting a value on customary behavior as such, over against the healing of abuses, it is already on the way out of the rut. Where the old has a semisacred value for its own sake, consciously or unconsciously, enormous evils may persist untouched.

Is there then no more rational standard than a conflict of forces between temperamental or professional radicals and temperamental or professional conservatives? It may be admitted that there is not, so long as men regard laws and institutions, oldness or newness, as ends in themselves, but as soon as men begin regarding anything as a means to an end, so soon they begin to weigh it more or less rationally against other means; and social institutions are no exception. Even the courts never actually reach the point of regarding the law and the constitution wholly as ends in themselves: indeed they are much freer than many people imagine to decide, for example, the constitutionality of labor laws, according to their judgment of what is demanded by the good society or the settled conviction of the people. And even the politician who advocates the laws merely to solidify his party, must present them to the voters as tools of social welfare.

The modern tendency is increasingly to view institutions as means to definite ends, and nothing can further this tendency more than a study of the particular economic gains and costs to society for which such institutions are responsible. This study the economist would seem to be specially qualified to make.

The whole problem of value to society is of course more than economic, and yet it seems to be one problem and not many separate ones.[14] While its economic aspect is far from exhausted, the chief thing to be striven for is that this central problem shall have all the light that can be thrown on it from all angles, and that problems of exchange should be treated with this aim constantly in mind.

NOTES

1. Cf. J. B. Clark, *Philosophy of Wealth,* p. 215 ff.

2. Cf. Ely, *Property and Contract,* passim.

3. Cf. *Philosophy of Wealth, op. cit.*

4. This sentence was inserted in final revision, 1936. Cf. *Social Control of Business* (1926), pp. 109-110.

5. These two classes of value cannot, of course, be treated as if wholly separate from each other. The "good of the greatest number" is of great importance to society as a whole.

6. J. B. Clark's concept of "social effective utility" clearly has this latter meaning combined with expressions pointing less certainly toward the former. *Distribution of Wealth,* Chap. XVI.

7. Cf. also the distinction made by Hadley between the social product of capital, which is held to explain the maintenance of the system of interest, and the private earning-power which is one of the forces determining the interest *rate.* This passage is so brief as to be sometimes misconstrued, and may perhaps be criticized as somewhat overemphasizing the element of rational calculation in a matter like the maintaining of a long standing custom, and also for omitting to develop the very real connection between increase of private earnings and increase of public wealth. A. T. Hadley, *Economics,* p. 268-269.

8. Cf. B. M. Anderson, *Social Value,* Chap. XIII. "Social value" can evidently mean more than one thing. Personal utilities and exchange values are of course social in the sense that they exist in society and result from the play of social forces.

9. Certainly if quality is considered!

10. Cf. *Social Value,* p. 151.

11. In all this my view is quite like Professor Anderson's, and I gladly acknowledge indebtedness to his writings. It is hardly necessary to add that my greater indebtedness is to our common source, the *Philosophy of Wealth.*

12. May not this be a necessary condition of a really vital connection between economics and sociology?

13. This conception is ethically neutral, accepting whatever standards are in force, and merely insists on distinguishing clearly (as the other concept does not do) to *what it is that the accepted standards are attached.*

14. Cf. Cooley, *Amer. Jour. of Sociology,* 19:192.

The Social Contract

Jean Jacques Rousseau

Man is born free; and everywhere he is in chains

The familiar opening line of Rousseau's *The Social Contract* expresses the dilemma he addressed. How can men remain free, while subject to the bondage of a necessary society? The answer lies in the concept of the social contract; an obedience to the General Will which the individual freely accepts for himself. Thus, liberty and obligation may coexist.

Why include the thoughts of an eighteenth century French philosopher in a twentieth century accounting book? Rousseau suggests direction for modern social accountants in a number of ways. First, the concept of the social contract itself suggests the imperative that social accountants must base their notions of social profit or loss on a societal concensus of what is or is not desirable.

If one is to attempt to ascertain a modern liberal democratic concept of social profit, what better source than one of the most influential writers at the time of the drafting of the American Constitution.

The Social Contract was first published in 1762. It exerted a profound influence on the founders of the new American Republic. A comparison of the writings of the advocates of the Constitution (for example, *Federalist* No. 10) and the separation of powers doctrine underlying that document, with the concepts in these selections show the deep relationship.

Rousseau also has a modern message. His notions of property, justice and the role of any political association, ". . . The preservation and prosperity of its members" suggest subtle arguments both for and against modern concepts of income redistribution. He appears to have predicted the problems of the increasing complexity of modern governments.

As with any powerful philosopher, there is danger in reading literally and extrapolating to modern circumstances. Rousseau was, at one time, even embraced by the Jacobins and Robespierre with whom, one assumes, he would have had little sympathy. Even today, one might contend that his renewal of the classic Platonic insistence that the community is the supreme teacher of morality would fit neatly with the doctrines of Mao Tse Tung and the Red Guards. Nevertheless, reasonably interpreted, his message is clearly relevant to a modern definition of social income.

CHAPTER VI: THE SOCIAL COMPACT

I suppose men to have reached the point at which the obstacles in the way of their preservation in the state of nature show their power of resistance to be greater than the resources at the disposal of each individual for his maintenance in that state. That primitive condition can then subsist no longer; and the human race would perish unless it changed its manner of existence.

But, as men cannot engender new forces, but only unite and direct existing ones, they have no other means of preserving themselves than the formation, by aggregation, of a sum of forces great enough to overcome the resistance. These

SOURCE: From *The Social Contract*, Jean Jacques Rousseau, 1762.

they have to bring into play by means of a single motive power, and cause to act in concert.

This sum of forces can arise only where several persons come together: but, as the force and liberty of each man are the chief instruments of his self-preservation, how can he pledge them without harming his own interests, and neglecting the care he owes to himself? This difficulty, in its bearing on my present subject, may be stated in the following terms—

"The problem is to find a form of association which will defend and protect with the whole common force the person and goods of each associate, and in which each, while uniting himself with all, may still obey himself alone, and remain as free as before." This is the fundamental problem of which the *Social Contract* provides the solution.

The clauses of this contract are so determined by the nature of the act that the slightest modification would make them vain and ineffective; so that, although they have perhaps never been formally set forth, they are everywhere the same and everywhere tacitly admitted and recognized, until, on the violation of the social compact, each regains his original rights and resumes his natural liberty, while losing the conventional liberty in favor of which he renounced it.

These clauses, properly understood, may be reduced to one—the total alienation of each associate, together with all his rights, to the whole community; for, in the first place, as each gives himself absolutely, the conditions are the same for all; and, this being so, no one has any interest in making them burdensome to others.

Moreover, the alienation being without reserve, the union is as perfect as it can be, and no associate has anything more to demand; for, if the individuals retained certain rights, as there would be no common superior to decide between them and the public, each, being on one point his own judge, would ask to be so on all; the state of nature would thus continue, and the association would necessarily become inoperative or tyrannical.

Finally, each man, in giving himself to all, gives himself to nobody; and as there is no associate over whom he does not acquire the same right as he yields others over himself, he gains an equivalent for everything he loses, and an increase of force for the preservation of what he has.

If then we discard from the social compact what is not of its essence, we shall find that it reduces itself to the following terms—

"Each of us puts his person and all his power in common under the supreme direction of the general will, and, in our corporate capacity, we receive each member as an indivisible part of the whole."

At once, in place of the individual personality of each contracting party, this act of association creates a moral and collective body, composed of as many members as the assembly contains votes, and receiving from this act its unity, its common identity, its life and its will. This public person, so formed by the union of all other persons formerly took the name of *city*,[1] and now takes that of *Republic* or *body politic;* it is called by its members *State* when passive, *Sovereign* when active, and *Power* when compared with others like itself. Those who are associated in it take collectively the name of *people,* and severally are called *citizens,* as sharing in the sovereign power, and *subjects,* as being under the laws of the State. But these terms are often confused and taken one for another: it is enough to know how to distinguish them when they are being used with precision.

Chapter VII: The Sovereign

This formula shows us that the act of association comprises a mutual undertaking between the public and the individuals, and that each individual, in making a contract, as we may say, with himself, is bound in a double capacity; as a member of the Sovereign he is bound to the individuals, and as a member of the State to the Sovereign. But the maxim of civil right, that no one is bound by undertakings made to himself, does not apply in this case; for there is a great difference between incurring an obligation to yourself and incurring one to a whole of which you form a part.

In fact, each individual, as a man, may have a particular will contrary or dissimilar to the general will which he has as a citizen. His particular interest may speak to him quite differently from the common interest: his absolute and naturally independent existence may make him look upon what he owes to the common cause as a gratuitous contribution, the loss of which will do less harm to others than the payment of it is burdensome to himself; and regarding the moral person which constitutes the State as a *persona ficta,* because not a man, he may wish to enjoy the rights of citizenship without being ready to fulfill the duties of a subject. The continuance of such an injustice could not but prove the undoing of the body politic.

In order then that the social compact may not be an empty formula, it tacitly includes the undertaking, which alone can give force to the rest, that whoever refuses to obey the general will shall be compelled to do so by the whole body. This means nothing less than that he will be forced to be free; for this is the condition which, by giving each citizen to his country, secures him against all personal dependence. In this lies the key to the working of the political machine; this alone legitimizes civil undertakings, which, without it, would be absurd, tyrannical, and liable to the most frightful abuses.

Chapter VIII: The Civil State

The passage from the state of nature to the civil state produces a very remarkable change in man, by substituting justice for instinct in his conduct, and giving his actions the morality they formerly lacked. Then only, when the voice of duty takes the place of physical impulses and right of appetite, does man, who so far had considered only himself, find that he is forced to act on different principles, and to consult his reason before listening to his inclinations. Although, in this state, he deprives himself of some advantages which he got from nature, he gains in return others so great, his faculties are so stimulated and developed, his ideas so extended, his feelings so ennobled, and his whole soul so uplifted, that, did not the abuses of this new condition often degrade him below that which he left, he would be bound to bless continually the happy moment which took him from it forever, and, instead of a stupid and unimaginative animal, made him an intelligent being and a man.

Let us draw up the whole account in terms easily commensurable. What man loses by the social contract is his natural liberty and an unlimited right to everything he tries to get and succeeds in getting; what he gains is civil liberty and the proprietorship of all he possesses. If we are to avoid mistake in weighing one against the other, we must clearly distinguish natural liberty, which is bounded only by the strength of the individual, from civil liberty, which is limited by the general will; and possession, which is merely the effect of force or the right of the first occupier, from property, which can be founded only on a positive title.

We might, over and above all this, add, to what man acquires in the civil state, moral liberty, which alone makes him truly master of himself; for the mere impulse of appetite is slavery, while obedience to a law which we prescribe to ourselves is liberty. But I have already said too much on this head, and the philosophical meaning of the word liberty does not now concern us.

. . . I shall end . . . this book by remarking on a fact on which the whole social system should rest: *i.e.* that, instead of destroying natural inequality, the fundamental compact substitutes, for such physical inequality as nature may have set up between men and equality that is moral and legitimate, and that men, who may be unequal in strength or intelligence, become every one equal by convention and legal right.

BOOK II

Chapter IV: The Limits of the Sovereign Power

If the state is a moral person whose life is in the union of its members, and if the most important of its cares is the care for its own preservation, it must have a universal and compelling force, in order to move and dispose each part as may be most advantageous to the whole. As nature gives each man absolute power over all his members, the social compact gives the body politic absolute power over all its members also; and it is this power which, under the direction of the general will, bears, as I have said, the name of Sovereignty.

But, besides the public person, we have to consider the private persons composing it, whose life and liberty are naturally independent of it. We are bound then to distinguish clearly between the respective rights of the citizens and the Sovereign, and between the duties the former have to fulfill as subjects, and the natural rights they should enjoy as men.

Each man alienates, I admit, by the social compact, only such part of his powers, goods and liberty as it is important for the community to control; but it must also be granted that the Sovereign is sole judge of what is important.

Every service a citizen can render the State he ought to render as soon as the Sovereign demands it; but the Sovereign, for its part, cannot impose upon its subjects any fetters that are useless to the community, nor can it even wish to do so; for no more by the law of reason than by the law of nature can anything occur without a cause.

We can see from this that the sovereign power, absolute, sacred and inviolable as it is, does not and cannot exceed the limits of general conventions, and that every man may dispose at will of such goods and liberty as these conventions leave him; so that the Sovereign never has a right to lay more charges on one subject than on another, because, in that case, the question becomes particular, and ceases to be within its competency.

When these distinctions have once been admitted, is is seen to be so untrue that there is, in the social contract, any real renunciation on the part of the individuals, that the position in which they find themselves as a result of the contract is really preferable to that in which they were before. Instead of a renunciation, they have made an advantageous exchange: instead of an uncertain and precarious way of living they have got one that is better and more secure; instead of natural independence they have got liberty, instead of the power to harm others security for themselves, and instead of their strength, which others might overcome, a right which social union makes invincible. Their very life, which they have devoted to the State, is by it constantly protected; and when they risk it in the State's defense, what more are they doing than giving back what they have received from it? What are they doing that they would not do more often and with greater danger in the state of nature, in which they would inevitably have to fight battles at the peril of their lives in defense of that which is the means of their preservation? All have indeed to fight when their country needs them; but then no one has ever to fight for himself. Do we not gain something by running, on behalf of what gives us our security, only some of the risks we should have to run for ourselves, as soon as we lost it?

Chapter XI: The Various Systems of Legislation

If we ask in what precisely consists the greatest good of all, which should be the end of every system of legislation, we shall find it reduces itself to two main objects, liberty and equality—liberty, because all particular dependence means so much force taken from the body of the State, and equality, because liberty cannot exist without it.

I have already defined civil liberty; by equality, we should understand, not that the degrees of power and riches are to be absolutely identical for everybody; but that power shall never be great enough for violence, and shall always be exercised by virtue of rank and law; and that, in respect of riches, no citizen shall ever be wealthy enough to buy another, and none poor enough to be forced to sell himself: which implies, on the part of the great, moderation in goods and position, and, on the side of the common sort, moderation in avarice and covetousness.

Such equality, we are told, is an unpractical ideal that cannot actually exist. But if its abuse is inevitable, does it follow that we should not at least make regulations concerning it? It is precisely because the force of circumstances tends continually to destroy equality that the force of legislation should always tend to its maintenance.

But these general objects of every good legislative system need modifying in every country in accordance with the local situation and the temper of the inhabitants; and these circumstances should determine, in each case, the particular system of institutions which is best, not perhaps in itself, but for the State for which it is destined.

BOOK III

Chapter IX: The Marks of a Good Government

The question "What absolutely is the best government?" is unanswerable as well as indeterminate; or rather, there are as many good answers as there are possible combinations in the absolute and relative situations of all nations.

But if it is asked by what sign we may know that a given people is well or ill governed, that is another matter, and the question, being one of fact, admits of an answer.

It is not, however, answered, because everyone wants to answer it in his own way. Subjects extol public tranquility, citizens individual liberty; the one class prefers security of possessions, the other that of person; the one regards as the best government that which is most severe, the other maintains that the mildest is the best; the one wants crimes punished; the other wants them prevented; the one wants the State to be feared by its neighbors, the other prefers that it should be ignored; the one is content if money circulates, the other demands that the people shall have bread. Even if an agreement were come to on these and similar points, should we have got any further? As moral qualities do not admit of exact measurement, agreement about the mark does not mean agreement about the valuation.

For my part, I am continually astonished that a mark so simple is not recognized, or that men are of so bad faith as not to admit it. What is the end of political association? The preservation and prosperity of its members. And what is the surest mark of their preservation and prosperity? Their numbers and population. Seek then nowhere else this mark that is in dispute. The rest being equal, the government under which, without external aids, without naturalization or colonies, the citizens increase and multiply most, is beyond question the best. The government under which a people wanes and diminishes is the worst. Calculators, it is left for you to count, to measure, to compare . . .

NOTES

1.   The real meaning of this word has been almost wholly lost in modern times; most people mistake a town for a city, and a townsman for a citizen. They do not know that houses make a town, but citizens a city . . . .

How Much Public Support to Private Business?

Loan Association V. Topeka (1874)

This frequently cited case involved the issuance of bonds, by a city government. The proceeds of the bonds were to be used by a private manufacturing company to help open a factory in that city. A local savings and loan association brought suit to prevent the city from making payments on the bonds.

In its opinion, the court considered a number of points which have a basic relevance to social accounting. What is the linkage between government spending for a given purpose and the manner in which it raises the funds? What are the limitations on the power of government, on the powers of the various branches of the government, and on the power of taxation? Finally, the case emphasizes the requirement that government funds be spent only for a public object, not for the aid of individuals or for strictly private enterprises.

Note that the criteria specified in the case permit the issuance of the currently popular industrial revenue bonds, so long as the payments on the bonds are not taken from general revenues.

This case has never been overturned. It is interesting to consider the recent legislation authorizing $250 million of federal loan guarantees to the Lockheed Aircraft Corporation in the light of this decision.

OPINION OF THE COURT

Mr. Justice MILLER delivered the opinion of the court. Two grounds are taken that the section of the statute on which the main reliance is placed to issue the bonds, is unconstitutional.

The first of these is, that by the constitution of that State it is declared that provision shall be made by general law for the organization of cities, towns, and villages; and their power of taxation, assessment, borrowing money, contracting debts, and loaning their credit, shall be so restricted as to prevent the abuse of such power.

The argument is that the statute in question is void because it authorizes cities and towns to contract debts, and does not contain any restriction on the power so conferred.

That proposition is that the act authorizes the towns and other municipalities to which it applies, by issuing bonds or loaning their credit, to take the property of the citizen under the guise of taxation to pay these bonds, and use it in aid of

---

SOURCE: *Loan Association* v. *Topeka,* 20 Wall, 655 (1874).

the enterprises of others which are not of a public character, thus perverting the right of taxation, which can only be exercised for a public use, to the aid of individual interests and personal purposes of profit and gain.

The proposition as thus broadly stated is not new, nor is the question which it raises difficult of solution.

If these municipal corporations, which are in fact subdivisions of the State, and which for many reasons are vested with quasi legislative powers, have a fund or other property out of which they can pay the debts which they contract, without resort to taxation, it may be within the power of the legislature of the State to authorize them to use it in aid of projects strictly private or personal, but would in a secondary manner contribute the public good; or where there is property or money vested in a corporation of the kind for a particular use, as public worship or charity, the legislature may pass laws authorizing them to make contracts in reference to this property, and incur debts payable from that source.

But such instances are few and exceptional, and the proposition is a very broad one, that debts contracted by municipal corporations must be paid, if paid at all, out of taxes which they may lawfully levy, and that all contracts creating debts to be paid in future, not limited to payment from some other source, imply an obligation to pay by taxation.

It follows that in this class of cases the right to contract must be limited by the right to tax, and if in the given case no tax can lawfully be levied to pay the debt, the contract itself is void for want of authority to make it.

If this were not so, these corporations could make valid promises, which they have no means of fulfilling, and on which even the legislature that created them can confer no such power. The validity of a contract which can only be fulfilled by a resort to taxation, depends on the power to levy the tax for that purpose.

It is, therefore, to be inferred that when the legislature of the State authorizes a county or city to contract a debt by bond, it intends to authorize it to levy such taxes as are necessary to pay the debt, unless there is in the act itself, or in some general statute, a limitation upon the power of taxation which repels such an inference.

With these remarks and with the reference to the authorities which support them, we assume that unless the legislature of Kansas had the right to authorize the counties and towns in that State to levy taxes to be used in aid of manufacturing enterprises, conducted by individuals, or private corporations, for purposes of gain, the law is void, and the bonds issued under it are also void. We proceed to the inquiry whether such a power exists in the legislature of the State of Kansas.

We have already said the question is not new. The subject of the aid voted to railroads by counties and towns has been brought to the attention of the courts of almost every State in the Union.

In all these cases; however, the decision has turned upon the question whether the taxation by which this aid was afforded to the building of railroads was for a public purpose. Those who came to the conclusion that it was, held the laws for that purpose valid. Those who could not reach that conclusion held them void. In all the controversy this has been the turning-point of the judgments of the courts. And it is safe to say that no court has held debts created in aid of railroad companies, by counties or towns, valid on any other ground than that the purpose for which the taxes were levied was a public use, a purpose or object which it was the right and the duty of State governments to assist by money raised from the people by taxation. The argument in opposition to this power has been, that railroads built by corporations organized mainly for purposes of gain—the roads which they built being under their control, and not that of the State—were private and not public roads, and the tax assessed on the people went to swell the profits of individuals and not to the good of State, or the benefit of the public, except in a remote and collateral way. On the other hand it was said that roads, canals, bridges, navigable streams, and all other highways had in all times been matter of public concern. That such channels of travel and of the carrying business had always been established, improved, regulated by the State, and that the railroad had not lost this character because constructed by individual enterprise, aggregated into a corporation.

We have referred to this history of the contest over aid to railroads by taxation, to show that the strongest advocates for the validity of these laws never placed it on the ground of the unlimited power in the State legislature to tax the people, but conceded that where the purpose for which the tax was to be issued could no longer be justly claimed to have this public character, but was purely in aid of private or personal objects, the law authorizing it was beyond the legislative power, and was an unauthorized invasion of private right.

It must be conceded that there are such rights in every free government beyond the control of the State. A government which recognized no such rights, which held the lives, the liberty, and the property of its citizens subject at all times to the absolute disposition and unlimited control of even the most democratic depository of power, is after all but a despotism. It is true it is a despotism of the many, of the majority, if you choose to call it so, but it is none the less a despotism. It may well be doubted if a man is to hold all that he is accustomed to call his own, all in which he has placed his happiness, and the security of which is essential to that happiness, under the unlimited dominion of others, whether it is not wiser that this power should be exercised by one man than by many.

The theory of our governments, State and National, is opposed to the deposit of unlimited power anywhere. The executive, the legislative, and the judicial branches of these governments are all of limited and defined powers.

There are limitations on such power which grow out of essential nature of all free governments. Implied reservations of individual rights, without which the social compact could not exist, and which are respected by all governments entitled to the name. No court, for instance, would hesitate to declare void a statute which enacted that A. and B. who were husband and wife to each other should be so no longer, but that A. should thereafter be the husband of C., and B. the wife of D. Or which should enact that the homestead now owned by A. should no longer be his, but should henceforth be the property of B.

Of all the powers conferred upon government that of taxation is most liable to abuse. Given a purpose or object for which taxation may be lawfully used and the extent of its exercise is in its very nature unlimited. It is true that express limitation on the amount of tax to be levied or the things to be taxed may be imposed by constitution or statute, but in most instances for which taxes are levied, as the support of government, the prosecution of war, the National defense, any limitation is unsafe. The entire resources of the people should in some instances be at the disposal of the government.

The power to tax is, therefore, the strongest, the most pervading of all the powers of government, reaching directly or indirectly to all classes of the people. It was said by Chief Justice Marshall, in the case of *McCulloch* v. *The State of Maryland** that the power to tax is the power to destroy. A striking instance of the truth of the proposition is seen in the fact that the existing tax of ten per cent imposed by the United States on the circulation of all other banks than the National banks, drove out of existence every State bank of circulation within a year or two after its passage. This power can as readily be employed against one class of individuals and in favor of another, so as to ruin the one class and give unlimited wealth and prosperity to the other, if there is no implied limitation of the uses for which the power may be exercised.

To lay with one hand the power of the government on the property of the citizen, and with the other to bestow it upon favored individuals to aid private enterprises and build up private fortunes, is none the less a robbery because it is done under the forms of law and is called taxation. This is not legislation. It is a decree under legislative forms.

Nor is it taxation. A "tax," says Webster's Dictionary, "is a rate or sum of money assessed on the person or property of a citizen by government for the use of the nation or state." "Taxes are burdens or charges imposed by the legislature upon persons or property to raise money for public purposes."†

We have established, we think, beyond cavil that there can be no lawful tax which is not laid for a *public purpose*. It may not be easy to draw the line in all cases so as to decide what is a public purpose in this sense and what is not.

It is undoubtedly the duty of the legislature which imposes or authorizes municipalities to impose a tax to see that it is not to be used for purposes of private interest instead of a public use, and the courts can only be justified in interposing when a violation of this principle is clear and the reason for interference cogent.

---

*Wheaton 431.
†Cooley on Constitutional Limitations, 479.

And in deciding whether, in the given case, the object for which the taxes are assessed falls upon the one side or the other of this line, they must be governed mainly by the course and usage of the government, the objects for which taxes have been customarily and by long course of legislation levied, what objects or purposes have been considered necessary to the support and for the proper use of the government, whether State or municipal. Whatever lawfully pertains to this and is sanctioned by time and the acquiescence of the people may well be held to belong to the public use, and proper for the maintenance of good government, though this may not be the only criterion of rightful taxation.

But in the case before us, in which the towns are authorized to contribute aid by way of taxation to any class of manufacturers, there is no difficulty in holding that this is not such a public purpose as we have been considering. If it be said that a benefit results to the local public of a town by establishing manufactures, the same may be said of any other business or pursuit which employs capital or labor. The merchant, the mechanic, the innkeeper, the banker, the builder, the steamboat owner are equally promoters of the public good, and equally deserving the aid of the citizens by forced contribution. No line can be drawn in favor of the manufacturer which would not open the coffers of the public treasury to the importunities of two-thirds of the business men of the city or town.

When is a Private Benefit a Public Benefit? The School Transportation Controversy

Everson V. Board of Education (1946)

The current crisis in the financing of private, usually religious affiliated, schools has intensified the debate over how much public assistance shall be given to non-public schools and their students. The issues were particularly well illuminated in this New Jersey case. It concerned a state scheme to reimburse the parents of children attending religious controlled schools for the students' transportation costs.

The opinion, written by Justice Hugo Black, one of the most rigorous defenders of individual rights ever to sit on the Supreme Court, is notable for its exploration of the church-state controversy in the United States and its history of the First Amendment. It is interesting to note that this 1946 court decision relied heavily on the writings of Jefferson and Madison, almost 300 years earlier.

In this abridged presentation of the majority opinion, a wealth of fascinating historical footnotes and other case precedents were necessarily omitted. The student or researcher interested in the subject should obtain the entire decision, along with the dissent by Justice Jackson.

Mr. Justice BLACK delivered the opinion of the Court. A New Jersey statute authorizes its local school districts to make rules and contracts for the transportation of children to and from schools. The appellee, a township board of education, acting pursuant to this statute, authorized reimbursement to parents of money expended by them for the bus transportation of their children on regular busses operated by the public transportation system. Part of this money was for the payment of transportation of some children in the community to Catholic parochial schools. These church schools give their students, in addition to secular education, regular religious instruction conforming to the religious tenets and modes of worship of the Catholic Faith. The superintendent of these schools is a Catholic priest.

The appellant, in his capacity as a district taxpayer, filed suit in a state court challenging the right of the Board to reimburse parents of parochial school students.

The only contention here is that the state statute and the resolution, insofar as they authorized reimbursement to parents of children attending parochial schools, violate the Federal Constitution in these two respects, which to some extent overlap. *First.* They authorize the State to take by taxation the private

SOURCE: *Everson* v. *Board of Education,* 330 U. S. 1 (1946).

property of some and bestow it upon others to be used for their own private purposes. This, it is alleged, violates the due process clause of the Fourteenth Amendment. Second. The statute and the resolution forced inhabitants to pay taxes to help support and maintain schools which are dedicated to, and which regularly teach, the Catholic Faith. This is alleged to be a use of state power to support church schools contrary to the prohibition of the First Amendment which the Fourteenth Amendment made applicable to the states.

First

The due process argument that the state law taxes some people to help others carry out their private purposes is framed in two phases. The first phase is that a state cannot tax A to reimburse B for the cost of transporting his children to church schools. This is said to violate the due process clause because the children are sent to these church schools to satisfy the personal desires of their parents, rather than the public's interest in the general education of all children. This argument, if valid, would apply equally to prohibit state payment for the transportation of children to any non-public school, whether operated by a church or any other non-government individual or group. But, the New Jersey legislature has decided that a public purpose will be served by using tax-raised funds to pay the bus fares of all school children, including those who attend parochial schools. The fact that a state law, passed to satisfy a public need, coincides with the personal desires of the individuals most directly affected is certainly an inadequate reason for us to say that a legislature has erroneously appraised the public need.

It is true that this Court has, in rare instances, struck down state statutes on the ground that the purpose for which tax-raised funds were to be expended was not a public one. *Loan Association v. Topeka,* 20 Wall. 655. But the Court has also pointed out that this far-reaching authority must be exercised with the most extreme caution. *Green v. Frazier,* 253 U. S. 233, 240. Otherwise, a state's power to legislate for the public welfare might be seriously curtailed, a power which is a primary reason for the existence of states. Changing local conditions create new local problems which may lead a state's people and its local authorities to believe that laws authorizing new types of public services are necessary to promote the general well-being of the people. The Fourteenth Amendment did not strip the states of their power to meet problems previously left for individual solution.

It is much too late to argue that legislation intended to facilitate the opportunity of children to get a secular education serves no public purpose. The same thing is no less true of legislation to reimburse needy parents, or all parents, for payment of the fares of their children so that they can ride in public buses to and from schools rather than run the risk of traffic and other hazards incident to walking or "hitchhiking." Nor does it follow that a law has a private rather than a public purpose because it provides that tax-raised funds will be paid to reimburse individuals on account of money spent by them in a way which furthers a public program. Subsidies and loans to individuals such as farmers and home-owners, and to privately owned transportation systems as well as many other kinds of businesses, have been commonplace practices in our state and national history.

Second

The New Jersey statute is challenged as a "law respecting an establishment of religion." The First Amendment, as made applicable to the states by the Fourteenth, commands that a state "shall make no law respecting an establishment of religion, or prohibiting the free exercise thereof . . . ." These words of the First Amendment reflected in the minds of early Americans a vivid mental picture of conditions and practices which they fervently wished to stamp out in order to preserve liberty for themselves and for their posterity. Doubtless their goal has not been entirely reached; but so far has the Nation moved toward it that the expression "law respecting an establishment of religion," probably does not so vividly remind present-day Americans of the evils, fears, and political problems that caused that expression to be written into our Bill of Rights. Whether this New Jersey law is one respecting an "establishment of religion" requires an understanding of the meaning of that language, particularly with respect to the imposition of taxes. Once again, therefore, it is not inappropriate briefly to review the background and environment of the period in which that constitutional language was fashioned and adopted.

A large proportion of the early settlers of this country came here from Europe to escape the bondage of laws which compelled them to support and attend government-favored churches. The centuries immediately before and contemporaneous with the colonization of America had been filled with turmoil, civil strife, and persecutions, generated in large part by established sects determined to maintain their absolute political and religious supremacy. With the power of government supporting them, at various times and places, Catholics had persecuted Protestants, Protestants had persecuted Catholics, Protestant sects had persecuted other Protestant sects. Catholics of one shade of belief had persecuted Catholics of another shade of belief, and all of these had from time to time persecuted Jews. In efforts to force loyalty to whatever religious group happened to be on top and in league with the government of a particular time and place, men and women had been fined, cast in jail, cruelly tortured, and killed. Among the offenses for which these punishments had been inflicted were such things as speaking disrespectfully of the views of ministers of government-established churches, nonattendance at those churches, expressions of non-belief in their doctrines, and failure to pay taxes and tithes to support them.

These practices of the old world were transplanted to and began to thrive in the soil of the new America. The very characters granted by the English Crown to the individuals and companies designated to make the laws which would control the destinies of the colonials authorized these individuals and companies to erect religious establishments which all, whether believers or non-believers, would be required to support and attend. An exercise of this authority was accompanied by a repetition of many of the old-world practices and persecutions. Catholics found themselves hounded and proscribed because of their faith; Quakers who followed their conscience went to jail; Baptists were peculiarly obnoxious to certain dominant Protestant sects; men and women of varied faiths who happened to be in a minority in a particular locality were persecuted because they steadfastly persisted in worshipping God only as their own consciences dictated. And all of these dissenters were compelled to pay tithes and taxes to support government-sponsored churches whose ministers preached inflammatory sermons designed to strengthen and consolidate the established faith by generating a burning hatred against dissenters.

These practices became so commonplace as to shock the freedom-loving colonials into a feeling of abhorrence. The imposition of taxes to pay ministers' salaries and to build and maintain churches and church property aroused their indignation. It was these feelings which found expression in the First Amendment. No one locality and no one group throughout the Colonies can rightly be given entire credit for having aroused the sentiment that culminated in adoption of the Bill of Rights' provisions embracing religious liberty. But Virginia, where the established church had achieved a dominant influence in political affairs and where many excesses attracted wide public attention, provided a great stimulus and able leadership for the movement. The people there, as elsewhere, reached the conviction that individual religious liberty could be achieved best under a government which was stripped of all power to tax, to support, or otherwise to assist any or all religions, or to interfere with the beliefs of any religious individual or group.

The movement toward this end reached its dramatic climax in Virginia in 1785-1786 when the Virginia legislative body was about to renew Virginia's tax levy for the support of the established church. Thomas Jefferson and James Madison led the fight against this tax. Madison wrote his great Memorial and Remonstrance against the law. In it, he eloquently argued that a true religion did not need the support of law; that no person, either believer or non-believer, should be taxed to support a religious institution of any kind; that the best interest of a society required that the minds of men always be wholly free; and that cruel persecutions were the inevitable result of government-established religions. Madison's Remonstrance received strong support throughout Virginia, and the Assembly postponed consideration of the proposed tax measure until its next session. When the proposal came up for consideration at that session, it not only died in committee, but the Assembly enacted the famous "Virginia Bill for Religious Liberty" originally written by Thomas Jefferson. The preamble to that Bill stated among other things that

Almighty God hath created the mind free; that all attempts to influence it by temporal punishments or burthens, or by civil incapacitations, tend only to beget habits of hypocrisy and meanness, and are a departure from the plan of the Holy author of our religion, who being Lord both of body and mind, yet chose not to propagate it by coercions on either . . . .; that to compel a man to furnish contributions of money for the propagation of opinions which he disbelieves, is sinful and tyrannical; that even the forcing him to support this or that teacher of his own religious persuasion, is depriving him of the comfortable liberty of giving his contributions to the particular pastor, whose morals he would make his pattern . . . .

And the statute itself enacted

That no man shall be compelled to frequent or support any religious worship, place, or ministry whatsoever, nor shall be enforced, restrained, molested, or burthened in his body or goods, nor shall otherwise suffer on account of his religious opinions or belief. . . .

This Court has previously recognized that the provisions of the First Amendment, in the drafting and adoption of which Madison and Jefferson played such leading roles, had the same objective and were intended to provide the same protection against governmental intrusion on religious liberty as the Virginia statute. Prior to the adoption of the Fourteenth Amendment, the First Amendment did not apply as a restraint against the states. Most of them did soon provide similar constitutional protections for religious liberty. But some states persisted for about half a century in imposing restraints upon the free exercise of religion and in discriminating against particular religious groups. In recent years, so far as the provision against the establishment of a religion is concerned, the question has most frequently arisen in connection with proposed state aid to church schools and efforts to carry on religious teachings in the public schools in accordance with the tenets of a particular sect. Some churches have either sought or accepted state financial support for their schools. Here again the efforts to obtain state aid or acceptance of it have not been limited to any one particular faith. The state courts, in the main, have remained faithful to the language of their own constitutional provisions designed to protect religious freedom and to separate religions and governments. Their decisions, however, show the difficulty in drawing the line between tax legislation which provides funds for the welfare of the general public and that which is designed to support institutions which teach religion.

The "establishment of religion" clause of the First Amendment means at least this: Neither a state nor the Federal Government can set up a church. Neither can pass laws which aid one religion, aid all religions, or prefer one religion over another. Neither can force nor influence a person to go to or to remain away from church against his will or force him to profess a belief or disbelief in any religion. No person can be punished for entertaining or professing religious beliefs or disbeliefs, for church attendance or non-attendance. No tax in any amount, large or small, can be levied to support any religious activities or institutions, whatever they may be called, or whatever form they may adopt to teach or practice religion. Neither a state nor the Federal Government can, openly or secretly, participate in the affairs of any religious organizations or groups and *vice versa*. In the words of Jefferson, the clause against establishment of religion by law was intended to erect "a wall of separation between church and State."

New Jersey cannot consistently with the "establishment of religion" clause of the First Amendment contribute tax-raised funds to the support of an institution which teaches the tenets and faith of any church. On the other hand, other language of the amendment commands that New Jersey cannot hamper its citizens in the free exercise of their own religion. Consequently, it cannot exclude individual Catholics, Lutherans, Mohammedans, Baptists, Jews, Methodists, Nonbelievers, Presbyterians, or the members of any other faith, *because of their faith, or lack of it,* from receiving the benefits of public welfare legislation. While we do not mean to intimate that a state could not provide transportation only to children attending public schools, we must be careful, in protecting the citizens of New Jersey against state-established churches, to be sure that we do not inadvertently prohibit New Jersey from extending its general state law benefits to all its citizens without regard to their religious belief.

Measured by these standards, we cannot say that the First Amendment prohibits New Jersey from spending tax-raised funds to pay the bus fares of parochial school pupils as a part of a general program under which it pays the fares of pupils attending public and other schools. It is undoubtedly true that children are helped to get to church schools. There is even a possibility that some of the children might not be sent to the church schools if the parents were compelled to pay their children's bus fares out of their own pockets when transportation to a public school would have been paid for by the State. The same possibility exists where the state requires a local transit company to provide reduced fares to school children including those attending parochial schools, or where a municipally owned transportation system undertakes to carry all school children free of charge. Moreover, state-paid policemen, detailed to protect children going to and from church schools from the very real hazards of traffic, would serve much the same purpose and accomplish much the same result as state provisions intended guarantee free transportation of a kind which the state deems to be best for the school children's welfare. And parents might refuse to risk their children to the serious danger of traffic accidents going to and from parochial schools, the approaches to which were not protected by policemen. Similarly, parents might be reluctant to permit their children to attend schools which the state had cut off from such general government services as ordinary police and fire protection, connections for sewage disposal, public highways and sidewalks. Of course, cutting off church schools from these services, so separate and so indisputably marked off from the religious function, would make it far more difficult for the schools to operate. But such is obviously not the purpose of the First Amendment. That Amendment requires the state to be a neutral in its relations with groups of religious believers and non-believers; it does not require the state to be their adversary. State power is no more to be used so as to handicap religions than it is to favor them.

This Court has said that parents may, in the discharge of their duty under state compulsory education laws, send their children to a religious rather than a public school if the school meets the secular educational requirements which the state has power to impose. It appears that these parochial schools meet New Jersey's requirements. The State contributes no money to the schools. It does not support them. Its legislation, as applied, does no more than provide a general program to help parents get their children, regardless of their religion, safely and expeditiously to and from accredited schools.

The First Amendment has erected a wall between church and state. That wall must be kept high and impregnable. We could not approve the slightest breach. New Jersey has not breached it here.

Affirmed

Is Private Enterprise the Business of Government?

Green V. Frazier (1920)

In contrast to *Loan Association* v. *Topeka,* this case considers the role and position of a governing body which actually enters business activities usually considered the domain of private enterprises. In this case, taxpayers in the state of North Dakota brought suit against the Governor and other officials, to prevent the state from entering several businesses, particularly those relating to the transportation and marketing of wheat.

The case is notable for its broad interpretation of the powers of a government to engage in usually private business fucntions, when these seem clearly compatible with the welfare of the governed group.

OPINION OF THE COURT

Mr. Justice DAY delivered the opinion of the court. The only ground of attack involving the validity of the legislation which requires our consideration concerns the alleged deprivation of rights secured to the plaintiffs by the Fourteenth Amendment to the Federal Constitution. It is contended that taxation under the laws in question has the effect of depriving plaintiffs of property without due process of law.

The legislation involved consists of a series of acts passed under the authority of the state constitution, which are:

1. An act creating an Industrial Commission of North Dakota which is authorized to conduct and manage on behalf of that State certain utilities, industries, enterprises and business projects . . . .

2. The Bank of North Dakota Act, which establishes a bank under the name of "The Bank of North Dakota," operated by the State.

3. An act providing for the issuing of bonds of the State in the sum of $2,000,000, the proceeds of which are to constitute the capital of the Bank of North Dakota. [Laws 191, c. 148.] The earnings of the bank are to be paid to the State Treasurer. Tax levies are authorized sufficient to pay the interest on the bonds annually.

4. An act providing for the issuing of bonds in the sum of not exceeding $10,000,000 . . . . These bonds are to be issued for the purpose of raising money to procure funds for the Bank of North Dakota . . . . the State Board of Equalization shall, if it appears that the funds in the hands of the State Treasurer are insufficient to pay either principal or interest, make a necessary tax levy to meet the indicated deficiency.

SOURCE: *Green et al.* v *Frazier, Governor et al.* 253 U. S. 233 (1920).

5. An act declaring the purpose of the State of North Dakota to engage in the business of manufacturing and marketing farm products, and to establish a warehouse, elevator, and flour mill system under the name of "North Dakota Mill and Elevator Association" to be operated by the State. The State shall engage in the business of manufacturing farm products and for that purpose shall establish a system of warehouses, elevators, flour mills, factories, plants, machinery and equipment, owned, controlled and operated by it under the name of the North Dakota Mill and Elevator Association."

6. An act providing for the issuing of bonds of the State of North Dakota in a sum not exceeding $5,000,000 for the purpose of carrying on the business of the Mill & Elevator Assocation.

7. The Home Building Act declares the purpose the State to engage in the enterprise of providing homes for its residents . . . . The price of town homes is placed at $5,000, and of farm homes at $10,000.

There are certain principles which must be borne in mind in this connection, and which must control the decision of this court upon the federal question herein involved. This legislation was adopted under the broad power of the State to enact laws raising by taxation such sums as are deemed necessary to promote purposes essential to the general welfare of its people. Before the adoption of the Fourteenth Amendment this power of the State was unrestrained by any federal authority. That Amendment introduced a new limitation upon state power into the Federal Constitution. The States were forbidden to deprive persons of life, liberty and property without due process of law. What is meant by due process of law this court has had frequent occasion to consider, and has always declined to give a precise meaning, preferring to leave its scope to judicial decisions when cases from time to time arise.

The due process of law clause contains no specific limitation upon the right of taxation in the States, but it has come to be settled that the authority of the States to tax does not include the right to impose taxes for merely private purposes.

The taxing power of the States is primarily vested in their legislatures, deriving their authority from the people. When a state legislature acts within the scope of its authority it is responsible to the people, and their right to change the agents to whom they have entrusted the power is ordinarily deemed a sufficient check upon its abuse. When the constituted authority of the State undertakes to exert the taxing power, and the question of the validity of its action is brought before this court, every presumption in its favor is indulged, and only clear and demonstrated usurpation of power will authorize judicial interference with legislative action.

In the present instance under the authority of the constitution and laws prevailing in North Dakota the people, the legislature, and the highest court of the State have declared the purpose for which these several acts were passed to be of a public nature, and within the taxing authority of the State. With this united action of people, legislature and court, we are not at liberty to interfere unless it is clear beyond reasonable controversy that rights secured by the Federal Constitution have been violated. What is a public purpose has given rise to no little judicial consideration. Courts, as a rule, have attempted no judicial definition of a "public" as distinguished from a "private" purpose, but have left each case to be determined by its own peculiar circumstances.

With the wisdom of such legislation, and the soundness of the economic policy involved we are not concerned. Whether it will result in ultimate good or harm it is not within our province to inquire.

We come now to examine the grounds upon which the Supreme Court of North Dakota held this legislation not to amount to a taking of property without due process of law. The questions involved were given elaborate consideration in that court, and it held, concerning what may in general terms be denominated the "banking legislation," that it was justified for the purpose of providing banking facilities, and to enable the State to carry out the purposes of the other acts, of which the Mill & Elevator Association Act is the principal one. It justified the Mill & Elevator Association Act by the peculiar situation in the State of North Dakota, and particularly by the great agricultural industry of the State. It estimated from facts of which it was authorized to take judicial notice, that 90 per cent of the wealth produced by the State was from agriculture; and stated that upon the prosperity and welfare of that industry other business and pursuits carried on in the State were largely dependent; that the State produced 125,000,000 bushels of wheat each year. The manner in which the present system of transporting and marketing this great crop prevents the realization of what are deemed just prices was elaborately stated. It was affirmed that the annual loss from these sources (including the loss of fertility to the soil and the failure to feed the by-products of grain to stock within the State), amounted to fifty-five millions of dollars to the wheat raisers of North Dakota. It answered the contention that the industries involved were private in their nature, by stating that all of them belonged to the State of North Dakota, and therefore the activities authorized by the legislation were to be distinguished from business of a private nature having private gain for its objective.

As to the Home Building Act, that was sustained because of the promotion of the general welfare in providing homes for the people, a large proportion of whom were tenants moving from place to place. It was believed and affirmed by the Supreme Court of North Dakota that the opportunity to secure and maintain homes would promote the general welfare, and that the provisions of the statutes to enable this feature of the system to become effective would redound to the general benefit.

As we have said, the question for us to consider and determine is whether this system of legislation is violative of the Federal Constitution because it amounts to a taking of property without due process of law. The precise question herein involved so far as we have been able to discover has never been presented to this court. The nearest approach to it is found in *Jones* v. *City of Portland,* 245 U. S. 217, in which we held that an act of the State of Maine authorizing cities or towns to establish and maintain wood, coal and fuel yards for the purpose of selling these necessaries to the inhabitants of cities and towns, did not deprive tax-payers of due process of law within the meaning of the Fourteenth Amendment.

This is not a case of undertaking to aid private institutions by public taxation as was the fact in *Citizens Savings & Loan Association.* v. *Topeka.* In many instances States and municipalities have in late years seen fit to enter upon projects to promote the public welfare which in the past have been considered entirely within the domain of private enterprise.

Under the peculiar conditions existing in North Dakota, which are emphasized in the opinion of its highest court, if the State sees fit to enter upon such enterprise as are here involved, with the sanction of its constitution, its legislature and its people, we are not prepared to say that it is within the authority of this court, in enforcing the observance of the Fourteenth Amendment, to set aside such action by judicial decision.

The Public Sector and the Public Interest

Peter O. Steiner

The development of a viable concept of social income is a virtual prerequisite for effective social accounting. Viewed in its most basic sense, any income concept defines what is good (revenues) and what is bad (expenses). Thus, the development of a notion of social income first requires a concept of that which is socially "good,"—of the public interest.

Steiner has attempted the almost monumental task of examining the basic nature of the public interest and the role of the public sector. In a society in which most goods and services are provided by a market system based on individual choices, what should be the role of collective action? "It is necessary to ask what it is that persuades or requires members of a group to seek a collective solution to some problem rather than to rely solely on individual action. It is also necessary to ask whether collective desires merit public support, public indifference, or public hostility."

Following the discussion of public, or collectively provided, goods, Professor Steiner discusses alternative views of the relationship between individual values and the legitimate demand for governmental, or collective, action. He attempts to define the amorphous concept of the "public interest" and the process by which the political system articulates that interest.

INTRODUCTION

If one starts at any point and place in history—say the United States in 1969—it is clear that the society has decided that there exist certain activities that are legitimately performed by governments. Many activities are by long tradition provided by various levels of government and are paid for by using the police powers of the state to raise funds. Others are left to the private sector. Without wishing to disparage the importance of the debate about the proper dividing line between private and public sectors, the fact is there is a large, relatively stable and broadly uncontroversial governmental "sector" of this economy, and of every other economy in the world.

In order to focus on certain critical issues I shall suppress some real distinctions and create some arbitrary ones. The most important simplification is to treat "government" as a single cohesive force, thus neglecting intergovernmental trans-

Peter O. Steiner is Professor of Economics and Law at the University of Michigan.

SOURCE: From the *Analysis and Evaluation of Public Expenditures:* The PPB System. A Compendium of Papers submitted to the Subcommittee on Economy in Government of the Joint Economic Committee, Congress of the United States (1969), Vol. 1, pp. 13-45. This paper is a modification and abridgement of a larger study to be published by the Brookings Institution. (43) Research underlying that study has been supported by the Brookings Institution, by the Graduate School of the University of Wisconsin, and by the Cook Foundation of the University of Michigan Law School.

fers as well as conflicts of authority and philosophy among Federal, State, and local governments. The most important complication is to pretend that the theory of public expenditure policy is in reality two very different sets of propositions. One of these may be called the theory of the marginal public expenditure. It takes as given the legitimacy of government activity, and is concerned with choicemaking of the public decisionmaker between competing demands for his limited resources. The other set of propositions may be called the theory of the public interest, and concerns the way in which demands for public activity arise, are articulated, and are legitimatized. It is this latter that I wish to discuss in this paper.

This is a separation of convenience, not of fact. For example, every marginal decision to expand some public program into a new area implies a legitimate public purpose in that area; thus proposed discrete extensions often pose the questions of public interest. Similarly, making a marginal decision requires rationally knowing what aspects of the public interest are being served.

There is one decisive reason for treating the theories separately. It is simply, that as of this date the available theories are of very different levels of adequacy in the two cases. For the marginal decision a well-developed, highly articulated and largely uncontroversial set of theories exists and awaits implementation into practice. In contrast, with respect to the nature of the public interest, it is we theorists who are the primitives in the sophisticated world of public decisionmakers. It is the theorists who know how to choose between two public housing proposals but not whether public housing is right and proper; while the bureaucrats and Senators have less difficulty deciding when public housing is required than in choosing between alternative schemes of public housing.

Definition of the public interest is genuinely difficult because the notion embodies at least two implicit distinctions. One is between collective action and individual action, the second between public (that is, governmental) action and private action. Each is important. It is necessary to ask what it is that persuades or requires members of a group to seek a collective solution to some problem rather than to rely solely on individual action. It is also necessary to ask whether collective desires merit public support, public indifference, or public hostility. Finally if collective desires are in some sense legitimatized the question remains as to what form of collective action is to be chosen. There is no simple dichotomy between individual private activities and collective public action. Instead there are various kinds of collectivities—clubs, unions, churches, political parties, as well as governments; various degrees of public involvement from outright prohibition of certain activities, to taxes or subsidies, to direct public provision of services.

The *desire* for collective action, which underlies many demands for public provision of goods and services, may arise any time a group feels it cannot achieve its objectives unaided. But mere demands (however genuine) are not enough. Aid to the needy aged (or unattractive prostitutes) may be the only effective device by which this portion of the population may be assured a subsistence level of living;

price supports may provide farmers (or retail grocers, or racetrack touts) with protection against excessive competition that they could not achieve without Government action; a program to place a man on the moon by 1970 (or to build a tunnel under Lake Michigan, or to commit genocide) can be visualized only as a collective program. Each of these activities transcends individual solution and thus requires collective solution or no solution, but that per se does not render them legitimate activities of Government. Most will find some of these proposed activities meritorious but some objectionable as spheres of public action.

Moreover, the required use of collective action is not only not sufficient to define public activities, it is not strictly *necessary*. We may have governments provide education, housing, transportation, and recreation even though private alternatives exist. Such a choice might rest upon considerations of efficiency but it might also reflect captions preference or even prejudice. What leads men to choose public provision from among alternative means of meeting particular ends?

Casual observation suggests that the public interest may be served by providing or encouraging provision of a variety of goods or services, and by nonprovision or discouragement of others. Let me loosely define these goods and services as vested with the public interest, or as *public goods*. Let us first look more closely at the nature of public goods.

THE NATURE OF PUBLIC GOODS

Serving the public interest may take many forms, among them providing of goods, subsidizing their private provision, passing laws that impede or prohibit their provision or constrain the form in which they are provided. Because of the focus of this compendium, I shall limit attention to policies that involve public expenditures. But it should be remembered that an important policy issue always concerns choice among alternative available means.

The goods and services provided by public expenditures or encouraged by public policies can be described and classified in a number of different ways. Though we speak of a single category, "public goods," any review of actual public goods are provided publicly or not at all because there exist no reasonable private alternative ways of providing them. This can happen (as in the case of national parks, national defense, or space research) because there exists no private mechanism to pay for the provision of these goods, or it can happen (as in the case of sewage disposal or justice) because compulsory use of the goods by all is required to permit its enjoyment by any group. Other public goods, such as public housing or public education, may be functionally similar to available private alternatives, but be qualitatively different in ways that society somehow prefers. Still other public goods may differ from private ones in no way other than in the distribution of beneficiaries and costs.

If the proper domain of public expenditure policy is public goods, their definition becomes vital. The concept has been defined in many ways, and for diverse purposes, and it is not surprising that definitions motivated by purposes other than ours—understanding the rationale and process of public expenditure policy—are not wholly satisfactory.

"A *public good* is any good or service which is *de facto* provided for or subsidized through Government budget finance. (Birdsall [5] p. 235).[1] This definition is neat but unhelpful. It is deficient in that it provides no guidance as to what attributes of a potential good or service a policymaker should look to in deciding whether to provide the goods. In this definition "publicness" is an act of congressional designation, not of any characteristics of the good or service.

In many ways, it would be desirable to have an intrinsic definition based upon technical characteristics of goods or services. One such definition of public goods is of the perfect collective consumption good. An impressive array of economists have so defined public goods including Samuelson [39], Strotz [45], Bowen [7], Breton [9], and most recently Dorfman [14]. Hear Dorfman:

> There are certain goods that have the peculiarity that once they are available no one can be precluded from enjoying them whether he contributed to their provision or not. These are the public goods. Law and order is an example, and there are many others too familiar to make further exemplification worth while. Their essential characteristic is that they are enjoyed but not consumed [and that their benefits are derived] without any act of appropriation. ([14], p. 4.)

This kind of very narrow definition was designed to demonstrate that there may be a type of activity that is socially desirable but that will not be achieved by the unaided private market. It serves well the purpose of showing the existence of public goods. It can prove a hindrance, however, if it leads to the view that such goods are *the only* class of goods which Government can legitimately provide. In fact, examples are hard to find, not ubiquitous, and the great bulk of (nondefense) public expenditures are for goods and services that do not meet the definition. Roads, schools, welfare payments, recreational facilities, housing, public power, irrigation (among others) are important classes of public expenditures that some can be precluded from enjoying, that can be consumed in whole or in part, and that technically can be made subject to user charges. The perfect collective consumption good, while sufficient to justify public expenditure, is neither necessary nor does it embrace much of what public expenditure policy concerns. What it does do is to identify certain characteristics such as nonconsumption, nonappropriation, and the existence of externalities that may give a good public goods aspect.

Externalities are very important, as has been recognized for a long time Wicksell (himself citing earlier authority) put it eloquently in 1896:

If the community or at any rate a sizable part of it has an interest in a particular utility accruing to an individual, then it would clearly be unreasonable to allow the creation of that more general utility to depend solely upon that individual: he might not value the state activity highly enough to make the sacrifice of paying the required fee or charge, or else ignorance may cause him or poverty force him to do without the service. Herein lies the chief justification of the modern demands for free or very cheap process of law, elementary education, and medical care, certain public health measures, and so forth.[2]

While they are important, it would be easy to follow externalities too far. Few goods fail to have some elements of externality in the sense of some benefits or costs that do not require an act of appropriation. But if few goods fail to meet this test it cannot provide guidance as to which goods ought to be candidates for public provision, nor to explain which goods are publicly provided.

Let me venture a definition of my own: *any publicly induced or provided collective good* is a public good. A "collective good" in my definition is not necessarily a collective consumption good. Collective goods arise whenever some segment of the public collectively wants and is prepared to pay for a different bundle of goods and services than the unhampered market will produce. A collective good thus requires (1) an appreciable difference in either quantity or quality between it and the alternative the private market would produce, and (2) a viable demand for the difference.

Collective goods may be privately or publicly provided. Co-ops, unions, vigilante organizations, country clubs, carpools, and trade associations are all examples of private organizations that arise in response to collective demands for private collective goods or services. When the coordinating mechanism for providing a collective good invokes the powers of the state I define the good as a public good. In this definition there is the requirement that a public good must meet the tests of being a collective good. Public provision by itself does not create public goods. This definition is virtually implicit in the discussions of Head [20], Musgrave [33], Olson [35], Weisbrod [50] and Margolis [30]. It provides something of a framework for considering various sources of public goods, as we shall see just below.

A most important aspect of this definition is that it makes "publicness" not an all-or-nothing attribute of a good, but an attribute that may apply merely to particular aspects of a good. While there are cases (for example, national defense) in which the choice is between public provision and no provision, and why we thus argue that the good is entirely a public good, the more common situation is for goods to provide a variety of services only some of which have the attributes of collective goods. When the aspects that are thus of collective interest become sufficiently important, we may be led to public provision either for those aspects, or of the entire good (including its noncollective aspects). Thus provision of smog control or river pollution attacks a particular externality of private production. In contrast public housing provides individuals with services they would otherwise have purchased privately, along with the peculiarly public services that public housing is supposed to entail.

Such mixed goods test and stretch definitions. "Public education" and "public housing" reflect both quantitative and qualitative differences from the privately produced or producible goods, "private housing" and "private education." If the differences are intended and desired, the differences constitute public goods in my definition.

This somewhat vague and embracing notion of public goods can be filled out by a more detailed classification of different types of public goods.

A CLASSIFICATION OF PUBLIC GOODS

I have (in effect) defined the vector of public goods as a vector of differences between the goods and services the private economy is motivated to provide and the goods and services the "public" wants, is willing to pay for, and expects its government to assist it in achieving.[3] This is, to an important degree, a normative definition, and much of the debate about the appropriate elements of the public goods vector is a normative debate. But there is a positive aspect as well: What is it about particular goods and services that makes them candidates for public consideration? What is it that makes certain activities the traditional province of governements?

It seems worth while to distinguish three types of public goods: (1) Those arising from intrinsic (perhaps technical) characteristics of specific goods that result in externalities that are not effectively marketed; (2) those arising from imperfections in the market mechanisms (rather than in the nature of the goods or services themselves); (3) those arising not from specific goods or services but from aspects concerning the quality or nature of the environment. These become increasingly elusive as we proceed from (1) to (3), but it is impossible to capture the flavor of actual government expenditure programs without all of them.

1. Public Goods Arising from Nonmarketable Services of Particular Goods

A discrepancy between public wants and private supplies often arises from externalities (or as they are alternatively called, spillover or third-party effects). Any time provision of a good or service provides side effects whose value is not reflected in the prices of the outputs sold or the resources used, external economies or diseconomies are produced. There can be many reasons for such externalities: Private producers may use resources they do not consider scarce, or produce byproducts that they do not consider valuable because they cannot control and market them. Familiar examples are discharges of noxious wastes into water or air, downstream navigational or flood control consequences of a private power dam, civic beautification or uglification incident upon building of private golf courses, factories, or slaughterhouses. Because some of the resources used or outputs produced are not correctly valued by the market there is every reason to expect the market to misuse them. Thus collective concern and public action may be required on simple efficiency grounds to allocate resources in accord with "true" valuations.

Whether the existence of such externalities (which must surely be present to some extent in every good) justifies public notice and action depends upon the benefits to be achieved measured against the costs of interference. Different people will have divergent views of the costs of interference but debate as to what the cutoff level should be is a different matter than debates about the nature and size of the externalities.

The perfect collective consumption good is really an extreme case of externalities: all of the output is regarded as individually unmarketable; all of the benefits are external. The outputs of those goods from which one cannot be excluded as a consumer—and thus for which one cannot be compelled to pay his share of the cost of provision—play a large role in the thinking of those who have been concerned with deriving a legitimate role for public activity. Defense, public health, law and order, hurricane watches, are familiar examples. It is common to list a few examples (and not press them very hard) and then say, "there are many other examples." This is close to fraudulent. If excludability implies no one can conceivably be excluded, the list of such goods is short indeed. One need not police the ghetto, nor defend Alaska. Television signals can be scrambled so as to exclude buyers who will not pay for the unscrambler. Movies, concerts, hospitals, and colleges all use walls to exclude those who will not meet the requirements placed upon their use.

Collective goods may arise because it would be relatively costly to exclude free riders rather than because it is impossible. If at any moment this cost is above a certain level there may be no effective supply of the good privately provided. But in other cases the cost of exclusion may be annoying rather than prohibitive and potential consumers may urge public action merely to avoid bearing the costs. Put differently, the cost of arranging exclusion may be an avoidable externality.

Implicit in this discussion is an important attribute of the public collective good: the willingness to appeal to the police power of the state. One can slide in imperceptible steps from situations where there is no viable alternative means of providing the good, to cases where the alternative seems unnecessarily costly, to cases where the alternative while not very costly is simply judged to be less desirable, to cases where the alternative differs only in who pays for it.

There is real purpose in downgrading the distinction between *inability* and *unwillingness* to provide a good privately. If there is to be a practical definition of specific collective consumption goods and services, it seems difficult to escape the view that a judgment is required about reasons for turning to the political process and the coercive power of the state, rather than dealing with the second best solution. These reasons must be judged meritorious by the social decision process. *If this is so, collective consumption goods are defined by the exercise of legitimate governmental decision processes as much as they define them.*

Among the positive issues that underlie the normative debate about whether a particular collective good ought to be publicly provided are (1) whether private market alternatives to public provision are impossible, impractical, merely costly or simply unwanted; (2) why the market solution is unsatisfactory to members of the group and to society as a whole; and (3) the identity of the group of beneficiaries. The last deserves a bit of comment.

A collective good need not provide joint benefits to all of a society's members, only to some subgroup. But which group? The larger the group the more persuasive its demand for public action is likely to be, or (put differently) the less willing will its members be to accept a costly alternative. There are bases other than size for weighing the merits of the demands of any group, and these may vary over time. Domestic producers of goods subject to foreign competition, farmers, labor unions, small businessmen, and minority groups are among the identifiable groups that have asked and received special treatment. Today, for example, we seem more responsive to the demands of the underprivileged than the wealthy; a half century ago it was clearly otherwise.

One reason many collective consumption goods lead to demands for public provision is because the potential willingness to pay of different consumers cannot be tapped by private suppliers. Weisbrod [50], is an important paper, suggests a further source of values for which there is no market: option demands.[4] Some examples: I value Yellowstone Park being there, though I hope I never have to visit it again; I value the Everglades because I may want to visit them (but probably will not); I value the existence of a first-rate tuberculosis sanatorium, though in all probability I shall never need its services. Were any of these threatened with extinction I should be the loser, but there is no market whereby my willingness to pay for the option of being able to use them can be translated into revenue to the providers.[5]

Weisbrod's most suggestive example concerns the standby availability of transport. How much is it worth to the New York-Washington air travelers to have a good rail alternative in case of snow or strike? Suppose it is worth enough to justify the rail service, but that the railroad has no way of being reimbursed by those whose option demands are critical to continuation of the services. In these circumstances, the public good may be provided by the government's insistence that the railroad's passenger service be maintained with or without subsidy. In this view governments may not have been irrational in trying to preserve passenger train service even in the face of inability of the carriers to find user charges equal to costs.

2. Public Goods Arising from Market Imperfections

There can be in practice no sharp distinction between market failure caused by technical characteristics of particular goods, and market failure caused by market imperfections. Inability to handle externalities, for example, may be regarded as a shortcoming of existing markets rather than as the absence of markets for specific services. But a distinction suggests additional sources of unsatisfactory private market performance that generate demand for public collective action. Efficient markets frequently support adequate information, sufficient competition, timely adjustment, and modest transaction costs. The absence of any of these may create motives to replace market determination by nonmarket provision, or to supplement markets with ancillary public goods.

a. Information

Suppose all conditions for ideal resource allocation are satisfied except that market signals are systematically not read or are misperceived by economic actors. An allocation of goods and resources will occur, but it will, in general, differ from the allocation that would occur without ignorance or misinformation. Information may be a collective good (and thus generate a demand for its public provision) because even if there is a well-articulated private desire to have information, there may be no effective market in which to buy it efficiently.[6] It may be a public good in addition because the externalities of misinformed traders may be judged to be socially undesirable.

b. Time lags

If resources respond to market signals surely but slowly, the market process may prove an expensive way to achieve resource shifts. If physicists are in short supply, their price may be expected to rise and this may motivate additional youngsters to undertake education leading to careers as physicists. Since education is a slow process, existing physicists may earn high rents over long periods due to the long supply lags. It may well be that public policy can increase the supply of physicists more quickly and more cheaply by fellowships, by research grants, etc.[7] than the unaided market. If increases in supply of physicists, but not increased incomes of existing physicists, are desired results, then such programs supply public goods.

There is a large and growing literature that is concerned with the extent and causes of factor immobility. Education is but one of the sources; others include unemployment rates, prejudice, institutional barriers such as seniority and pension laws and State laws affecting eligibility for relief. Whenever markets work to reallocate resources sufficiently slowly, there may be a collective demand to supplement the market mechanism, or to replace it. Retraining programs, moving allowances, public employment services and even attacks on prejudice may be public goods if they serve to reduce the lags that the market economy accepts.

c. Monopoly power

Noncompetitive imperfections need little comment here. Public activities to encourage or compel competitive behavior, or to replace monopolistic private by public provisions are further sources of public goods.

d. Transaction costs

We have seen that an important aspect of collective goods concerns the inability of the market to translate potential willingness to pay into revenues. Related is the situation where the private market is technically able to collect revenues, but at a high cost. Collection of user tolls on interurban roads and urban bridges may or may not be both feasible and efficient, but intraurban toll roads would surely involve even larger collection costs and time losses. Prohibitive transaction costs of collecting revenues for intraurban toll roads make high-speed roads of that kind public goods. Metering costs may be justified for high unit value commodities such as gas and electricity, but not for sewage (and, in some high population density areas, for water).

Where these high transaction costs inhere in the particular service they are simply an externality; where they reflect the institutional arrangements of the market they are a potential additional source of collective concern. The higher cost of attempting to gear a pricing system to an individual's willingness to pay is a repeated source of turning away from the market. For many goods, willingness to pay may be regarded as rising at least proportionally with income. Most private services are not provided on a basis that reflects income, because of the enormous costs of administration that such pricing would entail. If such a basis of payment is appropriate, reliance on the income tax, and thus on State provision, may appear desirable.

3. Public Goods Arising Because of Concern with the Quality of the Environment

To this point public goods have been discussed in terms of market failure; failure either because of the absence or the imperfections of private markets. This is the grand tradition of classical economics. But even perfectly functioning markets for all goods and services would not eliminate the desire for market interference. Men may choose to reject the market solutions to allocative problems with respect to the distribution of income, the nature or quality of goods produced, or the patterns of consumption that markets produce.

The most compelling examples of collective public goods have always seemed to me to be national defense, law and order, and public health. What is their particular appeal? Is it that they are collective consumption goods? So is television. It is not in the specific planes, rockets, soldiers, policemen, vaccines, or nurses that are their elements—each of which can be readily provided as private goods to private users—but rather in the fact that they are part of and condition the *environment* of the society. Even the criminal who detests the legal framework is affected by it. Looked at this way they suggest other things that affect the environment and thus create externalities not linked to particular goods: for example, the literacy rate, the level of unemployment, the crime rate, the rate of technological progress, and importantly, the pattern of distribution of income and wealth.

a. Distribution of income[8]

Accept this assertion: it is fully feasible to charge users for use of parks and playgrounds, to charge parents for school bus service and school lunches, to charge fishermen for fishing privileges. Suppose in each of these cases that there is sufficient willingness to pay and ability to collect so as to assure private provision of parks, playground, school buses, school lunches, and fishing opportunities. Should these functions be left to private provision?

To answer this question we must decide whether we are concerned merely with the distribution of income or instead with the pattern of consumption. When we provide subsidized public housing to the urban poor do we desire to provide more or better housing to users who would be excluded by private provision (or who would exclude themselves) or do we simply choose to increase their share of national consumption and use public housing instead of a cash income supplement for some obscure reason? (One might use indirect means, for example, in order not to impair the feelings of self-respect of the recipients.)

It is sometimes argued that purely redistributional objectives which reflect a dissatisfaction with the initial situation of ownership of wealth and resources ought to be satisfied by income transfers rather than by provision of goods and services in order not to distort resource allocation. This familiar argument is unpersuasive if one regards as legitimate a desire of a society to interfere with the *pattern of consumption* that would result from market determinations. A society may choose to affect jointly with income distribution and the pattern of consumption. Provision of housing, education, milk, and recreation for underprivileged children may be public goods because of the externalities which children so treated bestow upon others. Public policies designed to provide aid for small business, for the family farm, for the needy aged, and for the slum child all reflect rejection of market determination, rather than denial of the possibility of market determination.

It is, of course, not clear that all actual interferences reflect a positive intention both to redistribute income *and* to change consumption patterns. In the United Kingdom (by way of contrast to the United States), fishing rights are sold, and it is an upper class form of recreation. On the other hand, virtually all Scottish golf courses are subsidized municipal ones, and in Scotland golf (but not fishing) is a working class recreation. But if some consumption distortions are fortuitous, others are intended.

b. Nature and quality of output

For some goods and services the quality and nature of the goods produced is of public concern, quite independent of any distributional considerations. Often the nature of the goods or service is affected by who provides it—for better or for worse. Government newspapers differ from private ones, public television and radio from commercial broadcasting, a system of public schools from a private school system, private research and development from public. In some of these examples both kinds of goods may coexist, in others an exclusive choice is made. But in all cases a choice among qualitatively different outputs may and can be made; the qualitative difference of public from private constitutes a public good or a public bad.

4. Public Goods: A Summary View

I have stressed the pluralistic nature of the sources of collective demands, as arising from technical characteristics of particular goods, from market imperfections and failures, and also from other divergences between collective and individual values. This time is long since past when we need to define public goods merely in order to establish the prima facie case for some public interference with private markets; instead we seek a framework to structure debate about whether particular activities merit inclusion in the public sector.

It seems to me worth identifying in each case what is the alleged source of collective concern. Does it depend upon a major qualitative difference between public and private provision, or does it merely seek some incremental output, perhaps by considering a particular neglected externality? In this distinction often lies an important policy choice between public provision on the one hand or a less fundamental public restructuring of private incentives. Similarly one wants an indication of whether public concern is specific to the particular good or service or is of a general environmental type. There are more ways to reduce overall unemployment than there are ways to retrain Appalachian miners. Again, the relevant alternatives are affected by what are the real objects of policy. A frequent issue concerns whether redistributional policies achieved by provision of specific goods and services are intended to bring about changes in consumption patterns or do so incidentally.

Next, having established the basis of *collective* concern, it is worth establishing the basis of *public* concern. Who are the alleged beneficiaries, and what is their claim to recognition? What is the "second best" that they face if their claims are rejected?

I believe that defining as specifically as one can the vector of differences between a private good and its public alternative to be a critical part of the public decisionmaking process. Neither de facto definitions (such as Birdsall's), nor neat but narrow ones (such as that of the perfect collective consumption good) prove very helpful for the critical problem of defining the scope of the public sector.

SOURCES OF A PUBLIC INTEREST: ALTERNATIVE VIEWS

To convert a collective interest of some group into the public interest requires a distinct act of legitimization. How does it occur? Views differ both with respect to what it is that is aggregated, and with reference to the requisite degree of consensus.

My dominant reaction to rereading the discussion among economists about the "public interest" is surprise at its defensive tone, as if we are somehow disloyal when we find a role for extramarket forces in the economy. Perhaps because economists have felt defensive, much of the economic discussion has revolved not around the issue of how to define the public interest, but rather how to demonstrate that there is a de minimis role of government activity that clearly benefits everybody. Much of welfare economics consists of such a possibility theorem. Possibility theorems are fine in their own way. If, however, they are misinterpreted they may greatly limit the scope of the phenomenon whose possibility they are concerned to establish. This has, I believe, been the problem and the fate of formal welfare economics. To document this view or to discuss the alternatives in any detail involves technical issues best avoided in this paper.[9] But it is possible to identify a variety of different points of view and the different implications that they may lead to.

1. The Point of View of Individual Utility

Those who hold this view consider the public interest of a society as being simply an appropriate aggregate of the private interests of the individuals who comprise the society. Each individual is assumed to seek his own utility (or satisfaction) by pursuing all avenues open to him. Assume as a rough distinction that he draws satisfaction from the consumption of two kinds of goods, private goods and collective goods. (He may, of course, derive utility not only from his own consumption but from the status of others, rejoicing in either their good fortune or their bad.) Let us distinguish initially the individual's wants reflected by his tastes and preferences and his effective demands, determined by his utility function *and* the constraints, such as income, that bind him

For private goods there is a market through which individuals can make their effective demands for goods felt, and in the context of an enterprise system whenever the aggregate of such individual demands warrant there is incentive for private producers to meet these demands. Collective goods differ in that (as we have seen) private markets fail to respond to real effective demands; thus *collective action* is required to satisfy *individual demands.* The devices of government can provide the form of collective action that substitutes for private markets in channeling resources to meet the aggregate of individual demands. (So far as the individual's utility depends upon others' consumption, it is likely to be outside of his individual ability to do much about; thus here is further motive for looking to the government.) In this attractively symmetrical view, government activity permits individuals better to achieve the individual objectives.

These assumptions have settled an issue of principle (that there may be a legitimate role of government) without having answered the practical question of which public goods the society should provide. Granted that individuals have demands for collective goods, how should individual preferences be aggregated to determine whether the aggregate welfare is sufficient to justify the total cost? Is this answer affected by the system of taxes used to raise the funds? These are among the critical questions of welfare economics.

A simple and uncontroversial solution is available in cases where unanimity prevails. Clearly, if some quantity of a particular new public good had the happy property that for every individual it added at least as much to his utility as his contribution to its cost detracted from his utility, such a good would be desirable. A totally de minimis view of the public interest would limit it to cases that fit this requirement. It is de minimis because, while it is conceivable that there are goods that satisfy this criterion, there cannot be many. In a many-person economy, if even one person had less use for the public good than his contribution to its costs no positive quantity of output would achieve unanimous consent.

Many public activities imply (often intentionally) a redistribution of income which leaves some individuals worse off and some better. Whatever the merit of establishing *at least* the quantity that might achieve unanimous consent as desirable, any implication that exactly that quantity is desirable seems quite unwarranted. Few economists, welfare or other, are content to rule out any change merely because it has redistributional consequences. To do so invests the initial distribution of society's resources with an overriding sanctity. Nor can we avoid this difficulty by assuming that an individual's utility function includes as an argument preferences about the distribution of income. For, unless an implied distribution were to be regarded as desirable by everyone, there would be no unanimous consent to it.

The struggle of formal welfare economics to escape this dilemma had been tortured and fruitless. The Kaldor-Hicks "compensation principle" wherein a change that benefited some but not all was justified if the gainers *could* compensate the losers even if they *did* not only encounters technical ambiguities[10] but implies an inherent neutrality toward redistributional consequences.

Neither am I impressed with the argument that we ought to be neutral toward redistribution in allocational decisions, on the ground that redistribution of income can be accomplished directly if it is desired. The inertia of social change is such that this would overweight the current distribution of income, and would serve in practice to limit the possibilities for redistribution.

Clearly we would be paralyzed by an operating rule that said: "provide no public good if it changes the distribution of income." But if we permit redistributions there is no reason why we cannot regard some as desirable and others as undesirable.

Clearly some reckoning of redistribution gains and losses is required if all proposals are not to be rejected. If one insists on basing decisions on individual utility functions this implies either assigning weights to the utility of individuals or being able and willing to measure and compare individual utilities. Making interpersonal comparisons is potentially unattractive,[11] unless it is itself subject to well-defined rules of procedure. Such rules might be formulated. For example, one may take a strict majoritarian view. But there is nothing inherently just or appealing about a rule that leads to the median effective demand of the society being dominant: indeed, without protections of minorities it would seem offensive to most people.

The major objection to a utility-consensus view of social welfare functions is that it is nonoperational and does not seem to provide guidance to the decisions of real societies. Certainly we *do* take decisions with less than unanimous consent. Certainly too, many public goods provide benefits in excess of their contributions only to very small minorities of the society, but with the evident acquiescence of sizable majorities. One can argue that, ex post, individuals are thus revealed to value the benefits which accrue primarily to others. But this rationalization leads us back to a de facto definition: whatever the Government does is revealed to be desired by the people.

Thus if formal welfare economics does not go beyond individual utility functions, it fails either because it justifies too little or because it justifies too much public expenditure. Viewed from the vantage point of welfare economics, public decisions about public goods appear to be impossible to make.[12] Fortunately, other economic views are possible: economists are saved the humiliation of abandoning as barren a fertile field. It is the wasteland of welfare economics, not the reality of public decisionmaking that is the mirage.

A partial escape from the wasteland can come from a pluralistic view of the individual. Suppose that each individual in addition to his personal evaluation of any proposed activity will also view it from the point of view of any one of a number of groups he belongs to, be it social club or trade union.[13] If he is willing to be bound by the consensus view of the members of the group, there is a much greater possibility of consensus, first because a significant clustering of views is likely to emerge, and second because logrolling between groups can create collections of activities that command dominant majorities. Suppose individuals are prepared to accept and to be taxed for things they consider socially worthwhile, such as (say) foreign aid, wars on poverty, and higher pay for Senators, even though they cost many individuals more in income foregone than they contribute to that individual's utility. They accept them as part of a package which they find adds to their own utility on an all-or-nothing basis.

The view that social choices may rest on collective values arrived at by causes rather than by simple aggregation is more than an escape from the general impossibility of deriving a social welfare function from individual values. It has positive merit in that it embraces a view of the individual which many find descriptively accurate and analytically helpful. In this view an individual functions in a pluralistic sense with loyalties, commitments, and valuations at many levels: to himself, his family, his church, his neighborhood, his employer—and possibly also to his race, religion, class, country, and political party. The pluralistic view is the heart of sociology, social anthropology, and much of economics. If it is accepted it suggests that individuals will be prepared to act on collective issues without inevitably tracing back to the explicit question: "What's in it for me?" They may ask instead; "What's in it for the Negro?" or the farmer, workingman, etc. If they do, they invite an analysis of the views of political pressure groups, which usually have highly articulate spokesmen and well-defined programs they are seeking to enact.

2. The Point of View of Willingness to Pay

The difficulties of deriving an aggregate preference ordering based on indivdiual utilities arise from the incommensurability of individual's utility indexes. Without unanimity of views or well-defined rules for assigning weights, consistent decisions become impossible to make.

A second view is to ask not how much an individual values a given collective good, but how much he is willing to be taxed to provide it. The differences between this view and the previous one may seem small but they may make a substantial difference in one's view of the scope of the public interest. In the first place a shift from every individual having a positive preference for some activity, to his being willing to tolerate it, is practically quite substantial, as the well-known political literature on the use of veto power makes clear. Second, the metric of value of the activity has been shifted from the inherently unmeasurable "utility," to the discernible, and interpersonally comparable, willingness of individuals to pay. To be sure we pay a price for this, in that an individual's willingness to pay reflects the status quo, and particularly his income and wealth. We must therefore, be all the more wary about distributional biases toward the status quo.

When applied to the collective consumption good this approach leads to the so called *pure theory of public expenditure*. This theory has a long life and is well articulated by Bowen [7] and Samuelson [38].[14] In barest essence the argument is that since demands of different individuals for a collective good are complementary rather than competitive we can add the willingness to pay of different individuals and if the aggregate sum exceeds the costs, the good is worth producing. For all quantities for which this is true, there exists a tax policy which would collect levels of taxes sufficient to cover marginal costs, and still leave all citizens satisfied.

Appeal to the "existence of tax policy such that . . . sounds very much like the compensation principle once again. And it is subject to a similar objection. If the tax structure is not (or should not be) malleable, there is no bliss in this solution. At independently determined tax rates some taxpayers are getting more than they are willing to pay for and are being coerced to provide what others want. If these others' needs are in some sense more meritorious than those of the reluctant taxpayers, this may be appropriate, but there is then no automatic stopping point. One cannot escape the distributional question, unless one insists on regarding it as irrelevant. If the collective good involves aid to the needy aged one may take a different view of the effects of the coercion than if it involves providing a civic yacht harbor.

Nor (in my view) are these difficulties with the optimal solution merely symptoms of imperfections in the taxing schema. Citizens have social values about appropriate tax policies too. Suppose we are building a public playground to be used by underprivileged children. If A is a rich misanthrope and B a poor Samaritan, there is no compelling reason why B should carry more of the tax burden, even though he may be willing to do so.

Notwithstanding these and other difficulties, some have argued that this approach offers the following rule as a usable rough guideline to public decision-making: if, in aggregate, effective demands exceed cost, the service should be provided whether or not payment is exacted. Unfortunately this opens the door to game strategic behavior. Suppose payment proportional to demand is not to be required. Any group that knows it will not be asked to pay more than a fixed share can exaggerate its valuation of a service it desires. If (on the other hand) proportional payment is to be required, every group will have an incentive to understate its real valuation as long as others value the service enough to get it provided.

3. The Point of View of an Aggregate Social Welfare Function

Society is necessarily made up of individuals, but it need be no simple aggregate of them. In looking at their behavior it may be that the interdependencies between people and their interactions are more important than the individual value structures. Nations, races, even football teams, acquire personalities and modes of behavior. While a search for collective values has until recently been more congenial to political scientists and sociologists than to economists, an increasing number of economists are moving toward the view that individuals voluntarily yield certain coercive power to a government which is somehow charged to discover, articulate and implement social priorities, or collective wants.

This, collective, view is broader than, not necessarily competitive with, the previous ones. It may be that social priorities are indeed arrived at by some aggregation process. But there are other possibilities as well. Political theory has long been concerned with the legitimacy of government and with the nature of the social contract among citizens or between a government and its citizens.

In this view a collectivity, *society* may be fruitfully viewed as an independent entity possessing its own value orderings. In Rothenberg's view [36], if I understand it, social valuation as opposed to solely individual valuation is an existent reality. This view has the great pragmatic value that it invites the search for revealed social priorities without insisting on a single source of them. If priorities with respect to income distribution (for example) are established, and consented to by the citizens, then the distributional consequences of particular public decisions become "benefits" or "costs" instead of barriers to either clear thinking or clear action. The formidable measurement issues—or quantifying the benefits, and assessing the costs—remain, but a major hurdle has been crossed. In this view one is aggregating not across individual utility, nor willingness to pay, but rather across individual political influence and tolerance. In so doing we vest to some extent the existing distribution of political power and influence, but possibly it can be argued that this is more nearly the result of a social contract than is the distribution of wealth.[15] The degree or consent that is required is whatever the political process demands.

Personally, I find this view of the problem both congenial and fruitful. It does not dispense with the individual and individual values, for one must ask how the political process articulates the public interest, but it does recognize that most individuals have a large range of things they will accept without opting out of the system, and will vent their approval or disapproval in some sort of orderly political process. It does not lead, inherently, to either a minimal or maximal role for government. It does not exclude distributional questions from policy, nor does it vest the existing distribution of income with a special status. What it lacks is any clear indication that one situation is superior to another in a wholly unambiguous sense. This does not mean that whatever society does is desired, rather it means that particular public decisions can be shown to be valid only in terms of particular value judgments. It tends to pose issues of public policy in terms of whether society does in fact hold certain value judgments rather than in terms of the demonstrable inherent legitimacy of certain activities. Some will regard this as retrogress. I am not so inclined. Economists have long sought a calculus of consent, but in the search have found it easier to derive a lower bound to public activities than to define their proper domain. If we are fruitfully to discuss public expenditure policy we must be prepared to go beyond this.

The central issue in this debate does not concern the logical correctness of looking at social choices on the one hand as an aggregation of individual values or on the other as a two-step procedure in which we first agree (some way, any way) on collective values and then use them to make social choices. Any perfectly understood aggregate behavior can be decomposed into its disaggregated elements. It is instead a matter of research strategy. Are we likely to achieve greater insight one way or the other? If there is stability in aggregate social values then basing policy on such aggregate values is likely to work. My own view is that at this stage in the development of our science there is more insight and less bias in the third view of the public interest than in either of the others. Many will disagree.

If one accepts the notion that aggregated social views must be discovered there remain two important questions to discuss. First, how these views get articulated and, second, how competing objectives get reconciled. It is convenient to treat them in reverse order.

THE PROBLEM OF WEIGHTING

It is increasingly the practice to treat the public interest (or "social welfare") as a function with several arguments. For example following Marglin [28] we might write:

$$U = U(Z_1, Z_2, Z_3, \ldots, Z_i)$$

where the Z's are different aspects of the public interest such as economic efficiency (or contribution to national income), the pattern of income distribution, the rate of economic growth, balance of payments equilibrium, economic stability, national security, and freedom. Whether one considers these as different aspects of a one dimensional index of utility, or as different dimensions of a multidimensional concept is more than a semantic issue. If for example, Z_1 and Z_2 are readily comparable in terms of a cardinal measure of their contribution to utility (e.g., market value of electric power and market value of irrigation water) they can easily be elements of a scalar measure of welfare. Their relative weights are given by the common yardstick used for measuring them. If on the other hand Z_1 and Z_2 represent efficiency and freedom each of which (let us suppose) may be meaningfully defined and ordinarily measured we may have no simple yardstick for comparing them. Thus the problem of trade-offs between these "separate dimensions" of a public interest vector remains to be solved. Because noncomparability of difficulties in comparison are a feature of many public choice problems, it seems to me convenient to regard the public interest as genuinely multidimensional, and thus to consider explicitly conflicts among objectives.

The number of dimensions and their definition is a matter of analytic and operational convenience. Because there are many different sources of a public (as distinct from private) interest there will be many forms of a proximate contribution to public welfare. Whether it makes sense to combine different effects into a single dimension or to treat them as separate dimensions of the public interest depends upon whether one believes there is an acceptable cardinal measure of their contribution to public welfare. If so it makes sense to combine; if not, it makes sense to keep them separate.

With a one dimensional objective there is a simple decision rule. If (for example) one is concerned solely with contribution to national income it is conceptually easy to choose between a dam in Oregon and a retraining program in West Virginia. But if one cares as well about who gets the income, such a simple rule can become simplistic. Given multiple objectives, it is inevitable that individual proposed actions will affect more than a single dimension. Inevitably also the objectives will often conflict. The definition of a multi-dimensional objective function neither creates nor resolves the conflicts, instead it identifies them.

The central aspects of choosing policies when faced with multiple objectives are how to define an appropriate measure of each objective, and how to resolve conflicts among objectives.

A very simple, indeed trivial, theorem says that if weights are left unspecified, any policy A may in general be made to appear less or more desirable after the fact than an alternative B (which may easily be "not A"), by specifying which objective is implicitly the important one. This theorem is important only because it is so frequently neglected.

Many forms of "implicit" weighting exist in practice. It is almost routine in lay discourse to argue that because a proposed policy advances *some* object of social policy, it is desirable: "The war on poverty will improve the distribution of income." Or to argue that because it retards some other objects it is undesirable: "The war on poverty extends the role of government and thus reduces individual freedom." Neither of these statements tells us whether the war on poverty is desirable.

Somewhat subtler is the implicit neglect of certain objectives by assuming the dominance of others. Much of the economist's traditional emphasis on efficiency has had the effect of giving it a very high weight relative to growth or distribution. Interestingly, Joseph Schumpeter, always treated as a giant with respect to his theories of development and cycles, is still regarded as a crank with respect to his views on monopoly, because he challenged orthodoxy by arguing that static efficiency considerations are overweighted relative to growth.

If objectives are genuinely multidimensional and not immediately comparable, some solution to the weighting problem is implicit or explicit in *any* choice, and that solution reflects someone's value judgment. Put formally, we now accept in principle that the choice of weights is itself an important dimension of the public interest. This choice is sometimes treated as a prior decision which controls public expenditure decisions (or at least should), and sometimes as a concurrent or joint decision—as an inseparable part of the process of choice.

1. Weight Selection Viewed as a Prior Decision

Several widely divergent views of the public decision process have in common a view that important aspects of the weighting decision should be regarded by the decisionmaker as given to him. Two of these virtually assume lexicographic ordering, objective "1" is dominant, but in case two choices are equivalent in terms of objective "1," choice is made upon the basis of objective "2," etc. (Listing in alphabetical order is the best known lexicographic procedure.)

One view of this kind is that efficiency, as measured by private market allocations, is the dominant criterion; if a project is efficient in this sense, it (or some substitute) is worth undertaking; otherwise not. Once a project is so legitimized, the decisionmaker is welcome to examine other, secondary objectives in project selection or design. This appears to me to be the view of McKean (27), Harberger (18), and Mishan (32) when they insist that the correct (really the only correct) discount rate for discounting future benefits and costs and for assessing the opportunity costs of public funds is some specified measure of the marginal productivities of capital in the private sector.[16] This view "solves" the weighting problem of assumption and makes many otherwise difficult decisions easy. Those who hold this view are repeatedly appalled at the obvious outrages performed by the public sector, and the apparent acquiescence therein of otherwise sensible men.

A different but no less arbitrary lexicographic view is that public budgets for particular activities reflect dominant social choices, and that while efficient allocation of the funds within such budgets is appropriate, efficiency considerations do not reflect sensibly on the size of the budget.[17]

While neither of these forms of solution-by-assumption of the weighting problem is likely to prove literally satisfactory in all situations, either might provide insight into how the public decisionmakers regard their actions as constrained by a society's underlying consensus view of key issues they face.

An alternative to taking weights as inherently given is to regard them as an explicit prior decision. It is conceivable to imagine the political system having a procedure whereby we decide upon and then announce a fixed set of weights that will be controlling in choosing among income, income distribution, and so on. No one suggests this is the procedure used, although both Chenery (12) and Marglin (29) urge this as a real possibility for economic planners. Chenery, for example, suggests the planners announce a national income equivalent to balance-of-payments effects, thus making for a fixed tradeoff.[18]

Eckstein [16], Haveman [19] and Weisbrod [15] among others, while more or less accepting the view that weighting decisions are relatively stable and pre-existing, do not wish to assume them nor to expect political leaders to articulate them. Instead they suggest attempting to infer the weights by an analysis of past choices. Eckstein [16] suggests we look at an issue such as differential tax rates in which a decision on distribution is at the heart of congressional intent in order to discover implied values Congressmen hold. Haveman [19] applies this approach to evaluating water resource investments with respect to a multidimensional objective. These approaches are suggestive, even if one is unwilling to go all the way and take congressional actions as perfectly revealing social consensus.

Weisbrod deals with a two-dimensional objective function covering efficiency and income distribution. He suggests that every example of choice of a less efficient over a more efficient alternative implies a minimum implicit weight to the redistribution that is involved. His hope is that analysis of many decisions would reveal a weighting scheme. The advantage of this procedure is the potentially large sample available. The hazard is that any irrational choices, any misestimates of efficiency, and any nonincluded objectives would all be imputed as distributional benefits. But the real test of Weisbrod's suggestion will depend upon whether it produces a clear and consistent pattern of implicit values. To my knowledge, it has not been tested as yet.

Yet another approach to weighting of objectives is to regard certain objectives as constraints. Suppose we would like to attain one objective, with the constraint that we cannot concentrate on that objective until certain other basic goals have been secured, at least to a minimum extent. Initially, then, these latter goals assume high priority, for we cannot turn our major attention to the former objectives without having satisfied the latter. Once the latter goals have been satisfied, they can be given shadow prices which reflect the price paid in assuring their achievement. This is often a useful (as well as a traditional) approach to allocational problems. It may, however, prove difficult to define which objectives are genuinely to be regarded as constraining.

2. Weights as the Outcome of Political Process

The discussion above treated the appropriate weighting scheme as a preexisting condition for the decision process. Dahl and Lindblom [13], Braybrooke and Lindblom [8], and Maass [25], Major [26], Banfield [2], Eckstein [16] among many others regard weights as generated by the process of decision. In this view the political process addresses weighting problems not abstractly but as a case-by-case confrontation. In each case need for a decision about what to do forces a discussion, or compromise, or struggle between competing objectives. To Maass, the essence of the *legislative* process is the making of choices between conflicting objectives. The decisions will be made upon the basis of the information (or prejudices) available, and the scope for the analyst in affecting the decision will be reasonably to identify the choices. Eckstein expresses the strong view (to which I find no academic dissent) that administrators and project analysts should not arrogate the weighting process and bury the choices within a single measure of benefit.

This whole area strikes an analyst as untidy. It is clear that choices among objectives must be made, and that the political process must somehow make them. But we appear to be undecided about whether it does so within narrowly confined limits of underlying consensus, or with substantial discretion. Is the alternative to the invisible hand the responsible arm or the visible paw? Perhaps more important is the source of such political discretion as exists; is it simply variance in underlying views, is it ignorance of indifference on the part of the citizen, or is it an explicit delegation of authority by the electorate? Answers to these questions critically affect subsequent research strategy. Banfield [2] appears to espouse the nihilistic view that discretion arises from such deep underlying ignorance and/or indifference that there are no effective limits on the wondrous ways of politicians. At the opposite extreme, if one assumes that politics is a mere veil that masks a variety of different underlying views, a key to understanding the outcome is to study the variance of underlying views. Downs [15] and to a lesser extent, Lindblom, embody this view. It has important precursors in an older political science literature on interest groups.[19]

What is particularly disturbing is that I can find virtually no disposition on the part either of economists or political scientists to engage in an empirical study of the decision process that will resolve these areas of debate. The large literature is almost entirely theoretical and assertive. Yet, survey data about public attitudes on issues exist and provide some sort of a base. Similar data about ex-post public reaction to political decisions and procedures might be developed. In fact we now ask such evaluative questions but only about things like a major war on the overall evaluation of a president or a party. Even to say more would take me further along the road than I care to go to design a study of how decisions are reached, and the extent to which they are responsive to public opinion. Such a study seems worth somebody's undertaking; it seems more promising than another decade of assertions in resolving our differences.

ARTICULATION OF THE PUBLIC INTEREST

There are divergent views about how the political structure articulates social priorities and the extent to which *process* determines outcome. It is helpful to start with a dichotomous classification that overstates differences in points of view. In one view the political process is a market-like mechanism that coalesces views that inhere in the members of the society. Here the political process is a facilitating and implementing one, not inherently a formative one. An efficient government, like an efficient market, quickly and accurately translates inherent preferences into explicit consensus. Just as a market may perform a mapping function (since people discover their preferences best by confronting real alternatives) so an efficient government serves to help people discover as well as fulfill their collective preferences. In principle (though, of course, not necessarily in practice) one should be able to simulate such a process, and simply add a government sector to a general equilibrium model of the society. Government (in this view) is a decisionmaker only in the limited sense of a reactor and processor of signals it receives. A properly functioning government will arrive at an optimal decision set without exercise of independent judgment.

The second view is that while individual social preferences clearly exist and play a role, they are sufficiently inchoate, ambiguous, or conflicting that the political process is required to force a public interest and it does so with substantial discretionary choice. Without knowledge of the motives of the governors, and of the political process itself, there is no indicated solution, nor accurate prediction of governmental action. In this view, to create a government sector it must be given objectives, procedures, and decisionmakers. However, the way in which individuals' preferences constrain or otherwise affect public decisionmakers must be made explicit.

The differences between the approaches are important not only in terms of the information each requires in order to permit prediction of outcomes, but in whether comparative static analysis is possible or must be replaced by a genuinely dynamic model of political decisions. I limit myself to a few dicta here, and refer to the interested reader to the fuller discussion in [43].

1. The Government as a Quasi-Market

In all market-type analyses of the political process, voting is the means by which individual values are translated into action decisions. Bowen's pioneer article [7] is of this type. If we assume that the tax-burden of any public expenditure on each individual is known to him, and if we assume everyone votes under simple majority rule we can predict the outcome of elections.

Abstracting from the effect of the tax structure on political choices, it is clear that so far as we can reduce preference to a single dimension, it is the median preference that dictates the outcome of majoritarian voting. The result thus depends wholly upon the pattern and variance of voters' preferences and the structure of taxes. The result may, but need not, yield the pure theory of public expenditure solution. That is based upon aggregate willingness to pay and thus, if tax burdens are equal, it depends upon the mean rather than the median willingness to pay. Bowen believes that the institutional facts are such that median and mean will tend to coincide because voters' preferences are symmetrically distributed. I know of no evidence with which to confirm this conjecture. Bowen does not suggest that a referendum on each proposed decision actually is the decision procedure, but rather that it is a decision procedure that might be used, and that perhaps roughly is represented by the institutions of democratic government.

A much more elaborate but broadly similar theory is presented by Downs [15] to whom government consists of men who like the emoluments and perquisites of their jobs and whose goal is reelection or reappointment by elected officials. The government is thus motivated to maximize its political support. The government is interested in a citizen's vote, not his welfare; it must, however, cater to his view of welfare to get his vote. Were it not for uncertainty, Downs' model would be fully mechanistic and predictable.[20]

A less mechanistic model is offered by Maass. He offers an explanation that to a major degree is a two-stage political market theory. In the first stage the voters choose men, who in their personal capacity, and in virtue of their character, are fitted to discharge the task of deliberation and discussion at the parliamentary stage.[21] In the second stage, these officials are held accountable for their political acts by the need to seek periodic reelection.

Maass' model gives rather more freedom to the politician than does Downs': officials are not worrying about the probability of reelection in every move, only in their overall performance. At the very least they are only constrained to be aware of their constitutents' sensibilities. Indeed if they regard their mandate as sufficiently general they have the need as well as the opportunity to crystalize their constitutents' values. Here Maass verges into a creative or formative view of government and the definition of public interest.

Market theories can be criticized from within or from outside the market framework. Most critics of the votes-as-market-signals approach to analysis of the political process have sought a more substantial discretionary role of government; we shall consider these just below. Within the market-analogy framework, Arrow [1], Black [6] and Buchanan [11] have questioned the ability of such a system to translate inherent preferences into rational social priorities, and the efficiency of such a quasi-market system.

Arrow's well-known demonstration of the paradox of collective choice is so simply illustrated that it bears repeating.

Individual	Individual's preference ordering
I	$A \to C \to B$
II	$C \to B \to A$
III	$B \to A \to C$

Even if each of the individuals has no difficulty ordering his preferences among three competing possibilities—A, B, and C—there may be no clear collective preference. In the example clearly two-thirds prefer A to C, and two-thirds prefer C to B. Thus, if they first choose between B and C and then between A and C, A will command a majority. But two-thirds prefer B to A and a different order of choice can produce any one of the choices.[22] Black [6] and Rothenberg [37] among others have explored the theoretic consequences of alternative voting and balloting schemes in producing outcomes, and both discover a purely political dimension to the politics of consent. To this we shall return.

Buchanan [11] in a paper stimulated by Arrow, identifies some important weaknesses in the market analogy. He accepts the voting process as analogous to the market mechanism, but is wary about drawing welfare implications from the analogy. Buchanan believes in the efficiency of decentralized market decisions and is concerned lest the loose analogy with voting give a similar blessing to voters' decisions. He notes:

1. Voting involves an extra dimension of uncertainty: consequences follow the collective vote, not the individual vote; therefore, the voter may not really vote his own best interests because he underestimates the possibility of the decision impinging on him. Indeed since in a collective vote there is a diffusion of responsibility for the collective decision, the individual may act in the mass as he would never act individually. A man may vote for prohibition, for capital punishment, or for a war policy while at the same he would not abstain from alcohol, invoke the death sentence, or opt for military service for himself or his son.

2. In voting, the individual is influenced by his sense of participation in social choice. A vote for open housing need not imply willingness to live in a racially mixed neighborhood: indeed many of the most ardent supporters of such laws have exercised their option to move further away from integrated neighborhoods. Men may be willing to do collectively unto others what they would not do individually nor consent to have done to them unless done to all.[23]

3. In voting, the individual is often faced with indivisible votes for mutually exclusive choices. He cannot make marginal choices, or influence very much the definition of candidate or choices. Often he votes for candidates some of whose policies he disapproves. Thus the mandate of a winning candidate is really misinterpreted.

4. Minority votes are wasted, whereas even minority preferences exert influences in the market. If fear of wasting their votes leads voters to vote for their second choices, even actual votes for candidates may fail to reflect the strength of the support their views have.[24] Nonvoting, an alternative form of expression, is not often easily interpreted.

5. Typically, voting provides equality of influence of individuals, instead of reflecting command over resources. Bowen is wrong: the weighting of individual choices is different in the marketplace and the polling booth. Buchanan here goes well beyond the point that it would require some remarkable coincidences to assure that the distribution of political and economic influence were perfectly correlated. He adopts (I think) a view of Frank Knight's [22] that market votes are in some sense superior to political votes.[25]

These critiques by Arrow and Buchanan serve to warn against too quick acceptance of an analogy of the political process with the market process. The practical question is whether the two situations are sufficiently similar that the economist's techniques of analysis and his theorems about market behavior can be applied directly and fruitfully to political decisionmaking. My own answer after reading in the political-market literature is "No." I certainly believe that individual citizen voters both influence and constrain political choices; but they do so within limits sufficiently broad that attention to choices *within the limits* needs, deserves, and repays analysis.

The important issue is, of course: how large are the limits? In the political choice arena, the limits seem to me sufficiently large that we cannot merely pay attention to voters' preferences. All of the following contribute to a substantial discretionary role of government: the variance in individuals' views; the fact that voters choose infrequently and among bundles of policies; the fact that many views are not held so strongly that a political leader who violates them is at once anthema; that many voters' preferences are inchoate, uncertain, and subject to change; that pressure groups can and do negotiate with governments; and finally that political leaders can, in fact, lead their followers on many issues. If these things are true, the choice set of the government while constrained by voters' preferences may be far from singular.

2. Government as an Organic Chooser of Ends

Dorfman [14] presents a suggestive model of the public sector that is close to the market analogy models while yet explicitly introducing governmental choice. He returns to an older view of the world in which individual views are oriented to and expressed by socioeconomic pressure groups. The government is in a sense a coalition of such blocs that cooperate in order to provide public goods. The constraint of coalition requires that no group be sufficiently badly treated that it is motivated to withdraw its support. In Dorfman's terminology each group has a potential voters' surplus: the excess of its self-perceived benefits from provision of the public good over the group's contribution to its provision. The imposed constraint is that this voters' surplus must be nonnegative for each group. But the government has multiple possibilities beyond this since it can weight the interest of the different groups unequally. Dorfman notes that the differences in political parties constitute, in effect, different weighting schemes, and members of the party in power have substantial freedom to pursue their own preferences, and to compete for the right to govern by catering to those groups that can generate sufficient support to keep them in power.

What is refreshing in this formulation is first the explicit statement of the constraint; second, the recognition of Governors as a group with ends of its own and some ability to pursue them; and third, the recognition of intermediate groups as a focus for articulating and coalescing individual values. What the behaviorial implications of this view are, are in dispute. Dorfman believes that the need to satisfy all (or most) groups imposes a downward pressure on public expenditure; I suspect that this same need is more likely to lead to logrolling and expenditure increases than to limit expenditures.

A more direct view of governmental search procedures can be represented by work of Maass [25] and Major [26]. Here the legislative process is centrally concerned to discover what agreement on objectives can be reached. Partly this is a matter of bringing together elected spokesmen for individuals and groups, but more basically it is a genuine search. The process of discussion is critically involved in a mapping function—it poses issues that permit both legislators and their constituents to discover their views about objectives. It may thus permit (via compromise and persuasion) the development of agreement on public objectives, which can serve for a time as the social objective function. This view continues to disquiet many economists, for it leaves a large element of slack within the governmental decision process that is not readily understood in terms of inputs into governmental decisions. Thus we are limited in our ability to predict Government decisions

Rothenberg [37] has an enormously elaborate model whose purpose is to remove this element of slack. Unfortunately it defies concise description. To quote his summary, in part, "The legislative process is seen as an n-person, nonzero sum, repeated cooperative game of strategy, for which no general solution exists

. . . unfortunately, manipulation of the model to elucidate its complication is beyond the scope of the present paper." I confess to being skeptical. Game theory, here as elsewhere, seems to me to provide a vocabulary for discussing a multiplicity of outcomes rather than proving a tool for predicting particular outcomes.

One aspect of Rothenberg's model picks up a strand that has characterized the work of Duncan Black [6] over two decades: the influence of the institutional rules of legislative decision on the outcome of the decision process. I shall neglect this fascinating literature only because the chief question this paper addresses is the choice of policies within a relatively fixed institutional framework, not with the influence on choices of changes in the institutional framework.

Banfield [2], like Maass and Black, is a political scientist, but unlike them he is profoundly skeptical of the utility of the type of analysis that characterizes economics: the solution of constrained maximization problems. His central point is that in the articulation of social values, the techniques of economics do not merely fail to predict behavior (because we need more information about individuals' values, or the nature of the constraints, etc.) but rather that they are inherently baised and bound to mispredict. As I understand Banfield's view, the alternating and intertwined activities of discussion, of struggle, and of arbitration, constitute the heart of the decision process and exhibit such variance in possible outcomes that they dominate the problem of explaining political behavior. To neglect these in favor of the inputs into the political hopper is to neglect the major sources of variance in favor of the minor ones. In effect he argues that the limits placed on decisionmakers by individual preferences are so wide as to be of no real interest.

Banfield's view might be expected to lead him toward the Black and Rothenberg analyses of process, or toward the literature by Schelling [40] and others on the strategy of conflict, or perhaps toward the organizational theorists. Here too, however, Banfield is pessimistic almost to the point of nihilism. His pessimism seems to me extreme, but it underlines the absence as yet of a compellingly effective set of predictive theories. Banfield's view that politics and thus also the prediction of its outcomes, is an art rather than a science, may prove right; at this stage neither the economists nor the bulk of the political scientists seem prepared to abandon the search for an explanation of public decisionmaking.

3. Evaluation of Alternative Views

This extended discussion of alternative views as to the nature of and means of articulation of the public interest clearly reveals no consensus. Indeed it is relatively easy to demonstrate why each approach is deficient. While one of these theories may with slight changes prove adequate, it is more likely we will have to await a more profound insight. It seems to me of prime importance to distinguish between the present inadequacy of our theories, and the presence of a phenomenon. Things need not be understood to exist; substantial agreement on certain social priorities may exist despite our inability (at any point in time) adequately to derive them from basic principles. Suppose we are today unable to *derive* from individual values a consistent set of social valuations that enable us to say "there is a clear collective demand for this activity." Are we constrained to act as if it does not exist, or to settle for the logic of the lowest common denominator of acceptable action, that which will command unanimous consent? The answer seems to me to be "No." To answer otherwise would make us prisoners of our ignorance. It is less elegant, but not less scientific, to take as a starting point for evaluating social actions, the revealed objectives of society instead of the derived ones.

Let me put the matter more strongly. Suppose one could prove that in some fundamental sense the prediction of social values is impossible from basic information about individuals and their political representatives. Would it then be necessary to quit the analysis of public decisionmaking? I think not. One might take the nature of social valuations as revealed by past actions and assume that such preferences have some stability. In other words it might be possible to infer dominant collective social priorities from social actions and the repudiation or nonrepudiation of them by the electorate.[26]

In the United States today it is hard to avoid a strong presumption in favor of believing there is a strong collective preference for certain public goods such as public aid to education, for improved highways, for redistribution of income in favor of the elderly, and in favor of farmers. Are these only today's choices of today's individuals or are they a reliable indicator of how Americans are likely to feel next year or even ten years hence? I think there is evidence of stability in some choices, and gradual change in others. In any period there are highly debatable issues that get resolved and stay resolved for generations, not unanimously, but sufficiently that legislators of each party are content to let them lie. Today the debates about minimum wages, and social security (even medicare), seem remote and (in this sense) resolved. We may ask about the appropriate level of the programs, but their existence is not likely to be subject to any serious challenge. On the other hand, I would not argue very strongly in favor of the presumption of similar preferences for or against integrated housing or schools, for foreign aid of nonalined or Eastern countries, for domestic gun control, or for international disarmament. At any time some issues are genuinely unresolved, for others the degree of consensus is uncertain.

Evidence on these matters is available even in the absence of analytic solution. Not only do elections provide some information about revealed preferences but enormous quantities of attitudinal information can be collected by the techniques of survey research. As theorists, we tend to denigrate stability and regularity in the absence of comprehensive theory. We should not. Men successfully and repeatedly circumnavigated the globe using navigational theories now regarded as naive and wrong. Today we can predict with enormous accuracy the tides along the Bay of Fundy but we do not begin to understand their differences from place to place. Closer to home, we can more accurately predict the aggregate effects of a tax cut, than the incidence of it.

In arguing so I do not mean to minimize or disparage the progress of the purely theoretical debate. Even our failures are more promising now, and we have come a long way beyond the emptiness of the new welfare economies. Most encouraging is the genuine joint dialog among social scientists of different fields as well as different persuasions.

CONCLUDING COMMENTS: THE ROLE OF EFFICIENCY

Economists traditionally place major emphasis on the efficient allocation of resources, and much of the public interest debate is also so phrased. This is particularly, but not exclusively, the case when dealing with the portion of the debate concerning the discount rate. In this paper I have stressed a multidimensional objective function rather than one involving only efficiency. Economists who disagree with this approach are not likely to do so on the grounds that efficient use of resources is the only sensible objective of social policy, nor on the grounds that efficient use of resources will never conflict with other objectives. Instead they may argue first, that any worthwhile objectives can be incorporated within an efficiency framework by an appropriate set of measurements of benefits and costs. Thus efficiency can embrace maximizing a utility function that may have several arguments. Or they may argue, second, that objectives like income redistribution not conveniently and conventionally included within the efficiency framework can and should be satisfied by lump sum taxes and transfers that do not serve to distort resource allocation.

Since either one of these arguments is, if correct, sufficient for use in the efficiency solution, the case for efficiency seems powerful and it has many adherents. Nevertheless, many economists, including this one, do not find these arguments persuasive.

The first argument has already been discussed at some length and constitutes a highly important question of research strategy: if there is a multi-dimensional objective structure, can it effectively be compressed into a single dimension by assignment of a measure of benefits? My view is that while it is possible so to compress it, it is not desirable to do so because it leads to submerging real issues behind a facade of faulty measurements. Bias can run either way: by overvaluing intangibles (see for example the characteristically shoddy imputation of secondary benefits), or by neglecting as benefits those differences in the vector of public and private goods that are not readily measured. There is, of course, no inherently correct answer to the question of what is the best form of response to difficulties in accurate measurement. I would rather measure only what I have confidence in measuring with some accuracy and leave "incommensurables" to be decided by explicit choice. It may be easy to choose between defense and education at a given time even though it is hard to express a price that equilibrates them.[27] If one does not use a uniform system of valuations (and I am arguing that one need not) there is a danger that one will make some inconsistent decision. But if one uses badly biased data there is a danger of making consistent but faulty decisions. As has been said in another connection, it may be better to be vaguely right than precisely wrong.

The second defense of efficiency fails to prove compelling if one believes that approximate lump sum transfers cannot be made, that they cannot be made without high transaction costs, or that they will not be made. These are factual questions but I have no real doubt about the facts. It might for example be possible to achieve indirectly for under-privileged urban residents what direct public action is today providing via urban redevelopment, and other poverty programs. But it is unlikely that in a political context the same results would have been achieved. The current effort to replace a myriad of welfare programs by a negative income tax provides contemporary test of how easy or difficult it will prove to achieve by taxes or transfers what might otherwise be provided by direct public action. Whether for good or ill it is frequently easier to do things one way than another. To limit the public policymaker to allocationally neutral tools constrains him, and thus changes the nature of the results he achieves. Whether the change is (as I believe) large or whether it is small is a factual matter on which one day we may have facts.

Obviously the question "What is the public interest?" has no simple answer Indeed, asking the question invites the sort of smile reserved for small children and benign idiots. Let me end this discussion by some wholly personal assertions. There is a role for measurement, a role for analysis and some need for explicit decisionmaking. We do our decisionmakers a disservice if we blur the roles. One such blurring occurs if we submerge real decisionmaking among competing objectives into a mere measurement problem by giving the advice: "assign benefits and costs and then pick the optimal set of projects." This provides too little help. One of the economist's most potent functions is honestly to identify what can be accurately measured and compared and what (on the other hand) involves such heroics of assumption that actual measurements are but concealed preferences. The advantage of articulating real choices over assigning measures that appear to obviate them is to make the decision explicit and subject to review. But having identified the scope for explicit choice does not mean public administrators have unconstrained choice. Within particular dimensions, departures from the efficient solution ought to be identified and justified.

Clearly all sorts of decisions do get made and not all of them are sensible. My conception of the analyst's role is to force an articulation of the proximate objectives served and of the conflicts between such obejctives. I should be willing to regard open decisions so arrived at by elected (or otherwise responsible) public officials as a reasonable approximation to the collective values that we call the public interest. I think at present that we conceal so many issues and conflicts, both among objectives and among alternative means, that we increase the discretion of the policymaker beyond that necessary or desirable.

NOTES

1.   Similar is Musgrave's definition of public goods as those produced under public management [33], p. 42. It should be noted that Musgrave recognized the need for a more complex classification which he provides.

2.   Knut Wicksell, "A New Principle of Just Taxation." Reprinted in [34].

3.   The identity of who the "public" is, is deferred for the moment.

4.   Millard F. Long [24] has recently challenged Weisbrod's concept.

5.   Option demands are in a sense much like consumers surplus: they arise because the price charged for the good or service is below the maximum each buyer would be willing to pay. Thus the option to buy at a low future price has present value. Weisbrod's insight, I think is that option demands are a significant source of demand for public action.

6.   Stigler [44] provides a conceptual analysis of the costs and benefits of obtaining information. Telser [46] deals with the problem of buying information in the form of advertising as a joint product with news, entertainment, etc.

7.   A Department of Health, Education, and Welfare study, [49] supplies some evidence on the incentive effects of subsidies to scientists and other academic personnel.

8.   See Freeman [17] for a recent effort to work out the implications of income distribution for public investment planning.

9.   They are discussed in [43].

10.   Scitovsky [41] demonstrated an inconsistency in the principle in the case in which price changes occurred: Baumo [4], Little [23], and Kennedy [21] questioned the use of potential compensation.

11.   Banfield ([2], p. 11) suggests the following as an extreme parable about a society that can make accurate interpersonal comparisons of the subjective states of individuals A and B:

> If A's preference is for putting B into a gas chamber, then 'bliss for the whole universe' is served by his putting him there, provided only that B's loss of satisfaction at being put there is less than A's at putting him there. Even if B claims that his loss of satisfaction will be at least as great as A's gain of it, the just and equitable society will tell him that he is mistaken and put him there anyway in the 'good cause of adding more to the rest of mankind's (that is to say, A's) well-being.' If perchance A and his friends constitute 51 per cent of the population and B and his friends only 49 per cent, the matter will be simple indeed.

12.   This is, of course, a conclusion of Arrow's "General Impossibility Theorem": "If we exclude the possibility of interpersonal comparisons of utility, then the only methods of passing from individual tastes to social preferences which will be satisfactory and which will be defined for a wide range of sets of individual orderings are either imposed or dictatorial." [1], p. 59. For discussion and criticism of this famous proposition, see especially: Little [23], and Tullock [48].

13. See Truman [47] for an extended discussion of groups in the political process.

14. A better historian of thought might define it as the Sax-Wicksell-Lindahl-Musgrave-Bowen-Samuelson . . . tradition, to recognize the apparently valued theorem that no one ever has an original idea. Samuelson is diligent in identifying his predecessors and Musgrave provides admirable summaries of earlier views. In an earlier day theories of this type were called voluntary exchange theories.

15. Buchanan and Tullock [10] develop an ingenious "economic theory of constitutions" in which individuals find it advantageous to agree in advance to certain rules even though they may work to the individual's disadvantage on occasion.

16. The discussion of the discount rate as an implicit weighting scheme involves technical issues best omitted from this paper. They are discussed in [43].

17. A paper on my own [42] is a good example of use of this approach.

18. One is not limited in principle to linear relationships. Chenery's tradeoff at time t could be a variable function of the size and sign of balance of payments disequilibrium at time t.

19. An admirable summary with an extended bibliography is found in Truman [47].

20. Uncertainty creates some scope for leadership, and for errors that give politics an interesting dynamics. It is not possible to pursue them now. See Downs [15], esp. chapters 5-8.

21. The words are Barker's [3], quoted with evident approval by Maass [25], p. 569.

22. The theorem proved is that transitivity in all individual orderings is not sufficient to assure a collectively transitive set of choices.

23. Margolis and Marglin offer yet a different view of this problem. A man may be willing to pay his share of a joint venture only if he can force his reluctant neighbors to do the same [35]. In this view a vote is an offer to sign a social contract if enough others also sign.

24. This phenomenon may be found in the market too. If buyers can be persuaded to accept second best, their true preferences may not be effective.

25. Knight points out that individuals may be unequally constrained by voting from utilizing their "normally available capacities for action." Evidently Knight feels that unequal constraints are more unfair than unequal initial distributions of wealth.

26. See Birdsell [5] for such an attempt.

27. Obviously once the dividing line between them is set, an implicit (shadow) price exists. But the price may be very different a few years hence. In any case I am arguing that it may be easier to make the decision (and thus imply the price) than in some objective sense to assign the price and thus determine the decision. Only at a purely formal level are these equivalent.

REFERENCES

1. Arrow, Kenneth J., *Social Choice and Individual Values,* 2d, ed., New York: John Wiley & Sons, 1963.

2. Banfield, Edward C., "'Economic' Analysis of 'Political' Phenomena: A Political Scientists' Critique," Harvard Seminar on Political-Economic Decisions, March 1967 (ditto).

3. Barker, Ernest, *Reflections on Government,* London: Oxford University Press, 1942.

4. Baumol, William J., *Welfare Economics and the Theory of the State,* 2d ed., London: G. Bell & Sons, 1965.

5. Birdsall, William C., "A Study of the Demand for Public Goods," in Richard A. Musgrave, ed., *Essays in Fiscal Federalism,* Washington: The Brookings Institution, 1965, pp. 235-292.

6. Black, Duncan, *The Theory of Committees and Elections,* Cambridge: Cambridge University Press, 1958.

7.   Bowen, Howard R., "The Interpretation of Voting in the Allocation of Economic Resources," *Quarterly Journal of Economics,* 58:27-48, November 1943.

8.   Braybrooke and Lindblom, *A Strategy of Decision,* New York: 1963.

9.   Breton, Albert, "A Theory of the Demand for Public Goods," *Canadian Journal of Economics and Political Science,* 32:455-467, November, 1966.

10.   Buchanan, James M., and Gordon Tullock, *The Calculus of Consent,* Ann Arbor: University of Michigan Press, 1962.

11.   —————, "Individual Choice in Voting and the Market," *Journal of Political Economy* 62:334-343, August, 1954.

12.   Chenery, Hollis B., "The Application of Investment Criteria," *Quarterly Journal of Economics* 67:76-96, February, 1953.

13.   Dahl, Robert A., and Charles E. Lindblom, *Politics, Economics, and Welfare,* New York: Harper & Row, 1953.

14.   Dorfman, Robert, "General Equilibrium with Public Goods," presented to International Economics Association Conference on Public Economics, September, 1966.

15.   Downs, Anthony, *An Economic Theory of Democracy,* New York: Harper & Row, 1957.

16.   Eckstein, Otto, "A Survey of the Theory of Public Expenditure Criteria," in James M. Buchanan, ed., *Public Finances: Needs, Sources and Utilization,"* National Bureau of Economic Research, Princeton: Princeton University Press, 1961.

17.   Freeman, A. Myrick, III, "Income Distribution and Planning for Public Investment," *American Economic Review,* 57:495-508, June, 1967.

18.   Harberger, Arnold C., "Survey of Literature on Cost-Benefit Analysis for Industrial Project Evaluation," *Inter-Regional Symposium in Industrial Project Evaluation,* sponsored by the Economic and Social Council of the United Nations, Committee for Industrial Development, Prague, October, 1965 (mimeograph).

19.   Haveman, Robert H., *Water Resource Investment and the Public Interest,* Nashville: Vanderbilt University Press, 1965.

20.   Head, J. G., "Public Goods and Public Policy," *Public Finance,* 17:197-220, No. 3, 1962.

21.   Kennedy, Charles F., "The Economic Welfare Function and Dr. Little's Criterion," *Review of Economic Studies,* 20:137-142, No. 2, 1953.

22.   Knight, Frank H., "The Meaning of Freedom," in Perry, C. M., ed. *The Philosophy of American Democracy,* Chicago, 1943.

23.   Little, Ian Malcolm David, *A Critique of Welfare Economics,* 2d, ed. Oxford: Oxford University Press, 1957.

24.   Long, Millard F., "Collective-Consumption Services of Individual-Consumption Goods: Comment," *Quarterly Journal of Economics,* 81:351-352, May, 1967.

25.   Maass, Arthur, "System Design and the Political Process: A General Statement," in *Design of Water-Resource Systems,* Cambridge, Mass.: Harvard University Press, 1962, pp. 565-604.

26.   Major, David C., *Decision-Making for Public Investment in Water Resource Development in the United States,* Harvard University, Graduate School of Public Administration, Harvard Water Program, August, 1965 (mimeograph).

27.   McKean, Roland N., "Cost-Benefit Analysis and British Defense Expenditures," *Scottish Journal of Political Economy,* 10:17-35; February, 1963.

28.   Marglin, Stephen A., "Objectives of Water-Resource Development: A General Statement," in *Design of Water-Resource Systems,* Cambridge, Mass.: Harvard University Press, 1962, pp. 17-87.

29.   —————, *Public Investment Criteria,* Cambridge, Mass.: Massachusetts Institute of Technology Press, 1967.

30.   Margolis, Julius, "Secondary Benefits, External Economies, and the Justification of Public Investment," *Review of Economics and Statistics,* 39:284-291, August, 1957.

31.   ——————, "The Structure of Government and Public Investment," *American Economic Review, Papers and Proceedings,* 54:236-242, May 1964, with discussion, pp.250-257, *ibid.*

32.   Mishan, E. J., "Criteria for Public Investment: Some Simplifying Suggestions," *Journal of Political Economy,* 75:139-146, April, 1967.

33.   Musgrave, Richard A., *The Theory of Public Finance,* New York: McGraw-Hill, 1959.

34.   ——————, and Peacock, Alan T., *Classics in the Theory of Public Finance,* Macmillan, 1958.

35.   Olson, Mancur, Jr., *The Logic of Collective Action,* Cambridge, Mass.: Harvard University Press, 1965.

36.   Rothenberg, Jerome, *The Measurement of Social Welfare,* Engelwood Cliffs, Prentice-Hall, 1961.

37.   ——————, "A Model of Economic and Political Decision Making," Harvard Seminar on Political-Economic Decisions, March, 1967 (ditto).

38.   Samuelson, Paul A., "Diagrammatic Exposition of a Theory of Public Expenditure," *Review of Economics and Statistics,* 37:350-356, November, 1955.

39.   ——————, "The Pure Theory of Public Expenditure," *Review of Economics and Statistics,* 36:387-389, November, 1954.

40.   Schelling, Thomas C., *The Strategy of Conflict,* Cambridge, Mass.: Harvard University Press, 1960.

41.   Scitovsky, Tibor, "A Note on Welfare Propositions in Economics," *Review of Economic Studies,* 9:77-88, November, 1941.

42.   Steiner, Peter O., "Choosing Among Alternative Public Investments in the Water Resource Field," *American Economic Review,* 49:893-916, December, 1959.

43.   ——————, "Public Expenditure Budgeting," The Brookings Institution, forthcoming, 1969.

44.   Stigler, George J., "Economics of Information," *Journal of Political Economy,* 69:213-225, June, 1961.

45.   Strotz, Robert H., "Two Propositions Related to Public Goods," *Review of Economics and Statistics, 40:329-331, November, 1958.*

46.   Telser, Lester G., "How Much Does it Pay Whom to Advertise?", *American Economic Review,* 51:194-205, May, 1961.

47.   Truman, David B., *The Governmental Process,* New York: 1962.

48.   Tullock, Gordon, "The General Irrelevance of the General Impossibility Theorem," *Quarterly Journal of Economics,* 81:256-270, May, 1967.

49.   United States, Department of Health, Education, and Welfare, *A Survey of Federal Programs in Higher Education,* 1962.

50.   Weisbrod, Burton A., "Collective-Consumption Services of Individual-Consumption Goods," *Quarterly Journal of Economics* 78:471-477, August, 1964.

51.   ——————,'. Income-Redistribution Effects and Benefit-Cost Analysis of Government Expenditure Programs," in Chase, Samuel B., Jr., ed. *Problems in Public Expenditure Analysis.* Washington: The Brookings Institution, 1968.

III
THE POLITICS OF SOCIAL ACCOUNTING

The Independence of the Social Accountant

Philip Green

A large literature has been devoted to the problem of obtaining and maintaining the independence of public accountants. The necessity for this independence seems virtually self-evident, however, the necessity for independence of the social accountant is perhaps less clear.

In this paper, Philip Green discusses the problems of the independence of social scientists, a group which encompasses accountants, and particularly social accountants. The problem of independence in social accounting may well be even more knotty than that encountered in the conventional environment. For example, who pays the accountant? As Green points out, the client of the social scientist is often a single party, the government. It is obviously more difficult to be independent of the one large client than a group of smaller ones.

However, the independence of the social scientist involves considerably more complexities than would be caused by a pecuniary tie to the client. As noted by several of the writers in this volume, social accounting must involve moral judgments. The social scientist cannot work in a moral vacuum; his judgments are not solely technological. But then, what if the values and moral judgments of the social scientist are different from those of the client? What if he views the client's actions as incompatible with his own values?

The work of the social scientist and the social accountant is often manipulative in two possible directions. The social scientist himself may be manipulated and his work may manipulate others. Obviously, independence becomes even more difficult. Finally, Green suggests that the trend towards the institutionalization of social science tends to undercut independence of thought and action.

One doubts that Green knows much about accountants, or that he even had them in mind when he wrote this paper. Nevertheless, his comments have direct applicability, not only to social accountants, but to the accounting profession as a whole.

Philip Green is a member of the Department of Government at Smith College.

SOURCE: From *The Annals,* Vol. 394 (March 1971), pp. 14-27, Copyright 1971 by The American Academy of Political and Social Science. This paper was originally titled "The Obligation of American Social Scientists."

SHALLOW: . . . if, sir, you come with news from the court, I take it there is but two ways: either to utter them, or to conceal them. I am, sir, under the king, in some authority.

PISTOL: Under which king, bezonian? speak, or die.

—Henry IV, Part 2

In the United States, discussions about the relationship between social scientists and the federal government are often not really discussions of that topic at all. Rather, they are thinly disguised attacks on or defenses of the policies and posture of that government, addressed essentially to our political beliefs. The thrust of such discussions is to suggest that before deciding whether and under what conditions to accept a government position, grant or consultantship, one must form a clear opinion on the proposition that the United States heads up a worldwide counterrevolution or, contrarily, represents fundamentally decent and progressive social forces.

This approach to the subject, tied down as it is to particular opinions about current policies, leads to essentially self-defeating analyses of the government's involvement in social science. Those who see the issue as simply one of boycotting an imperialist or racist government doom themselves to a position of comparative ineffectuality, since they are unable to give *any* reasons for being chary of such involvement to those who disagree with them politically.[1] On the other hand, to make the constructive potential of American policy an assumption that underlies all discussions of this relationship, can desensitize the observer to a whole range of very real concerns. Most especially, attention gets shifted to the narrow vocational concern with "government interference," an invidious phrase with which scientists try to discredit the perfectly reasonable desire of those who pay for research to insure that they will get what they are paying for. The clear implication of most such commentaries is that if only government watchdogs would leave social scientists alone, professional laissez-faire would take care of all ethical problems—or, rather, none would be found to exist, since any research done freely is automatically ethical.[2]   But just as a laissez-faire economy can "freely" generate wage slavery, so laissez-faire social science can freely generate what Conor Cruise O'Brien calls "counterrevolutionary subordination"—or any other kind.[3] O'Brien's complaint is chiefly against the willingness or desire of social scientists to subordinate themselves and their work to the implementation of a destructive American foreign policy. But from a perspective in which it is important to maintain the intellectual independence of social science *any* subordination—revolutionary, counterrevolutionary, or conventional—is potentially harmful, and voluntary subordination to good men may be just as damaging as that which is coerced by bad men.

THE PROBLEMS

It is appropriate, therefore, to forget for a moment one's judgment of American foreign and domestic policies, and look instead at the general relationship between government and social science. When one does this, certain problems present themselves—and they are problems that do not vanish simply with a change in administration, or war, for they stem from the generally laudable but seductive desire of social scientists to make themselves useful.

The nature of these difficulties can perhaps be seen most clearly if we ask the following question: Under what conditions would research in the social sciences be most likely to have a successful policy application? To begin with, it seems obvious that if social science is to have a practical short-run application, a given research problem must be defined in terms which are familiar to public officials, and suggestions for action or potential solutions must be phrased so as to be politically acceptable—that is, must be "constructive" rather than "negative," and consensus- rather than conflict-creating. The ramifications of this need are many, and dangerous in their implications for the future condition of social science.

Generally, it is a commonplace observation that policy-makers tend to have a particular view of "the real world"—a view which in our society sees the dominant forces in political life as a competing tyrannies of public opinion, organized interest groups and their official allies, and the bureaucrats' narrow conception of administration feasibility. The policy-makers' world, in other words, is the familiar one of incremental change and political prudence; the world in which one proposes nothing startlingly innovative until the last possible moment, so as to avoid making enemies and mobilizing centers of resistance.

This world view may perhaps be a wise one when held by the politician or administrator, but it is deadly to the development of social science.[4] Insofar as political leaders become their own instinctive theoreticians, they operate in this "real world" as vulgar empiricists, taking the accumulation of current "facts" to be synonymous with the whole of existence. Unhappily, this concern with what "is" and neglect of what may be, could be, or will be, makes the creation of explanatory or critical social theory impossible; with such a focus one can never do more than predict that tomorrow will be like today, with a few minor changes. Such typical instances of realism as the exercise of prudent foresight about next year's elections are no more an adequate substitute for social theory than the calm conviction that the sun will rise tomorrow is an adequate substitute for astrophysics. There are plentiful pressures, as it is, to produce a present-ridden social theory: witness the failure of mainstream social science to foresee *any* of the major crises that now threaten the stability of the United States. One cannot help but trace at least some part of this failure to the coincidence of perspectives between American social scientists and our governing elites; to honor in any sense—as policy-oriented research necessarily does—the wisdom of the "practical man" is therefore but to institutionalize that unfortunate coincidence.[5]

On the face of it, of course, there is no necessity for research sponsored by the government to follow the conventional wisdom. But the pressures are immense, and some are bound to go unrecognized unless special care is taken to be conscious of them and to compensate for the effect. This is especially true of the internal pressure within social scientists: the urge to reform and the concomitant belief that more knowledge is always better than less, which only the most dedicatedly conservative among us escape. The belief in the progressive role of knowledge carries with it the conviction that anyone who offers a chance to pursue knowledge is conveying an indubitable benefit, and the reformist urge further makes an ally of anyone who promises to put that knowledge to effective use. The government-as-sponsor, therefore, comes with impressive credentials, and the temptation to fall into the traps of practicality and "relevance" is correspondingly great. There are many ways, some barely noticeable, which the conjunction between the policy-maker's need for assistance on his own terms, and the scientist's desire to be helpful, may deflect the work produced by social scientists from the paths it might otherwise follow.

COMPROMISES WITH INDEPENDENCE

At the technical level, for instance, that kind of collaboration may entail procedural compromises with the independence of research, such as accepting the severe time limits and short-run orientation with which governments operate as a constraint on one's research, or accepting the categories of official statistics. To take one example of the latter difficulty, a researcher employed to seek out structural patterns underlying the occurrence of interpersonal aggression ("violent crimes") could not study the subject thoroughly without taking account of two types of behavior that never appear in official records: police violence, and at least some kinds of military violence.[6] But no study which took those two categories seriously could be of use to any government officials, and that obvious fact is likely to affect a research design created with an eye to catching official interest.

Similarly, there are pressures to accept not just official categories but official terms of intellectual discourse as well. It is possible, for example, that social scientists may propose an understanding of foreign policy that goes well beyond the traditional Cold War approach, and receive a respectful hearing; but at present that is likely only if the analyst pays lip service to, and thus once more reconfirms, the anti-Communist rhetoric that has helped fuel the cold war in the first place. More generally, even if the nation outgrows this particular bias in its international attitudes, it will remain desirable for scientific advisers to work with the assumption that commonsense versions of the national interest and national security take precedence over all other considerations in the analysis of their government's relations with other nations.[7]

There are yet deeper ways in which the association with government can affect the work of social scientists. In an outburst of enthusiasm, one prominent social scientist has written that ". . . eventually the entire complex of social prestige and social status will be rooted in the intellectual and scientific communities." That judgment is possible only on the assumptions that war and the space race have brought about "the acceptance of planning and technocratic modes in government," and that elites perceive the academic and scientific communities as places where theoretical knowledge is sought, tested, and codified in a disinterested way."[8] Realistically, though, "intellectuals" will seem properly "disinterested" and "technocratic" only if they do not issue any kind of challenge, partisan or otherwise, to the political realism of the governing elites. Practically speaking, this means that they must cast their research and their findings in the familiar rigid mold that maintains an epistemologically indefensible distinction between "facts" and "values," and provide their patrons only with what purport to be the former.[9] Already several of those academics who move easily between the university and government have taken steps to encourage such a distinction, by proclaiming "the end of ideology" and arguing that America's major social problems are now mostly "technical" in nature. The adoption of this terminology is hardly neutral in its effect. Since neither major American political party is currently committed to massive income redistribution, it becomes "unrealistic" and (by simple deduction) "value-laden," non-disinterested, and non-technocratic to see redistribution as a reasonable option for dealing with social issues. Similarly, neither party is committed to explicit public planning, or to a serious invasion of the sphere of private profit; it thus becomes unrealistic to define social problems and their potential solutions in a way that might suggest that particular kind of government activity as a reasonable option. Allegedly "disinterested" and "theoretical" analysis, then, produces a thoroughly truncated version of social science—or what comes to pass for social science.

PUBLIC DOCUMENTS AFFECTED

The concrete results of this transfiguration are evident in some of the public documents that social scientists have recently produced for various government agencies. In *Toward a Social Report,* for example, the concept of "social progress" is present in such a way that it seems to consist of discrete advances in a number of separate areas: health, social mobility, education, participation, and alienation, for instance. These are discussed in virtual isolation from each other; and thus the assumption is implicitly made that these are separable problem areas, not related aspects of the same problem. It is, therefore, further implicitly assumed that no single, over-all strategy commends itself for dealing with these discrete "problems," although the same data as are presented in the *Report* could be reworked by a "disinterested" observer so as to suggest a strategy of, say, income equalization combined with increased popular participation in political decision-making.[10]

Similarly, in a paper on "The Current Status of the Planning-Programming-Budgeting System" submitted to the Joint Economic Committee of Congress, Jack Carson describes a series of "analytic studies" of urban transportation undertaken by the Department of Transportation which, though at first glance astonishing, is ultimately quite unsurprising. In each of these studies an aspect of the urban transportation problem is considered and potential solutions presented; in each case, the data seem to suggest, indeed demand, a "strong" solution in the realm of greater public planning, ownership, and control; and in each case the investigators finally recommend "further study," or incremental additions to current policies, such as "demonstration projects." That is to say, in each case they recommend the exact course of action that would be chosen by any budget-conscious congressman who had never heard of social science, the result being not only that a measurable portion of the nation's intellectual resources has been wasted, but that the prejudices of "commonsense" have been reinforced.[11] Although surely some social scientists will always be able to produce work, no matter for whom, that escapes this fate, it is equally certain that many of them will be unable to resist the peculiar institutional pressures that government service carries with it.

Again, part of the problem of "realism" is the necessity of finding a feasible social context for one's research—feasible, that is, from the point of view of those from whom research support is being solicited. This constraint may be hardest of all to escape. For instance, at least in a democracy, it is difficult to conduct publicly sponsored studies of the politically powerful, be they (rarely) a self-conscious majority, a powerful and well-organized minority, or members of the governing elite themselves. Thus, government sponsorship can only emphasize the existing tendency in the social sciences to concentrate attention on the personality structures of the least influential of all constituencies—the apathetic, unorganized mass—while ignoring the physchic ills and antisocial characteristics to be found among those who really do rule. Of course, there are many studies of the overt activities of organized pressure groups and their congressional allies. But even these, for the most part, take the activities of their subjects at face value; that is, they assume that their subjects are rational economic and political men—a friendly assumption never remotely applied in studies of social outcasts and others among the powerless. Thus, the perspective attributed to sociologists by Martin Nicolaus—walking around with their eyes "turned downwards, and their palms upwards"—can only be further entrenched by an extension of direct government support for applied social research.[12]

SOCIAL SCIENCE BECOMES MANIPULATIVE

These last comments, moreover, suggest the most basic way in which the commingling of social science and government must be expected to affect the kind of contribution that scientific intellectuals make to society. Government policy-makers at all levels are prone to adopt, quite rationally from their stand-point, an attitude which sees the contribution of social science as essentially manipulative.

The official, that is, has a mandate to implement particular laws or even current opinion. Not being a political theorist, he does not ask if the "representative" system producing this mandate has been fairly and truly representative of all the interests, whether those of majorities or minorities, affected by it; conversely, if he is confronted with an overwhelming popular prejudice, he does not (publicly) ask if the demands it makes on him are perhaps unintelligent and uninformed. In either event, the policy has been authorized; let it be done, as efficiently and painlessly as possible. From this perspective, then—from the inside looking out—the official, replicating either mass intolerance or the political system's "mobilization of bias,"[13] will tend to see deviance, disaffection, dissidence, and similar types of social behavior as ills to be cured, "problems" to be solved. The development of some new form of social control, or the refinement of an old one, is most likely to be proposed as a solution: morale must be raised, violence cooled down, the disorganized reorganized, dissidence placated, policies "explained" (that is, sold). Rarely indeed will the government official see phenomena of social upheaval or dislocation as elliptical but fundamentally correct indictments of the system that employs him, as a challenge to stop taking for granted the composition, structure, or legitimate authority of his own or any other government agency. Rarely, in other words, will he imagine that opposition and alienation express interests opposed to *and properly superior* to his own;[14] and it is hard to believe, either abstractly or on the record, that he will welcome evidences of that kind of imagination in the social scientists whose skills he buys.[15]

As it is, an incredible amount of work in the social sciences has managed to be thoroughly anti-popular and manipulative, even without external encouragement. This intellectual habit, perhaps the worst one from which social scientists suffer, can only be strengthened as more of their work gets tailored to the requirements of those for whom manipulation is not merely a habit, but a positive vice. And as the profession of social science is overtaken by that fate, it will more and more come to be dominated by an elitist bias, which, regardless of how one judges it in

comparison with other biases, can hardly be confused with the political independence and detachment that social science presumably seeks.

PROJECT CAMELOT WAS TYPICAL

On reflection, finally, one is led to the significant conclusion that the notorious
Project Camelot, which social scientists have mostly treated as an unfortunate
aberration, in fact embodied almost all the defects referred to here, and was thus
thoroughly typical of what we must expect when government concerns are inter-
mixed with those of social science. (Only the obvious volatility of the research
design was atypical, thus lending to the affair its dramatic aspect.) Most especially
the adjustment which social scientists must make to a realist estimate of the
government's interests, and to officialdom's obvious preference for guides to
manipulation over other kinds of social science, are both evident in the design of
that project. Although several of the social scientists engaged in it have argued
persuasively that that design was entirely of their own creation, none deny having
accepted the funding agency's definition of the goals of the study, which in one
document were defined as follows:

... to identify with increased degrees of confidence those actions which a government might take to relieve conditions which are assessed as giving rise to a potential for internal war ... [16]

But when one chooses to view revolutionary discontent in this way, as a problem affecting the interests of those who prefer "order"[17] (which must mean those
already benefiting from some existing political arrangements), an important choice
has been made. Citizens have been conceived of as mere objects. To conceive of
them as the *subjects* of one's work would require accepting *their* definition of
the research problem rather than, as in this case, the Pentagon's. Clearly, these
two approaches to the subject matter are decisively different, and in choosing between them one must absolutely determine the ultimate nature of one's findings—
a question about which it is hard to image a government sponsor being neutral.
Of course, not all agency-funded social science research is initiated by academi-
cians bidding, like entrepreneurs, for a contract drawn up to government specifica-
tions.[18] But the kind of subordination to the realistic and manipulative interests
of government exposed in Project Camelot, is only the most overt and extreme
example of a constraint which in other cases social scientists are likely to impose
on themselves voluntarily, in order to impart practical value to their publicly
sponsored work.

In the light of the preceding analysis, what can one say about the responsibilities of the social scientist who wishes to maintain his own independence or, more
particularly, that of his discipline? At first thought, it is tempting to repeat
Julien Benda's passionate denunciation of "the treason of the intellectuals":

To have as his function the pursuit of eternal things and yet to believe that he becomes greater by concerning himself with the State—that is the view of the modern "clerk." . . .

Today the game is over. Humanity is national. The layman has won. But his triumph has gone beyond anything he could have expected. The "clerk" is not only conquered, he is assimilated. The man of science, the artist, the philosopher are attached to their nations as much as the day-laborer and the merchant. Those who make the world's values, make them for a nation . . .

This appears to me to be the true order of things: The "clerk," faithful to his essential duty, denounces the realism of States; whereupon, the States, no less faithful to their duty, made (*sic*) him drink the hemlock. The serious disorganization in the modern world is that the "clerks" do not denounce the realism of States, but on the contrary approve of it; they no longer drink the hemlock.[19]

To know that the truths we seek have nothing to do with party, or state, or nation . . . Unfortunately, to adopt this view one must believe what Benda also believed: that there is, finally, one Truth for all scientists and intellectuals, rather than a heterogeneous collection of many truths; that this religious Truth is ultimately universal by nature and therefore inimical to the interests of any one secular order; and that any kind of scientific method not leading directly to this Truth must be spurious. And even if one believes all this, one must remember what Benda himself had already perceived long ago, that in the modern world the universalist view is but one very ineffectual morality among a host of competitors: most social scientists, after all, *really do want* what the State wants. Thus, to adopt Benda's perspective will be to perpetuate an unhappy division in the intellectual world. On the one hand there will be a multiple of dependent technicians, performing "technical" operations on other people's values, maintaining the engine of public policy without asking any embarrassing questions about the condition of the vehicle; and on the other hand there will be a tiny minority of independent "philosophers," who ask irrelevant questions to which nobody listens.

It is more appropriate, therefore, to assume that since transcendence and universality no longer have a real existence in Western civilization, the intellectual laborer must remain in the secular world of competing, partial forces that lack, most of them, the slightest impulse toward truth-seeking. Moreover, since any important work he does will certainly have relevance to somebody's interests, he willy-nilly attaches himself to one or more of those forces. In the Wars of the Roses, only the identity of the true king is uncertain. The social scientist's situation is more extreme: there is no king, and many pretenders; under which king ought we to serve?

To this question there is one immediately appealing answer that seems to be implicit in the work of, for example, those social scientists who produced the document, *Toward a Social Report,* and who argue for a permanent Council of Social Advisers. If the interest to which the social scientist consciously addresses himself are public, it seems to be suggested, then that scientist ought to make certain that his knowledge will somehow reach, in usable form, the institutionalized repository of the *public* interest. In a democracy, that will be the coordinate branches of government in general, but most particularly the office of the Chief Executive; if the social scientist can't help but subordinate himself to some interest, that is the one he ought voluntarily to choose.

It is one thing, though, to argue that any group of offices or any one office, such as the Presidency or the executive branch generally, is the location in which the public interest will most likely be found to reside[20]; quite another to establish that it actually ever does reside there. Certain difficulties arise when we try to visualize the real political arrangements for which a conclusion of this sort would be true. It would be true, I should think, in a neo-classical polity, administered in its upper echelons by the best—wisest—men, for by definition they would be most likely to know what the public interest required. It would also be true in a Jeffersonian or Rousseauian democracy, about which we could accept two premises: that the will of the majority always genuinely ruled on matters of public policy, and that, on the average, the best way to pursue wisdom would be to seek out that popular will.

Surely, however, it is unnecessary to belabor the proposition that American democracy—any modern democracy—incarnates the wisdom neither of *aristos* nor *demos*.[21] Most of the time, rather, as political scientists from Arthur Bentley to Theodore Lowi have suggested, democratic governments merely express through their policies the desires of various competing and fragmentary private interests.[22] No doubt, as critics of group theory have made clear, the representative position of a president and his administration (or a court) may give them a perspective which surmounts the clash of private interests and, when effectuated, creates genuinely public policy. But it is equally true that very often the hope that this will happen, either in the office of the President or elsewhere, is only a vain one.[23]

To take but one example of the conceptual difficulty involved in any position that seeks to identify a permanent abode of the public interest, when President Kennedy refused to support Senator Kefauver in his challenge to the drug industry, the thalidomide scandal promptly proved the Senator right, and the President wrong, about where "the public interest" lay. With how much confidence then, could one possibly assert the proposition that, but a short time later, the President was right and the Senator wrong about the nature of the public's interest in the Communications Satellite dispute? How, indeed could one make such a judgment about any of the issues daily confronted by the various arms of our government, and the various voices of our citizenry?

Undoubtedly, the Presidency is better organized than any other office for producing and presenting something that might pass as an aggregate will; but in a social system as permeated by powerful private interests as contemporary democracy, no political institution—particularly not one as disunited as the American executive branch—can escape being their frequent captive. The fact is that our institutions are very poorly structured both to discover a general popular majority and to link that majority's sentiments and interests to the actions of political leaders. For this reason, the only way in which a president or even a dynamic congressional figure can be certain of relating his actions to the wishes of the general public is to exploit those vast and temporary waves of mass mood that disfigure modern societies. To respond to such currents of popular opinion may be somehow "democratic" (in the classical sense of mob rule), and the response somehow characterizable as an expression of "the public interest"; but no profession dedicated to the increase of intelligence can possibly justify subordinating itself to such a conception for even a moment.

To repeat, there is, then, no office or combination of offices in modern democracies whose occupants may safely be presumed to be acting in the public interest. For the social scientist, that means concretely that there is no single institution which can perform for us the task of linking together the demands of our subject matter, our own values, and the general good. Apostles of technocratic intelligence to the contrary, the priestly vocation for which Benda felt a hopeless nostalgia cannot be replaced by that of the scientist/intellectual. The nation-state is even less universalist than the church, and the President less authoritative than the Pope.

WHITHER THE SOCIAL SCIENTIST?

In such a situation it is tempting to say that there is nothing to be said, that every social scientist must choose for himself what use to make of his knowledge and where to sell his services. No doubt, laissez-faire in the intellectual realm has an attractiveness it has long since been found to lack in the economic realm. And yet, the drawbacks of sheer individualism are really the same everywhere.[24] Monopoly at the one extreme, and gross inequality at the other, are the inevitable result of a marketplace approach to the selling of expertise, for the market is rigged: the kinds of resources needed to buy that expertise are distributed no more equally than are the resources needed, say, to publish a daily newspaper. Moreover, except perhaps for the work of the macro-economists, whose advice supposedly keeps the economy functioning at a mediocre but passable level, social science is usually a luxury: only rarely can important results of its application be immediately seen and appreciated. Like any luxury, therefore, it will be budgeted out of economic fat; the national administration and corporate oligopolies will—already do—dominate the market on the buyer's side. Whatever benefits social science does convey, it will therefore convey unevenly. Most important of all, since those whose work is appreciated tend to give loyalty to those who appreciate it, the loyalty of some of the community's most intelligent and persuasive citizens will be channelled in the direction of certain partial interests and away from others. No more than executive-oriented nationalism, then, will sheer voluntarism, through the operations of some "invisible hand," manage to amalgamate the many biases of social scientists into a body of knowledge neutrally serving all interpretations of the general good.

In such circumstances, I think, it ought to be the primary professional commitment of social scientists (at least those whose work has some public resonance) to work in every conceivable way to "de-rig" the social science marketplace, and thus make possible to all social classes and groups the enjoyment of equal benefits from their intelligence. In a socially diverse society whose supposedly pluralist political institutions are often a facade masking a very unequal distribution of power, social scientists surely ought to make their own contribution to public life genuinely pluralist; and in a plural world where nationalism fosters a similar kind of inequality among nation-states, they ought surely to make their own contribution to the body of human knowledge genuinely internationalist.

What does this mean, practically speaking? Certainly there will always be a need for social scientists to translate their arcane knowledge into a language comprehensible to policy-makers and the attentive public, to gather and organize data about societies and their resources, and, where possible, to provide through research the kind of intelligence that corrects the misinformation of common sense. But all these benefits ought to be available in a usable form at the bottom of society as well as at the top, to the obstructionist as well as to the reformer, to the ideologue as well as to the technocrat, to those who are investigated as well as those who commission the investigation. Furthermore, this prescription does not imply that social intelligence ought to be more equally distributed only as among levels of government—that might easily amount to nothing more than recentralizing it in the state and cities.[25] Rather, what is implied is that social intelligence ought also to be dispersed away from government altogether, to organizations—unions, community groups, and the like—which are attempting to speak for those who are unrepresented or underrepresented in the national political process. Of course, if there are government agencies that have such groups for their clientele, and really do represent them, then they too should be favored. The main point is a general one: social science should become, in the familiar phrase, a countervailing power; only in that way can it justify its pretensions to the special respect, and degree of freedom in choosing its working conditions, that it has so far obtained.

This prescription, no doubt, is more difficult to put into practice than it is to state. Social scientists cannot be forced, after all, to work for the black or the poor or a Senator Kefauver rather than for a president's council of social advisers. There are, however, certain things that social scientists can do, *as an organized body,* to neutralize (and compensate for) the political effects of their research.

THE GOVERNMENT AND BASIC RESEARCH

For example, they should contest the notion that government agencies with their own interests can be accepted as sources of support for "pure" or "basic" research. Often, as we have seen, the desire to meet the preconceptions of a grant-ing agency will force aspects of research into a mold not of the investigator's own making.[26] Even when that does not happen, such grants are not politically neutral, since a funding agency by the very act of disbursing its funds justifies the size of its research budget and furthers its own interests in the competitive strug-gle to establish research priorities.[27] Thus, to the extent that the government re-mains an important superior of "basic" research, organized social science should lobby vigorously for a diversion of funds away from policy-oriented agencies and contractual relationships and toward outright grants to such relatively inde-pendent patrons as the National Science Foundation or (potentially) the universities.

As for that great bulk of government-supported research which will, as we have said, necessarily continue to be "applied" (that is, more or less openly tailored to the needs of a public or private client), social scientists should support all legislative initiatives to diversify the sources of their public patronage, whether the work in question is original research or mere data collection. Only if agencies with conflicting interests can offer their support will unorthodox approaches to applied research become more common and a more widespread and equitable diffusion of knowledge become somewhat more possible. Indeed, in the absence of such a decentralization policy, social scientists ought to offer their aid to those legislators who attack the size of the federal government's research budget, whether overall or in particular agencies; for, as I have suggested above, in the in-cremental world of the budget, this year's expenditure is taken as justifying next year's at a slightly higher level, and thus only the meat-axe approach can combat the process by which power is even further accumulated at the centers of government.

More immediately, it is crucial that social scientists should oppose all efforts to institutionalize social reporting and data collection *at the Presidential level,* in imitation of the Council of Economic Advisers (and they should equally oppose any expansion in the powers of those bodies such as the CEA, that already exist to give the President intellectual assistance). In the United States today, centra-lized social reporting carries with it the implication not only that problems exist and solutions are needed, but that the federal government through its executive branch ought to take the lead in articulating and implementing those solutions. Conversely, if such reporting were to become institutionalized, the further impli-cation would be that any social need *not* reported on at all, or casually dismissed, simply did not exist.[28] All these implications can be resisted, no doubt, but only with a great deal of difficulty. And in any event, it will be even more diffi-cult to resist the tendency, described by me earlier, for the choice of research goals to be affected by the source of the researcher's support, and for knowledge to be so perceived, categorized, and catalogued that it cannot be used except in ways that are congenial to some political interests and not to others. For these reasons, then, social scientists ought to lobby on this issue too, resisting the no-tion of a "Council of Social Advisers"—except perhaps in a form much more decentralized and less oriented to the executive than is suggested by current proposals.

Admittedly, social scientists have but a limited amount of the kind of access needed to promulgate such a policy successfully, in the face of so many opposed interests. But however little they may be able to accomplish in the overtly political arena, at the very least they are capable of adopting their own canons of professional responsibility, thereby discouraging certain types of work and encouraging others. In fact, this is done all the time. Graduate departments, for example, ardently embrace the laissez-faire ethic and the pretenses of scientism; professional associations, by the nominations they make to award-granting agencies and the kinds of public and private bodies to which they lend their talents, distribute rewards as certainly as though they were the Pulitzer Prize Committee. It is not, then, that the social science professions make no attempts to channel or allocate the work of their members, but rather that they do so indirectly; and the resulting allocation is roughly in harmony with the preferences of existing political and economic elites.

A POSTURE OF COUNTERVALENCE

As a start, therefore, it is essential that the graduate schools, with the encouragement of the professional associations, abandon the attitude of sham laissez-faire with regard to the sources of research funds, and help future social scientists to realize that every acceptance of a project grant is as much a political choice as a scientific one—a choice having to do not so much with what current policies one favors as with what social interests seem to be in greatest need of intellectual assistance.[29] Beyond this, the various associations of social scientists should make it their organizational business to adopt and foster this posture of countervalence in whatever ways are possible. This would mean, *inter alia,* that the associations monitor both their own activities and those of the governments and foundations that fund social research on behalf of the principles outlined here: seeking professional assistance, internships, and research support for needy public agencies in preference to flourishing ones; needy private groups in preference to wealthy ones; international agencies in preference to American ones; and poor nations rather than rich ones.

Will these approaches to public policy and professional reorientation overcome the difficulties outlined in the earlier part of this essay? Not with certainty, of course; yet it seems to me that, on the whole, social science can only improve itself if we follow such a path. For example, the possibility of voluntary subordination by the individual social scientist to his paymaster will always remain, no matter what—but we can hope to avoid the subordination of a whole profession, or the bulk of it, to one social interest.[30] In the same way, we may hope that by dispersing their activities social scientists will also, as a group, avoid the parochialism and the particular bias fostered by too intimate an involvement with governing elites. To be sure, we cannot today follow Marx or Sartre in thinking that knowledge in the service of the proletariat will produce a truly universalistic science. But, at the very least, a closer association with political outsiders will introduce more social scientists to differing versions of "the real world"; to value systems that do not merely reify current social relationships: to perspectives in which tomorrow may be different from today, not merely its replication; and, in sum, to a diversity of interests which, though each of them taken simply may be narrow, together make up a much richer field of investigation than we are accustomed to. In addition, and even more important, a social science oriented to the needs of the *dis*established will tend to breed a healthy negativism and skepticism in place of our present penchant for elaborating policy proposals much more concrete and definite than can possibly be justified by the weak theoretical underpinnings of our science.

Above all, the greatest step the various social science professions could take toward justifying our claims to intellectual and political independence would be to proclaim and enforce a code of professional conduct that would treat manipulative social science as, prima facie, unethical. From their first introduction to our techniques, future social scientists ought to be instructed that, for example, every behavioral investigation or attitude survey potentially affects the interests of its subjects; and that no people, except on their own terms, ought to be made an object of the kind of study that could lead to the further rationalization of social controls over them.

Carried to an extreme, perhaps proposals like all those made here might lead to an enfeeblement of intelligence for government, such that by any definition the public interest would be suffering; and perhaps some day we would wind up worrying about the monopolization of skills by small-city mayors, or the Young Lords, or the cloistered academy. But that outcome is almost unimaginable; at present it takes a leap of faith to think that the tendency toward government coöptation of social science can even be stemmed, let alone reversed. As far as we can foresee, surely, our current situation provides more than enough dangers to worry about; and it is against these dangers that social scientists ought presently to be on their guard.

NOTES

1.   Conor Cruise O'Brien has this difficulty in "Politics and the Morality of Scholarship," his contribution to the volume edited by Max Black, *The Morality of Scholarship* (Ithaca, N. Y.: Cornell University, 1967).

2.   See, for example, Ralph L. Beals, "Who Will Rule Research?" *Psychology Today* (September, 1970), p. 44.

3.   An account of alleged "counterrevolutionary subordination" is unfolded by David Ransom in "The Berkeley Mafia and the Indonesian Massacre," *Ramparts* 9 (October, 1970), p. 27.

4.   See the important critique of "political realism" by J. Peter Euben, "Political Science and Political Silence," in Philip Green and Sanford Levinson, eds., *Power and Community* (New York: Pantheon, 1970).

5.   Thus, Gabriel Almond and Sidney Verba, in *The Civic Culture* (Princeton, N. J.: Princeton University Press, 1963), could consider the American mix of apathy and involvement a balanced and healthy one only because they perceived the state of American society as being itself relatively balanced and healthy. Had they instead perceived the level of involvement as being appallingly *low,* they would have been out of step with the conventional wisdom of the time, but they would be honored today for having produced a potential contribution to democratic theory, instead of an obsolescent study of temporary states of public opinion in five countries.

6.   Perhaps one should even consider the willful violation of health and safety regulations by employers and manufacturers as instances of "criminal violence." For a general commentary on the defects of some official statistical categories, see Albert D. Biderman, "Social Indicators and Goals," in Raymond A. Bauer, ed., *Social Indicators* (Cambridge, Mass.: M. I. T. Press, 1967).

7.   Elsewhere I have remarked at length on this phenomenon; see Philip Green, "Science, Government, and the Case of RAND: A Singular Pluralism," *World Politics* 20 (January, 1968), pp. 301-326.

8.   The quotations are from Daniel Bell's "Notes on the Post-Industrial Society: Part I," *The Public Interest* (Winter, 1967), pp. 24-35.

9.   Critical literature on the supposed fact/value distinction is so extensive that only the tip of the iceberg can be exposed here. Two especially convincing demonstrations of the impossibility of making that distinction, written from quite different philosophical standpoints, are Michael Polanyi's *Personal Knowledge* (Chicago, Ill.: University of Chicago Press, (1958); and Jean-Paul Sartre's *Search for a Method* (New York: Knopf, 1963). Specific instances of ways in which the interpretation of data can be biased by the presumption that factual analysis and value analysis are separable are contained in Green and Levinson,op. cit.; William Connolly, *Political Science and Ideology* (New York: Atherton, 1967); and William Connolly, ed., *The Bias of Pluralism* (New York: Atherton, 1969).

10.   U. S. Department of Health, Education, and Welfare, *Toward a Social Report* Washington, D. C.: U. S. Government Printing Office, 1969). Daniel Bell was co-chairman of the panel that produced this Report.

11.   For Carlson's paper, see U. S. Congress, Subcommittee on Economy in Government of the Joint Economic Committee, *The Analysis and Evaluation of Public Expenditures: The PPB System,* 91st Congress, First Session, 1969, Vol. 2, especially pp. 676 ff.

12.   Martin Nicolaus, "The A. S. A. Convention," *Catalyst* (Spring, 1969), p. 104. In an article entitled "Social Science or Ideology?" *Social Policy* 1 (September/October, 1970), pp. 30-36, David Horowitz notes an extreme example of the problem mentioned here: There exist no independent academic studies of the Standard Oil Company of New Jersey, and organization central to the political economy of half a dozen countries in the underdeveloped world and at least as many American states, and whose agents and their associates (from groups such as the Rockefeller Foundation) have dominated the State Department, and been an important influence in the C. I. A., since the first Eisenhower Administration. The more social scientists that are occupied with government-sponsored projects, the less the likelihood, surely, that that kind of lacuna in our knowledge of American social forces will be filled.

13.   The phrase is E. E. Schattschneider's, from his *The Semisovereign People* (New York: Holt, Rinehart, and Winston, 1960), especially ch. 2.

14.   Chief Justice Taney explained, *inter alia,* the necessity of this position from a court's point of view in his opinion in *Luther v. Borden,* 7 Howard 1, 12 L. Ed. 581 (1849), a well-

known case (growing out of "Dorr's Rebellion" in Rhode Island), in which the Supreme Court held that only the political agencies could decide whether a state had a lawful, republican form of government.

15.   Consider the descriptions of government-sponsored research in Gene Lyons, *The Uneasy Partnership* (New York: Russell Sage Foundation, 1969), ch. 4.

16.   The basic source of public information about Project Camelot is Irving Louis Horowitz, ed., *The Rise and Fall of Project Camelot* (Cambridge, Mass.: M. I. T. Press, 1967). The quotation is from a description of Project Camelot released through the Office of the Director of the Special Operations Research Office of the American University in Washington, D. C. As Horowitz puts it, "It was sent to scholars who were presumed interested in the study of internal war potentials. . . ." (See p. 47 of the Horowitz book for both quotations.)

17.   See p. 52, ibid.

18.   The results of such contracted work can at times be amusing. In *Communist China and Arms Control,* a Hoover Institutions study for the Arms Control and Disarmament Agency (Palo Alto, Calif.: Stanford University Press, 1968), the authors issue a disclaimer that the views expressed in the report are solely their own and not those of the A. C. D. A., and follow it with a summary of their A. C. D. A. contract's "Statement of Work," that "requires the contractor" to assess seven specific aspects of Chinese Communism, with their "implications for United States Arms Control Policy" (p. v).

19.   Julian Benda, *The Treason of the Intellectuals,* translated from the French *La Trahison des Clercs* by Richard Aldington (New York: Norton, 1969), pp. 47, 182, 217. The translator explains his use of the word "clerk" in a "Translator's Note."

20.   See Gene Lyons' essay in this volume for a general discussion of this question, from a somewhat different standpoint than that expressed here.

21.   With regard to the possibility of considering the American system as one which incarnates and represents popular wisdom, social scientists have built up a copious literature about, on the one hand, the delusions of mass opinion, and on the other, the failures of the majority principle to work as it is supposed to. On the latter point, perhaps, Schattschneider, op. cit., and Robert A. Dahl, *A Preface to Democratic Theory* (Chicago, Ill.: University of Chicago Press, 1956), should be mentioned specifically.

22.   Bentley's primary intention, of course, was to argue that anyway there can't be such a thing as a public interest "spook," to use his language. This position, which is not at all the one I mean to imply here, is subjected to devastating criticism by Leo Weinstein, "The Group Approach: Arthur F. Bentley," in Herbert J. Storing, ed., *Essays on the Scientific Study of Politics* (New York: Holt, Reinhart & Winston, 1962), pp. 151-224; Stanley Rothman, "Systematic Political Theory: Observations on the Group Approach," *American Political Science Review* 54 (March, 1960), pp. 15-33; and Robert Paul Wolff, *The Poverty of Liberalism* (Boston: Beacon Press, 1968), chs. 4 and 5.

23.   Undoubtedly, the best description of how American liberalism fails to represent anything that might be recognizable as the public interest is Theodore J. Lowi's *The End of Liberalism* (New York: Norton, 1969). Although there are serious conceptual difficulties inherent in the system of "juridical democracy" that Lowi proposes as an alternative to interest-group liberalism, his proposal should be studied carefully, as an example of how a representative government would have to behave before social scientists could contribute their intelligence to it with easy consciences.

24.   Professional laissez-faire is criticized in Howard Zinn's essay, "History as Private Enterprise," reprinted in his *The Politics of History,* Boston: Beacon Press, 1970, pp. 15-34.

25.   Compare Grant McConnell's analysis of state and local government oligarchy in his *Private Power and American Democracy* (New York: Knopf, 1966), especially ch. 6.

26.   To return to a point mentioned earlier, the Defense Department encouraged those social scientists solicited for Project Camelot to think of their work as model-building, in the realm of "pure," theoretical social science. But the claims of those social scientists that that is what they were doing simply disappear in the face of their own descriptions of the Project. See the essays by Boguslaw and Bernard in Horowitz, op. cit.; and see fn. 18 above.

27.   For this reason, individual social scientists should rethink their explanations of why it is acceptable to take funds for "harmless" research from an agency which, from the scientist's own perspective, admittedly engages in some projects that are *not* totally harmless.

28.   In *Toward a Social Report,* the chapter on "Social Mobility" concludes with this paragraph: "What can we conclude about social mobility in America? We have seen that there is opportunity for the great majority of our citizens to improve their relative occupational status through their own efforts. Yet we are far from achieving true equality of opportunity. Economic and social status in our society still depend in a striking way on the color of a man's skin. Until we can eliminate this barrier to full participation, we will not have been faithful to our historic ideals" (p. 26). The implied conclusion that *whites* have achieved "full equality" (a conclusion totally unjustified by the data) is startling; more subtle in its effect is the authors' apparent offhand acceptance of the popular prejudice that severe "economic and social status" differentiations are reasonable as long as there is upward mobility for everyone.

29.   One implication of this proposal is that it should be considered beyond the pale of responsible professional behavior for social scientists to do secret government work. Since the primary purpose of what we call alternately, "scientific method" or "scholarship" is to make information publicly available in a form such that our hypotheses about its meaning can be verified, secret information can never be social science; and its dispenser is not a social scientist.

30.   In this context it might be helpful to encourage the continued use of independent—not necessarily presidential—commissions as public collectors of social science, since they may be less tied down to specific interests than social scientists in the direct employ of a government agency. Not even those commissions escape the difficulties created by association with government; and they also have the special drawback that by studying an issue they certify it to the public consciousness as a "problem." In this way even the recent Pornography Commission, despite its recommendation that the anti-smut laws be relaxed, helps spread somewhat the notion that pornography, as opposed to, say, advertising, is a potential social evil that people ought to be thinking about.

The Freedom to be Bad

Carl Cohen

Mr. Cohen approaches a major social issue within the framework of analysis of the rationale for a tax exemption. The right of supposedly "private" groups to exclude other members of the public from membership or participation in their activities has become particularly controversial in recent years. With the increasing pervasiveness of government participation in all sectors of the economy, virtually all "private" groups (possibly even including the family unit) are dependent to some degree, on governmentally conferred privileges. Civil rights groups have found that the attribution of supposed government benefits to private groups has been a successful lever in the legal destruction of exclusionary barriers. Cohen argues, however, that there are different types of relationships between government and private groups. Only in certain cases should a linkage to the government force a private group to give up its rights to discriminate; in others, the relationship does not change the private nature of the activity. Cohen uses the privilege of tax exemption, in its various forms, to demonstrate the point. His method of analysis suggests implications for accounting calculations in a similar manner.

Shall a purely social club be permitted to restrict its membership to whites only, or to blacks only? What if such a club enjoys tax benefits? Shall a club restricted to Polish-Americans be granted a liquor license? May the Harvard Club restrict the use of some of its facilities to men only? Cultural pluralism and heterogeneity on one side, egalitarian justice on the other—in this tension is the dialectic of American society now manifest. To achieve reasonable synthesis, what principles should guide us?

See the moral dilemma. On the one hand, we cherish the right to assemble with whom we please, for the mutual pursuit of such lawful purposes as may interest us. We are free to choose our own associates and our own objectives— charitable, recreational, religious, whatever. Within reasonable limits, we need not answer to anyone, in or out of government, for the worth or character of our private business, jointly pursued. If a just and representative government is the warp of a good society, real freedom of private action, individually and in groups, is its woof. This far, the libertarian side.

On the other hand, we cherish the right of all to equal treatment. Irrelevant considerations of race, religion, sex, national origin, or any other must certainly not be allowed to interfere with the universal right to participate effectively in the life of the community, or in the allocation of educational opportunities, or in the

---

Carl Cohen teaches philosophy at the University of Michigan, Ann Arbor.

SOURCE: From *The Nation* (January 22, 1973), pp. 111-114.

120

distribution of any goods which, in principle, are offered or guaranteed to citizens generally. This far, the egalitarian side.

Concretely, then, how far into the private activities of voluntary associations should the legal protection of equal treatment reach? Respecting admission to schools, or the rental of privately owned but publicly offered housing, the question is not very difficult. The hard cases arise in the sphere of private, voluntary associations, with special functions, whose activities are neither official nor public, yet which play a consequential role in the community.

Actual cases get very sticky, and now reach the courts with some frequency. But judges, no less than the rest of us, need general principles to resolve conflicts equitably, and none thus far developed adequately serve the serious and competing social interests. Single-minded appeals—either to equality or to freedom—are sure to yield results both distorted and painful.

I propose to bring some order to these complicated matters, first by identifying the kinds of questions that need to be asked; second, by identifying the categories needed to give the answers; and third, by formulating some general principles for the guidance of action.

Questions of two very different kinds need to be asked about any particular case in controversy. The first concerns the kind and degree of *support by the government* given to a private association, and the consequent right of that government to impose standards regarding membership policies, and the like. Direct government subsidies, for example, may be made contingent upon meeting such standards. But other so-called benefits—corporate charters, liquor licenses, the use of public parks and buildings, tax-exemption of income, and tax-deductibility of gifts, raise close yet important questions.

A second set of questions looks not to the kind or degree of government support, but to the *nature of the private association* itself. Private associations differ greatly in kind and function, and these differences bear directly upon the right of such associations to discriminate on the basis of race, religion, etc., in their internal business.

I deal first with the somewhat easier issues of the latter sort, where what is chiefly needed is a fine taxonomy of private associations. I offer only a rough taxonomy, distinguishing seven categories in three groups; but the distinctions here are central, I suggest, in deciding whether particular cases of discrimination are the community's business. And I offer some conclusions based on the distinctions drawn.

Group A comprises those private associations which:

1. Offer goods or services to the public at large—e.g., hotels and retail stores, barbers and automobile clubs.

2. Offer no service to the public at large, but perform some official or quasi-official functions in the public interest—e.g., medical and bar associations, real estate boards and athletic associations—which set standards or control opportunities in business, or recreation, or the professions.

3. Offer no general public service, and have no quasi-official function, but operate in fact as a place of public accommodation—e.g., a fraternal order in whose clubhouse public dances are commonly held, or a club adjoining city hall in which, informally, much public business is transacted.

Private organizations in these first three categories present few serious theoretical problems. Racial, religious, or sexual discrimination is obviously not relevant to the public or quasi-public functions that are really being served by such organizations, and must therefore not be permitted to interfere with the just fulfillment of those functions. Of course, deciding whether a given club or organization is *in fact* serving an important public function through its membership or within its precincts may sometimes prove difficult. Still, that determination can be made.

Much harder to deal with are private associations in Group B, being those which:

4. Serve genuinely recreational purposes—e.g., private hunting lodges, swimming clubs, or bowling leagues.

5. Are based on special avocational or intellectual interests—e.g., stamp clubs, debating societies, or the local historical association.

6. Are purely social, forming wholly around the personal attraction of the members for one another.

Recreational or intellectual activities (categories 4 and 5) sometimes rely upon facilities that are unique in the community—its only lake, or its historical archives. Because all citizens, regardless of race, religion, sex, etc., are entitled to the enjoyment of such community assets, all citizens (with appropriate avocational qualifications) have an equal claim to membership in organizations which control the use of such facilities. Barring circumstances of that sort, I hold that in all of Group B, discrimination in membership or participation on grounds of race, religion, sex, etc., even where we may think it highly objectionable on moral grounds, ought not to be prohibited by law. The freedom to assemble or associate must not be conditioned upon its use in certain approved ways. As in the case of free speech we do not ask what will be said to determine whether it may be said, so with freedom of association, we ought not, as a community, to ask first with whom the association will be to determine whether the association may be formed or allowed to continue. If that freedom is contingent upon its being exercised, in certain approved ways, no *right* of free association remains; what is left is a privilege for only those who act in ways the authorities deem acceptable. Whether the supervision by those authorities should prove (in substance) honorable or despicable, the mere exercise of such supervision must damage the freedom of that community.

Group C comprises all those private associations which:

7. Are based openly upon special religious or ethnic affiliations—e.g., Afro-American clubs, or Catholic confraternities. Here discrimination is relevant to an honorable social function and ought to be cultivated rather than despised.

Cultural diversity is a contribution to American life greatly undervalued, in my view. Lip service to it, of course, is not in short supply. But real pluralism, preserving genuine differences of language and custom, embodied in games and feasts and rituals—and most of all in a feeling of identified belonging—can thrive only when supported concretely by organizations. Such organizations—together with the principles of exclusion they entail—must therefore be protected, even if that protection carries with it the equal protection of evil men in their private exercise of irrational prejudice. Where freedom is real it is enjoyed by all members of the community, including the nasty ones.

Questions of the first general kind mentioned above concern the support or assistance given by the government to any private organization whose policies are in question. What benefits, direct or indirect, have been received from the community at large? And what rights of inspection and supervision of membership policy do the varieties of governmental assistance justify? Here matters become quite intricate.

In the tangle of real community life virtually all private associations receive some variety of support from the government—most of it not in the form of direct subsidy. Tentatively, and by no means exhaustively, I distinguish seven categories of government assistance which have been held by some to justify the legal prohibition of discrimination. Among these are the most difficult cases: (1) outright subsidy; (2) essential services—fire and police protection, etc.; (3) incorporation; (4) liquor licenses; (5) the use of public facilities—parks, streets, meeting halls, etc.; (6) tax-exemption of income; (7) tax-deductibility of gifts.

Using these categories I shall put forward a set of principles that answer partially the questions raised above. Some of my conclusions require a more detailed justification than I give here; and some borderline cases will remain puzzling whatever the set of principles defended; but a little progress is better than none.

1. Outright subsidy, the extreme case, is easy. If the community offers grants from the public treasury to a private organization—a school, or an orchestra, etc.—it may surely do so upon the condition that public policy not be flouted in the use of those grants.

2. Essential services—fire protection, health inspection, etc.—are not provided to private organizations as special benefits, but in the interests of all. The well-being of the entire community is protected by such services. The membership policies of private groups, therefore, cannot justify the withdrawal of such services.

3. A corporate charter, although not essential in the way that fire and police protection are, is vital to many associations. Some argue, therefore, that such charters give a kind of state authorization, and (moreover) bring the financial advantage of limited liability, and that the grant of a charter is thus a benefit properly withheld from organizations that discriminate. This argument is mistaken; it misapprehends the basic function of the charter. The "authorization"

that a corporate charter provides is no more than the concrete realization of the right to association and assembly; it is the practical condition of the exercise of that right. Nor does any special advantage accrue, for there is no limit to the number of corporate charters a state can grant, and such charters are available to all, individuals as well as groups, on an equal basis. No approval or inspection of membership policy by government ought to be involved in the matter of incorporation.

4. Liquor licenses are more problematic. There is, first of all, obscurity and uncertainty regarding the justification of state licensing in general, and of state liquor licensing in particular. These matters cannot be entered here; but I underscore the assumption, rarely questioned, that the health and safety of the community require restrictions upon place, time and manner of liquor sales.

The number of available liquor licenses being now sharply limited, the award of such a license to sell to the public is clearly a financial benefit not available to all. A private club that really functions as a public tavern, and benefits financially thereby, may rightly have its liquor license conditioned upon nondiscriminatory service. That, in effect, has been the recent holding of the Supreme Court. But where a club license serves merely to insure that alcohol consumption by members, in their own clubhouse, goes on within regulations laid down by the state for all such consumption, its award is not basically a financial issue. Community health and safety may be involved, but special benefits are not in question. I conclude that, in applications for such a license, the conduct and opinions of the applicants in matters not relating to the health issues which justify the licensing should not even enter consideration. ·

5. The use of the streets, public parks, meeting halls and the like, must not be selectively withdrawn from any persons or groups. Conditions for the use of such facilities may be reasonably formulated, of course, but they must be conditions which bear only upon the forms of use intended (noise level permitted, size of audience expected, whether the activity be suitable for the facility, etc.) and upon the fair distribution of the opportunity to use those facilities (rotation of users, or first-come-first-served, etc.). To require that groups holding public meetings, parades, demonstrations, etc., adopt some government-approved membership policies in order to receive permission for the use of such facilities, is to violate the right of free assembly. If public facilities are for all, they are for bad guys as well as good guys—supposing we could tell them apart.

Since the use of public facilities, on the same basis for all, is the essential practical foundation of the right of free association and assembly, it must not be withdrawn, however much we may despise the views of those assembled. Government approval of our objectives must not become a condition of their effective joint pursuit—precisely because government itself is often the target at which citizens are obliged to direct their attack. We must not be lured into granting supervisory powers whose exercise may ultimately prove disastrous. Real freedom does not wax or wane with the (alleged) morality of those exercising that freedom, singly or collectively. I conclude that the use of the parks, or the rental of public halls, etc., ought not to be refused to organizations whose membership policies are discriminatory, even invidiously so. Such organizations should be given no special support; but they lose no rights to assemble because the majority think them pernicious.

A cautionary note. Discriminatory membership policies should not disqualify organizations from the use of public facilities, but under some circumstances the actual use of those facilities must not be discriminatory. For example, at any meeting to which the general public is invited (e.g., candidates' night at a public school, or a lecture in a park) or to which tickets are publicly sold, admission must not be exclusionary whoever may be the sponsor, or whatever the views espoused by that sponsor. Public places and public facilities must be open to the use of all on the same terms.

(6) and *(7)* Tax benefits are very consequential, and very complicated. I address here two issues only within this muddy area: First, what are the differing controversial forms of tax relief for private organizations? Second, which of these forms of tax relief may properly be withdrawn if the organization is proved to employ discriminatory policies in membership or function?

It must be seen that the benefit of tax-*deductibility* for gifts received, and the benefit of tax-*exemption* of income are importantly different both in theory and result. Permitting any donor to deduct from his income, for purposes of tax computation gifts made to a private organization, is a deliberate instrument of public policy. Philanthropic activity of certain kinds is strongly encouraged thereby—either because the recipients are considered intrinsically worthy of support (e.g., the Boy Scouts, the YMCA), or because the recipients satisfy public needs that would have to be shouldered by the community to the degree that they were not met privately (e.g., sectarian old-age homes; private medical research; private disaster relief, etc.). Governments do not authorize the tax-deductibility of contributions to any cause an individual taxpayer happens to think worthy; quite otherwise, contributions are deductible only when made to organizations of clearly identified kinds, meeting carefully laid down requirements, and only after being specifically cleared for such deductibility. Tax-deductibility for gifts unavoidably involves a government stamp of approval. It is therefore reasonable for the government to demand that the recipient of the deductible gift comply with current standards of nondiscrimination.

That argument does not apply to tax-exemption. The dues income of non-profit associations—chess clubs, for example, or country clubs—is exempt from taxation for quite different reasons. Here individuals come together to pursue jointly objectives that would be impossible or inconvenient to pursue singly. Income from dues (I emphasize this restriction) flows from the members themselves, is used by them for themselves, with any residues belonging still to them alone. Income of the form normally subjected to taxation has not been generated in such a nonprofit group. Money has been shifted from the individual to the collective pocket—but the same people are wearing the pants. The tax-exemption of such income is not a special benefit; those who suppose that it is assume that if the exemption had not been granted moneys would be in the public treasury which are not now there. In fact, there would be virtually no such moneys, because most such organizations simply would not exist if so taxed. And even if they could survive taxation (which the worthiest among them could not) the general right to associate is seriously damaged if we tax the joint pursuit of an activity that would be untaxed if pursued singly.

It is important to realize that (unlike the case of deductibility) no process of approval or inspection is called for in granting such tax-exemption to private nonprofit groups. That exemption is awarded simply as a recognition of the right of citizens to band together for the pursuit of their common ends, without penalty. The claim that discriminatory membership policies, or other unacceptable policies, justifys the withdrawal of tax-exemption, necessarily introduces government judgments on private conduct which, properly, have nothing to do with the right of citizens to associate and organize.

The merest introduction of such questions is a serious danger, in view of the constant supervision of private activities by government agents that the need for official approval would necessarily ordain. Much private business would inevitably become public business. Better by far, I submit, to let some private organizations whose practices we detest receive the same tax-exemption granted in blanket form to all nonprofit groups, and that private citizens be spared the supervision and snooping of bureaucrats.

Private organizations and associations lie beyond the legitimate concern of the state, or other public authorities. They are, and ought to be, constitutionally protected against government interference; they are, and ought to be, insulated, so far as reasonably they can be, from governmental inspection and approval. Clearly, when private associations serve public or official functions they take on public or official obligations. When they manifest no such public purposes private organizations must be free to carry on activities, and practice policies, which might well be unconstitutional if sponsored by the government or its agencies.

In groups as well as singly we must be free to be bad. If bad men have not the same rights as good men to speak, assemble, associate, and mind their own business, the community is not really free.

Construction of Large Accelerators: Scientific and Political Aspects*

W. Heisenberg

Heisenberg's paper suggests some novel approaches to the problems of evaluating large expenditures for basic research projects. Particularly unique is his contention that the principal responsibility for this social resource allocation should lie with the experimenters themselves, in this case, the physicists, and not with the government. He suggests that centralized resource allocations, for instance, comparison of defense requirements with those of basic particle physics, are essentially impossible. The physicists must assess the incremental costs and benefits of new proposals, as compared with the total resources that they believe they can validly claim from society.

In addition, the author explores the influence of changing technology on the costs of basic research, and on the relative necessity for speeding progress on particular projects. One wonders what would have been the cost and time frame of the American space program had Heisenberg's analysis been applied during President Kennedy's administration. Also, the author's discussion of the economics of centralized or politically balanced locations for research facilities has obvious applicability to the space program.

During the past years, there has been much talk of a large accelerator to be constructed by the combined efforts of the governments, engineers, and physicists of various European countries. The question of the urgency of the project, its financing, and its location have been the subject of public controversy and discussions. Finally, however, an agreement was reached to build the accelerator at the European Center of Nuclear Research (CERN) in Geneva, with a number of European states participating in its financing and completion, such as France, Great Britain, Italy, and the German Federal Republic. All important decisions with respect to this controversial project have thus been taken, and I believe that the majority of the participants—meaning the physicists as well as the representatives of the participating governments, in the Federal Republic as well as in the other European countries—are well satisfied with the result. Just for this reason, it may be of interest to recall the guidelines which have played a role in the decision, since we may expect similar large cooperative projects in the future,

W. Heisenberg is at the Max Planck Institute for Physics and Astrophysics, Munich, German Federal Republic. He received the Nobel Prize in Physics in 1932.

SOURCE: From *Science*, Vol. 179 (February 16, 1973), pp. 643-647, Copyright 1973 by the American Association for the Advancement of Science. Based on a speech delivered at the twenty-first meeting of the Nobel laureates at Lindau, Germany, in July 1971.

*This article was translated by Sonja Bargmann.

and the same questions of the relationship between science and society and of the conditions for international scientific collaboration will then arise again. Therefore, one may learn a good deal from the discussions which led to the decision, and I should like to express some thoughts of a more general nature about the relationship between government and science and their possible collaboration, which were stimulated by these discussions.

PROGRESS THROUGH LARGE ACCELERATORS

Let me start with a few words about the physical problems to be investigated with the help of the large accelerator. Progress in atomic physics during the last hundred years has been closely connected with the construction of ever larger accelerators—using the word "accelerator" in its very general meaning. In ordinary discharge tubes, such as those used in advertisements, the electrons have to traverse a potential difference of only a few volts to be sufficiently accelerated so that they may modify the atomic shells of gas atoms with which they collide and excite these atoms to radiation. Such electrons with energies of a few electron volts have been used to investigate the atomic shells and to uncover, finally, the regularities of their structure. Atomic shell stands here for the totality of the electrons surrounding the atomic nucleus.

In the atomic nuclei the binding energies are about 1 million times larger than in the electronic shells. In the beginning of the 1930's. Cockroft and Walton in Cambridge built a high-voltage machine with which they were able to accelerate protons up to energies of the order of 1 million electron volts. Very soon thereafter, Lawrence and Livingston in the United States constructed their first cyclotron, which produced particles of about the same energy. With such machines it became possible to affect light atomic nuclei, to knock elementary particles out of them, or to attach other particles to them. In this manner one learned in the course of the 1930's to understand the structure of atomic nuclei, which—as has been well known ever since—consist of two kinds of particles, protons and neutrons.

The next group of such machines, which may already be called large accelerators, was built in the 1950's. In these machines protons were to be accelerated up to the order of several billion electron volts (Gev). With their help it was hoped to modify also the elementary particles known at the time, possibly to break them up into still smaller fragments, to find still smaller elementary building blocks. These large accelerators, too—among them those in Berkeley, Geneva, Hamburg, Brookhaven, Serpuchov—have fully measured up to expectation. It turned out that it is, indeed, possible to modify elementary particles, to raise them to excited states, to split them into many parts. But—and this was definitely new—the fragments are no smaller than the particles which were made to collide.

It is no longer properly a question of division, but rather of the generation of matter from energy. In such energetic collisions the resulting elementary particles all belong to the same family. One might say that the elementary particles are simply different forms which energy can assume in order to become matter; but there are no particles which are more elementary than the ones we already know. Such was the state of experimental research some years ago, and on the basis of this knowledge it had to be decided whether or not to build still larger accelerators with energies of the order of several hundred billion electron volts and of correspondingly high costs.

FACTORS INVOLVED IN BUILDING LARGER ACCELERATORS

In favor of this step spoke first of all the simple consideration that, as was pointed out above, each transition from smaller to larger accelerators resulted in new discoveries. Why shouldn't it go on this way? Entering a new energy region cannot fail to lead to new information, and nobody can exclude the possibility that part of this information will be highly interesting and quite surprising. But even setting aside such surprises, it may be important to learn how, for example, the interaction responsible for radioactivity behaves at high energies. The experimental evidence now available does not permit us to form a reliable conjecture, and it is quite possible that knowledge of the behavior at yet higher energies will bring about fundamental advances in understanding the spectrum of elementary particles.

I wish to emphasize at this point the central importance of these problems for all of physics. It is likely that, in the last analysis, all laws of physics will be reducible to the laws governing the behavior of the smallest material particles; hence, it is crucial to determine these laws. But apart from the importance of large accelerators for the extension of elementary particle physics, their construction will lead to new technical experiences, which may become valuable in entirely different fields. With such accelerators one will have to go to the extreme limits of what is feasible, and what is learned may have practical applications. I may remind you, for example, of the recently developed technique of superconducting magnets, which may well be utilized in the construction of a new large accelerator. Thus, there are many reasons in favor of building large accelerators with energies of the order of 300 Gev or more, and if it were possible to construct such machines for a few million marks, nobody would doubt that it should be done. Unfortunately, however, the costs run into billions. This is why it was necessary, considering the other needs of the state, to ask whether such enormous expenditures could be reduced or, at least, postponed. Are they really absolutely necessary?

To start with, it must be admitted that the reasons for expecting new basic results with higher energies are not entirely conclusive. Nature has given us a new and unexpected answer to our attempts to divide the elementary particles, which is that in these processes we are no longer dealing with division, but with a transformation of energy into matter. Probably, it will be the same with still higher energies, and hence we must take into account the possibility that, however much we increase the energy, nothing essentially new is going to happen. In fact, extremely energetic particles up to about 1 million Gev have been observed in cosmic radiation, and no basically new phenomena have been found. Hence, it is possible that the large body of experimental data on elementary particles accumulated so far suffices to comprehend the laws of nature in this field, and that we do not require a further extension to higher energies. Indeed, it is hard to imagine that a theory, hypothetical at its inception, although able to account correctly for all existing experiments within their limits of accuracy, might yet break down in the unexplored region of still higher energies. But even if one considers experiments in the range of high-energy physics as absolutely necessary, one might entertain the hope that within several years or decades it will be possible to build a large accelerator at much lower cost because by that time technology, for example that of super-conducting magnets, will have advanced far enough or new principles of construction will have been found. Applying such reasoning, one could have argued for postponing the construction of a large accelerator, at least for a few years. You will realize that physical and technological arguments could hardly have sufficed to make a clear-cut decision, and hence it is also necessary to weigh the factors relating to broader questions of science and of foreign affairs which affect such a decision.

Let us start with the effects of such a decision on education and research in our own country. The amount to be spent on an accelerator of 300 Gev or more is so large that it cannot be easily raised in addition to the existing research budget, not even for an international cooperative project. Thus, quite embarrassing questions of priority come up for society or the government, for instance in this form: Should we build another university in view of the fact that the number of our institutions of higher education is insufficient or, instead, participate in a large international accelerator project? Or put in another way: Should we spend several millions per annum on the protection of our environment, against the pollution of rivers, lakes, and air, or should we use them on elementary particle physics? Such questions are embarrassing because totally incommensurable goals have to be compared with respect to their priority. On the one hand stands the pursuit of pure research concerning the problems of physics and science, which later on may have, although only indirectly, important economic consequences, and on the other an immediate practical concern of everyday life, such as the possibility for our children to attend college or the provision of a healthy environment for them. How does one decide such questions?

ATTITUDES AND INFLUENCE OF SCIENTISTS

It seems to me, first of all, that those physicists who wish to construct the large accelerator, who want to work with it, ought to realize the great difficulties inherent in these problems. It is not enough to dispose of these questions by shifting the responsibility for them to the government, to say casually that the necessary sum should be taken out of the defense budget. For those responsible for the commonwealth the question of the security of this commonwealth must have higher priority than participating in a large project for the study of elementary particles. In other words, a decision to build a large accelerator involves questions of politics which even physicists cannot simply ignore.

An excellent example of the proper attitude in such a situation was given by the British physicists. If I am correctly informed, the British physicists made the following proposal to their government: that it participate in the European accelerator project, but that it also cut correspondingly the national budget for elementary particle physics in order to balance the costs. It was even considered to shut down a great and distinguished research institute in the same field, the Rutherford Laboratory in Cambridge. Such a proposal is based in part on the conviction that the experiments to be performed with the new European giant accelerator will be more interesting and important than those that can be made with the smaller machines in the Rutherford Laboratory, and in part on the recognition that during the past decades physicists have already put high demands on the economy of their country, and hence ought to be circumspect in making any further requests. The British physicists were paying careful attention to the welfare of their community while putting forward their wishes.

Let me make here a general remark which goes beyond the immediate subject of this article. It seems to me an unfortunate phenomenon of our time—not only in our country and certainly not only among physicists—that many of us are tempted to make demands on the government without reciprocating or sacrificing something of our own. It may be a question of demanding an education, grants, having a voice in difficult questions, or simply of demanding a lot of leisure time, extensive vacation trips, material well-being. I am afraid that again and again the tendency manifests itself to consider it unnecessary to justify these demands by one's own sacrifices. The good example of the British physicists points to the more general question of what the relationship of the physicists, and scientists in general, to their government ought to be.

Most people seem to agree that in our time the government needs the advice of scientists. Science and technology play such an important role in modern life, in the economy, in questions of education, and in the preparation of political decisions, that advisory committees of scientists and engineers are indispensable in order to render the work of the government easier. Such advisory committees have, indeed, been established in all modern industrial countries. In the Federal

Republic, advisory councils exist on several levels, helping the government in the distribution of public funds for research purposes, in decisions on large research and development projects, in problems of higher education, and so forth. Examples are the Atomic Energy Commission the Scientific Council of the Ministry of Economic Affairs, and the Advisory Council for Research. Lately, the reorganization of these advisory committees has been much discussed.

Quite apart from all this, the government in Bonn is naturally surrounded by lobbies of certain economic interest groups, in industry or in agriculture, who wish to make themselves heard. This too is entirely legitimate in a democracy since it is the task of the government to find as just a balance as possible between the various interests of the citizens of the country. Therefore, it is important for the government to be informed about these interests.

It seems to me extremely important, however, that the distinction between advisory committees and special interest groups remain clearly marked. The moment an advisory committee becomes also an interest group, it ceases to be useful as an advisory committee. The government can only profit from an entirely unbiased council. The government's participation in a large international scientific-technological project such as the large accelerator project leads, therefore, to a difficult dilemma. On the one hand, a counseling by specialists in the field of high-energy physics is indispensable because they are the only ones capable of correctly judging the details. On the other hand, these specialists are necessarily also an interested party since they or their students will want to work with the large accelerator. This difficulty cannot be avoided. Clearly it was also felt by the British physicists, and they tried to sacrifice some of their interests so they would be able to play the role of adviser with a clear conscience.

But even if one assumes that all participants fully appreciate these problems, the task of evaluating the priority of such a scientific-technological project over others remains extremely difficult. How important is scientific knowledge? How important is it to obtain it soon, and not in 10 or 20 or 30 years? Those who spent their lives being active in science will give high priority to scientific knowledge and are in a position to adduce many sound and weighty reasons. But a politician who, before entering politics, was a businessman or a farmer may consider questions of economy or of environmental protection more important, and he, too, will be able to find many convincing arguments for his point of view. Or, on the contrary, he may be in danger of overvaluing scientific knowledge because science appears awesome and strange and because, impressed by modern technology, he overrates its potentialities.

In view of this unavoidable uncertainty of the politician, it is the first duty of the adviser to provide the authorities with a completely factual, unvarnished picture of the scientific plans and their expected significance. All arguments in favor, but also all those against the project, must be presented and elucidated as objectively as possible so that the politician will be supplied with the best information obtainable. In expounding the reasons for or against such a project it is important to put the burden of proof where it belongs. If it is a question of a billion-mark project, which will require sacrifices in other areas, the proponent of such a project is the one to bring proof of its urgency, of the results expected from it. It is not up to the opponent to prove that the project is not all that important. It will never be possible to prove that a scientific project breaking new ground will not produce startling and important new discoveries. But this alone can never provide sufficient reason for spending billions. Hence, the burden of proof must definitely lie with those who want to claim such extremely large public funds.

But even if such proof is furnished, it will be difficult enough for the politicians to make up their minds. It facilitates their work that similar decisions must, after all, be made in other countries as well and that they can take their bearings from them. In the case of an international project, such as the European giant accelerator, other countries which may take part in it have to deal with exactly the same problems. In such a situation, the decision will have to be taken more or less jointly.

COOPERATION OF EUROPEAN STATES

The international character of such a large project introduces some new aspects which have not yet been dealt with. We all agree, I think, that it is extremely important for the future of our continent to form a true community of all the small European states. A large scientific project whose importance is accepted by everybody, but which because of the high costs involved can no longer be carried by a single European country alone, represents an ideal case of such a cooperative effort. When it is a question of pure science, economic and political competition are no longer significantly involved, results and technical know-how do not have to be kept secret. A common interest in fascinating scientific problems unites young physicists and technicians from different countries in fruitful work; without any further effort, a steady exchange of opinions takes place and an unconscious assimilation of interests results, the importance of which cannot be over-emphasized with regard to the future goal, the unity of Europe. Large international projects should, therefore, be supported if only because they are international. In view of this unifying potential one should not be overly critical and skeptical with respect to the scientific possibilities and arguments.

As a matter of fact, during the post-war years several such international projects and installations have come into being in Europe, which have been significant examples of scientific cooperation. The best institution of this kind is the nuclear center, CERN, in Geneva. Since 1959 its proton-synchrotron of 30 Gev has been in use and has made possible a number of highly interesting experiments. Last year the large intersecting storage rings were put in operation, corresponding—with respect to the collision energy of two protons—to an accelerator of about 1700 Gev. It will be the only machine of its kind in the world. Shortly afterward, it was decided to build a new European giant accelerator of several hundred billion electron volts in Geneva. Europe will thus be in a position to play a leading role in high-energy physics for the next 10 to 20 years, provided as good use will be made of these machines as has been made of the protron-synchrotron. In Trieste, on Italian soil, a very successful international center for theoretical physics has been created; it is supported not only by European countries, but also by non-European ones, and maintains particularly good contacts with Eastern Europe and Asia. In Ispra on Lake Maggiore, also in Italy, developmental and research problems in the field of reactor technology are being carried out on behalf of the European Atomic Energy Community (EURATOM). This, again, is a large international cooperative project supported by several European countries. In Grenoble, France, a reactor with a very high neutron flux has been installed through French and German cooperation, where scientific and technical investigations can be made about the behavior of materials under the influence of strong irradiation. Similar international installations in other fields, for example, for space research, exist in Belgium and Holland.

There is, indeed, great interest in international scientific collaboration, and one may be fully satisfied with the successful results obtained in the various institutions. Nevertheless, when a decision to found another such international scientific installation is taken, difficult new problems arise concerning its site, in particular, but also its financing, the distribution of contracts, and appointments to the leading positions. The question of location is by far the most difficult one because, as a rule, it must be decided from a political rather than a purely objective point of view. It is true that the technical or scientific purpose to be achieved will often impose certain conditions which greatly restrict the choice of location. For a large accelerator, for example, a large level surface must be available which is geologically stable, that is, which does not become deformed by ground motions or distorted by atmospheric conditions, and the amount of earth moving required for the erection of the accelerator must not be too costly. Moreover, the installation must be conveniently located, schools and colleges must be easy to reach, and so on. Thus, there are quite a number of conditions which must be satisfied, but as a rule, it is not too difficult to find sites in different parts of Europe which satisfy all of them.

In the final account, it is necessary to make a political decision, and the question is which factors play the most important role. Since all of these international scientific centers are erected through cooperative European efforts, it seems to me that these installations ought to be more or less uniformly distributed over Europe. One may, of course, debate the meaning of this vague concept "more or less uniformly." But glancing at a map of Europe and looking over the spatial distribution of the international scientific installations built until now, it is evident that their distribution is still rather uneven and should in the future become more uniform. This argument is sometimes countered by pointing out that one aim ought to be the United States of Europe, in which case the location within Europe would no longer matter. But the case of the United States of America demonstrates that this is not so, that even in such a large, politically unified country one must pay attention to a uniform distribution of scientific institutions. Thus, the latest American giant accelerator, which is to furnish approximately 400 Gev, was built at Batavia, Illinois, not far from Chicago, whereas the two former centers for high-energy physics were constructed in the West, in California, and in the East, at Brookhaven, New York. In Europe, the question of the site played an important part in the debates about the giant accelerator. But the possibility of making use of the already existing infrastructure at CERN, and thus of considerably reducing the costs of the new installation, finally won out over the other possibility, to create the new European research center in a region far removed from other centers of this kind. Let us hope, however, that future installations will contribute to a more uniform distribution over Europe.

OBSOLESCENCE IN PHYSICS

There was another reason for locating the new giant accelerator at CERN. Another European center for high-energy physics independent of Geneva would have tied down a staff of thousands to work at the new site. Many young and talented physicists and technicians would have turned to this very specialized field of elementary particle physics and accelerator technology. During the coming years they would probably have been so fascinated by the problems in this field that it would have been difficult for them to change later on to another one. On the other hand, the preoccupation with the special problems of elementary particle physics will sooner or later come to an end, just as it has happened with so many other branches of physics which have been absorbed—together with their applications—by technology. If one projects "the end of elementary particle physics" to a very remote point in time, as some physicists do, one may feel justified in not giving any thought to the future activity of elementary particle physicists. But the United States has already closed down some of its accelerator installations and dismissed physicists and technicians working there. This shows that one does these young people an injustice by not taking an interest in their future after having involved them in this specialized field. For this reason, it was a wise decision to build the new large accelerator in Geneva, where the proton-synchrotron and the large intersecting storage rings were built. Although in Geneva, too, personnel will be considerably increased, this will not happen to the same extent as in a completely new accelerator station. The dangers for the distant future have thus been somewhat reduced by choosing Geneva as the site. Still another argument, rather incidental: the spatial restriction of the site, which the choice of

Geneva entails, has technical consequences. It forces the designers to make use of the latest technical developments, for example superconducting magnets, in order to obtain such high energies within so little space. The new project will, therefore, necessarily be much more modern than the one planned earlier.

I think I have presented most of the arguments which played a part in the final decision. Let me repeat them in a few words. First of all, there is the satisfaction of working on a meaningful cooperative project, but also uncertainty with respect to the forthcoming results with the new instrument, the question whether the experience gained with the earlier accelerators may not suffice to comprehend the world of elementary particles. There is the further question of progress in technology; might it not be the case that in a few years accelerators with the required energies can be built much more cheaply than now by using new technical processes? An additional difficulty was the necessity for the participating nations to come to a fair decision with respect to the site, and for each of the individual governments to renounce plans or projects of their own in favor of the international accelerator. It seems to me that in view of all these difficulties the final decision is a very good solution, an appropriate compromise between the various interests, and a valuable contribution to the strengthening of the European community.

MOTIVES BEHIND THE BUILDING OF GIANT ACCELERATORS

In conclusion, however, let me leave this level of practical considerations, scientific reasoning, and political negotiations and, descending to a somewhat deeper level, ask: Why, after all, do we humans make such strenuous efforts to build a large accelerator, why do we spend billions on a scientific instrument which, at least for the moment, does not promise any economic return? When I once put this question to the American ambassador in Bonn, I received the following reply: In ancient Egypt pyramids were built, in the Christian Middle Ages magnificent cathedrals, and in our time we are building scientific instruments. In ancient Egypt the royal ancestors represented a bond to the deity, and the trust in help and support deriving from this bond manifested itself in the erection of these giant tombs. In the Christian Middle Ages the believers went into the cathedrals firmly convinced of obtaining deliverance from their suffering. In our time we trust almost blindly in science and rational thought, and we are bringing enormous material sacrifices to further science, to increase our knowledge of the world. The American ambassador's comparison contains without doubt part of the truth, and if we mean by religion in a very general way the center of trust forming the kernel of a society, it must be admitted that religious motives are the driving force behind the building of these giant accelerators. Still, one must ask oneself here whether the power of the goddess "Reason" is, indeed, as large as it was hoped at the time of the French Revolution. The experiences of our century seem to indicate that it is rather limited. However one may judge this power, our minimal demand must be that we do not blindly commit ourselves to it, but that we act sensibly and critically if it is a question of investing enormous funds in large scientific projects. This has certainly been the case with regard to the Geneva giant accelerator, and it must be hoped that in the future, too, similar scrupulous care will be taken in deciding on such large projects.

International Environmental Politics: Declaration on the Human Environment* and The Stockholm Conference: U.S. Appraisal†

It is clear that the environmental issue raises economic consequences for many parties, and that these economic effects will be translated into a political dimension. The controversy over the Alaska pipeline may be the classic example of this situation. It is less evident, however, that environmental politics may clearly extend into the international dimension. The developing countries, having less pollution than developed economies, may have less fear of pollution. Indeed, it is sometimes viewed as a symbol of progress. On a more tangible level, the use of the national resources of developing countries by the developed produces a host of contradictory forces. For example, the developed countries buy and use the crude oil of the developing countries thus helping to deplete the resources that should later be available to the developing country for its own production. On the other hand, the purchase of the oil provides capital needed for immediate development. When the developed country decides that the crude oil it buys is too high in sulfur content—and is a pollutant—the developing country finds itself rather confused as to an appropriate reaction.

The United Nations Conference was enmeshed in these problems from the start. The final document, reproduced here, provides fascinating evidence of the compromises that may be necessary to deal with the pollution problem on an international level. The Bulletin of the National Foreign Trade Council sums up the U. S. position on the U. N. document, and pinpoints the political issue with somewhat less subtlety than the U. N. document.

DECLARATION ON THE HUMAN ENVIRONMENT

Having met at Stockholm from 5 to 16 June 1972, and

Having considered the need for a common outlook and for common principles to inspire and guide the peoples of the world in the preservation and enhancement of the human environment,

Proclaims

1.   Man is both creature and moulder of his environment which gives him physical sustenance and affords him the opportunity for intellectual, moral, social and spiritual growth. In the long and torturous evolution of the human race on this planet a stage has been reached when through the rapid acceleration of science and technology, man has acquired the power to transform his environ-

---

*SOURCE: Declaration on the Human Environment adopted at Stockholm by the United Nations Conference on the Human Environment on June 16, 1972.

†SOURCE: *National Foreign Trade Council, Inc.,* Bulletin No. 3469 (August 29, 1972).

ment in countless ways and on an unprecedented scale. Both aspects of man's environment, the natural and the man-made, are essential to his well-being and to the enjoyment of basic human rights—even the right to life itself.

2. The protection and improvement of the human environment is a major issue which affects the well-being of peoples and economic development throughout the world; it is the urgent desire of the peoples of the whole world and the duty of all Governments.

3. Man has constantly to sum up experience and go on discovering, inventing, creating and advancing. In our time man's capability to transform his surroundings, if used wisely, can bring to all peoples the benefits of development and the opportunity to enhance the quality of life. Wrongly or heedlessly applied, the same power can do incalculable harm to human beings and the human environment. We see around us growing evidence of man-made harm in many regions of the earth: dangerous levels of pollution in water, air, earth and living beings; major and undesirable disturbances to the ecological balance of the biosphere; destruction and depletion of irreplaceable resources; and gross deficiencies harmful to the physical, mental and social health of man, in the man-made environment, particularly in the living and working environment.

4. In the developing countries most of the environmental problems are caused by under-development. Millions continue to live far below the minimum levels required for a decent human existence, deprived of adequate food and clothing, shelter and education, health and sanitation. Therefore, the developing countries must direct their efforts to development, bearing in mind their priorities and the need to safeguard and improve the environment. For the same purposes, the industralized countries should make efforts to reduce the gap between themselves and the developing countries. In the industrialized countries, environmental problems are generally related to industralization and technological development.

5. The natural growth of population continuously presents problems on the preservation of the environment, and adequate policies and measures should be adopted as appropriate to face these problems. Of all things, in the world, people are the most precious. It is the people that propel social progress, create social wealth, develop science and technology, and through their hard work, continuously transform the human environment. Along with social progress and the advance of production, science and technology, the capability of man to improve the environment increases with each passing day.

6. A point has been reached in history when we must shape our actions throughout the world with a more prudent care for their environmental consequences. Through ignorance or indifference we can do massive and irreversible harm to the earthly environment on which our life and well-being depend. Conversely, through fuller knowledge and wiser action, we can achieve for ourselves and our posterity a better life in an environment more in keeping with human needs and hopes. There are broad vistas for the enhancement of environmental

quality and the creation of a good life. What is needed is an enthusiastic but calm state of mind and intense but orderly work. For the purpose of attaining freedom in the world of nature, man must use knowledge to build in collaboration with nature a better environment. To defend and improve the human environment for present and future generations has become an imperative goal for mankind— a goal to be pursued together with, and in harmony with, the established and fundamental goals of peace and of world-wide economic and social development.

7.   To achieve this environmental goal will demand the acceptance of responsibility by citizens and communities and by enterprises and institutions at every level, all sharing equitably in common efforts. Individuals in all walks of life as well as organizations in many fields, by their values and the sum of their actions, will shape the world environment of the future. Local and national Governments will bear the greatest burden for large-scale environmental policy and action within their jurisdictions. International co-operation is also needed in order to raise resources to support the developing countries in carrying out their responsibilities in this field. A growing class of environmental problems, because they are regional or global in extent or because they affect the common international realm, will require extensive co-operation among nations and action by international organizations in the common interest. The Conference calls upon the Government and peoples to exert common efforts for the preservation and improvement of the human environment, for the benefit of all the people and for posterity.

Principles

States the Common Conviction that

1.   Man has the fundamental right to freedom, equality and adequate conditions of life, in an environment of a quality which permits a life of dignity and well-being, and bears a solemn responsibility to protect and improve the environment for present and future generations. In this respect, policies promoting or perpetuating *apartheid,* racial segregation, discrimination, colonial and other forms of oppression and foreign domination stand condemned and must be eliminated.

2.   The natural resources of the earth including the air, water, land, flora and fauna and especially representative samples of natural ecosystems must be safeguarded for the benefit of present and future generations through careful planning or management as appropriate.

3.   The capacity of the earth to produce vital renewable resources must be maintained and wherever practicable restored or improved.

4.   Man has a special responsibility to safeguard and wisely manage the heritage of wildlife and its habitat which are now gravely imperilled by a combination of adverse factors. Nature conservation including wildlife must therefore receive importance in planning for economic development.

5.   The non-renewable resources of the earth must be employed in such a way as to guard against the danger of their future exhaustion and to ensure that benefits from such employment are shared by all mankind.

6.   The discharge of toxic substances or of other substances and the release of heat, in such quantities or concentrations as to exceed the capacity of the environment to render them harmless, must be halted in order to ensure that serious or irreversible damage is not inflicted upon ecosystems. The just struggle of the peoples of all countries against pollution should be supported.

7.   States shall take all possible steps to prevent pollution of the seas by substances that are liable to create hazards to human health, to harm living resources and marine life, to damage amenitites or to interfere with other legitimate uses of the sea.

8.   Economic and social development is essential for ensuring a favourable living and working environment for man and for creating conditions on earth that are necessary for the improvement of the quality of life.

9.   Environmental deficiencies generated by the condition of under-development and natural disasters pose grave problems and can best be remedied by accelerated development through the transfer of substantial quantities of financial and technological assistance as a supplement to the domestic effort of the developing countries and such timely assistance as may be required.

10.   For the developing countries, stability of prices and adequate earnings for primary commodities and raw material are essential to environmental management since economic factors as well as ecological processes must be taken into account.

11.   The environmental policies of all States should enhance and not adversely affect the present or future development potential of developing countries, nor should they hamper the attainment of better living conditions for all, and appropriate steps should be taken by States and international organizations with a view to reaching agreement on meeting the possible national and international economic consequences resulting from the application of environmental measures.

12.   Resources should be made available to preserve and improve the environment, taking into account the circumstances and particular requirements of developing countries and any costs which may emanate from their incorporating environmental safeguards into their development planning and the need for making available to them, upon their request, additional international technical and financial assistance for this purpose.

13.   In order to achieve a more rational management of resources and thus to improve the environment, States should adopt an integrated and co-ordinated approach to their development planning so as to ensure that development is compatible with the need to protect and improve the human environment for the benefit of their population.

14.   Rational planning consitutes an essential tool for reconciling any conflict between the needs of development and the need to protect and improve the environment.

15.   Planning must be applied to human settlements and urbanization with a view to avoiding adverse effects on the environment and obtaining maximum social, economic and environmental benefits for all. In this respect projects which are designed for colonialist and racist domination must be abandoned.

16.   Demographic policies, which are without prejudice to basic human rights and which are deemed appropriate by Governments concerned, should be applied to those regions where the rate of population growth or excessive population concentrations are likely to have adverse effects on the environment or development, or where low population density may prevent improvement of the human environment and impede development.

17.   Appropriate national institutions must be entrusted with the task of planning, managing or controlling the environmental resources of States with the view to enhancing environmental quality

18.   Science and technology, as part of their contribution to economic and social development, must be applied to the identification, avoidance and control of environmental risks and the solution of environmental problems and for the common good of mankind.

19.   Education in environmental matters, for the younger generation as well as adults, giving due consideration to the underprivileged, is essential in order to broaden the basis for an elightened opinion and responsible conduct by individuals, enterprises and communities in protecting and improving the environment in its full human dimension. It is also essential that mass media of communications avoid contributing to the deterioration of the environment, but, on the contrary, disseminate information of an educational nature on the need to enable man to develop in every respect.

20.   Scientific research and development in the context of environmental problems, both national and multinational, must be promoted in all countries especially the developing countries. In this connexion, the free flow of up-to-date scientific information and transfer of experience must be supported and assisted, to facilitate the solution of environmental problems; environmental technologies should be made available to developing countries on terms which would encourage their wide dissemination without constituting an economic burden on the developing countries.

21.   States have, in accordance with the Charter of the United Nations and the principles of international law, the sovereign right to exploit their own resources pursuant to their own environmental policies, and the responsibility to ensure that activities within their jurisdiction or control do not cause damage to the environment of other States or of areas beyond the limits of national jurisdiction.

22.   States shall co-operate to develop further the international law regarding liability and compensation for the victims of pollution and other environmental damage caused by activities within the jurisdiction or control of such States to areas beyond their jurisdiction.

23. Without prejudice to such criteria as may be agreed upon by the international community, or to the standards which will have to be determined nationally, it will be essential in all cases to consider the systems of values prevailing in each country, and the extent of the applicability of standards which are valid for the most advanced countries but which may be inappropriate and of unwarranted social cost for the developing countries.

24. International matters concerning the protection and improvement of the environment should be handled in a co-operative spirit by all countries, big or small, on an equal footing. Co-operation through multilateral or bilateral arrangements or other appropriate means is essential to effectively control, prevent, reduce and eliminate adverse environmental effects resulting from activities conducted in all spheres, in such a way that due account is taken of the sovereignty and interests of all States.

25. States shall ensure that international organizations play a co-ordinated, efficient and dynamic role for the protection and improvement of the environment.

26. Man and his environment must be spared the effects of nuclear weapons and all other means of mass destruction. States must strive to reach prompt agreement, in the relevant international organs, on the elimination and complete destruction of such weapons.

THE STOCKHOLM CONFERENCE: U. S. APPRAISAL

The United Nations Conference on the Human Envrionment, which met at Stockholm June 5-16, 1972, laid a foundation for international cooperation in dealing with common environmental problems. The Conference was attended by 1200 representatives of 113 nations—with the notable exception of the Soviet bloc, which boycotted the meeting in a dispute over the seating of East Germany. The Conference adopted a Declaration on the Human Environment (text attached); and approved 109 recommendations to be embodied in an international Action Plan setting out guidelines—for governments.[1] The Conference theme: "Only One Earth."

Convened by a decision of the UN General Assembly taken in 1968 on the initiative of Sweden, the Conference will submit its recommendations and Declaration to the General Assembly for approval at its 27th session, which opens September 19 in New York.

The National Foreign Trade Council, expressing views of the U.S. International business community, has commended the organization of the Stockholm Conference as an important basis for developing international approaches for dealing with environmental problems.

"There is reason for hope that the Stockholm Conference, although it cannot solve all the problems of international pollution, can provide an initial framework for approaching solutions," NFTC President Robert M. Norris said in a communication on March 17, 1972 to the Secretary of State's Advisory Committee on the UN Conference on the Human Environment.

Actions of Major Importance

Summarizing major accomplishments at Stockholm, President Nixon said: "The Conference achieved nearly all of the goals which the United States had urged in advance.[2] He said that, specifically, the participating nations:

1.   Reached agreement on the establishment of a permanent new organization within the United Nations to coordinate international envrionmental activities.
2.   Agreed to the establishment of a United Nations environmental fund to be financed by voluntary contributions from UN member governments. I shall ask Congress to authorize and approve $40 million as our Nation's share of a five-year $100 million fund.
3.   Endorsed completion of a convention proposed by the United States to control ocean dumping of shore-generated waste. The favorable prospect for international action heightens the urgency of passing the domestic legislation. I have proposed to curtail ocean dumping from our shores.
4.   Approved an "earthwatch" program for worldwide environmental monitoring.
5.   Endorsed in principle a convention on endangered species, designed to protect species of plants and animals threatened with extinction by imposing control in international shipment, import and export.
6.   Endorsed our recommendation for a ten-year moratorium on commercial whaling. (Despite vigorous U.S. efforts, this moratorium was not agreed to by the International Whaling Commission at its recent meeting, although we were successful in achieving substantially reduced quotas and other protective measures.)
7.   In addition, a proposal which I made in 1971 for a World Heritage Trust—to give uniquely important historic, cultural and natural areas of the world special international recognition and protection—was strongly supported at Stockholm. When established, the Trust will provide vital new international dimension to the national park concept.

"I am hopeful about the prospects of international cooperation in the environmental field. The U. S. will continue to provide leadership in developing such cooperation," the President said.

A State Department press release[3] rounding up actions taken at Stockholm summarized Conference actions considered by the United States to be of major importance. In addition to the actions noted by the President, the round-up release also listed these:

8.   Recommended steps to minimize release of such dangerous pollutants as heavy metals and organochlorines into the environment.

9.   Called for world programs to collect and safeguard the world's immense variety of plant and animal genetic resources on which stability of ecosystems and future breeding stocks depend.

10.   Recommended creation of an Environmental Referral Service to speed exchange of environmental know-how among all countries.

11.   Urged steps to prevent national environmental actions from creating trade barriers against exports of developing countries.

12.   Recommended higher priority for environmental values in international development assistance, e.g., more emphasis on conservation, land use planning, and quality of human settlements.

13.   Urged greater emphasis on population policy and accelerated aid to family planning in countries where population growth threatens environment and development goals.

14.   Issued a Declaration on the Human Environment containing important new principles to guide international environmental action, including Principle 21 that states are responsible to avoid damaging the environment of other states or of the international realm.

United States Delegation

The sixty-three-member U. S. delegation, including twenty-eight technical advisors, went to Stockholm with a coordinated position developed in consultation with many U. S. Government agencies concerned with environmental issues. The delegation was headed by Russell E. Train (Chairman), Chairman of the Council on Environmental Quality; Christian A. Herter, Jr. (Vice Chairman), Special Assistant to the Secretary of State for Environmental Affairs, and Senator Howard Baker (R.-Tenn.), Chairman, Advisory Committee on the UN Conference on the Human Environment.

Maurice F. Strong, a Canadian, was *Secretary-General* of the Conference. Ingemund Bengtssen of Sweden served as Conference President.

International Trade Relations

One of the six major subject areas considered at Stockholm was entitled "Development and Environment" (Subject Area V). Several recommendations in this area were presented under the heading, *International Trade Relations.*[4] The United States supported some of these recommendations and opposed others. Specifically:

Area V, Paragraph 32—the United States *abstained* on this paragraph as a whole. However, the U. S. *supported* the key principle that participating countries not use environmental actions as a pretext for discriminatory trade practices; the proposal that existing machinery of GATT be used to examine trade and environment questions; the principle that environmental standards in given products or processes need not be uniform in all countries where environmental disruption to other countries is not involved; and that the purpose of these standards is to protect the environment, not to gain trading advantage.

The U. S. *opposed* other sections of Paragraph 32, which:

—Call for "compensation" to exporting countries (especially developing countries) when environmental actions hamper their exports. The U. S. pointed out that many forces affect export earnings and to single out any of these, such as environmental actions, for compensatory treatment would be wrong in principle and a disincentive to environmental responsibility, but stated readiness to deal with any complaint that its environmental actions violate GATT obligations.

—Call for advance consultation on planned environmental actions affecting trade, and assistance aimed at removing obstacles to trade which these actions create. The U. S. said the recommendation is too vague and general to permit effective implementation.

The U. S. *supported* Paragraph V-33, which recommends that UN agencies identify environment and export problems and remedies; also help governments negotiate international standards on traded projects; also Paragraph V-34, which recommends that GATT and UNCTAD monitor and report on trade barriers arising from environmental policies.

Paragraph V-36, *World distribution of industry,* recommends, (A) that developing countries consider establishing industries in which their environmental situation may confer comparative advantages, but avoid creating the environmental pollution problems in the process; and (B) that the UN review the implications of environmental concerns for future world distribution of industry, especially in developing countries.

The U. S. *abstained* on this recommendation, noting that the study called for in (B) would be meaningless generalities if made on a global basis, since relevant factors vary so widely from country to country.

U. S. Appraisal

In general, the U. S. appraisal[5] was:

"One of the most important insights that emerged from the Conference was the recognition by developed and developing countries alike that economic development at the expense of the environment imposes heavy costs in health and in the quality of life. The United States stressed that it is much less costly and more effective to build the necessary quality into new facilities and new communities from the outset than it is to rebuild or modify old facilities.

"On the interrelationship between environment and economic development, the industrialized countries agreed that economic progress does not have to be paid for in the degradation of cities and exhaustion of resources, while the developing countries were more appreciative of the fact that environmental quality and resource conservation do not have to be paid for in economic stagnation and inequity."

Declaration on the Human Environment

The Declaration on the Human Environment, consisting of a preamble and 26 principles, was adopted almost unanimously, with the exception of the People's Republic of China, at the closing meeting of the Conference.

The Conference adopted the first 25 principles by acclamation, with formal reservations on various points as registered by individual nations to go on the official record later. The Chinese objected to No. 26, dealing with nuclear weapons, and this was adopted separately.[6]

The final text, although uneven in the view of the U. S. Delegation, preserves a number of important principles in the draft declaration[7] as submitted by the 27-nation Preparatory Committee for the Stockholm Conference headed by Keith Johnson of Jamaica.

Chief among these is Principle 21, which declares that States have "the responsibility to ensure that activities within their jurisdiction or control do not cause damage to the environment of other States or of areas beyond the limits of national jurisdiction."

Agreement could not be reached on a draft principle, opposed by Brazil, which has been referred to the UN General Assembly for action. This principle read: "Relevant information must be supplied by States on activities or developments within their jurisdiction or under their control whenever they believe, or have reason to believe that such information is needed to avoid the risk of significant adverse affects on the environment in areas beyond their national jurisdiction."

United States Reservations

The record of the Conference will include the following U. S. statement of interpretation regarding four of the 26 principles of the declaration.

"Principle 2. The U. S. places emphasis on the word 'representative' which, in our view, ensures that the phrase means retention of a complete system with all of the complex interrelationships intact not a portion thereof. Moreover, the size of the sample must be sufficient to represent the size of the whole.

"Principle 12. The U. S. does not regard the text of this principle or any other language contained in the Declaration, as requiring it to change its aid policies or increase the amounts thereof. The U. S. accepts the idea that added costs in specific national projects or activities for environmental protection reasons should be taken into account.

"Principle 21. The U. S. considers it obvious that nothing contained in this principle, or elsewhere in the Declaration, diminishes in any way the obligation of states to prevent environmental damage or gives rise to any right on the part of states to take actions in derogation of the rights of other states or of the community of nations. The statement of the responsibility of states for damage caused to the environment or other states or of areas beyond the limits of national jurisdiction is not in any way a limitation on the above obligation, but an affirmation of existing rules concerning liability in the event of default on the obligation.

"Principle 26. The U. S. fully supports the purpose, aspirations and ultimate goals contained in this paragraph. We are constantly striving to meet such goals in all relevant fora including for example SALT which has recently achieved such success. We regard our commitment under this principle as identical to the treaty obligation we have assumed in connection with the treaty on the non-proliferation of nuclear weapons, specifically Article VI including the requirement of 'strict and effective international control.' We believe it obvious that agreements called for in the principle must be adequately verifiable or they will not be soundly enough based to achieve the purpose of this principle."

NOTES

1.   UN Press Release HE/78/Rev. 1, June 19, 1972. Representatives of 110 States, whose credentials were approved, attended the Conference. Chad, Haiti and Yemen attended the opening meetings.

2.   Message to the Congress Transmitting the third Annual Report of the Council on Environmental Quality, August 7, 1972.

3.   Results of the U. N. Conference on the Human Environment at Stockholm,'' Department of State News Release, Bureau of International Scientific & Technological Affairs, Office of Environmental Affairs, June 21, 1972.

4.   A/CONF.48/10, Reproduced in "Background Papers, UN Conference on the Human Environment," NFTC Ref. No. M-328, May 9, 1972.

5.   State Department News Release, "Stockholm Conference on the Human Environment,"   July 28, 1972.

6.   "UN Parley Ends by Adopting Guide to Pollution War," New York Times, June 17, 1972.

7.   A/CONF. 48/4. Also NFTC M-163, January 19, 1972.

The Public Accountant in a Public Dispute

The 12,000 licensed taxicabs in New York City transport about 800,000 passengers each day; almost 300 million per year. In as much as the taxis constitute a significant portion of the city's public transportation system, the fares are obviously a matter of considerable public concern.

In 1967 and again in 1970, when the New York City Council was considering proposed changes in the rate structure for the taxi industry, which it regulated, several studies were ordered to provide added information. The results of these studies conducted by certified public accountants were to be considered in evaluating the merit of a general fare increase.

Taxis are often considered an upper-class mode of transportation. In New York, however, they serve as a primary source of intracity mobility for the elderly, the handicapped, and workers keeping odd hours. Many people residing in high crime areas will often take a taxi to and from the subway stations. These latter, often low-income groups have a strong and determined interest in holding fares down, and they make their views known to their political representatives.

Thus, with taxi fares of great public concern, the public accountants who were called upon to provide independent studies, evaluations, and projections for the taxi industry found themselves in the midst of a major public controversy. The reports of the CPAs were subject to widespread public comment, and criticism in several nonfinancial publications. A number of questions for public accountants and the public were raised. Among them were:

1.   Should the public accountant involve himself in certification of circumstances outside the normal financial area?
2.   What standards should be applied to such work, assuming it is undertaken?
3.   How active or passive should the CPA be in his report on social issues? How active or passive *can* he be?
4.   Do the economics of non-recurring, social-type engagements permit the standard of work expected in normal, recurring financial audits?
5.   How is the work of public accountants in this area to be evaluated?
6.   What steps can, and should, the CPA take to protect himself in accepting such "community-conscious" assignments?

The public's view of the fare controversy came largely through the newspapers. Several articles appeared, in which comments *from* the reports of the CPAs and *about* their reports were featured. The following article, by Frank J. Prial of *The New York Times* is representative.

Thereafter, excerpts from the Price Waterhouse report and the report of the accountants of the City Transportation Administration are given, to enable readers to evaluate the fairness of the comments in the article.

In reference to Councilman Merola's comments, the monthly charge for a garage in midtown Manhattan was about $60. In the outlying areas of the Bronx and Brooklyn—where taxi garages are usually located—the monthly charge was about $25 to $30.

Final Result

At the time of this dispute the New York City taxi fares were the lowest of the twelve largest cities in the United States (exclusive of Washington, D. C. which has a zoned fare and cannot be compared). During 1971 the New York rates were raised to a level which made them the highest in the United States.

CAB FINDINGS QUESTIONED—CRITICS SAY ACCOUNTING DODGES OBSCURE THE ISSUE: IS FARE RISE REALLY NEEDED?

The financial report on which the proposed taxi fare increase is in part based has come in for considerable criticism by some members of the City Council and by others knowledgable about the fleet taxi business.

The report, prepared by the accounting concern of Price Waterhouse & Co., contends that the fleet taxi industry is in poor financial health. In effect, the report endorses the industry's contention that it needs the fare increase of some $41-million a year included in the taxi bill before the Council.

The critics contend, among other things, that the industry is in far better shape than the figures indicate and that the fleets use a variety of accounting dodges to conceal their true financial condition.

As approved by the Consumer Affairs Committee of the Council, the proposed fare calls for a rise in the average fare to about $2 from $1.35.

Rise in Meter Rates Asked

At present the meters read 45 cents for the first sixth of a mile plus 10 cents for each additional third of a mile. The proposed rate would be 60 cents for the first fifth of a mile and 10 cents for each fifth thereafter.

The financial data that some City Councilmen and others are questioning are included in the 13-page Price Waterhouse report prepared late last year at the request of the fleet owners.

Based on data for the year ended last June 30, the report asserts that the taxi industry here is losing $7-million a year, or $2.81 on each cab each day.

The fare was raised 16 per cent in 1968 (after a similar Price Waterhouse report), but costs have risen 23 per cent since then, the accounting firm says.

In preparing its most recent report, Price Waterhouse said, it audited the books of three of the city's 72 taxi fleets, made spot checks on the books of seven others and looked at some statistics of 40 fleets.

Survey Called 'Representative'

"The large cross-section, "the accounting firm said, "is believed to be representative to the entire fleet taxicab industry" because the "principal financial operating factors" of the 50 apply equally to the rest.

Price Waterhouse noted in the covering letter of its report that it did "not express an opinion" on the books of fleets it had not examined.

In its survey for the taxi industry in 1967, after which fares were raised, Price Waterhouse's disclaimer was more pronounced. It noted that the figures had been supplied by the fleets—48 fleets. The firm said:

"As you understand, we did not perform an examination of the 48 fleets, and therefore cannot express an opinion as to whether the financial operating data for each individual fleet has been fairly presented."

Taxi industry spokesmen defended the new report briskly, however, Bronx Councilman Mario Merola, chairman of the Council's Finance Committee and a supporter of the proposed fare increase, said the Price Waterhouse report "is impossible to evaluate."

"How can you take samples and make projection," he asked, "when the industry you are dealing with has no uniform accounting procedures?"

Both the Taxi Board of Trade and spokesmen for Benjamin Botwinick & Co., regular accountants for the board, insist that the industry does have a uniform system of bookkeeping and has had for many years.

Garage Fees Disputed

"If the Price Waterhouse figures are correct," Mr. Merola said, "the fleet owners are paying $75 to $85 a month to garage their cabs. Maybe on Park Avenue," he went on, "but in a garage in the South Bronx?"

The Bronx Councilman said that many of the fleet owners owned the garages and were

SOURCE: Frank J. Prial, *The New York Times,* February 15, 1971.

paying themselves the high parking fees.

In fact, Price Waterhouse comments on this "multicorporate structure" of the taxicab fleets. The "fleet" is actually a management corporation, "which usually operates the taxicabs, receives the fare income and pays the operating and maintenance expenses."

The taxicab companies that make up the fleet, are, Price Waterhouse notes, normally owned by the same principals who own the management company."

In some instances," the report says, "real estate companies owning the garage rented by the fleet are controlled by the same principals who own the fleet."

Another vocal critic of the taxi industry's financial report is Councilman Theodore S. Weiss of Manhattan. Agreeing with Mr. Merola that the Price Waterhouse report provided little usable information, Mr. Weiss said he had found more information in an audit of the fleets done recently by the City Transportation Administration.

The city audit was done on four fleets, Mr. Weiss said totaling 650 cabs. It found that 200 of the 650 accounted for 80 per cent of the losses of the entire group.

The losses for that group were averaged out and projected for the entire fleet industry, Mr. Weiss said, and the figure came to around $7-million.

80 PCT Believed 'Doing Well'

"I think that about 20 per cent of the industry accounts for most of the losses," Mr. Weiss said, "with the rest of the owners doing quite well."

Some critics of the taxi industry charge that the fleet owners actually make more from interest charges than from fares and management fees. In such cases, these critics say, the taxi management companies make loans, at high interest, to the taxi owning companies—which are often one and the same.

"The industry is almost 100 per cent financed," Mr. Merola said: "What other business is operated that way?"

Price Waterhouse says in its report that the fleets incur "significant" debt, in part because of the need to replace battered cabs every 18 to 24 months. The report estimates the average debt per cab at about $8,400, and the average interest rate in the industry at about 11 per cent.

Other sources contend that the smaller, higher-risk cab owners may pay as much as 20 per cent interest for new cabs and medallions.

PRICE WATERHOUSE & CO.

60 BROAD STREET

NEW YORK 10004

November 6, 1970

Metropolitan Taxicab Board of Trade, Inc.
1775 Broadway
New York, N. Y.

Dear Sirs:

We enclose our report on the financial survey of the fleet-owned taxicabs in New York City which we conducted in September and October 1970. This survey was made at your request for the purposes of (1) accumulating financial operating results and related data that would be representative of the operations of the fleet taxicab industry in New York City and (2) summarizing the information obtained and making such adjustments as appeared necessary in order to provide a basis for the City Council of New York City to review the reasonableness of the current taxicab fare rates.

The accompanying report is based upon the financial operating data for the year ended June 30, 1970 which we obtained for 50 taxicab fleets operating 5,426 taxicabs and representing 80% of the fleet taxicabs. We reviewed the data for each fleet for reasonableness and comparability with both the data for the other fleets and the information and understanding we developed in visiting and examining the records and operations of 10 fleets and in performing other tests as further described in Section II. The purpose of our review and tests was to provide a basis for summarizing the industry data and adjusting it as appropriate to reflect the current operating conditions of the industry. For this purpose we did not believe it necessary to examine operating results of each fleet included and accordingly we do not express an opinion on the financial data for fleets not so examined.

- 2 -

The results of our survey indicate that the fleet taxicab industry as a whole is presently operating at a loss of about $7 million a year. This and other factors disclosed in our survey indicate that the industry is facing serious financial difficulty.

Since our previous survey in 1967, the financial operating results of the industry detericrated significantly, as the fare increase in 1968 which increased revenues 16% has proved inadequate in relation to the increases in employee compensation and the inflation in other operating costs which increased 23%. Correspondingly, it should be noted that the fare rates in New York City are lower by as much as 44% than in other major cities, as summarized in Exhibit B.

Yours very truly,

Price Waterhouse & Co.

NEW YORK CITY FLEET TAXICAB INDUSTRY—FINANCIAL SURVEY, OCTOBER 1970

            *   *   *

Asterisks indicate sections or material omitted

Licensing of Taxicab Industry:

. . . . The license to operate a taxicab in New York City is issued by the Hack Bureau of the New York City Police Department, and is evidenced by a "medallion" which is affixed to the taxicab. Fleet medallions must be owned in multiples, while individual owner medallions must be owned singularly. The total number of medallions authorized is 11,787 (including 8 unrenewed medallions) which has been unchanged since 1937 except for the limited additional number made available after World War II to former owners who had sold their medallions prior to entering the armed forces. The medallions have to be renewed annually but otherwise have an indefinite life and are transferable under the jurisdiction and restrictions of the Hack Bureau.

The transfer value of fleet medallions has been declining steadily in recent years. In 1965 fleet medallions were transferred at a price of $34,500. By 1967 this value had declined to $16,000. There have been only a very limited number of transactions in the past year, usually involving the assumption of bank loans and other liabilities. Based on these transactions the current value appears to be about $14,000, but there does not appear to be any significant interest in purchasing medallions, except by established fleets who are already operating the facilities needed to serve and manage additional cabs.

            *   *   *

Organization of Taxicab Fleets:

Taxicab fleets are normally a multicorporate structure, consisting of:

—A single management company, which usually operates the taxicabs, receives the fare income and pays the operating and maintenance expenses with a few exceptions. The net income of the management company is distributed, usually on a per cab basis, to the taxicab-owning corporations.

—Various taxicab-owning corporations, which typically own two or three taxicabs, pay such expenses as licenses, insurance, interest and minor other unpooled expenses. They are normally owned by the same principals who own the management company, but in several instances include corporations owned by others.

In some instances real estate companies owning the garage rented by the fleet are controlled by the same principals who own the fleet. The rent charged in such situations noted in our survey bore a close relation to the depreciation, taxes and interest related to the garage.

This corporation structure affords several advantages, including facilitating the pooling of separately owned taxicabs into larger fleets, limitation of liabilities for accidents to each taxicab-owning corporation, and possible reductions in federal income taxes. For purposes of this survey the financial data for the management and taxicab-owning corporations in each fleet has been combined. . .

*   *   *

Financing of Taxicab Fleets:

Our survey indicates that the majority of the taxicab fleets are financed to a significant extent by borrowings, usually from one of several New York City banks, and related to the purchase of a new fleet of vehicles, which takes place most frequently in 18 to 24-month cycles, and the purchase of additional medallions. The loans are normally secured by the entire fleet of vehicles, the medallions, and the capital stock of the corporations and are guaranteed by the principals operating the fleet.

In the typical situation the vehicle and medallion purchase loans are repayable in installments over 18 to 24 months, which amortize a portion of the loan over that period, with the unpaid balance refinanced at the end of the period. Personnel of major lending banks have informed us that they will re-finance already existing medallion loans if necessary but they are reluctant to extend new lines of credit for the purchase of fleets.

The average loan balance, based on information received from the principal lending banks representing 3,149 cabs (46% of the taxicab fleet industry), approximates $8,400 per cab. Banks are generally charging interest at 6% discounted (equivalent to over 11% effective rate) on vehicle loans and 11% add-on interest on the medallion loans. The overall average effective interest rate on existing loans appears to be approximately 11%.

*   *   *

II – Combined Financial Operating Results

*   *   *

To afford us a basis for making a review of the financial operating results submitted to us and to gain insight to operations of the fleet industry, we examined in accordance with generally accepted auditing standards the income statements of three representative fleets, independently selected by us. Such examinations included review and testing of revenues, examinations of selected disbursements for propriety and reasonableness, checking of payrolls and employees, and examination of taxes and contractual obligations, including payments to affiliated real estate companies. As a result of these examinations we concluded that the financial operating results furnished to us for these three fleets fairly presented results of the operations in accordance with generally accepted accounting principals consistently applied.

To extend the scope of our understanding we then selected an additional seven fleets, which represented a cross section of fleet sizes and ranges of financial results, to visit and carry out a review and tests of their financial operating results. These reviews augmented and supported our conclusions as to the reasonableness of the data furnished to us by the industry members.

We also reviewed the financial operating results for the remaining 40 fleets included in the survey and questioned any unusual or disproportionate variation from the results of the fleets reviewed in greater detail.

Statement of Combined Financial Operating Results:

The information presented in the statement of combined financial results (Exhibit A), in the first column, represents an accumulation of the financial statements for the 50 fleets obtained by us, except for interest expense and taxes which are discussed below. In reviewing the operations of the fleets included in our survey by categories (up to 49 cabs, 50 to 99 cabs and 100 and over cabs) we noted only marginal differences among their operating results, indicating the aggregate results are typical for all segments of the fleet taxicab industry. In addition, we did not note any material nonrecurring item of income or expense in our survey which would make the year ended June 30, 1970 not representative.

Interest expense of the fleets is not included in the fleets combined operating data because not all fleets account for interest on the same basis, and in some cases information was not ascertainable for the year ended June 30, 1970. Consequently, we obtained from major lending banks information for fleets operating 3149 taxicabs. From this information we determined the average interest expense per taxicab paid to banks by these fleets and projected this average for the entire 50 fleets. Interest expense projected on this basis amounts to $4,992,000.

No federal income tax provision was included in Exhibit A. The income tax structure in the industry is complex and inconsistent; for example, the election by a fleet operator to have a corporation treated for federal income tax purposes as a "Subchapter S" Corporation would have the effect of eliminating any tax on the corporation and instead its income would be included in determining the personal federal income tax of the stockholders of the fleet. Although we recognize that some fleets or corporations individually may be subject to federal income taxes for the survey period, other fleets or corporations as a result of their losses may be able to claim a refund of prior years taxes. However, because of the limited amount of taxes subject to refund this could not be done on a continuing basis. In view of the foregoing and the indicated major loss sustained by the industry in total, we have considered all federal income tax provisions as not being representative of continuing operations at the present time.*

III – Adjustments to Combined Financial Operating Results

As a result of our review of the financial operating results for the 50 fleets shown in Exhibit A and related examination procedures, we believe that certain adjustments should be made to the reported operating results in order to present them on a basis that will be most meaningful for evaluating the reasonableness of the current fare rate structure.

These adjustments are of two types, as follows:

a. Adjustments to include public liability insurance and interest income on an estimated or projected basis which is considered to be more appropriate for rate evaluation purposes than the actual amounts reported for the reasons stated herein and in Section II (Adjustments #1 and #2).

b. Adjustments to give a full year's effect to certain increases in costs occurring during the year ended June 30, 1970 that are of a continuing nature and will accordingly affect future operations (Adjustments #3 through #5)

The explanation and amount of each of these adjustments are described below.

Adjustment #1 – Public Liability Expense:

Most taxicab fleets are self-insured for public liability claims involving personal injury or property damage. The expense they report in their financial statements is usually related to the claims paid in a period rather than to the losses incurred in the period. At the present time when the backlog of claims and litigation awaiting settlement is growing and the cost of settlements is inflating, we do not believe that the claims settled during a period properly reflect the true public liability expense; rather, it is essential to recognize in the expense provision the added costs of claims that are delayed in settlement. To accomplish this we have obtained data from six legal firms who represent a major portion of the fleet taxicabs and from two insurance carriers who write the major portion of the industry's insurance coverage, as to the current cost of settling public liability claims. Based on this information it appears that currently the average cost is at least $150 per month per cab and accordingly we have adjusted the reported public liability expense by $2,410,000 to equal $150 per month per cab.

*A part of this report not reprinted here notes a provision for minimum NYS and NYC corporate taxes payable even in the absence of any profits, in the amount of $222,000.

Adjustment #2 – Interest Income:

Fleets which are self-insured for public liability claims are required to make a deposit with a bonding agent to cover claims outstanding against the fleets. The self-insured fleets have deposited securities for this purpose, most frequently non-taxable municipal securities. Since the accounting for this income varies among the corporations we have projected, for consistency purposes, the income to the fleets in our survey based upon information received for 31 of the 50 fleets. Applying a 5% interest rate (which approximates the yield on high-grade, tax-free municipal bonds) interest income was projected to be $377,000.

Adjustment #3 – Workmen's Compensation Insurance:

Workmen's compensation insurance rates increased on policies renewed after January 1, 1970 from $3.80 per $100 of drivers' earnings to $4.00 per $100, an increase of $.20 per $100. To give effect for the entire year to the increased premium rate, workmen's compensation expense, as recorded, was increased by $340,000. It should be noted that, effective July 1, 1970, the premium rate was further increased to $4.50 per $100. Had this increase been recognized an additional $259,000 adjustment would have been necessary.

Adjustment #4 – Maintenance and Garage Salaries:

Under the terms of the collective bargaining agreement currently in effect an increase of 5% in maintenance salaries and garage salaries became effective November 17, 1969. To give effect for the entire fiscal year to the increased salaries together with social security tax thereon, reported maintenance and garage salaries were increased by $94,000 and $30,000, respectively. We have also provided a $75,000 adjustment to administrative salaries to put them on a corresponding basis.

Adjustment #5 – Tire Leasing Expenses:

Tire leasing charges were increased by 10% effective May 1970 by the two tire leasing companies serving a major part of the industry. To give effect for the entire year to the increased tire costs, reported tire expense was increased by $114,000.

Exhibit A
Statement of Combined Financial Operating Results for the Fleet Taxicab Industry
for the Year Ended June 30, 1970
(Unaudited)

Fleets in survey (50 fleets; 5,426 cabs)

	Combined operating	Adjustments Dr.	(Cr.)		Combined operating data adjusted	Per cab per day	% of gross fare income	Projected industry totals (72 fleets 6,816 cabs)
Gross fare income	$132,619,182				$132,619,182	$66.97	100%	$165,773,978
Operating expenses:								
Drivers cost	78,544,077	$ 340,000		(3)	78,884,077	39.83	59.5	98,605,096
Vehicle operation	11,486,814	114,000		(5)	11,600,814	5.86	8.7	14,501,018
Depreciation	8,598,836				8,598,836	4.34	6.5	10,748,545
Public liability	7,509,353	2,410,000		(1)	9,919,353	5.01	7.5	12,399,191
Maintenance	8,513,143	94,000		(4)	8,607,143	4.35	6.5	10,758,929
Garage	4,371,485	30,000		(4)	4,401,485	2.22	3.3	5,501,856
General and administrative	11,493,454	75,000		(4)	11,568,454	5.84	8.7	14,460,568
Interest expense	4,992,000				4,992,000	2.52	3.8	6,240,000
Nontaxable interest income		(377,000)		(2)	(377,000)	(0.19)	(0.3)	(471,250)
Net Loss	($ 2,889,980)	$2,686,000	(377,000)		($ 5,575,980)	($ 2.81)	(4.2%)	($ 6,969,975)

Exhibit A-1
Combined Financial Operating Results
As Reported by the 50 Taxicab Fleets
For the Year Ended June 30, 1970
(Unaudited)

Details of Expenses	
Vehicle operation:	
Tires	$ 1,248,569
Gasoline	8,835,628
Licenses	1,130,874
Other	271,743
	$11,486,814
Maintenance:	
Salaries	$ 4,739,926
Parts and supplies	3,280,693
Outside repairs	437,666
Other	54,858
	$ 8,513,143
Garage:	
Salaries	$ 1,584,276
Rent	1,716,543
Other	1,070,666
	$ 4,371,485
General and administrative:	
Salaries	$ 4,007,285
Executive salaries	2,846,429
Legal and accounting	577,755
Life and medical insurance	231,196
Payroll taxes	579,450
Other (miscellaneous insurance, association dues, taxes, telephone, office supplies and expenses, etc.)	3,251,339
	$11,493,454

TRANSPORTATION ADMINISTRATION
Office of the Administrator
40 WORTH STREET, NEW YORK, N. Y. 10014
Telephone: 566-4112
CONSTANTINE SIDAMON-ERISTOFF, *Administrator*

First Deputy Administrator John G. deRoos   NOV 1 0 1970

Transportation Administration

40 Worth Street

New York, New York 1001

Dear Commissioner de Roos:

At your request, we have examined the financial statements, books, and records of the companies specifically selected by you, in your memorandum dated October 27, 1970, and their affiliated operating companies:

        1. Star Maintenance Corporation

        2. Helen Maintenance Corporation

        3. Terminal Systems, Inc.

        4. Affiliated Taxi, Inc (a merger of Lenox Maintenance

            Corporation and Transportation Maintenance Coporation).

In addition, we have reviewed the report prepared by Price Waterhouse and Company, Certified Public Accountants, covering their examination of the statements, books and records of approximately 80 per cent of the fleet taxi industry in New York City. We note that included in their report are the specific companies covered by our examination.

For comparative purposes, income statements of the companies we examined were recast to reflect a common fiscal year ending June 30, 1970. This was done in order that our data would be on a comparative basis with the data presented in the Price Waterhouse Report, and to

enable us to reach some independent conclusions regarding the financial
condition of the taxi fleet industry, on the basis of our limited sample
of the 72 fleet companies in operation in New York City.

Within the time frame allotted we could not conduct a detailed
examination of the records of the companies covered by this report.
Consequently the focus of our examination has been to develop, on the
basis of a system survey, tests of the accuracy of selected Ledger
accounts and other techniques deemed appropriate under the circumstances,
an opinion with respect to the operating statements prepared for the
aforenamed companies by Certified Public Accounts.

It is our opinion that the statements (Exhibit A) examined by us
present fairly the income and expenses as reflected on the books and
records of the companies for the fiscal years indicated.

For the period ending 6/30/70 our examination (after recasting the
operating statements to a common fiscal year) indicates a combine net
operating loss (before taxes) of $395,737.54 (Exhibit B). Among the
individual companies the loss varied from $2,298.96 to $193,784, reflecting differences in fleet sized and management expertise. On a per
cab basis we have completed a net loss per cab of $615. (395,737,54
divided by 643 cabs in the combined fleets).

In order to get some idea of the order of magnitude of the fleet
industry loss for the period ending 6/30/70, we have projected our
sample findings, unadjusted. This computation indicates a fleet industry
loss of the order of $4,194,975 before provision for income or franchise
taxes (Exhibit C).

On Friday, November 6, 1970, we received a copy of the Price
Waterhouse repo_t. In order to test our findings against the conclusions
presented therein with respect to the projected industry loss, we examined
and evaluated the adjustments to operating expenses. In our opinion their
adjustments as noted below* appear to be appropriate and correct for
purposes of forecasting the future operating results of the fleet industry.
Accordingly we increased our industry wide net loss by the amount of the
adjustments set forth in the Price Waterhouse report. As compared to the
$6,969,975 reported by Price Waterhouse we calculate an industry loss of
$6,880,956. Consequently, the Price Waterhouse projected industry loss
appears compatiable with our calculations.

Ed. Note: Scope of Audit Section Omitted

*   *   *

On the basis of the foregoing, the income and expenses of the
operating statements submitted appear to be in good order with respect
to survey and report submitted by Price,Waterhouse. Using our own
criteria and methods we appear to have arrived at the same approximate
conclusion with regard to the future financial position of the industry
under the existing rate structure.

We wish to state that all times we received maximum cooperation from
the industry, its accountants and employees.

Respectfully submitted,

Planning, Programming, and Budgeting: The Agencies and the Congress

Senator William Proxmire

The comments of Senator Proxmire served as a foreword to the three volume PPB (planning, programming, budgeting) study from which several other papers in this book have been taken. They provide some interesting insights into several aspects of social accounting.

The PPB process, as described by the Senator, bears a striking resemblance to conventional accounting techniques for the planning and control of business enterprises. Somewhat more substantive is the discussion on the difficulties of applying objective decision-making techniques within the peculiar political framework of the Congressional budgetary process. Because it is doubtful that the existing political structure is going to accommodate itself to the aspirations of social accountants, it seems incumbent on the accountants to accommodate their techniques to the political environment.

It is now three and a half years since all major Federal agencies were instructed to develop and implement planning-programming-budgeting systems. During this period there has been great activity in connection with program analysis and evaluation and a tremendous amount of discussion and debate. There has not been, however, any systematic look at how the application of the tools of economic and systems analysis has worked out in practice. There has been no comprehensive study of the lessons which have been learned, the changes which have been made, and the policies which should be followed in the future. Because of increasing interest in efforts to develop a more rational decision process, it seemed appropriate for the Joint Economic Committee to try to fill this gap.

The form chosen is that of a compendium, a collection of papers by both scholars and practitioners in the areas of public finance, systematic analysis, and program budgeting. The reason for this choice is, I think, fairly obvious—perceptions and conclusions differ widely, and there is no way to produce a "definitive"

Senator Proximire is Chairman of the Joint Economic Committee and Chairman, of the Subcommittee on Economy in Government.

SOURCE: From *The Analysis and Evaluation of Public Expenditures: The PPB System.* A Compendium of Papers submitted to the Subcommittee on Economy in Government of the Joint Economic Committee, Congress of the United States (1969) Vol. 1, pp. v-xiv. This paper has been adapted from a speech given by Senator Proxmire to the Agency Program Planning Officers Group luncheon meeting on Thursday, April 24, 1969. Budget Bureau Director Robert Mayo introduced Senator Proxmire.

work. To attempt to do so would mean forcing a developing field of public policy analysis into a limited and artificial mold, something that we certainly wished to avoid.

Instead, our hope was that by combining the thoughtful efforts and differing perspectives of a diverse group we would produce a work that would be valuable both to Government officials interested in improving the policymaking process and to students of Government decisionmaking and innovation. As I read through the contributions made to the compendium, I am confident that this hope has been fulfilled.

THE PPB SYSTEM AND RATIONAL DECISIONMAKING

It should be emphasized that the use of PPB and systematic analysis in the Government is not a partisan issue. While originally implemented pursuant to the instruction of President Johnson, it also is supported by the new administration. As Budget Director Robert Mayo has stated, it is now quite clear that any administration needs techniques of program evaluation if it is to make effective decisions on resource allocation.

The absence of partisan dispute over the use of PPB points to the recognition by responsible Government officials that we must be rational in our approach to public policy decision. For, to use PPB to obtain information about the gains and losses to be anticipated from a decision is to demand no more than that the decision be rational. Properly defined, PPB is the most basic and logical planning tool which exists: it provides for the quantitative evaluation of the economic benefits and the economic costs of program alternatives, both now and in the future, in relation to analyses of similar programs.

Any decisionmaker, whether he be the head of a household or the head of a business firm, must rely on the comparison of the gains and costs of his decisions if he is to be successful at achieving his objectives. To ignore the careful consideration of gains and losses is equivalent to saying that he has no objective at all; no goal which he is attempting to achieve. While the objectives of the Federal Government are less tangible and more complex than those of a household or a business firm, they do exist, and analysis should be carried out to determine which of our alternatives will allow us to satisfy these objectives at least cost. I would add that the very effort of attempting to evaluate alternatives is of substantial assistance in determining what our objectives really are.

I have never been able to understand why we are only now getting around to the task of developing such a system of analysis and evaluation. It is even more difficult for me to understand why many official and private groups sometimes object so violently to the application of this logic to public sector choices. Obviously, they themselves demand such information before they buy a new car or trade 15 shares of one common stock for seven shares of another.

THE CONGRESSIONAL BUDGETARY PROCESS

As a U. S. Senator, I also have a strong interest in the potential of PPB for improving decisionmaking in the legislative branch as well as in the executive. This is a very important possibility because, in my view, the legislative resource allocation process is sorely in need of improvement. In a very real sense, the congressional appropriation process is a classic example of an *explicit, closed,* and *uninformed* decision process. This does not mean that the executive budgetary process is perfect, or even that it is, in fact, very good on any absolute scale of values. But it is both informed and open compared with the budgetary process which exists in the legislative branch.

In the Congress, with its appropriations committees and subcommittees there is very little explicit consideration of program objectives or tradeoffs, of alternative means of attaining objectives, or of the benefits and costs of budget proposals this year and in the future. In short, Congress does not really give the budget a meaningful review because it fails to ask the right questions. Perhaps the primary reason for this is the traditional policy of executive branch dealings with the Congress. The executive branch comes to Congress with only one budget, with only one set of program proposals, and typically with no quantitative information on the benefits and the costs of even their own proposals. In fact, the only program area in which the Congress is presented with substantive cost-benefit evaluation information is that for water resources development. Since the Flood Control Act of 1936, project proposals in this area have been accompanied by a benefit-cost ratio. This number enables Congressmen and Senators to get some sense of the economic value of the choices which they are making and of the implicit costs involved when they choose to accept a project with a low benefit-cost ratio despite the fact that one displaying a higher ratio is available. (Even so, the usefulness of these analyses has been impaired by the use of artificially low discount rates in computing the present values of benefits over time. This has made bad projects look far better than they should.)

A second reason why the Congress has performed so badly in the budgetary and appropriations area has to do with the interests of Congressmen and Senators. Many in the legislative branch have little interest in or patience for careful deliberations on budgetary matters. The careful consideration of alternatives requires much effort and concentrated study of the relative merits and demerits, the costs and the gains, of alternative policy proposals. This is hard and grubby work. Those not used to thinking in such terms find it easier simply to rely on the executive agencies. Unfortunately, these agencies are often more interested in selling their programs, regardless of merit, than in having Congress analyze them.

A final reason for Congress' poor performance in this area is the severe staffing constraints under which the legislative branch operates. Currently, we do not have the staff either to interpret or to evaluate the analysis done by the executive branch were it presented to us, nor does Congress have the staff to do policy analysis of its own. Indeed, in my judgment, this is one of the primary barriers to the ability of the Congress to fulfill its mandate as controller of the public purse. Dr. Jack Carlson, who is Assistant Director of the Bureau of the Budget, stated this well in his recent testimony:

> You [the Congress] have some outstanding people who can provide program evaluation, but very few. I frankly think that Congress is not very well equipped to provide that evaluation.

Nonetheless, even if the interest and the staff existed, there would still be substantial organizational problems to hinder an effective public expenditure decision process. A primary difficulty is the organization and structure of the Appropriations Committees. In considering appropriations requests from the executive, we in the Congress have organized ourselves into appropriations committees and subcommittees with each subcommittee having control over a particular portion of the budget. The subcommittees consider the executive's proposed budget, deliberate on it, perhaps amend it, and ultimately report out an appropriations bill. The structure of this arrangement is such that the powerful people on the appropriations subcommittees—the Chairmen—almost inevitably desire to see the budgets which they oversee rise. They are not interested in careful scrutiny and evaluation of their own budgets. Other budgets should be cut, of course, but everyone knows that defense (or agriculture, or space, or public works, as the case may be) is "absolutely necessary" to the further growth and prosperity of the Nation.

I happen to be on the steering committee of the Democratic Party. It is this committee which assigns the Democratic membership to the available committee vacancies. In the deliberations of this committee, there are enormous pressures to place those Senators whose States benefit from, say, public works appropriations on either the Senator Interior Committee or the Public Works Subcommittee of the Appropriations Committee. In fact, a Senator who is from a State which benefits substantially from these programs is, at least in the short term, rather clearly serving his own best interests and those of at least some of his constituents if he attains a seat on one of these committees. The net result of all of this, however, is that the committee structure develops a built-in bias toward higher budgets. Because the people who serve on each committee have an interest in seeing the budget for which they are responsible increase, they often fail to encourage careful evaluation and analysis of expenditures.

An example of the bias which results from this process is clearly seen by observing the State membership of the Senate Committee on Interior and Insular Affairs. The Democratic members on that committee are from Washington, New Mexico, Nevada, Idaho, Utah, North Dakota, South Dakota, Wisconsin, Montana, and Alaska. The Republican membership is from Colorado, Idaho, Arizona, Wyoming, Oregon, Alaska, and Oklahoma. With the exception of my able colleague, Gaylord Nelson, there is no Senator on this committee representing holds in the Public Works Subcommittee of the Senate Appropriations Committee. The Democratic membership of this committee represents Louisiana, Georgia Arkansas, Washington, Florida, Mississippi, Rhode Island, Nevada, West Virginia, and Wyoming. Again, a substantial concentration of Senators from those Southern and Western States which receive major water resource appropriations. Much the same is true with the Republicans on that subcommittee, although I should add that at least two of these are from the Eastern States—Maine and New Jersey.

Largely as an outgrowth of this built-in committee bias, the relationships between the staffs of the committees and subcommittees and their counterparts in the executive agencies is hardly one of arms-length dealings. The degree of mutuality of interest between the executive staff and those on legislative branch committees is substantial. I would add that this problem is not peculiar to legislative-executive relationships. The serious colleagiality between Budget Bureau examiners who work on the military budget and their counterparts in the Pentagon has recently been the cause of much concern.

TOWARD AN IMPROVED APPROPRIATION PROCESS

Given the institutional constraints which inhibit change in this situation, is there anything which can be done to improve the congressional budgetmaking process? In my judgment, there are a number of important steps which can be taken. Many of them entail the bringing to bear of additional PPB-type information on the appropriations process. Congressmen and Senators who are concerned with national priorities and efficiency in Government must have the information and data necessary to raise and debate the right basic questions about program effectiveness and worth.

Building a Capability To Ask the Right Questions: The First Step

The most basic and elementary step which the Congress needs to take in improving the appropriation process is to develop a capability to ask the right questions. Whether this means a substantial increase in staff capability or a special office of budgetary analysis or an increase in the PPB capability of the General Accounting Office is not clear. What is clear, however, is that the Congress cannot respond to the demands of the people, cannot establish proper national priorities, cannot improve the quality of its decisions, cannot properly scrutinize the executive budget unless it equips itself to ask the right questions.

The right basic questions are those having to do with the outputs of a program and its inputs and the economic values of each. They are questions concerning the total costs of program decisions, and not just the given year costs. They are questions having to do with the distribution of a program's costs and benefits among the people. We must, for example, determine the economic losses which will be sustained (or gains which will be foregone) if program X is reduced by ten or fifty per cent, or increased by ten or fifty per cent.

The following are a few examples of the kinds of questions which I have in mind:

What, for example, are the real national security costs of removing Southeast Asia from the primary defense perimeter and what are the budgetary savings from its removal? On the basis of very little evidence and information, I am inclined to say that the costs of removing Southeast Asia may well exceed the value of the budgetary savings which we would experience. However, I cannot make a rational decision on this matter, nor can my colleagues in the Congress, unless we have the best analysis available on the costs and gains of such a policy alternative.

What would be the national security impact of a thirty per cent reduction of total U. S. ground forces, and what would be the budgetary savings from this reduction? An article in the *Congressional Quarterly*** claimed that $10 billion could be cut from the defense budget with no loss of national security effectiveness. Over fifty per cent of this suggested $10 billion cut was in the area of manpower. The efficiency of the Department of Defense in the handling of manpower policy is very low. Indeed, the national security costs of reducing ground forces by thirty per cent may well be zero. In any case, it is evidence—data and information—on the costs and gains of that sort of decision which Congress requires if the level of rationality is to be increased.

What are the total costs of adding a nuclear carrier force with all of its required support to our existing fifteen-carrier complex? What would be the gain in national security? How much elementary and secondary education could we purchase for the dollar cost of the new carrier?

What national economic benefits would the Nation sacrifice and what national costs would it avoid, if the Trinity River project is not constructed? This project involves the creation of a channel from Dallas-Forth Worth to the Gulf of Mexico. Some observers have argued that it would be cheaper to move Dallas-Fort Worth to the Gulf than to construct this channel.

What benefits are available from manned space flights that are not available from unmanned flights? What are the incremental costs of manned over unmanned flights? The space agency is now asking us for funds for ten moon landings and for the exploration of still additional planets. Those planets are going to be there ten years from now, or even twenty years from now. On what basis can we justify the current expenditure of these funds in view of the other social objectives which we would obtain if these

---

* Congressional Quarterly, June 28, 1968.

funds were not allocated to the space program? Moreover, some scientists believe that all of the information that we need from space flights can be obtained from unmanned flights, that manned flights are not necessary for this purpose. We need hard analysis of this decision.

What are the real costs to the American economy of specific protectionist measures that are sought by industry, such as the oil import program? What, in hard economic terms, do similar measures by other countries cost us? Such information is essential for effective bargaining.

How much do we spend to maintain the military capability to keep open important transportation bottlenecks, such as the Panama Canal, Gibraltar, or the Straits of Malacca? What costs would be incurred if such bottlenecks were not open?

What is the relationship between resources put into Federal criminal investigation, prosecution and judicial activities and the outputs of those activities in terms of cases actually processed? What are the benefits obtainable through Federal payments for increasing the number of State and local law enforcement personnel versus those obtainable from increasing the support available to existing personnel? In particular, to what extent are trained police officers now used less than optimally because of a lack of subprofessionals, dictating equipment, vehicles, cameras, or other fairly elementary support items?

Which policy of preschool education produces greater benefits: a policy which is going to reach all poverty children to at least some extent, or a program of intensive work with fewer children?

What economic losses will be incurred in the future—in terms of loss of productivity and increased welfare costs—that could be prevented by child nutritional and health care programs? How do the benefits available from such programs compare with the benefits available from further extension of the medicare program? For each type of program, upon whom would the costs and benefits fall or accrue?

What are the costs and benefits involved in the construction of mass transit systems in cities which do not presently have them? What should be included in our calculation of benefits, and how accurate can we be in our judgments? In the Northeastern United States, are the costs of constructing a high-speed ground transit system for intermediate intercity journeys less than those of constructing additional airport capacity?

What is the likely yield from the Government's investment in fast breeder reactor R. & D., and how does it compare with the return that the relevant private sector would demand? Are there possibilities for international cooperation that would avoid the overlap between this work and similar work in other countries?

These are the kinds of questions that Congress needs to ask, and for which responsible executive branch agencies must develop and supply answers. In my judgment, concerned Congressmen and Senators can reduce much gross waste from our budgets if we can first develop enough information to ask the right questions, and second, have the cooperation of the executive branch in getting answers.

In this same vein, it seems to me that the current ABM discussion which is going on in the Congress is one of the few examples of careful policy analysis by the legislative branch. It is a case in which Congress—the whole Congress—is asking the right questions about the benefits which will be achieved from this decision, about the costs which it will entail. As in good policy analysis, the question of objectives is being explicitly discussed and the interrelationships between the program proposal and the attainment of objectives is being investigated with some care. It is my belief that with more PPB-type information, the Congress can do this kind of policy analysis on increasing numbers of issues and expenditure proposals.

Gaining Access to Appropriate Data and Analysis: A Second Step

In addition to developing the capability to ask the right questions, the Congress needs to be provided with certain basic kinds of PPB-type information on an ongoing basis. The executive branch must be asked to develop this information and submit it to the Congress in appropriate form. The Bureau of the Budget must assume the leadership in this effort. Let me describe a few specific kinds of information which are essential to a more open and explicit congressional decision process.

Overview Information

The first of these items of analysis and data I will call "Overview Information." We need a display of each program in the Federal budget and an estimate of its benefit-cost ratio—that is, the efficiency impact of that program. We also need information on the distributional pattern of project outputs by income level, race, and geographic location—its equity impact. This information is often as important to those of us in the legislative branch as is the efficiency information. We can frame good policy only if we have knowledge of who we are helping when we appropriate money and who is bearing the cost. Even though many of these estimates would have to be rough, they would generate a major improvement in the appropriation process by giving Congress a better perspective on the probable impacts of these public expenditures. I urge the agencies to develop this kind of information, and I urge the Bureau of the Budget to collect and supply it to the Congress for individual programs and in summary form. I should note that in recent hearings before the Subcommittee on Economy in Government, Dr. Jack Carlson of the Bureau of the

Budget presented us with a sample format for this overview information and some preliminary data. The format is an excellent one. We now need the calculations to be made and the tables completed.

Budget Projections

A second body of information which Congress requires is out-year budget information. For each program, what are the expenditures to which we are committed over the next 5 years because of decisions which we have already made? For each new program proposal, what are the total five- or ten-year costs entailed by the decision? An example of what happens when we do not have this kind of information is the Higher Education Act of 1965 (Public Law 89-329). In this legislation, we provided thousands of student scholarships for the first year without really recognizing that to maintain our commitment the funding would have to double in the second year, triple in the third year, and quadruple in the fourth. By keeping the program at its present level, and refusing to honor the implied commitment, we have placed college and university administrators in an impossible position. They now either have to reduce the scholarship aid for the class which entered school last year, or they have to completely eliminate scholarship aid from this source for students currently entering school. If Congress had been oriented towards explicit consideration of the future costs of present decisions I think it would have avoided this bind.

I urge the executive branch to formulate a framework and procedure to develop this out-year budget information across the Federal Budget and to present it to the Congress. Moreover, I would propose that the President use the out-year budget framework which is developed to convey his budgetary priorities to the Congress. The numbers which he would place in the appropriate slots in this framework would not commit him, and would change over time. However, they would show the level of program outlays for which commitments have already been made as well as the budgetary areas to which the President would like to see uncommitted funds devoted. They would give the Congress an ongoing description of how the President hoped to allocate the Federal budget over the next several years and how much discretionary room remains in the budget if existing laws remain unchanged. They would give the Congress a bird's-eye view of the Executive's plans and priorities. I would hope that the Bureau of the Budget could play the leadership role in developing this information.

Quantitative Analysis of Alternatives

The final type of information which is essential to improvements in Congress' performance of its budgetary function entails the quantitative economic analysis of alternatives. As stated earlier, when the administration comes to Congress with a new program, it typically comes with a single recommendation. If Congress is to effectively carry out its decisionmaking role, it must do more than simply accept or reject an administrative recommendation. The Congress needs to be presented with a number of alternatives which would achieve a given objective. These alternatives should be accompanied by quantitative analyses of the benefits and the costs of each. It is only slightly less than absurd that the Congress is expected to participate meaningfully in the policymaking process when it is not asked not to consider alternatives, but only to approve or disapprove or to amend slightly at the margins. This problem is especially severe in the area of defense spending and military budgets. The development of a changed policy on the part of the executive branch in this area will, I suspect, be long in coming. Current policies are rooted in the concrete of both tradition and realistic gamesmanship. Nevertheless, it is something that we should work hard to change.

THE FURTHER DEVELOPMENT OF THE PPB SYSTEM

All of these improvements in PPB in the legislative branch are tied to the further development of the PPB system by the executive.

As is obvious, I am a strong supporter of program analysis. I also think the efforts that have been made recently to strengthen the process are important. In particular, the narrowing of the number of issues which receive special analytic attention was an important step, as is the insistence that these issues deal with the larger budget questions. Hopefully, agencies will be able to respond with more quantitative and more pointed analyses on the reduced list of issues. I also support the goal of increasing the role of agencies in the PPB process.

In my judgment, of high priority to the further development of PPB systems is the issuance by the Bureau of the Budget of a number of guideline documents to insure consistency in the economic analysis of public expenditures applied throughout the Federal Government. Last year, the Subcommittee on Economy in Government learned of the enormous divergence in the discounting analysis of public investment programs. The interest rates used ranged from zero per cent in some programs to twenty per cent in others. In testimony before the subcommittee, we learned from reputable economists that the discount rate to be used by public agencies should be at least eight per cent. This would eliminate the economic waste of diversion of resources from the private sector, where they are producing at least this return, to the public sector where, if rates of discount lower than this are applied, they will be likely to produce less. As stated earlier, I am well aware that the equity aspects are as important as the efficiency ones. However, one should not think that programs with low rates of return automatically produce equity, because they do not. Nor do I doubt our ability to find programs which meet both sets of criteria.

In the report of the Subcommittee on Economy in Government, we recommended that (1) the Bureau of the Budget should require all agencies to develop and implement consistent and appropriate discounting procedures on all Federal investments entailing future costs or benefits; and (2) the Bureau of the Budget, in conjunction with other appropriate Government agencies, should immediately undertake a study to estimate the weighted average opportunity-cost of private spending which is displaced when the Federal Government finances its expenditures. In response to these recommendations, the Bureau of the Budget has assured us that it is developing a guideline document to insure consistency in discounting practices across the Federal Government. I am anxious to see how the subcommittee recommendations are going to be implemented by the Bureau and Federal agencies.

On the basis of recent hearings before the Subcommittee on Economy in Government, I judge that Federal Government practice in benefit estimation is also extremely disparate. The issuance of a guideline document on the procedures for benefit estimation is also necessary. We need to develop a consistent concept of program benefits viewed from a national accounting stance. We need to establish a consistent procedure for handling benefits such as regional effects and secondary impacts, which are not appropriately considered from a national economic viewpoint.

In addition to increasing the role of consistent analysis through the issuance of guideline documents, the executive branch should build explicit procedures for the ongoing evaluation and appraisal of programs into new and experimental social programs. The Congress should require that provision for ongoing evaluation be included in appropriations for these programs. We know little about the kinds of inputs and program structures which will yield the outputs we desire and if we ever hope to generate improvements in programs in the areas of education, health, labor retraining, and so on, we must have followup evaluation. This information must be available to Congress on an ongoing basis as these programs evolve.

Finally, we need a new budget analysis which breaks down and evaluates the economic impact of tax expenditures, as well as direct expenditures. In testimony before the Joint Economic Committee, Joseph Barr, former Secretary of the Treasury, pointed out that the special provisions, exceptions, and deductions in the Federal structure cause an enormous reallocation of the Nation's resources. The volume of these tax expenditures is huge; in some of the functional categories of the Federal budget they outweigh direct expenditures. So far we have little analysis of these expenditures; we know very little about the kinds of outputs which they are producing, and the kinds of resource diversions they entail. The Federal budget should include information on these items, as well as the information which it currently includes. I call upon the Bureau of the Budget to develop a new budget format to include a description of both direct and tax expenditures.

CONCLUSION

In this compendium of papers, a large number of additional proposals for improving the analysis of public expenditures are made. In my view, these papers will make a valuable contribution to the quest for an effective system of policy analysis and program evaluation in both the Congress and the executive branch. They should serve to focus attention on the importance of applying economic analysis to Government decisions, and on the extent to which the public interest suffers in the absence of such analysis. The views presented on many facets of this issue should provide valuable insights into the problems involved in rationalizing the budget process and the evaluation of policy alternatives, and should point to possible solutions to some of the difficulties currently encountered. It is my hope that this compendium will stimulate greater efforts on the part of both congressional and executive decisionmakers to enhance the effectiveness of the public policy decision process.

IV

CORPORATE SOCIAL ACCOUNTING AND REPORTING

U.S. Securities and Exchange Commission Requirements for Environmental Accounting

By 1971 the SEC (Securities and Exchange Commission) recognized that environmental problems could have material effects on the financial position of corporations, and it adopted a modest set of disclosure guidelines at that time. The 1973 amendments, reproduced here, provide far more comprehensive requirements for recognition of the financial effects of present and anticipated environmental impacts in the filings of publicly held corporations.

With specific reference to concepts of social *accounting*, the commission has not limited itself to requiring only disclosure of existing or contemplated legal proceedings against a company. Companies must also state the impact—on earnings and capital expenditures—of conformity to pollution control and similar laws. Of particular interest is that the requirement relates to estimated *future* impacts of conformity to current legislation. This would suggest some immediate use for the application of many of the techniques described in this volume.

For those not familar with SEC filings, Form S-1 and 10 are utilized in connection with new issues of securities. Form 10-K, however, is an annual report to the SEC, while Form 8-K is required whenever there are material changes in a number of areas related to the financial condition and operations of a company. The requirements for environmental disclosures and calculations included in these forms will, therefore, make such social accounting calculations into recurring, normal operations.

SECURITIES ACT OF 1933
Rel. No. 5386/April 20, 1973
SECURITIES EXCHANGE ACT QF 1934
Rel. No. 10116/April 20, 1973

SOURCE: From Securities Act of 1933, Release No. 5386, April 20, 1973 Securities Exchange Act of 1934, Release No. 10116, April 20, 1973.

NOTICE OF ADOPTION OF AMENDMENTS TO REGISTRATION AND REPORT FORMS TO REQUIRE DISCLOSURE WITH RESPECT TO COMPLIANCE WITH ENVIRONMENTAL REQUIREMENTS AND OTHER MATTERS

The Securities and Exchange Commission today adopted amendments to its registration and reporting forms to require more meaningful disclosure of certain items pertaining to business and litigation, and particularly as to the effect upon the issuer's business of compliance with Federal, State and local laws and regulations relating to the protection of the environment. The forms which are amended are Forms S-1, S-7 and S-9 under the Securities Act of 1933 and Forms 10, 10-K and 8-K under the Securities Exchange Act of 1934. This action is being taken pursuant to the provision of these acts and pursuant to the National Environmental Policy Act ("NEPA").

The Commission notes that Section 105 of the NEPA states that the policies and goals set forth therein are supplementary to those in existing authorizations of Federal agencies. Having considered the public comments on Securities Act Release No. 5235 (February 16, 1972) it is the Commission's opinion that the amendments will promote investor protection and at the same time promote the purposes of NEPA.

The amendments adopted herewith will require as a part of the description of an issuer's business, appropriate disclosure with respect to the material effects which compliance with environmental laws and regulations may have upon the capital expenditures, earnings and competitive position of the issuer and its subsidiaries. Other amendments describe the extent to which litigation disclosures should contain specific descriptions of environmental proceedings. These amendments obviate the need for the environmental disclosure guidelines set forth in Part I to Securities Act Release No. 5170 (July 19, 1971), and accordingly these amendments will supersede such guidelines.

I. DESCRIPTION OF BUSINESS

The description of business items in the forms require information concerning business done and intended to be done with respect to the development of business during prior years and in future periods. The amendments emphasize the possible future effect of environmental statutes and regulations, and proceedings thereunder, on the issuer, and they specify the information to be furnished in connection with the description of business. Under the description of business items, the amendments require disclosure of the:

> material effects that compliance with Federal, State and local provisions regulating the discharge of materials into the environment, or otherwise relating to the protection of the environment, may have upon the capital

expenditures, earnings and competitive position of the registrant and its subsidiaries.

The Commission is aware that the amendments do not specify any minimum or maximum time period in the future required to be described. However, inasmuch as environmental compliance programs for different industries may involve substantially differing lead times, the Commission feels the time period is best left unspecified. If management has a reasonable basis to believe that future environmental compliance may have a material effect on the issuer's expenditures, earnings or competitive position in the industry, then such matters should be disclosed.

Expenditures solely attributable to compliance with environment provisions should be disclosed if material. When expenditures are partly for the replacement, modification or addition of equipment of facilities, and partly for the purpose of complying with any environmental provisions, management should estimate the cost of environmental compliance when there is a reasonable basis to segregate such amount. Such disclosures should be based and stated on an annual basis when such would diminish the apparent materiality of the expenditures or result in non-disclosure.

II. LEGAL PROCEEDINGS

The amendments include several revisions relative to disclosure requirements for legal proceedings. It is noted that some of the forms have a separate item for legal proceedings; others contain requirements or instruction under the business caption.

A.   Item 12 of Form S-1 now generally requires information as to material legal proceedings "know to be contemplated by governmental authorities." The Commission has adopted amendments the same as those published for comment to include a requirement similar to that in Form S-1 in Item 10 of Form 10 and Item 5 of Form 10-K. The requirement is applicable to proceedings relating to environmental matters as well as to other types of proceedings.

B.   The existing requirements in the various forms pertaining to disclosure of litigation generally call only for a "description" of certain proceedings. The Commission has adopted amendments to Forms S-1, 10, 10-K and 8-K, as published for comment, to require a description of the factual basis of the proceedings and the relief sought. The Commission notes that nothing in the amendments alters the present practice permitting in disclosures of legal proceedings, counsel's opinion as to the meritorious character of the claim and as to the validity of alleged defenses or cross-claims.

C.   Heretofore, instructions under Item 12 of Form S-1, Item 10 of Form 10, Item 5 of Form 10-K, and Item 3 of Form 8-K have stated that a legal proceeding is not "material" if it involves primarily a claim for damages and if the amount involved does not exceed fifteen per cent of the issuer's current assets on a consolidated basis. The amendments adopt the proposals published for comment to reduce this standard of economic materiality to 10 per cent of current assets, as being a more realistic test of materiality and one which conforms to other similar standards appearing elsewhere in the Commission's rules and forms. This reduction will apply to all forms of litigation, regardless of whether it is related to the environment.

D.   Presently, the instructions to the items of the forms mentioned in the preceding paragraph state that even though a legal proceeding does involve damages in an amount meeting the standard of economic materiality, information need not be given if the proceeding is considered "ordinary routine litigation incidental to the business." The Commission has adopted amendments to the instructions to the litigation items to state that administrative or judicial proceedings arising under any Federal, State or local provision regulating the discharge of materials into the environment, or otherwise specifically relating to the protection of the environment, shall not be considered "ordinary routine litigation incidental to the business," and shall be described if such proceeding is material to the business or financial condition of the registrant or if it involves primarily a claim for damages and the amount involved, exclusive of interest and costs, exceeds 10 per cent of the current assets of the registrant and its subsidiaries on a consolidated basis.

E.   At the present time, the Commission's disclosure forms contain no specific requirement for obtaining descriptions of environmentally-related proceedings, although certain descriptions are called for in Securities Act Release No. 5170. Securities Act Release 5235 proposed a revision to the litigation items to indicate, generally, that any environmentally-related administrative or judicial proceeding by governmental authority shall be deemed material and shall be described. The Commission at this time believes that the proposal on this matter is too broad and that the disclosures elicited by the proposal generally would cause the disclosure documents filed with the Commission to be excessively detailed without commensurate benefit to average investors. Accordingly, the Commission has revised the proposal published for comment to indicate that detailed disclosure of each such proceeding need not be given. Instead, issuers may set forth groupings of similar proceedings, specifying the number of such proceedings in each group, giving generic descriptions thereof, stating the issues generally involved, and, if such proceedings in the aggregate are material to the business or financial condition of the issuer, describing the effect of such proceedings on the issuer. Any such single proceeding, whether public or private, involving a claim for damages in excess of ten per cent of the issuer's current assets on a consolidated basis, or which otherwise may be material, should be individually described. The proposals under the instructions to the litigation headings included the following sentence: "Any such proceedings by private parties shall be described if material." Under the amendments adopted, that sentence is deleted as being redundant; other provisions of the amendments establish that private environmentally-related proceedings shall be described if they are material. The Commission intends to review the disclosures resulting from this requirement to determine whether subsequent modification is appropriate, in the public interest and for the protection of investors in such a manner as will promote the purposes of NEPA.

III. General

Under amendments to the description of business and the litigation items, the types of environmental provisions dealt with are those "regulating the discharge of materials into the environment, or otherwise relating to the protection of the environment" The Commission recognizes that this description, particularly the last clause thereof, is broad. Also, with respect to certain types of provisions, the description may not give a precise answer as to whether or not a given provision lies within the description quoted. To provide assistance to issuers, the staff will be available to respond to written inquiries.

The text of the amendments follows:

FORM S-1

I. Item 9(a) of Form S-1 is amended by adding thereto a new Instruction 5 reading as follows:

5. Appropriate disclosure shall also be made as to the material effects that compliance with Federal, State and local provisions which have been enacted or adopted regulating the discharge of materials into the environment, or otherwise relating to the protection of the environment, may have upon the capital expenditures, earnings and competitive position of the registrant and its subsidiaries.

II. Item 12 of Form S-1 is amended to read as follows:

Item 12. Legal Proceedings

Briefly describe any material pending legal proceedings, other than ordinary routine litigation incidental to the business, to which the registrant or any of its subsidiaries is a party or of which any of their property is the subject. Include the name of the court or agency in which the proceedings are pending, the date instituted, and the principal parties thereto, a description of the factual basis alleged to underlie the proceeding and the relief sought. Include similar information as to any such proceedings known to be contemplated by governmental authorities.

Instructions. 1. (No change)

2.   No information need be given with respect to any proceeding which involves primarily a claim for damages if the amount involved, exclusive of interest and costs, does not exceed ten per cent of the current assets of the registrant and its subsidiaries on a consolidated basis. However, if any proceeding presents in large degree the same issues as other proceedings pending or known to be contemplated, the amount involved in such other proceedings shall be included in computing such percentage.

3.   (No change)

4.   Notwithstanding the foregoing, administrative or judicial proceedings arising under any Federal, State or local provisions regulating the discharge of materials into the environment or otherwise relating to the protection of the environment shall not be deemed "ordinary routine litigation incidental to the business" and shall be described if such proceeding is material to the business or financial condition of the registrant or if it involves primarily a claim for damages and the amount involved, exclusive of interest and costs, exceeds ten per cent of the current assets of the registrant and its subsidiaries on a consolidated basis. Any such proceedings by governmental authorities shall be deemed material and shall be described whether or not the amount of any claim for damages involved exceeds ten per cent of current assets on a consolidated basis and whether or not such proceedings are considered "ordinary routine litigation incidental to the business;" provided however, that such proceedings which are similar in nature may be grouped and described generically stating: the number of such proceedings in each group; a generic description of such proceedings; the issues generally involved; and, if such proceedings in the aggregate are material to the business or financial condition of the registrant, the effect of such proceedings on the business or financial condition of the registrant.

FORM S-7

III.   Item 5(a) of Form S-7 is amended to read as follows:

(a)   Identify the business done and intended to be done by the registrant and its subsidiaries. In the case of an extractive enterprise, give appropriate information as to development, reserves and production. Appropriate disclosure shall be made with respect to (i) any portion of the business which may be subject to renegotiation of profits or termination of contracts or subcontracts at the election of the Government, and (ii) the material effects that compliance with Federal, State and local provisions which have been enacted or adopted regulating the discharge of materials into the environment, or otherwise relating to the protection of the environment, may have upon the capital expenditures, earnings and competitive position of the registrant and its subsidiaries.

IV.   Item 5(e) of Form S-7 is amended to read as follows:

(e)   Briefly describe any pending legal proceedings to which the registrant or any of its subsidiaries is a party which may have a substantial effect upon the earnings or financial condition of the registrant, and any administrative or judicial proceedings (i) now pending or (ii) known to be contemplated by governmental authorities arising under any Federal, State or local provisions referred to in (a) (ii) above, including the name of the court or agency, the factual basis alleged to underlie the proceeding and the relief sought.

FORM S-9

V.   Item 3 of Form S-9 is amended by adding thereto the following new paragraph (c):

(c)   Appropriate disclosure shall be made as to the material effects that compliance with Federal, State and local provisions regulating the discharge of materials into the environment, or otherwise relating to the protection of the environment, may have upon the capital expenditures, earnings and competitive position of the registrant and its subsidiaries.

FORM 10

[Note: Form 10 amendments are similar to requirements for Form S1]

FORM 10-K

VIII. Item 1(b) of Form 10-K is amended by adding thereto a new paragraph reading as follows:

(7)   The material effects that compliance with Federal, State and local provisions which have been enacted or adopted regulating the discharge of materials into the environment, or otherwise relating to the protection of the environment, may have upon the capital expenditures, earnings and competitive position of the registrant and its subsidiaries.

IX.   Item 5 of Form 10-K is amended as follows:

Item 5.   Legal Proceedings

Briefly describe any material pending legal proceedings, other than ordinary routine litigation incidental to the business, to which the registrant or any of its subsidiaries is a party or of which any of their property is the subject. Include the name of the court or agency in which the proceedings are pending, the date instituted, the principal parties thereto, a description to the factual basis alleged to underlie the proceeding and the relief sought. Include similar information as any such proceedings known to be contemplated by governmental authorities.

Instructions. 1. (No change)

2. No information need be given with respect to any proceeding which involves primarily a claim for damages if the amount involved, exclusive of interest. and costs, does not exceed ten per cent of the current assets of the registrant and its subsidiaries on a consolidated basis. However, if any proceeding presents in large degree the same issues as other proceedings pending or known to be contemplated, the amount involved in such other proceedings shall be included in computing such percentage.

3. (No change)

4. Notwithstanding the foregoing, administrative or judicial proceedings arising under any Federal, State or local provisions which have been enacted or adopted regulating the discharge of materials into the environment or otherwise relating to the protection of the environment, shall not be deemed "ordinary routine litigation incidental to the business" and shall be described if such proceeding is material to the business or financial condition of the registrant or if it involves primarily a claim for damages and the amount involved, exclusive of interest and costs, exceeds ten per cent of the current assets of the registrant and its subsidiaries on a consolidated basis. Any such proceedings by governmental authorities shall be deemed material and shall be described whether or not the amount of any claim for damages involved exceeds ten per cent of current assets on a consolidated basis and whether or not such proceedings are considered "ordinary routine litigation incidental to the business"; provided however, that such proceedings which are similar in nature may be grouped and described generically stating: the number of such proceedings in each group; a generic description of such proceedings; the issues generally involved; and, if such proceedings in the aggregate are material to the business or financial condition of the registrant, the effect of such proceedings on the business or financial condition of the registrant.

FORM 8-K

[Note: Form 8-K amendments are similar to 10-K requirements]

The foregoing amendments are adopted pursuant to Sections 6, 7, 8, 10 and 19(a) of the Securities Act of 1933 and Sections 12, 13, 15(d) and 23(a) of the Securities Exchange Act of 1934. The amendments shall be effective with respect to reports and registration statements filed on or after July 3, 1973.

By the Commission.

Ronald F. Hunt
Secretary.

A Comprehensive Corporate Social Reporting Model

Ralph W. Estes

Estes' paper represents one of the most ambitious attempts so far, to develop a corporate social reporting model. The model is distinguished by a considerably more fastidious effort to classify relevant social costs and benefits than has typically been the case in other attempts.

One of the most interesting contributions of this paper is the distinction Estes draws between social costs which should be attributed to producers and those which are appropriately allocated to users. Thus, he suggests that it is the motorist who is responsible for most automobile pollution, not the manufacturer. The importance of this distinction should not be underestimated; it could result in a totally different appraisal of the social performance of many producer companies. On the other hand, one must consider if Estes' analysis exonerates the producer from a burden he should bear; the responsibility for the manufacture of a product which could be less detrimental to society when it is used.

Efficient (in a Pareto optimal sense) and equitable (in a social welfare sense) allocation of a society's resources requires information. The information set should systematically reflect the worth of all resources consumed, including those resources or values which are free to the consuming entity (non-internalized costs, or external diseconomies); and the worth of all benefits produced by each entity, including those which provide no compensation to the producing entity (external economies).

Information presently available—in annual reports, press releases, advertising, and federal reports required by the Securities and Exchange Commission, Environmental Protection Agency, Occupational Safety and Health Act, and Equal Employment Opportunities Commission—is neither complete nor integrated. It is also in many instances one-sided and self-serving.

Several reporting models have recently been proposed which, although lacking comprehensiveness, would include additional environmental and social information. These are briefly evaluated, and a comprehensive social reporting model is then proposed which seeks to overcome the major deficiencies of these earlier models by including *all* costs and benefits.

But first, the meaning of a few troublesome terms must be clarified.

Ralph W. Estes is Professor of Accounting at Wichita State University, Wichita, Kansas.

SOURCE: Prepared for presentation in the Quantitative Systems for Social Performance Evaluation session of the TIMS XX International Meeting, Tel Aviv, Israel, June 24-29, 1973.

DEFINITIONS

Social resource. Anything—tangible or intangible—with a net positive value to society. Thus clean air is a resource, as are minerals, land, buildings, highways, clean waterways, and equipment. Even though it lacks intrinsic value, money is treated as a resource when considering transfers between a reporting entity and the rest of society. The value of any resource depends on the existence of some social welfare function; no particular function is specified or assumed in this paper, but it is recognized that measurement of any benefit or cost reflects such a function.

Value. Quantified worth or utility.

Social benefit. Any benefit to society (or to specific elements of society), whether economic or noneconomic, internal or external. Thus social benefits include those benefits provided by an entity for which it is compensated as well as those external economies for which no compensation (or inadequate compensation) is received.

Social cost. Any cost, sacrifice, or detriment to society, whether economic or noneconomic, internal or external. For example, the use of land by an entity results in a cost to society in that society sacrifices the next best alternative use of that land, even though rent may be paid by the using entity; the rent in turn represents a social benefit. Most economists net the cost and the benefit in such a case, resulting in no net benefit or cost. In the model proposed in this paper, netting is avoided; all factors are reported gross.

Of course consumption or damage by an entity for which no compensation is rendered (external diseconomies) are also social costs. Traditionally the term "social cost" has been used in this restrictive sense to refer only to external diseconomies—costs to society with no associated pecuniary cost to the offending or consuming entity, and thus not internalized by it. The reader should be careful to note the broader, more inclusive meaning assigned in this paper.

REVIEW OF SOCIAL REPORTING MODELS

Corcoran and Leininger, Linowes, and Abt have proposed relatively formal models. Other, less formal proposals for extension of corporate social reporting, such as those of Beams and Fertig,[1] Marlin,[2] Clausen,[3] and the American Accounting Association's Committee on Environmental Effects of Organization Behavior[4] will not be discussed here.

Corcoran and Leininger's Environmental Exchange Report[5]

The Corcoran and Leininger proposal (Exhibit I) reflects inputs and outputs of human and physical resources. Several metrics are used, such as number of indi-

Exhibit I.
XYZ Company: Environmental Exchange Report
for Year Ended December 31, 1970

INPUT

Human Resources:

Time—During the year, 100 individuals were hired, bringing total employment to 1,000. Employees made available 2,000,000 man-hours to the firm, and there were no layoffs during the year. 75,000 man-hours were lost because of sickness or other personal reasons, and employees earned 100,000 man-hours of paid vacation.

Time With Firm	Percentage of Employees	Education* Level	Percentage of Employees	Age of Employees	Percentage of Employees
under 1 yr.	10%	under 12 yrs.	20%	18 to 25	20%
1–3 yrs.	15%	12 yrs.	40%	26 to 30	23%
3–5 yrs.	42%	13–14 yrs.	10%	31 to 40	27%
5–10 yrs.	30%	college degree	30%	41 to 50	19%
over 10 yrs.	3%			51 to 65	11%

*The firm invested $50,000 in assisting employees further their education.

Physical Resources:

Direct Materials—
(A)   500 tons of cast iron (35% of which is recycled scrap metal)
(B)   100 tons of steel (30% of which is recycled scrap metal)
         The firm pursues a policy of purchasing from manufacturers who not only produce quality products but are also leaders in the area of pollution control.
(C)   200,000 board feet of lumber
         The supplier of the lumber estimates that it took 35 years to grow the lumber. This lumber is used in the end product and for packaging and is not recoverable.

Indirect Materials—
(A)   500 tons of oil and related products
(B)   5,000,000 gallons of water
(C)   60 tons of paper and related products (20% of which is recycled scrap)

OUTPUT

Human Resources:
10 employees were dismissed, 25 terminated voluntarily, and 13 retired with annual pensions ranging from $3,500 to $10,400 with a mean of $5,200.

Exhibit I. (Continued)

Annual Earnings	Mean	Average Increase	Percentage of Employees	Percentage Holding Other Employment	Mean Unemployed Dependents	Mean Years With Firm
under $5,000	$ 4,750	$500	15	75	2.1	2
$4,000-7,499	$ 7,200	$600	20	42	4.1	5
$7,500-9,999	$ 8,900	$600	40	20	4.3	8
$10,000-14,999	$11,700	$720	20	5	4.8	11
over $15,000	$18,000	$840	5	0	3.8	15

Source: W. Wayne Corcoran and Wayne E. Leininger, Jr., "Financial Statements—Who Needs Them?" Financial Executive, 46–47 (August, 1970).

Physical Resources:

End Product—500,000 widgets with two-year guarantees, and estimated life of five years. It is thought that the bounty offered for recovery of widgets will result in the return of 75% of the widgets and that 80% of raw materials contained in the recovered widgets will widgets will be reprocessed for future use. 100,000 board feet of lumber are not recoverable.

Water—5,000,000 gallons were removed from the Blue River, and 4,000,000 gallons were returned. The installation of several cooling ponds eliminated appreciable thermal pollution to the river. The Massachusetts Department of Natural Resources has certified that the water returned to the river was in all aspects purer than the water removed. The remaining 1,000,000 gallons were dissipated into the atmosphere in the form of steam.

Air—5 tons of solid material in the form of dust were unavoidably emitted into the atmosphere. During the month of June, the firm was fined $3,000 for excessive emissions into the air caused by the breakdown of our air pollution control system. Management decided against suspending production during the breakdown period.

Waste—Packaging of product resulted in 50 tons of paper and plastic waste, and 100,000 board feet of lumber that are not recoverable. 15 tons of solid waste resulted from the production process and are not recoverable in any form.

Financial:

Taxes Paid	By Firm	By Employees
Federal	$1,000,000	$1,200,000
State	500,000	200,000
Local	450,000	800,000

Contributions		
Colleges and Universities	40,000	20,000
United Fund	10,000	20,000
Massachusetts Social Action Board	10,000	unknown

viduals hired during the period; man-hours used; tons of cast iron and steel used; units of product produced; number of gallons and condition of water returned to a waterway; air pollution emissions and fines; and solid waste generated. The omission of dollar cost information makes evaluation difficult. Further, the report includes practically no information on economic performance, and thus does not present a comprehensive picture of the entity's performance and effect on society. The model is relatively simple, however, and involves measurements already available or obtainable with moderate difficulty.

Linowes' Socio-Economic Operating Statement[6]

The Linowes model (Exhibit II) contains three sections: relations with people, relations with environment, and relations with product. Improvements, detriments, and a net figure are reported within each section, and a net total (improvements or deficit) is also reported for the entity for the period. This net total is then added to "net cumulative socio-economic improvements" as of the beginning of the period to produce "grand total net socio-economic actions to December 31, 19xx." Improvements are defined as expenditures made voluntarily (not required by law or union contract) for such matters as product safety, employee welfare, and environmental protection. Detriments are measured by the cost of actions *not* taken when a need is brought to the entity's attention by a responsible authority.

All the models discussed in this paper involve subjective judgments to some degree, but the definition of detriments in the Linowes model appears to permit an unreasonable degree of subjectivity. Furthermore, measuring detriments at the cost of actions not taken may grossly understate the cost to society. For example, it may cost a company $10,000 to install equipment which would eliminate $160,000 in pollution damage; if the equipment is not installed, this model would reflect a detriment of $10,000 instead of $160,000. Like the Corcoran and Leininger model, Linowes' Socio-Economic Operating Statement omits information on economic performance; it does, however, use a matching mode which reflects a net result.

Abt's Social Audit[7]

The Abt model* is the most comprehensive of the three, and includes both a "social balance sheet" and a "social income statement;" such reports were actually

---

*See following selection where Abt report is reproduced in full on page 205.

Exhibit II.
XXXX Corporation: Socio-Economic Operating Statement
for the Year Ending December 31, 1971.

I *Relations with People:*

  A. *Improvements:*

1. Training program for handicapped workers	$ 10,000	
2. Contributions to educational institution	4,000	
3. Extra turnover costs because of minority hiring program	5,000	
4. Cost of nursery school for children of employees, voluntarily set up	11,000	
Total Improvements		$ 30,000

  B. *Less: Detriments*

1. Postponed installing new safety devices on cutting machines (cost of the devices)	$ 14,000	
C. Net Improvements in People Actions for the Year		$ 16,000

II *Relations with Environment:*

  A. *Improvements:*

1. Cost of reclaiming and landscaping old dump on company property	$ 70,000	
2. Cost of installing pollution control devices on Plant A smokestacks	4,000	
3. Cost of detoxifying waste from finishing process this year	9,000	
Total Improvements		$ 83,000

  B. *Less: Detriments*

1. Cost that would have been incurred to relandscape strip mining site used this year	$ 80,000	
2. Estimated costs to have installed purification process to neutralize poisonous liquid being dumped into stream	100,000	
		$180,000
C. Net Deficit in Environment Actions for the Year		($ 97,000)

III *Relations with Product:*

  A. *Improvements:*

1. Salary of V.P. while serving on government Product Safety Commission	$ 25,000	
2. Cost of substituting lead-free paint for previously used poisonous lead paint	9,000	
Total Improvements		$ 34,000

Exhibit II (Continued on next page)

Exhibit II. (Continued)

B. *Less: Detriments*
   1. Safety device recommended by Safety Council but
      not added to product   22,000
C. Net improvements in Product Actions for the Year $ 12,000

Total Socio-Economic Deficit for the Year   ($ 69,000)

Add: Net Cumulative Socio-Economic Improvements
    as at January 1, 1971 $249,000

GRAND TOTAL NET SOCIO-ECONOMIC ACTIONS
TO DECEMBER 31, 1971 $180,000

SOURCE: David F. Linowes, "An Approach to Socio Economic Accounting," Conference Board Record, P. 60 (November, 1972)

produced and included in Abt Associates' 1971 and 1972 annual reports. The balance sheet reports assets available to society (social assets) of staff, organization, research, and the excess of taxes paid over public services consumed (curiously labeled "public services consumes, net of tax payments"); and social commitments, obligations, and equity consisting of staff committed to contracts or internal administration, organizational requirements, environmental obligations (including an obligation for pollution), and "society's equity." The social income statement reports social benefits and costs to the staff, to the community, and to the general public, with a "bottom line" figure for "net social income to staff, community and public." The 1971 social income statement also reported separately the social benefits of services provided to clients and their related costs; these items were omitted from the 1972 statement pending further research to more rigorously quantify the benefits.

As noted above, the Abt model has been used as a basis for published reports. In this respect it differs materially from the other models which have only been proposed. This model is also unique in that it includes certain financial information, such as retained earnings, land, buildings, and equipment.

The Abt model is commendably ambitious, it seeks to present stocks as well as flows, and it has been used on a real if unrepresentative company (Abt Associates is a service and consulting organization which neither manufactures nor sells a tangible product). But it suffers from several serious deficiencies: it is difficult to understand; it's treatment of primary and secondary effects is inconsistent (for example, solid waste resulting from paper used by Abt is not recognized, but water pollution resulting from the initial manufacture of such paper is); it is still incomplete with respect to certain benefits and costs; the articulation between the social balance sheet and the social income statement is unclear; and it is not designed for manufacturing or merchandising concerns.

A COMPREHENSIVE SOCIAL BENEFIT/COST MODEL

Complex economic systems rely on specialization among entities to increase output, rather than having each user produce everything he needs. Resources are allocated—or find their way—to producers who are expected to return benefits with values at least equal to but hopefully in excess of the values of the resources used. The allocation process is sometimes quite formal (federal research grants, for example), usually rather informal (the price/market system), and in some cases completely unstructured (consumption of clean air, silence, and highways).

Maximization of net social benefits (taking some unspecified social welfare function as given) requires effective allocations which depend on complete and valid information. This information should include at least identification of and preferably a valuation for each significant social benefit provided and social cost incurred by an entity, to reflect the full effect of the entity on society. Allocations at present depend heavily on information provided through the financial accounting model which excludes certain benefits (external economies) and detriments (external diseconomies). The financial accounting model, as well as the three models discussed above, generally reflects the vantage of the entity looking out, toward society; benefits (products and services) provided to society are thus indicated by the surrogate of revenues received, while costs are measured only by the entity's expenditures. Improved social reporting would result from a different vantage, that of society looking toward the entity; benefits to society would then be measured by the values or utilities actually received by society (which may differ from the amount paid to the entity); while costs would reflect the full detriments to society, and not only those for which the entity pays. The vantages are illustrated in Exhibit III, and are reflected in the Abt model discussed earlier.

Exhibit III.

Social Reporting Vantages

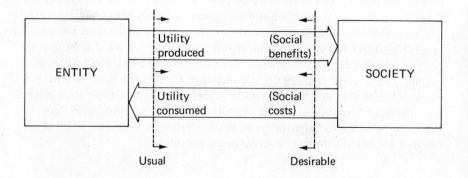

To provide the information required for rational resource allocation, a model of the following simple structure is thus proposed:

$$SS = \sum_{i=1}^{n} B_i - \sum_{j=1}^{m} C_j$$

where:

SS = social surplus or deficit

B_i = the ith social benefit

C_j = the jth social cost

A comprehensive social report for a manufacturing firm, based on this model, is presented in Exhibit IV.

Care must be taken in defining the reporting entity or system. The corporation or other organization, as legally constituted and publicly recognized, is the starting point. Included are all activities of employees carried on in behalf of the entity and while "on-duty." Activities of a board of directors and of stockholders acting collectively for the entity are included. Excluded from the system for reporting purposes are personal activities of employees including commuting, activity of customers including use of misuse of the product, and all other secondary or indirect effects.

This point should perhaps be amplified. The proposed model is a comprehensive report of the direct effects of a single entity on society. It is not designed to show what would happen (how society would be better or worse off) if the entity had not existed during the reporting period; this would require the reporting of such indirect and secondary effects as a pro-rata share of pollution caused by suppliers and detriments produced by users of the entity's products. A model including such information would certainly be useful but could not be additive and could not result in a single net result.

The present model could in fact reflect secondary effects, but only if they were internalized (i.e., built into the entity's cost and rewards structure). This would occur if (a) *each* element of society accurately measured and reported all social benefits and costs created; (b) each element was periodically assessed or rewarded an amount equal to its net social surplus or deficit; and (c) each element then adjusted the prices of its goods and services upward in response to assessments or downward for rewards. Of course these conditions do not presently obtain; consequently the proposed model would reflect significant secondary effects only in footnotes.

The report should be prepared for the entire entity i.e., it should be "consolidated." In addition, reports should be prepared when possible for each community in which a component of the entity operates, reflecting the social impact on that community alone. Local government bodies, citizens, and other concerned elements of a community need to know the effects of a corporate division on

Exhibit IV.
The Progressive Company
Corporate Social Report
For the Year Ended December 31, 1984

Social Benefits:

Products and services provided		$ xxx
Payments to other elements of society —		
Employment provided (salaries and wages)	$ xxx	
Payments for goods and other services	xxx	
Taxes paid	xxx	
Contributions	xxx	
Dividends and interest paid	xxx	
Other payments	xxx	xxx
Services to employees		xxx
Improvements in environment		xxx
Staff services donated to others		xxx
Equipment and facility services donated		xxx
Other benefits		xxx
Total Social Benefits		$ xxx

Social Costs:

Human services used		$ xxx
Raw material purchases		xxx
Building and equipment purchases		xxx
Other goods and materials used		xxx
Payments from other elements of society —		
Payments to company for goods and services	$ xxx	
Additional capital investments	xxx	
Loans	xxx	
Other payments	xxx	xxx
Environmental damage —		
Terrain damage	$ xxx	
Air pollution	xxx	
Water pollution	xxx	
Noise pollution	xxx	
Solid waste	xxx	
Visual pollution	xxx	
Other environmental damage	xxx	xxx
Public services used		xxx
Public facilities used		xxx
Work-related injuries and illness		xxx
Other social costs		xxx
Total Social Costs		xxx
Social Surplus (Deficit) for the Year		$ xxx
Accumulated Surplus (Deficit) for Company, December 31, 1983		xxx
Accumulated Surplus (Deficit) for Company, December 31, 1984		$ xxx

Exhibit IV (Continued on next page)

Exhibit IV. (Continued)

Standard Footnotes:
1. Significant secondary effects associated with inputs.
2. Significant secondary effects associated with outputs.
3. Environmental protection outlays and activities.
4. Employment and promotion of minorities and women.
5. Bases for measurements and estimates.

their community; they are less interested in and have less need for information regarding the corporation's national or world impact.

As noted previously, all significant costs and benefits are reported "gross," netting is avoided. For example, the cost to society of human services used by the reporting entity and the benefit to society (i.e., the workers themselves) from compensation paid might logically be netted against each other, but in the proposed report each would be separately disclosed. This approach permits the disclosure of *total* benefits and *total* costs—useful information for evaluating the total impact of the organization on society. The report may thus appear to count the same item twice but this appearance is illusive, resulting from the presentation of both sides of each activity or transaction.

It should be emphasized that this model is highly idealistic, and not presently practical for all firms; the objective here is to suggest a standard, a goal, for social reporting. Nevertheless, much of the information is presently available in every corporation, and a serious effort should produce adequate estimates for completion of the report in many corporations.

The components of the model will now be discussed in some detail.

Social Benefits

1. Products and Services Provided

Corporations generally exist to provide products and services; these are purchased by customers, providing prima facie evidence of benefit to society. The starting point for valuing such benefits is the exchange prices usually arrived at in response to demand and supply factors. In other words, an automobile which sells for $4000 presumably is expected to provide benefits to the purchaser, one element of society, with a present value of at least $4000. Included in this category of benefits are interest and dividends received by the reporting entity for providing capital for use by other entities, and rent received for providing facilities, equipment, space, etc., to other elements of society.

Upward adjustments will be required when exchange prices do not adequately measure benefits. Consumer surplus should be estimated and added to the exchange price. Care must be exercised, however, to value only primary effects from the products and services provided. Suppose the automobile referred to above provides utility to the purchaser with an estimated present value of $4200 and he in turn uses the auto to provide free transportation to and from work for several neighbors, resulting in additional benefits to the neighbors (but not to the owner) estimated at $500. The amount to be reported by the selling corporation is $4200, not $4000 or $4700 (the automobile owner could report social benefits provided of $500). Significant secondary and tertiary effects should be reported in footnotes, but not integrated into the model since they are not actually provided by the reporting entity.

Downward adjustments will be required when the exchange price exceeds the utility provided. This can occur when purchasers have inadequate information, when products are dangerous or unsafe, when benefits are exaggerated through improper advertising and promotion, or when artificial barriers to free price movements exist (such as monopoly power, price fixing, and the use of threats and extortion).

It is tempting to argue that downward adjustments should be made for products which pollute or in other ways are detrimental to society. The responsibility for such detriments rests primarily on the *user,* not the producer, and double-counting would result if both the user and the producer were charged for such detriments. Air pollution caused by automobiles is a good example of this problem. Producers can be induced (or required) to develop low pollution-generating automobiles, but users sometimes disconnect the control devices—or they simply fail to maintain them in proper condition and adjustment. If automobile users were assessed for pollution generated (perhaps using sealed odometers and annual inspections in conjunction with license renewal), users would then have incentives to (1) purchase automobiles with efficient pollution control devices, (2) maintain such devices in good working order, and (3) drive fewer miles thus generating less pollution.[9]

2. Payments to Other Elements of Society

We usually think of raw material consumption as a cost or detriment to society, and indeed it is—but when such materials are paid for by the user benefits are provided commensurate with the amount of payment received. Thus corporations render benefits to various elements of society as they pay for goods and services used.

The value of employment provided should be separately disclosed; that is, payments to employees represent a social benefit in the amount of money transmitted to such employees and available for their use. Discrimination in employment should be dealt with here. Assuming a norm of zero discrimination, any discrimination practiced should be valued (perhaps at the amount of lost income to minorities and women) and deducted from the gross benefit provided through employment; conversely, extra efforts going beyond simple fair employment to compensate for past discrimination and discrimination practiced in other areas of society could be assigned a positive value in addition to the benefit provided through normal employment.

Other significant payments included in this section might include taxes, contributions, dividends, interest, fines and assessments. It should be noted that the benefit provided by the corporation disbursing money is the money disbursed itself; what the recipient entity does with that money should be credited to that separate entity. This is especially important for charitable contributions. Here again, significant secondary and tertiary effects might be reported in a footnote but should not be integrated into the model.

3. Services to Employees

The value of most fringe benefits should be reported in this category. So should the value of experience provided, training programs, special opportunities provided, and rewarding work which provides utility to the employee over and above the monetary renumeration.

This category involves unusual measurement problems. What is the value to participants of a company-sponsored bowling league? a company cafeteria? executive washrooms? The proper valuation is the utility provided to employees, *not* the cost to the company (which is reflected separately as an outlay). Employee surveys, shadow pricing, and a variety of surrogates should be helpful in reaching estimates of these values.

4. Improvements in Environment

When corporations restore previously strip-mined areas, plant trees, landscape eroded terrain, and clean polluted lakes, benefits may accrue to society. Valuation is difficult for these benefits, and is probably *not* accurately reflected by the amount of outlay (which is a separate benefit provided, as noted above). Community surveys, shadow pricing, and economic studies might be used to develop suitable estimates.

As noted below in the section on social costs, the corporation will be charged for current damage done; hence it should receive credit for benefits provided through restoration of a previously damaged environment.

5. Staff Services Donated to Others

As corporations loan employees to charitable, social, and other community organizations benefits are provided separate from the compensation paid to the employees. These benefits might be measured at the cost which would have been incurred by the outside organization if it had hired persons with the qualifications required. Such required qualifications may be less than the qualifications actually possessed by employees on loan, in which case the value of the benefits provided to the outside organization will be less than the compensation actually paid by the reporting entity.

6. Equipment Facility Services Donated

Corporations sometimes allow community groups to use otherwise idle equipment and facilities. Benefits may thus be provided even though there is no incremental cost to the corporation. The value of these benefits may be estimated at the amount of rent the user organizations would have paid if they had rented other facilities. This may be different from, and probably less than, the amount of rent the corporation could obtain for the facilities if rented to a profit-making organization.

7. Other Benefits

Corporations may provide benefits to society not falling within the above classes. These would include such programs as free daycare centers, special assistance to minority enterprises (other than donated staff services), and sponsorship of public interest television programs at a cost exceeding the advertising value.

Social Costs

1. Human Services Used

The cost to society of human services used by an entity is the value which could be generated in alternative use of such services. This raises extremely difficult measurement questions: what would be the most valuable alternative service? what would be its value? would the employee be working at all if not employed by the reporting entity? Furthermore, the answers to these questions will vary with the level of unemployment, technological developments, and cultural changes such as reverence for the work ethic. When these measurements involve excessive subjectivity, however, it seems reasonable to simply value employee services at the amount paid for them (the amount shown in the benefits section). Instead of appearing as a social cost, the effect of discrimination is treated as a reduction of the benefits provided by employment.

2. Raw Material Purchases

Raw materials acquired by an entity represent a sacrifice to society to the extent of their value in alternative use. Some raw materials are fixed in supply and cannot be replaced or regenerated for eons (fossil fuels, for example); others can be replaced over several years or perhaps a generation (hardwood trees); while still other resources can be regenerated in as little as a year (such as food crops). Feasibility of replacement is a major consideration in valuation of such materials.

So is the substitutability of other resources. For example, solar energy may eventually become readily and cheaply available, and might thus devalue fossil fuels.

These factors only suggest the difficulty of measuring the sacrifice or cost to society from the consumption of raw materials. An operational approach might be to value materials with short replacement cycles at their exchange prices, while adjusting the value of those with longer cycles to reflect world supply and long-term prospects for development of substitutes.

3. Building and Equipment Purchases

When the reporting entity acquires a building or piece of equipment, the utility from that item is lost to the rest of society for the item's entire useful life. This cost to society should be reflected in the exchange price, although market imperfections may result in some divergence which must be estimated.

Note that in this approach there is no cost to society as the capital assets are used by their owner. The full cost occurs at the moment of transfer from the rest of society to the reporting entity, and is measured by the discounted present value of the future stream of benefits which other elements in society would have received and which were sacrificed in the exchange.

4. Other Goods and Materials Used

This category includes not only other purchased materials, such as office and manufacturing supplies, components, and parts, but also utility contained in goods and materials the corporation may consume which are not purchased. These might include donated goods, certain "public" goods (such as those taken from the oceans), stolen goods, and those accidentally or even purposely destroyed for which payment is not made.

5. Payments from other Elements of Society

Customers, lenders, investors, and others may make payments to the reporting entity; in so doing they are sacrificing the utility which such purchasing power could command. This sacrifice is a cost to society vis-a-vis the reporting entity. Payments from customers might be netted against the value of the products and services provided, but the proposed unnetted or gross disclosure is more informative—especially when market imperfections result in the value of products or services being significantly different from the amount paid.

6. Environmental Damage

The entity imposes damage on the environment most noticeably through the production and waste disposal processes, but damage is also done by delivery trucks, salesmen's automobiles, construction, and some advertising. The damage comes in several forms: air and water pollution, noise, plant life destruction, terrain damage (and drainage modification), trash and litter, and even "visual pollution." (Solid waste damages the environment when it is disposed of in open dumps; when solid waste is recycled, incinerated, used in landfills, or otherwise processed by governmental agencies, the social cost would be recognized under the "public services used" and "public facilities used" categories below.)

In measuring environmental damage, the objective is to estimate the utility lost to society through the entity's activities (or omissions). For water pollution estimates may be sought for lost recreational utility, value of fish and plant life destroyed, increased treatment costs down stream, and impairment of living conditions proximate to the waterway. Air pollution may require estimates of lost utility due to pollution-related illness (medical cost, lost productivity, shortened life span, pain), damage to exterior finishes, impairment of living conditions, and plant life damaged or destroyed. The social cost of noise might be based on an estimate of the current discomfort resulting from the noise. Terrain damage might be estimated at the lesser of lost utility (including some value for landscape attractiveness) and cost of restoration to an original, unimpaired condition.

Several efforts have been made to place a value on environmental damage. These were reviewed in an earlier paper,[10] and include estimates of the cost of smoke damage in Pittsburgh in 1913 (extended to the entire United States in 1959), shadow pricing of outdoor recreational facilities, estimates of the cost of "noise pollution" near an airport, and water pollution in the Genossenschaften system of Germany's Ruhr area.

7. Public Services Used

This category includes the reporting entity's share of police and fire protection, the legislative and judicial systems, and government activities at all levels. Many of these services are so pervasive as to make estimation of one entity's share impractical. The amount of taxes paid might be used as a starting point, but this amount should be adjusted for unusual costs caused by unsafe plants, inadequately secured assets, exceptionally high value merchandise, etc. In addition industry studies might be undertaken to produce guidelines or adjustment factors for firms within the industry.

8. Public Facilities Used

Separate disclosure of the cost of public facilities used might be useful. This category would include damage done to streets and highways, bridges, parks, public buildings, and the life.

Estimation of the relevant cost of public services and facilities used presents perhaps the greatest measurement problems to be encountered in this model,

Imagination and research will produce a variety of techniques, some clever and some unrealistic. Reporting entities may have little feasible choice but to use taxes paid as a surrogate for these two costs, at least until better and more realistic measures are developed.

9. Work Related Injuries and Illness

Any injuries and illnesses which would not have occurred if the entity had not existed should be charged to it and reported as a social cost. This cost can of course be reduced by installation of safety devices, elimination and unhealthy conditions, and similar efforts.

The cost of an injury or illness might be estimated at the value of lost services, probably using the employee's salary or wage rate, plus an amount representing pain and discomfort, frustration, and delayed experience. While some will balk at such a crass approach, especially when death is involved, failure to make a serious attempt at cost estimation may result in personal and emotional impressions which play down or magnify the loss. Absence of a cost estimate may in fact lead some to implicitly assume a cost of zero.

10. Other Social Costs

This catchall category is of course intended to include any costs omitted above, and especially to provide flexibility to allow use of the model in many industries and under varying circumstances. One particularly important but unusual social cost, which belongs in this category but unfortunately will never be reported unless the report is prepared or at least audited by an external and independent entity, is the damage caused by political bribes, price-fixing, sabotage of competitors, and other law violations.

Standard Footnotes

Several standard footnotes are proposed to report significant secondary or indirect effects and additional information relevant in judging an entity's effect on society, but not additive in the model.

1. Significant Secondary Effects Associated with Inputs

Any social costs of goods and services used which are not reflected in exchange prices should be disclosed in this footnote. Examples are water pollution caused by paper manufacturers in the production of office supplies used by the reporting entity, and air pollution caused by employees driving to work. As noted earlier, if complete social costs and benefits were internalized and integrated into the pricing structure of every entity, prices would reflect all social costs and this note would not be necessary.

2. Significant Secondary Effects Associated with Outputs

Pollution, injuries, solid waste, and other social costs resulting from the use of the reporting entity's products should be estimated and reported here. For example, the air pollution caused by automobiles should be noted here in the report of an automobile manufacturer; since the pollution is not caused by the manufacturer directly it is not included in the "cost" section of the report. Additional benefits should also be reported. For example, this footnote is the proper place for disclosure by a producer of air pollution control equipment of the additional benefits to society derived from use of his products by customers; the direct benefit to the customers is of course included in the "benefits" section of the report and is not included in this footnote.

3. Environmental Protection Outlays and Activities

This footnote should disclose the activities the entity is engaged in to reduce the pollution costs reflected in the body of the report. For example, placement of an order for pollution abatement equipment or pollution-reducing changes in the production process might be disclosed.

4. Employment and Promotion of Minorities and Women

This footnote should contain actual statistics and not platitudes. Comparative data for two years should be disclosed as a minimum (but not merely rates of change, such as "this year we employed seventy-five per cent more women than last year").

5. Bases for Measurements and Estimates

While standardized measurement techniques are available or can be developed for many of the items in the body of the report, several items will always require ad hoc techniques developed by the reporting entity. These should be described to permit the reader to judge the reliability of the reported data.

MEASUREMENT CONSIDERATIONS

While numerous measurement problems have been mentioned, much of the information needed for the proposed model is readily available in present corporate financial systems. Additional information can be systematically gathered with relatively minor system modifications. Some of the information needed, however, will require extensive system changes or expensive ad hoc studies. This disadvantage is partially offset by the likelihood that replications of studies are often much less expensive, and some studies can be done for an entire industry (possibly on a pooled cost basis or through an industry organization).

Discounted present values should be used whenever the reporting entity's activities generate any benefits or costs which will be realized in future periods.

Employee and citizen surveys were suggested as a way of estimating certain benefits and costs. Numerous problems are associated with such surveys, and these are well covered in the appropriate literature. One is especially relevant here, however: personal attitudes are fluid—they change, sometimes abruptly. This requires special alertness on the part of those producing social reports; studies recently completed may have to be replicated.

Finally, reference must be made to the problem of comparing interpersonal utilities. This very complex question has also received extensive attention in the literature, with many concluding that interpersonal utilities cannot be compared. In this paper it has been assumed that general measures of utility can be obtained.

SUMMARY

A social reporting model is proposed which matches benefits and costs generated by an entity, resulting in a net social surplus or deficit. The proposed model differs from the present financial reporting model and various proposed extensions primarily in its comprehensiveness; all significant benefits and costs would be reported including those not presently internalized, such as consumer surplus and air pollution. The model also differs in its vantage point; society's vantage is taken, rather than the firm's. Thus reported benefits and costs reflect benefits and detriments to society, not to the firm.

The objective of the proposed model is to report fully the direct effects of the reporting entity on other elements of society and on society collectively. Complete information should result in better evaluation of organizations by investors, policy makers, consumers, and citizens generally, and should thus contribute to more efficient resource allocation. Eventually the model might be used as a basis for a system of assessments and rewards to entities for their reported social surpluses or deficits, thereby internalizing present externalities.

While much of the information to be reported is already available or easily obtained, several items are not presently capable of reliable measurement. Fortunately research and experimentation on possible measurement approaches is currently being pursued by a variety of groups, but complete implementation of the proposed model must await further progress on this front.

While it must thus be viewed as largely conceptual at the present time, the proposed model should still serve as a useful framework for internal reporting in organizations concerned with social responsibility issues and interested in determining their full impact on society.

NOTES

1.   Beams, Floyd A., and Paul E. Fertig, "Pollution Control Through Social Cost Conversion," *The Journal of Accountancy,* (November, 1971), 37-42. Also see Floyd A. Beams, "Accounting for Environmental Pollution," *The New York CPA,* 657-661, August, 1970.

2.   Marlin, John Tepper, "Accounting for Pollution," *The Journal of Accountancy,* 41-46, February, 1973.

3.   Calusen, A. W., "Toward an Arithmetic of Quality," *The Conference Board Record,* 9-13, May, 1971.

4.   Committee on Environmental Effects of Organization Behavior, "Report of the Committee on Environmental Effects of Organization Behavior," *The Accounting Review,* 72-119, Supplement to Vol. XLVIII, 1973.

5.   Corcoran, A. Wayne, and Wayne E. Leininger, Jr., "Financial Statements—Who Needs Them?" *Financial Executive,* 34-38, 45-47, August, 1970.

6.   Linowes, David F., "An Approach to Socio-Economic Accounting," *Conference Board Record,* 58-61, November, 1972.

7.   *1972 Abt Associates Inc. Annual Report + Social Audit.* Cambridge: Abt Associates Inc.

8.   Materials related to Footnote 8 are not included here.

9.   Solid waste is a more difficult question than air or noise pollution. Cost of disposal processing, or recycling is primarily a function of design, and the purchaser has limited choice in this regard. He can of course seek to buy beer in returnable bottles, cereal in biodegradable packaging, and automobiles with longer expected lives, but his choices are generally quite limited in such respects, and in some cases nonexistent. Disposal costs should probably still be charged to users for *reporting* purposes, but society may then elect to assess or tax producers. A distinction must be made between proper reporting in terms of direct responsibility (the objection of the proposed model) and equitable or workable solutions to problems (which must reflect social welfare and political considerations).

10.   Estes, Ralph W., "Socio-Economic Accounting and External Diseconomies," *The Accounting Review,* 284-290, April, 1972.

The Social Audit Concept Applied: Abt Associates Annual Report

The Abt Associates 1972 annual report represents one of the few actual attempts to implement the social audit concept to a going corporation. The Estes' paper preceding this selection contains a discussion of the model and its implications.

It is of interest to note that there may be some degree of enlightened self interest involved in this project. Abt's heavily illustrated annual report indicates that its services include: education, human development, social experimentation and research, employment and management systems, training and personnel systems, health systems, technology management, and a number of other services closely related to the idea of the measurement of social performance. The unique annual report received considerable publicity in major business publications; the result was certainly not adverse to the company's business. Equally interesting, Abt is a privately held company, under no obligation to publish and publicly disseminate a formal annual report.

That there may have been some direct gain to the company from this supposed experimentation should not influence an evaluation of the methodology. To the contrary, it suggests that comprehensive social reporting may not become a reality until it is profitable for companies to do so.

SOURCE: Annual Report and Social Audit, Abt Associates, Inc., 1972.

Abt Associates Inc.
balance sheet
December 31, 1972 with comparative figures for 1971

Assets	1972	·1971
Current assets		
Cash	$ 364,535	$ 99,046
Accounts receivable, less allowance for doubtful		
accounts $26,000 ($20,000 in 1971)	1,284,945	984,025
Unbilled contract costs and fees	1,538,536	651,815
Other current assets	45,534	44,057
Total current assets	3,233,550	1,778,943
Property and equipment, at cost (note 1):		
Land	307,429	128,358
Buildings	1,736,825	270,622
Improvements	151,907	94,168
Equipment, furniture and fixtures	136,638	43,042
	2,332,799	536,190
Less accumulated depreciation	111,343	59,700
	2,221,456	476,490
Office building under construction and related land	–	1,300,539
Net property and equipment	2,221,456	1,777,029
Other assets (note 6)	88,832	8,630
	$5,543,838	$3,564,602

Liabilities and Shareholders' Equity	1972	·1971
Current liabilities:		
Notes payable (note 2)	$1,111,475	$ 154,700
Accounts payable	538,644	99,884
Accrued expenses		
Payroll and accrued vacation pay	324,508	150,234
Other	270,970	161,956
Total accrued expenses	595,478	312,190
Federal income taxes	78,000	167,000
Total current liabilities	2,323,597	733,774
Deferred Federal income taxes	35,000	19,000
Long-term liabilities:		
Notes payable (note 2)	756,564	519,483
Leasehold interest in property (note 1)	127,226	126,146
Construction loan	–	162,806
Total long-term liabilities	883,790	808,435
Shareholders' equity (notes 3 and 4):		
Common stock, $1.00 par value per share. Authorized		
1,000,000 shares, issued 195,384 Series A and 99,700		
Series B shares	295,084	295,084
Additional paid-in capital	1,490,684	1,490,684
Retained earnings	515,683	217,625
Total shareholders' equity	2,301,451	2,003,393
Commitments and contingencies (notes 5 and 6)		
	$5,543,838	$3,564,602

·1971 figures reclassified to conform to 1972 presentation.
See accompanying notes to financial statements.

·I   II

Abt Associates Inc.
statement of earnings and retained earnings
Year ended December 31, 1972
with comparative figures for 1971

	1972	1971
Contract revenues (note 1)	$6,994,543	$4,587,902
Direct contract costs	3,847,067	2,123,100
Indirect contract costs, general and administrative expenses	2,447,266	1,944,436
Total contract costs	6,294,333	4,067,536
Operating profit	700,210	520,366
Other deductions, net:		
Interest	106,806	24,817
Miscellaneous, net	23,346	65,110
Total other deductions, net	130,152	89,927
Earnings before Federal income taxes	570,058	430,439
Provision for Federal income taxes:		
Current	256,000	167,000
Deferred (note 1)	16,000	19,000
Total provision for Federal income taxes	272,000	186,000
Net earnings	298,058	244,439
Retained earnings (deficit) at beginning of year	217,625	(26,814)
Retained earnings at end of year	$ 515,683	$ 217,625
Earnings per share of common stock based on weighted average shares outstanding	$ 1.01	$ .83

See accompanying notes to financial statements.

III

IV

Abt Associates Inc.
statement of changes in financial position
Year ended December 31, 1972
with comparative figures for 1971

	1972	1971*
Funds provided:		
Net earnings	$ 298,058	$244,439
Add expenses not requiring outlay of working capital:		
Depreciation and amortization	57,073	20,264
Deferred Federal income taxes	16,000	19,000
Funds provided from operations	371,131	283,703
Increase in long-term debt, principally mortgage notes	403,161	496,170
Total funds provided	$ 774,292	$779,873
Funds applied:		
Additions to property and equipment	501,500	621,757
Reduction of notes payable and construction loan	327,806	–
Purchase of treasury stock	–	3,750
Change in other assets	80,202	(8,933)
Total funds applied	909,508	616,574
Increase (decrease) in working capital	$ (135,216)	$163,299
Summary of changes in working capital:		
Increase in current assets:		
Cash	265,489	58,866
Accounts receivable, net	300,920	288,041
Unbilled contract costs and fees	886,721	746
Other current assets	1,477	29,024
	1,454,607	376,677
Increase (decrease) in current liabilities:		
Notes payable	956,775	54,000
Accounts payable	438,760	(119,575)
Accrued expenses	283,288	111,953
Federal income taxes	(89,000)	167,000
	1,589,823	213,378
Increase (decrease) in working capital	$ (135,216)	$163,299

*1971 figures reclassified to conform to 1972 presentation
See accompanying notes to financial statements

V   VI

Abt Associates Inc.
notes to financial
statements
December 31, 1972

(1) Summary of accounting policies:

Contracts Substantially all of the Company's services are performed under cost-plus-fixed-fee or fixed price contracts. The Company recognizes revenue substantially in proportion to the percentage of the total contract completed. Any excess of costs, including estimated costs to complete, over total contract revenue is charged to income immediately. Contracts with the U.S. Government, which constitute a major portion of the Company's operations, are subject to audit and possible adjustment of allowable costs. Such contracts have been audited by the Government through 1971 and no material adjustments were required.

Property and equipment – depreciation policies In general, the Company depreciates property and equipment over the estimated useful lives of such assets using the straight-line method.

The estimated useful lives of property and equipment are summarized as follows:

	Estimated useful lives
Buildings	20-45 years
Improvements	5-12 years
Equipment, furniture and fixtures	3-8 years

Upon the sale or retirement of property and equipment the applicable cost and accumulated depreciation are eliminated and the gains or losses reflected in income. Maintenance and repairs are expensed as incurred.

In the Company's income tax returns accelerated methods are used to compute depreciation. Deferred taxes have been provided as applicable.

Leasehold interest in property The Company rents land under a lease which contains an option to purchase. The agreement provides for annual payments of approximately $7,500 through May 1976, and $8,000 through May 1996. The lease has been accounted for as a purchase based upon the discounted value of payments to be made through 1981 under the terms of the agreement.

(2) Notes payable

Notes payable consist of the following:

	December 31, 1972	
Description	Current	Long-term
6% and 6¼% unsecured thirty to ninety-day notes	$1,100,000	$ —
6½% and 7% mortgage notes payable in varying monthly instalments through 1988	875	20,622
9% mortgage note payable in direct reduction monthly instalments through August 1995	10,600	735,942
	$1,111,475	$756,564

(3) Common stock and additional paid-in capital

On November 9, 1972 the Company's then outstanding Class A and Class B common stock, no par value, was reclassified into one class of Common Stock, $1.00 par value per share. Within this class there are two series, Series A and Series B, with the Series A shares having a liquidation preference of $2.00 per share and the power to elect a minority of the Board of Directors, and the Series B shares having the power to elect a majority of the Board of Directors. Upon a vote of the majority of the Series B shares, the Series B shares are convertible into Series A and upon such conversion, the distinctions between the series (and the series designations themselves) are abolished. In addition, the Company retired 600 Class A and 300 Class B shares previously held in the treasury. The financial statements for 1971 and 1972 included herein reflect this recapitalization.

The additional paid-in capital represents the excess of book value over par value of the shares of common stock, par value $1.00 per share, issued in the recapitalization.

(4) Stock options

The Company has reserved 25,000 shares of Common Stock, Series A (5,000 of which were reserved during 1972) for issuance to certain key employees under its formal qualified stock option plan. Options under this plan are granted at market value at date of grant and become exercisable cumulatively in equal annual instalments over a period of five years. The qualified plan provides that options granted thereunder will expire five years after date of grant.

auditor's opinion

With respect to the qualified plan, options to purchase 19,500 shares were outstanding at December 31, 1972 of which 6,100 were granted in prior years at $20.00 per share and 13,400 were granted in 1972 at $15.00 per share, and of which 4,180 were exercisable at December 31, 1972.

In addition to the Company's formal qualified stock option plan, there were options outstanding and exercisable at December 31, 1972 to purchase 4,000 shares of common stock at $20.00 per share. Such options expire at various dates through 1977.

Also outside of the qualified plan, the Company in 1972 reserved 11,000 shares of common stock for grant of options at a price set by the Directors approximating market value to key individuals who are not eligible to participate in the qualified plan. These options are to be exercised over a period of four years commencing one year from date of issue. The Company has adopted a commitment to grant options to purchase 6,500 shares of the 11,000 shares so reserved, contingent on the completion of the public stock offering mentioned below (note 6), the option price to be 120% of the offering price of the stock. No options were exercised in 1972.

(5) Lease commitments

With respect to long-term leases, the Company leases office facilities under agreements which provide for annual rentals of approximately $30,000. Of this amount $25,000 expires in 1974 and the balance in 1975. Certain of these facilities have been sublet at an annual rental of $10,500.

(6) Public offering

The Company has filed a Registration Statement with the Securities and Exchange Commission in contemplation of a possible public offering of 100,000 shares of common stock. Certain costs incurred in connection therewith have been deferred, and will be charged against the proceeds of the issue if consummated.

PEAT MARWICK MITCHELL & CO
CERTIFIED PUBLIC ACCOUNTANTS
ONE BOSTON PLACE
BOSTON MASSACHUSETTS 02108

The Board of Directors
Abt Associates, Inc.:

We have examined the balance sheet of Abt Associates, Inc. as of December 31, 1972 and the related statements of earnings and retained earnings and changes in financial position for the year then ended. Our examination was made in accordance with generally accepted auditing standards, and accordingly included such tests of the accounting records and such other auditing procedures as we considered necessary in the circumstances.

In our opinion, such financial statements present fairly the financial position of Abt Associates, Inc. at December 31, 1972 and the results of its operations and changes in its financial position for the year then ended, in conformity with generally accepted accounting principles applied on a basis consistent with that of the preceding year.

Peat, Marwick, Mitchell + Co.

February 19, 1973

IX   X

social audit

Abt Associates pioneered its social audit in the 1971 annual report. A social balance sheet and a social income statement was prepared which tabulated the effects the Company had on "society," defined as staff, the local community clients, and the general public. For the sake of comparability, the same format is used in this report, with updated figures to show changes in condition from last year to this. Also presented is a newly-developed format which integrates measures of social performance into the financial report. This allows the estimation of **financial return on social investment**, a concept drawn from Company efforts in the last year to advance the state-of-the-art in social accounting.

The pages that follow present the 1971 and 1972 social balance sheet and income statement, notes explaining the rationale and calculations supporting those statements, the integration of social and financial statements, comments on the results of this new presentation and explanatory notes on that presentation.

These statements must be considered separately from the company's regular financial statements. Generally accepted auditing procedures have not been developed with respect to such statements, and accordingly our independent auditors are unable to express an opinion thereon.

The social balance sheet and income statement are "society's statements" and not the Company's, in that they show the net social assets and net social benefits "owned" by society as a result of the Company's activities. The main categories of social assets are: **staff assets** made available by the company to society; **organization assets**, representing the cost which society would have to incur if it reconstituted the Company in 1972; **research assets** having social value; and taxes paid net of public services consumed.

Social liabilities or commitments include staff and organization commitments to **non-socially productive contracts** and **environmental pollution**. On the social income statement, social benefits include extraordinary benefits to staff in the last period, net of social costs imposed on staff; social benefits to the community, net of social cost; and social benefits to the general public, net of social costs imposed on the public.

Because the "net social income" from the income statement is considered to be a social dividend paid out to staff, community and general public, it does not accrue to the social net worth shown on the balance sheet. Other normal accounting flows from balance sheet to income statement, such as conversion of assets and liabilities to revenue and expense, have not yet been encompassed by these social accounting methods

XII

Abt Associates Inc.
social balance sheet
Year ended December 31, 1972 with comparative figures for 1971

	1972	1971
Social Assets Available		
Staff		
Available within one year (Note G)	$ 4,166,125	$ 2,594,390
Available after one year (Note G)	12,566,700	6,368,511
Training Investment (Note H)	1,008,548	507,405
	17,741,373	9,470,306
Less Accumulated Training Obsolescence (Note H)	247,541	136,995
Total Staff Assets	17,493,832	9,333,311
Organization		
Social Capital Investment (Note I)	2,192,685	2,192,685
Retained Earnings	515,684	219,136
Land	307,430	285,376
Buildings at Cost	1,736,825	334,321
Equipment at Cost	136,638	43,018
Total Organization Assets	4,889,262	3,074,536
Research		
Proposals (Note J)	37,898	26,878
Child Care Research	6,629	6,629
Social Audit	18,130	12,979
Public Services Consumed, Net of Tax Payments (Note E)	160,514	90,452
Total Research and Tax Assets	223,171	136,938
Total Social Assets Available	22,606,265	12,544,785
Social Commitments, Obligations and Equity Staff		
Committed to Contracts within one year (Note K)	29,451	43,263
Committed to Contracts after one year (Note K)	88,836	114,660
Committed to Administration within one year (Note K)	57,538	62,598
Committed to Administration after one year (Note K)	173,558	165,903
Total Staff Commitments	349,383	386,424
Organization		
Financing Requirements (Note L)	1,463,438	415,156
Facilities & Equipment Committed to Contracts		
and Administration (Note K)	182,398	37,734
Total Organization Commitments	1,645,836	452,890
Environment		
Pollution from Paper Production (Note M)	5,345	1,770
Pollution from Electric Power Production (Note N)	41,451	10,601
Pollution from Automobile Commuting (Note O)	20,130	10,493
Total Environmental Obligations	66,926	22,864
Total Commitments & Obligations	2,062,145	862,178
Society's Equity		
Contributed by Staff (Note P)	17,144,449	8,946,887
Contributed by Stockholders (Note Q)	3,243,426	2,621,646
Generated by Operations (Note R)	156,245	114,074
Total Equity	20,544,120	11,682,607
Total Commitments, Obligations and Equity	$22,606,265	$12,544,785

XIII   XIV

Abt Associates Inc.
social income statement
Year ended December 31, 1972 with comparative figures for 1971

	1972	1971
Social Benefits and Costs to Staff:		
Social Benefits to Staff:		
Health Insurance, Life Ins., Sick Leave	$ 193,560	$ 93,492
Career Advancement (Note A)	331,872	345,886
Company School & Tuition Reimbursement	1,326	6,896
Vacation, Holidays, Recreation	304,932	207,565
Food Services, Child Care, Parking	122,305	57,722
Quality of Life (Space and its Quality)	84,268	61,002
Total Benefits to Staff	1,038,263	772,563
Social Costs to Staff:		
Layoffs and Involuntary Terminations (Note B)	14,849	9,560
Overtime Worked but Not Paid (Note C)	882,721	654,000
Inequality of Opportunity (Note D)	26,000	–
Total Costs to Staff	923,570	663,560
Net Social Income to Staff:	$ 114,693	$109,003
Social Benefits and Costs to Community:		
Social Benefits to Community:		
Local Taxes Paid (Note E)	$ 71,352	$ 38,952
Environmental Improvements	22,053	10,100
Local Tax Worth of Net Jobs Created	39,886	20,480
Total Benefits to Community	133,291	69,532
Social Costs to Community:		
Local Taxes Consumed (Note E)	66,848	55,700
Net Social Income to Community:	$ 66,443	$ 13,832
Social Benefits and Costs to General Public:		
Social Benefits to General Public:		
Federal Taxes Paid (Note E)	$ 272,000	$165,800
State Taxes Paid (Note E)	61,750	55,500
Contributions to Knowledge (Publications, etc.)	17,700	14,100
Federal & State Tax Worth of Net Jobs Created	173,674	69,800
Total Benefits to Public:	525,124	305,200
Social Costs to General Public:		
Federal Services Consumed (Note E)	128,880	83,000
State Services Consumed (Note E)	46,368	31,100
Total Costs to Public:	$ 175,248	$114,100
Net Social Income to General Public:	$ 349,876	$191,100
Net Social Income to Staff, Community & Public: (Note F)	$ 531,012	$313,935

notes to the social balance sheet and social income statement

Note A: Career advancement is expressed as the added earning power from salary increases for merit and/or promotion. In 1972, 97 employees (22% of total staff) were promoted, compared to 49 (18% of staff) in 1971. In 1972 67% of employees earned merit or promotion increases versus 79% in 1971.

Note B: The social cost of layoff is estimated to be one month's salary for each layoff, i.e., the mean time to next employment is one month.

Note C: Staff-contributed overtime worked but not paid is equal to approximately 33% over the required 40 work hours. This represents a social cost to staff in free time foregone.

Note D: Equality of opportunity is defined in terms of the costs to individuals of the inequality of opportunity for appropriately remunerative work and advancement, as measured by the income loss equal to the difference between what the minority individual earns and what a majority individual doing the same job with the same qualifications earns. The $26,000 social cost of inequality of opportunity was incurred entirely by women, as a result of a strongly discriminatory labor market that company policy was not completely able to overcome within national wage-price policy constraints. No inequality of opportunity cost was incurred by ethnic minorities. Minority advancement of blacks, Chicanos, Indians and Orientals promoted in 1972 was 14% compared to 13% in 1971, and 24% of women were promoted in 1972 compared to 25% promoted in 1971. This should be compared with 25% of white males promoted in 1972 and 10% in 1971, and a company average of 22% promotions in 1972, and 18% in 1971. The aggregate ethnic minority and female staff promoted in 1972 was 21% of total minority and women compared to 22% in 1971. The total minority and female staff was 66% of the entire staff (287 of 432) in 1972, compared to 55% (150 of 271) in 1971.

Note E: Taxes paid are considered a social contribution or benefit while public services paid for by taxes that are consumed by the company are considered social costs. When the company does not consume public services paid for in part by company paid taxes, a net social income contribution is produced. Federal and state public services consumed are calculated by multiplying the ratio of company revenues to total federal or state corporate revenues times the total of federal or state tax collections. The company's share of local services consumed is computed by multiplying the ratio of company

population to total local population times the total local taxes, on the assumption that local services used is roughly in proportion to the number of people using local services. This share is then reduced by the percentage (29%) of the local budget devoted to services not consumed by the company (local schools). The balance sheet item "public services consumed, net of tax payments" consists of the net of total (federal, state, and local) taxes paid over total services consumed; this is carried as an asset for one year's time. The counter entry is an addition to society's equity generated by operations. This represents a change in treatment from the 1971 statement; the 1971 figures are restated to reflect the change from a liability to an equity account.

Note F: In its 1971 social audit, the company showed an addition to social income calculated as "benefits to clients." This was defined as quantifiable social benefits resulting from specific projects which exceeded the contract revenues net of social costs imposed by contracts. This was calculated at $17,765,041 in 1971. This item is omitted in 1972 because research is still underway to more rigorously quantify these benefits. The measurement problem addressed by this research is a common delay between project completion and the occurrence of social benefits. Methods are being developed to estimate benefits on a time basis consistent with the company's fiscal accounting period.

Note G: That portion of company staff engaged in social research is considered a social asset. The valuation of the asset is based on the year-end staff payroll, discounted to present value, the discount rate a function of mean staff tenure and pay raise rate. The discount rate for 1972 was .9634 for staff available within one year and 2.906 for those available after one year, based on a mean staff tenure of 4.59 years. For 1971, mean staff tenure was 5.45 years. (Note K)

Note H: Training investment is estimated at 25% of first year salary for all staff. Training obsolescence is based on a straight-line depreciation of training investment over the mean staff tenure. (See Note G)

Note I: The social capital investment is equated with the capital cost of reconstituting the organization. It is computed by weighting the capital stock account from 1965 (the year of the company's founding) to the present, by the consumer price index (1967 = $1.00) expressed in current year dollars.

the integration of social and financial balance sheets

Note J: A portion of the research carried out by the firm is performed in connection with the preparation of proposals submitted to prospective clients. The cost of this research is estimated at $37,898 in 1972 and $38,280 in 1971. This cost is reduced by the costs associated with proposal resulting in client contracts, in which the research developed was exploited, and any remaining amount is written off at the end of one year.

Note K: The total staff payroll was used (Note G) to calculate staff assets available. Since part of the staff is engaged in administrative and contract activities not considered socially productive, these liabilities or commitments are created counter to clients. They are equated here to the mean of the financing outstanding during the year.

Note L: The company's financing requirements are considered an opportunity cost to society. They are equated here to the mean of the financing outstanding during the year.

Note M: A substantial portion of the company's activities are expressed in tangible form through the printed word. The company used 102 tons of paper in 1972 and 26 tons of paper in 1971. The company recognizes an obligation to society based on the cost of abatement of the water pollution created by the manufacture of this paper. This cost is estimated at $35 per ton.

Note N: The company consumed 1,542,524 KWH of electric power in 1972 and 476,053 KWH in 1971. The company recognizes an obligation to society based on the cost of abatement of the air pollution created by the production of this power. This cost is estimated at $.02 per KWH.

Note O: The company generated 783,750 commuting trip miles in 1972 and 615,960 miles in 1971. The obligation to society based on the air pollution thus created is estimated at $.01 per mile.

Note P: Staff assets available less staff commitments.

Note Q: Organizational assets available less organizational commitments.

Note R: Research and tax assets less environmental obligations.

The financial statements presented on the previous pages are "society's statements," showing the assets, liabilities, costs and benefits accruing to various segments of society from the company's operations.

In the socially-motivated company, decision-making requires a comparison of social investment with financial return and of financial investment with social return, as well as the usual comparison of financial investments and returns. Some of the net social investment of the company is expected to have a beneficial financial result, while some of it may affect the company's financial performance negatively, or not at all. These effects are netted out and evaluated by integrating the company's net social investment into its own financial statement.

This treatment "internalizes" social costs and benefits. The pages which follow internalize social assets net of liabilities. All of the net asset is considered "social equity" in the restated net worth. On the page following the integrated statement, this restated net worth is discounted, in recognition that only a portion of it is likely to produce a return.

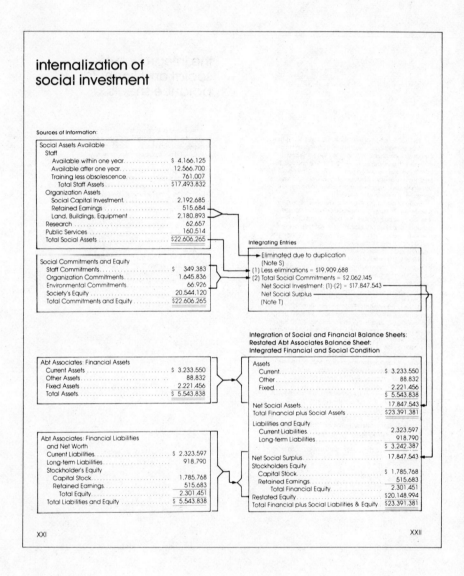

internalization of social investment

Sources of Information:

Social Assets Available
Staff
Available within one year............ $ 4.166.125
Available after one year............ 12.566.700
Training less obsolescence............ 761.007
Total Staff Assets....................... $17.493.832
Organization Assets
Social Capital Investment.............. 2.192.685
Retained Earnings...................... 515.684
Land, Buildings, Equipment 2.180.893
Research 62.657
Public Services 160.514
Total Social Assets $22.606.265

Social Commitments and Equity
Staff Commitments....................... $ 349.383
Organization Commitments............... 1.645.836
Environmental Commitments............. 66.926
Society's Equity 20.544.120
Total Commitments and Equity $22.606.265

Integrating Entries

Eliminated due to duplication
(Note S)
(1) Less eliminations = $19.909.688
(2) Total Social Commitments = $2.062.145
Net Social Investment: (1)-(2) = $17.847.543
Net Social Surplus
(Note T)

Integration of Social and Financial Balance Sheets:
Restated Abt Associates Balance Sheet:
Integrated Financial and Social Condition

Abt Associates: Financial Assets
Current Assets .... $ 3.233.550
Other Assets 88.832
Fixed Assets 2.221.456
Total Assets............................... $ 5.543.838

Assets
Current............................... $ 3.233.550
Other................................... 88.832
Fixed................................... 2.221.456
$ 5.543.838
Net Social Assets.......................... 17.847.543
Total Financial plus Social Assets $23.391.381

Liabilities and Equity
Current Liabilities...................... 2.323.597
Long-term Liabilities.................... 918.790
$ 3.242.387

Abt Associates: Financial Liabilities
and Net Worth
Current Liabilities....................... $ 2.323.597
Long-term Liabilities.................... 918.790
Stockholder's Equity
Capital Stock............................ 1.785.768
Retained Earnings....................... 515.683
Total Equity............................ 2.301.451
Total Liabilities and Equity .... $ 5.543.838

Net Social Surplus...................... 17.847.543
Stockholders Equity
Capital Stock........................... $ 1.785.768
Retained Earnings....................... 515.683
Total Financial Equity................. 2.301.451
Restated Equity.......................... $20.148.994
Total Financial plus Social Liabilities & Equity $23.391.381

XXI   XXII

notes to integrated balance sheet

Note S: Retained earnings and land, buildings and equipment are found on both the social and financial balance sheets. They are eliminated here so that they will not be double-counted.

Note T: Net social surplus reflects the total potential increase in the "worth" of the company due to the company's "investment" in net social assets. It is recognized that part of this may not be realized in financial terms. The return on investment calculations discussed on page XXIV reflect this.

comments: the social audit as a decision-making tool

The company believes that its performance should be judged on both financial and social grounds because in reality the two are always linked. Management needs the tools to assess the financial consequences of social investment and policy decisions, and the social consequences of financial decisions, which, in turn, lead to further financial results.

The financial earnings of the company result from both the financial and the social assets. Therefore, the integrated financial and social statements on the previous page recognize a "net social asset" which, together with financial assets, affect the company's financial return. Calculation of the "return on social investment" of "net social asset" thus becomes feasible, offering a new performance measure to use as a policy guide for maximizing overall return on investment.

Before such a social performance measure can be applied, however, some social and financial interactions must be clarified. It is necessary to determine what part of the social investment yields how much of the financial return, over what time periods, and vice versa. This we have tried to do by segregating social investments with and without financial consequences, and financial investments with and without social consequences.

In AAI's industry, the most important asset is staff. The return on "staff investment," if monitored over time, is an indication of the efficiency of that asset's use. Staff assets available within one year have been compared to the company's annual financial net income; an analysis of assets available beyond one year would necessitate projecting net income. The change from 1971 to 1972 in financial return on "staff assets available within one year" shows:

1971: Staff assets (within one year) available at midpoint of year: $2453K. Return after taxes: $244K. ROI: 9.9%
1972: Staff assets available: (midpoint of year) $3380K. Return after taxes: $298K. ROI: 8.8%

Thus, there has been a drop in ROI from one year to the next, accompanying a substantial increase in investment. One interpretation of this is that the company has increased its investment in staff — a social asset — and has seen the financial return as that and other assets decline. An improvement in short-run social impact through staff assets has been accompanied by a decline in financial return on the staff assets.

Another view is gained by an examination of the composition of "staff assets available." The increase in that asset value obscures the fact that the staff turnover rate increased in 1972, as measured by a reduction of mean staff tenure from 5.45 in 1971 to 4.59 years in 1972. Thus, a growth in company size is reflected by a larger payroll, but the mean projected "life" of the staff has declined. Since we assume that the staff is benefiting society as long as it remains on the payroll, we have increased the benefit, but have provided the benefit less efficiently than in the past. An increased turnover rate would tend to depress profit, if no corrective action were taken. The loss of "social efficiency" referred to would be matched by a loss in financial efficiency as well, all other things being equal.

A continuing analysis of the return on staff assets should enable corporate management to balance social and financial goals. The history to date shows:

	1972	1971
Financial Return on Equity	13.8%	13.0%
Financial Return on Staff assets within one year	8.8%	9.9%

The corporate goal should be to increase the financial return on equity while keeping the return on staff assets within an acceptable range. Too high a return on staff assets will indicate too great a concentration on financial over social performance. Too low a return will show the opposite.

Abt Associates Inc. was incorporated under the laws of the Commonwealth of Massachusetts in 1965 and has its executive offices at 55 Wheeler Street, Cambridge, Massachusetts 02138. The Company's telephone number is 617-492-7100.

The transfer agent for Abt Associates Inc. is the State Street Bank and Trust Company, Boston, Massachusetts.

Abt Associates Inc. owns and uses facilities totaling 32,000 square feet and rents for its use an additional 58,100 square feet, including branch and field office facilities.

Piecemeal Social Accounting:
Eastern Gas and Fuel Associates

While few corporations have attempted the comprehensive approach to social accounting of an ABT Associates, several have moved to a less complete, piecemeal approach. These presentations have varied from a few paragraphs or pictures in the annual report discussing the company's good works, to somewhat broader attempts. The insert included in the 1972 annual report of Eastern Gas and Fuel Associates is a good example of such a piecemeal effort. The company's performance in each of several apparently "social" areas is appraised in the company's own terms. In addition, the shareholders are given an opportunity to suggest other areas for inquiry.

So far, this company has limited its efforts largely to the employment area. One might question why an enterprise whose product is so closely involved in questions of pollution control has totally ignored that critical area?

SOURCE: Insert for the 1972 Annual Report of Eastern Gas and Fuel Associates.

Toward Social Accounting

TO OUR SHAREHOLDERS:

There has been much talk in recent years of corporate social responsibility and of the need to develop some sort of social accounting to gauge how well a given firm is performing – not just as an economic unit, but as a citizen. Indeed, some have suggested that these measures of corporate performance beyond net profit should be subjected to an independent social audit.

This insert for the 1972 Annual Report of Eastern Gas and Fuel Associates has been designed as an experimental exploration of two aspects of social accounting for "self-auditing" purposes:

(1) What are some internal topics on which management can presently assemble and organize reasonably accurate and coherent data?

(2) Which issues of social accountability are of external interest, and to what extent are shareholders in particular interested, if at all?

To explore the first of these aspects we have gathered statistical information that covers four topics from among the many that are currently of concern to those studying corporate social responsibility:

- industrial safety
- Minority employment
- Charitable giving
- Pensions

To explore the second aspect we have included, at the end of this insert, a short questionnaire which, if you will mail it back, will serve as a useful measure of shareholder concern with corporate social responsibility and the reporting of it. No generally accepted standards or methods of presentation have been developed for shareholder reporting on such topics nor is there clear evidence as to shareholder interest.

The topics for this first report were not chosen because they are necessarily the most important ones, or the ones that might make us look good, but because they are the most readily measurable, because our goals with respect to them are comparatively simple and clear, and because they lie in areas where management can rather directly influence results. In addition, managerial decisions on these topics can have a significant impact on earnings per share.

In the process of making this first consolidation of social data from our various operations, we found that our records were less complete and less certain than we had believed. We also found that even inadequate disclosure begins to exert a useful pressure on management to comply with new public expectations as to the conduct of large corporations. It may also be some of the best evidence that management is sincerely concerned and making an effort to meet proper expectations.

Four major recurring principles for the quantification of social responsibility have been suggested:

The first is that our priorities have been changing with some rapidity. Many of our political, economic and commercial measures of progress have become obsolescent. We need a new kind of social accounting that goes beyond GNP for the nation and goes beyond net profit for the firm.

Second, while we think of our current economic and accounting measures of GNP and net profit as very precise, when you really get into the nitty gritty of how they are put together, their certainty is delusive.

Third, many proposed imprecise measures of social accounting can be sufficiently accurate to be instructive. They are not hopelessly less accurate than GNP or net profit, and so they can be quite useful, even though they lack precision, for many purposes for which we cannot use GNP and net profit.

And finally, while our efforts to calibrate our concerns by social accounting will reflect this new sense of priorities, without personal observation in the field and a weighing of the figures that we create with moral concerns, social accounting itself becomes only a new numbers game.

As we proceed with these early attempts to develop some form of internal social accounting, we should acquire additional useful insights into this new art.

Eli Goldston

Eli Goldston, *President*

1 INDUSTRIAL SAFETY

Recent legislation has demonstrated that a major current public concern, especially in the heavy industries in which Eastern is involved, is the health and safety of employees.

Our industrial accident record in recent years has not been very good. One standard measurement is the accident frequency rate (number of accidents versus hours worked), and our rate has almost doubled in the last three years, going up most dramatically in gas operations. It is clear that our safety performance has been slipping. In addition it seems that our record is poorer than that of a number of firms with whom we have compared specific records. Just where we stand in our various industries is difficult to gauge because meaningful comparative figures are not available.

ACCIDENT FREQUENCY RATE
(Lost time accidents per million employee hours)

	1970	1971	1972
Coal & Coke	43	61	78
Gas	14	26	30
Marine	34	41	43
EGFA Avg.	36	50	64

Another measure of safety performance is the severity rate, which takes into account time lost as a result of accidents. Here Eastern's record has been steadier, and apparently more in line with other firms for our industries. But much room for improvement remains.

ACCIDENT SEVERITY RATE
(Employee days lost per million employee hours)*

	1970	1971	1972
Coal & Coke	2,948	3,427	4,209
Gas	222	191	303
Marine	1,707	2,015	1,423
EGFA Avg.	2,225	2,516	3,033

*Excluding days charged for fatalities.

Frequency and severity rates, either for a single firm or for an industry, are rather elusive statistics. They may appear worse simply from improved reporting, or may appear better if excessive pressure to improve the record results in variable reporting practices. Comparisons are complicated by numerous variables. Our river towboat crews, for instance, live aboard the boats and so are at their workplace even when not actually working. A greater awareness by both employees and management of the importance of safety may increase the number of reported accidents. Improved benefits could encourage accident reporting. Comparisons are also difficult because of different bases of reporting. We are trying for 1973 to improve both our performance and our ability to supply managers with comparable industry statistics.

Job related fatalities, of course, are the most salient and tragic accidents. We require full reports to top management on all serious injuries and fatalities along with proposals to prevent recurrence. At Eastern we are constantly trying to develop more effective ways to impress on all our people the need to guard against the ever present hazards in their particular line of work. Here is our recent record of fatalities:

FATALITIES

	1970	1971	1972
Coal & Coke	8	3	4
Gas	0	0	0
Marine	1	1	2
EGFA Total	9	4	6

Critics of industry often assume that management has more ability to reduce accident frequency and severity and to eliminate fatalities than may be the case. We do not accept at all the rationalization that "accidents just happen" and we would be the last to suggest that a victim alone is at fault. But it is obvious that we need to be better persuaders and to improve training, motivation and enforcement when it is considered that in at least five of the six 1972 fatalities, the victim was an experienced employee who was clearly violating a standard safety work rule of the company at the time of his death. The need for and difficulty of broad safety indoctrination is evidenced by the fact that 11 employees were fatally injured in 1972 in accidents off the job.

The economics of safety reinforces our social/humanitarian concerns. Compensation of employees injured on the job cost Eastern at least $3,600,000 last year, or about 20¢ in earnings per share.

We are continuing to increase our commitment of men and money to ongoing safety programs in all operations. One of our headquarters officers has been assigned to regular field checks of safety practices and the compilation and analysis of accident statistics. Eastern Associated Coal Corp. has further strengthened its existing safety program by engaging the highly respected safety department of a firm in another industry to help us improve our safety performance in coal operations. In Boston Gas Company, a safety campaign has commenced that focuses not only on safe work habits but also on continuing "defensive" use of equipment and procedures to avoid dangerous situations.

2 MINORITY EMPLOYMENT

An important thrust of Eastern's social concerns effort is to respond positively to the apparently clear national desire to bring an end to discrimination in employment and promotion because of race, religion or other difference from that elusive notion of "the majority."

It is difficult to generalize fairly and judiciously about Eastern's minority employment statistics. Numerically, minority employment in the company has increased in recent years, but has not quite maintained its percentage proportion. This has been particularly noticeable in coal operations, but in this instance, the increased employment has come in areas where there has been a smaller minority proportion in the local population. And it may be that the improving employment prospects for minority members either with our competitors or in fields previously closed to them have reduced the relative attractiveness of jobs with us. Boston Gas has had an excellent record of integrating its work force, but the addition of new territory with a different population mix has appeared to slow the trend.

MINORITY EMPLOYMENT

	1970	1971	1972
Coal & Coke			
Total	5,703	6,050	6,448
Minority	526	544	517
% Minority	9.2%	9.0%	8.0%
Gas			
Total	1,466	1,500	1,611
Minority	66	96	115
% Minority	4.5%	6.4%	7.1%
Marine			
Total Employees	1,077	1,332	1,358
Minority	64	84	79
% Minority	5.9%	6.3%	5.8%
EGFA*			
Total Employees	8,349	8,995	9,526
Minority	659	727	716
% Minority	7.9%	8.3%	7.5%

*Includes Boston Office

Measuring progress in integration is further complicated by the fact that companies were forbidden to record the race of employees until quite recently. Many of our operations are so geographically scattered that it is difficult to determine in many cases if our percentages of minority employment are in line with the minority population in reasonably relevant areas, although this does seem to be true.

MINORITY EMPLOYMENT LEVELS

	1971	1972	1972 Total in Category	1972 % of Total
Officers & Managers	15	12	1,229	1%
Professional & Technical	19	34	648	4.9%
Clerical	58	56	895	6.1%
Skilled	364	398	5,091	7.8%
Unskilled	271	216	1,663	1.3%
	727	716	9,526	

Passing over complicated matters of definition, the figures seem to indicate that Eastern has done a reasonable job but still has some distance to go in reaching a fair proportion of minorities in the work force and in levels of employment. Our effort in recruitment and advancement is to give due recognition to merit and performance while still showing concern for the need to achieve appropriate representation of minorities. There are local instances in our operations which will require continuing attention and prodding if this is to be accomplished.

3 CHARITABLE GIVING

The figures we present below on our charitable giving through The Eastern Associated Foundation are far from complete. Although most charitable gifts of $500 and over have been made by all operations through the Foundation, a good many smaller gifts are made directly from operating funds. In addition, there are expenditures that get classified as personnel expense or sales expense in Eastern that could properly be considered charitable giving. For example, we provide recreation directors for several of our mining communities and we subsidize a summer camp for the children of mine employees. Particularly in the mining areas, equipment is donated or the use of it given to various causes. In addition, company employees are sometimes loaned or assigned to assist in charitable campaign drives or social service projects.

CHARITABLE GIVING BY THE
EASTERN ASSOCIATED FOUNDATION

	1970	1971	1972
Total Contributions	$185,442	$210,320	$216,429
1% of Pre-Tax Income	336,450	240,750	225,250
$ per Employee	23.77	23.11	22.78
Earnings per Share	1¢	1¢	1¢

The Federal Income Tax law permits contributions to the extent of 5% of taxable income; many studies, however, have shown that the majority of large public corporations make charitable gifts of about 1% of pre-tax income. We have been using this 1% figure as a guide so far as Foundation gifts are concerned.

We have employed outside professional consultants to help us decide how (a) to respond thoughtfully to the charitable concerns of the communities with which we are related and (b) to balance the interest of numerous applicants. On the basis of their suggestions we have considered it appropriate to channel Foundation giving about one-half to health and welfare, one-fourth to higher education, and one-fourth to civic and cultural causes. Costs of educational assistance to active employees is in addition to this giving.

PER CENT OF FOUNDATION GIVING BY CATEGORY OF INTEREST

	1970	1971	1972
Health and Welfare	56.3%	57.1%	53.8%
Higher Education	26.4	20.7	22.8
Civic and Cultural	17.3	22.2	23.4
Total	100.0%	100.0%	100.0%

Charitable giving budgets are established annually by each of the operations and are reviewed along with our other business plans to be sure they are adequate and balanced. Through a matching gifts program, where the company matches an employee's gift to an educational institution, employees can themselves help determine the scale and direction of company assistance to higher education.

4 PENSIONS

Where at one time company retirement plans had been an accepted, almost competitive, way to attract and keep employees, current thinking turns more to their adequacy of coverage and fiscal soundness. In both of these areas it is virtually impossible to generalize about the pension arrangements for Eastern's employees.

In the matter of coverage, all of our employees are, of course, covered by Social Security, with the employee and the employer paying their equal shares. In 1972 each paid 5.2% of the first $9,000 of an employee's earnings but this has since increased to 5.85% of the first $10,800. In addition, substantially all of Eastern's employees participate in one of the 23 separate formal retirement plans to which the company and its subsidiaries are a party.

Eastern's pension arrangements involve very substantial amounts of money. Total Social Security payments by the company in 1972 amounted to about $4,300,000. The expense for the various types of pension and welfare plans supplemental to Social Security has climbed to more than $12,500,000 annually in recent years. Social Security, health and retirement costs thus add an average of almost $2,000 per employee to the average of $10,000 a year paid to an Eastern employee.

ANNUAL COST OF PENSION & WELFARE PLANS
($000)

	1970	1971	1972
Union Welfare & Pension Plans	$5,814	$5,724	$ 8,904
Other Formal & Informal Plans	2,693	2,967	3,649
	$8,507	$8,691	$12,553

(Costs charged to income in the fiscal year of the company)

Eighteen of the formal retirement plans are maintained by negotiations in collective bargaining with various labor unions. In most of these we have no control over management of the funds or the amount of the benefits. We participate in the control of others to varying degrees.

So far as we know, none of these funds has been challenged as to the competence of its management except the Health and Welfare Fund of the United Mine Workers. Contributions to this fund, based on a per tonnage contribution made by all unionized operators, including our Eastern Associated Coal Corp., have been brought under Federal court jurisdiction because of alleged mismanagement.

So far as fiscal soundness is concerned, we annually charge as an expense against income an amount which reflects the actuarial obligations of the current year. In addition, the past service obligations that existed when various funds were established or resulted from amendments, are being charged to the current year on the basis of 30-year amortization periods.

We have been funding each negotiated plan in accordance with the relevant collective bargaining agreement. In the case of Eastern's Retirement Plan for Salaried Employees, which is non-negotiated and non-contributory, funding has recently been brought up to the level for which concurrent tax deductibility is permitted. This plan is fairly well funded compared to the plans of most companies.

An accrued total liability of almost $35,000,000 is funded by assets in trust with a market value of about $27,000,000. The additional $8,000,000 must be paid to the Trustees or earned through fund investment income in excess of annual expenditures in order for the plan to be considered fully funded.

STATUS OF EGFA SALARIED PLAN FUNDING

Fiscal Year Ending June 30, 1972
($000)

Liability for Retired Employees	$18,872
Liability for Active & Terminated Employees	15,825
	$34,697
Accrued Liability	$34,697
Plan Assets at Market Value	26,671
Unfunded Liability @ Market	$ 8,026

It is difficult to determine how adequately funded the various negotiated plans are since many cover other companies in addition to our own companies and, with continuing changes in benefits, actuarial assumption, and market value of assets, there will be variations which defy simple explanation.

We are regularly reviewing both our negotiated pension arrangements and our salaried plan, using an independent insurance firm as consultants when appropriate. We believe that the expense, the benefits and vesting provisions of our numerous retirement plans are reasonably in line with those of the different industries in which we operate. Since the Health and Welfare Fund of the coal industry is portable within that industry, some of the issues as to portability do not apply to our single largest employee group. There may be continuing pressure to require us and other employers to liberalize vesting and portability. These are, no doubt, desirable pension changes, but they must be recognized as being increases in actual pension cost.

* * * * *

The compilation of this report has helped to clarify Eastern's goals in these areas of social concern.

Our goal in industrial safety is to reverse an unfavorable trend and to significantly reduce the frequency and severity of industrial accidents.

Our goal in minority employment is to achieve full equality of opportunity for all and to adequately reflect in our work force the minority proportion in the population of the areas of our operations without sacrificing performance standards.

Our goal in charitable contributions is to maintain, possibly to increase, a level of about 1% of pre-tax income as an appropriate amount of support for various social causes.

Our goal in our retirement programs is to make certain that company benefits are adequate and that promises to employees are secured through proper funding.

SHAREHOLDER COMMENTS

The attached questionnaire has a number of specific questions and also an opportunity for general comments. We will greatly appreciate your detaching it, filling it in and mailing it to us. We hope to be able to make a preliminary report at the shareholders' meeting on April 26, 1973 as to any significant shareholder opinion.

Please fill out, detach and mail

Questionnaire

1. Should this sort of social accounting report be:
    - ☐ enlarged
    - ☐ continued in about same manner
    - ☐ condensed
    - ☐ omitted

2. Should such reports cover:
    - ☐ Industrial Safety
    - ☐ Minority Employment
    - ☐ Charitable Giving
    - ☐ Pensions
    - ☐ Environment
    - ☐ Female Employment
    - ☐ Consumer Rights
    - ☐ Other (please list)

3. How does our record on industrial accidents seem to you?
    - ☐ Good, taking problems into account
    - ☐ Fair
    - ☐ Mediocre
    - ☐ Poor

4. Should the company continue to move ahead of legal enforcement pressures in the following areas:
    Employment and promotion of minorities
    ☐ Yes   ☐ Moderately   ☐ No

    Preferential hiring of minorities
    ☐ Yes   ☐ Moderately   ☐ No

    Special counselling, training for minorities
    ☐ Yes   ☐ Moderately   ☐ No

5. In charitable contributions, should the company give:
    - ☐ Present level of about 1% as is common practice
    - ☐ Up to permitted tax deductible level of 5% of taxable income
    - ☐ Above 5% even though not deductible
    - ☐ Nothing, letting individuals choose their own charities

6. Should company charitable contributions be:
    Limited to programs likely to serve our own employees and families   ☐ Yes   ☐ No
    Limited to social welfare programs such as hospitals or United Funds   ☐ Yes   ☐ No
    Include urban or minority programs
    ☐ Yes   ☐ No

7. Should the company continue its "Matching Gifts" program as a way of bringing employees into charitable giving decisions
    ☐ Yes   ☐ No

    (continued on other side)

Please add your own comments below:

Investment Selection on a Social Basis: The Dreyfus Third Century Fund

The Dreyfus Third Century Fund is the largest of several mutual funds that have been formed to invest in companies that, in one way or another, act in a socially desirable manner. The excerpt from the prospectus provides a description of the general investment goals of the Fund. The 1973 annual report provides some indication of the methodology used by the Fund and lists some of the questions it asks companies. It includes the list of investments held by the Fund, which presumably meet its social investment criteria. The Fund's financial statements have also been included to give some idea of its performance.

To place that performance in some perspective, it should be noted that the Dow Jones Index declined by 6.2% during the year ending May 31, 1973, while the Standard & Poors Index of 500 stocks declined 4.2% for the same period. It is interesting to note that about 1/3 of the Fund's total assets were invested in short-term debt securities. Whether this position indicates a shortage of socially desirable investments or merely reflects the depressed condition of the stock market at the end of May, 1973, is not made clear in the annual report.

SOURCE: From The Dreyfus Third Century Fund Prospectus, March 22, 1972, and Dreyfus Third Century Fund, Inc., Annual Report 1973.

PROSPECTUS   March   , 1972

The Dreyfus Third Century Fund, Inc.

2,500,000 Shares Common Stock ($1 Par Value)

The Dreyfus Third Century Fund, Inc. (the "Fund") is a mutual fund seeking capital growth through investment in companies which, in the opinion of the Fund's Management, not only meet traditional investment standards, but also show evidence in the conduct of their business, relative to other companies in the same industry or industries, of contributing to the enhancement of the quality of life in America as this nation approaches the Third Century of its existence. See "The Fund — Special Considerations." In making this latter assessment, the Fund intends to consider performance by companies in the areas of (1) the protection and improvement of the environment and the proper use of our natural resources, (2) occupational health and safety, (3) consumer protection and product purity and (4) equal employment opportunity. In addition, special consideration will be given to those companies which have, or are developing, technology, products or services which, in the opinion of the Fund's management, will contribute to the enhancement of the quality of life in America.

Capital growth is the primary objective of the Fund, and income is a secondary objective. Fund shares should be purchased only by those who consider the Fund's primary objective of capital growth to be consistent with their own investment objectives and to whom the Fund's special standards are important factors in selecting securities for investment. The Fund's special standards tend to limit the availability of investment opportunities more than is customary with other investment companies. At February 10, 1972, The Dreyfus Corporation, the Fund's Manager (the "Manager"), managed approximately $2.8 billion of assets. The Fund pays the Manager a management fee of ¾ of 1% per annum of the average value of its net assets as computed daily. This fee is in excess of that paid by most other funds. See "Management of the Fund — Management Fee." The Fund's address is 767 Fifth Avenue, New York, New York 10022. The minimum purchase of shares offered by this Prospectus is 100 shares ($1,250). Retain this Prospectus for future reference.

THESE SECURITIES HAVE NOT BEEN APPROVED OR DISAPPROVED BY THE SECURITIES AND EXCHANGE COMMISSION NOR HAS THE COMMISSION PASSED ON THE ACCURACY OR ADEQUACY OF THIS PROSPECTUS. ANY REPRESENTATION TO THE CONTRARY IS A CRIMINAL OFFENSE.

	Price to Public (a)	Underwriting Discount (a)(b)(c)	Proceeds to the Fund (a)(c)
Per Share	$12.50	$1.09	$11.41
Total	$31,250,000	$2,725,000	$28,525,000

(a) Assuming these shares are sold in single transactions involving less than 400 shares each ($5,000). In larger transactions, the offering price and the 8.75% underwriting discount per share are reduced. See "Underwriting."
(b) The Fund and the Manager have agreed to indemnify the Underwriters against certain liabilities, including liabilities arising under the Securities Act of 1933. See "Underwriting."
(c) All expenses of organizing the Fund and making this offering will be borne by The Dreyfus Sales Corporation and the Representatives of the several Underwriters.

The Fund will not offer its shares between the Closing Date and June 20, 1972 when the Fund will commence a continuous offering of its shares at an offering price equal to the then net asset value per share plus a maximum sales charge of 8.75%. See "Continuous Offering of Fund Shares."

BACHE & CO.
Incorporated

REYNOLDS SECURITIES INC.

KIDDER, PEABODY & CO.
Incorporated

THE DREYFUS THIRD CENTURY FUND, INC.

THE FUND

The Dreyfus Third Century Fund, Inc. (the "Fund") is a mutual fund primarily seeking capital growth, with income as a secondary objective. The Fund's investment policy involves investment risk and there can be no assurance that the Fund will achieve its investment objectives. The Fund is a diversified open-end investment company with its shares redeemable at net asset value at the option of the holders. See "Redemption of Fund Shares." The Fund is managed by The Dreyfus Corporation, which also manages The Dreyfus Fund, Inc., The Dreyfus Leverage Fund, Inc., The Dreyfus Special Income Fund, Inc., and other mutual funds. See "The Manager—The Dreyfus Corporation."

The Fund was organized under the laws of the State of Delaware on May 6, 1971, with its offices at 767 Fifth Avenue, New York, New York. Its telephone number is (212) 935-6633.

Special Considerations

The Management of the Fund believes that investment by the private sector can become a positive force to encourage social progress in America. The Fund will invest in companies which, in the opinion of the Fund's Management, not only meet traditional investment standards, but also show evidence in the conduct of their business, relative to other companies in the same industry or industries, of contributing to the enhancement of the quality of life in America as this nation approaches the Third Century of its existence. In making this latter assessment, the Fund intends, as a matter of fundamental policy, to consider performance by companies in the areas of (1) the protection and improvement of the environment and the proper use of our natural resources, (2) occupational health and safety, (3) consumer protection and product purity and (4) equal employment opportunity. In addition, special consideration will be given to those companies which have, or are developing, technology, products or services which, in the opinion of the Fund's Management, will contribute to the enhancement of the quality of life in America. The Management of the Fund further believes that the foregoing special standards are relevant to attaining the Fund's primary objective of capital growth in that the Management of the Fund believes that the ability to meet these standards will generally be an indication of companies which are well managed and which, therefore, present opportunities for capital growth.

The Manager, initially guided by legal requirements which prescribe standards of commercial and social conduct in the areas of concern to the Fund, has developed, and is continuing to develop, techniques for measuring relative performance in these areas. It must be recognized, however, that there are few generally accepted measures of performance in these areas, and that therefore the development of suitable techniques to measure such performance will be largely within the discretion and judgment of the Management of the Fund. Currently, development of these techniques and evaluation of companies with respect to these areas are the responsibility of a full-time special research staff of the Manager.

The following paragraphs describe the process by which the Fund's Management selects securities for the Fund's portfolio. At the outset, on the basis of traditional investment considerations, the Manager directs the special research staff to investigate specific industries and specific companies within those industries which present likely investment possibilities. The number of companies investigated will depend on the industry being examined. This investigation usually will include personal interviews with company officials, inspection of facilities and the collection of qualitative and quantitative data. Additional quantitative data is obtained from information publicly available in reports filed by each such industry and company under applicable laws.

2

As a result of this special research, the companies investigated are ranked according to their relative performance in the areas of special concern to the Fund. Companies will generally be evaluated on the basis of their current performance. The rankings, together with the special staff's comments, are presented to the Board of Directors of the Fund. The Board then determines the overall level of performance in these areas which must be met in each industry investigated in order for a company to be eligible for investment by the Fund and decides which companies of those examined have attained the level of performance set for its particular industry. Depending on the industry, a company that scores in the lower half of the industry sample would not generally be eligible for investment by the Fund although such a company may become eligible if special circumstances are present. The Board of Directors does not intend to disqualify companies because of past actions not in keeping with the Fund's special standards so long as it has been ascertained that current company policies and actions attain the requisite level of performance. At present, Management does not intend to attempt to evaluate indirect or secondary implications of corporate activities; for example, in investigating insurance companies the Fund will not evaluate their lending practices.

Finally, within the group of securities which meets the Fund's special standards, the Fund purchases and sells securities based on traditional investment considerations, including technical market factors as well as Management's opinion of the fundamental value of a security. Securities which may be desirable for the Fund to purchase or to retain solely for traditional investment reasons are not purchased unless the issuers thereof meet the Fund's special standards and are sold if at any time the Board of Directors determines they cease to meet such standards.

Although the Fund's investment objectives and its consideration of the special standards discussed above are fundamental policies of the Fund and cannot be changed or added to without approval by the holders of a majority of the outstanding shares of the Fund, the required overall levels of performance in the areas of special concern may be varied by the Board from time to time. The Board will periodically review the performance of companies in these areas in order to determine whether previously ineligible companies then meet the required overall level of performance which has been established for their industries or whether previously eligible companies have become ineligible.

It should be noted that the Fund's special standards tend to limit the availability of investment opportunities more than is customary with other investment companies, including others managed by the Manager. However, the Management of the Fund believes there are sufficient investment opportunities among the companies which will meet the Fund's special standards to permit it, if Management believes it desirable, to be fully invested in securities which meet the Fund's primary investment objective of capital growth.

Fund shares should be purchased only by those who consider the Fund's primary objective of capital growth to be consistent with their own investment objectives and who believe that the Fund's special standards are important factors in selecting securities for investment. The distinguishing features of this Fund, in the opinion of Management, are the special standards being applied and the method used in selecting companies whose securities are eligible for inclusion in the Fund's portfolio. Because the number of investment opportunities is finite, at any one time the investment portfolio of other growth funds may, to a degree, overlap with the portfolio of the Fund.

It will be the policy of the Fund to communicate with its shareholders in its reports with respect to the special standards which it is applying. From time to time, when, in the judgment of the members of the Board who are not interested persons of the Fund or the Manager (as defined in the Investment Company Act), the views of shareholders would be of use in their deliberations, questionnaires, including those which may appear as part of a report to shareholders, will be prepared and distributed at the expense of the Fund. Although the cost of the questionnaires cannot be estimated, it is not expected to be significant. Such questionnaires will be for the information of the Board only, and Management of the Fund will retain the responsibility for making all decisions necessary to the operation of the Fund.

3

Investment Techniques

The Fund intends to diversify its security holdings among various industries and among various issuers within such industries. The Fund will normally invest in common stock or securities convertible into common stock. Investment policies will vary, however, with current financial and economic conditions. When Management believes that an increase in the Fund's defensive position is desirable, the Fund may invest in investment grade corporate bonds, United States Government securities, high grade commercial paper, bank certificates of deposit and cash or cash equivalents, without limit as to amount.

Generally, the Fund's policy is to purchase marketable securities which are not restricted as to public sale and to invest in companies with a continuous operating history (including that of predecessors) of at least three years, although the Fund may invest up to 10% of the value of its total assets in securities whose public sale is subject to registration under the Securities Act of 1933 and up to 5% of such assets in securities of companies having less than three years of such history. See Investment Restrictions Nos. 3 and 9 below. It is expected that investments by the Fund will be made primarily in securities listed on national securities exchanges.

The Fund will not seek to realize profits by anticipating short-term market movements and intends to purchase securities generally for capital growth. While the rate of portfolio turnover will not be a limiting factor when Management deems portfolio changes to be appropriate, it is anticipated that, in light of the Fund's investment objectives, its annual portfolio turnover rate will not generally exceed 60%. Market conditions, however, could result in portfolio activity at a greater rate than anticipated.

Even though investment decisions for the Fund are made independently from those of the other funds managed by the Manager, securities of the same issuer may be purchased, held or sold by the Fund and such other funds because the same security may be suitable for the investment objectives of more than one fund. When two or more funds managed by the Manager are simultaneously engaged in the purchase or sale of the same security, the transactions are averaged as to price and allocated as to amount in accordance with a formula believed to be equitable to each fund. In some cases, this procedure may adversely affect the price paid or received by the Fund or the size of the position obtainable for the Fund.

Common Stock Portfolio Changes*
for the six months ended May 31, 1973

New Commitments Were Made in the Following Securities:

Century Laboratories

Charles River Breeding Laboratories

Columbia Broadcasting System

Corometrics Medical System

Dun & Bradstreet

General Electric

National Semiconductor

RCA Corporation

Xerox Corporation

Additions to Existing Positions Were:

Chicago Bridge & Iron

Chubb Corp.

Coherent Radiation

General Automation

Mine Safety Appliances

New England Nuclear

Spectra-Physics

UAL Inc.

Union Camp

Washington Post-Cl.B.

Weyerhaeuser Company

Eliminations Were:

American Airlines

Bankers Trust

Baxter Laboratories

Bell & Howell

Brown & Sharpe Manufacturing

Champion International

Colonial Penn Group

Fairchild Camera and Instrument

Federated Department Stores

Federal National Mortgage Association

First Charter Financial

Grace (W. R.)

Great Western Financial

Howard Johnson

International Paper

Ionics Incorporated

Lea-Ronal

Macy (R. H.)

Marcor Inc.

Narco Scientific

Sears Roebuck

Southern Railway

Storer Broadcasting

Teleprompter Corp.

Texaco Inc.

Reductions Were:

Envirotech Corporation

Instrumentation Laboratory

Stauffer Chemical

Travelers Corporation

Eliminations of Securities Acquired During the Six Months Ended May 31, 1973:

American Home Products

Exxon Corp.

Honeywell Inc.

Kennecott Copper

Zenith Radio Corp.

---

*Not shown above are securities included in investments as "Other" where the Fund has acquired a new commitment and had not completed its initial position. Increases resulting from stock dividends or splits are also not shown.

The Dreyfus Third Century Fund, Inc.
Statement of Investments May 31, 1973

Shares	Common stocks— 69.3 per cent	Market or fair value[a]	Diversification of $10,000 of net assets
	Companies Enhancing the Quality of Life by the Conduct of their Business		
	Air Transport—1.0%		
10,000	UAL, Inc.	$ 207,500	$ 102
	Chemicals—5.1%		
21,420	Air Products & Chemicals, Inc.	819,315	401
5,000	Stauffer Chemical Company	228,750	112
		1,048,065	513
	Communications—3.1%		
17,500	Columbia Broadcasting System, Inc.	625,625	306
	Instruments and Components—7.9%		
26,000	General Automation, Inc.	773,500	378
10,000	National Semiconductor Corporation	297,600	146
3,250	Raychem Corporation	539,500	264
		1,610,500	788
	Insurance—7.4%		
23,500	Chubb Corp. (The)	1,086,875	532
15,000	Travelers Corporation (The)	427,500	209
		1,514,375	741
	Multi-market—6.2%		
17,000	General Electric	1,011,500	495
10,000	RCA Corporation	251,250	123
		1,262,750	618
	Office Equipment—1.4%		
2,000	Xerox Corporation	295,250	145
	Paper—5.8%		
10,000	Union Camp Corp.	430,000	210
13,200	Weyerhaeuser Company	745,800	365
		1,175,800	575
	Printing and Publishing—7.5%		
10,000	Dun & Bradstreet, Inc.	747,500	356
33,900	Washington Post Company (The)—Cl. B	788,175	385
		1,535,675	751
	Retail Stores—1.5%		
10,000	Safeway Stores, Incorporated	308,750	151
	Companies Enhancing the Quality of Life Through the Development of New Technology, Products or Services		
	Environment—3.3%		
17,000	Chicago Bridge & Iron Company	1,245,250	609
10,600	Combustion Equipment Associates, Inc.	196,100	96

The Dreyfus Third Century Fund, Inc. Statement of Investments May 31, 1973
(Continued on next page)

The Dreyfus Third Century Fund, Inc. (Continued)

Shares	Common Stocks— (continued)	Market or Fair Value[a]	Diversification of $10,000 of Net Assets
6,600	Envirotech Corporation	$ 195,525	$ 96
40,000	Pennzoil Louisiana and Texas Offshore, Inc. Cl. B	142,500	70
3,000	Thermo Electron Corporation	130,500	64
		1,909,875	935
	Occupational Health and Safety—3.4%		
16,900	Mine Safety Appliances Co.	701,350	343
	Health—8.7%		
50,000	Century Laboratories, Inc.	91,919[b]	45
10,000	Charles River Breeding Laboratories, Inc. (The)	325.000	159
7,000	Coherent Radiation	67,375	33
6,000	Corometrics Medical System, Inc.	112,500	55
7,600	Instrumentation Laboratory Inc.	153,900	75
13,300	New England Nuclear Corporation	400,662	196
5,000	Northrup, King & Co.	182,500	89
23,500	Spectra-Physica, Inc.	434,750	213
		1,768,605	865
	0% — 10%	201,000	98
	TOTAL COMMON STOCKS	$14,165,121	$ 6,931

Amount Payable at Maturity	Bank Certificates of Deposit— 25.7%	Market or Fair Value[a]	Diversification of $10,000 of Net Assets
$ 500,000	Bank of America National Trust & Savings Association, 7-1/8% due 7/23/73	$ 500,000	$ 245
500,000	Bank of America National Trust & Savings Association, 7-1/4%, due 7/2/73	500,000	245
500,000	Bank of New York (The), 7.20%, due 7/9/73	500,000	245
1,000,000	Bankers Trust Company, 7.30%, due 7/10/73	1,000,000	489
750,000	Chase Manhattan Bank, N.A., 7.55%, due 7/30/73	750,000	366
1,000,000	Chemical Bank, 7.30%, due 6/29/73	1,000,000	489
500,000	Manufacturers Hanover Trust Co., 7%, due 7/6/73	500,000	245
500,000	Manufacturers Hanover Trust Co., 7-1/4%, due 6/26/73	500,000	245
	TOTAL BANK CERTIFICATES OF DEPOSIT	$ 5,250,000	$ 2,569

The Dreyfus Third Century Fund, Inc. Statement of Investments May 31, 1973
(Continued on next page)

The Dreyfus Third Century Fund, Inc. (Continued)

Amount Payable at Maturity	Short-Term Corporate Notes— 10.9%	Market or Fair Value[a]	Diversification of $10,000 of Net Assets
$ 500,000	Charter New York Corp., 7%, due 7/10/73	$ 491,250	$ 241
1,000,000	Montgomery Ward Credit Corp., 7.10%, due 6/18/73	993,886	486
250,000	Penney (J.C.) Financial Corp., 6-7/8%, due 6/4/73	247,803	121
500,000	Penney (J.C.) Financial Corp., 7.30%, due 7/19/73	494,930	242
	TOTAL SHORT-TERM CORPORATE NOTES	$ 2,227,869	$ 1,090
	TOTAL INVESTMENTS — 105.9%	$21,642,990	$10,590
	LIABILITIES, LESS CASH AND RECEIVABLES — (5.9%)	$(1,205,539)	$ (590)
	NET ASSETS — (100.0%)	$20,437,451	$10,000

Notes

[a]Marketable securities, unless otherwise noted, are valued at the last sales price on May 31, 1973, for securities listed on an exchange or, in the absence of recorded sales and for securities traded in the over-the-counter market, the average of the closing bid and asked prices on that date, except for bank certificates of deposit and short-term corporate notes, which are stated at cost.

[b]Securities restricted as to public resale. The security is carried at fair value, as determined by the Board of Directors of the Fund, computed both at the date acquired and at May 31, 1973 at a discount of 45.5% from the equivalent value of unrestricted securities of the same class. The security was acquired at a cost of $210,000 on December 29, 1972, the date the Fund first obtained an enforceable right to acquire the security. The aggregate market quotation for an equivalent number of shares of unrestricted securities of the same class amounted to $412,500 on the date the purchase price was agreed to and $385,000 on the date the security was acquired. The issuer has agreed to register the security at the request of the Fund, and to bear the expenses of registration.

The Dreyfus Third Century Fund, Inc.
Statement of Investment Income and Expense
for the year ended May 31, 1973.

INCOME

Cash dividends	$249,678	
Interest	246,604	
TOTAL INCOME		$496,282

EXPENSES

Management fee—Note B	163,214	
Directors' fees—Note E	70,000	
Transfer and dividend disbursing agent's fees	38,674	
Custodian fee	16,790	
Auditing fees	15,000	
Legal fees	7,000	
State and local taxes	20,023	
Stockholders' reports	3,681	
Miscellaneous	4,327	
TOTAL EXPENSES		338,709
NET INVESTMENT INCOME—Note A (3)		$157,573

The accompanying notes are an integral part of this statement.[a]

---

[a]The original notes are not included in this book.

The Dreyfus Third Century Fund, Inc.
Statement of Assets and Liabilities May 31, 1973

ASSETS

Investments at market or fair value—see statement			$21,642,990

	Cost	Market or Fair Value	
Common stocks	$15,389,780	$14,165,121	
Bank certificates of deposit	5,250,000	5,250,000	
Short-term corporate notes	2,227,869	2,227,869	
	$22,867,649		

Cash in bank		246,033
Receivable for subscriptions to capital stock		3,814
Interest, dividends and other receivables		67,276
		21,960,113

LIABILITIES

Payable for securities purchased (including $37,809 to The Dreyfus Sales Corporation)	$ 1,402,727	
Due to The Dreyfus Corporation for management fee	4,776	
Payble for capital stock repurchased	33,691	
Accrued expenses and taxes	81,468	1,522,662

NET ASSETS at market or fair value, applicable to 2,191,355
shares of $1 par value capital stock, equivalent to $9.33 a share
(20,000,000 shares authorized) $20,437,451

The Dreyfus Third Century Fund, Inc.
Statement of Changes in Net Assets for the year ended May 31, 1973

	Shares		
Net assets at May 31, 1972 (including $32,505 undistributed income)			$24,171,568
Net investment income			157,573
Net realized (losses) on sales of investments, identified cost basis—on the basis of average cost ($3,657,393)— Note A (3)			(3,650,180)
Unrealized (depreciation) of investments for the year · ·			(1,338,137)
Capital Stock issued and redeemed—Note D:			
Amounts received on issuances:			
Shares sold	330,844	$ 3,659,429	
Exchanges	114,676	1,272,820	
	445,520	4,932,249	
Amounts paid on redemptions:			
Shares redeemed	324,849	3,473,916	
Exchanges	34,917	351,706	
	359,765	3,835,622	
Net increase	85,754		1,096,627
Net assets at May 31, 1973 (including $190,078 undistributed income)			$20,437,451

The accompanying notes are an integral part of these statements.[a]

---

[a]The original notes are not included in this book.

Management Accounting Alternatives in Airline Pollution Control Requirements

Selig Altschul

Most discussions of the economics of pollution control are concerned with the proportions of costs that will or should be borne by the different segments of society. Mr. Altschul's article, however, analyzes the internal decisions to be made by a corporation required to conform to higher pollution control standards. Pollution control standards may be met by various modifications of existing equipment, involving different costs and performance effects or, alternatively by the replacement of existing equipment with newer devices. These two alternatives must be modified by further considerations of the remaining service and economic lives of both new and existing equipment, financing demands, and financial reporting requirements.

AIRLINES HEFTING EXTRA LOAD: ECOLOGY COSTS

Simmering in the minds of airline managements and certain to boil into a problem by next year is the vexing question of how their industry can finance compulsory ecology improvements. At this point, near total confusion reigns.

Measures designed to reduce aircraft noise and emission levels are being advanced by the Environmental Protection Agency for processing and implementation by the Federal Aviation Administration. The aircraft noise-reduction proposals will have the greatest financial impact. The new aircraft smoke-emission standards are less troublesome.

While the grand design for ecological improvement has been drawn, the methods and devices for accomplishment have yet to be clearly defined.

This has led to a murky estimate of the total cost in effecting the necessary modifications ranging anywhere from $1-billion to $3-billion over a span of four to five years. This is the area of expenditures that will have to be financed by the United States airline industry and ultimately paid for, in one form or another, by the users of air transport services.

Sometime before the end of this year, the F.A.A. is expected to issue a notice to modify Federal Air Regulations, Part 36.

Selig, Altschul is President of Aviation Advisory Service, Inc.

This will be a procedure leading to proposed modifications of the rules dealing with the aircraft noise requirements of all United States certificated airplanes. All interested parties, primarily the airlines and ecology groups, will come forward during the subsequent 60 to 90 days with their views and suggestions as to how the proposed regulations should be modified.

After a period of proper digestion, by mid-1974 at the earliest, the F.A.A. will issue its final pronouncement for aircraft noise reduction and programs to achieve the stated objectives in the new and modified Part 36 regulation.

Preliminary indications are that an immediate freeze will be placed on increases in an air carrier's fleet noise level, and a 50 per cent average noise reduction would be required by July 1, 1976. By July 1, 1978, an airline's fleet noise level would have to meet the new Part 36 requirements.

Preliminary plans call for the final Part 36 regulation to require a reduction of 10 or more "effective perceived noise levels" in sideline noise, a reduction of about 10 in take-off noise and a reduction of approximately 7 or 8 in approach noise.

The acoustic modification method now available and likely to be utilized at the outset is sound absorbing material. Kits of this type are being designed to meet the power plants for specific aircraft types and will require separate certification.

In anticipation, the twin-engined 737 powered by the Pratt & Whitney JT-8D could have its modification kit of sound absorbing material certificated by October, 1973. With a 15-month lead time, orders placed at that time could result in the necessary hardware emerging by the end of 1974.

Present estimates for the cost of this modification kit are placed at about $200,000 a unit. This excludes labor installation costs and consequences of down time. Moreover, installation could run for a period of three to four years for completion of an airline fleet. This time span for installation will apply for modifications involving sound absorbing material on all separate type of aircraft fleets.

The same type power plant is utilized in the twin-engine DC-9 series and the tri-engine 727 group of aircraft. No modification kit has been ordered for this group of aircraft as yet. The same 15-month lead time, however, will be required from the date of certification to obtain the necessary hardware or parts. In view of the multiplicity of aircraft types involved, the cost of kits is estimated to range anywhere from $127,500 to $175,000 each in this group.

The aircraft noise reduction program for the larger four-engine DC-8's and 707's, powered by the P.&W. JT-3D series, entails far greater modifications and hence costs. The variation in types of this aircraft group places the estimated cost for the necessary kits of sound absorbing material from $1-million to $1.5-million per unit. The F.A.A. has yet to evolve a definitive program for these larger jets.

The family of wide-body jets, the 747-200 series, DC-10's and L-1011's, powered respectively by the P.&W. JT-9D, GE-CF-6 and Rolls-Royce RB-211, are currently believed to meet presently anticipated aircraft noise level requirements.

Interestingly enough, these modifications when finally accomplished are not expected by industry sources to decrease aircraft noise appreciably. Ironically, this modification is expected to lead to reduced performance of anywhere from 0.5 per cent to 2 per cent while increasing specific fuel consumption per airplane, thus compounding problems elsewhere.

There is a much more sophisticated method being refined which has the potential of effecting more significant aircraft noise reduction than the sound-absorbing material approach.

This is the "new front fan" method. This entails modifications revising versions of the engine where the fan becomes larger, providing more thrust from the fan. It is expected that such an installation may also show improved cost performance but not necessarily be compensatory.

The National Aeronautics and Space Administration and the aircraft engine manufacturers are working on this concept.

Much work remains to be done to effect acceptable fan-modifications. At this stage, preliminary estimates for developing the necessary modification hardware for the separate aircraft types (excluding labor installation costs) are quite fuzzy but currently run as follows:

737 . . . . $1-million (plus $500,000 for landing gear adjustment)
727 . . . . $1.5-million
DC-9 . . . . $1-million
707 . . . . $1.5-million to $2-million
DC-8 . . . . $2-million

The aircraft smoke-emission standards that the Environmental Protection Agency ordered, while adding to the capital costs of the airlines, have not caused any serious problems. As of March 31, 1973, 95 per cent of some 3,000 JT-8D's powering the 737, 727, and DC-9 have been modified to meet the new standards. Completion of all modifications in this category must be accomplished by Jan. 1, 1974.

A major problem in this respect, however, exists for the JT-3D engines powering the 707 and DC-8. These aircraft must meet the smoke standards by Jan. 1, 1978, which is two years later than the original deadline proposed. Nevertheless, no effective modification kit has evolved. The difficulties encountered in this development are highlighted by potential costs, estimated to range anywhere from $50,000 to $300,000 per aircraft.

The cost of engine modifications for smoke-emission control on these aircraft may be too prohibitive to warrant modifications and instead lead to some retirements, particularly in the light of the existing age of many of those 707's and standard DC-8's

Depending upon the firming up of the technological changes ultimately to be ordered for aircraft noise reduction by the F.A.A., the airline industry will have a clearer concept of the magnitude of the additional financial requirements needed to meet modifications decreed by ecological improvement edicts during the next five years or so.

Even a billion dollars, at the lower end of the scale, in additional funds for this requirement will put quite a strain upon industry finances. Placed in perspective, this would compare with an estimated $3.1-billion to be expended for about 271 aircraft delivered and on order for 1973 and beyond. (This includes 159 of the new generation of the quieter and "cleaner" wide-body jets valued at $2.73-billion.)

The Environmental Protection Agency has recognized the pressures upon the airline industry's finances as a consequence of these ecological-ordered modifications. As a result, the E.P.S. is known to be planning to request Congress to develop a method to pay for its programs to reduce aircraft (and airport) noise. Among the measures likely to be advanced would be the following:

Passenger head and freight tax imposed as a surcharge on tickets and freight invoices.

Expanded use of Airport and Airways Development Act of 1970 trust funds for grants to airports and airlines for noise abatement

Surcharge on aircraft fuel tax.

General fare increase

With surcharges now being imposed on individual tickets for airport security measures, the airline industry is opting for a "large measure of public financing." What is likely to emerge, as the extent of the financing costs for aircraft noise reduction is more clearly defined, is a general fare and tariff increase. This will shift these costs to the backs of the air transport users.

There will be other major ripples flowing from these E.P.A.-inspired programs upon airline finances, accounting practices and reported earnings.

The airlines are likely to capitalize the cost of these modifications and amortize them over the remaining life of the aircraft involved.

For example, Eastern's fleet of 35 DC-9's has been in service for an average of five years and was carried at a depreciated cost of $77.3-million, as of December 31, 1972. These aircraft are being amortized over a 15-year period.

Hence, the estimated modification cost for aircraft noise control of about $6,125,000 for the fleet would be added to the existing cost base of the fleet and amortized to the extent of $61,250 annually. This amount, of course, becomes an added cost of operation to the airline, which must be absorbed by increased revenues.

There is still another tantalizing aspect of this modification exercise. It may well develop that the modification effected may extend the serviceable life of the aircraft involved.

This determination must await a judgment sometimes in the future and will depend largely on circumstances then prevailing. Among other considerations will be the possibility of newer aircraft types emerging to replace the current generation of modified aircraft.

If no such replacement is in sight for the DC-9, say, five years hence, Eastern may well find justification for extending the serviceable life of this aircraft another five years.

At that point, the annual depreciation charges on the DC-9 fleet would be about $4.2-million annually as compared with the approximately $8.34-million annual amortization which was projected for the preceding five-year period after giving effect to the required aircraft modifications.

Once the airlines get over the major hurdle of arranging financing for the aircraft modifications inspired, by the Environmental Protection Agency, there can be some positive benefits surfacing in reported results some years down the line.

V

ENVIRONMENTAL ACCOUNTING

Environmental Protection at Minimum Cost: The Pollution Tax

William J. Baumol

Professor Baumol's paper sets forth, with elegant simplicity, the arguments that a tax on polluters will produce environmental protection at a minimal cost to society.

Accountants will have little difficulty agreeing with the logic and conclusions of the paper. Baumol, quite appropriately, however, does not consider the actual implementation and application problems of a pollution tax—what is the "cost" of pollution, and how is the tax to be levied, assessed, and collected? These would seem to be rather fundamental accounting issues. The Kneese reading (which follows) provides an example of an actual test of the pollution tax, with possible answers to these questions.

The great public outcry for the protection of the environment is unlikely to prove a transitory matter. The mounting flow of trash, the increasing pollution of the atmosphere, the growing level of noise will constitute unremitting irritants capable of maintaining political pressure that governments will be unable to ignore.

The issue is whether one can devise measures that will prove effective in protecting environmental quality and whether these are, in fact, likely to be adopted. This is of interest not only as a matter of general public welfare. It is important for those who are concerned with investments in pertinent economic activities—in pollution control devices, in noise abatement equipment, etc. It is obviously relevant also for the industries whose operations contribute to the basic problems.

William J. Baumol is Professor of Economics at Princeton University.

SOURCE: From Fourth Annual Report, Economic Policy Council and Office of Economic Policy, Department of the Treasury, State of New Jersey (May 1971), pp. 13-19.

This paper describes one of the proposals most widely advocated by economists for the control of pollution and other environmental problems. The proposal seeks to minimize the use of direct controls and to provide effective encouragement to industry to take appropriate remedial action. Its approach is the imposition of effluent charges in the most general sense—the taxation of activities that contribute to environmental problems and remission of taxes on activities that help to remedy them. The method claims for itself a number of advantages, not the least among them being efficiency (in terms of cost) in the achievement of whatever goals are adopted in the area. Moreover, the program in question has another considerable virtue. Unlike most other measures that have been advocated for the purpose, it need not add to the financial burdens of the state and local governments. Given the tremendous and growing financial pressures to which the public sector of our economy finds itself subjected, it is not implausible that methods of the sort discussed here will be employed ever more frequently by harassed governments under constant pressure to do something about the environment, but in no position to devote large quantities of money for the purpose. Already at the federal level there is a bill calling for a system of effluent charges to protect our waterways, and the President has advocated a tax on leaded gasolines. A number of states have just enacted related measures, and they are under consideration in many others.

Even where a new tax is under consideration primarily because of revenue needs, it is tempting to achieve two goals for the price of one—to increase the flow of revenues to the public treasury in a way that provides very powerful incentives for improvements in the quality of life. Once experience confirms the efficacy of these measures, their popularity seems very likely to increase.

ALTERNATIVE POLICY PROPOSALS

A variety of policies have so far been proposed for the protection of the environment. Clearly, any effective policy has to be flexible and must employ a variety of instruments. The bulk of the methods that have been proposed so far, however, are, *by themselves,* simply incapable of doing the job. In fact, one sees evidence that this is beginning to be realized by policy makers, many of whom are now turning to the methods that some economists have been advocating since 1911, long before the issue had become very fashionable.

The standard approaches consist, essentially, of three measures offered in varying dosages. The first of these is moral suasion; the appeal to the conscience of the businessman and the general public to adopt a new and finer code of virtue. The second is increased public investment. When something isn't working well the obvious solution seems always to call for the government to spend more money. In this case it is proposed to have the public sector build more disposal plants, clean up slag heaps, undertake the control of oil spills, etc. In effect, the government is asked to undertake a gigantic sanitation operation, cleaning up after the activities of industry. The third approach, which is perhaps the most popular of all, is outright prohibition by law.

THE APPEAL TO CONSCIENCE

Moral suasion has its limitations, not because businessmen are less moral than other people but because asking businessmen to bear the brunt of the task on a voluntary basis is a request to do the impossible. If the firm is to devote on a voluntary basis the huge resources that will be needed to deal with the environmental issues, it must undertake to spend the stockholder's money in a way the stockholder has not authorized. More important, it requires management to put its enterprise at a severe competitive disadvantage, perhaps thereby even undermining the viability of the firm.

GOVERNMENTAL OUTLAYS TO PROTECT THE ENVIRONMENT

The second of the popular proposals for the protection of the environment is the government expenditure approach. More will have to be spent on waste-treatment plants, and something will have to be done to clean up the enormous mess inherited from our predecessors and to which we still continue to contribute at most alarming rates. But we once again ask the impossible if we expect the government to cope in this way with, for example, the flow of garbage as it grows at its massive exponential rate. The fact is that waste-treatment plants are generally inadequate before they are completed, and sometimes even before they are planned. Man simply cannot cope with the problem unless, simultaneously, something is done to decelerate the flow of garbage that his society generates.

DIRECT CONTROLS

The third method of environmental control, direct prohibition, suffers from a variety of problems, many of which are, no doubt, brought to mind by the term *prohibition* itself. The effectiveness of such measures clearly depends upon the vigor of the enforcement mechanism. We have seen, for example, the workings of laws forbidding the use of incinerators in apartment houses under which landlords are occasionally subjected to token fines on something like a random basis.

They then simply continue to run their incinerators because it is far cheaper to pay the fines than to undertake alternative measures for waste disposal. Thus, the incinerators continue to emit their noxious fumes even though incineration has been prohibited absolutely and categorically.

Also, enforcement depends on policing, and this in turn offers all sorts of temptations and leads in too many cases to outright corruption.

Even in those cases where direct controls have made a difference, their effects are all too likely to prove transitory. In the first blush of public enthusiasm the severity of standards is increased and enforcement is relatively effective. However, several years later, when public attention has focused on other issues and the subject is no longer in the headlines, the strength of its enforcement mechanism ebbs. The regulatory agency then takes on the Characteristic lassitude that is most easily compatible with self-preservation and the avoidance of trouble.

Finally, direct controls suffer from a serious *economic* disadvantage. Even when they achieve their purpose—a reduction in the smoke content of the atmosphere or the noise level near an airport or in the number of substandard houses in a slum neighborhood—they are likely to do so in a manner that is highly inefficient, wasting the resources of society in the process.

Suppose that an agency has been directed, say, to cut by sixty per cent the total emission of certain pollutants into a river into which many plants are pouring industrial wastes. As a matter of fairness, if for no other reason, the regulatory agency is likely to assign a similar quota to each of the offending plants—to prohibit any plant from emitting more than forty per cent of its former flow per unit of time. Any other basis for the setting of quotas would seem discriminatory; yet a little thought shows that the procedure is apt to prove quite inefficient. Some of the plants, very likely those that are relatively new and adaptable, can decrease their efflux at very little cost to themselves. In others, the cost of reducing the outflow of pollutants by some given amount will be very high. Consequently, one would expect that the cost-minimizing assignment of reductions in pollution will normally not involve proportionate decreases in emissions. To minimize total costs a plant which can decrease its pollution outflow cheaply and easily might be asked to effect an eighty per cent reduction in its effluents, while another whose adaptation cost is high might be assigned only a twenty per cent reduction. And yet, as we have noted, an assignment of such uneven quotas is likely to be considered discriminatory, and is therefore likely to be unpalatable to a regulatory agency.

ENVIRONMENTAL PROBLEMS AND THE PRICE SYSTEM

Put very briefly and very superficially, many economists argue that the source of the environmental problem is the fact that the price system simply is not applied to many of society's resources. Its fresh air, its clean rivers, its good neighborhoods are resources that can be used up in the productive process just as coal, electricity, and steel are consumed. But while a price related to cost of production is charged for fuel and raw materials, the air and our other environmental resources can be used up without payment for the privilege. The economist is impressed by the efficiency with which the economy utilizes resources that are supplied under the rules of the price system. Industry uses its raw materials with a degree of care and efficiency that is perhaps unparalleled in economic history. Yet, at the same time, the air supply deteriorates progressively, the rivers are transformed into sewers, and the neighborhoods into slums. What has gone wrong?

Experience tells us what happens when costly resources are supplied free of charge.

TAX INCENTIVES FOR ENVIRONMENTAL PROTECTION

The proposal that the economist, consequently, makes is a very simple one. He maintains that there is no excuse for supplying expensive resources free. He says that those resources should be provided at an appropriate price just like the resources supplied by private industry. More specifically, he calls for a reorientation of the tax system, one that does not necessarily increase the overall burden of taxes. An example will, once again, help to clarify the issue.

Suppose it were decided that the oil industry were currently paying the right total amount in taxes, but that taxation were to be used to help get the lead out of its products. For this purpose one could reduce by, say, $0.03 a gallon the tax on unleaded gasoline and increase it by a similar amount on leaded gasolines. This is clearly not punitive. On the contrary, it gives the industry the opportunity to recoup its money by behavior consistent with social goals. Nor does this procedure constitute a drain on the public budget or a subsidy to industry. Given the efficiency with which private enterprise is able to proceed in the pursuit of profits I suspect the speed of the resulting changeover to lead-free fuels will truly be impressive. Similarly, in the neighborhood of airports much can be accomplished by a substantial differential in landing fees depending on the noise level and pollution emission level of the airplane. In the same way, the flow of trash can be reduced by imposing a significant tax on no-deposit-no-return containers, perhaps matched by a reduction in excise tax on items in returnable containers. Or, to give yet another illustration, there is much to be said for a reorientation of taxes on rental property which offers some material advantage to the improvement of buildings, and under which the landlord who pollutes his neighborhood by creating a slum—by failure to maintain his property or by abandoning his property outright—has to pay the cost that he imposes on society.

In each of these cases the basic notion is the same. By giving virtue its just (financial) reward the rules of the game are changed so that industry is induced to accomplish what society wishes of it.

Besides its obvious attractions, this approach has several additional virtues. In many cases, it is virtually self-enforcing. Its instrument is typically the meter rather than the police inspector. For example, the proposed tax on leaded gasoline requires no more than a record of how much of each type of gasoline has been sold, and the tax can be collected just as it is today. The emission of pollutants by a factory can also be metered and billed. There are no crimes to be discovered, no courtroom hearings, and no legal battles over level of fines. Enforcement is consequently not sporadic—it is continuous, predictable to the business planner and, consequently, effective. In this respect it differs markedly from the reality of outright prohibition.

The taxation approach to the protection of the environment also has the virtue of longevity. That is to say, because it is automatic, because it is self-enforcing, it will still be effective five, ten, and twenty years after it was enacted, when public interest in the subject has waned. A tax on smoke emission which is billed monthly will continue to exert its influence on managerial decisions indefinitely. Unlike a program dependent on the vigor or a regulatory agency, the tax incentive does not require continued enthusiasm for the cause. It can, thus, transform a transient public outcry into a permanent influence that affects significantly the behavior of the economy.

The tax approach, at least in principle, achieves its reductions in effluents in noise, and in smoke in a manner that minimizes the total cost of the changeover. Without assigning quotas to anyone, or interfering in the operations of the individual enterprise, it provides the incentives for each firm to make those decisions which in the aggregate will make the cost of pollution control as low as possible.

To illustrate consider the earlier case where it had been decided to reduce the total influx of pollutants into a river by sixty per cent. Suppose that instead of assigning a quota to each company with a plant on the river, a tax on the discharge of wastes is imposed, a tax sufficiently high to achieve the desired reduction in the pollution content of the river. The firm for which it is very cheap to reduce emissions will find it profitable to cut down on its effluents substantially because, for it, the installation of the required equipment will be less costly than the taxes. On the other hand, the firm for which such a changeover is very expensive will find it cheaper to pay the tax than to undertake a substantial conversion. The first firm may then find it most profitable to cut its discharges by eight or ninety per cent, while the second company may end up with no more than a ten or a twenty per cent reduction. Thus, the difficult task of assigning emission quotas to the various plants in accord with the requirements of efficiency is taken care of automatically by the tax incentive approach. It does so without direct interference in the decision processes of the individual firm and without recourse to direct controls.

CONCLUSIONS

In sum, the tax reorientation approach offers a variety of attractive features. It is equitable—it charges only those who engage in the activities that threaten the environment and bases the charges on the extent of the taxpayer's contribution to the environmental problems; it is automatic and self-enforcing; it minimizes the need for enforcement machinery and the temptations for corruption; it does not increase the financial problems of state and local governments; it is effective and makes full use of the productive efficiency of the free enterprise system; its effects are long lived, and it promises to achieve its goals at minimum overall cost to the economy.

Society has been giving away, free, too many of its precious resources for too long. It is not as scandalous as it sounds to decide that everything has its price. The real scandal lies in setting that price at zero or at some token level that invites us all to destroy and to despoil. Unless we recognize the legitimate role of taxation in this area, we may end up with our sense of morality intact but our environment in ruins.

Water Quality Management by Regional Authorities in the Ruhr Area

Allen V. Kneese

In the previous article, Baumol provided the theoretical rationale for a pollution tax. In this paper, Kneese describes the operation of an existant pollution tax system, that of the Ruhr Valley. In particular, the paper emphasizes the technical problems of cost determination and measurement that are fundamental to the accountant's role in such a system.

It is interesting to contemplate whether such a system could be applied to any of the major river systems in the United States. Would the heavy dependency of states bordering the river systems on tax revenues from polluters, and the frequent competition between states for industrial locations permit the operation of this, or a similar tax system? Could a federal pollution tax be levied if it affected only polluters on certain river systems?

PART I—BACKGROUND AND CONCEPTS

Water quality management is coming to dominate the problem of planning for development and use of water resources in many parts of the United States. Moreover, it has become widely recognized that water quality is a problem which, in most respects, can be best analyzed and dealt with on a regional basis. This is seen in the creation of the Delaware River Basin Commission, one major function of which will be the management of water quality, the United States Public Health Service Comprehensive Planning Studies for the various river basins and the establishment of numerous watershed and metropolitan authorities.

The recent report of the Senate Select Committee on National Water Resources helps give perspective to the possible magnitude of the water quality management task in the various water resource regions. Indeed it replaces the prevalent image of quantitative shortage on a nationwide scale with the conclusion that in most areas water supply is more than sufficient to meet the various projected uses which man will make of concentrated supplies. But it also concludes that presently dependable supplies are generally far from adequate to provide dilutions or projected future municipal and industrial waste discharge. Based on its analysis, the

Allen V. Kneese is an economist on the staff of Resources for the Future.

SOURCE: From *Papers and Proceedings of the Regional Science Association* Vol. II (1963), pp. 109-129.

committee concluded that maintaining comparatively clean streams in the various regions might require a national investment of an additional $100 billion by 2000 A.D. This is indeed a huge sum. By contrast the cost of completing the Bureau of Reclamation program of multi-purpose western water resources development is estimated at a mere $4 billion after 1954.

The estimates of the committee cannot be viewed as more than broad indicators of the potential magnitude of various aspects of water supply problems. *They do suggest, however, that achieving fairly clean streams throughout the United States, in view of expected future economic-demographic development, will involve public investment far higher than in any other field of resources development or conservation.*

Despite the fact that some institutions have been created whose major or primary function is to plan for optimum water quality management on a regional basis, there is as yet little institutional, economic or engineering scientific analysis aimed explicitly at the problems of regional water quality management in the watersheds and river basins of the United States.

For example, questions concerning the appropriate spatial jurisdiction and appropriate powers of an authority responsible for water quality in a region have hardly been addressed. There are many such questions. For example, should a single authority be made responsible for the water resources of a small watershed, a river basin or a whole system of river basins? If there are different authorities, what coordinating devices are available? Should authorities only make general framework plans or should they be directly responsible for their execution by (say) constructing and operating facilities (dams, treatment plants, etc.)? How should the obvious interdependencies between land use patterns (especially industrial and municipal location decisions) and water quality problems be handled? Where land use planning is undertaken should it be under the same authority as water resources? If not, what functional division of powers is appropriate? What information should the authorities provide each other? What incentive or disincentive devices should they have available to see to it that social costs which occur in their area of responsibility are reflected in decisions of fiscally independent decision makers?

In light of increasingly pressing questions of this kind, it is useful to examine the experience of an area where these problems have long been confronted and regional institutions have been developed for dealing with them. The area in question is the Ruhr industrial area of West Germany. Indeed, the Ruhr with its extremely concentrated economic and demographic development and with the extraordinarily heavy burden which its urban-industrial area-society puts on water resources, reflects the type of situation numerous areas in the United States are just beginning to face.

The aim of this paper is to provide a brief review and assessment of the regional quality management activities of the water authorities in the Ruhr area. Special emphasis is placed upon the methods used to articulate the system planning and operation activities directly under their control, with often equally important decisions impinging upon water quality but under the control of other private and public or semipublic decision makers. It will be seen that the cost assessment and distribution methods used have played a prominent role in this regard.

Before undertaking a discussion of water quality planning in the Ruhr area, I would like to make a few generalizations concerning the economics of resource allocation especially pertinent to water quality management. This will provide a setting for the subsequent discussion. Economists will readily understand that unrestricted waste disposal into "common" water courses produced technological external diseconomies. Since putting wastes into water courses gives rise to costs which occur primarily "offsite," the cost and production structure tends to be distorted. There is no inducement to undertake waste water treatment, and other abatement measures, materials recovery, process adjustments and other measures to reduce waste loads generated are not implemented to an optimum degree. The effectiveness of process engineering and materials recovery processes in reducing waste loads has been richly demonstrated by various instances in this country and perhaps even more strikingly in the Ruhr area. Moreover, industry accounts for over two thirds of the organic waste load in the United States and a far higher proportion of most other pollutants. This emphasizes the importance of regional water resources authorities providing the appropriate incentives for reduction of industrial waste loads by in some fashion causing off-site costs to be reflected in waste generation and disposal decision.

Indeed the traditional tax subsidy solution of welfare economics to externality problems of this kind lays exclusive emphasis upon the incentives provided by means of a redistribution of opportunity costs. I have elsewhere reviewed the circumstances under which this suggested solution might work in practice and some approaches to the complex measurement and computational problems that are encountered, including such matters as difficult to value as damages, interrelationships between wastes, hydrological variability, etc. The general principle is, however, that an effluent charge equal to downstream damages (resulting from increased water supply treatment and value of physical damages) would be imposed on the decision unit responsible for the outfall. The decision unit would then take measures to reduce its waste discharge by an optimum combination of measures—process and product adjustments, waste treatment and perhaps others, until the marginal cost of an additional unit of abatement equals the marginal cost of damages imposed in the affected region. At this point the cost associated with the disposal of wastes in the region would be minimized. Several things may be noted (without elaboration here) about this solution with a view to the literature on external diseconomies: 1. Since "water flowth whither it listeth," the reciprocal effects which have recently come under discussion and which may destroy the possibility of achieving approximately optimum results via the charges or taxes route are not involved, at least in the case of streams. Pollution damage is essentially a serial phenomenon. 2. In order to obtain an efficient (cost minimizing) solution, the damaged parties need not be compensated. If the charge levied upon the waste discharger produces optimal water quality in the stream, the water users will be induced to adapt optimally to it. (This result may not be considered equitable but this paper offers no criteria or equity.) 3. Solely from the viewpoint of efficiency, the desired (cost minimizing) result can be achieved with a subsidy (for reducing effluent) based on damages. The subsidy must be paid to the waste dischargers since, for the reason indicated in (1), only they control the water quality available to downstream users. The significant thing is that the upstream waste discharger must view downstream costs as opportunity costs. The present discussion will, however, proceed in terms of effluent charges. 4. Effluent charges have not been used on a regional basis in this country. In some instances effluent "standards" have been proposed and used. Charges appear to have certain advantages over standards which cannot be examined here. Both, however, can be viewed as devices for redistributing opportunity costs with attendant effects on treatment, process and product adjustments, and industrial location decisions. 5. If there are economies of scale in abatement measures, which cannot be realized by individual waste dischargers, the "classical" tax approach (or analogous procedures) cannot achieve an optimal solution.

The last point requires some additional comment since it is basic to further discussion of the work of the German water authorities. When economies of scale exist in abatement measures "system design" arises as a problem confronting a regional authority, in addition to seeing to it that opportunity costs are distributed in such a way as to induce efficient behavior. This is true, for example, when economies of large scale exist in waste treatment which permit wastes from diverse sources to be brought together for collective treatment, or where measures such as augmentation of low steam-flows by reservoir releases or artificial reaeration of streams are efficient alternatives or supplements to treatment over certain ranges, or where the entire flow of a stream can be advantageously treated. In other words, the problem of system design presents itself when economical abatement measures exist which cannot be undertaken by individual polluters.

In virtually all highly developed regions efficient ways of controlling pollution will be available, the use of which cannot be induced by levying the net offsite costs of their waste disposal on the waste disposers. It is to such regions that the present paper is especially relevant.

In these areas a social cost-minimizing solution will demand planning of the system by an organization which can comprehend the significant large-scale alternatives and supervise their operation. Such an organization is thus confronted with a set of problems. These include designing the system, operating some elements of it and making charges (or using other devices) to induce efficient use of alternatives, the construction and operation of which it does not control directly. The latter would ordinarily, and probably should, include *at least* process and production adjustments by manufacturers' pretreatment of wastes, and decisions with respect to specific locations of industries.

If the objective of a regional authority is to minimize the sum of the costs associated with waste disposal in the region, the economic design criterion would be to equalize the costs of all alternatives *including the costs of pollution damages* at the margin. This would be accomplished by a combination of direct construction and operation of abatement measures and by effluent standards or charges. The latter can be shown to lead to more efficient industry responses than arbitrarily selected standards, and are especially advantageous in inducing adjustment to shortrun changes in social cost. The abatement facilities actually constructed and operated by the authority must take into account the response of the waste load generated to the system of charges. The optimal mix between measures planned and executed by the regional authority and those induced on the part of other decision makers will of course depend upon the degree to which economies of collective measures can be realized. This in turn will largely depend upon the extent of development of the basin.

One of a number of difficulties in actually designing and operating a system which minimizes costs is that certain values diminished or destroyed by water pollution are exceedingly difficult to measure. Prominent among these are the value of aesthetic and recreational amenities. Where these values are not actually quantified, specific judgments concerning their physical requirements or standards can be made. In a formal sense they can be considered constraints on the objective (which we have taken to be the minimization of costs associated with waste disposal). For example, costs may be minimized provided that dissolved oxygen does not fall below four parts per million (ppm) in the stream (a generally accepted minimum level for fish life). There are various formal methods by which such constrained optimum problems can be solved. In general, the economic criteria for an optimum with such constraints are analogous to those indicated earlier (i.e. the equalization of marginal costs in all directions). In other words, the optimum system is not attained until a situation is reached in which it is impossible to make marginal "tradeoffs" (say, between waste treatment and pollution damages) which lower costs without violating the constraints. The marginal costs affected by the constraint (say, waste dilution) now, however, have a shadow price which derives from the limited supply of the constrained input (say, dissolved oxygen).

These general points have been made not to imply that *precisely* optimum (given the objective) regional water quality management systems are possible or even desirable goals but to provide a conceptual framework for discussion of the German experience.

PART II—THE GENOSSENSCHAFTEN

There are seven large water resources Cooperative Associations called Genossenschaften in the highly industralized and heavily populated area generally known as the Ruhr. These organizations were created by special legislation in the period from 1904 to 1958.[1] There are thousands of water Genossenschaften in Germany, most of them created for special purposes such as the drainage or flood protection of specific plots of land. The large Genossenschaften in the Ruhr region were given almost complete multipurpose authority over water quantity and quality in entire watersheds by their special laws. These organizations are henceforth referred to simply as *the Genossenschaften*. They have for up to fifty years made comprehensive plans for waste disposal, water supply, flood control and land drainage (a problem of great significance in the coal mining areas). The Genossenschaften are comparable to cooperatives (in the Anglo-American sense) but with voting power distributed in accordance with the size of the contribution made to the associations' expenditures and with compulsory membership. Members of the associations are principally the municipal and rural administrative districts, coal mines and industrial enterprises.

General public supervision over the Genossenschaften is in the hands of the Ministry of Food, Agriculture and Forestry, of the state of North-Rhine Westphalia. The Ministry's supervision is, however, almost completely limited to seeing that the associations comply with the provisions of their constitutions.

The Genossenschaften have the authority to plan and construct facilities for water resources management and to assess their members with the cost of constructing and operating such facilities. A process of appeal (internal appeal to special boards and final appeal to the federal administrative courts) is available to the individual members.

Statutes creating the Genossenschaften are limited to a few brief pages. Accordingly, the goals and responsibilities of these organizations are set forth in highly general terms. This has left the staffs and the members free to adapt to changing conditions and to develop procedures and concepts in line with experience. Perhaps one general provision of the statutes, the meaning of which has developed greater and greater specificity in the course of time, has proved most central to successful and efficient operation. This provision specifies that the costs of constructing and operating the system are to be paid for by those members whose activities make it necessary and by those who benefit from it. Comparatively elaborate procedures for fulfilling this directive have been developed in regard to the costs of land drainage, waste disposal and water supply. In the course of time these procedures have come to be accepted not only as rational and equitable but have played an important role in the efficient operation of the system.

The area of the Genossenschaften contains notable cities such as Essen, Bochum, Muelheim, Dortmund, Duisburg and Gelsenkirchen and is one of the most concentrated industrial areas in the entire world—containing some forty per cent of German industrial capacity. The industrial complex consists heavily of coal mining, iron and steel, steel fabrication, and heavy chemicals. By far the dominant industries are coal, coke, iron and steel. Between eighty and ninety per cent of total German production in these industries is in the Ruhr area. There are some eight million residents in the region, which contains about 4,300 square miles of land area—roughly one-half the size of the Potomac River watershed in the U. S.

Water resources are extremely limited if one excludes the Rhine River (to which the Ruhr area streams are tributaries). The Rhine has a mean flow roughly comparable to that of the Ohio but is drawn upon to supply water to the Ruhr area only during periods of extreme low flow. There are two reasons for this. First, the Rhine itself is of very poor quality where the Ruhr enters it, and secondly, the water from the Rhine must be *lifted* into the industrial area. With present installations, it is possible to "back-pump" the Ruhr as far up as Essen by means of pump stations installed in dams creating a series of shallow reservoirs in the Ruhr. Back pumping was carried on during the extreme drought of 1959. A large new reservoir for the augmentation of low flows which is nearing completion on a tributary of the Ruhr will even further reduce the already modest dependence of the area on the use of Rhine water.

The Ruhr area has been dependent upon the waste-carriage capacity of the Rhine to a much more far-reaching extent than for water supply. A large proportion of the wastes discharged from the industrial region into the Rhine receives comparatively little treatment. However, the construction of a large new biological treatment plant on the Emscher (a highly specialized stream described in more detail subsequently), will mean that virtually all effluents reaching the Rhine are given far-reaching treatment and the contribution of this area to the pollution of the Rhine will be comparatively modest.[2]

Five small rivers constitute the water supply and water-borne waste carriage and assimilative capacity of the industrial area proper. In descending order of size, these are the Ruhr, Lippe, Wupper, Emscher and the Niers. The *annual* average low flow of all these rivers combined is less than one third of the *low flow of record* on the Delaware River near Trenton, New Jersey, or one half of the *low flow of record* on the Potomac River near Washington, D. C.

The three rivers serving the main industrial area—the Ruhr, the Lippe and the Emscher—run roughly parallel. The Ruhr and the Wupper Rivers are mountain streams suitable for damsites and both have some developed storage with more under development and/or planned. An indication of the amazing load which these rivers carry is the fact that in the Ruhr, which is heavily used for household and industrial water supply and which in general serves these uses well, at annual low water flow, the volume of river flow is only about 0.8 as large as the volume of wastes discharged into the river. A frequently used rule of thumb is that in order for a river to be generally suitable for reuse, each unit of waste discharge must be diluted by at least eight parts of river water.

How was such an extensive industrial complex successfully built upon a comparatively minute water supply base with considerable attention to the recreational and aesthetic amenity of water resources and at relatively modest cost?[3] Broadly the answer lies in the design and operation *of a generally efficient system,* which because of the regional purview of the Genossenschaften, and the dense development of the area, *can make far-reaching use of collective abatement measures and stream specialization.* Moreover, so-called indirect measures (waste reclamation, process engineering and influence on the selection of industrial sites) play a large role in controlling the generation of industrial wastes and the expense of dealing with them.

In the present discussion references to the Genossenschaften may be taken to mean either the Ruhrverband-Ruhrtalsperrenverein (RV-RTV) or the Emschergenossenschaft-Lippeverband (EG-LV) unless a specific organization is indicated. While the EG-LV and the RV-RTV are nominally four organizations, the two linked pairs are each under a single management. These are by far the largest Genossenschaften with both the most complex physical water resource systems and the most sophisticated methods of assessing costs.

The regional system of waste disposal which these organizations have established is very interesting. However, time permits only a few general comments to be made about it here. While the process of design was done with little or no explicit attention for formal optimizing procedures, the systems are designed and operated with the explicit objective of minimizing the costs of attaining certain standards in the rivers. Moreover, there is explicit recognition of the equimarginal principle in the planning procedures. Perhaps most important, the Genossenschaften provide an institution which permits a wide range of relevant alternatives to be examined systematically within a functionally meaningful planning area. However, it is also recognized that in some instances efficient solutions require a super-regional view. This is illustrated by the recent German law forbidding the sale of "hard" detergents after October 1964. Scientific investigation and cost assessment of alternatives leading to this legislation were primarily carried out in the laboratories of the Genossenschaften.

In the Ruhr itself the objective of the system generally is to maintain water quality suitable for recreation[4] and municipal-industrial water supply. In the Lippe the objective is much the same. The Emscher, by far the smallest of the three streams, is used exclusively for waste dilution, degradation, and transport.

The Emscher has thus been converted to a single-purpose stream, and is sometimes referred to as the *cloaca maxima* of the Ruhr area. It is fully lined with concrete, and the only quality objective with respect to it is the avoidance of aesthetic nuisance. This is sufficiently accomplished by primary or, as the Germans say, mechanical treatment of effluents which largely removes materials in suspension. Since the Emscher cannot be used for purposes other than effluent discharge,[5] the area is dependent upon adjoining watersheds for water supply and waterbased recreation opportunities. The feasibility of this system is enhanced by the small size of the area and the fact that the streams are parallel and close together. Actually, as an aid to protecting the quality of the Ruhr, some of the wastes generated in the Ruhr basin are pumped over into the watershed of the Emscher. By the use of plantings, gentle curves of the canalized stream, attractive design of bridges, etc., care is taken to give the Emscher a pleasing appearance and to blend it gracefully into the surrounding countryside.

Near its mouth the entire dry weather flow of the Emscher up to about 1,000 cfs is given primary treatment thus realizing scale economies in treatment to a very far-reaching extent. The heavy burden put on the Rhine both from upstream sources and from the Ruhr industrial area (largely via the Emscher) has caused great downstream costs.[6] Consequently the Emschergenossenschaft is now laying detailed plans for biological treatment of the Emscher. As experimental plant indicates that this treatment will be highly successful. When the new plant is built, the contribution to Rhine river pollution on the part of the Ruhr industrial area will be substantially mitigated and the area will come quite near to being a closed water supply-waste water system.

While formal optimization procedures have not been utilized by the Genossenschaften, they probably have realized the major gains from viewing the waste disposal–water supply problem as one of a system character rather than solely as a matter of treating wastes at individual outfalls. They have made extensive use of scale economies in treatment by linking several towns and cities to a single treatment plant when the cost of transporting effluents to the plants were less than the saving due to additional scale economies that could be realized—in the case of the Emscher they have, in fact, linked an entire watershed to a single treatment plant. They have utilized opportunities for more effective treatment of wastes which accrue through combining industrial and household wastes. They have made use of stream specialization for recreational and water supply purposes, and artificial ground water recharge for quality improvement purposes. They have at various times and places used flow-augmentation, and direct aeration of streams. They have explicitly considered the differential ability of streams to degrade wastes at various locations (resulting from the opposing effects on oxygen balance of waste degradation and natural reaeration) both in determining location of treatment plants and in influencing the selection of industrial plant sites. Where scale economies, or special technical competence of Genossenschaft staff,[7] merited it, they have established their own waste recovery plants (phenols). They have, in other instances, induced waste recovery or process changes by levying charges for effluent discharge based on quantity and quality of waste water and by acting as a cooperative marketing agency for recovered waste products. While not always in a comprehensive manner, decisions between different alternative ways of achieving objectives have, at least in a rough and ready fashion, been based upon consideration of cost "tradeoffs" between them. Finally, and of considerable importance, they have provided for monitoring of the streams (especially those used for water supply) and operation of facilities to take account of changing conditions in a more or less continuous fashion.

Whether, in view of the value of recreation use, the conversion of the Emscher into an open sewer, or the very heavy use of waste degradation capacity on certain stretches of the Ruhr is optimal, cannot be determined because explicit valuations of recreation use have not been made. Actually, outdoor recreation is quite impressively catered to in the Ruhr area. This is probably due to the considerable power which the communities and counties exercise in both the water Genossenschaften and the Siedlungsverband (the latter is the agency responsible for land use planning in the Ruhr area and eighteen major cities are in its planning jurisdiction). Coordination of the work of the Siedlungsverband and the Genossenschaften is significant not only in producing an explicit weighing of recreational and aesthetic values against others in the development and use of water resources, but also in providing explicit consideration of industrial location (especially with respect to areas of compact industrial development) as a variable in water use and waste disposal planning. In other words, planning procedures which provide for cooperation between the staffs of the water and land use authorities make sure that a variety of costs and benefits involved in patterns of land use and water quality alteration are reflected in the planning process, even though neither takes a comprehensive view in all its details. Moreover, once a general pattern of development is laid out, the water authorities continue to influence more specific industrial location decisions as well as process engineering and waste recovery through their systems of charges.

PART III—COST ASSESSMENT PROCEDURES

It is of course clear that solely from the point of view of resource allocation, the method of pricing adopted, or indeed whether effluent charges are made at all, would be relatively unimportant if waste loads delivered to the system were unresponsive to the charges imposed on them. This would appear in general to be the case with respect to household effluents, since there is comparatively little households can do to diminish their waste loads. However, through product and process adjustments, through waste recovery, through separation of wastes and various forms of pretreatment, industrial waste loads can be altered over very wide ranges.

Numerous adjustments, especially in process design, are being made by the industrial plants in the Ruhr area as a consequence of the Genossenschaften's methods which force industry to bear at least a significant portion of the social costs of waste disposal. In general indirect methods of reducing wastes such as recovery and process changes are considered on a par with treatment in the work of the Genossenschaften. This is one of the reasons why the giant North-Rhine-Westphalian industrial complex can operate on a water base which is tiny by United States standards.

The vast variety and potentially large effect which recovery processes and process design can have on waste loads point to the important role which a correctly planned system for the assessment and distribution of costs may play in restricting to an optimum degree the amount of waste products which industrial society produces. This being the case, a closer look at the methods of cost assessment used by the Genossenschaften is in order.

PART IV—COST ASSESSMENT AND EFFLUENT CHARGES

A. Description

The question confronting both these organizations is how the diverse wastes produced by industrial enterprises can be assessed with an appropriate portion of costs.

Very briefly put, the Emschergenossenschaft procedure is roughly as follows: 1. There is estimated first an amount of water necessary to dilute a given amount of waste materials subject to sedimentation (no distinction is made between organic and inorganic material) in order that they not be destructive to fish life under the conditions of the area. An amount of dilution water required by such materials in a given effluent is then computed on that basis. 2. An analogous calculation made for materials subject to biochemical degradation (and which therefore exert an oxygen demand) but which are not subject to sedimentation. 3. The amount of dilution required under specified conditions in order that the toxic material in the effluent not kill fish is computed by direct experimentation. 4. Certain side calculations having to do with water depletion, heat in effluent, etc., are made. The derived dilution requirements are added together for the effluent and form a basis for comparison with all other effluents. In principle, costs are distributed in accordance with the proportion of aggregate dilution requirements accounted for by the specific effluent. One might say that this procedure is based on a particular physical objective, *i.e.* not to "kill fish." However, the result of the method is used as an "index" of pollution even when effluents are discharged to streams in which lower or higher standards prevail than needed to preserve fish life.

The Ruhrverband method is also based on a physical objective but on a different one. Again, the details are described elsewhere. In essence, however, the method is founded on the concept that toxic wastes by killing bacteria and slowing down the rate at which wastes are degraded have somewhat the same effect on treatment plant effluents and the level of BOD in streams as an *increase* in the amount of degradable material. On the basis of laboratory tests, an equivalence is formed so that toxic as well as degradable wastes are converted into a standard unit—a "population equivalent BOD."

These procedures can be criticized on technical as well as economic grounds. They are indeed recognized as less than ideal by the Genossenschaften but are generally defended as being readily understandable and relatively inexpensive to administer. Further development of cost assessment procedures along even more meaningful lines appears possible, however, especially in light of new technology which has recently become available or is now under development and which points to an easing of certain measurement problems.

Three areas will be briefly commented upon: 1. A formula for the assessment of costs based upon a physical objective will tend to lead to some misallocation of costs. 2. The procedure distributes average costs rather than assessing marginal costs. 3. Important economies might be achieved by an application of peak load pricing.

B.   Comments

1.   Deficiencies in the Use of Physical Objectives in Cost Distribution

The minimization of costs either in the limited sense of minimizing costs for given objectives or in the broader sense of minimizing the social costs associated with waste disposal, has been taken to be the general objective of a regional water quality control system. This objective logically implies that both the system design criteria and the cost distribution criteria must be based on *costs*, not directly upon *physical effects*. Thus in the matter of system design it is *costs* which must be balanced at the margin.

Similarly, in the matter of cost distribution, a procedure based upon physical results alone (as are the Emschergenossenschaft and the Ruhrverband procedures) will, in principle, not allocate costs properly. For example, a substance may be very destructive to fish (and thus merit a high weight in the Emschergenossenshaft's method) but be relatively inexpensive to treat or to deal with by other means. In this instance a disproportion between the costs of dealing with waste substances and costs allocated to those producing them will arise. This would be true even if the sole objective of the system were to avoid killing fish.

In the broader context of multipurpose water use a practical illustration of substances which are not handled at all adequately by either method is the phenols. Phenols are produced in the distillation of petroleum and coal products. In low concentrations (a few parts per million) they do not exert much oxygen demand nor are they very toxic to fish. But even in the smallest concentrations they pose the most serious problems in the preparation of drinking water. When water containing minute amounts of phenols is chlorinated in order to kill bacteria, extremely evil tasting chlorophenols are formed.

Phenolic substances present a problem in all the world's great industrial complexes. The recommended limit for phenols in the latest revisions of the United

States Public Health Service recommended drinking water standards is an infinitesimal 0.001 mg/1. Unless water supplies drawn from surface sources are to be very unpalatable, phenols must be kept out of waste water or else removed at great expense by the application of activated carbon at the water plant. Moreover, very small amounts of phenols in streams can impart an unpleasant "carbolic" taste to fish which may as effectively destroy their value as though they were actually killed. If a stream standard is imposed (say, instead of attempting to balance the cost of damages and abatement at the margin), this may mean farreaching treatment or recovery processes are necessary for the phenol containing effluents. Clearly the cost of those procedures and/or damages is not reflected in the allocation procedures used by the Genossenschaften. This follows because in one instance the implied objective of the cost allocation procedure is not to kill fish and in the other not to kill bacteria.

Where substances do involve a large disproportion between the costs they impose on the system and the costs allocated to them by the methods, side calculations are generally made to take this aspect into account. The basic point, however, is that the cost assessment procedure is not fully consistent with the design objective.

2. The Appropriate Concept of Costs

As earlier indicated, in principle, charges made for effluent discharge should equal full opportunity costs including increased water supply costs and foregone productive opportunities downstream. If there is no separate system design problem, imposition of these costs on waste discharges would tend to produce an allocation of resources which maximizes social product.

If scale economies introduce a separate problem of system design, levying only the (appropriately defined) costs of a correctly designed system would tend to accomplish the resource-allocation objective. The appropriate process, product and location adjustments would be induced even though the costs of residual damages (which most probably would exist in an optimum system) are not specifically imposed on, the waste discharger. This remains true even if the objective is to accomplish minimum cost of achieving certain standards. Consequently, basing the charges on costs actually incurred by the system as the Genossenschaften do, is not *per se* incorrect.

A number of different possibilities exist with respect to the elements of a system which are directly constructed and operated by a regional authority and those left in the hands of fiscally independent decision makers. However, in general a charge set equal to marginal cost, at their optimum level of utilization, of those abatement measures directly undertaken by the authority will be appropriate.[8] (In essence each discharger is subjected to a "last added" test). This is because the marginal costs of induced measures will tend to be equated with the charge per unit of waste discharge and consequently with the marginal cost of other alternatives.

It is clear, however, that the Genossenschaften distribute average costs to the dischargers, not marginal costs. Thus, if the system displays declining costs the charges as levied will generally be too high, whereas if increasing costs are incurred, the opposite will generally be the case. The efficiency argument against average cost pricing in this context is that it will not induce appropriate use of measures controlled by fiscally independent decision makers.

3.   Cost Variation Over Time

For purposes of planning, costs properly include all capital costs of new facilities. The system of abatement (ideally) should be expanded to the point where an additional unit of abatement (optimal combination of measures) for any given pollutant, or combination of pollutants, raises the expected present value of total abatement costs as much as it diminishes the expected present value of pollution damages. Or if there is a constraint, or a standard, until the constraint is met and the expected present value of marginal total cost of all alternative measures for achieving the constraint are equalized.

However, at any given time with an established abatement system, only current operating costs and opportunity costs internal to a multipurpose system are relevant. These systems costs tend to vary strongly over time due to hydrological variability. This is true whether the objective is to equate marginal abatement costs and marginal damage costs or to minimize the costs of meeting a standard. This suggests the possible desirability of attempting to base prices on a rather short-run variation in costs.

The cost distribution methods of the Genossenschaften fail to take account of the fact that waste disposal costs (in the broad sense) are highly variable through time. As already mentioned, this variability results from the fact that the dilution and degradation capacities of streams show strong variation over time. For example, the long-term average discharge of the Delaware River at Trenton, New Jersey, is about 12,000 cfs, the mean annual flow is roughly ¼ that and the low flow of record about 1/10 of the average flow. The average flow of the Ruhr is about 2,600 cfs and the average annual low water flow is only about 140 cfs. If the costs of waste discharge to the polluter do not vary in accordance with flow, there is no incentive to reduce discharges during low flow periods, even though the concentration of pollutants, attendant damages and the costs of optimally operating abatement works tend to rise sharply during low stream stages.[9]

If it were clearly uneconomical to change the amount and/or quality of waste discharge over short periods of time, it might not be a matter of great concern whether or not costs levied upon polluters varied correspondingly over time. However, it appears probable that measures to change the pattern of discharge would enter economically into a quality control system designed to minimize costs.

For example, depending upon the location of a manufacturing concern and upon attendant land values, it may be less expensive for the company to withhold its waste discharge temporarily in a lagoon rather than bear its share of the costs of storing and, at long intervals, releasing a much larger volume of river water. In some instances, especially where the product is storable, it may be more economical to reduce or halt production during low flow periods rather than to provide additional treatment or dilution capacity for an unchanged effluent. In other instances it may pay the manufacturer to provide temporary treatment (like chemical neutralization of acids) rather than meet the full costs of putting his effluents into the receiving water during low flow periods. In the light of such possibilities, incentives should be provided to use them to an optimal degree.

The method of peak pricing has been extensively carried out by electrical utilities, hotels, resorts and theaters, among others. It regards the service performed (in this case pollution abatement) as different according to the heaviness of the load on the system. In the case of electrical utilities, this necessitates a price varying by time of day and the season. In the case of pollution probably no more than seasonal variations could be justified.

In assessing the merits of applying "peak load" pricing principles to effluent discharges, the costs of determining variation in the quality and quantity of effluent over the relevant period must of course be considered. Presently, the Genossenschaften generally establish by sampling an effluent quality which is taken to be typical for the year. The quantity effluent discharged during the year is ordinarily based upon measurements reported by the plant.

The costs of operating analysis sampling programs along present lines would mount sharply if an effort were made to determine quality and quantity variation with sufficient continuity to permit peak load pricing. Fortunately in recent years progress has been made in the development of automatic monitoring devices. Such variables of river quality as dissolved oxygen, acidity-alkalinity, salinity, specific conductance (dissolved solids), temperature and turbidity can be continuously measured with fairly simple devices. Some measurements are already successfully carried out on effluents and there is considerable promise that others can be developed. Optimism appears justified that accurate and comparatively simple devices for continuous measurement of a wide variety of water quality characteristics can be worked out.

In some instances an occasional rather thorough laboratory test may have to be done in order to establish relations which will permit the use of certain continuously measurable characteristics as surrogates for those which can only be measured with difficulty. For example, if fish toxicity is an important variable (as it is for example in the Emschergenossenschaft cost allocation method), a relation may be established between certain measurable substances in the effluent and fish skills; thus over specified periods of time this would permit the surrogate measurement to substitute for a direct toxicity test.

It is probably not excessively visionary to foresee a time when a number of important quality characteristics can be continuously recorded, at a central point, for every major outfall in an entire basin at comparatively modest cost.

NOTES

1. All of the Genossenschaften with one exception were established before 1930. The Erftverband (Verband and Genossenschaft are used interchangeably in this context) was created in 1958 primarily to deal with problems resulting from a massive pumping down of ground water tables by the coal industry in the area of Erft river, west of the Rhine.

2. Except for saline pollution from the coal mines in the area. The Lippe carries considerable natural salinity and additional saline water is pumped up from the mines. Another major source of salinity in the Rhine is the potash industry, particularly in France. Effective arrangements for reducing salinity have not yet been made.

3. Despite rather impressive attention to amenities and recreation, the combined expenditure of the Genossenschaften (which build and operate all water treatment plants, dams, pump stations, etc.) amounts to about sixty million dollars a year (exclusive of capital investments), somewhat over half of which is for land drainage. The largest water works in the area (which is a profit-making enterprise and which contributes heavily to the costs of the facilities on the Ruhr) delivers water for household and industrial use at thirty cents per thousand gallons (official exchange rates used in making conversions).

4. However, the quality of the Ruhr varies considerably along the course of its flow. At the head of the Hengsteysee (a shallow reservoir in the Ruhr built essentially as an instream treatment plant) the quality of the water is very poor. Neutralization, precipitation and oxidation occur in the Hengsteysee, and further stabilization takes place in the Harkortsee, a similar instream oxidation lake. By the time the water reaches the Baldeneysee (a third such lake) the quality has improved to such an extent that the water is suitable for general recreational use. This is true despite the fact that there are further heavy discharges of treated wastes between the Hengsteysee and the Baldeneysee. These waste discharges are generally given far-reaching treatment, frequently by means of treatment plants which double biological stages (activated sludge and trickling filters).

5. One reason why such stream specialization may be advantageous is that the rate at which oxygen passes into the stream through the air-water interface is directly proportional to the size of the oxygen deficit (*i.e.* the amount by which actual dissolved oxygen (D.O.) falls below saturation level). Thus a stream in which dissolved oxygen is heavily drawn on has a much larger capacity to degrade organic wastes than a stream with sufficient dissolved oxygen to support fish life or provide drinking water.

6. Especially in Holland where even recently introduced large-scale ground water recharge projects are failing to supply suitable quality water.

7. Administrators of the Genossenschaften place great emphasis on the economies which result from a single staff planning, building, operating, and supervising the water resources facilities of an entire basin. The Ruhrverband operates eighty four effluent treatment plants (to which, on the average, four new ones are added each year), four large detention lakes, twenty seven pumpworks, 300 km of trunk-sewer, run-of-the-river power plants, six dams (one in addition is under construction), power plants associated with the dams, and their own electricity distribution systems with a total staff (including laborers, apprentices and janitorial help) of 780 persons.

8. If some action is taken by the authority for each pollutant.

9. Oxygen conditions are especially likely to deteriorate radically during such periods because high temperatures (which cause bacteriological activity to increase and the oxygen saturation level of water to decline) ordinarily correspond with low flows. The combination of high concentrates of toxins and low oxygen levels can easily be fatal to fish. If oxygen

levels are below several parts per million, oxygen deficiency itself will kill fish and if oxygen becomes exhausted extreme nuisance conditions accompany the development of anaerobic processes in a stream.

The concentrations of substances which alter Ph value of water, affect its hardness, create tastes and odors, cause dissolved solids content to rise—all tend to be higher during periods of low flow. This leads to rising municipal and industrial water supply treatment costs and a variety of pollution-caused damages to facilities and equipment. The point is that the social costs of pollution rise strongly during periods of low flow.

An authority controlling a going waste disposal system and attempting to operate it in such a way as to equate the relevant marginal costs would necessarily incur much greater costs of operation during low flow periods than during higher flows.

During the critical periods such measures as increased aeration in activated sludge plants and the addition of chemicals which aid precipitation in all types of treatment plants might be undertaken, leading to an increase in operating costs. During such periods artificial reaeration of streams may be done directly in the stream or through the turbines of hydro plants which in the first instance involves direct costs, and in the second, indirect costs because power plant efficiency is cut down. During low stream stages the augmentation of flow from reservoir storage offers the opportunity to increase waste dilution and if there are alternative uses for the stored water (say, peak power generators, or for recreation), an opportunity cost (internal to the water resources system) is incurred.

It is thus quite clear that costs are strongly related to time of discharge. In fact the social costs of a given quantity of a pollutant discharged at one time may easily be a multiple of those at another. Indeed, during periods of high stream flow waste disposal into the stream is likely to be virtually without downstream damages. During such periods the only justification for operating treatment plants at all may be to avoid the aesthetic nuisance of floating materials in the water.

Multiple Source Analysis of Air Pollution Abatement Strategies

Ellison S. Burton and William Sanjour

This paper illustrates how social cost can be reduced through the establishment of rigorous mathematical models. The authors stress that by using the least cost algorithm in their Washington study, they have shown further reduction of the air pollution abatement cost from the original proposal of $5 million to less than $50 thousand.

In addition, in the Kansas City study the lowest cost solution is shown as approximately $700 thousand lower than the present rate and produces less pollution. The law of diminishing returns is dramatically illustrated in Figure 5.

---

1. INTRODUCTION AND SUMMARY

In attacking the problem of air pollution, the Federal Air Quality Act of 1967 mandates a decentralized approach to abatement. State and local air pollution control agencies must develop abatement programs to achieve Federally-approved "air quality standards" for each pollutant posing a threat to people and property.

While abatement programs could be expected to contain detailed procedures for collecting information on the character of local pollution and to provide legal procedures for hearings, appeals, and penalties, at the heart of an abatement program is the requirement for specified source-by-source reduction in pollutant emissions. Who should abate, by how much, and who should pay for it will depend on the abatement philosophy or strategy of the control agency. For example, a strategy of issuing ordinances setting industry emission standards has legal, economic, and air quality implications which can be far different from a strategy banning the use of certain fuels in a region. Since there may be hundreds, or even thousands, of controllable sources of the more common pollutants in large urban areas, with several ways of controlling the emissions of each source, the choice of an abatement strategy for each pollutant requires careful study to ensure that the choice can produce the goals sought. Five factors in particular affect the feasibility of an abatement strategy:

Ellison Burton and William Sanjour are both with the Policy Analysis Division of the Environmental Protection Agency, Washington, D. C.

SOURCE: *The Federal Accountant,* Vol. XVIII, Number 1 (March 1969). Copyright by The Federal Government Accountants Association, pp. 48-69.

1. The phasing of mandated emission reductions
2. The source-by-source costs of emission control options and their economic burden on the sources required to reduce emissions
3. The effect of individual emission controls on local and regional air quality
4. The control agency resources required to enforce an abatement program
5. The political acceptability of the controls mandated.

While factor 5 cannot be quantitated to the extent of the other four, it is reasonable to assume that economic self-interest plays an important role in motivating acceptance or rejection of an abatement program.

This paper discusses an approach to air pollution abatement planning which can provide most of the detailed cost-effectiveness estimates needed to evaluate the five factors listed above for any quantifiable abatement strategy. The primary basis for evaluating a candidate strategy is the least-cost strategy for achieving stated air quality goals, defined in terms of emissions or concentrations of the pollutant of interest. The least-cost strategy permits the economic efficiency of a candidate strategy to be assessed. Some results of applying this approach to Kansas City, Kansas-Missouri and to Washington, D.C. are examined in terms of the five factors above.

2. ANALYTICAL APPROACH

The analytical approach developed uses interrelated computer programs, data files, and special techniques to simulate the source-by-source control of air pollution in a geographic area so that any number of prospective abatement strategies can be compared for cost and effectiveness.

There are four major parts to the approach:

Inputs
Abatement analysis
Meterological analysis
Final analysis.

In the following explanation of these parts below, refer to the Analytical Flow Diagram.

Inputs

There are four types of inputs:

1. Data on emission control alternatives for each pollutant considered: types, sizes, applicability, effectiveness, and capital and operating costs.
2. Data on the availability and cost of fuels in the geographic area under construction.

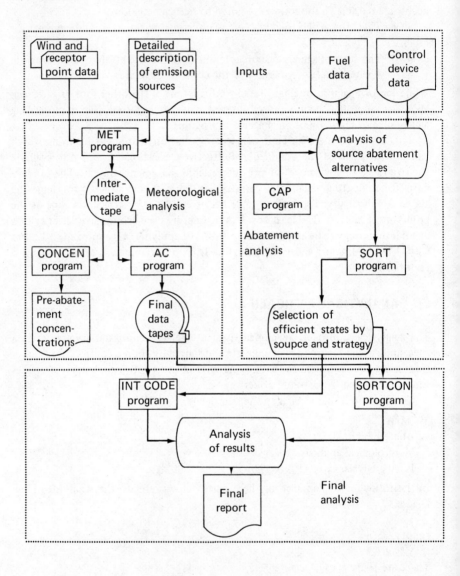

3.   A detailed emission inventory of the pollution sources in the geographic area, including coordinate grid location, emissions of all relevant pollutants, smoke stack height, number and types of furnaces, process description, existing control devices, rate of gaseous emission, hours of operation, and similar factors for each major source.

In addition, small emission sources can be aggregated by fuel use or activity class, such as coal users, oil users, open burning, gasoline vehicles, aircraft, etc.

4.   Receptor point grid locations and frequency distributions of wind vectors.

Abatement Analysis

Analyzing abatement alternatives usually comprises the major effort. Depending on the pollutants of interest, a comprehensive analysis may include not only stationary sources, but mobile sources as well. Abatement analysis begins with a listing of the emission control alternatives, such as fuel substitution and control devices, to be applied to a model of each source. Although some of the cost analysis is computerized in the CAP program, most of the analysis is manual because some peculiarity is usually involved in applying control alternatives to the specific source models. This part of the analysis results in estimates of the annual cost and the effectiveness of the emission control alternatives available to each source. These alternatives are usually broken down by several levels of control. For example, a coal-fired combustion source of particulate and sulfur dioxide might have the following breakdown of feasible emission controls, assuming the present coal is 2.5% sulfur by weight:

Control Alternative	Control Level
1. Substitute low sulfur coal (reduces SO_2 emissions)	1. 2% sulfur 2. 1.5% sulfur 3. 1.0% sulfur
2. Install precipitator (reduces particulate emissions)	1. Low efficiency 2. Medium efficiency 3. High efficiency
3. Switch to oil (reduces SO_2 and particulate)	1. 2% sulfur 2. 1.5% sulfur 3. 1.0% sulfur
4. Switch to natural gas (reduces SO_2 and particulate)	1. Interruptible (95% gas, 5% light oil) 2. Firm (100% gas)

In this example, while there are 11 discrete levels among the 4 alternatives, there are actually 17 distinct control combinations available because alternatives 1 and 2 can be used together. Listing all the possible combinations with their corresponding emissions and cost variances is done in the SORT program. The most efficient states are selected from the SORT output to be used in the final analysis.

Meteorological Analysis

The MET program is a computerized meteorological diffusion model developed by personnel of the Environmental Sciences Administration and the Public Health Service for determining the concentration of a pollutant at any arbitrary receptor point per unit emission from each source point. The output of the MET program can be used by the CONCEN program to determine pre-abatement concentrations at all receptor points. MET output can also be used in the AG program for totaling the pollution contribution of small sources by user type. For example, in the Washington, D. C. study 1,000 area sources were aggregated into twelve fuel use and activity classes, such as distillate oil burners, diesel trains, open burning, etc. These classes can then be treated in the same fashion as point sources in detailing control alternatives and states.

Final Analysis

In the SORTCON program, one emission control state is selected for each source in conformance with the abatement strategy being simulated. The program then computes the resulting concentrations and costs answer such questions as "What reduced emissions and concentrations of SO_2 result if all sources use fuels of no more than 1 per cent sulfur content by weight?" or "What would be the cost and effectiveness of having all power plants burn natural gas?"

The INTCODE program is a zero-one integer program which can answer maximization or minimization questions such as "What is the cheapest overall way to reduce pollution at every receptor point to at least 0.015 parts of sulfur dioxide per million parts of ambient air and seventy-five micrograms of particulate per cubic meter of air?" or "What is the greatest sulfur dioxide reduction that can be achieved at a cost of $10 million per year?" INTCODE allows an abatement problem to be bounded on many sides: least total cost to the community to meet a goal, most ambitious goal which can be achieved for a given total cost, most ambitious goal which can be achieved for any total cost, and so on. Sets of solutions can be computed for any combination of cost and emission constraints on individual sources and for a great variety of constraints on costs, emissions, and pollutant concentrations. The ability to compute the optimum abatement strategy under any set of constraints provides the basis for assessing the economic efficiency of any candidate strategy.

3.   SOME APPLIED RESULTS

The approach described has been applied to an analysis of some prospective strategies for abating sulfur dioxide and suspended particulate (airborne soot, flyash, and other respirable solid particles) in Kansas City, Kansas-Missouri, and Washington, D. C.[1] The discussion below concerns mainly the Kansas City analysis, but some comparison with Washington results is given.

Inputs

The Kansas City and Washington, D. C. studies came from agencies of the Federal, state, and local governments, manufacturers of emission control equipment, public utilities, process industries, trade associations fuel suppliers, consultants, and others. The U. S. Public Health Service in particular provided for study purposes detailed data on surveyed emission sources and all meteorological inputs.

Meteorological Analysis

Figure [1] depicts the estimated pollution levels of suspended particulates superimposed on a map of the Greater Kansas City area. The heavy contours are called iso-intensity lines and connect points of equal annual mean concentrations in micrograms per cubic meter ($\mu Gms/M^3$). These iso-intensity lines are based on the Public Health Service emission survey data mentioned which show over 59,000 tons of particulates emitted annually in the study area. The computerized meteorological diffusion model mentioned earlier translated the surveyed emissions into concentrations on the ground at selected receptor points on the basis of a wind rose of sixteen mean annual wind vectors. By adding up the concentrations contributed by all sources to each of the receptor points, the iso-intensity lines were interpolated. The estimated annual mean concentrations of suspended particulates range from less than 50 $\mu Gms/M^3$ to over 150 $\mu Gms/M^3$. Notice that several high concentrations correspond well to actual observations near those points. The highest predicted particulate concentration supported by actual observations is about 184 $\mu Gms/M^3$.

Figure [2] shows the estimated annual mean iso-intensity lines for sulfur oxides based on the same meteorological diffusion model. The concentrations here range from less than 0.015 parts per million (ppm) to over 0.045 ppm. A peak annual mean of 0.046 ppm was estimated by the model which corresponds well to observed data. The annual emissions of sulfur oxides in the area mount to over 124,000 tons.

Figure 1.

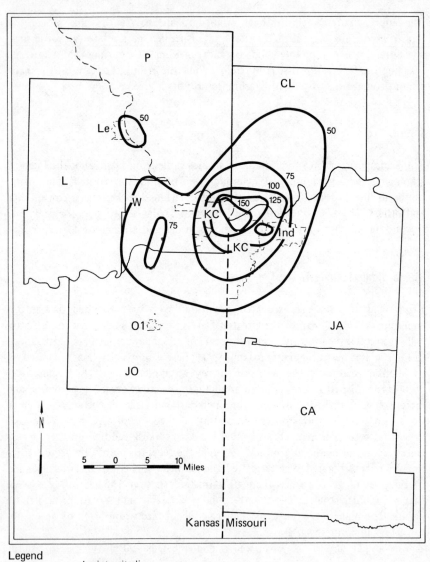

Legend

$\mu Gm/M^3$

Iso-intensity line
  micrograms per cubic meter
  (annual average)

Kansas City Study Area

CA	Cass County	L	Leavenworth County
CL	Clay County	Le	Leavenworth
Ind	Independence	Ol	Olathe
JA	Jackson County	P	Platte County
JO	Johnson County	W	Wyandotte County
KC	Kansas City		

Figure 2.

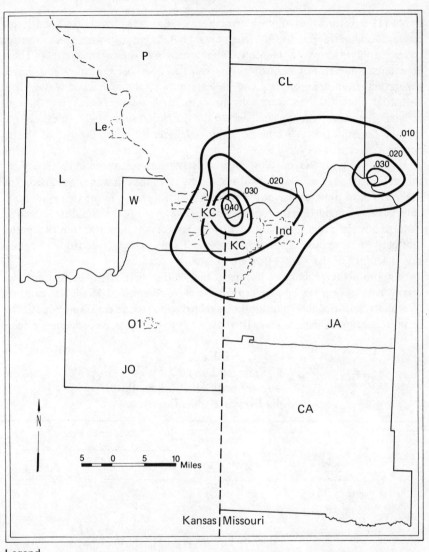

Legend

PPM — Iso-intensity line, parts per million (annual average)

Kansas City Study Area

CA	Cass County	L	Leavenworth County
CL	Clay County	Le	Leavenworth
Ind	Independence	Ol	Olathe
JA	Jackson County	P	Platte County
JO	Johnson County	W	Wyandotte County
KC	Kansas City		

Abatement Analysis

Table [1] lists the types of emission sources of suspended particulates and sulfur oxides found in the Kansas City study area. These aggregated sources account for the percentages shown of the total annual tonnages of the two pollutants. These emissions come from combustion of fossil fuels for space heating and power generation, from open burning and incineration of solid and liquid waste, from industrial processes, and from miscellaneous small sources. Stationary sources account for over eighty-six percent of the particulates and over ninety-six per cent of the sulfur oxides emitted in this area according to the Public Health Service emission survey.

Figure [3] gives the emission control alternatives postulated in this study for the stationary sources. Control of mobile source emissions was not studied. The fuel and hardware alternatives for emission control shown in the figure are available to major combustion sources presently using either coal or residual oil and to major industrial process sources. A major source emits over 100 tons of a pollutant per year. One hundred twenty-nine major sources were included in the emission inventory of the Kansas City study area.

Suppose a source is now burning a high sulfur coal, then the figure shows several paths which can be taken to achieve reduced emission levels. Substitution of a lower sulfur coal would result in reduced sulfur oxide emissions but in little or no reduction in particulates. To reduce the particulates, a mechanical device,

Table 1
Emission Sources of
Particulates (P) and Sulfur Oxides (SO$_x$)
in the Greater Kansas City Area

	% Total Emissions	
Source Type	P	SO$_x$
Power Plants	10.2	51.9
Process Industries	36.5	34.5
Waste Disposal	27.7	0.3
Aggregated Small Sources	25.6	13.3
	100.0	100.0
Total Annual Particulate Emissions:	59,000 tons	
Total Annual Sulfur Oxide Emissions:	124,000 tons	

Source: U.S. Public Health Service

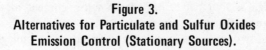

Figure 3.
Alternatives for Particulate and Sulfur Oxides
Emission Control (Stationary Sources).

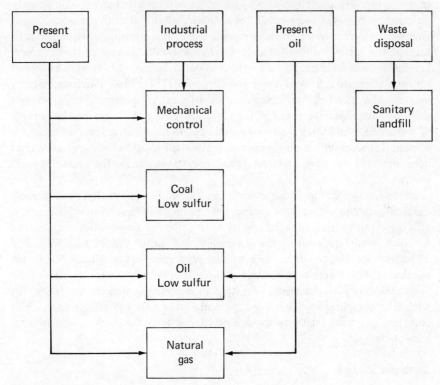

a multiple cyclone, could be installed. Another device, an electrostatic precipitator, could be added in series with the collector to increase particulate reduction to as much as 99.5 per cent of the uncontrolled emissions of a coal-fired source. Other alternatives were also postulated. For example, a possibility for one power plant in the Kansas City area is to retain the present high sulfur, high ash coal but to install a stack gas cleaning system. Another possibility is for a coal or residual oil user to switch to natural gas. Some alternatives were not considered, such as relocation of a source, switching to atomic energy, or building a high smoke stack. For the thousands of small fuel sources in the model, the only alternative stipulated was for coal users to substitute a coal with as low as one per cent sulfur by weight. No mechanical controls were allowed for small sources because of prohibitive costs. It was assumed that the sulfur content of the coal presently used ran as high as four per cent, and the sulfur content of the residual oil presently used as high as 2.5 per cent.

In reality, no two emission sources are identical, and seemingly small differences in physical plant can imply, for some control alternatives, significantly different problems of technical and economic feasibility. For this reason, control alternatives were selected to be compatible with the principal characteristics of each of the major sources listed in the Public Health Service emission survey. Present levels of emission control were considered. Ranges of cost were estimated for each alternative, broken down into cost per BTU for fuels, purchase, installation, maintenance and operating costs for mechanical equipment, boiler conversion costs for switching types of fuels, and the cost of terminating the burning of waste and substituting sanitary landfill operations. A fifteen-year depreciation of capital equipment has been assumed. An amount equal to the depreciation has been included to cover interest, insurance, taxes, and other miscellaneous charges.

Since fuels of different sulfur levels can be used in combination with an array of mechanical equipment, each component of which can have a different designed efficiency, there can be as many as fifty different possibilities which exist for each source to control the particulate and sulfur oxides emissions. For 129 major sources, therefore, an astronomical number of combinations exist for simulating the reduction of the two pollutants over the Kansas City study area. Some selectivity is obviously necessary in choosing abatement strategies, for while the computer may be able to calculate the cost and effectiveness of all combinations, only relatively few are of interest from the point of view of area-wide abatement.

Strategies Studied

The following abatement strategies were selected for analysis and comparison:

1.   Maximum control of particulate and sulfur oxides emissions
2.   Maximum control of particulate emissions alone
3.   Equi-proportional (EP) reductions of all major sources of particulate to at least twenty, forty, sixty, and eighty per cent of each source's uncontrolled emissions.
4.   Prohibit the use of fossil fuels of greater than two per cent sulfur content by weight.

The basis of comparison in each case is the least-cost combination of emission controls which achieves the same measure of effectiveness as the selected strategy. The primary measure of effectiveness computed for each strategy is the highest concentration of each of pollutants after application of the emission controls compatible with the strategy. A concomitant measure of effectiveness is the percentage reduction in total area-wide emissions of each of the pollutants. Thus, we are interested not only in how much the peak concentration of the mountain of pollution is reduced compared to the pre-abatement situation (Figures [1] [2]), but also how much the whole mountain of emissions is reduced.

The estimated annual cost of a strategy is defined as the annual capitalized purchase and installation cost of equipment plus the estimated annual maintenance and operating cost of emission controls to all the appropriate emission sources of a pollutant. Control agency costs to implement a strategy are not included in these estimates.

Because the maximum control strategy bounds the problems at the top, it is interesting to study a picture of its effect, at least for particulate, which is the pollutant of major concern in Kansas City.

It will be recalled from Figure [1] that the present maximum annual mean concentration of suspended particulates was estimated to be 184 μG ms/M^3. The maximum control strategy reduces the maximum concentration to 85 $\mu Gms/M^3$. Figure [4] shows the resulting iso-intensity lines. To achieve this, the total annual emissions of particulates are reduced sixty-nine percent from 59,000 tons to less than 19,000 tons. This strategy simultaneously reduces the peak sulfur oxides concentration sixty-nine per cent from 0.046 ppm to 0.015 ppm. The associated total annual emissions of sulfur oxides are reduced eighty-one per cent from 124,000 tons to less than 24,000 tons. The estimated least cost to achieve this maximum abatement strategy is $26,400,000 annually. As it happens, this is also the highest cost for any of the abatement strategies studied. Since there is only one way to achieve maximum emission control, other than closing everything down, the least-cost strategy and the maximum control strategy are the same. We shall see shortly, however, that in terms of air quality other least-cost strategies achieve approximately the same results at greatly reduced cost.

4. THE EFFICIENCY OF SELECTED STRATEGIES

For comparison purposes we have plotted in Figure [5] all of the principal strategies simulated in this study and a summary of their effectiveness.

The vertical axis is estimated annual cost in millions of dollars; the horizontal axis is the predicted maximum annual average concentration of suspended particulates at any point in the Kansas City study area. The topmost point in this figure locates the maximum control strategy already discussed. The bottommost point locates the lowest cost strategy. The lowest cost strategy results in an estimated total cost, reduction of over $700,000 from the base conditions but without changing the pollution values significantly. While this may be surprising, it is explained by the fact that based on present fuel costs some sources can apparently effect operating reductions by buying fuels which are cheaper than those now being used.

Figure 4.

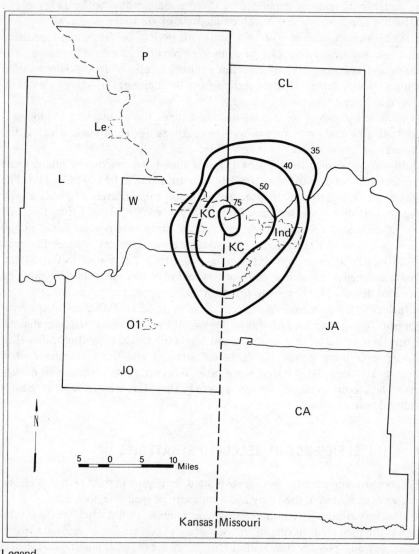

Legend

$\mu Gm/M^3$ Iso-intensity line,
microgram per cubic meter
(annual average)

Kansas City Study Area

CA	Cass County	L	Leavenworth County
CL	Clay County	Le	Leavenworth
Ind	Independence	Ol	Olathe
JA	Jackson County	P	Platte County
JO	Johnson County	W	Wyandotte County
KC	Kansas City		

Figure 5.
Comparison of Simulated Abatement Strategies
for Kansas City Study Area.

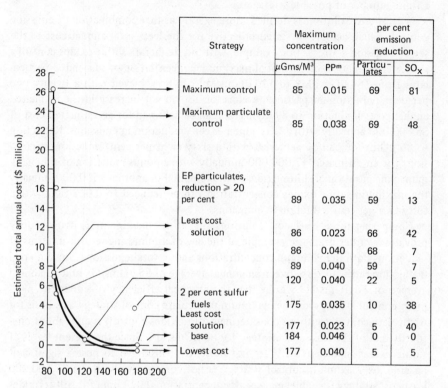

Strategy	Maximum concentration		per cent emission reduction	
	μGms/M³	PPm	Particu-lates	SOₓ
Maximum control	85	0.015	69	81
Maximum particulate control	85	0.038	69	48
EP particulates, reduction ⩾ 20 per cent	89	0.035	59	13
Least cost solution	86	0.023	66	42
	86	0.040	68	7
	89	0.040	59	7
	120	0.040	22	5
2 per cent sulfur fuels	175	0.035	10	38
Least cost solution base	177	0.023	5	40
	184	0.046	0	0
Lowest cost	177	0.040	5	5

Maximum concentration of suspended particulates (annual average, μGms/M³)

The individual controls comprising any simulated strategy represent only possibilities, not certainties, unless, of course, the means of control itself is mandated—an unlikely event. A number of factors may dictate against the actual implementation of any particular control action in practice. For example, because of cost-versus-savings trade-offs a fuel user may not elect to interrupt his operations while converting a boiler to take advantage of a cheaper fuel alternative.

The curve connecting the cost of the maximum control strategy to the lowest cost contains all of the least-cost solutions for reducing the maximum concentration of suspended particulates without deliberately controlling sulfur oxides.

The curve which merges with it connects all the least cost strategies for reducing the maximum concentration of suspended particulates while requiring that the initial maximum concentration of sulfur oxides, 0.046 ppm, be reduced by half to 0.023 ppm. We show these least-cost curves as smooth curves for convenience; they are actually made up of a large number of discrete steps, since there are only a finite number of possible strategies.

A least-cost solution is defined more exactly as that combination of emission controls which achieves a stated objective for the least total annual cost to the set of emission sources. For example, with no deliberate sulfur oxides control a simulated reduction of the initial maximum concentration of suspended particulates from $184 \mu Gms/M^3$ to $120 \mu Gms/M^3$ can be achieved with a twenty-two per cent reduction in particulate emission for no net increase in the estimated annual cost. Reduction to $89 \mu Gms/M^3$ can be achieved for an estimated cost of $5,000,000 annually with a fifty-nine per cent reduction in emissions. Reduction to $86 \mu Gms/M^3$ can be achieved, with a sixty-eight per cent reduction in emissions for an estimated $7,000,000 annually with a bonus reduction of the maximum concentration of sulfur oxides to 0.040 ppm. For another $500,000 annually the maximum sulfur oxides concentration can be reduced to 0.023 ppm with a forty-two per cent reduction in emissions.

Comparing these least cost solutions first to the maximum control strategy provides a rather dramatic example of the law of diminishing returns in terms of reductions both in maximum concentrations and in total emissions. Since no real distinction can be made between an annual average of $85 \mu Gms/M^3$ and an annual average of $86 \mu Gms/M^3$ we see that the practical efficiency of either the maximum control strategy or the maximum particulate control strategy as a basis for particulate control (without considering sulfur oxides control) is only about one-fourth that of the least-cost strategy for $86 \mu Gms/M^3$. Since the present levels of sulfur oxides in Kansas City are not presently considered to pose a significant hazard, the maximum control strategy is not competitive with the $7,500,000 least-cost strategy for achieving a peak concentration 0.023 ppm for sulfur oxides in addition to the $86 \mu Gms/M^3$ peak concentration for particulate: neither the extra reduction of the peak to 0.015 ppm nor the doubling of sulfur oxides emissions reduced to eighty-one per cent would justify the extra cost ($18,900,000) at the present level of hazard.

It is true, of course, that a least-cost solution selects those emission sources which can get the most abatement per dollar, so that some sources may not be affected. Is there, then, a more equitable, if perhaps more costly, strategy? Suppose that every source is required to reduce its particulate emissions in concert with all other sources successively by at least twenty, forty, sixty, eighty, and maximum per cent of its base emissions. The results of at least a twenty per cent reduction show that the maximum concentration of suspended particulates is reduced to $89 \mu Gms/M^3$ with a fifty-nine per cent reduction in total annual particulate emissions for an estimated cost of over $16,000,000 annually. The corresponding least cost solution has an estimated annual cost only one third of that and, therefore, three times the efficiency. (The reduction in sulfur oxides obtained under both strategies is a bonus resulting from controls affecting both pollutants, e.g., switching from oil to natural gas.) Table [2] compares the simulated emission reductions obtained by the major types of sources under the two strategies. This table shows what percentage of emission reduction is obtained by each of the major emission source types for each strategy and the associated costs. It is apparent that while the least cost strategy is more highly selective, the so-called equi-proportional strategy has the more disproportionate impact on the emission sources in terms of both emission reduction and cost. The reason for this is that it costs no more for many sources to control their particulate emissions to the maximum than it does to control precisely twenty per cent. Except for process changes or improved process operation, which were not considered, most mechanical equipment for particulate control has collection efficiencies in excess of eighty per cent. Thus, the first step in control for many sources takes them to maximum control. This is demonstrated further by Figure [5]. Note that for an additional $9,000,000 annually the maximum particulate control strategy effects only a sixteen per cent increase in particulate emission reduction over the first equi-proportional step. This implies that on a cost-effectiveness basis many sources in the simulation went to maximum control in that first step. The simulated equi-proportional emission reductions of forty, sixty, or eighty per cent do not generate further significant reductions either in concentrations or in total emissions; the only significant change is increased cost.

Table 2
Comparison of Particulate Reductions for
Each Source Type Under Equi-Proportional (EP)
and Least Cost (LC) Strategies

| | Source Emissions % Reduction and Cost ($ Millions) | | | |
| | LC | | EP | |
Source Type	%	$	%	$
Power Plants	68	0.2	53	0.2
Process Industries	81	0.7	71	8.6
Waste Disposal	81	4.1	100	6.4
All Other	-0-	-0-	1	0.8
Total Emissions	59	5.0	59	16.0

A strategy of current interest in several cities for controlling the emissions of sulfur oxides is to ban the use of high sulfur fuels. In the Kansas City study, a restriction of the sulfur content of fuels to two per cent by weight or less was evaluated. The estimated cost is $3,500,000 annually in increased fuel costs. This strategy reduces the sulfur oxides peak concentration to 0.035 ppm and effects a thirty-eight per cent reduction in the total tonnage of sulfur oxides emitted, while providing a bonus reduction of ten per cent in particulate emissions. In contrast, we note a least-cost solution which halves the peak concentration to 0.023 and reduces sulfur oxides emissions by forty per cent with an apparent net reduction in cost over the base conditions. This can be explained by some sources in the simulation changing to fuels which are both cleaner and cheaper than their present fuels.

A one per cent sulfur fuel restriction strategy was simulated in the Washington study with similar results. In that case, the fuel restriction reduced the peak from 0.06 to 0.035 ppm at a cost of $5,000,000 annually. The corresponding least-cost solution also involves an apparent reduction in annual cost over the base conditions. These results strongly suggest that restrictions on the sulfur content of fuels have limited ability to reduce urban pollution levels and are very inefficient relative to the least-cost strategy achieving the same air quality.

Sulfur fuel restrictions are probably cheaper for a control agency to enforce than abatement strategies involving selective sulfur oxides emission standards, since in the former case, controls are, in effect, applied to a few fuel suppliers instead of the many fuel users. But in view of the limited pollution reduction obtained, the relatively high cost to the users of low sulfur fuels, and the adverse impact on high sulfur coal producing areas and the railroads servicing them, sulfur fuel restrictions do not appear to be economically attractive as abatement strategies.

We have used least-cost solutions to evaluate the economic efficiency of proposed abatement strategies, but are least-cost strategies themselves impractical? The question really involves the enforcement cost and the political acceptability of a strategy. Referring again to Table [2], note that the cost of control for each source type is less than the corresponding costs for the equi-proportional strategy. If the politically important sources, as a class, pay less under a least-cost, or near-least-cost, strategy than under any other, then at least the economic motivations affecting political acceptability can be stimulated. As to enforcement costs, it may be feasible to write a few ordinances controlling the emissions of all sources of a certain type and channel enforcement through quasi-official industry abatement groups staffed partly by abatement agency personnel and partly by industry personnel. Cooperation and conformance with the spirit of the abatement ordinances would reduce enforcement costs for both industry and government. In any case, least-cost, or near-least-cost, strategies, should not be written off as academic.

5.   CONCLUSIONS

The kind of comprehensive analytical approach presented can supply most of the detailed cost-effectiveness data needed to evaluate the economic impact of urban air pollution abatement strategies. The impact of a strategy on urban air quality permits rapid determination of the feasibility of attaining certain air quality standards. By providing estimates of the emission reductions and costs incurred source-by-source, an abatement agency also has a detailed basis for assessing the enforcement costs and the political acceptability of an abatement strategy.

The cost estimates presented here do not take into account future price fluctuations, deterioration of equipment, availability of low sulfur fuels, and several other factors which would have to be reckoned with in a precise determination of costs. It should also be emphasized that the results would have to be modified for conditions other than those assumed and for different geographic definitions. The approach has great flexibility as a systems analysis tool, however, and can be applied to other geographies and other pollution conditions.

NOTE

1.   Under Contract No. Ph 86-68-37 the U. S. Public Health Service, Department of Health, Education, and Welfare.

The Cost of Clean Air

The Clean Air Act requires a number of reports documenting various aspects of the pollution problem. The first report in accordance with Section 305 (a) of the Act provided data on pollution concentrations and technology. The second report, from which these excerpts are taken, is an attempt to determine the *cost* of the enactment of the pollution standards in the law.

While an accountant might wish for greater detail in the calculations here, there is enough to provide some assessment of the measurement methodology. Section 1.1.2 describes briefly the cost methodology and some of its problems. The excerpts from chapter three (stationary sources—steam powerplants) give a better idea of the methodology, and also suggest some of the perils of shadow pricing. The report assumes that the additional cost of using desulfurized residual fuel oil can be used as a proxy for the (unknown) cost of controlling particulates and sulfur oxides. It is interesting to contemplate how the validity of that assumption was affected by the general oil shortage that developed in late 1973.

PREFACE

This report is the second submitted in accordance with section 305(a) of Public Law 90-148, the Clean Air Act, as amended, which reads as follows:

SEC. 305. (a) In order to provide the basis for evaluating programs authorized by this Act and the development of new programs and to furnish the Congress with the information necessary for authorization of appropriations by fiscal years beginning after June 30, 1969, the Secretary, in cooperation with State, interstate, and local air pollution control agencies, shall make a detailed estimate of the cost of carrying out the provisions of this Act; a comprehensive study of the cost of program implementation by affected units of government; and a comprehensive study of the economic impact of air quality standards on the Nation's industries, communities, and other contributing sources of pollution, including an analysis of the national requirements for and the cost of controlling emissions to attain such standards of air quality as may be established pursuant to this Act or applicable State law. The Secretary shall submit such detailed estimate[s] and the results of such comprehensive study of cost for the five-year period beginning July 1, 1969, and the results of such other studies, to the Congress not later than January 10, 1969, and shall submit a reevaluation of such estimate[s] and studies annually thereafter.

Like the first report,[1] this one gives estimated costs of applying control techniques to meet selected standards as well as implementing governmental air pollu-

SOURCE: Excerpts from The Second Report of the Secretary of Health, Education, and Welfare, in compliance with PL 90-148, The Clean Air Act, as amended, March, 1970.

tion control programs; however, it covers a larger number of pollutants, stationary sources, and metropolitan areas, and it bases the cost estimates on different emission control regulations.

CHAPTER 1.   OVERVIEW

1.1   Background and Purpose

Section 305(a) of the Clean Air Act, as amended in November 1967, calls for a series of annual reports on the prospective costs of implementing the act's provisions for governmental and private efforts to control air pollution. This report, the second one submitted under section 305(a), is an extension and modification of the first one, which was submitted to the Congress in June, 1969. It provides estimates of the costs of implementing governmental—Federal, State, and local—air pollution control programs and applying air pollution control measures to selected stationary sources. Unlike the first report, this one does not include estimates of the cost of motor vehicle pollution control; no new data were available on costs associated with the control techniques currently in use.

1.1.1   Sources and Locations

Twenty-one types of stationary sources are discussed under three major categories. The section on solid waste disposal, not included in the first report, gives estimates of the costs of controlling air pollution arising from open burning and incineration. Four types of fuel combustion sources are covered: Steam-electric powerplants, industrial boilers, commercial-institutional heating plants, and residential heating plants; the last was not included in the first report. The third category is industrial process sources. Both reports include processes within the following industries: Kraft (sulfate) pulp, iron and steel, gray iron foundry, sulfuric acid, petroleum refining, asphalt batching, and cement. The second report covers nine additional industries: Primary nonferrous metallurgical smelting, phosphate fertilizer, lime, coal cleaning, petroleum products storage, grain milling and handling, varnish, rubber (tires and inner tubes), and secondary nonferrous metallurgical recovery. Thus, the report contains cost estimates for sixteen industrial processes.

This report gives the estimated costs of controlling four types of pollutants: Particulates and sulfur oxides, the two covered in the first report, plus carbon monoxide and hydrocarbons. Solid waste disposal sources emit primarily particulates and hydrocarbons; fuel combustion sources, particulates and sulfur oxides; industrial processes, particulates, sulfur oxides, hydrocarbons, and carbon monoxide. In some of the source categories considered in this report, there are other pollutants that are significant problems; to estimate the additional cost of controlling their emissions is beyond the scope of this report.

Control costs were estimated for the twenty-one types of stationary sources in one hundred metropolitan areas that comprise sixty per cent of the Nation's population. For the purpose of estimating these costs, the one hundred metropolitan areas were treated as though they had been or will be designated air quality control regions (AQCR's) during the timespan (fiscal years 1971-75) covered by this report. Appendix I* lists the one hundred areas and explains their status in relation to actual or projected AQCR's. Also, for the purpose of estimating control costs, certain assumptions were made about the timing of air quality standard-setting, development of implementation plans, phasing of actual control action, and so on; Appendix II discusses these assumed schedules in greater detail.

1.1.2 Cost Estimations

Control costs are reported in terms of the initial investment required to establish control and the continuing annual expenses related to that investment. The investment cost is the total expense of purchasing and installing control equipment. The annual cost is the sum of yearly charges for capital-related costs (interest on the investment funds, property taxes where applicable, insurance premiums, and depreciation charges) plus operating (labor, utilities, and supplies) and maintenance costs.

The estimates for both investment and annualized costs are reported in a manner to indicate their expected accuracy. In addition to the expected cost which is the estimate calculated from the data and assumptions available, lower and upper limits to the costs are given. The difference between the expected cost and the limits is a measure of the possible error in the estimate of the expected cost.

Two significant changes have been made in the methodology used to estimate control costs. In the first report, the levels of control used to make cost estimates were based on the expected requirements of pollution reduction in terms of percentages; but for this report, they were based on selected emission control regulations which are either identical or similar to comparable types of regulations in effect in various places in the United States; Appendix III contains a detailed description of the selected regulations.

The other significant change in methodology was to estimate control costs separately for two broad groups of sources: Those that were operating when the November, 1967 amendments to the Clean Air Act became law and newer sources that have begun operations since that time or are expected to do so by

---

*The Appendixes are not reproduced here.

June 30, 1975. This latter group was calculated on the basis of industry production and capacity data as well as relevant information on industry growth patterns.

In general, stationary source control costs were estimated by calculating the expenditure required to increase the levels of emission control from an assumed baseline level to the level required for compliance with the selected emission control regulations described in Appendix III. This approach is based on the premise that the stationary source control costs properly attributable to the implementation of the Clean Air Act, as amended, are those costs incurred in reaching levels of control above those commonly being achieved at the time the 1967 amendments to the act were passed.

The number and type of installations currently controlling pollutants, the level of efficiency each is achieving, the location of all sources, their capacity, and other characteristics are bases for determining the extent and types of control methods needed to meet the selected standards. This information, derived from published data, trade association reports, and interviews with industry contacts, varied greatly in the number of underlying assumptions and accordingly in the accuracy of the cost estimates that were derived; however, even the least accurate estimates are considered sufficient to predict the magnitude of the total control cost for a particular source category.

In summary, many important assumptions are necessary to estimate emission control costs. These assumptions, including the set of control regulations and the implementation schedules, are identified in this report. Obviously then, the results in terms of emissions and control costs that are tabulated depend heavily on the underlying assumptions. If the assumptions hold, then the results as estimated will follow.

1.2 Report Organization

Chapter 2 outlines the probable course, scope, and interrelationships of local, State, regional, and Federal programs. It also gives an estimate of expenditures for fiscal 1970-1975 for governmental research and development activities and for abatement and control efforts to implement the Clean Air Act, as amended.

Chapter 3 covers all three major source categories—solid waste disposal, fuel combustion, and industrial processes. For each category, it gives information about the total amounts and types of emissions and the average level of control for facilities operating in the 1967 calendar year in the one hundred metropolitan areas; the number of sources and methods of emission control; and the associated cost estimates for achieving the expected degree of control required by the assumed regulations.

Section 3.5 summarizes, by metropolitan area, the projected costs of implementing control plans and applying emission control measures to the twenty-one stationary sources in the period fiscal 1971-1975 for facilities operating in calendar year 1967.

Section 3.6 gives projections of the additional (growth) facilities expected to be operating during fiscal 1968-1975 in the total one hundred metropolitan areas and the estimated costs and emissions at specified control levels.

1.3 Summary of Report

This report presents estimates of costs which will be incurred by some parts of government and industry pursuant to the Clean Air Act, as amended. Summary table [1] covers the National Air Pollution Control Administration's research and control program, State and local programs, and abatement of all pollution from Federal facilities. Expenditures for research and development by Federal agencies other than the National Air Pollution Control Administration are not included.

To estimate costs for controlling selected non-Government operations, a certain emission control regulation was assumed for each of four pollutants of this report. More specifically, the costs estimates apply to the control of particulates, sulfur oxides, hydrocarbons, and carbon monoxide for twenty-one source categories in the one hundred metropolitan areas. The estimated costs cover those facilities operating during 1967 and new facilities that have or will have come into operation in the period from 1967 to the end of fiscal 1975. These costs are summarized in two tables.

Summary Table [2] presents the total costs, as investment and annual costs for all one hundred metropolitan areas by stationary source category for both the facilities operating in 1967 and those facilities added or expected to be added in the period to fiscal 1975. Summary table 1-3 tabulates emission levels and combined costs for both periods (1967 and fiscal 1968-1975) by source category. Emissions estimates for fiscal 1975 are given at levels that might exist if the Clean Air Act, as amended, were not in effect. The reported costs are estimates of the financial requirements of each industry in decreasing those projected 1975 emission levels by the corresponding reported percentages.

In general, the annual cost to control these four pollutants is a very very small percentage of the value of shipments in each of these industries—usually less than one per cent. To control air pollution from solid waste disposal operations, about $0.39 per ton of waste will be required; the cost for steam-electric powerplants is estimated at 1.3 mils per kilowatt-hour.

CHAPTER 3. STATIONARY SOURCES

3.1 Introduction

This chapter presents analyses of twenty-one categories of stationary sources of air pollution. The analyses cover the combustion or manufacturing processes of

Summary Table 1
Projected Expenditures for Governmental
Air Pollution Programs
[in millions of dollars]

| Fiscal year | Type of activity | | Total, program costs |
	Research and development	Abatement and control	
1970	50.0	82.0	132.0
1971	85.0	106.6	171.6
1972	84.5	138.6	223.1
1973	109.9	180.2	290.1
1974	142.9	234.2	377.2
1975	185.8	304.6	490.4
Total	638.1	1,046.3	1,684.4

each category, their emissions in terms of type and quantity, and methods and costs of controlling emissions to comply with the standards selected (Appendix III) for this report.

The twenty-one categories of stationary sources are discussed under three groupings—solid waste disposal (Section 3.2), fuel combustion (Section 3.3), and industrial processes (Section 3.4). Section 3.5 presents tabulations of control cost estimates for each of one hundred metropolitan area; these tabulations reflect the yearly pattern of expected investment and annual costs for fiscal 1971-1975. Section 3.6 covers the growth in emission sources in the period since 1967 and to the end of fiscal 1975; emissions from these additional facilities and the estimated costs to control their emissions are presented in the tables of this final section.

Since most of the tables in this chapter show totals for both investment and annual costs and because they both appear on the same line in the tables, further explanation of the meaning of these data is necessary. In essence, annual costs are the chargeable expenses for the year in which they are reported and they include a charge for investment on an annualized basis (i.e., depreciation). Investment cost estimates, on the other hand, indicate only the amount of capital outlay for a given source category during a specific year to install equipment or implement control measures that are anticipated. The total of the investment cost column, similarly, shows the estimated total capital requirement for that source category during the fiscal 1971-1975 period. Annual costs for a specific year do not necessarily correspond to the investment made that year but rather result from the cumulative control installations made in the current and prior

Summary Table 2
Projected Costs for Controlling Facilities in 100 Metropolitan Areas[1]
[Millions of Dollars]

Fiscal year	Costs by source category for facilities operating in calendar year 1967								Costs by source category for facilities expected to be operating at end of fiscal year 1975[2]							
	Solid waste disposal		Fuel combustion		Industrial processes		Total area control cost		Solid waste disposal		Fuel combustion		Industrial processes		Total area control cost	
	Invest-ment	Annual	Invest-ment	Annual	Invest-ment	Annual	Invest-ment	Annual	Invest-ment	Annual	Invest-ment	Annual	Invest-ment	Annual	Invest-ment	Annual
1971	10	5	65	70	41	21	116	96	17	8	82	107	78	37	177	152
1972	45	27	268	359	208	108	521	494	56	35	291	445	261	147	608	627
1973	67	60	416	765	344	237	827	1,062	80	74	443	912	410	303	933	1,290
1974	39	79	306	1,000	224	317	569	1,396	50	98	331	1,200	278	404	659	1,710
1975	10	84	123	1,090	65	340	198	1,514	18	107	142	1,330	104	443	264	1,880
Total	171	255	1,178	3,284	882	1,023	2,231	4,562	221	322	1,289	3,994	1,131	1,334	2,641	5,659

[1]Projected costs (Investment; Annual) are the initial investment expenditure (for purchasing and installing control equipment) and the sum of continuing annual costs (for interest, property taxes, insurance, depreciation, etc., and for operating and maintaining equipment). The 100 areas are defined in Appendix 1.
[2]These costs include control expenditures for 21 sources (Chapter 3) with facilities operating in calendar year 1967 plus additional facilities expected to be operating by the end of fiscal year 1975.

years of the fiscal 1971-1975 period. The five-year total of annual cost, then, is the total cost that is expected to be incurred during the fiscal 1971-1975 period.

The expected costs are tabulated with lower and upper limits. The possible error in each estimate varies: the limits were calculated to indicate the possible range of costs and to reflect the error involved.

All of the tables entitled "Estimates of Reduced Emission Levels and Associated Costs," include a column headed "Associated emission control level." The percentages shown in this column reflect estimates of the extent to which potential emissions are controlled. For example, in Table [3], pertaining to solid waste disposal, the 844,000 tons of particulate emissions in 1967 are estimated to be about 46.5 per cent of potential emissions of particulate matter from solid waste disposal operations. If there had been no control of particulate emissions, the emission level would have been 1,815,000 tons. Thus, 53.5 per cent (one hundred per cent minus 46.5 per cent) is the associated emission control level.

3.3 Fuel Combustion

3.3.1 Introduction

The combustion of fossil fuels (coal, oil, and gas) causes a significant portion of the Nation's air pollution problem. In 1967, stationary combustion sources accounted for over 3.9 million tons of particulates and about 12.5 million tons of sulfur oxides released within the one hundred metropolitan areas. The emission control lamp projected in this study would reduce the particulate emissions by ninety-one per cent and the sulfur oxides by fifty-nine per cent of the 1967 emission levels.

The stationary combustion sources covered in this report are: steam-electric powerplants, industrial boilers, commercial-institutional heating plants, and residential heating plants. Together, these four account for about thirty-two per cent of the particulates and seventy-four per cent of the sulfur oxides emitted in the nation by all sources. The other two pollutants of concern, hydrocarbons and carbon monoxide, are not emitted in significant quantities when the combustion equipment is operating properly. Table [4] indicates the amounts of these two pollutants contributed by each of these four types of combustion sources in the one hundred metropolitan areas.

For this study two standards were selected as the basis of estimating the cost of controlling emissions from fuel combustion sources. The first is the State of Maryland's combustion regulation, which limits particulate emissions on a graduated basis depending upon the heat rating of the boiler. The regulation sets a maximum limit on the quantity of particulates emitted per hour; the requirements increase in stringency for increased boiler capacity. The standard used in this study for sulfur oxide emissions from fuel combustion sources limits such emissions to 1.46 pounds of sulfur dioxides per million BTU input.

Summary Table 3
Projected Emission Levels and Relative Effects of the Act by the End of Fiscal Year 1975[1]
(100 metropolitan areas)

Stationary emission source	1975 emission level without the act[3] (thousand tons per year)				Expected results and costs					
					Decrease in emission level[2] (per cent)				Total area control cost (million dollars)[3]	
	Part	SOx	HC	CO	Part	SOx	HC	CO	Investment	Annual
Solid waste disposal	947		204	2,089	30.0		76.4	86.2	221	322
Fuel combustion:										
Steam-electric powerplants	2,550	8,520			91.0	63.6			161	2,430
Industrial boilers	1,980	4,780			96.4	63.0			547	1,180
Commercial-institutional heating plants	69	736			51.5	14.0			31	17
Residential heating plants	173	1,100			67.3	51.2			550	376
Totals	4,722	15,136							1,289	4,003
Industrial process:										
Kraft (sulfate) pulp plants	164				80.5				7	7
Iron and steel plants	1,420				90.5				412	823
Gray iron foundries	129			1,720	88.6			93.9	238	195
Primary nonferrous metallurgical plants	29	175			43.8	97.6			81	75
Sulfuric acid plants	55	561			40.0	86.0			37	7
Phosphate fertilizer plants	16				67.0				5	5
Petroleum refineries	63	1,130	719	1,323	45.5	20.6	86.4	91.0	103	5
Asphalt batching plants	306				60.0				34	78
Cement plants	723				92.8				19	16
Lime plants	289				90.0				1	2
Coal cleaning plants	47				87.3				3	3
Petroleum products storage plants			779				46.8		84	0
Grain mills and elevators	1,350				98.4				46	45
Varnish plants							87.8		1	3
Rubber (tire and inner tube) plants									5	12
Secondary nonferrous metallurgical plants	65				90.2				55	59
Total	4,656	1,866	1,498	3,043					1,131	1,335

[1] Clean Air Act, as amended. Blanks in the table indicate the emission levels meet applicable regulations (Appendix III); levels for rubber plants could not be estimated due to lack of data.

[2] Particulates (part.), sulfur oxides (SOx), hydrocarbons (HC), carbon monoxide (CO).

[3] Projected costs (inventory; annual) are the initial investment expenditure (for purchasing and installing control equipment) and the sum of continuing annual costs (for interest, property taxes, insurance, depreciation, etc., and for operating and maintaining equipment). The 100 areas are defined in Appendix I.

Summary Table 4
Estimated Emission Levels for Fuel Combustion Sources[1]
Nationally and in 100 Metropolitan Areas

Type of source	Total number of sources		Total quantity of emissions[2] (thousand tons/year)			
			United States		100 areas	
	United States	100 areas	Part	SO_x	Part	SO_x
Steam-electric powerplants[3]	410	252	5,550	15,000	2,190	6,860
Industrial boilers (thousands)	307	219	3,000	5,260	1,540	3,970
Commercial-institutional heating plants (thousands)	999	607	105	1,110	64	675
Residential heating plants (millions)	58	35	314	1,530	163	1,040
Total	([4])	([4])	8,970	22,900	3,960	12,500

[1] Totals for facilities in operation in 1967.
[2] Particulates (part.); sulfur oxides (SO_x).
[3] Plants of 25 megawatts and greater using coal and/or oil.
[4] Not applicable.

The use of low-sulfur oil to comply with the selected sulfur oxides regulation allows fuel combustion sources to meet the above-mentioned particulate regulation at the same time, In this report, NAPCA has assumed that the cost of controlling particulates and sulfur oxides can be approximated by using the estimated cost of desulfurized residual fuel oil. This selection should not be interpreted as a general recommendation for the control of air pollution from fuel combustion operations; such as interpretation would overlook the problems of supply and distribution of the large quantities of low-sulfur content oil that would be required.

3.3.2 Steam-Electric Powerplants

3.3.2.1 Introduction

Steam-electric powerplants consume twenty-one per cent of the Nation's fuel including sixty-four per cent of the coal; as a result, they produce tremendous quantities of air pollutants. Nationally, they contribute about twenty per cent of the particulates and forty-nine per cent of the sulfur oxides, which are essentially not controlled. In 1967, there were about 252 plants in the one hundred metropolitan areas that had capacities of twenty-five megawatts or greater and that burned coal and/or fuel oil. They generated 420 billion kilowatt-hours of electricity. The estimates do not include the Tennessee Valley Authority powerplants.

3.3.2.2 Control of Emissions

Present control practice for particulates is to use electrostatic precipitators, sometimes in combination with high efficiency mechanical collectors. The present level of industry control of particulate emissions is estimated at eighty-six per cent. Reduction of sulfur oxide emissions has been accomplished only in a few locations, generally by substituting low-sulfur content fuel for high-sulfur fuel of the same type or by switching to another type of fuel.

Sulfur oxide emissions can be reduced by changing from high-sulfur content coal or oil to natural gas or low-sulfur content coal or oil. Use of gas or oil has the additional benefit of normally obviating the need for control of particulates. Natural gas and low-sulfur coal and oil are limited in either supply or distribution. Both coal and oil can be processed to reduce their sulfur content. It is also possible to remove a substantial amount of sulfur oxides from stack gas; techniques for doing this are being studied, but some technical problems must be resolved before widespread use.

It is likely that a variety of alternatives will ultimately be used by the industry to meet sulfur oxide control requirements. But, since it appears, as indicated above, that the cost of controlling both particulates and sulfur oxides can be approximated by using the estimated cost of desulfurized residual fuel oil, this approach was used in calculating cost estimates; the resulting estimates are thought to approximate the costs of other alternatives or a combination of other alternatives. Many of the boilers involved would require conversions in order to burn oil; an estimate of the investment cost of conversion was made. Annual costs of control, based on the change from high-sulfur content coal or oil to desulfurized residual fuel oil, were estimated by using metropolitan area fuel price differentials and by adding a charge of $0.40 per barrel for desulfurizing the oil to an average of 1.14 per cent sulfur content. This will enable steam-electric plants to meet the selected sulfur oxides regulation for fuel combustion sources. The cost estimates are given in Table [5].

3.4.2   Kraft (Sulfate) Pulp Industry

3.4.2.1   Introduction

The pump industry manufactures pulp from wood and other materials for use in making paper and related products. The several methods by which pulp can be produced are generally classified as either chemical or mechanical. Only the chemical methods, however, cause significant air pollution problems. Among the chemical pulp production methods, sulfite and sulfate (kraft) pulp plants account for the majro proportion of pulp production, about seventy-five per cent of the total industry output. Emissions from sulfite pulp plants can be recovered at a net benefit; therefore, sulfite pulp mills are not included in this report.

In kraft pulp mills, four major processes emit significant amount of particulates: recovery furnaces and smelt dissolving tanks in the form of process chemicals, lime recovery kilns in the form of lime, and bark boilers in the form of bark char. Recovery furnaces also emit sulfur oxides, but the best available estimates indicate that these emissions do not exceed the 500 ppm regulation limit assumed for this analysis.

3.4.2.2   Control of Emissions

Table [8] indicates the estimated costs to control particulate emissions from the four above-mentioned processes to meet the process weight regulation for particulates. The necessary reductions in emissions can be accomplished with gas-cleaning equipment. The application of these devices will allow more than ninety-six per cent collection efficiency compared with the 1967 level of eighty-one per cent.

NOTE

1.   "The Cost of Clean Air," first report of the Secretary of Health, Education, and Welfare to the Congress of the United States, June 1969.

Table 5
Steam-Electric Powerplants—Estimates of Reduced Emission Levels and Associated Costs[1]
(100 metropolitan areas)

Year	Expected emission level (thousand tons per year)[2]				Associated emission control level (per cent)[2]				Control costs (million dollars per year)						
									Investment cost			Annual cost			
	Particulates	SO$_x$	HC	CO	Particulates	SO$_x$	HC	CO	Lower limit	Expected	Upper limit	Lower limit	Expected	Upper limit	
1967	2,190	6,860			86.0	0									
Fiscal year 1971	2,050	6,577			86.8	4.1			5.4	6.7	8.0	32.8	41.0	49.2	
Fiscal year 1972	1,500	5,361			90.4	21.9			31.8	39.7	47.6	174.0	217.0	260.0	
Fiscal year 1973	719	3,640			95.4	47.0			51.9	64.9	77.9	371.0	466.0	559.0	
Fiscal year 1974	292	2,707			98.1	60.6			31.4	39.2	47.0	481.0	601.0	721.0	
Fiscal year 1975	198	2,500			98.7	63.6			8.6	10.8	13.0	505.0	631.0	757.0	
Total									129.1	161.3	193.5	1,563.8	1,956.0	2,346.2	

[1] Cost estimates are for the control of only those facilities in operation in calendar year 1967. These areas are defined in Appendix I.
[2] For levels of particulates, sulfur oxides (SO$_x$), hydrocarbons (HC), carbon monoxide (CO). Blanks in the table indicate the emission levels meet the applicable regulations (Appendix III) without additional control.

Table 6
Estimated 1967 Emission Levels for Industrial Process Sources (Nationally and in 100 Metropolitan Areas)[1]

| Type of Source | Total number of sources | | Total quantity of emissions[2] (thousand tons per year) | | | | | | | |
| | United States | 100 areas | United States | | | | 100 metropolitan areas | | | |
			Particulates	SO_x	HC	CO	Particulates	SO_x	HC	CO
Kraft (sulfate) pulp plants	113	16	633				109			
Iron and steel plants	141	115	1,490				1,060			
Gray iron foundries	1,279	661	217			3,200	94			1,250
Primary nonferrous metallurgical plants	64	12	95	3,848			22	144		
Sulfuric acid plants	212	102	60	750			40	480		
Phosphate fertilizer plants	171	19	20				11			
Petroleum refineries	262	134	96	2,100	[3]932	2,000	48	923	[3]587	1,080
Asphalt batching plants	1,500	903	522				206			
Cement plants	176	92	908				525			
Lime plants	135	67	450				251			
Coal cleaning plants	691	109	160				27			
Petroleum products storage plants	29,664	6,130			1,100				636	
Grain mills and elevators	14,013	1,996	1,210				1,200			
Varnish plants	230	216			5				5	
Rubber (tire and inner tube) plants	159	102								
Secondary nonferrous metallurgical plants	793	690	48				45			
Total			5,909	6,698	2,037	5,200	3,638	1,547	1,228	2,330

[1] Totals for facilities in operation in 1967. Blanks in the table indicate the emission levels meet applicable regulations (Appendix III); levels for rubber plants could not be estimated due to lack of data.

[2] Sulfur oxides (SO_x), hydrocarbons (HC), carbon monoxide (CO).

[3] Hydrocarbon emissions from storage evaporation, transfer operations, and catalytic cracking.

Table 7

Expected Annual Control Costs Relative to Capacity and Shipments of Industrial Process Sources[1]
[1967 base; 100 metropolitan areas]

Type of source	Source totals			Cost ratios	
	Capacity (millions of units)	Value of shipments (billions of dollars)	Annual control cost (millions of dollars)	Cost per unit of annual capacity (dollars per unit)	Cost per dollar of shipment (per cent)
Kraft (sulfate) pulp plants (tons)	4.1	0.4	2.5	0.61	0.63
Iron and steel plants (tons raw steel)	116.0	10.5	104.0	1.76	1.94
Gray iron foundries (tons castings)[2]	10.0	1.7	49.1	4.91	2.89
Primary nonferrous metallurgical plants (tons)[2]	3.4	0.6	23.5	6.91	3.52
Sulfuric acid plants (tons)	24.4	0.2	2.2	0.09	1.10
Phosphate fertilizer plants (tons P_2O_1)	3.5	0.4	5.5	1.57	1.39
Petroleum refineries (barrels)[4]	2,530.0	13.5	1.4	0.00	0.01
Asphalt batching plants (tons paving mixture)[4]	250.0	0.6	18.6	0.74	3.10
Cement plants (barrels)	279.0	0.6	5.7	0.02	0.95
Lime plants (tons)	9.6	0.1	0.5	0.05	0.50
Coal Cleaning plants (tons)	61.4	0.3	0.5	0.01	0.17
Petroleum products storage plants (gallons)[5]	5,140.0	9.8	0.0	0.00	0.00
Grain mills (tons)	43.9	3.7	7.9	0.18	0.21
Grain elevators (bushels)[6]	1,330.0	(7)	7.5	0.01	(7)
Varnish plants (gallons)	52.0	0.1	0.8	0.02	0.80
Rubber plants (tires and tubes)	170.0	2.5	2.5	0.01	0.10
Secondary nonferrous metallurgical plants (tons)	2.4	1.4	11.9	4.96	0.85

[1] Costs for controlling particulate, sulfur oxide, hydrocarbon, and carbon monoxide emissions from facilities operating in calendar year 1967. The areas are defined in Appendix I.

[2] Capacity is calculated assuming 1,000 operating hours per year.

[3] Tons applies to copper, lead, zinc, and aluminum smelters; for copper and lead, capacity is input material.

[4] Capacity is calculated assuming 1,000 operating hours per year.

[5] Capacity is in million gallons of gasoline storage space.

[6] Capacity is in million bushels of storage space.

[7] Not applicable.

The Effects of Pollution Abatement on International Trade

It is obvious that environmental legislation—in fact, all social legislation—may have significant impacts on the cost structure of business enterprises, and on the relative competitive positions of different companies. Somewhat less attention has been devoted to the way in which environmental legislation may alter the international competitive position of companies and ultimately, of the United States. A section of the Federal Water Pollution Control Act amendments of 1972 is concerned with this problem. It requires the Department of Commerce to prepare reports on such impacts. The following reading is an excerpt from the first report under this law.

In addition to a preliminary analysis of the impacts of U.S. legislation, it contains descriptions of environmental legislation in several other countries.

I. SUMMARY

This is excerpted from the initial report prepared in accordance with Section 6 of Public Law 92-500, the Federal Water Pollution Control Act Amendments of 1972. Under this section, titled "International Trade Study," the Secretary of Commerce is required to report initially to Congress within six months of the date of enactment on the potential economic impacts of the evolving pollution control programs in the U.S. and abroad. Subsequent reports are required on at least an annual basis. Specifically, Section 6 provides that:

(a) The Secretary of Commerce, in cooperation with other interested Federal agencies and with representatives of industry and the public, shall undertake immediately an investigation and study to determine—

> *(1) the extent to which pollution abatement and control programs will be imposed on, or voluntarily undertaken by, United States manufacturers in the near future and the probable short- and long-range effects of the costs of such programs (computed to the greatest extent practicable on an industry-by-industry basis) on (A) the production costs of such domestic manufacturers, and (B) the market prices of the goods produced by them;*

> *(2) the probable extent to which pollution abatement and control programs will be implemented in foreign industrial nations in the near*

SOURCE: U.S. Department of Commerce

future and the extent to which the production costs (computed to the greatest extent practicable on an industry-by-industry basis) of foreign manufacturers will be affected by the costs of such programs;

(3) the probable competitive advantage which any article manufactured in a foreign nation will likely have in relation to a comparable article made in the United States if that foreign nation—

(A) does not require its manufacturers to implement pollution abatement and control programs,

(B) requires a lesser degree of pollution abatement and control in its programs, or

(C) in any way reimburses or otherwise subsidizes its manufacturers for the costs of such programs;

(4) alternative means by which any competitive advantage accruing to the products of any foreign nation as a result of any factor described in paragraph (3) may be (A) accurately and quickly determined, and (B) equalized, for example, by the imposition of a surcharge or duty, on a foreign product in an amount necessary to compensate for such advantage; and

(5) the impact, if any, which the imposition of a compensating tariff or other equalizing measure may have in encouraging foreign nations to implement pollution abatement and control programs.

(b)   The Secretary shall make an initial report to the President and Congress within six months after the date of enactment of this section of the results of the study and investigation carried out pursuant to this section and shall make additional reports thereafter at such times as he deems appropriate taking into account the development of relevant data, but not less than once every twelve months.

Although P.L. 92-500 is the most extensive U.S. water pollution legislation that has been enacted, Section 6 does not specify particular types of pollution for the assessment of the economic implications of abatement costs. Accomplishing the tasks set out in Section 6 for a given industry may require aggregation of the direct impact of types of pollution control, combined with the cost impacts passed on by all of its suppliers. These and other complex data collection and methodological problems will have to be resolved, especially with respect to foreign data and analyses, before specific competitive advantages due to pollution abatement programs can be identified.

Some attempts have been made to determine industrial costs related to pollution control requirements. In 1971, a series of industry studies on the costs of environmental controls was carried out under the joint sponsorship of the Council on Environmental Quality, the Environmental Protection Agency, and the Department of Commerce. An additional set of industry studies designed to determine the economic impact of anticipated water pollution controls was sponsored by the Environmental Protection Agency in 1972. These two sets of studies covered over forty industries, including steel, copper, aluminum, inorganic chemicals, foods, energy and automobile manufacturing. The studies have been reviewed in depth as background for this report under Section 6. The specific data and findings they contain were based on early projections of pollution control standards. These standards are now largely out of date since most have been superseded by stricter controls. Therefore, the specific data in the reports have not been directly useful for the types of analyses required under Section 6. These studies covered capital investments and direct operating costs related to air or water pollution abatement in the industries surveyed, and they provide a useful base of experience in this regard. However, indirect costs (e.g., those imposed on suppliers) were not covered, so Section 6 analyses will have to start with a new methodology to cover these important factors. The following report identifies and discusses the major considerations related to this and other tasks called for by Section 6.

To assist in carrying out its responsibilities under Section 6, the Department of Commerce would appreciate receiving comments on this report, and any data, analyses, or other materials related to the specific requirements of Section 6. Communications should be addressed to Director, Bureau of Competitive Assessment and Business Policy, U.S. Department of Commerce, Washington, D.C. 20230.

II. DOMESTIC CONTEXT OF SECTION 6

The first assignment in Section 6 requires the Secretary of Commerce to *under-take immediately an investigation and study to determine—*

(1)   the extent to which pollution abatement and control programs will be imposed on, or voluntarily undertaken by, United States manu-facturers in the near future and the probable short- and long-range effects of the costs of such programs (computed to the greatest extent practicable on an industry-by-industry basis) on (A) the pro-duction costs of such domestic manufacturers, and (B) the market prices of the goods produced by them. . .

The requirements of this mission are twofold—first, the identification of U.S. industrial pollution abatement programs, and second, the identification of the probable short- and long-range U.S. industrial cost effects of these programs.

A. U.S. Industrial Pollution Abatement Programs

Federal mandatory pollution abatement programs are now in effect for a wide range of pollutants, including air, water, noise, and radiation. In addition, there are Federal programs for the management of coastal zones and public lands which will impose additional environmental controls.

These antipollution laws provide for implementation by regulations that set out standards for industrial compliance. For most of the recent enactments, however, the standards development has only begun. Specific conclusions about cost impacts will have to await further steps in this process.

The statutory basis for these Federal programs is briefly described in the following section.

B. U.S. Industrial Cost Effects

Taken together, the regulatory requirements will have significant economic consequences. They have important implications for the future scope and character of business decision-making, and for the profitability and viability of particular firms and industries. They impose cost burdens that must be accommodated in one manner or another—for example, by resource substitutions in manufacture, by productivity gains, by reduction of profit margins, by price rises, by diminished increases in real wages, or, at worst, by plant shutdown or relocation. The size of the costs to be absorbed or shared depends not only on the technical standards of purity that are adopted but also on such factors as the nature and scale of the production process, the degree of success already achieved in pollution abatement, the age and adaptability of plant and equipment already in place, and the comparative expensiveness of (a) new construction, and (b) the installation of antipollution systems in existing facilities.

In Section 6 of P.L. 92-500, the concern of Congress over the aggregate economic implications of pollution control is directed at the resulting production costs and market prices. The costs of pollution control could be considerable, for at least two reasons. First, stringent pollution controls could involve substantial capital expenditures, compressed into a short span of years, with possible strain on company resources and on capital markets. Second, some firms and industries—and the geographic areas in which they are located—will be less able than others to carry the new economic load imposed by an intensive national antipollution effort.

To identify the costs involved, consideration must be given to the combined impact of all types of pollution control requirements on firms, and on their suppliers. While the direct cost impact of any particular pollution control requirement might be modest, the combined impact of all types of pollution controls and the effect of such controls on all suppliers, not just for the end-product industry, could be substantial. Thus, higher prices due to pollution control requirements (in, e.g., the glass, plastics, and steel industries) have to be accumulated at end-product levels (e.g., automobiles and appliances) before the true impact on international markets can be known. Pollution abatement costs in industries which have little or no international trade, such as electric power, are therefore relevant to the requirements of Section 6.

Development of a consistent methodology for an industry to determine pollution abatement effects on costs and prices will involve simulation of the response of cost accounting and budgeting criteria for additional capital and operating costs associated with compliance. Allocation of these costs on an industry or product basis will require either a knowledge of, or some reasonable assumption concerning, these decision rules. The complexity of this particular calculation is evident from the variety of feasible costing approaches available— e.g., standard, actual, job, or process, each of which may cover either "full" or "variable" costs. The existence of multidivision or multiproduct companies further complicates the determination of actual costs on a product basis. In addition, the proprietary nature of information on production costs and their implications for an industry's competitive position will hamper the direct collection of detailed information from companies. Synthetic or calculated estimates will probably have to be developed for a number of plausible alternative situations, or a set of "representative" costs would have to be adopted.

The translation of production costs into actual market prices is equally difficult. It involves assessment of likely incremental financial returns and premises regarding the performance and service standards of the market. The structure of an industry and the quality of competition are major influences on pricing. Estimated probable price increases must take account of customary profit margins, the target return on investment, and the return on equity sought by firms within the particular industry. Furthermore, intercompany and interindustry variations in these criteria will result in a range of prices for the given decision rules.

To be complete, the production cost and market price determinations for an industry or product line must include indirect costs. This means that pollution-related material and labor inputs to the industry must be traced throughout the industrial infrastructure. The use of input-output tables may be feasible, but this requires assumptions regarding price elasticity, shifts in markets due to substitutability, and other factors before final prices can be determined. In addition, as price effects are projected through time, the original input-output table becomes outmoded. Consequently, the assumptions underlying the analysis become more tenuous.

A tracing of these costs through the industrial structure should be accompanied by statistical analyses of errors arising from the dispersion of the observed data.

The final result would thus yield a set of average values for cost and price effects, rather than point estimates.

These are formidable methodological problems. They will not be solved easily, or soon. However, to some extent, these problems will diminish as the cost effects of pollution control rise with the aggregation of strict regulations for several types of pollution within a given industry. The general level of these cost impacts should thus be easier to identify over time. These opportunities to develop beginning, comprehensive, order-of-magnitude effects will be pursued further in subsequent reports.

III. POLLUTION CONTROL IN FOREIGN COUNTRIES

The second requirement in Section 6 specifies that the Secretary of Commerce *shall undertake immediately an investigation and study to determine...*

> *(2) the probable extent to which pollution abatement and control programs will be implemented in foreign industrial nations in the near future and the extent to which the production costs (computed to the greatest extent practicable on an industry-by-industry basis) of foreign manufacturers will be affected by the costs of such programs...*

The requirements of 6 (a) (2) are similar to those contained in 6 (a) (1), namely, the identification of foreign industrial pollution abatement programs and their probable effect on foreign production costs.

A. Foreign Industrial Pollution Abatement Programs

An initial examination is presented in the Appendix* to this report of the pollution control programs of nine other industrialized nations. The countries reviewed are:

Belgium	Japan
Canada	Netherlands
France	Sweden
Germany	United Kingdom
Italy	

In 1971, fifty-eight per cent of total U.S. exports of merchandise went to these countries, and they, in turn, provided sixty-five per cent of total U.S. imports.

Within the data limitations cited in connection with the discussion in Chapter II of this report, the country profiles provided in the Appendix summarize each country's pollution problems, environmental awareness, abatement policies and

---

*The Appendix is not reproduced here.

programs, pollution costs, governmental assistance and future programs. The highlights of the environmental policies and programs of these countries concerning air and water pollution only are noted briefly below. While all the countries evidence concern regarding air and water pollution abatement, their performance to date varies from comprehensive to nonexistent controls.

Belgium recently has enacted comprehensive laws for dealing with air and water pollution. Water pollution regulations are to be issued in 1973. Air pollution standards for industrial and power generating plants are being developed. After August 5, 1973, all fuel oils produced and used in Belgium for domestic heating must have no more than one per cent sulfur.

Canada has comprehensive water resources legislation, which when fully implemented, will rely on regional water resource management agencies to control all aspects of water use, including the setting of environmental water quality and discharge standards. At present, the Canadian Federal Government has set national effluent discharge limits for the pulp and paper industry, and is also developing similar standards for several other industries. Air quality standards are set by the provincial governments, taking into consideration national air quality objectives set by the Federal Government for specified pollutants. At present, the Province of Ontario has strict air pollution regulations, while the less industrialized provinces have done little to curb industrial air pollution.

In *France*, authorities may impose conditions regarding the quality and content of gaseous emissions into the air prior to the construction of an industrial plant. These standards are rigorously enforced in nationalized industries and utilities, generally less so with respect to private firms. France also has established laws for surveying and controlling river pollution and the power of water management agencies is being strengthened.

In *Germany*, the States have the constitutional authority to regulate air and water pollution. While the Federal Government may recommend emission and discharge standards, it must rely on the States to adopt and to enforce them. As such, standards and enforcement vary widely. Amendments to the German constitution to centralize environmental control authority are now under consideration, as are ambitious federal legislative proposals to control air and water quality.

Italy has no water pollution legislation, but does have a 1972 air pollution law which provides for the establishment of emission standards regulating heating installations, industrial plants and motor vehicles. The development and enforcement of standards vary region-by-region, but on the whole there is only minimal control at present.

Japan recently has enacted fourteen new environmental laws providing, *inter alia*, for comprehensive controls of air and water pollution. Whether and to what extent these new efforts will be effective in abating Japan's serious pollution problems must await their implementation and enforcement.

The Netherlands has a comprehensive water pollution program which includes the prohibition of discharging effluents into surface water without a permit. The permits specify what water quality or discharge standards must be met. Air pollution is controlled through the imposition of emission standards for manufacturing and service plants. To assist in the enforcement of these standards, a national network of 250 monitoring stations and ten regional measuring centers is under construction and scheduled for completion in 1973.

Sweden regulates both industrial air and water pollution through a license procedure required of firms using specified production processes. Emission limits, which follow national recommended standards, and other operating conditions for the protection of the environment, are set forth in the operating license of each firm and are legally enforceable. The terms of each license are negotiated with the Government, taking into consideration the economic ability of the firm to meet the recommended national standards. However, the burden of proof lies with the firm if it believes that it is unable to meet the applicable standards.

In the *United Kingdom*, local and regional authorities set and enforce emission standards on a case-by-case basis, applying a "best practicable means" standard in determining the extent to which a firm is technically and economically capable of meeting the established standards. While enforcement is not consistent, significant progress has been made in abating smoke, grit and dust emissions. All water discharges must be approved by the river authorities. Their responsibility includes conserving, redistributing and augmenting water resources as well as determining effluent standards for new and existing sources.

Tracking the levels of control in these and other nations, and their changes over time, amount to major technical efforts. Several international organizations have similar interests in this area, and one or more may become a continuing source for this information on a global basis.

B. Foreign Pollution Control Costs

In Chapter II of this report, the difficulties that will be encountered in developing good domestic cost data on pollution control were described. This situation is further complicated at the international level by such additional factors as incompatible industrial classifications, differences in cost accounting practices, language barriers, and data verification problems. Some of these difficulties can be overcome by the development and use of standardized methodologies. The likelihood that these developments will occur under one or more international organizations will be examined in subsequent reports.

An initial international pollution cost study for a few industries has been carried out by the staff of the twenty-three nation Organization for Economic Cooperation and Development (OECD), but the reports are currently restricted by the OECD. The OECD is now in the process of developing plans for several additional cost studies under the auspices of its Environmental Committee. As the results of these efforts become available, they will be reviewed in this series of reports.

In addition, the U.S. State Department is currently completing an ad hoc review of the pollution costs in three foreign industries—steel, pulp and paper, and non-ferrous metals. The results of this effort will also be carefully reviewed for future reports under Section 6.

IV.   INTERNATIONAL COMPETITIVE CONSIDERATIONS

The remainder of Section 6 (a) requires that the Secretary of Commerce *shall undertake immediately an investigation and study to determine . . .*

(3)   *the probable competitive advantage which any article manufactured in a foreign nation will likely have in relation to a comparable article made in the United States if that foreign nation—*

   (A)   *does not require its manufacturer to implement pollution abatement and control programs,*

   (B)   *requires a lesser degree of pollution abatement and control in its programs, or*

   (C)   *in any way reimburses or otherwise subsidizes its manufacturers for the costs of such programs;*

(4)   *alternative means by which any competitive advantage accruing to the products of any foreign nation as a result of any factor described in paragraph (3) and be (A) accurately and quickly determined, and (B) equalized, for example, by the imposition of a surcharge or duty, on a foreign product in an amount necessary to compensate for such advantage; and*

(5)   *the impact, if any, which the imposition of a compensating tariff or other equalizing measure may have in encouraging foreign nations to implement pollution abatement and control programs.*

A.   Competitive Advantages as a Result of Pollution Abatement Programs

The inadequate data and methodology described in previous sections preclude any specific computation at the present time of competitive advantages due to the factors cited in numbered paragraph (3) above. However, since the United States is in the relatively early stages of application of the strict environmental controls enacted in the recent past, it may be some time before the most substantial cost effects reach the international marketplace in the form of higher prices. In water pollution control, for example, the strictest industrial controls will not be applied until the late 1970s and early 1980s.

Any foreign competitive advantages will occur as these and other U.S. pollution control programs simultaneously impose costs of domestic manufacturers, and their suppliers. These advantages may be due to lower foreign levels of pollution control, or foreign government actions which subsidize industrial compliance.

Each of the nine countries reviewed in this report, and the U.S., are members of the Organization for Economic Cooperation and Development and all have adopted the OECD's "polluter-pays" principle. Some assistance, however, is usually provided by governments to industries for costs imposed by pollution control regulations, as may be seen in the "Government Assistance" sections of each of the country profiles contained in the Appendix.

Depreciation allowances on pollution control equipment, for example, are generally more favorable in other countries than in the U.S., as may be seen from Figure [1]. In the U.S., amortization of the entire cost of such equipment over five years is permitted, but the investment tax credit does not apply in this case, and straight-line depreciation must be used.

Figure 1
Special Depreciation Allowances for Pollution Control Equipment:
Selected Foreign Countries and the United States

Country	Percentage and Time	Comments
Canada	100% in 2 years	Equipment purchased 1965–1973
France	50% in 1 year	Facilities built 1968–1974; in addition to normal accelerated depreciation
Germany	50% in 5 years	In addition to straight-line depreciation
Italy	None	—
Japan	50% in 1 year	In addition to accelerated depreciation
Sweden	None	—
United Kingdom	None	—
United States	100% in 5 years	Equipment purchased after 1970 for plants built before 1969; 5 year period must be amortized on straight-line basis; no investment tax credit permitted

In future reports, an attempt will be made to isolate for special attention the instances where the most serious international market dislocations will occur under the considerations set forth in Section 6. This attempt will require an identification of those U.S. products which (a) will be impacted most severely by aggregated pollution control requirements, and (b) are involved in substantial trade flows with countries exercising lesser control, or which offer high subsidies for industrial compliance.

B.   Equalization Measures

Provisions of P.L. 92-500 other than Section 6 call for Federal action to encourage international harmonization of standards at least to the same extent as required by U.S. laws, and its Declaration of Goals and Policy proposes that the President cooperate with other nations in a quest for this uniformity. Section 101 (c), which is part of the Declaration, further provides:

> . . .that the President, acting through the Secretary of State and such national and international organizations as he determines appropriate, shall take such action as may be necessary to insure that to the fullest extent possible all foreign countries shall take meaningful action for the prevention, reduction, and elimination of pollution in their waters and in international waters and for the achievement of goals regarding the elimination of discharge of pollutants and the improvement of water quality to at least the same extent as the United States does under its laws.

Section 7 provides for international agreements and for participation in international forums, including the United Nations, on behalf of harmonization:

> The President shall undertake to enter into international agreements to apply uniform standards of performance for the control of the discharge and emission of pollutants from new sources, uniform controls over the discharge of pollutants into the ocean. For this purpose the President shall negotiate multilateral treaties, conventions, resolutions, or other agreements, and formulate, present, or support proposals at the United Nations and other appropriate international forums.

Adoption of the "polluter-pays" principle by all twenty-three members of the Organization for Economic Cooperation and Development (OECD) in May 1972 represents a significant step toward harmonization. This principle is strongly supported by the U.S. Government. Thus, in his 1973 State of the Union Message on Natural Resources and Environment, President Nixon reaffirmed that "the costs of pollution should be more fully met in the marketplace, not in the Federal budget." A similar view of cost allocation was adopted by OECD to prevent trade distortions that would result if the cost burdens were more or less widely diffused in some countries in the first instance, but imposed directly upon industry in others.

Determination of equalization procedures other than harmonization would have to be based on cost comparisons which take account of many complex factors, including abatement techniques, governmental assistance programs, the aggregation of pollution-control costs for products manufactured from multiple raw material sources, and environmental costs associated with energy production. No means are available at present for obtaining and combining this information "accurately and quickly." Accomplishing this requirement of Section 6 is one of the most difficult assignments presented in P.L. 92–500. The data and methodological problems discussed throughout this report are involved, at both domestic and foreign levels. A determination of the feasibility and design of approaches to accomplish this task will be a major topic in future reports in this series.

Federal Environmental Laws, 1872-1983

U.S. Department of Commerce

The first federal laws concerning the environment were enacted over one hundred years ago, although concern with such matters has been increased in recent years. This section lists and describes significant federal legislation in the environmental area since 1872. It is interesting to note that some of the older dormant legislation, such as the Refuse Act of 1899, has recently been utilized as the basis for new actions against polluters. This summary was extracted from a U.S. Department of Commerce report.

1. AIR POLLUTION ABATEMENT

Air Pollution Act of 1955 (69 Stat. 322)

Authorizes research and data collection program by Public Health Service; establishes policy of state and local responsibility for air pollution under Federal Government leadership.

Clean Air Act of 1963 (77 Stat. 392)

Federal Government authorized to set standards for motor vehicle pollution; expands federal research.

Air Quality Act of 1967 (81 Stat. 485)

Establishes procedures for issuance of air quality criteria; establishment of atmospheric areas and air quality control regions; provides for setting of standards by states or Federal Government.

Clean Air Amendments of 1970 (84 Stat. 1676)

Major provisions are:

EPA required to prescribe national standards for each air pollutant with an adverse effect on public health and welfare.

States are required to submit plans for implementing and enforcing primary and secondary standards within nine months after promulgation of a national ambient air quality standard; Administrator must approve within four months after submission.

SOURCE: From The Second Report of the Secretary of Health, Education, and Welfare, in compliance with PL 90-148, The Clean Air Act, as amended, March, 1970.

Figure 1
Federal Environmental Legislation

Year of Enactment and Implementation

Type of Program	Pre-1900–1950	1951–1960	1961–1970	1971–1975	1977	1983
MR		Air Pollution Control of 1955	Clean Air Control Act of 1963 Air Quality Act of 1967 Clean Air Amendments of 1970	State Implemented plans by 1975		
Noise				Noise Control Act of 1972 Final regulations by 1974		
Public Land Resources		Watershed Protection and Flood Prevention Act of 1954 Flood Control Act of 1956 Multiple Use—Standard Yield Act of 1960	Wilderness Act of 1964			
Radiation		Atomic Energy Act of 1954				

Figure 1 (Continued)

	Year of Enactment and Implementation					
Type of Program	Pre-1900–1950	1951–1960	1961–1970	1971–1975	1977	1983
Solid Waste			Solid Waste Disposal Act of 1965 Resource Recovery Act of 1970			
Water	Rivers and Harbors Act of 1899 Public Health Services Act of 1912 Oil Pollution Act of 1924 Water Pollution Control Act of 1948	Amendments of 1953 Federal Water Pollution Control Act of 1956	Amendments of 1961 Water Quality Act of 1965 Clean Water Restoration Act of 1966 National Environmental Policy Act of 1969	Federal Water Pollution Control Act Amendments of 1972	Effluent limitation standards are to be achieved by 1977 for public sources; and for non-public sources using "best practicable control technology"	Establish effluent limitation standards by 1983 for public sources using the "best practicable control technology" over plant life" and for non-public sources using the "best available control technology"

Implementation of state plans by not later than three years after approval; Administrator may grant a further two-year extension.

EPA to set such plan if not provided by state, or if not acceptable to EPA.

EPA to suggest ways of achieving standards.

EPA authorized to adopt standards for stationary sources of pollution, and for hazardous air pollutants.

Emissions of carbon monoxide and hydrocarbons from new motor vehicles in the 1975 model year must be reduced by ninety per cent from emissions permitted under regulations applicable to the 1970 model year; same reduction is mandated for oxides of nitrogen by 1976 as compared with emissions permitted under regulations applicable to the 1971 model year.

Various penalties provided, including fines of up to $25,000 per day and/or one year imprisonment.

2. NOISE POLLUTION ABATEMENT

Noise Control Act of 1972

Establishes mechanism within EPA for control of noise (except aircraft noise). Major provisions are:

Within nine months, EPA authorized to develop and publish criteria on noise.

Within three months thereafter, EPA must publish information on the levels of environmental noise which should be maintained to protect public health and welfare with an adequate margin of safety.

Within six months thereafter, EPA must publish reports identifying products that are major sources of noise and techniques for control reflecting "best available technology" as well as cost of complying.

By April 28, 1974, initial regulations are to be proposed.

By October 28, 1974, final regulations are to be published.

Penalties of up to $25,000 per day are provided.

Authorized expenditures are provided of $3 million (fiscal 1973), $6 million (fiscal 1974) and $12 million (fiscal 1975).

3. PUBLIC LAND RESOURCES MANAGEMENT

A number of laws have been enacted to deal with specific areas of and management and in particular with government owned land. Several agencies are authorized to administer federally owned lands:

Interior Department (National Park Service; Bureau of Land Management)
Department of Agriculture (Forest Service)
Department of Defense

The following summarizes applicable legislative efforts:

Public Land Law Review Commission

Created in 1964 to recommend necessary changes in federal laws and regulations; dissolved December 31, 1970 pursuant to law of creation.

Multiple Use-Sustained Yield Act of 1960 (74 Stat. 215)

Promotes use of national forest for wildlife, grazing, mining, and recreation as well as to assure timber supplies.

Wilderness Act of 1964 (78 Stat. 890)

Provides protection from exploitation of designated wilderness areas.

Watershed Protection and Flood Prevention Act of 1954 (68 Stat. 666)

Provides for Federal Government cooperation with states for the purpose of preventing erosion, floodwater, and sediment damages in U.S. watersheds and of furthering the conservation, development, utilization, and disposal of water.

Flood Control Act of 1954 (68 Stat. 1256)

Various works of improvement are enumerated for the benefit of navigation and the control of destructive floodwaters; no modification of any project herein is allowed without a report by the Chief of Engineers, U.S. Army.

Mining Law of 1872 (17 Stat. 91)

Declares all valuable mineral deposits in public lands to be free and open to exploration and purchase by U.S. citizens; sets out standards for possession and obtaining patents to land.

Mineral Lands Leasing Act of 1920 (41 Stat. 437)

Provides for granting of leases and prospecting permits to U.S. citizens for exploration and exploitation of various enumerated minerals in public lands; limitations on possessory rights are set forth at length.

Coastal Zone Management Act of 1972 (86 Stat. 1280)

Provides for establishment of a national policy and development of a national program for management, beneficial use, protection, and development of the land and water resources of the Nation's coastal zones; grants authorized to be made to coastal states for development and administration of management programs; Secretary of Commerce vested with authority under this Act and authorized to convene a Coast Zone Management Advisory Committee to assist him in his evaluation of state programs.

4. RADIATION POLLUTION CONTROL

Atomic Energy Act of 1954 (68 Stat. 919)

AEC is established and authorized to control the possession, use, and transfer of licensed material; establish protection standards; require appropriate monitoring devices; criminal penalties are provided.

5. WATER POLLUTION ABATEMENT

Refuse Act of 1899 (30 Stat. 1151)

Prohibits discharge of matter into navigable waters except in liquid state from streets and sewers; primarily designed to prohibit impediments to navigation; violators subject to $2,500 and/or thirty days imprisonment.

Public Health Service Act of 1912 (37 Stat. 309)

Authorizes investigations of water pollution related to diseases and impairment of man.

Oil Pollution Act of 1924 (43 Stat. 604)

Controls discharge of oil from vessels in coastal waters which may damage health, aquatic life, harbors, and docks.

Water Pollution Control Act of 1948 (62 Stat. 1155)

Recognizes water pollution as national problem; best dealt with at local level with federal government assistance; authorizes $22.5 million annually (for five years) for low interest loans for municipal abatement facilities but limited to lower of one-third of cost of $250,000.

Amendments of 1952 (66 Stat. 755)

Extends Act to 1956.

Water Pollution Control Act Amendments of 1956 (70 Stat. 498)

Extends and strengthens 1948 law; administered by Surgeon General.

Federal Water Pollution Control Act Amendments of 1961 (75 Stat. 204)

Designates Secretary of HEW to administer the Act; abatement enforcement extended to intrastate navigable waters; enforcement procedures strengthened; authorizes $100 million annually for construction and $25 million total for research.

Reorganization Plan No. 2 of 1966

Transfers FWPCA to Interior Department.

Clean Water Restoration Act of 1966 (80 Stat. 1246)

Provides $3.9 billion for construction grants to build sewage plants and for research; removes previous ceiling limits to provide grants for large cities.

National Environmental Policy Act of 1969 (83 Stat. 852)

Establishes Council on Environmental Quality (CEQ) to analyze trends in environment and effect of Federal programs; provides for "impact statements" to precede every federal action which significantly affects the quality of the environment.

Reorganization Plan No. 3 of 1970

Consolidates many previous agencies into EPA with responsibility for:
1. establishing and enforcing standards
2. monitoring and analyzing the environment
3. conducting research and demonstrations
4. assisting local and state control programs
5. administering Federal programs dealing with air and water pollution, disposal of solid waste, pesticides regulation, and noise.

Executive Order 11574 (December 23, 1970)

Establishes new permit program for industrial discharge under Refuse Act of 1899; administered by Army Corps of Engineers.

Federal Water Pollution Control Act Amendments of 1972 (86 Stat. 816)

Replaces previous Acts (1961, 1965, 1966, and 1970), all of which were amendments to the original Water Pollution Control Act Amendments of 1956. Major provisions of the 1972 Amendments are:

The Act provides a national goal of complete elimination of discharged pollutants into navigable waters by 1985; interim goal of water quality suitable for the protection and propagation of fish and wildlife and for water recreation by 1983.

Title I

EPA authorized to prepare comprehensive programs for preventing and eliminating pollution in navigable and ground waters; authorizes appropriation of funds to assist states in administering programs.

Title II

EPA authorized to make grants to states and local governments of up to seventy-five per cent of the construction costs of public owned treatment plants.

Title III

EPA to establish effluent limitations:

By July 1, 1977: for all non-public stationary sources employing "the best practicable control technology currently available"

By July 1, 1983: additional effluent limitations for above sources employing "the best available technology economically achievable"

By July 1, 1977: for publicly owned treatment facilities; all must be operational by June 30, 1978

By July 1, 1983: additional effluent limitations for all publicly owned treatment works employing "the best practicable waste treatment technology over the life of the works"

EPA to issue new source standards for some twenty-seven designated industries, and for any discharge of toxic pollutants.

Penalties provided are up to $10,000 per day (civil) and $2,500 to $25,000 per day or $50,000 per day (criminal).

Title IV

Requires permit to discharge any pollutant into navigable waters from stationary source (replaces permit program under Refuse Act of 1899).

VI
ACCOUNTING FOR HUMAN LIVES AND RESOURCES

The Value of a Human Life

Social accounting may be distinguished from conventional accounting by the extra-ordinarily high degree of subjectivity that characterizes the calculations. The subjectivity occurs not only in the usual sense of a bias that intrudes in difficult or unclear measurements, but in the attitudes of the social accountant. For example, measurement of the effects of redistribution may be affected by the accountant's view of the desirability of such redistribution. Perhaps the area of the greatest, but unavoidable, subjectivity is that which involves attributing costs or values to a human life.

Human lives are shortened or extended by most of the actions with which social accounting is concerned. It is doubtful that many will dispute that lengthening human lives represents a social benefit, or that shortening lives is socially undesirable. Thus, accident reduction is desirable; unhealthy pollution is clearly not wanted. But, accident prevention and pollution control have costs, therefore so do the lives saved. If rational social decision making and resource allocation is to take place, some costs or values will have to be attributed to human lives.

The three articles in this section suggest somewhat different views of this problem. The NHTSA approach, described in the *Business Week* article, is reasonable, but only when alternatives are clearly comparable, and only when the single factor of a human life is considered.

The FAA approach—based on the lost productivity of an average individual, plus the associated marginal costs of a death—provides an absolute number for comparison in varying circumstances.

The Washington Area Accident Study also utilizes earnings as a basis for the value of a human life, but instead of an average, it aggregates the computed individual and therefore different values of the persons involved in the accidents. Thus, accidents involving high income people supposedly cost more—a concept that may not sit well, morally, with many people, even accountants.

Obviously, the value of a *specific* human life, particularly to that individual, is not susceptible of rational calculation. However, social calculations would rarely, if ever, include the consideration of the value of any *specific* lives. Far more likely, in pollution, health, accident prevention and similar areas, is the probability that the human lives involved—taken or given—are randomly distributed throughout the population. It might be logical to modify that assumption in certain geographically localized situations, such as the Washington area, or in the case of differentiated populations, for example, air travelers. More frequently, however, the random selection assumption seems valid.

With this in mind, it might be suggested that society has already performed calculations of the valuation of a human life, and that it performs such calculations continuously. Note, for example, the Ibsen quote on the frontispiece of this volume. Multitudes of decisions are

317

made daily; whether to add an emergency room to a hospital, to buy a kidney machine, to erect a guard rail, to install a traffic light, to place a new safety device on an airplane, in which the saving of human lives (or the failure to do so), as in *An Enemy of the People,* is the decision factor. It would be interesting, but not easy, to conduct a survey of a representative sample of such decisions, to see of the value of a life so derived is consistent enough to provide a "concensus" measure of the value of a life.

THE COST-BENEFITS OF SAVING LIVES

Absolutely safe transportation is no more possible to attain than absolute safety in a bathtub. There is inherent risk in any activity. Says a Federal Aviation Administration official: "The safest way to operate aircraft is to keep them in the hangar." And the same is true of operating boats, trains, automobiles, buses, bicycles, or pogo sticks. Moving people and goods always entails some exposure to danger, and eliminating that exposure would result in complete and unacceptable immobility. Even lessening the danger could result in skyrocketing costs that might have the same effect of cutting off the free flow of people and freight that makes the economy tick.

The question is one of cost effectiveness. What constitutes an acceptable cost for trying to provide transportation safety? Put another way: What is the minimum degree of safety the public has a right to expect whatever the cost?

There are no easy answers when cost-benefit formulas have to take into account the value of human lives. For the National Transportation Safety Board, which is charged with investigating conditions that affect the safety of individuals, saving even one life is a paramount consideration. The transport administrative agencies, though, are required to weigh considerations other than safety in carrying out their responsibilities of promoting and maintaining a sound national transportation system. Inevitably this means that the NTSB and the administrative bodies are often at loggerheads.

An example of the difference in approach of the two kinds of agencies grew out of a truck-auto collision on June 19, 1970, near Washington, D.C. Two persons in the automobile, a Mustang, were killed when it ran under the rear of a truck that stopped short. The NTSB accident report issued in August, 1971, found that the absence of rear "underride" protection on the truck was not the cause of the accident but was the probable cause of the two deaths. Ironically, shortly before the NTSB report appeared, the National Highway Traffic Safety Administration, also a part of the Transportation Dept., had dropped a five-year study of underride protection. The agency had decided that improving such protection was not economically feasible. The board's report recommended that NHTSA reopen its investigation, but the NHTSA, thus far, has not done so.

SOURCE: From *Business Week* (October 14, 1972), p. 41. Copyright © 1973 by McGraw-Hill, Inc.

Worth

The decision to drop the study was based on a cost-benefit study that determined that putting steel bars under the rear ends of all trailers would cost $5-million for each life saved—an amount considerably higher than the $200,000 figure NHTSA statistician figured society could reasonably be expected to pay to protect a life. The $5-million-per-life-saved figure was derived by multiplying the cost per vehicle of the device by the number of vehicles affected, and then figuring the cost-per-death by dividing the number of deaths into the aggregate cost.

The NTSB looked at the figures in a different way. It determined that it would cost only $175 per truck to install the device and an additional $540 a year to maintain it. In a sharply critical letter to Douglas W. Toms, administrator of the NHTSA, John H. Reed, chairman of the NTSB, said: "Cost-benefit analysis should continue to be employed to aid in determining priorities among methods of reducing fatalities, but not for determining whether the goal is worthwhile." Reed also indicated that it is part of the public interest to help even the odds that are heavily weighted against car occupants in a collision with a truck.

Toms, in response to the NTSB recommendation replied: "It is certainly true that in almost every collision that mixes cars and heavy trucks, the car will come off second best." But based on NHTSA's cost-benefit studies he added: "Rulemaking on underride guards is not attractive" from an economic standpoint. That is where the matter now stands.

THE COST OF A LIFE IN WASHINGTON, D.C.

Cost Elements

The total cost of reported in-area involvements in traffic accidents relating to Washington area residents was $50,660,655 for the study period (Table 2). Delineation of the various elements of direct cost associated with these traffic accidents was an important aspect of the project. One or more of twenty-four individual elements of direct cost were recorded where applicable. Ten of them pertain to property damage costs of an involvement, and fourteen relate to personal injury costs. Differences in cost elements also were established according to accident severity.

Table 3 summarizes the number of reported involvements and direct costs associated with each of the applicable cost elements. Property damage costs

SOURCE: This selection is an excerpt from a larger study, "Motor Vehicle Accident Costs in the Washington Metropolitan Area," by Gerard L. Drake and Merwyn A. Kraft. Tables and figures are not reproduced here. The Washington Area Motor Vehicle Accident Cost Study was sponsored by the District of Columbia Department of Highways and Traffic and several other groups, in cooperation with the U.S. Bureau of Public Roads.

represented only about two per cent of the total cost in fatal injury involvements, whereas loss of future earnings accounted for ninety-one per cent. In nonfatal injury cases, the costs were evenly divided between property damage losses and personal injury costs (Figure 4).

Considering all reported involvements regardless of severity, 45.2 per cent ($22,883,000) of the $50,661,000 total cost concerned damages to vehicles, 26.7 per cent ($13,525,000) was the present value of loss of future earnings, and all other cost elements combined accounted for 28.1 per cent ($14,253,000). Of the latter amount, the value of work time lost accounted for $3,651,000; legal and court costs amounted to $2,475,000; doctor bills accounted for $1,952,000; hospitalization costs added $1,494,000; and all other costs amounted to $4,681,000.

The Washington Area Motor Vehicle Accident Cost Study was the first study of its type to include in the cost determinations the present value of loss of future earnings for persons fatally injured or permanently impaired. Potential earnings based on age, sex, employment status, education level, the extent of disability, and other factors were considered in these calculations. The procedure required that the potential earnings of the deceased person be considered had he or she enjoyed a normal work life; any reductions in long-term earning capabilities of injured persons also were considered. Anticipated earnings were based on Bureau of the Census data obtained from special tabulations prepared for the District of Columbia. Estimated 1964 wage and salary data related to education, race, and sex classifications of employed persons were utilized.

Loss of future earnings incurred by Washington area residents in fatal injury cases amounted to nearly $63,000 per involvement, and almost $36,000 per involvement in nonfatal injury cases. Damages to the case vehicle averaged $996 in fatal injury cases compared with $427 for nonfatal injury cases and $197 for cases involving property-damage-only. Considering all severity classes combined, damages to vehicles averaged $270 per vehicle.

Legal and court costs averaged about $100 per vehicle involvement for cases involving property-damage-only, but over $500 for nonfatal injury cases and $3,400 for those involving a fatal injury. Including all relevant cost elements, the average cost related to all 202 persons fatally injured in the involvements covered by this study was $59,200, and the average for all 21,477 nonfatally injured persons was about $600.

Doctor bills averaged $127 per person, and hospitalization costs averaged $136 for persons who incurred these costs. Funeral expenses averaged slightly less than $1,000 per person.

ECONOMIC CRITERIA FOR FEDERAL AVIATION EXPENDITURES

Fatalities and Injuries

The purpose of this inquiry to estimate the value of human life lost or injuries suffered in aviation accidents is to derive some guidelines useful in making decisions relating to investment or expenditure for aviation facilities or procedures. Consideration of this problem flows from the view that in our society it is important for the government to attempt to maximize the welfare of all its constituents. Welfare here includes not only material factors, but also all the noneconomic satisfactions which the individual may attain. Ideally, then, in constructing a measure of value for human life, insofar as possible, one should take account of both economic and noneconomic factors. This estimation, therefore, involves several differences from a calculation designed to derive an equitable amount for compensation.

Because the concept of "value" used here involves both economic aspects, some of which can be assigned approximate dollar amounts, and noneconomic values which cannot be translated into sums of money, this inquiry is useful in setting a floor for the value of a human life lost in an airplane accident, but in no sense can it indicate a ceiling. In practice, the expenditures that can be devoted to the purpose of attempting to save human lives will be affected by the availability of resources and the benefit-cost relationship in alternative uses rather than simply by considering the value of human life. Specific alternatives involving varying costs and expected fatality rates should be compared with each other to see which yields the highest benefit-cost ratio.

This discussion will proceed by considering the value of the individual's life to those persons or groups affected by his death. Computations are based on 1960 dollars and upon presently prevailing conditions, using current estimates relating to air travel and costs.

The Individual Himself: The value of an individual's life to himself is basically a noneconomic one and depends to a large extent on his personal view of himself and on whatever underlying philosophical orientation is presupposed. (It should be noted here that the value an individual might place on his life under particular circumstances—such as that involved in the contemplation of suicide—may not be equal to an objective valuation of his life.) In crude terms, the value of life for the individual concerned can be expressed as the net satisfactions, economic and noneconomic, that he would have realized had he lived his normal term.

Although a person's satisfactions from life are extremely individualistic, as a minimum amount we might assign to them the present value of his earning stream. For persons involved in fatal airplane accidents, this amounts to an average of $210,000.[1] The present value of the individual's total income, rather than only that segment directed toward his personal consumption, is used in this calculation since the individual derives satisfactions from all uses made of his income. For example, the individual is presumed to allocate his income

SOURCE: From *Economic Criteria for Federal Aviation Expenditures* (June 1962), pp. VI 20-25. Prepared under FAA Contract No. FAA/BRD-355 by Gary Fromm, Director of Economic Research, United Research Inc.

between personal and family uses in that manner which best enhances his net satisfactions.

The Individual's Family: The individual's family suffers both a noneconomic and an economic loss. The family loses the net value of such things as the love, companionship, direction, and support which the passenger would have provided had he lived, and the satisfactions derived from their sharing his pleasures with him.

In the case of the death of an earning member of the family, the family also loses the discounted value of the family's consumption stream that would have been derived from the member's earned income and its prorated share of the member's contribution toward the family's increase in asset position. (This is an element similar to, but separate from, the satisfactions an individual derives from that part of his income devoted to his family.) It is reasonable to estimate that approximately two-thirds of the average earned income of individuals killed in airplane accidents is devoted to the consumption of other family members and toward increasing their prorated share of total family assets. The individual's family, therefore, suffers a loss of $123,000. To this should be added the economic costs concerned with burial, mourning, and other last rites, reduced by the present value of such expenses had the individual lived his normal term.

It should be noted here that any amounts that the family may receive in insurance payments (as in the case of aircraft hull insurance) do not enter into the calculations since these are transfer payments and so do not have a positive net over-all economic effect (the gains of the beneficiary are the losses of the insurance company and its stockholders and clients) in the calculation of the value of a human life lost in an airplane accident.

The Individual's Friends and Community: The individual's friends and his community lose the net noneconomic satisfactions that they would have derived from the individual had he lived. They also suffer an economic loss equal to the net value of the noncompensated services the individual would have rendered to them. (The magnitude of this loss is especially apparent in the case of a man who renders such significant community service as that connected with heading up a Community Chest drive.) Assuming that the average individual contributes an amount equal to approximately fifteen per cent of his working time to noncompensated services for friends and community, the present value of this economic loss amounts to $28,000.

The Individual's Employer: At a minimum, the individual's employer loses the economic costs of restaffing to fill the dead passenger's position compared with what the situation would have been under conditions of normal turnover. On an average, such costs might approximate one-third of the yearly income of individuals lost in airplane accidents, or approximately $4,000.

The employer might also suffer a further economic loss if the individual had certain unique characteristics so that the employer could not secure an equivalent replacement for him.

The Economy as a Whole: To the extent that the occurrence of airplane accidents resulting in fatalities influences a percentage of the traveling public to forego what otherwise would have been economically valuable trips or to travel by less efficient modes, the economy as a whole suffers a net economic loss. It is not possible to calculate this amount.

Furthermore, insofar as the average individual killed in an airplane accident is paid less than is economically merited (in economic terms: less than his marginal product), the economy suffers a further loss from his death.

The Government: The Federal Aviation Agency and the Civil Aeronautics Board incur costs directly concerned with accident investigation. An approximate figure for the cost of this activity per fatality is arrived at by imputing the expenses of accident investigation, allocating a proportion of these expenses toward the examination of fatalities as opposed to injuries, and dividing this figure by the annual number of fatalities. The total cost per fatality of FAA and CAB investigation approximated $4,000 in 1960. (Costs involved in preventing accidents are not included in this computation because these should not be ascribed to fatalities which have occurred but to those potential fatalities which it is assumed have been prevented by such action.)

The government also incurs economic and noneconomic losses due to the decline in prestige resulting from having an air transportation system in which there has been loss of human life.

Air Carriers: Airlines incur a direct economic cost for accident investigation and other related costs which can be estimated at $4,000 per fatality. (Money paid in settlement of claims is a transfer payment and so is not included here.)

Owing to the occurrence of air accidents, individuals shift from air to other forms of transportation. Assuming this results in the average load factor on *all* transportation facilities being lower than it would have been, there is a net economic loss to transportation agencies, since greater over-all investment is required for the same number of revenue passenger-miles.[2]

In conclusion, then, the minimum economic cost per fatality in 1960 amounted to $373,000.[3] There are also other economic losses incurred from passenger fatalities for which it is not possible to assign a specific value. Furthermore, this sum does not include a number of noneconomic values which can not be directly translated into economic terms but which have great importance in our society. The figure of $373,000 then should be looked upon only as a floor in calculating the value of a human life lost in a 1960 air carrier accident.[4]

The analysis for the determination of serious injury costs is similar to that for loss of life. The individual is unable to work and earn his salary and, in addition, must pay medical expenses. His family loses their share of the income too. (Again, as above, any insurance or other compensation for the accident is irrelevant, since it represents a transfer of assets and the gains of the passenger and his family from this source is matched by the losses of others.) There are accident investigation costs to be borne by government agencies and the airlines, and the community loses the services of the passenger for a period of time.

It has been assumed that, on the average, this interval is one year. That is, the injured passenger requires a year to recuperate completely from the accident.[5] Thus, per serious injury in 1960, the passenger's loss was $13,000, the family lost satisfactions worth $8,700, and the community was denied services valued at $3,800. Airlines and government agencies, on an average basis, are assumed to spend as much for the investigation of serious injury accidents as for fatalities (this is logical since both are frequently found in the same accident), $4,000 per person for each group. The remaining cost is for medical expenses which are estimated to total an average of $50 per day for one year, or $18,250. No provision has been made for any employer costs due to the loss of an employee for one year. It is presumed that responsibilities, such as management, sales, etc., will temporarily be realigned to accommodate the individual's absence. This would result in some additional charges.

Taking all the above costs into account, the estimated total cost per serious aviation injury in 1960 was $51,750. This, of course, does not include an allowance for the suffering endured by the injured passenger, which, if it were added, would substantially raise the figure shown. As in the case of minor or no damage to aircraft, no estimate was prepared for the cost of minor injuries because their extent is unknown, many result from nearly uncontrollable causes (e.g., turbulence) and the total value involved in probably negligible.

Forecasts of U.S. Air Carrier Accident Costs

Forecasts of air carrier accident costs have been prepared for the years 1960–1975 and are presented in Table [1]. Annual cost increases of two per cent have been utilized for items other than those which derive their value from passenger income. For the latter, the assumed annual salary increment is 2½ per cent. This corresponds to the rate of increase evidenced by passengers' income in the air travel surveys cited previously in this chapter.

General Aviation

Property Damage

Property damage stemming from general aviation accidents is more extensive than that arising from air carrier incidents because the number of accidents is far

Figure 1
Unit Costs for United States Air Carrier Accidents: 1960-1975

	1960	1965	1970	1975
Value of Human Life				
Direct Costs				
Employer	$ 4,000	$ 4,500	$ 5,100	$ 5,800
Government Accident Investigation	4,000	4,400	4,900	5,400
Airline Accident Investigation	4,000	4,400	4,900	5,400
Indirect Costs				
Passenger and Family	333,000	376,700	426,300	482,200
Community Services	28,000	31,700	35,800	40,600
Total Cost per Fatality	$373,000	$421,700	$477,000	$539,400
Serious Injury				
Direct Costs				
Medical Expense ($50 per day)	$ 18,250	$ 20,100	$ 22,200	$ 24,600
Government Accident Investigation	4,000	4,400	4,900	5,400
Airline Accident Investigation	4,000	4,400	4,900	5,400
Indirect Costs				
Passenger and Family	21,700	24,500	27,700	31,400
Community Services	3,800	4,300	4,900	5,500
Total Cost per Injury	$ 51,750	$ 57,700	$ 64,600	$ 72,300
Average Value of Aircraft				
Destroyed	$770,000	$1,270,000	$1,260,000	$1,440,000
Substantially Damaged	385,000	635,000	630,000	720,000

greater in the former case. In 1960 there were 4,540 general aviation accidents as contrasted with 97 for air carriers. Of these, 438 and 18 respectively were of a fatal nature. The damage caused by an air carrier crash, of course, is more extensive than that of a similar general aviation catastrophe. Unfortunately, as was true above, no data is available on the value of the property damage arising from general aviation accidents.

Destruction of Aircraft

The method of calculating the value of aircraft destroyed or substantially damaged (as before, no estimate of the cost of minor or no damage was made) is identical to that employed for air carriers. The general aviation fleet was disaggregated into its component aircraft types, the numbers within each category estimated, and market prices attached to the quantity statistics. Cross-multiplication, summation, and division of the total value by the number of aircraft in the fleet then yielded an average value per aircraft of $8,700 in 1960.

Future year values were derived by grouping the planes into three major categories, forecasting (by least squares trends) the number of planes in each class, and depreciating prices for used aircraft at the following rates: piston equipment, five years to a twenty-five per cent residual; turbine equipment, ten years to a fifteen per cent residual; and rotorcraft, five years to a thirty per cent residual. The 1960 average age of these planes was taken into account. New aircraft were added at 1960 prices and an annual inflation factor of two per cent was introduced. As in the case of air carriers, substantial damage repair costs were assumed to equal fifty per cent of the average value of planes in the general aviation fleet.

It should be noted that the future values may be somewhat understated in that strong market demand for general aviation planes in recent years has caused used aircraft prices to decline at slower rates than normal depreciation. Also, no provision has been made for the addition of DME or other similar navigation equipment to future planes or those currently in the fleet. Thus, the estimates for average aircraft values in the later years are conservative.

Fatalities and Injuries

The analysis of the value of human life lost and injuries suffered in general aviation accidents is the same as for air carriers, with the exception that the average income of the individual involved is higher. The 1960 income of business general aviation passengers was previously estimated at $20,000. For personal flying a lower figure, $13,000, has been selected as representative of pilot or passenger income (this corresponds to the average income of passengers on air carrier flight).

Data on the incomes of professional business general aviation pilots[6] and assumptions (based on these statistics) about the incomes of persons engaged in commercial and instructional general aviation activities led, where properly weighted by the number of flying hours in each category,[7] to an estimate of an average 1960 income of $12,000 for these individuals. Weighting the above incomes by flying hours in each class resulted in an average 1960 income of $15,000 for persons utilizing general aviation.

Therefore, the losses resulting from fatalities in general aviation in 1960 were estimated to be: for the individual, $242,000; for his family, $142,000; to the community, $32,000; and to his employer, $4,500. Government accident investigation costs were assumed to be $1,500 per fatality.[8] Thus, the total loss per fatal injury equalled $422,000.

Similarly, application of the techniques employed to evaluate the losses arising from serious injury in air carrier accidents leads to an estimated cost of $49,150 per general aviation serious injury in 1960. This figure is composed of $25,000 to the individual and his family, $18,250 in medical expenses, $4,400 in community services and $1,500 for government accident investigation. Again, as above, no permanent handicap is assumed.

Forecasts of General Aviation Accident Costs

Forecasts through 1975 of general aviation accident costs are presented in Table [2]. As can be seen, given 2½ per cent annual income increments and two per cent cost increases for government accident investigation, the total cost

Table 2
Unit Costs for General Aviation Accidents: 1960-1975

	1960	1965	1970	1975
Value of Human Life				
Direct Costs				
Employer	$ 4,500	$ 5,100	$ 5,800	$ 6,500
Government Accident Investigation	1,500	1,700	1,950	2,200
Indirect Costs				
Individual and Family	384,000	434,500	491,600	556,200
Community Services	32,000	36,200	41,000	46,300
Total Cost per Fatality	$422,000	$477,500	$540,350	$611,200
Serious Injury				
Direct Costs				
Medical Expense ($50 per day)	$ 18,250	$ 20,100	$ 22,200	$ 24,600
Government Accident Investigation	1,500	1,700	1,950	2,200
Indirect Costs				
Individual and Family	25,000	28,300	32,000	36,200
Community Services	4,400	5,000	5,600	6,400
Total Cost per Injury	$ 49,150	$ 55,100	$ 61,750	$ 69,400
Average Value of Aircraft:				
Destroyed	$ 8,700	$ 12,700	$ 16,100	$ 19,400
Substantially Damaged	4,350	6,350	8,050	9,700

per fatality rises from $422,000 in 1960 to $611,200 in 1975. Serious injury costs run from $49,150 in the former year to $69,400 in the latter.

Military Aviation

No accident cost figures have been prepared for military aviation because projections of the number and type of accidents could not be made due to lack of data. Military aviation safety too, for the most part, falls outside the scope of ineffectiveness of the aviation support system.

Summary

The unit costs of physical aviation support ineffectiveness have been ascertained in this chapter. These may be utilized to determine the value of the physical ineffectiveness. Before turning to that task, however, the impact of air travel disruptions on the demand for aviation services will be measured.

NOTES

1.   The present value of the individual's earning stream is computed by assuming an average (mean) salary of $13,000, a yearly increase of 2½ per cent in salary, assets of $25,000, 40 as the average age at death (a lower age would raise expected lifetime earnings and the present value), and taking a discount rate of 6 per cent. (These figures are all on the basis of 1960 dollars. They are URI estimates; in the case of "average salary" and average age at death," they are based on the *Fortune Magazine* air travel survey and studies conducted for the Travel Research Association and Port of New York Authority.) Calculations are made on a pretax basis since it is assumed that benefits equivalent to the amounts paid are derived from the disposition of tax money.

Of this amount, $185,000 also represents the loss to the economy in the form of decreased output. The assumption is made that individuals are paid their marginal products (if they are exploited, the loss to the economy is even greater), but it is not necessary to assume that there is full employment since the incremental losses in efficiency at each stage after the chain of substitution of personnel has taken place would probably approximate the passenger's salary.

2.   For the airlines themselves, if the loss in passenger-mile levels due to the incidence of fatalities amounts to one per cent of present levels, this amounts to approximately $60,000 per fatality. Under present load factor conditions, there is a direct decrease in profits equal to the bulk of this figure.

3.   This figure is the sum of the economic value of the individual's life to himself, $210,000; the economic loss to his family, $123,000; to his friends and community, $28,000; to his employer, $4,000; to the government, $4,000; and to airlines, $4,000. It does not include the losses the airlines sustain from the decrease in passenger-mile levels which result from fatalities.

4.   Further discussion on the significance of this figure may be found in Chapter VIII.

5.   Because of lack of information on the extent of injuries, it is assumed that the recovery is complete and not marred by life-long physical or economic impairment of the individual's physical functions or earning power. If these occur, however, they should be taken into account by raising the loss in the expected earnings stream and including a satisfactions diminution allowance for the handicap.

6.   National Industrial Conference Board, "Executive Aircraft Practices," *op. cit.*

7.   Departure weights would have been desirable, but are unavailable.

8.   Government accident investigation costs were derived by dividing the sum of CAB expenditures for the Bureau of Safety plus twice that amount for FAA accident outlays, by the total number of air carrier and general aviation fatalities and serious injuries. Air carrier fatalities and injuries were accorded twice the weight of those in general aviation because of the greater complexity of aircraft accidents, and causal determinations in the airline field. This method of allocation, of course, provides no funds for the investigation of incidents involving minor or no injury to passengers and little or no damage to aircraft. However, since the total cost of analyses in this area is probably low, the error introduced by distributing the money for these investigations to fatal accident examinations is minimal.

Effectiveness in Saving Lives as a Resource Allocation Criterion

Robert N. Grosse

The brief *Business Week* excerpt, describing the NHTSA accident study, suggests a policy of decision making based on the cost of saving a human life. In the following section, Professor Grosse presents a somewhat more sophisticated approach, utilizing an incremental notion of the cost of a life saved as a basis for resource allocation in health care and research. This selection is a portion of the larger paper, *Problems of Resource Allocation in Health.*

If the first step toward rational decisionmaking is a good information system, the second is a strong capability for analyzing the consequences of alternative courses of action. In the past two years HEW has undertaken a series of analytical studies of existing health programs and possible alternatives.

One of the first analytical studies of the PPB era at DHEW was a study of disease control programs [1]. Considerable work had been done during the last ten years in estimating the economic costs of particular diseases. Among the best known of these are Rashi Fein's *Economics of Mental Illness* [2], Burton Weisbrod's *Economics of Public Health* [3] in which he estimated the costs of cancer, tuberculosis, and poliomyelitis, Herbert Klarman's paper on syphilis control programs [4], and Dorothy Rice's studies covering the international classification of diseases [5], A generation earlier Dublin and Lotka's classic explored the impact of disease and disability and their relation to changes in earning power [6]. The economic implications of disability were, of course, a matter of central interest in the area of workmen's compensation insurance [7]. It was not surprising, then, that when systematic quantitative analysis of government programs and policies began to spread from defense to civilian applications, one of the first analytical studies was a study of disease control programs.

The basic concept of the study was a simple one. HEW supports (or could support) a number of categorical disease control programs, whose objectives are

---

Robert N. Grosse is Professor of Health Planning at the School of Public Health of the University of Michigan.

SOURCE: From *The Analysis and Evaluation of Public Expenditures: The PPB System.* A Compendium of Papers submitted to the Subcommittee on Economy in Government of the Joint Economic Committee, Congress of the United States (1969) Vol. 3, pp. 1208-1225.

Chart 1
Cancer Control Program: 1968–1972

	Uterine-cervix	Breast	Head and neck	Colon-rectum
Grant costs (in thousands)	$97,750	$17,750	$13,250	$13,300
Number of examinations (in thousands)	9,363	2,280	609	662
Cost per examination	$10.44	$7.79	$21.76	$20.10
Examinations per case found	87.5	167.3	620.2	496.0
Cancer cases found	107,045	13,628	982	1,334
Cost per case found	$913	$1,302	$13,493	$9,970
Cancer deaths averted	44,084	2,936	303	288
Cost per death averted	$2,217	$6,046	$43,729	$46,181

Chart 2

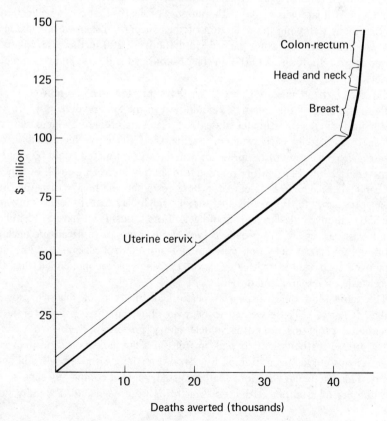

Deaths averted (thousands)

to save lives or to prevent disability by controlling specific diseases. The study was an attempt to answer the question: If additional money were to be allocated to disease control programs, which programs would show the highest payoff in terms of lives saved and disability prevented per dollar spent? The study defines "disease" liberally. Motor vehicle accidents were included along with tuberculosis, syphilis, cancer, and arthritis.

I'm talking here not about research, but where a technology exists and the problem is whether to put the same, more, or less Federal funds behind these control programs to support activities in hospitals, States, and communities. The question we address is where should we allocate the resources available for this purpose.

Chart 1 illustrates the approach to one set of diseases, cancer. We looked at cancer of the uterine cervix, breast, head and neck and colon-rectum. We estimated cost per examination, and the probably number of examinations that would be required for each case found. From this was derived the number of cases that would be found for an expenditure level, and estimates of the cost per case found. An estimate was made of the number of deaths that could be averted by the treatment following the detection of the cancers and then we calculated the cost per death averted which ranged from about $2,200 in the case of cervical cancer up to $40,000 to $45,000 in the case of head and neck and colon-rectum cancer.

On the vertical axis of Chart 2 we have plotted the program costs; this includes the cost of the treatment in addition to the Federal detection program. On the horizontal axis estimates of deaths averted are ordered by increase in cost per death averted in each program. Segments of the curve identified to each disease cover the extent of the program which it was estimated could be mounted in the years 1968–1972 before running into sharply increasing costs. In concept, the cervical cancer curve is cut off where costs become higher than the breast cancer program, etc. From this analysis one might say that if there is only available $50 million, cervical cancer should get all the funds. If we have $115 million, then breast cancer control programs look quite competitive. Head and neck and colon-rectum cancer detection program as major control programs did not look attractive when viewed in this context. The analysts recommended that they concentrate on research and development.

The same kind of analysis was performed for each of the five programs studied (Chart 3). There seemed to be a very high potential payoff for certain educational programs in motor vehicle injury prevention trying to persuade people to use seatbelts, not to walk in front of a car, and so on. And then as we move up this curve, again ordered by cost of averting death we begin adding the others. This particular criterion, deaths averted, was not completely satisfactory. The number of fatalities attributed to arthritis were negligible. Secondly, there

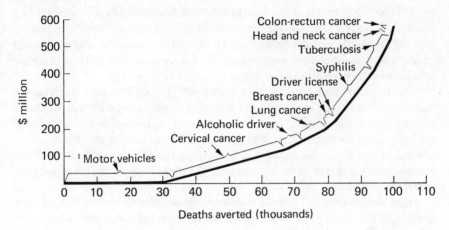

Chart 3

^{1} Seat belt, restraint
Pedestrian injury

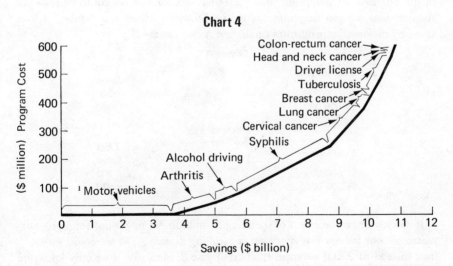

Chart 4

^{1} Seat belt, restraint
Pedestrian injury

is the question, did it matter who died? Did it matter whether it was a thirty-year-old mother or a forty-year old father of a family or a seventy-five-year-old grandfather? On Chart 4, dollar savings summing avoided medical treatments and a crude estimate of the average (discounted) lifetime earnings saved are plotted as a variable in place of deaths averted. There are two changes in results: Cervical cancer and syphilis control programs change places in priority order, and we are able to introduce the arthritis program.

Allocations of resources to programs are developed from such analyses by using information such as this and the preceding charts as an additional insight to give an additional feel for what were relatively high-priority and what were relatively low-priority programs, and then to feed these insights into the decision-making process which also considers existing commitments, the political situation, feasible changes in the rates of spending, the ability to get people moving on programs, and so on.

These studies were not greeted with universal acclaim. Criticisms focused on a number of problems. First, with almost no exception the conclusions were based on average relationships. That is, the total benefits were divided by the total costs. There was little evidence of what the actual impact of increasing or decreasing programs by small amounts might be. If we actually believed the average ratios to be valid at the margin, ought we not to put all our funds into the program with the highest benefit-cost or deaths averted per dollar ratios?

Let me illustrate with a hypothetical example how such marginal information might be used to determine the preferred mix of disease control programs. Assume that we can determine as in the following tables the number of lives saved by different expenditures on disease A and disease B:

Disease A

Expenditures	Lives Saved
$ 500,000	360
$1,000,000	465

Disease B

Expenditures	Lives Saved
$ 500,000	200
$1,000,000	270

If we only knew the effect of spending $1 million, we might opt for a program where all our money was spent on controlling disease A, as we could save 465 lives instead of 270 if we spent it all on disease B. Similarly, if we only knew the effects of programs of a half million dollars, we would probably prefer A, as we'd save 360 rather than only 200 lives.

But if we knew the results for expenditures of both half a million and 1 million dollars in each program, we would quickly see that spending half our money in each program was better than putting it all in one assuming we have $1 million available:

Our calculations would be:

Expenditures			Lives Saved
$1,000,000 on A			465
$1,000,000 on B			270
$1,000,000	{ $500,000 on A	360 }	560
	{ $500,000 on B	200 }	

But suppose we had still more discrete data, as in the following tables which give us the effect of each hundred thousand dollars spent on each control program:

Disease A

Expenditures	Lives Saved
$ 100,000	100
$ 200,000	180
$ 300,000	250
$ 400,000	310
$ 500,000	360
$ 600,000	400
$ 700,000	430
$ 800,000	450
$ 900,000	460
$1,000,000	465

Disease B

	Lives Saved
$ 100,000	50
$ 200,000	95
$ 300,000	135
$ 400,000	170
$ 500,000	200
$ 600,000	225
$ 700,000	240
$ 800,000	255
$ 900,000	265
$1,000,000	270

We could then spend the million dollars even more effectively:

	Lives *Saved*
$ 600,000	400
$ 400,000	170
$1,000,000	570

The lack of marginal data resulted from both a lack of such data for most programs, together with a lack of economic sophistication on the part of the Public Health Service analysts who performed the studies. Despite the theoretical shortcomings, the results were useful when applied with some common sense.

Practical obstacles of existing commitments made it almost impossible to recommend *reductions* in any program. So the decisions dealt with the allocation of modest increments.

In the case of oral and colon-rectum cancers, the average cost per death averted seemed so high that the Department recommended emphasis on research and development, rather than a control program to demonstrate and extend current technology.

In cervical cancer, investigation indicated a sizable number of hospitals in low socioeconomic areas without detection programs which would be willing to establish these if supported by Federal funds. The unit costs of increasing the number of hospitals seemed to be the same as that of those already in the program. Shifting the approach to reach out for additional women in the community would increase costs per examination, but not so high as to change the relative position of this program. At most, it raised costs to about those of the breast cancer control program.

Despite the seeming high potential payoff of some of the motor vehicle programs, there was considerable uncertainty about the success. As a consequence recommendations were for small programs with a large emphasis on evaluation for use in future decisions. The same philosophy was applied to the arthritis program.

What resulted then, was a setting of priorities for additional funding, based on the analytical results, judgment about their reliability, and practical considerations.

A second type of criticism of the analysis described above was concerned with the criteria, especially the calculation of benefits [8]. They were considered inadequate in that they paid attention to economic productivity alone, and omitted other considerations. In particular, they were thought to discriminate against the old who might be past employment years, and women whose earning were relatively low. It was also feared that the logic, if vigorously pursued, would recommend reductions in any program. So the decisions dealt with the allocation medicare, but also programs aimed at assisting the poor whose relative earning power is low by definition.

in actual practice in the programs studied, these concerns were only hypothetical. The programs for cervical and breast cancer looked to be good despite their being for women. As for the poor, most of the programs considered, especially cervical cancer, syphilis, and tuberculosis were aimed primarily at them, and projects were usually located to serve low income residents.

Another type of objection was raised not against the technique of analysis, but against its being done at all. Choices among diseases to be controlled and concern with costs of saving lives can be viewed as contrary to physicians' attitudes in the care of an individual patient. Yet, such decisions are made, analysis or no. Prior decisions on allocations to various health problems rested upon a combination of perception of the magnitude of the problem and the political strength organized to secure funding, e.g., the National Tuberculosis Association.

The disease control cost-benefit analyses suggest that additional considerations are very relevant. Given scarce resources (and if they are not, there is no allocation problem), one ought to estimate the costs of achieving improvements in health. If we can save more lives by applying resources to a small (in numbers affected) problem than a large one, we ought to consider doing so.

A somewhat separate issue is that of the disease control approach to personal health. This is too large an issue to deal with in this paper, but it may make more sense to develop programs of delivering comprehensive health care, including preventive services, than to maintain categorical disease programs.

The following year a number of additional control studies were performed. One of the most interesting and important was on kidney diseases [9]. This analysis was launched at a time when the public was becoming conscious of a new technique, the artificial kidney (chronic dialysis), which could preserve the life and productivity of individuals who would otherwise die of end-stage kidney disease. About 50,000 persons a year do so die. It is estimated that about 7,500 of these were "suited" by criteria of age, temperament, and the absence of other damaging illnesses for dialysis treatment. The national capacity could handle only about 900, who would remain on intermittent dialysis the rest of their lives. About ninety per cent would survive from one year to the next. The operating cost of dialysis treatment in hospitals was estimated at about $15,000 per patient per year. A home treatment approach might reduce this to about $5,000 per year.

The Federal Government was under great pressure to expand the national capacity, which was limited not only by the large money costs, but also by shortages of trained personnel and supplies of blood. Indeed, at the same time as this analysis was being performed, an advisory group to the U.S. Bureau of the Budget was studying the problem of end-stage kidney disease. This group came in with the recommendation for a massive national dialysis program [10].

The HEW program analysis was somewhat more broadly charged, and took a more systems oriented approach. It concerned itself not only about the 7,500 annual candidates for dialysis, but also about the other 40,000 or so who would suffer the end-stage disease, but were unsuited to dialysis. If some way could be found to reduce the numbers falling into the pool of end-stage patients, perhaps a larger number of people could be helped. Chart 5 illustrates the classes of kidney diseases leading to end-stage disease. If these could be better prevented or treated we might keep down the number of patients requiring dialysis or transplantation.

The analysis group, therefore, examined a number of mechanisms or program components. Among these were:

1. Expanded use of existing preventive techniques.

2. Expanded use of existing diagnostic techniques.

3. Expanded use of existing treatments, including chronic dialysis, kidney transplantation and conservative management (drugs, diets, etc.)

4. Laboratory and clinical research to produce new preventive, diagnostic, therapeutic and rehabilitative methods.

5. Increased specialized scientific medical and paramedical training to provide the manpower needed for the research and treatment attack on the kidney disease problem. This also includes continued postgraduate education to train practicing physicians in the use of the latest diagnostic modalities.

Chart 5
Schematic of Transplant and Dialysis Patients

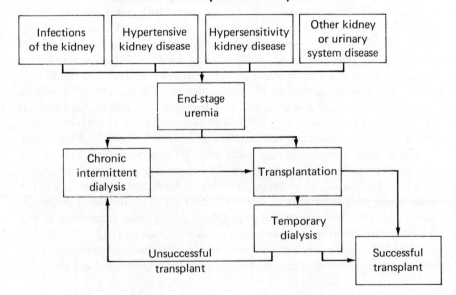

6.   Increased public education to alert potential victims of kidney disease to seek medical help at the earliest possible emergence of warning signs.

7.   Provision of specialized facilities not currently in existence which are essential for the execution of any of the above programs.

It must be understood from the outset that these program components are interdependent in most cases. For example, preventive techniques exist that need further research to make them maximally effective for broad application. New treatment methods are useless if existing diagnostic techniques are not being applied in medical practice. Because of the present inadequacies of existing treatments, be they dialysis, transplantation, or conservative management, a considerable research effort is called for to increase their efficacy and economy to make them more broadly useful.

Time does not permit a detailed description of the analysis. Costs we estimated for relevant public and private expenditures for the nationwide treatment of kidney disease. The latter includes cost of physician care, hospital care, nursing home care, and other professional services for diagnosis and therapy of kidney diseases, as well as the cost of drugs and net insurance costs. In addition, the cost was estimated for ongoing research efforts, for demonstration, screening and detection programs, for education and training efforts, and for that portion of the cost of construction of hospital and medical facilities which can be prorated to the use of patients with kidney disease.

Based on the substantive information obtained and statistical and economic data collected, estimates were made of the benefits to be gained by different approaches to the solution or amelioration of the overall national kidney disease problem at different expenditure levels of HEW funds.

Several different funding levels were assumed, and estimates were made assuming both the current state-of-art and an expected advanced state-of-art in 1975.

Each program consisted of a hypothetical situation where a specific level of HEW program funding was divided among a rational mix of program components (screening, diagnosis and treatment, research, training, etc.) based on the particular characteristics of the specific disease group involved, and was applied to specifically involved or particularly vulnerable groups or, as the case may be, to the entire population. The benefits accruable from these programs were their estimated and stated in terms of overall reduction of mortality, prevalence, and morbidity due to kidney disease.

Benefit indices were quantified in terms of the reduction in annual mortality, the reduction in annual morbidity (number of sick days per year) and in terms of the disease prevalence in the total population due to the specific type of kidney disorder analyzed, which would accrue thanks to the impact of the various program components—such as research advances, disease prevention and improved treatment.

The analysis group avoided estimates of the impact on economic productivity in their results, although such calculations have been made independently [11].

The HEW study concluded that concentration in future programs merely on the treatment of end-stage kidney disease is not likely to solve the problem of annual deaths due to irreversible uremia unless unlimited funds are available for an indefinite continuation of such a program. Thus, steps must be taken to decrease the number of people who enter the irreversible fatal stage each year by a systematic prevention or treatment of the primary kidney diseases which initiate their progressive downhill course. It is obvious from the analysis in the three major kidney disease groups—infectious, hypersensitive, and hypertensive—that the otherwise inevitable annual reservoir of patients with irreversible kidney failure can be diminished considerably through vigorous programs activated to deal with each of these groups. The application of relatively minor funds in the group of infectious kidney diseases to stimulate systematic screening of high-risk groups followed by diagnosis and treatment, even within the current state-of-the-art and without awaiting additional advances due to ongoing or future research, can bring about a significant future reduction in the number of end-stage patients. Continued and expanded research activities will be necessary to increase the percentage of patients ultimately benefited by this approach.

In the area of hypersensitivity diseases involving the kidney there appears to be no promising mode of attack in sight except for the launching of a systematic research effort intended to increase our knowledge of the disease mechanisms involved. Here, the sooner this effort is started the greater the likelihood of a reduction of the number of end-stage victims in the near future. The promise for benefits to be derived from this type of research effort is such that it should not be postponed—particularly since any new effective treatment or prevention modality would produce major benefits in the entire field of hypersensitivity diseases, such as rheumatic heart disease, rheumatoid arthritis and others.

In the group of hypertensive diseases of the kidney an immediate start, within the current state-of-the-art, of screening, diagnosis and treatment can begin to diminish the number of patients who will eventually require end-stage treatment because of their progressive renal involvement. Simultaneous research efforts are likely to make this particular portion of the overall program more effective as time goes by, in the same fashion in which the new antihypertensive drugs developed during the last ten years have succeeded in decreasing by about fifty per cent the mortality due to malignant hypertension.

Thus, a meaningful Federal program to reduce the annual mortality due to kidney disease and aimed at a general reduction of the prevalence of the various kidney diseases must perforce be a multifactorial one which brings into play all of the program components—research, prevention, treatment and education—available in our arsenal. An optimally proportioned mix of these program components must be present to yield maximum benefits in overall number of lives saved. This last concept includes not only deaths avoided today but deaths to be prevented in the years to come. Needless to say, such a total program, to be meaningful and productive, must be aimed at all three major primary kidney diseases, as well as at end-stage kidney failure.

Chart 6 shows a hypothetical program mix that might come from such conclusions. Note the early emphasis on research to affect the state-of-the-art, and the growth in allocations to the prevention and treatment of primary kidney diseases as relative allocations to dialysis are diminished.

In 1966, HEW also did a rather different type of analysis in the field of health: a study of alternative ways of improving the health of children [12]. The President had focused public attention on the problem of child health and expressed a desire to introduce new legislation in this field. The HEW study was an attempt to assess the state of health of the Nation's children (to what extent the children have correctable health problems and in what groups in the population were the problems concentrated) and to estimate the cost and effectiveness of various kinds of programs to improve the health of children.

Chart 6
Effect of Advancing State of the Art on Future Program Composition
(Percentages are wholly arbitrary and merely serve to illustrate shifting trends.)

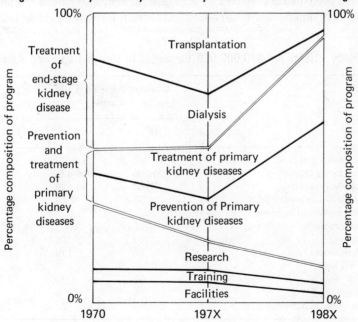

This study proved more difficult than anticipated. Hard information on the state of health of children is hard to come by. Surprisingly, estimates of improvement in health attributable to medical care are almost nonexistent. It is not easy to demonstrate statistically that children who see doctors regularly are healthier than children who do not.

In regard to maternal and child care programs the stated goal was to make needed maternal and child health services available and accessible to all, in particular to all expectant mothers and children in health depressed areas. Health depressed areas could be characterized as areas with excessive infant mortality rates. There is no universal index of good or bad health among children. Two measurable areas were selected—mortality and the prevalence of chronic handicapping conditions. Over a dozen possible programs aimed at reducing these were examined. On Chart 7, three selected programs addressed to the problem of coverage of maternal and child health are illustrated, two of them comprehensive programs of care to expectant mothers and children. This table shows the annual effects of spending the same amount of money, $10 million a year, in different ways. The analysts examined comprehensive care programs covering up to age eighteen and up to age five with estimates based on the best assumptions derived from the literature and advisers on the probabilities of prevention of maternal deaths, premature deaths, infant deaths, and mental retardation, and handicapping conditions prevented or corrected by age eighteen. They also looked at a program of early case finding and assured treatment which focused on children at ages

Chart 7
Yearly Effects per $10,000,000 Expended in Health Depressed Areas

	Comprehensive programs to age		Case finding of treatment
	18	5	0, 1, 3, 5, 7, 9
Maternal deaths prevented	1.6	3	
Premature births prevented	100-250	200-485	
Infant deaths prevented	40-60	85-120	
Mental retardation prevented	5-7	7-14	
Handicaps prevented or corrected by age 18:			
Vision problems:			
All	350	195	3,470
Amblyopia	60	119	1,140
Hearing loss:			
All	90	70	7,290
Binaural	6	5	60
Other physical handicaps	200	63	1,470

four days and again every other year until they were nine. Expending the same amounts, where you put the money yields different results. With respect to reduction of infant mortality, several other programs had higher payoffs than these. For example, a program of intensive care units for high-risk newborns was estimated to reduce annually 367 deaths if we put all our money in that basket— it would cost about $27 thousand per infant death prevented. The programs shown cost about four times that, but they do other good things too.

The HEW analysts also looked at programs with a given amount of money (Chart 8) aimed at reducing the number of children who will have decayed and unfilled teeth by age eighteen. Fluoridation programs in communities which do not possess this, will, for the same amount of money, give us close to 300,000 fewer children in this condition, compared to 18,000 or 44,000 fewer in other programs noted. Fluoridation looks like a very attractive program. It was so attractive that it could be inferred that a program as cheap as this is not being inhibited by lack of financial support by the Federal Government; there are other factors at work.

One other program, additional funds on family planning, looked like a very good way not only to reduce the number of infant deaths, but also the rate of infant mortality in high-risk communities.

Despite the information difficulties, several conclusions emerged clearly from the study. Two of these conclusions resulted in new legislation being requested from Congress. First, it seemed clear that a program of early casefindings and treatment of handicapping conditions would have considerable payoff. It was also clear that if the large number of children who do not now have access to good medical care were to be provided with pediatric services, an acute shortage of doctors would be precipitated. Ways have to be found to use medical manpower more efficiently. The Social Security Amendments of 1967 include provision for programs of early casefinding and treatment of defects and chronic conditions in children, and for research and demonstration programs in the training and use of physician assistants.

These condensed discussions of some of HEW's applications of cost-benefit analysis to disease-control programs illustrate both the usefulness and limitations of such analyses for decisionmaking [13]. Issues are sharpened, and quantitative

Chart 8
Reduction in Number of 18-year-olds with Decayed and Unfilled Teeth per $10,000,000 Expended in Health-Depressed Areas

Fluoridation	294,000
Comprehensive dental care without fluoridation	18,000
Comprehensive dental care with fluoridation	44,000

estimates are developed to reduce the decisionmakers' uncertainty about costs and effects. Nevertheless, the multiplicity of dimensions of output, and their basic incommensurabilities both with costs and the outputs of other claimants for public expenditure, still requires the use of value judgments and political consensus.

Prior to the introduction of the planning-programing and budgeting system, long-range planning in HEW was sporadic and generally not departmentwide. No mechanisms existed for focusing attention on longer range objectives, deciding which types of programs should be given highest priority over the next several years, and then drawing up a budget consistent with those objectives and priorities.

In 1967 and 1968, the Department experimented with a new procedure for making budget decisions in the context of a long-range plan.

The procedure involves several steps. First, very early in the calendar year the planning and evaluation staff drew up a list of significant issues which would have to be addressed in formulating the budget and legislative program. This list of issues was discussed within the Office of the Secretary, with the operating agnecies, and with the Bureau of the Budget. Decisions were made as to which of these issues seemed likely to be illuminated by analytical work, and studies of many of them were initiated.

The second step in 1967 was the development of a set of tentative departmental objectives for 1973. The operating agencies were asked to formulate their objectives for 1973 in program terms. Each agency was given two ceilings by the Secretary for 1973—a "low" which implied continued budget stringency, and a "high" which implied somewhat greater availability of funds. Each of them was asked to answer the question: How would you allocate these sums in 1973 among existing programs or new programs which could be developed between now and then?

The agencies took this assignment seriously, despite the difficulties of forcing busy administrators to take the time away from daily crises to think five years into the future. The 1973 objectives which the agencies sent back to the Secretary reflected considerable thought and effort on the part of agency heads and their bureau chiefs.

The agency 1973 objectives were reviewed by the Secretary and his staff and a set of departmental objectives for 1973 was formulated.

In both the agency plans and those of the Department, the tentative results of analyses were considered. For example, the study of the delivery of health services to the poor made recommendations which involved policy decisions with respect to the coverage of the medicaid program, the training of physician assistants and family health advisers, reorganization of delivery systems (especially those dealing with ambulatory care), hospital-community links, and comprehensive care versus categorical control programs. The departmental objectives, reflecting the Secretary's judgment about priorities for 1973, were then transmitted back to the operating agencies as guidance for formulating their fiscal year 1969 budget submissions and fiscal year 1969–1973 suggested program and financial plan, and legislative program. These were reviewed for conformance to Department objectives, and a Department program and financial plan (1969–1973), fiscal year 1969 budget and framework for legislative proposals were then developed and transmitted to the Bureau of the Budget.

The HEW system has proven of some use. A better understanding of the health programs of the Department and their interrelationships have been achieved. This was true not only at the Office of the Secretary, but also at the Bureau of the Budget. The primitive analyses have assisted the dialog on budget and legislative programs. The five-year planning system has enabled the Secretary and his staff to control the processes somewhat more by testing budget and legislative proposals against the Secretary's program and financial plan.

Problems, of course, remain. One of the greatest is inadequate program evaluation [14]. Very little is really known of the impact of programs. Partly this is because of the complications in sorting out Federal funding impacts from all the others. Partly it is because health effects take considerable time to become evident. But a large measure of the reason is because it has not been a matter of high interest to program managers. This is beginning to change. New health legislation increasingly contains authorization of a portion of the funds for evaluation. For example, Public Law 90-174, the Partnership for Health amendments of 1967, contains wording affecting formula grants to the States, project grants, and training and demonstration grants in the following manner:

> . . .such portion of the appropriations for grants under this subsection as the Secretary may determine, but not exceeding 1 percentum thereof, shall be available to the Secretary for evaluation (directly or by grants or contracts) of the program authorized by this subsection.

Under the direction of the Office of the Secretary, agencies are developing evaluation plans which may lead to significant gains in information for policy decisions.

REFERENCES

1.   U. S. Department of Health, Education, and Welfare, Office of the Assistant Secretary for Program Coordination: *Motor Vehicle Injury Prevention Program,* August, 1966; *Arthritis,* September, 1966; *Selected Diseases Control Programs,* September, 1966; and *Cancer,* October, 1966.

2.   Rashi Fein, *Economics of Mental Illness.* New York: Basic Books, Inc., 1958. For later study using a new conceptual framework resulting in cost estimates almost 10 times higher see Ronald Conley, Margaret Cromwell, and Mildred Arrill, "An Approach to Measuring the Cost of Mental Illness," *American Journal of Psychiatry,* 63-70, December, 1967.

3. Burton A. Weisbrod, *Economics of Public Health: Measuring the Economic Impact of Diseases.* Philadelphia: University of Pennsylvania Press, 1961.

4. Herbert E. Klarman, "Syphillis Control Programs," *Measuring Benefits of Government Investments,* edited by Robert Dorfman. Washington, D.C.: The Brookings Institution, 367-410, 1965.

5. Dorothy P. Rice, *Estimating the Cost of Illness,* Public Health Service Publication 947-6, Washington, D.C., May, 1966; Jacob Cohen, "Routine Morbidity Statistics as a Tool for Defining Public Health Priorities," *Israel Journal of Medical Sciences,* May, 1965, pp. 457-460, estimated the weighted impact of twenty five mass diseases on deaths, loss of life years under sixty five, hospitalization, days of hospitalization and cases in Workers' Sick Fund.

6. Louis J. Dublin and Alfred J. Latka, *The Money Value of a Man,* New York: Ronald Press, 1930.

7. See, for example, Earl F. Cheit, *Injury and Recovery in the Course of Employment,* New York and London: John Wiley, 1961.

8. For discussion of some of these issues see Dorothy P. Rice, "Measurement and Application of Illness Costs," *Public Health Reports,* February, 1969, pp. 95-101; T. C. Schelling, "The Life You Save May Be Your Own," *Problems in Public Expenditure Analysis,* edited by Samuel B. Chase, Jr., The Brookings Institution, 1968, pp. 127-176; and Pan American Health Organization, *Health Planning: Problems of Concept and Method,* Scientific Publication No. 111, April, 1965, especially pp. 4-6.

9. U. S. Department of Health, Education, and Welfare, Office of the Assistant Secretary (Planning and Evaluation), *Kidney Disease,* December, 1967.

10. The Bureau of the Budget convened an expert Committee on Chronic Kidney Disease. See *Report* by this committee, Carl W. Gottschalk, chairman, Washington, September, 1967. Herbert E. Karlman, John O'S. Francis, and Gerald D. Rosenthal, "Cost Effectiveness Analysis Applied to the Treatment of Chronic Renal Disease," *Medical Care,* vol VI, No. 1, January-February, 1968, pp. 48-54, analyzed by the committee's data to explore what is the best mix of center dialysis, home dialysis, and kidney transplantations. The authors restricted their beneficiaries to those in end-stage kidney disease, and concluded that transplantation is economically the most effective way to increase life expectancy of persons with chronic kidney disease, although they recognize the factors that constrain the expansion of transplantation capability.

11. Jerome B. Hallan and Benjamin S. H. Harris, III, "The Economic Cost of End-Stage Uremia," *Inquiry,* volume V, No. 4, December, 1968, pp. 20-25, and J. B. Hallan, B. S. H. Harris, III, and A. V. Alhadeff, *The Economic Costs of Kidney Disease,* Research of Triangle Institute, North Carolina, 1967.

12. U. S. Department of Health, Education, and Welfare, Office of the Assistant Secretary for Program Coordination, *Maternal and Child Health Care Programs,* October, 1966.

13. Other studies included U. S. Department of Health, Education, and Welfare, Office of the Assistant Secretary (Planning and Evaluation): *Delivery of Health Services for the Poor,* December, 1967; *An Economic Analysis of the Control of Sulfur Oxides Air Pollution,* December, 1967; *Nursing Manpower Programs,* March, 1968; Public Health Service, Bureau of Health Services, *Recommendations and Summary: Program Analysis of Health Care Facilities.*

14. A useful reference to the existing literature on evaluation is Willy De Dyndt and Karen B. Ross, *Evaluation of Health Programs—An Annotated Bibliography,* Systems Research Project, University of Minnesota, comment series No. 8-9(9).

VII
PROBLEMS IN THE DEVELOPMENT OF AN ACCOUNTANT'S CONCEPT OF SOCIAL INCOME

On the Discount Rate for Public Projects

William J. Baumol

The determination of the appropriate discount rate to be used in the evaluation and selection of investment projects occupies a major portion of conventional managerial accounting and corporate finance literature. There is general agreement that the marginal cost of capital to the enterprise is the most logical rate, although there are, of course a number of problems in the practical determination of that figure.

In this significant paper, Baumol explores the social accounting analog of the conventional problem: what discount rate should be used in the selection of public sector investments? The analysis is couched in a familiar framework: what rate will produce the most efficient allocation of (total social) capital? The conclusion is that the appropriate social discount rate is the weighted average rate of return of the suppliers of government capital, that is, the private sector.

The article then treats the problems of corporate income taxes, risk, and externalities.

Baumol's logic is based on an unstated assumption of the nature of government as an agent of the citizenry. Thus, it is bound by their opportunity cost of capital. (Note the neat fit with the social contract theory.) If, on the other hand, the government is endowed with a separate existence, distinct from that of the citizenry, might not it have its own, separate discount rate, for example, the discount rate on government bonds?

William J. Baumol is Professor of Economics at Princeton University.
SOURCE: from*The Analysis and Evaluation of Public Expenditures: The PPB System.* A Compendium of Papers submitted to the Subcommittee on Economy in Government of the Joint Economic Committee, Congress of the United States (1969) Vol. 1, pp 489-503.

1.   SIGNIFICANCE OF THE DISCOUNT RATE

It is generally recognized that the discount rate is a critical datum for the evaluation of any proposed Government project. Even where there is little basic disagreement about the investment's prospective costs and benefits, the choice of discount rate figure may make the difference between acceptance and rejection. A project which seems to yield substantial net benefits when evaluated at a three per cent rate may well appear extremely wasteful if the rate is five per cent.

Yet despite the critical nature of this parameter, in some calculations it is assigned a value almost cavalierly, with little attempt to show that the selected figure is not chosen arbitrarily and capriciously. One sometimes encounters discount figures in cost-benefit calculations whose sole justification seems to be that similar figures were used in the past. Of course that can never be an acceptable argument, first because the earlier figure may have had as little justification as the one presently employed and, second, because changing circumstances change the appropriate value of the discount rate.

At stake in the choice of an acceptable discount rate is no less than the allocation of resources between the private and the public sectors of the economy. The discount rate, by indicating what Government projects should be undertaken, can determine the proportion of the economy's activity that is operated by governmental agencies, and hence, the proportion that remains in the hands of private enterprise.

Moreover, even given the decision on resource allocation between the private and the public sectors, the choice of discount rate can affect profoundly the type of projects undertaken by Government agencies. When the discount rate is low this will encourage highly durable investments, the bulk of whose benefits will become available only in the distant future. Thus, when the economy is beset by urgent and immediate investment needs a relatively high discount rate will tend to be appropriate.

With so much at issue it is well worth exploring in some detail the principles that should be employed in arriving at a discount figure, and the rationale that underlies them. This paper undertakes to do so without heavy reliance on the jargon of technical economics.

2.   THE BASIC CRITERION: OPPORTUNITY COST

The observation that the discount rate is the arbiter of the allocation of resources between private and public enterprise is the key to the principles which underlie the choice of an acceptable discount figure. The right discount rate becomes that number which indicates correctly when resources should be transferred from one sector to another.

More specifically, suppose one is considering the construction of a dam which will employ x man-hours of labor, y tons of cement, and z kilowatt hours of electricity. In an economy in which the level of employment is high, if those resources are made available to the Government they must be transferred out of the private sector. Just as in the guns versus butter case, each item added to the public sector involves some corresponding reduction in the volume of resources in private hands.[1]

We may now establish a rather obvious criterion to test the desirability of the proposed resource transfer. If the resources in question produce a rate of return in the private sector which society evaluates at r per cent, then the resources should be transferred to the public project if that project yields a return greater than r per cent. They should be left in private hands if their potential earnings in the proposed government investment is less than r per cent. The logic of this criterion is self-evident. It states no more than the minimal dictate of efficiency: Never take resources out of a use where they bring in (say) nine per cent in order to utilize them in a manner which yields only six per cent!

The standard which has just been described is the concept economists call *opportunity cost.* We have stated, in effect, that the proper criterion on which to judge the desirability of a governmental project, from the point of view of the general welfare, is the value of the opportunities which the private sector must pass by when the resources are withdrawn from that sector. A government project is desirable if and only if the value of the net benefits which it promises exceeds the cost of the lost productive opportunities which that investment causes.

It follows almost immediately that *the correct discount rate for the evaluation of a government project is the percentage rate of return that the resources utilized would otherwise provide in the private sector.* That is, the correct discount rate is the opportunity cost in terms of the potential rate of return in alternative uses on the resources that would be utilized by the project. An example will readily show why this must be so. Suppose these resources are capable of returning our hypothetical nine per cent in the private sector. Consider three proposed government projects: Project A which offers an average rate of return of twelve per cent, project B whose expected return is nine per cent, and project C whose anticipated yield is seven per cent. It should be obvious that if we discount the returns of project C at the opportunity rate of nine per cent we will end up with a negative net present value figure (i.e., seven per cent discounted at nine per cent comes out to less than the principal invested). If we discount project B's expected returns at nine per cent we will obtain a zero figure for the present value of net benefits (the returns will just cover the cost of the investment). Only project A, when discounted at nine percent, will be assigned a positive net benefit figure. Thus the discount rate calculated at the opportunity rate works just as it should: it passes projects whose yield is greater than its resources could earn in the private sector and turns down projects whose benefits are not equal to the earnings the resources could provide in private hands.

The same illustration also shows immediately how an incorrect choice of discount figure—one not equal to the opportunity rate—can result in decisions harmful to the general welfare. For example, consider two extreme possibilities in terms of our hypothetical figures—a discount rate that is much too high (say, fifteen per cent) and one that is much too low (say, five per cent). At the excessive fifteen per cent figure the usual cost-benefit criterion would reject all three projects, even project A. The Government would then fail to undertake an investment that clearly represents an efficient use of society's resources. On the other hand, a five per cent discount rate would, on a cost-benefit criterion, lead to the construction of all three projects. Thus even investment C would be undertaken even though it uses resources that should better be left in private hands. For it takes resources from employments in which they return nine per cent and puts them into an occupation in which they bring in only seven per cent, a palpable two per cent net loss to the community.

The upshot is perfectly clear. Any discount rate that is clearly above or clearly below the opportunity cost rate is indefensible because either of these will lead to decisions that reduce the general welfare. We must turn therefore to an investigation of the opportunity cost rate of resources, for once we have determined this we will have the requisite information for the choice of discount rate to be used in the evaluation of Government projects.

3. REASONS FOR DIFFERENCES IN OPPORTUNITY COSTS

Matters would be relatively simple if any batch of resources withdrawn from the private sector were to incur the same (percentage) opportunity cost as any other batch. If an opportunity cost of r per cent were to apply throughout the economy, to determine the social discount rate one would simply proceed to estimate this number, r, and the resulting figure would then be the discount rate.

Unfortunately, for a variety of reasons, the magnitude of the opportunity cost varies with the source from which a project's resources are obtained. As we will see, resources which might otherwise have been used by a corporation will generally incur a higher opportunity cost than do resources drawn from direct consumer use.

In some sense, differences in opportunity costs of resources taken from different sectors of the economy are all a manifestation of imperfections in the market. In principle, if capital could flow without restriction to any sector of the economy where its earnings would be increased and all returns on capital were to accrue to its investors, resources would be forced by the market process to yield the same rate of return in every use. The standard argument is easily summarized. Suppose in such an economy that there were two industries, one of which returned k per cent on capital while the other yielded some higher return, say *2k*. In that case investors would find it profitable to withdraw funds from the first of these industries and put them to work in the second. But the growing scarcity of capital in the first industry would tend to reduce its outputs, raising its prices and (therefore) its rate of return. Similarly, in the second industry the influx of capital would expand production, and force prices and returns downward. This transfer of capital would continue so long as any substantial difference in the two rates of return persisted. The flow of capital would cease only when the rate of return in the first industry had risen sufficiently and that in the second had fallen enough to make the two rates of return equal. At that point, clearly, capital withdrawn from the one sector would have exactly the same rate of return as capital withdrawn from the other—their opportunity cost rates would be identical.

Why does such equalization generally not occur in practice? There are two broad reasons: First, part of the return to capital may not accrue to the investor. A prime example of this is provided by taxation which siphons part of that return off to the Government, and since the burden of taxation varies from industry to industry, from one corporate to the noncorporate sector, and so forth, it means that opportunity costs will vary accordingly. A second broad reason for such variation lies in impediments, such as monopoly, to the influx of capital into some productive activities.[2] Specifically, we will consider three broad sources of such divergence because they must be taken into explicit account in the determination of the social rate of discount. These elements are the following: (a) taxes, (b) risk, (c) divergence between private and social benefits (externalities). Let us examine them in turn.

4. THE ROLE OF TAXES: ANALYSIS

As already indicated, the burden of taxes will vary from industry to industry, from one class of producer to another, depending on its mode of organization—that is, corporation, partnership, or do-it-yourself production by the consumer himself.

However, let us, to begin with, assume for simplicity that there are only two classes of producer: The corporation, which pays a fifty per cent corporate income tax, and the private individual who produces certain items for his own use, and who pays no taxes on this production process. Assume, also that there are available for sale riskless Government bonds offering a rate of return of, say, five per cent.

In our example, it is easy to determine the opportunity cost of resources withdrawn from the corporate sector. Corporations must yield to their investors an after-tax return of five per cent. For otherwise investors would be unwilling to provide any funds to the corporations and would instead put all their money into the safe Government bonds. But the required after-tax return of five per cent on corporate capital means that these firms must earn ten per cent on capital *before* payment of the fifty per cent corporate profit tax. In other words, the presence of special taxes on the output of this sector means that resources invested in it must produce goods and services valued at a level sufficiently high to yield a ten per cent return. The corporation can then engage only in the production of consumers' or producers' goods whose purchasers value them sufficiently to pay a price that yields a ten per cent return on corporate investment. A withdrawl of resources from the corporation, then, will cause a reduction in output whose opportunity cost in terms of consumer valuation is given by that figure: ten per cent.

Notice in evaluating resources from the corporate sector in this way, it does not matter whether the resources are used by the firm to produce consumers' goods or producers' goods (e.g., machinery). So long as the output in question is supplied by a corporation, the resources used in its manufacture will have a ten per cent opportunity cost. The relevance of this consideration will be clear presently.

Let us turn now to the more difficult problem, the opportunity cost of resources withdrawn from the other productive sector in our imaginary economy, the do-it-yourself consumers.

Since goods produced by consumers for their own use do not provide a rate of return that is measureable directly it is necessary to find some indirect means by which their opportunity cost can be inferred. Fortunately there is a straightforward way in which this can be done. When a consumer voluntarily purchases one of the bonds available in our imaginary economy he is indicating that their five per cent rate of return compensates him for giving up the use of that money in his do-it-yourself operation. Put another way, if this investment in his own production were worth more than five per cent to him he would not buy the bond, while if his investment in his own work were worth less than five per cent to him he would purchase more bonds than he does. Thus without any conscious calculation on his part, a consumer's security purchases reveal something about what the rate of return of investment in the production of goods for his own consumption is worth to him—the opportunity cost incurred when a dollar's worth of resources is prevented from going to him and is transferred to a Government investment project.

What about consumers who do not buy any bonds? It follows from the preceding discussion that their opportunity cost must be at least as high and probably higher than it is for bond purchasers.[3] To a man who chooses *not* to purchase bonds at five per cent, the purpose for which he uses his money must by definition be worth more than five per cent. This is no less true for a man who fails to purchase bonds because "he cannot afford them." That phrase merely implies that his consumption dollar means a great deal to him—perhaps even survival itself, and is therefore certainly more valuable than five per cent.

We may summarize by saying that the opportunity cost of present consumption to nonbondholders must be at least as great as the figure for bondholders, and that to bondholders the opportunity cost of resources is indicated by the rate of return on their bondholdings.

In practice, of course, there is a broad spectrum of earnings tax conditions, among which are included the untaxed do-it-yourself productive process and corporate production with its (roughly) fifty per cent profits tax. We have seen that the opportunity cost of resources from the untaxed sector (assuming the absence of risk and other such complications) is, roughly, r per cent. In the corporation, half of whose earnings are taxed away, the opportunity cost rate is $2r$, where r is the bond rate of interest. Similarly, if the earnings of a partnership in a particular industry were reduced by, say, one-fourth through taxation, that firm would also have to earn enough before taxes to yield r per cent after taxes to its investors. This company's pretax rate of return, call it s per cent, must then satisfy the relationship

$$s - (1/4)s = r, \quad \text{that is,} \quad (3/4)s = r \quad \text{or} \quad s = (4/3)r.$$

This figure, which obviously lies between r and $2r$, will then be the opportunity cost rate for resources withdrawn from a firm paying $1/4$ of its earnings in taxes.

5.   TAXES AND THE SOCIAL DISCOUNT RATE: GENERAL PRINCIPLES[4]

We may then generalize our results as follows:

(a)   For production that is not subject to taxation the opportunity cost rate will generally be no lower than, and as an approximation, be equal to the r per cent rate of return on riskless bonds.

(b)   For production whose returns are taxed at a rate such that the fraction $1/k$ of the returns *remains* after taxes, then the opportunity cost rate for resources withdrawn from this sector will be kr per cent. Thus, in the preceding example, $1/k$, the fraction of the partnership's pretax returns remaining after taxes, is $3/4$. Therefore, the opportunity cost rate for its resources is $kr = 4/3r$ per cent.

What can be done with the diverse opportunity cost figures for resources drawn from different sectors in calculating a single discount rate for the evaluation of a Government project? The answer is simple. Suppose the Government is to withdraw some resources from the one type of productive activity and some from the other. Suppose, for example, twenty per cent of these resources would have come from do-it-yourself production yielding a five per cent return, and eighty per cent from the corporate sector with its ten per cent opportunity cost yield. Then the Government project will offer a net benefit to society if on the whole it can produce a rate of return equal to their weighted average:

$$(20/100) \times 5\% + (80/100) \times 10\% = 9\%.$$

More generally, we have as a third rule:

(c)   The correct social discount rate for a project will be a weighted average of the opportunity cost rate for the various sectors from which the project would draw its resources, and the weight for each such sector in this average is the proportion of the total resources that would come from that sector.[5]

The preceding rule, incidentally, will be seen to hold where there are differences in opportunity cost rates whatever their origin, whether produced by variation in the tax treatment of different economic sectors, or differences arising from any other source. The three rules (a), (b), and (c) also hold for an economy with many more than the two sectors in our simple illustration.

Before turning to the next general topic, it should be emphasized that the preceding analysis was couched entirely in terms of productive sectors and had nothing to do with the distinction between consumption and investment goods. A corporation can produce either or both of these two types of output and the same opportunity cost rate will apply to both. This means, if the analysis is valid, that the correct social discount rate will tend to be considerably higher than it would appear to be on the basis of some of the more standard modes of calculation[6] which, in terms of our simple example again, would employ the bond rate r for the discounting of all relevant consumers' goods production and the corporate rate only to (corporate) investment. An illustration will make the difference clear. Suppose the opportunity cost rates for our two sectors were the figures in our previous illustration (five and ten per cent), and suppose the resources to be employed in the proposed project would otherwise have been divided into the following proportions:

	Per cent
Consumers' goods production by consumer sector	20
Consumers' goods production by corporate sector	70
Producers' goods production by corporate sector	10

Since the conventional calculation applies the five per cent bond discount rate to all consumers' goods, its weighted average calculation of the social discount rate would be

$$[(20 + 70)/100] \times 5\% + [10/100] \times 10\% = 5.5\%.$$

But, as has been shown, even consumers' goods produced by the corporate sector must yield a ten per cent return on investment, and hence the correct weighted opportunity cost rate must be (as before)

$$[20/100] \times 5\% + [(70 + 10)/100] \times 10\% = 9\%$$

a very substantial difference.[7] It may be noted, incidentally, that the orders of magnitude of the figures are not totally unrealistic.

A final conclusion to be derived from the analysis is the implication that the appropriate discount rate may vary from one proposed Government project to another. If they derive their resources from different sectors or vary in the proportions in which they draw upon the different sectors, then their opportunity costs may vary. Consequently, it may sometimes be possible to reduce the opportunity cost rate for the project by careful planning of the means by which its resources are obtained. In particular, as has already been noted, a project designed to draw heavily on resources which would otherwise be unemployed will for this reason incur an opportunity cost that is particularly low.

6.   THE ROLE OF RISK

Risk will also typically vary from industry to industry and from firm to firm. This produces further differences in reported rates of return. A risky industry may be expected to offer comparatively high profit prospects in order to be attractive to investors. That is why returns on stocks are typically higher than bond yields and why the rate of interest on a corporate bond is normally higher than that on a comparable Government security.

The nature of the issue this poses for the calculation for a social discount rate as well as its resolution can be brought out clearly with another simple example. Suppose two firms which are in all other aspects alike produce respective rates of return before taxes of ten and twelve per cent. The two per cent excess in the return of the riskier firm is, in effect, an insurance premium to compensate investors for the greater gamble involved in offering funds to the less safe of the two companies. The question then is whether resources withdrawn from the second firm incur an opportunity cost of twelve per cent, or whether the true (riskless) opportunity cost is merely ten per cent as it is for the other firm.

One may argue that in fact the two companies yield the same real rate of return to their investors. Since the latter's two per cent higher return merely covers investors' risk, as already noted, the real loss to investors of withdrawal of a unit of resources will therefore be equal.

However, a number of noted economists (see, e.g., Arrow [1], Hirshleifer [6] and Samuelson [14] have argued with considerable cogency that the risk for the investment in an individual project taken by itself does not necessarily correspond to the risk it contributes to society's investment as a whole.[8] A bankrupt firm which continues to operate in the hands of its receivers is a loss to its investors but not to society. More important, because in the economy a very large number of projects are underway at any given time, the insurance principle, that is, the statistical "law" of large numbers, applies to them if their prospects for success are largely independent. It is true that because a recession can produce serious consequences for a large number of investment projects simultaneously, the prospects for their success are not completely unrelated. But if, as an approximation, we ignore this complication it can be shown that the larger the number of projects involved the smaller the risk contributed to total social return by any one of them. Taken as a whole, from the viewpoint of society, they become virtually riskless.

This is essentially the principle on which a life insurance company operates. It cannot tell when any one of its policyholders will expire and, taken by itself, the risk of insuring him is enormous. But when it insures a large body of policyholders the operation becomes *virtually riskless.* That is, barring calamities such as epidemics or wars, the insurance company can forecast with virtual certainty how many of its policyholders will die in any given year, and the residual risk approaches zero as the number of policyholders increases.

Viewed in this way, we must conclude that while the risk involved in any individual investment project is apt to be substantial for the supplier of capital, it may be negligible from the point of view of society as a whole.[9]

Only one more step is needed to see what these considerations imply for the role of risk in the evaluation of the social discount rate. Going back to our illustration, consider once again the twelve per cent rate of return of our riskier firm. The two per cent differential between this return and that of the safer company represents, as we saw, no net gain to the investor who is merely compensated thereby for his risk relative to investment in the other company. But since to society either firm's investment program is virtually riskless, it follows that the social rates of return of the two are *not* equal. One produces a riskless twelve per cent while the other yields a riskless ten per cent. This means that the corresponding social discount rate of resources drawn from these two firms would be a weighted average of these two rates, in accord with rule (c) of the preceding section.

Specifically, it means that in the social discount rate calculation there should be no deductions for a risk component in the rates of return observed in practice. When a corporation produces a before-tax yield of sixteen per cent, six per cent of which might be judged as a risk premium, from the point of view of the social discount rate the corresponding opportunity cost rate is sixteen and not ten per cent. For here risk plays the same role as taxation in its effects on the social rate of return. Private risk forces the firm to invest only in opportunities which offer a yield of sixteen per cent. The social opportunity cost is therefore correspondingly high.

We conclude that the correct discount rate is a weighted average, over all tax and risk circumstances, of the rates of return that would otherwise be earned by the resources to be used in a Government project. As already stated, rule (c) then holds, at least approximately, for variations in rates of return resulting from differences in risk as well as from disparities in tax rates.

7. EXTERNALITIES

There is one other element important for the social discount rate calculation, though we may treat it rather briefly. It is a matter that has been given considerable emphasis in the economic literature, and justly so. This is the issue of externalities—the differences between social and private costs and benefits of an investment program, of which risk compensation is a special case, as we have just seen.

The point is easily made with the aid of the most standard of illustrations of an externality. The firm whose output pollutes the atmosphere obviously provides a net social return significantly lower than the figure given by the yield on its capital. Similarly, the company that produces external benefits; perhaps training of the underprivileged, yields a social product greater than is indicated by its financial returns. In calculating the social discount rate, corresponding adjustments naturally have to be made in the discount figure. The polluting firm's rate of return figure has to be adjusted downward in order to base the calculation on its true social yield, and a corresponding upward adjustment is required to obtain the true social opportunity cost of the company whose operations provide training to the unskilled.

This principle is one that would no doubt be accepted by virtually all economists. Yet one must not overlook some reservations relating to its implementation. First, one must recognize difficulties that beset the evaluation of externalities. The cases where investigators have succeeded in providing some quantification of external costs and benefits are extremely rare. Many types of externality (that is, the impairment of health that is caused by pollutants) simply are not readily translated into financial terms; for example, into a numerical evaluation of their consequences for the social rate of return. Even where such a translation is possible, the effects are typically so widely diffused among the population that an estimate of their aggregate value becomes very difficult. These remarks are of course not meant to question the validity of the principle under discussion—the need to adjust the discount rate for the *social* costs and benefits of the resources concerned. It does however suggest that anything but the roughest sort of implementation of this principle will not be very easy.

A second comment on the externalities issue is the fact, not often alluded to in the literature, that governmental projects can also produce externalities. Army trucks pollute the air as effectively as private vehicles, and government work also can, as a byproduct, teach skills to ghetto residents. This means that in judging the desirability of a proposed Government project adjustments for externalities must be made on both sides of the ledger—the estimated yields of both the private and the governmental projects competing for resources must be revised in order to arrive at *net* social contribution.

8. SUBSIDY FOR THE FUTURE

There is one argument in the literature which has been used to maintain that the weighted average rate of return such as that proposed in rule (*c*) yields too high a social discount rate. This view maintains that private citizens tend systematically not to invest enough from the viewpoint of the Nation's future. It concludes that the discount rate should be kept very low in order to induce an increase in investment today, as a contribution to the Nation's welfare tomorrow.[10] A low discount rate will clearly lead to approval of a large number of governmental investment projects, and the greater the number of investment projects undertaken, the greater is the contribution to the Nation's prosperity.

Such a position is, however, questionable in several respects. First of all, there is no basis for the presumption that a transfer of resources from the private to the public sector will necessarily produce a net increase in the amount of investment undertaken by the economy. The increase in the amount of governmental capital construction is very likely to be offset, a least in part, by a decline in private investments in plant and equipment.

Surely, if society's investment for the future is considered to be inadequate the appropriate remedy is to institute simultaneous inducements to both private and public capital formation.[11] As we have seen, an arbitrarily low discount rate on public projects is certainly not the instrument for that purpose. Such artificially low discount rate on public projects introduce serious inefficiencies into the investment process by causing the withdrawal of resources from areas of use in which their yield is high and leading to their transfer to areas in which their return is low. This is a most peculiar way to encourage more effective investment in the future.

In any event, those who maintain that there is inadequate provision for the future draw incorrect general inferences from irrelevant particular cases. It is difficult to quarrel with the conservationist's view that the destruction of irreplaceable natural resources imposes a heavy cost on our posterity. The destruction of a portion of a canyon, the extinction of a species of wildlife, the erosion of soil all are matters of serious concern because once done they cannot be undone, and this is precisely the legitimate ground on which conservationists urge increased care in avoiding depletion of our resources.[12]

But it is not legitimate to jump from the valid point that one generation has no right to use up wastefully the resources that cannot be replaced by its successors, to the questionable conclusion that each generation is constrained to engage in overall efforts to support its posterity beyond the level that is indicated by the free market. For that is precisely what is involved in a program of low discount rates or any other program of special inducements to investment.

The basic issue is whether it is desirable to subsidize in this way the commitment to the future of resources which could otherwise serve society today. Considerable real investment is already provided by the private sector and by the program of government projects which can pass the standard cost-benefit test utilizing the discount rate that has already been described. Is there any justification for a program of subsidies designed to produce an even greater overall commitment of resources to the future?

A little thought shows that the grounds for such a program are tenuous at best. Our economy is characterized by a long run rate of growth of GNP of the order of three to four per cent per year, compounded, and in recent years the growth rate has been even greater. Per capita income has risen persistently throughout our history and there is every reason to expect the rise to continue. We are therefore wealthier than our predecessors and it can quite safely be predicted that our successors will be richer than we. In effect, then, the subsidization of a program of added investment amounts to an inducement for the transfer of additional resources from the poor to the rich. It would take inputs whose product would be available for consumption today and make them available tomorrow when the supply of consumer goods is likely to be so much more abundant than it is at present.[13]

It should be made clear that the preceding discussion is not meant to imply that there is no need for increased activity by the public sector. The crisis of our cities, the problems of the impoverished and the underprivileged minorities and a variety of other critical issues may well require for their resolution governmental activity on an increased scale. But these all call for investments whose yield is obtainable quickly, not long-term investments, the bulk of whose benefits will become available in the more distant future. Advocacy of a very low discount rate in these circumstances is tantamount to the view that these immediate problems are not very pressing, and that society's resources are better transferred to the service of the future generations who in any case will surely be wealthier than we.

9.   THE PROBLEM OF THE SECOND BEST

One technical problem besets the analysis of the social discount rate presented in this paper. This is the well-known problem of the second best. We have seen how taxes, risk, and externalities produce discrepancies in the rates of return earned by various parts of the private sector. This means that capital simply is not allocated optimally within that sector. Society could obviously benefit by a transfer of capital from areas in which its social rate of return is relatively low to other parts of the economy offering a higher social return.

It is, then, not necessarily true that the rules of optimal investment procedure for the public sector are applicable, unless they are simultaneously put into operation in the private portion of the economy as well. For it has long been shown (see [9]) that if an optimality rule is enforced in one sector of the economy alone it can actually make matters worse.

In the present case, however, it does not seem plausible that this problem will be very serious. By the nature of the opportunity cost test, it calls for a transfer of resources only from a use in which its yield is relatively low to one where its return is comparatively high. This implies that the social welfare can be expected to increase in the process, assuming of course that there has been adequate adjustment for differences between private and social returns, so that the yield and opportunity cost figures take into account the more indirect contributions of the resources in question.

10. CONCLUDING COMMENT

There always remains a formidable task of implementation even after the basic principles in an area have been enunciated. But a rational decision process does require examination of those principles. It is primarily to this task that this paper has addressed itself. It has proposed what is, in appearance, a relatively simple formula for the evaluation of the social discount rate, the weighted average of the rates of return in the various productive sectors from which resources would be withdrawn for the government project under consideration.

But the simplicity of this expression is deceptive. It is not easy to determine in practice from what productive sector a given project will be drawn, or even from where governmental investment as a whole obtains its resources. What one seeks in trying to obtain this information is the catalog of the decrements in the outputs of the various portions of the private sector which would result from a governmental investment program. When the matter is put in this way, its difficulties should be obvious.

Nor is it easy to judge the rate of return figures for the various sectors of the economy. A corporation offers different nominal rates of return on its various types of debt and equity and, as the recent literature on corporation finance has brought out so forcefully, it is not easy to arrive on the basis of these figures at a single number representing the rate of return on the company's capital. Perhaps a reasonable rule of thumb is the traditional weighted average of the rates of return on a firm's stocks, its bonds, and it other securities, where each of these sources of funds is weighted by the proportion of the company's total finances which it contributes.

In sum, the calculation of the social rate of discount is not something that can be left simply to traditional practices and conventions. The underlying principles should enable us, by a reasonable process of approximation to arrive at operational procedures that represent a significant improvement over current procedures. I have sought to emphasize the complications in order to avoid the impression that all the issues have been settled and can readily be reduced to routine. But I believe firmly that with the help of the prinicples and the data now available one should be able to arrive at reasonable approximations to the social rate of discount. Certainly it should be possible to derive figures considerably more defensible than the conventional calculations that are all too often utilized to justify projects not all of which are clear in their economic merit.

NOTES

1.   On the other hand, if any resources used by the Government project would otherwise be totally unemployed, now and in the future, their use obviously incurs no opportunity cost in the private sector. In an economy such as that of the United States since World War II employment of resources has usually been so high that this consideration is often largely irrelevant to the facts of the matter, except when a project is designed specifically to make use of idle resources, e.g., to provide jobs to the unemployed. However, some types of project, or projects undertaken to particular sectors of the economy may well utilize a relatively large proportion of resources and particularly labor, that might otherwise go unused. For a discussion of this phenomenon and its consequences see [5].

2.   For the relevance of monopolistic elements to the social discount rate calculation, see [2], p. 791, footnote 2.

3.   In particular, the do-it-yourself producer may not only invest his own money in his productive activity, but may in fact borrow to help in its financing. In that case his productive activity must to him be worth at least as much as the rate of interest on the funds that he borrows, for otherwise he would not be willing to pay that amount for a loan. Since the rate of interest on loans to an individual can be expected to exceed the yield on a government bond of comparable life, the basic proposition enunciated in the text still holds for such a borrower—the opportunity cost of resources coming from him must be at least as high as the bond rate of interest (and it may well be significantly higher).

4.   This section draws heavily on an unpublished note [13] by Professor David D. Ramsey of the University of Missouri. That note pointed out some shortcomings in an earlier version of my analysis [2].

5.   The weighted average expression for the social discount rate can be derived by the following elementary argument. Let k dollars be invested in the Government project and let v be its value (including benefit flow) one year later. Suppose, if the project had not been built, that the proportion p of the investment would have been employed in an activity yielding r per cent, and that the remainder $(1-p)$, would have been used in an investment with an s per cent yield. In total, at the end of the year the alternative use would then have yielded the total value

$$pk(1+r)+(1-p)k(1+s)=k[1+pr+(1-p)s].$$

The Government's use of the k dollar investment will therefore be socially preferable to the private use if and only if

$$v>k[1+pr+(1-p)s], \text{ i.e., } k<\frac{v}{1+[pr+(1-p)s]}.$$

Thus, the discount rate is given by $pr+(1-p)s$, the weighted average of the returns in the two sectors described in rule (c) in the text. This argument obviously also applies directly to the case where resources are taken from more than two economic sectors.

6.   See, for example, Krutilla and Eckstein [8] and Eckstein [3]. On the other hand, I suspect that the radically different discount rate calculation recommended by Harberger [4] will yield results very similar to those that would be obtained by the methods proposed in the text. There also seems to be no conflict between these methods and the views expressed in the Joint Economic Committee's report ([7], pp. 13-14), which are deliberately (and, no doubt, wisely) vague on this issue, stating "while advocating the opportunity cost of displaced private spending as a correct conceptual basis for the Government discount rate, the subcommittee does not presume to advocate a precise method for calculating this rate. . . . We agree with the Bureau of the Budget's reluctance to 'adopt . . . the rate of return on private investment foregoing alone because government funds are withdrawn from both consumption and investment.' " The text of this paper obviously recognized the relevance of the distinction between consumption and investment but maintains that the proper role of consumption in the discount rate of calculation is not quite what it is sometimes taken to be.

7.   The recommended procedure does of course conflict with the approach that has been taken in a number of highly reputable studies. It is therefore important to be very clear about the case for taking the opportunity cost of consumers' goods produced by a corporation to be dependent on the corporate income tax. The argument can be put very simply: assume that without a corporation tax all consumers' goods are associated with an r per cent opportunity cost rate. Then the imposition of such a tax will lead the corporate sector to reduce its outputs and hence to arise the marginal utility of these goods to their consumers. Therefore a reduction of c units of corporate output of consumers' goods after the tax has gone into effect will incur a greater loss of consumer profit than the same c units of decrease in output would have caused before the tax. Hence if the opportunity cost was r when there was no tax it *must* exceed r per cent after the tax has taken effect.

The argument clearly runs into all sorts of complications in practice in a world of risk and imperfect competition. But if the corporations were perfect competitors in a riskless economy it would apply precisely. Then the imposition of a tax would lend a sufficient number of firms to leave the production of any consumers' good to raise the pretax rate of return to $2r$ where r is the pure rate of interest. The marginal cost of a unit of output (excluding marginal return to capital) would, in equilibrium, equal price minus $2r\Delta k$ where Δk is the incremental capital needed to produce the output, and hence the opportunity cost per unit of capital moved out of this productive activity must then be $2r$.

Note that this argument is independent of the incidence of the tax, i.e., it must hold whether or not price has gone up by the amount of the tax, or has even gone up at all.

8.   It should be noted, incidentally, that risk affects governmental as well as private investment projects. For example, many abandoned canals were no doubt built in the anticipation that their use would continue much longer than it did. And just as bankruptcy may prevent the completion of a private investment project, a change in administration after an election may result in the abandonment of some unfinished public undertaking.

9.   I have made this point elsewhere in a slightly more formal manner (see [2], p. 794-795). Note that on this point my position differs somewhat from that of the Joint Economic Committee ([7], pp. 13-14) which calls for a special allowance in the discount rate applied to a particular public project for the risk to which that project is subject. On the argument in the text, the *incremental* risk contributed by any one such project may plausibly considered negligible, and hence requires little or no discount rate adjustment.

10.   This view is clearly associated with the work of Pigou. See [12], part 1, chapter II. Among others Marglin also seemed to take such a stand in an earlier paper [10]. In a more recent discussion [11] his position is hedged considerably more. He argues "that individuals may not have unique preference maps, that instead preferences may depend on the role they play. . . . The preferences with respect to present and future which individuals hold in their political life as citizens may differ from the preferences they hold in their economic roles as consumers and producers." (Pp. 15-16). However, he does not indicate whether he believes the difference between the two follows any consistent pattern, one way or the other.

11.   This viewpoint is also taken by the Joint Economic Committee report ([7], p. 11). There are of course important cases where it is considered socially desirable to stimulate governmental output of goods and services which cannot be provided effectively by the private sector. Education, elimination of pollution and national defense are all services whose supply, it is generally felt, should not be left exclusively in the hands of the private sector. In such cases Government subsidy, and in some cases complete Governmental financing, is entirely appropriate because of the external benefits contributed by these activities. But this only requires us to take explicit account of such externalities in our cost-benefit calculations. It does not justify a particularly low *discount rate* on the Government project which would distort the allocation of resources between short- and long-term investments. If we need more expenditure on education now—better books and better teachers—a reduction in the discount rate would not provide them. It would only stimulate the construction of durable school buildings, the long-term investment portion of educational-expenditure.

12.   Paradoxically, in practice a low discount rate will probably increase the destruction of such resources. In the past low discount rates have been used to provide a cost-benefit justification for precisely those engineering projects which have constituted, at least according to conservationists, the most serious threats to national parklands, recreation areas and other such resources.

13.   This argument is based on Tullock [15]. For a similar position, see also the Joint Economic Committee report [7], p. 11.

REFERENCES

1.   K. J. Arrow, "Discounting and Public Investment Criteria," in A. V. Kneese and S. C. Smith, eds., *Water Research,* Baltimore, 1966.

2.   W. J. Baumol, "On the Social Rate of Discount," *American Economic Review,* 788-802, September, 1968.

3.   Otto Eckstein, *Water Resources Development: The Economics of Project Evaluation,* Cambridge, Massachusetts, 1961.

4.   Arnold Harberger, "Statement," in *Hearings Before the Subcommittee on Economy in Government of the Joint Economic Committee of the Congress of the United States,* July 30-August 1, 1968, Washington, 1968.

5.   R. Haveman and J. V. Krutilla, "Unemployment, Excess Capacity, and Benefit-Cost Investment Criteria," *Review of Economics and Statistics, 49,* No. 3, August, 1967.

6.   Jack Hirshleifer, "Investment Decisions Under Uncertainty: Applications of the State-Preference Approach," *Quarterly Journal of Economics, 80,* 252-277, May, 1966.

7.   Joint Economic Committee, *Economic Analysis of Public Investment Decisions: Interest Rate Policy and Discounting Analysis,* Washington, 1968.

8.   J. V. Krutilla and O. Eckstein, *Multiple Purpose River Development, Studies in Applied Economic Analysis,* Baltimore, 1958.

9.   R. Lipsey and K. Lancaster, "The General Theory of the Second Best," *Review of Economic Studies, 24,* 11-32, 1956.

10.   S. A. Marglin, "The Social Rate of Discount and the Optimal Rate of Investment," *Quarterly Journal of Economics, 77,* 95-112, February, 1963.

11.   ———, "The Discount Rate in Public Investment Evaluation" (unpublished) December, 1968.

12.   A. C. Pigou, *The Economics of Welfare,* 4th ed., London, 1932.

13.   D. D. Ramsey, "On the Social Rate of Discount: Comment," 1968 (unpublished).

14.   P. A. Samuelson, "Principles of Efficiency: Discussion," *American Economic Review,* Proc., *54,* 93-96, May, 1964.

15.   Gordon Tullock, "The Social Rate of Discount and the Optimal Rate of Investment : Comment," *Quarterly Journal of Economics, 78,* 331-336, May, 1964.

The Treatment of Risk and Uncertainty[*]

Jack Hirshleifer
and
David L. Shapiro

   While the existence of uncertainties provide the rationale for the transfer of some private sector activity to the public sector, there is very little understanding of how Government should adjust to the existence of risk and uncertainty when evaluating alternative public undertakings. Indeed, existing practice in the Federal Government has been extremely disparate, reflecting both the conceptual difficulties in dealing appropriately with uncertainty and the state of economic thought on this matter.

   Professors Hirshleifer and Shapiro attempt to integrate the substantial progress made in economic theory in recent years "with traditional viewpoints, so as to provide a framework for the evaluation of ongoing practices with respect to risk and uncertainty." Following a review of the basic propositions on which the economic analysis of public investments rests, they discuss the different meanings of the terms "risk" and "uncertainty" and the implication of the different varieties of each for public investment analysis. They find the literature of economics which deals with the problem of risk and uncertainty to contain "a good deal of confusion." For example, while some observers see risk to be a social cost, others have argued that "risk premiums observed in the market are not socially relevant." In part, the controversy concerning the size of the appropriate public discount rate has revolved about these different views of the social relevance of risk and uncertainty. In the final section of their paper, Professors Hirshleifer and Shapiro discuss some recent theoretical developments and present a "model of time-state preference" as a framework for appropriate public sector response to the existence of risk and uncertainty. This model leads them to the conclusion that the application of a riskless rate of interest in discounting is inappropriate and would result in the adoption of inefficient projects. Rather, the observed "risky rate" implicit in the evaluation of comparable private projects provides an appropriate guide to governmental evaluation practice.

I.   THE PROBLEM

We live in a world all too obviously dominated by risk and uncertainty. Facing the issue of risk and uncertainty, in the analysis of public investment decisions, is therefore no mere theoretical flourish. Rather, it is very close to the heart of the matter. Unfortunately, the conceptual difficulty of the problem is very great, and the "state of the art" in economics does not yet provide for its full

Jack Hirshleifer is Professor of Economics at the University of California at Los Angeles. David L. Shapiro is Assistant Professor of Economics at the University of California at Los Angeles.

SOURCE: *From the Analysis and Evaluation of Public Expenditures: The PPB System.* A Compendium of Papers submitted to the Subcommittee on Economy in Government of the Joint Economic Committee, Congress of the United States (1969) Vol. 1, pp. 505-530
[*]Research and clerical assistance furnished by the Water Resources Center, University of California, is hereby acknowledged.

solution. In consequence, benefit-cost investigations typically employ the artificial model of a world of certainty—with perhaps some intuitive or rough-and-ready *ad hoc* adjustments. Thus, costs may contain an item for "contingencies," benefits may be said to have been evaluated "conservatively," or a time-discount rate higher than the "pure" (riskless) rate of interest may be employed. These procedures are not necessarily incorrect, and may in fact be quite unavoidable, but the entire enterprise shows the need of a firmer theoretical foundation.

In the past decade, theoretical economists have made very substantial progress in dealing with risk and uncertainty. This progress has not yet been fully absorbed by the economists who specialize in the applied area of cost-benefit analysis, and of course even less so by practitioners and administrators in the field. The present paper represents an attempt to integrate recent theoretical development with traditional viewpoints, so as to provide a framework for the evaluation of ongoing practices with respect to risk and uncertainty.

Any analysis must be conducted within certain "ground rules." These are a set of propositions, which might themselves be debatable or even more or less clearly in violation of "the facts," but which are taken as useful and acceptable simplifications for the sake of the argument. Among such ground rules for this discussion are:

(1) *The principle of cost-benefit analysis.* This principle asserts that policy ought to be determined by a systematic comparison of costs and benefits—rather than, for example, by inspired intuition or by the interplay of political pressure groups.

(2) *The efficiency criterion.* This criterion asserts that costs and benefits are to be calculated in terms of the overall achievement of individual desires, as expressed in the valuation of goods and services (commodities) produced or foregone. Maximizing the difference between the values of benefits and costs represents a goal akin to maximizing real national income, except that the value placed by individuals upon voluntarily chosen leisure is counted along with the values of material consumption and investment. The *distribution* of the net benefits is not taken into account, presumably because a larger total income could in principle be redistributed so that everyone benefits in comparison with whatever could be attained with a smaller aggregate income. The serious questions and objections that can be raised concerning the efficiency criterion have been discussed to some extent in other papers and will not be considered here.

(3) *Reduction to dollar values.* Actual projects may involve the production or sacrifice of a great variety of different commodities: familiar goods like wheat and electric power, as well as less obvious ones such as leisure and collective goods (e.g., national defense), and "intangibles" like better neighborhoods. For this paper, the problems

involved in the treatment of multiple commodities—as well as the difficult questions connected with the evaluation of "externalities" and the consequences of market imperfections—are presumed to have been solved. (Again, these topics have been very fully discussed in a number of the other papers.) In consequence, we will need only to deal with risk and uncertainty as related to the dollar totals of costs and benefits associated with investment alternatives.

We can now consider the meaning of the terms "risk" and "uncertainty." While the words have rather different connotations ("risk" suggests the potential variability of the objective configuration of events, while "uncertainty" underlines our subjective lack of knowledge as to which configuration will obtain), no formal distinction between them will be made here. Both terms will be used to express a situation in which, whether for objective or subjective reasons, analysis requires us to take into account the possibility of a number of alternative outcomes or consequences of actions. There is one tradition in the literature that attempts to formulate a distinction between risk and uncertainty on the basis of ability to express the possible variability of outcomes in terms of a probability distribution (Knight [18 : 225-231]). According to this tradition, when we do not know the specific outcome but do know the probability distribution, we have "uncertainty." This distinction has proved to be sterile. And indeed, we cannot in practice act rationally without summarizing our information (or its converse, our uncertainty) in the form of a probability distribution)Savage [28]).

There are two different senses of the word "risk" that are often confused. In the first sense, risk is the danger that reality might somehow fall short of overoptimistic beliefs or promises. Thus, an investment adviser might say: "There is a high risk that this railroad bond, though promising a ten-per cent coupon, may be defaulted." On the other hand, there is a more neutral use of the word in the technical literature. In this latter sense risk refers to the fact of variability of outcome, whether favorable or unfavorable. Thus, the same adviser might say: "Common stocks are riskier than Government bonds," by which he means that the investor holding the former might either do much better or much worse than an investor holding the latter.

This distinction may be clarified by introducing the concept of *expected value* (or *mathematical expectation*). Given a probability distribution of numerical (dollar) outcomes, the expected value is the probability-weighted average. Thus, the expected value in the toss of a single die is 3.5—the average of the equally probable outcomes 1, 2, 3, 4, 5, 6. The ten-per cent coupon yield was an optimistic if-all-goes well estimate of the actual yield from holding the railroad bond mentioned above; allowing for the probability of default, the mathematical expectation of yield might be only five per cent. Use of the mathematical expectation is an adjustment allowing for the risk of unfavorable outcomes. It can be regarded as a *correction for optimistic bias,* and must not be confused with adjustments that might be made to allow for attitudes toward risk in the sense of variability.

In dealing with variability risk, we are no longer in a position to make allowances or corrections merely in terms of mathematics. For, an element of taste enters in: the investor's degree of risk-aversion (if he dislikes risk) or risk-preference (if he likes risk). In the case of the railroad bond with ten per cent nominal but five per cent expectation of yield, consider the alternative of a Treasury bond yielding five per cent with certainty. An individual characterized by risk-aversion would prefer the latter, an individual with risk-preference would prefer the former. Whereas taking the *expected value* represents a correction or allowance for bias, allowance for risk-aversion (or risk-preference) leads to the concept of the *certainty-equivalent value* of an uncertain outcome. Thus, for an individual characterized by risk-aversion, the railroad bond above might have a certainty-equivalent yield of only four per cent—that is, be indifferent to a Treasury bond yielding four per cent, even though the railroad bond has a mathematical expectation of yield equal to five per cent.

One important issue, where the two concepts of risk have caused some confusion, concerns the ability of Government to "pool" a large number of independent investments and therefore (it has been alleged) to "ignore risk." The underlying idea here rests upon the statistical law of large numbers. This law states that, if there are a large number of independent experiments, the average outcome obtained will be very close to the mathematical expectation of outcome. It will be immediately clear that the thrust of the argument is that Government may sometimes be in a position to "ignore risk" in the sense of *variability*—the mathematical expectation of return on Government investments may become almost a certainty overall. But if the risk in question is due to the fact that returns from Government projects are typically stated in an overoptimistic way, the fact that Government engages in many such projects will in no way tend to counteract or eliminate this bias.

II.   THE RISKLESS CASE*

Consideration of the principles of investment decision in the world of risk and uncertainty is best preceded by a review of the principles that would be applicable in an artificial but simpler world of certainty. For, some of the errors and confusions that bedevil analysis of the more complex case can be dispelled by a thorough understanding of the simpler certainty model.

---

*Further discussion of this issue is found in the preceding article by Baumol.

In this certainty model we of course need not take any account of risk-preferences. But as we are dealing with intertemporal choices (investment decisions), the *time*-preferences of the members of the community are relevant. Indeed, given the assumed reduction to dollar values, we are in effect dealing with a one-commodity model in which the only distinguishable objects of choice are consumption claims now and in the future. Coordinate with the taste information summarized under the heading of time-preference is the technological information that can be summarized under the heading of time-productivity. Time-preference refers to the *willingness* of consumptive decisionmakers (individuals and households) to exchange units of current consumption for units of future consumption; time-productivity refers to the ability of productive decisionmakers (firms and governments) to physically convert potential consumption of the present date into potential future consumption. It is conventional to measure both time-preference and time-productivity in terms of the percentage premium in the exchange of future claims for current ones. Thus, if an individual is just willing to give up $1 of current consumption for $1.10 of consumption one year from now, his marginal 1-year rate of time-preference is said to be ten per cent. And if a producer can convert (invest) $1 of current consumption so as to return $1.20 one year from now, his marginal rate of time-productivity is said to be twenty per cent. Finally, if in the market $1 of titles to current consumption exchanges against $1.05 of titles to consumption one year off, we say that the market *rate of interest* is five per cent.

Standard economic theory leads to a number of conclusions that will be relevant to our present discussion. These are summarized briefly below. The wording runs in terms of comparisons between present consumption claims and future claims dated one year from now. The generalization to a multiplicity of future dates, while not without its complications, does not introduce any really novel problems.

(1) *The principle of rational intertemporal consumptive decision.* Each consumptive decisionmaker will distribute his wealth between current and future consumption in such a way that his marginal rate of time-preference is just equal to the market rate of interest. For if there were any disparity between the consumptive premium and the market premium, it would pay him to modify his consumption plans by lending or borrowing on the market.

(2) *The principle of rational intertemporal productive decision.* Each productive decisionmaker will continue to invest until his marginal rate of time-productivity is just equal to the market rate of interest. For, if there were any disparity it would pay him to adjust his production plans by increasing or decreasing the scale of investment.

(3) *The principle of market equilibrium.* The interaction of rational consumptive and productive decisionmakers leads to a market equilibrium characterized by an interest rate that simultaneously measures (is equal to) the marginal rates of time-preference and the marginal rates of time-productivity everywhere in the economy. For, if the latter conditions failed for even one decisionmaker, he would be trying to engage in additional transactions—the economy would not be at equilibrium.

The principles above represent "positive" conclusions from the standard behavioristic postulates of economic theory. That is, given such assumptions as rational individuals, perfect markets, etc., the statements above can be inferred as scientific predictions to be tested against observation. The fourth principle below, however, is a "normative" conclusion or policy recommendation—based on value judgments in addition to purely scientific elements.

(4) *The present-value rule for government investment decision.* The government ought to adopt that set of investment projects which maximizes the net balance of the values of aggregate present sacrifice and aggregate future return, where the future return is "discounted" at the market rate of interest.

To explain this principle, it will be convenient to introduce some formal symbolism. We will denote current investment of an economic unit by i_O, and the return on investment one year from now by q_1 (thus, the subscript represents time from the present). The present value of the entire set of productive investments undertaken by the unit in question is defined as V_0 in:

$$V_0 = -i_0 + \frac{q_1}{1 + r_1} \tag{1}$$

Here r_1 is the market rate of interest effective for exchanges between present and future funds (borrowing and lending).[a] A particular project will involve some increment Δi_0 of investment and Δq_1 of future return, so the present value of the project is defined as:

$$\Delta V_0 = -\Delta i_0 + \frac{\Delta q_1}{1 + r_1} \tag{2}$$

Consequently, the present-value (PV) rule can be expressed in two essentially equivalent forms: (a) Maximize overall present value V_0, or (b) Adopt any and all projects whose present values ΔV_0 are positive.[1]

The justification for the PV rule runs in terms of the positive conclusions listed above, together with the value-judgment as to the efficiency criterion listed among the "ground rules" in section I. For, if the goal is to be maximization of the net balance of costs (investment) and benefits (returns from investment), and if the relative values placed by consumers upon the commodities current and future consumption are to be accepted (in the form of the ruling market rate of interest used as a discounting factor), then the government should also in its sphere attempt to maximize the value of its net output in the interests of its ultimate clients—the consumers.[2]

The present-value rule could be challenged either by the rejection of the efficiency criterion as a value judgment, or by the rejection of one or more of the positive principles listed above. Thus, consumer irrationality would cast great doubt upon the significance of the market rate of interest as representative of marginal time-preferences, while producer irrationality would have the same effect with regard to marginal time-productivities. And market disequilibrium would mean, in effect, that there is no single rate of interest serving the function of representing these magnitudes. But we will be holding to the efficiency criterion as a ground rule,[3] as for the positive principles of individual behavior, we need not discuss their "realism" in the artificial certainty model since the issue will arise even more forcefully in the context of risk and uncertainty.

One noteworthy aspect of the present-value principle is its *objective* nature. No subjective considerations of the productive decisionmakers' *personal* time-preferences enter into their decisions—but only the integrated weight of all individuals' preferences as they interact in determining the market rate of interest. It is this feature that facilitates the voluntary organization of many individuals for combined production through instrumentalities like the corporation.

Since the present-value principle would also be naturally used by private firms in maximizing wealth of their owners, a question arises that may be put in the following form: If private firms and government agencies are both to be using exactly the same decision rule, does this model leave any real role for government as a distinct type of social agency? The point of the question is that, since there surely is a real role for government, there must be something wrong with the present-value principle. This inference would be incorrect. Private firms and government agencies can be both using the PV rule, but may be valuing benefits and costs differently. In particular, private firms would be expected to take into account only benefits and costs expressing themselves in market valuations. But government is in a position to separate the provision of the commodity or service from the attendant financial receipts and outlays. Consequently, it is able to take into account, on either the cost or benefit side, the values placed by consumers upon nonappropriable goods (e.g., national defense), positive or negative spillovers (as in water-resource management), etc. Of course, our postulated reduction to dollar values combines goods of all kinds in one analytical category, but this was solely for expository convenience. The real differences in appropriability or marketability of goods suffice to provide a role for government as a distinct productive agency.[4]

III. REVIEW OF THE LITERATURE

In the enormous literature on cost-benefit analysis for public investment decision, the problem of risk and uncertainty has received only sparse coverage.[5] Some authors raise the topic only to deny its relevance; others propose more or less specific "adjustments," but without substantial attempts at theoretical justification. (The recent development of the concept of "State-preference" does, however, provide an analytical basis for the treatment of risk—this topic will be reserved for sec. V below.)

The problem of risk obtrudes itself upon the analyst or decisionmaker when he tries to determine "the" interest rate r_1—or more generally, the temporal sequence of interest rates $r_1, r_2, \ldots, r_7$—for use in present-value formulas like those of section II. For, in the world of reality we observe not a single rate but a bewildering variety of interest rates, even between a given pair of dates. Two main hypotheses come to mind in connection with this diversity. The first calls on *market imperfections* to explain why, for example, consumers must pay more for personal loans than savers receive on time deposits (e.g., Eckstein [7 : 503]). The other school of thought maintains that the divergences of observed yields conceal an underlying harmony represented by the systematic and in principle predictable influence of risk (see, for example, Sharpe [29]). In the nature of the case, this issue can probably never be fully resolved; the hypotheses are programmatic statements rather than empirical generalizations. We shall be concerned here mainly with those analysts who do regard the divergences of realized interest rates as having at least something to do with differential risk and uncertainty.

The major analytical controversy that has occupied the literature is the following: Does the risk compensation sought by individuals—in the form of a "risk-premium" over and above the riskless rate of interest—represent a social as well as a private cost? There are also subcontroversies concerning the policy implications of each of the basic conclusions on the main issue. All these topics will be reviewed here. It should be kept in mind, however, that the risk-premium representing compensation for risk-aversion (reluctance to bear variability of outcome of investments) must always be distinguished from compensation for risk in the sense of optimistic bias in the statement of costs and benefits. Unfortunately, failure to make this distinction has been responsible for a good deal of confusion in the literature.

Does Risk-Aversion Exist?

Before turning to the main issue, there is a prior question that ought to be settled. If individuals were on balance "risk-lovers," they would be willing to accept a discount to bear variability risk—rather than insisting on a market premium. And in fact, there is a tradition in economic thought which so maintains. Thus, Adam Smith declared:

> The chance of gain is by every man more or less overvalued, and the changes of loss is by most men undervalued, and by scarce any man who is in tolerable health and spirits, valued more than it is worth. ([30], Book I, Ch. 10.)

And of course, the phenomenon of gambling is further evidence along this line. On the other hand, Alfred Marshall came to the opposite conclusion ([22], Book V, Ch. 7 and Book VI, Ch. 8). And the institution of insurance is evidence in favor of his viewpoint.

There have been a number of attempts to explain the seeming conflict here (see Friedman and Savage [11], Markowitz [21], Hirshleifer [14]). All of these tend to support the conclusion that gambling is likely to be a relatively minor perturbation, with the bulk of substantial investment behavior subject to the influence of risk-aversion. And indeed, that risk-aversion predominates does not appear to be a matter of controversy in practice. Risk-aversion is almost always taken for granted not only in the cost-benefit literature for government investment decision, but in theoretical and applied works in the area of corporate finance and security markets (see, for example, Modigliani and Miller [24]).

Risk-Aversion Not a Social Cost—The Pooling Argument

The major support for the viewpoint that private risk aversion, accepted as a fact, is or ought to be socially irrelevant stems from the pooling argument. As indicated above, this argument is based upon the operation of the law of large numbers in making the mathematical expectation of outcome almost a certainty where there are many independent experiments. The position is well expressed by Vickrey:

> But insofar as riskiness is concerned, the reason risky investments carry an expected return greater than that of secure investments is that in the market, facilities for pooling of risks are imperfect, so that investment by private investors in risky investments given a limited portfolio and a certain indivisibility in the market, is unavoidably associated with a considerable dispersion of individual incomes. Given a certain risk aversion

on the part of individuals . . . maximization of expected utility leads naturally to a bias against risky investments . . . . On the social level however, the risk associated with a given public venture is inevitably pooled and averaged over the entire population of the country in some fashion, along with the risks of other projects, and this pooling or averaging of risks for public projects is accomplished without any cost of extra financial transactions [32 : 89].

And at the same meeting, Samuelson supported Vickery's view:

One can look at much of government as primarily a device for mutual reinsurance. General Motors can borrow at a lower rate than American Motors because it is a pooler of more independent risks. It would be absurd for G.M. to apply the same high risk-interest discount factor to a particular venture that A.M. must apply. The same holds for We, Inc. which is a better pooler of risks than even G.M. [27 : 96].

The pooling argument will be vigorously evaluated in terms of the model of State-preference in seciton V. A few remarks may be in order here, however, Vickery's contention shows awareness of the fact that the argument does depend in some unspecified sense upon market imperfections. However, these authors do not seem to fully appreciate that there is at least one other condition necessary for the validity of the argument. The second condition is that the returns on the private and Government investments being compared are not correlated with social variability of outcome. If the higher risk premium on American Motors is due largely to, for example, a higher correlation of outcome with the general business cycle—one type of "social risk"—it would be incorrect to say that private A.M. risks do not reflect social costs. And similarly, if the returns on Government investments vary systematically in procyclical fashion, the existence of many Government projects will not eliminate this source of variability. Kenneth Arrow [1] is aware of both of these necessary conditions, but nevertheless defends the pooling argument. He maintains that markets for reinsurance of private risks do not exist and that the returns on new investments tend to be uncorrelated with social risks. It would seem that both of these contentions are rather extreme. Diamond has indicated recently that Arrow underestimates the efficiency of security markets in effectively pooling the private sector's risks [5]. And it would seem preferable to explicitly account even if only approximately for the procyclical or anticyclical impact of particular Government investments rather than making an unwarranted assertion of neutrality on this score.

Policy Implications of Socially Irrelevant Risk

For the proponents of the argument that private risk aversion is a socially irrelevant cost of investment, the policy implications are treated as straightforward.

Arrow's statement is typical:

> . . . the proper procedure is to compute the expected values of benefits and costs, and discount them at the riskless rate . . . [1 : 28].

As will be seen below, this also would seem to provide the rationale for the existing procedures of many Government agencies.

The effect of this procedure is to encourage the expansion of public investment in the place of the private investment deterred by socially irrelevant risk. That this is the best method of coping with the problem has been challenged. For, granted the premises, it would clearly be more efficient for the Government to induce, by subsidy if necessary, adoption of the higher-expected-yield private investments not being undertaken [14 : 270]. Indeed, as will be shown below, it is hardly a question of subsidy but rather a correction of the effect of a tax that places an enormous burden upon private risky investment—the corporate income tax. Opposition to a policy of divergence between public and private discount rates has also been expressed by Baumol*:

> Thus, nothing said so far argues for or against a low rate of discount. It states merely that society will not benefit if it increases long term investment in a wasteful and inefficient manner, by forcing the transfer of resources from employments with a high marginal yield to uses with a low marginal yield. For that is exactly what can be expected to result from the usual sort of figure of say 5 per cent for discount rates on public projects when the corporate rate of return is perhaps three times that high [3 : 797].

Students of economics will recognize herein the familiar "second best" problem of welfare theory. In this context the "first-best" solution is the expansion of the deficient risky *private* investment, by correction of the influence of a discriminatory tax—or by subsidy, if necessary. If for some reason the "first-best" solution is unfeasible, we may want to consider "second-best" policies. But the exapnsion of risky *government* investments is a very inefficient "second-best," since some of the funds so used are preempting more productive investments in the private sector. Even if it were impossible to do anything to favor risky private investment, which is evidently not the case, government discounting at higher than the riskless rate is indicated—to strike a balance between the desired expansion of risky investment in general but the undesired preempting of more productive private investment.[6]

---

*Further discussion of this issue is found in the preceding article by Baumol.

Views That Risk is a Social Cost

Those who argue that the risk premiums observed in the market are not socially relevant have reference. of course, to premiums for bearing variability risk. We have noted earlier, however, that part of what is regarded as the market risk premium may be a correction for the optimistic bias of the borrower. We refer here to the "premium" of higher nominal yield that must be offered on securities considered risky by investors. Those who advocate the riskless rate for government investment are generally concerned, of course, that optimistic bias be eliminated from the cost-benefit stream (see Samuelson [27 : 96]). Where the issue is made explicit, economists seem unanimously to agree that risk in the sense of optimistic bias of proposed government investments is a social cost and must be allowed for. Some authors would prefer, however, to make the adjustment through the discount rate. Bain, Caves, and Margolis declare:

> The only general justification for introducing a "risk allowance" of one sort or another into investment calculations would be that some or all water agencies seem to have shown a propensity to make unjustifiably optimistic estimates of future benefits of projects; thus, reducing their estimates by such a means as increasing the rate of discount by two or three percentage points would compensate for their optimistic bias in estimating [2 : 272].

These authors argue against tampering with the cost and benefit streams directly.

Turning to authors who seem to accept implicitly or explicitly that aversion to variability risks is a social cost to be considered in Government investment decision, the vast majority agree that adjustment has to be via the discount rate. One important exception, however, is Fred Hoffman, who as Assistant Director of the Bureau of the Budget testified:

> While I certainly do not wish to argue that Government programs are riskless—on the contrary they are often subject to considerable risk—I believe that better decisions are likely to result from considering the risks explicitly by adjusting the expected costs and benefits than by attempting to relate the average risk of peculiarly public programs to "similarly risky" investments in the private sector [17 : 27].

Most other authors, while possibly agreeing that such a procedure might be desirable in principle, rule it out as impractical (Hirshleifer, DeHaven, and Milliman [16 : 144] or as lacking any foundation in traditional approaches to uncertainty (Dorfman [6 : 149]).

The mainstream of debate on the evaluation of risky Government investment projects has turned upon the selection of the appropriate rate of discount to allow for "optimism bias" and/or "variability risk." Here the different views may be classified according to whether they presume that divergences in observed interest rates fundamentally represent (a) the influence of market segmentation or other imperfections or (b) the systematic and predictable influence of differing riskiness. Any such classification cannot be entirely hard-and-fast. Some authors may maintain an intermediate position, and others may not pose the issue clearly one way or the other. Nevertheless, it is possible at least to a first approximation to classify those whose views are primarily based upon the "market imperfections" hypothesis on the one hand, or the "harmony" hypothesis on the other.

For those thinking in the former terms, the inclination is to apply some across-the-board discount rate for all Government projects. Thus, Eckstein proposes a general risk premium of from one-half to one per cent [9 : 86]. In another work, Krutilla and Eckstein [19] conduct an elaborate analysis to determine the social cost of Federal financing. Clearly presuming market segmentation, they examine the differential impact upon the various investing and consuming sectors of ways of securing Federal funds. This is done in order to provide weights for the averaging of typical interest rates or yields in these various sectors. The Government discount rate derived by this procedure incorporates some unknown average degree of risk-premium—in both the optimistic-bias and variability senses of the term. A somewhat analogous estimation procedure has been adopted by Harberger, who however recognizes the need for an explicit risk adjustment [12].

Those authors thinking primarily in terms of the harmonistic hypothesis are led to seek discount rates in the market that are somehow related to or reflective of the same sort of risks as the Government projects considered. Thus Hirshleifer, DeHaven and Milliman:

> ... attempt to determine the *real marginal opportunity rate* which the market insists upon in providing capital to *private* companies whose investment decisions are most comparable to those of public agencies in water supply, namely, corporations in the public utility fields [16 : 146].

And Professor Harberger testified:

> A third and still better approach would be to try to identify especially risky Government investments, investments of medium risk, and investments of demonstrably low risk and to make separate risk adjustments for each of these three categories. If we could simply identify investments in those three classes and have a higher than average discount rate for those that bear the earmarks of being highly speculative and a lower than average discount rate for those of types with assured histories of proven payoffs, we would be doing a decent job, though obviously not the best conceivable job [12 : 73].

Bains, Caves, and Margolis seem to espouse a similar harmonistic viewpoint:
  Briefly, however, it would appear that, in order to secure the optimal or best attainable suboptimal allocation of resources to water development (given existing organization and performance in the private sector, including the organization of markets for funds), the appropriate rate of discount should be roughly equal to the *marginal* rate of return in marginal long-term investment in the private sector, and also equal to the marginal rate of time preference of the taxpayers of agency constituents who ultimately finance the bulk of investment in water projects. These two rates tend generally to coincide and to be approximated by the going net rate of interest on private savings invested in real estate [2 : 268].

Note that the first and third citations here select rather different private investment classes as relevant and comparable in riskiness to public investment in the water-supply field. Still another related viewpoint is that of Stockfisch, who takes the estimated overall rate of return in the private sector as the comparable rate for military investment decisions [34]. A very important practical consideration here is whether rates are to be computed gross or net of corporate income tax—a point which will be taken up in Section VI.

  There are a number of other viewpoints worthy of notice, though not conveniently classifiable in terms of the categories above. McKean regards risk as an "intangible," and leaves its resolution to the sphere of judgment [23 : 64]. Dorfman attempted to apply statistical decision theory to the water-resource field, but came up with pessimistic conclusions as to the present applicability of these ideas [6 : 144]. He did suggest one modification of traditional risk-adjustment approaches: to choose projects on the basis of minimizing probability of experiencing a specified disaster outcome. Finally, Haveman has advocated an interesting variant of discounting procedures ([13], Appendix B). He would add a premium to the riskless rate when discounting benefits but would use a rate lower than the pure rate in discounting costs. The basic idea is that risk-aversion dictates writing *down* the present-value estimate of future benefits but writing *up* the present-value estimate of future costs. Moreover, in view of the greater uncertainty of benefits, the former adjustment should be larger than the latter. However, this discussion does not lead to a specification of how the discount rates are to be determined. Doing so would require a theoretical model of risk. The state-preference analysis of Section V, which provides such a model, indicates that it is not actually necessary to separate the two rates—as will be seen below, it is possible in principle to determine a single risky discount rate that will generate the correct present certainty-equivalent value of an investment project. However, as a practical matter Haveman's two-rate proposal would probably be a defensible and workable improvement, in comparison with using a single discount rate that purports to be related to the average riskiness of the separate cost and benefit streams.

Summary of Quantitative Recommendations on Discount Rates

The discount rates shown in Table 1 represent estimates and proposals by different authors for Government investment decisions. The figures are not fully comparable, since they were made at varying dates in a period of changing conditions in the financial markets. Also, in some cases differing types of Government decisions were under consideration, so that the "comparable" private rates would not be expected to be the same.

Against all these should be kept in mind the recommendation of some authors that the *riskless* rate be used. This is usually interpreted as the government borrowing rate for the appropriate (usually long term) period of investment. This rate has varied in recent years between five and 5¾ per cent. However, it is clear that the figures here include an adjustment for inflationary expectations; the anticipated real riskless rate has probably been rather steady in the neighborhood of four per cent.[7]

Table 1
Discount Rate Recommendations—Risky Rates

Author	Year	Recommendation
Krutilla and Eckstein [19]	1958	5 to 6 per cent
Eckstein [9]	1958	½- to 1-per cent risk premium
Eckstein [8]	1968	8 per cent
Hirschleiter, DeHaven, and Milliman [16]	1960	10 per cent
J. A. Stockfisch [34]	1967	13.5 per cent
Bain, Caves, and Margolis [2]	1966	5 to 6 per cent
Harberger [12]	1968	10.68 per cent

IV. PAST AND PRESENT GOVERNMENT PRACTICE

The analytical controversy over whether premiums paid in the market to overcome individuals' risk-aversion represent a social as well as a private cost of investment, finds its counterpart in the practices of Government agencies.[8] The issue was epitomized in the testimony of the Comptroller General:

> One school of thought holds that the rate should be determined by and be equal to the rate paid by the Treasury in borrowing money. A second school of thought holds that the rate should be determined by what is foregone; namely, the return that could have been earned in the private

sector of the economy when the decision is made to commit resources to the public sector [31 : 6].

The first position cited by the Comptroller General clearly corresponds to the prescription of discounting by the riskless rate; the second to discounting by a risky one.

It is very worthy of note that some Federal agencies do not discount future benefits (and costs) at all, while others employ only a haphazard method for doing so. A recent study by the Comptroller General (see Table 2) showed that only ten of twenty-three agencies surveyed employed the discounting technique in evaluating agency investment. Of the remaining thirteen, eight do have plans to employ discounting in the future. Some agencies engage in a form of implicit discounting by imposing an arbitrary cutoff date on future benefits. The Department of Labor, for example, is said to use a one-year time horizon even though its program benefits are thought to continue for periods of five to twenty-five years. This method is equivalent to a zero discount rate up to the cutoff date, and an infinite discount rate thereafter. Other agencies that simply cumulate costs and benefits regardless of data are in effect employing a zero discount rate throughout.

In an effort to standardize analytical procedure, particularly among water resource agencies, the "Green Book" [35] was produced in 1950 by a committee of several agencies. With regard to the question of risk, the Green Book followed Frank Knight in attempting to distinguish between "predictable risk" and "nonpredictable risk."[9] Examples cited of predictable risk were fires, storms, pests, and diseases. Examples of nonpredictable risk were fluctuations in the level of economic activity, and innovations and technological change. For predictable risk the Green Book recommended what were in effect expected-value adjustments of the cost-benefit stream. For nonpredictable risk, a variety of adjustments were recommended: conservative estimates of net benefits, safety margins in planning, or the inclusion of a risk component in the discount rate. The rather surprising last possibility was advocated because of the impracticability in some cases of arriving at risk-free estimates of benefits.

The quantitative recommendation of the Green Book included the use of 2½-per cent discount rate on government costs. (It must be remembered that, at the date of the Green Book, interest rates were far lower than those we have since become accustomed to. And, furthermore, they were then regarded as abnormally high and due for a fall toward the more "normal" ranges experienced in the 1930s.) A rate of not less than four per cent was recommended for private costs and all benefits. This higher rate was justified on the ground that it would:

... approach the rate of return needed to induce private investment and participation. This rate corresponds to the minimum current costs to

private borrowers for obtaining funds through mortgage loans secured by
real property or other substantial assets [35 : 23].

The report even contemplated that still higher rates would be used in certain
circumstances. Thus, the Green Book actually went a considerable distance
toward the risky-rate prescription for discounting—the premise being that the
projects under consideration were at least comparable in risk to "mortgage loans
secured by real property or other substantial assets."

This advice went unheeded, however, Later revisions were made in the discount rate but the quest was merely for a representative riskless rate. In 1962 an
ad hoc council appointed by President Kennedy recommended a formula for
calculating such a rate. This provided:

> The interest rate to be used in plan formulation and evaluation for
> discounting future benefits and computing costs . . . shall be based upon
> the average rate of interest payable by the Treasury (i.e., *the coupon
> rate*) on interest bearing marketable securities of the United States out-
> standing at the end of the fiscal year preceding such computation which,
> upon original issue, had terms to maturity of fifteen years or more [36:12].

In 1968, another revision was sought and the most current proposal is:

> The interest rate to be used in plan formulation and evaluation for
> discounting future benefits and computing costs, or otherwise converting
> benefits and costs to a common time basis, shall be based upon the
> average yield during the preceding fiscal year on interest–bearing market-
> able securities of the United States which at the time the computation is
> made, have terms of fifteen years or more remaining to maturity: Pro-
> vided, however, that in no event shall the rate be raised or lowered more
> than one-quarter per cent for any years [4 : 13].

The intent of the proposed reform is to eliminate the influence of historical
coupon rates in favor of the yield data that reflect the current state of the funds
markets. The net effect of the proposal was to raise the rate from 3 1/4 to 4 5/8
per cent. While this has the salutary effect of bringing the rate more up-to-date,
it is clear that the intention remains to discount at a riskless rate.[10]

Many agencies follow this lead and employ the Treasury's borrowing cost (see
[33], App. 1). Other Government agencies, however, have used rates that at
least implicitly include a risk premium. The leader and prime mover in this area
is the Department of Defense, which employs a discount rate of ten per cent.
This rate was selected:

> To reflect the amount of time preference for current versus future
> money sacrifices that the public exhibits in nongovernmental transactions.
> The ten-per cent rate is considered to be the most representative   point

Table 2
Discounting Practices of Federal Agencies

I. Federal agencies not using discounting in the analysis of individual programs in fiscal
    year 1969

   A. *Agencies that plan to use discounting in future—*

      1. Department of Housing and Urban Development

      2. Federal Power Commission

      3. Peace Corps

      4. National Science Foundation

      5. National Aeronautics and Space Administration

      6. Department of Labor

      7. Post Office Department

      8. Federal Communications Commission

   B. *Agencies that have no stated plans to use discounting or had no comments on their
    plans—*

      1. Interstate Commerce Commission

      2. Veterans Administration

      3. Department of the Treasury

      4. Export-Import Bank of Washington

      5. Department of Commerce

II. Agencies Employing Discounting—

      1. Tennessee Valley Authority

      2. General Services Administration

      3. Department of Agriculture

      4. Office of Economic Opportunity

      5. Department of Transportation (Federal Aviation Administration)

      6. Atomic Energy Commission

      7. Department of Defense

      8. Agency for International Development

      9. Department of the Interior

    10. Department of Health, Education, and Welfare

NOTE: Survey did not cover agencies involved in water and related land resources programs that come within the purview of the Budget Circular A-76 entitled "Policies for
Acuiring Commercial or Industrial Products and Services for Government Use." Source:
[33:47].

within a range of plausible rates obtained from and considering this public
time preference [33 : 57].

We see that Government practice is highly varied. This is not surprising when
it is realized that the establishment of the discount rate is left to administrative
decision rather than being the subject of legislative direction. Not only are
Government planners given considerable discretion and latitude in the estimation
of benefits and costs, they are also left to exercise discretion regarding the
applicable rate of discount. The potentialities for optimistic distortion are

evident, if only because the decisionmakers within any given agency tend to be enthusiastic about and committed to its own particular goals. This review would seem to indicate the desirability of constraining the now-excessive degrees of freedom of the agencies, in the interests of a more efficient balance of investment within the Federal Government.

V.   RECENT THEORETICAL DEVELOPMENTS: THE MODEL OF TIME-STATE PREFERENCE

In the past decade, theoretical economists have made considerable advances in the direction of an exact theory of risk. While many problems remain, this theoretical development now makes possible a better understanding and pinpointing of the unresolved issues in the traditional literature reviewed in Section III above.

The key idea of the recent theoretical development is the picturing of an uncertain future as a set of hypothetical alternative "states of the world" at each date. Although one and only one of these states will in fact occur at each date, decisionmakers now, in the present, must contemplate and allow for all the possibilities if they are to act rationally. In so acting, they will naturally take into account, where relevant, their beliefs as to the probabilities of the several states, the values they place upon larger and smaller income claims, and their time-preferences. The interaction in the market of individual decisions will in effect determine a set of market prices for contingent claims to income at each future time-state. It is as if these contingent claims themselves become the elementary commodities that are traded in markets, although in reality trading occurs in sets of claims packaged into the forms we call *securities.*

These concepts can be elucidated with a simple model. In expounding the nature of the riskless solution, we dealt with the elementary case of choice between consumption now and consumption one year from now. The minimal extension of this model to allow for risk is the case in which there is no uncertainty about the present, but at a single future date (one year from now) just one of two alternative states of the world "a" or "b" (e.g., war or peace, depression or prosperity) must come about. Given the reduction to dollar values, there are in this situation three objects of choice: claims to present consumption, claims to future consumption valid if and only if the state "a" obtains, and claims to future consumption valid if and only if state "b" obtains.

In the riskless case, the market was said to determine the interest rate r_1 as a discounting factor for future claims. But it is possible to express this in another way: we can say that the market determines the relative price ratio between future and present claims. Thus, taking the price of current claims P_0 as unity, the price of future claims P_1 is given by the discount factor: $P_1 = 1/(1 + r_1)$. This permits us to rewrite the present value equation (1) for the certainty case in the instructive form:

$$V_0 = -P_0 i_0 + P_1 q_1 \qquad (1')$$

In the simple model of risk dealt with here, the market will determine the price ratios among the three objects of choice. Again taking the price of current claims P_0 as unity, the prices of the future contingent claims $P_{1a} P_{1b}$ will be determined. As before, a number of conclusions will follow from standard economic theory: there will be a principle of rational consumer behavior, of rational producer behavior, of market equilibrium, and a normative rule for Government investment decisions. The extension of the "positive" principles to this risky model is reasonably clear, and they need not be explicitly restated here. But it will be important to specify the *present certainty-equivalent value rule* for Government investment decision as the generalization to risky situations of the present-value rule of the riskless model. This rule is that the Government ought to adopt that set of projects maximizing the net balance V_0 of the market values of present sacrifice and future returns in the several states of the world contemplated:

$$V_0 = -P_0 i_0 + P_{1a} q_{1a} + P_{1b} q_{1b} \qquad (3)$$

Or,[11] that each and every project should be adopted for which the incremental present certainty-equivalent value ΔV_0 is positive, where ΔV_0 is given by:

$$\Delta V_0 = -P_0 \Delta i_0 + P_{1a} \Delta q_{1a} + P_{1b} \Delta q_{1b} \qquad (4)$$

As in the case of the riskless rule, the present certainty-equivalent value (PCEV) is strictly *objective*. It does not depend at all upon the decisionmaker's personal time-preference (or even probability beliefs), but only upon the net integration of all individuals' preferences and beliefs as expressed in the market in the form of prices present and future claims.

A numerical illustration may be helpful at this point. Suppose that, with P_0 set at unity, the market-equilibrium prices for contingent claims are $P_{1a} = 0.3$ and $P_{1b} = 0.5$. Now imagine a government decisionmaker considering an investment project involving a current outlay of \$1 and the future receipt of \$3 conditional upon state a coming about (and returning zero otherwise). This opportunity may be suggestively symbolized in the form $[-1, \substack{3 \\ 0}]$. Its present certainty-equivalent value ΔV_0 is $-1 + 3(0.3) + 0(0.5) = -0.1$; this project, if adopted would decrease overall PCEV and so should be rejected. Alternatively, consider the opportunity symbolized by $[-1, \frac{2}{2}]$. Here a dollar outlay in the present leads to $2 return regardless of which state obtains one year from now (this is a riskless investment). Since $-1 + 2(0.3) + 2(0.5) = +0.6$, the project has positive PCEV and so should be adopted. Note the strictly objective nature of the determination of acceptability of projects.

While productive decisionmakers need not consider subjective preferences or beliefs, as in the riskless case the *consumptive* decisionmakers will take these into account in distributing consumption (within their wealth constraints) over the available objects of choice. This, an individual might desire to purchase and hold more claims to future consumption in state *a* because he thinks state *a* is very likely, or because he is already well covered if state *b* comes about, or because he is generally satiated with consumption in the present, and so forth. All these factors will enter into the supplies and demands for the several objects of choice, and thus into the determination of the market prices.

In the certainty model, we saw that the simple relationship $P_1 = 1/(+ r_1)$ holds between the rate of interest r_1 and the price of future claims P_1. It is possible to generalize this relationship to the risky case by expressing the value of a future *certain* claim as P_1 in:

$$P_1 = P_{1a} + P_{1b} \tag{5}$$

That is, a unit of future consumption can be purchased with certainty by combining unit future claims for each state of the world. This leads directly to the definition of a *riskless rate of interest* r_1 *in an uncertain world*, in the form:

$$P_{1a} + P_{1b} = \frac{1}{1 + r_1} \tag{6}$$

In terms of the numerical illustration above, with $P_{1a} = 0.3$ and $P_{1b} = 0.5$, it is evident that the price of a future certain claim $P_1 = 0.8$, so that the riskless rate of interest r_1 is 25 per cent..

We can now employ this theoretical development to reconsider the key issues debated in the literature review in Section III. The first and most central issue is: Is risk (in the sense of variability) a social cost, or a merely private cost that government ought to ignore? The latter view rests, of course, upon the "pooling" argument. Since government is in a postiion to undertake many independent projects, it can treat the mathematical expectation of yield as in effect certain. Operationally, proponents of this position would take the mathematical expectations of the benefits and costs at each date, and then discount with the riskless rate of interest r_1. In contrast, the view that private risk aversion is reflective of a real social cost leads operationally to discounting the mathematical expectations of net benefits by a "risky interest rate" r_1^* suitable for the characteristic pattern of risk of the investment in question. Since we know that the present certainty-equivalent value rule gives correct results, the question may be posed in terms of the consistency of each of these operational procedures with that rule.

The difference between the recommended procedures can be illustrated by the respective evaluations of the project symbolized above by $[-1,_0^3]$. In this numerical example, as before, we let P_{1a} = 0.3 and P_{1b} = 0.5 But let us now assume in addition that the two states can be considered equiprobable; thus, $\pi_{1a} = \pi_{1b} = 1/2$. Then, the mathematical expectation of the future return is 1.5 With a *riskless* interest rate of twenty-five per cent, the discounting equation takes the form $-1 + (1.5/1.25) = +0.2$. But we know that this is a project whose PCEV is negative $(= -0.1)$ and which should *not* be adopted. Thus, the example shows that the recommendation to use the riskless rate in discounting the mathematical expectation of future returns cannot be correct in general. For the contrasting recommendation, the key problem is the question of how to determine the "suitable" risky rate r_1^*. Waiving for the moment the source of this figure, it is possible to verify numerically that 66-2/3 per cent is the correct discount rate to employ. That is, $-1 + (1.5/1.667) = -0.1$, which equals the PCEV.

More formally, the procedure recommended by those supporting the pooling argument—discounting the mathematical expectation of future return by the riskless rate—would indicate adoption of an incremental project when the $\Delta V_0'$ is positive, ΔV_0 being defined in terms of the state probabilities π_{1a} and π_{1b} as follows:

$$\Delta V_0' = -\Delta i_0 + \frac{\pi_{1a}\Delta q_{1a} + \pi_{1b}\Delta q_{1b}}{1 + r_1} \tag{7}$$

It is intuitively evident that this procedure is correct—i.e., is logically equivalent to the PCEV rule—*if and only if the probabilities assigned to states are proportional to the prices of the state claims.*[12] In terms of the numerical example, if the state probabilities were 3/8 and 5/8, respectively, the mathematical expectation of future return would be 3(3/8) + 0(5/8) = 9/8, so that $\Delta V_0' = -1 + (9/8/1.25) = -0.1$, the correct result.

Can we assume that the prices of state-claims must be proportionate to the state-probabilities? No; because for one thing the consumers might simply have a disproportionately intense preference for consumption in one state rather than in another. A still more important, because systematically predictable, consideration is the following: Prices of future state-claims will depend not only upon relative probabilities but on the relative *scarcities* of income in the several states.

If individuals are predominantly risk avoiders, claims to incremental consumption in a given state will be more highly valued, the probability being the same, if that state is associated with low overall income.[13] And indeed this prediction is borne out empirically by the relatively high realized percentage yield (implying relative low prior valuation of income) earned by procyclical securities like industrial equities in comparison with stable or anticyclical securities like government bonds.

Returning to the procedure of discounting mathematical expectation of future return by a risky interest rate, the correct r_1^* is given by the condition:[14]

$$1 + r_1^* = \frac{\pi_{1a}\Delta q_{1a} + \pi_{1b}\Delta q_{1b}}{P_{1a}\Delta q_{1a} + P_{1b}\Delta q_{1b}} \tag{8}$$

It is important to note that the suitably risky rate is dependent only upon the *proportional* state-pattern of future returns. Thus, the projects symbolized by $[-1,_0^3]$, $[-1,_0^2]$, $[-3,_0^5]$ would all be discounted at the same rate; i.e., they constitute a "risk class" in the terminology of Modigliani and Miller [24 : 268]. Note also that the riskless interest rate can be regarded as a special case of the more general logical category of risky interest rates; specifically, as the rate applicable to the certainty "risk class" represented by projects like $[-1,_2^2]$ or $[-5,_6^6]$.

We may now begin to consider some of the problems of practical application by asking the question: If the suitable risky discount rate is determined by consistency of results with those yielded by the PCEV rule, why go through this roundabout procedure? Why not simply evaluate all projects on the basis of incremental ΔV_0, calculated directly as in equation (4) from the outlay Δi_0, receipts Δq_{1a} and Δq_{1b}, and objective market prices P_{1a} and P_{1b}? Here it is necessary to reveal the skeleton in the closet! In actuality, the number of imaginable states even at a signle date is enormously great. There do not exist in fact a complete set of securities in the form of elementary state-claims whose prices would directly provide the needed data for the use of the PCEV rule directly, Actual securities—e.g., stocks and bonds—represent more or less complex packages of claims to income distributed over many different states and dates. It may sometimes be possible to draw inferences from the pattern of prices for securities about the implicit prices for time-state claims, but it seems unlikely that all the necessary prices could be so inferred.

This does not mean, however, that we are completely helpless in practice. Here is where the concept of a "risk class" comes to our aid. For, it may well be that a proposed government project can reasonably be placed in the same risk class as a private project. It is then only necessary to estimate what risky discount rate r_1^* the market imposes on expected returns from such private projects.

Concretely, the procedure would work as follows: Suppose we are evaluating a public power project, and there seems to be no reason to assume that the project is not in the same risk class as private power projects in general. Let us suppose that the latter are typically financed half and half by stocks and bonds, and that market prices for securities are such that the mathematical expectation of yield on the stocks is eight per cent and the bonds five per cent. Then the suitable r_1^* for use in discounting expected returns of the comparable government project would be 6.5 per cent.[15] (Actually it is not strictly necessary to know mathematical expectations of returns; provided that the degree of bias in the private and public estimates of returns were the same, the implied private discount rate could still be employed.)

Low discount rates tend to make investment projects look good; high interest rates tend to make them look bad. In this connection, it is of some importance to appreciate the fact that the "risky" interest rate, while usually higher, could conceivably turn out to be lower than the "riskless" interest rate. Consider our earlier numerical example, with state probabilities still $\pi_{1a} = \pi_{1b} = 1/2$, prices $P_{1a} = 0.3$ and $P_{1b} = 0.5$, but where we now have a project whose state pattern of returns is the reverse of that considered earlier; to wit $[-3, {}^0_3]$. Direct calculation from equation (4) shows ΔV_0 to be +0.5, while equation (8) shows the suitable "risky" rate r_1^* to be zero per cent! This figure is *lower* than the riskless rate r_1 of twenty-five per cent. The explanation for this possibly surprising result is that the riskless rate is calculated in terms of a state–pattern of returns yielding *equally in the two states*, while in the present example we have a situation in which the returns fall disproportionately (entirely, in fact) in the relatively more highly valued state. Proponents of government investment programs often argue that government should ordinarily employ a lower discount rate than does private industry in evaluating investment projects. Such a recommendation would be valid in this model if it were the case that returns from government projects tend to fall disproportionately in such highly valued states, in comparison with private industry. Thus, the "typical" private investment would, on this argument, not be "comparable" one (in terms of risk class) from which the correct risky rate r_1^* is to be caluclated.

Even among those who support the idea that the market's reflection of private risk aversion represents a real social cost, there is a school of thought opposed to *adjustment* for risk through the discount rate. One argument in this connection says that risk need not be a simple compounding function of time, and so no single overall interest rate adjustment would be suitable. The argument is correct, in that in principle r_2^*—the discount rate appropriate for moving claims dated two years from now one year closer in time—need not be the same as r. But, of course, there is nothing in the theory developed here that precludes the use of a series of different rates for discounting returns through time; we dealt only with r_1^* above merely because of the simplicity of the expository model used here. Furthermore, it will always be possible to find a single time-averaged discount rate $\bar{R}_T^*$ that will give the same results as calculating with a series of one-year discount rates $r_1^*, r_2^*, \ldots r_T^*$.

The alternative to use of the risky interest rate for discounting future uncertain returns would be to attempt to determine at each date, the *certainty equivalent* of the net return at that date. If this could be done, the riskless interest rate could then be employed to discount these future certainty equivalents into a present certainty-equivalent value. However, the calculation of these future certainty-equivalent values seems to require direct knowledge of consumers' utility functions, and so is not a feasible procedures.

VI.   UNRESOLVED ISSUES AND DIRECTIONS OF FUTURE RESEARCH

It may seem surprising that the "pooling" argument fails so completely, in view of the plausible arguments that can be made in its favor. One can, in fact, construct a model in which the pooling argument does make more sense. The key is to distinguish between private and social states. To take the most extreme case, suppose that on the social level the amount of income at the single future data is constant; the only thing that may vary is its distribution over individuals. For concreteness, suppose that the individuals can be grouped into equally numerous "even" and "odd" categories. Imagine that each individual has an investment opportunity of the form $[-1, {}_0^3]$ and define state a as the situation where the evens obtain three and the odds obtain zero, while state b is the reverse situation. Then, we can see, private risk aversion may make every individual disciplined to undertake his personal investment project—whereas, on the social level, there is no risk at all.

The crucial point of this example, and the hidden assumption in the usual pooling argument, is that *the two classes of individuals cannot trade* state-a for state-b claims. For, if they traded at par, say, they could all convert their respective investment opportunities into the form $[-1, {}_{1.5}^{1.5}]$ which would be *privately as well as socially* riskless. Given risk aversion, everyone would benefit from such an exchange. Why then do they not make the exchange? The same argument can be generalized to a situation where there are multiple social states (*some* degree of social risk exists), but where the investment opportunities available to individuals have private state-patterns of returns that are all uncorrelated with these social states. Again trading among individuals should eliminate all private risk that is not reflective of social risk.

The pooling argument rests ultimately for support upon market imperfections—which hinder the trading that would otherwise tend to eliminate private risks (unbalanced state-patterns of returns) not reflective of social risks. Now the number of conceivable time-state contingencies is enormous, far greater than the number of distinct securities traded. This disparity is not surprising, given that there are real costs of providing markets. Thus, imperfect marketability of time-state claims is a fact, and so there is a degree of validity in the pooling argument. On the other hand, imperfect ability of Government to distribute time-state claims in accordance with consumers' marginal preferences is surely an equally significant fact.[16] As a practical matter, the present authors believe that the use of the "comparable" risky rate of discount from the private sector is the best general guide—though the justification falls short of being airtight.

As a final note, let us consider the role of the corporate income tax.* The existence of this tax makes an enormous difference in the computation of the net returns from investment, and therefore in the calculation of risky interest rates for use in evaluation of Government projects comparable to those in the private sector. In the example above of a project to be equally financed with bonds of an expected yield of five per cent and stocks of an expected yield of eight per cent, in the absence of tax the required real yield for the project to be profitable would be 6.5 per cent. But with corporate income tax at a fifty per cent rate, the real yield would have to be 10.5 per cent.[17] Thus, the tax places at an enormous disadvantage the risky projects that have to be financed in whole or in part from equity investment.[18] It is therefore, just the reverse of the policy that might be suggested by the degree of validity in the pooling argument: namely, that risky investment ought to benefit from a subsidy. *The effect of the corporate income tax is very likely greater than imperfection of capital markets in deterring private risky undertakings.*

Now it may be that the corporate income tax in its present form reflects some kind of "social judgment" that private individuals are *excessively* inclined to undertake risky investment. If that is the case, then the effective required market yield (10.5 per cent in the example) is the one that represents the suitable risky interest rate for use in evaluating a comparable government project. That is, the "social judgment" presumably says that the risk–class of projects that individuals would be inclined to undertake at a 6.5 per cent expected yield ought not to be undertaken unless they yield 10.5 per cent—and this would hold true for Government projects as well. On the other hand, if the bias against risky private investments is to be taken as a mistaken or merely accidental results of policies adopted for other ends, presumably some figure between the 6.5 per cent and the 10.5 per cent is to be used in discounting Government investments (as a "second best" to the more desirable policy of modifying the tax law). The precise balance would have to depend upon the degree to which the public project under consideration absorbed funds that

---

*Further discussion of this issue is found in the preceding article by Baumol.

would be invested otherwise in higher-yielding private projects. For, here the "market segmentation" hypothesis is indeed validated. The Government tax places a wedge between the real productive rate of return on investment and the after-tax rate in terms of which investors make their time-preference decisions.

The main contentions of the last two sections can be briefly summarized. The model of time-state preference leads to the present certainty-equivalent value (PCEV) criterion as the generalization of the present-value (PV) criterion applicable in a world of certainty. Within the framework of this model, the "pooling argument" is incorrect. That is, discounting the mathematical expectation of future return by the riskless rate of interest r_1 may result in the adoption of projects of negative PCEV (or failure to adopt projects of positive PCEV). For discounting mathematical expectation of return, the model shows how a "risky rate" r_1^* appropriated for the risk class of the proposed investment should be calculated. In practice we do not actually have enough data to *calculate* this r_1^*. However, it can usefully be approximated by *observing* the r_1^* implicit in the evaluation of private projects in the same or closely comparable risk class. Any validity that the pooling argument has must rest upon market segmentation that prevents trading of time-state claims. Such market imperfections do indeed exist. But it seems unlikely that government has the ability to distribute time-state claims more in accordance with consumer desires than even these admittedly imperfect capital markets. Indeed, one form of government intervention— the corporate income tax— is an enormous deterrent to the risky private investment whose alleged insufficiency is what the "pooling argument" seeks to correct.

NOTES

a.   The generalization to multiple future-time periods leads to an equation of the form:

$$V_0 = -i_0 + \frac{q_1}{1 + r_1} + \frac{q_2}{(1 + r_2)(1 + r_1)} + \ldots + \frac{q_r}{(1 + r_r)\ldots(1 + r_2)(1 + r_1)}$$

Here $r_1, r_2, \ldots, r_r$ are successive one-year interest rates up to the economic horizon T.

1.   The two formulations are strictly equivalent only when projects are independent. In the sense that adoption of any one does not affect the investment required or the returns yielded by any others. There are many possible patterns of interdependence: projects may be mutually exclusive, or one may be prerequisite to another, etc. For interdependent projects, the version (a) of the present-value principle remains valid and thus is the more fundamental conception.

2.   Here again the statement is true in simplest form only if an independence condition holds, in this case independence between the productive costs and returns on government and private projects. Should this condition fail, it might pay the government to adopt projects of negative present value in themselves, but having favorable "spillover effects" on projects of private firms (or, conceivably, of other levels of government). In principle, such spillover effects are already allowed for in the established procedures of government cost-benefit calculations.

3.   Among economists, the most prominent deviating school of thought accepts efficiency as a goal but rejects the valuation of temporal consumption that runs in terms of the supposedly biased preferences of the *present* generation—the only one in a position to cast "dollar votes." For varying points of view on this issue of "social time-preferences," see: Pigou [25], Marglin [20], Feldstein [10], Hirshleifer [15]. For the purposes of this paper, we need only assume that government takes appropriate measures (by a system of taxes on present consumption and subsidies on investment for future consumption) to correct the market expression of these biased preferences. If this were done, the remainder of the analysis now running in terms of the "corrected" time-preferences would remain valid.

4.   In some cases the goods produced may be perfectly marketable, but the underlying desire is to achieve a wealth redistribution by not maximizing the attainable commercial provision of the service.

5.   See, for example, the recent review of cost-benefit analysis by Prest and Turvey [26].

6.   Essentially the same point arises in the "social time-preference" argument, which maintains that there is inadequate provision for the future since only the current private generation casts "dollar votes" on the disposition of current resources. Attempts to overcome this supposed distortion by an expansion of government investment alone lead once more to the same sort of difficulty (Hirshleifer [15]). In general, it is necessary to compromise between the objectives sought.

7.   Although the nominal rate on long-term Government bonds has ranged from five to 5¾ per cent in recent years, the rate of inflation in the economy has grown from one to about 3½ per cent. This implies that the rate of return on these bonds has fallen from four per cent to as low as two per cent at the present time. However, the erosion of *realized* real returns by inflation appears to be systematically underestimated by investors. It seems reasonable to infer, therefore, that the *anticipated* real rate of return that enters into investors' calculations has remained in the neighborhood of four per cent.

8.   Attention here will be restricted to agencies of the Federal Government.

9.   In Section I above, we discarded this distinction as sterile.

10.   The current rates on money loans do reflect, however, the market's state of inflationary expectation. Since price-level increases of around 1 to 3 per cent per year have been experienced in recent years it is reasonable to infer that the market's estimate of the *real* riskless rate of interest must be somewhat lower than the Treasury's borrowing rate. It follows that if future benefits are calculated at today's prices without allowance for inflation, the current Treasury borrowing rate really is too high to be a riskless rate. However, this result seems to be inadvertent, and not a concession in the direction of use of a risky discount rate.

11.   As in the simple PV rule, the two forms here are equivalent given project independence.

12.   If $\dfrac{\pi_1 a}{P_{1a}} = \dfrac{\pi_1 b}{P_{1b}}$, then their common ratio equals $\dfrac{\pi_1 a + \pi_1 b}{P_{1a} + P_{1b}} = \dfrac{1}{P_1}$. Then $V_0' = \Delta_{i_0}$ + $\dfrac{\Delta q_{1a}\,(P_{1}a/P_1) + \Delta q_{1b}(P_1 b/P_1)}{1 + r_1}$. This reduces immediately to the PCEV, ΔV_0, upon making the substitution $P = 1/(1 + r_1)$.

13.   This is sometimes described as the condition of "diminishing marginal utility of income."

14.   This condition leads to the r_1^* yielding the correct PCEV in

$$\Delta V_0 = \Delta_{i_0} + \frac{\pi_{1a}\Delta q_{1a} + \pi_{1b}\Delta q_{1b}}{1 + r_1^*}.$$

This equation is the discounting version of equation (4).

15.   This discussion omits the problem of dealing with the corporate income tax, a complication that may be of great practical importance. Its role will be reconsidered in Section VI below.

16.   This point was made in private correspondence by Peter A. Diamond.

17.   The real yield would be the average of 16 per cent gross of tax (8 per cent net) yield to pay on equity, and 5 per cent yield to pay on bonds.

18.   On the other hand, it should be mentioned that the personal income tax has a partially counterbalancing opposite effect. The returns on risky securities can often be taken in the forms of capital gains that benefit from a reduced tax rate.

REFERENCES

1.   K. J. Arrow, "Discounting and Public Investment Criteria," in A. V. Kneese and S. C. Smith, eds., *Water Resources Research,* Baltimore: Johns Hopkins Press, 1966.

2.   J. S. Bain, R. E. Caves, and J. Margolis, *Northern California's Water Industry,* Baltimore: Johns Hopkins Press, 1966.

3.   W. J. Baumol, "On the Social Rate of Discount," *American Economic Review, 58,* September, 1968.

4.   H. P. Caulfield, Jr., Statement of Henry P. Caulifield, Jr., Executive Director, Water Resources Council, before Subcommittee on Economy in Government, Joint Economic Committee, *Economic Analysis of Public Investment Decisions: Interest Rate Policy and Discounting Analysis,* 90th Congress, 2nd Session.

5.   P. A. Diamond, "The Role of a Stock Market in a General Equilibrium Model with Technological Uncertainty," *American Economic Review, 57,* September, 1967.

6.   R. Dorfman, "Basic Economic and Technologic Concepts: A General Statement," in A. Maass, M. Hufschmidt, R. Dorfman, H. A. Thomas, Jr., S. A. Marglin, and G. M. Fair, *Design of Water Resource Systems,* Harvard University Press, 1972.

7.   O. Eckstein, "Reply by Mr. Eckstein" (to Comments of J. Hirshleifer), in National Bureau of Economic Research, *Public Finances: Needs, Sources, and Utilization,* Princeton University Press, 1961.

8.   O. Eckstein, Statement of Otto Eckstein before Subcommittee on Economy in Government, Joint Economic Committee, *Economic Analysis of Public Investment Decisions: Interest Rate Policy and Discounting Analysis,* 90th Congress, 2nd Session.

9.   O. Eckstein, *Water Resource Development,* Harvard University Press, 1958.

10.   M. S. Feldstein, "The Social Time Preference Discount Rate in Cost Benefit Analysis," *Economic Journal, 74,* June, 1964.

11.   M. Friedman and L. J. Savage, "The Utility Analysis of Choices Involving Risk," *Journal of Political Economy, 56,* August, 1948.

12.   A. Harberger, Remarks before Subcommittee on Economy in Government, Joint Economic Committee, *Economic Analysis of Public Investment Decisions: Interest Rate Policy and Discounting Analysis,* 90th Congress, 2nd Session.

13.   R. H. Haveman, *Water Resource Investment and the Public Interest,* Vanderbilt University Press, 1965.

14.   J. Hirschleifer, "Investment Decision Under Uncertainty: Applications of the State-Preference Approach," *Quarterly Journal of Economics, 80,* May, 1966.

15.   J. Hirshleifer, "Preference Social a l'Egard du Temps," *Recherches Economiques De Louvain, 34,* 1968.

16.   J. Hirshleifer, J. C. DeHaven, and J. W. Milliman, *Water Supply: Economics, Technology, and Policy,* University of Chicago Press, 1960.

17.   F. S. Hoffman, Statement before Subcommittee on Economy in Government, Joint Economic Committee, *Economic Analysis of Public Investment Decisions: Interest Rate Policy and Discounting Analysis,* 90th Congress, 2nd Session.

18.   F. H. Knight, *Risk, Uncertainty, and Profit,* Harper & Row, 1965.

19.   J. V. Krutilla and O. Eckstein, *Multipurpose River Development,* Baltimore: Johns Hopkins Press, 1958.

20.   S. A. Marglin, "The Social Rate of Discount and the Optimal Rate of Investment," *Quarterly Journal of Economics, 78,* May, 1964.

21.   H. Markowitz, "The Utility of Wealth," *Journal of Political Economy, 60,* April, 1952.

22.   A. Marshall, *Principles of Economics,* 8th ed., London: Macmillan, 1964.

23.   R. N. McKean, *Efficiency in Government Through Systems Analysis,* New York: Wiley, 1958.

24.   F. Modigliani and M. H. Miller, "The Cost of Capital, Corporation Finance, and the Theory of Investment," *American Economic Review, 48,* June, 1958.

25.   A. C. Pigou, *The Economics of Welfare,* 4th ed., New York: Macmillan, 1960.

26.   A. R. Prest and R. Turvey, "Cost-Benefit Analysis: A Survey," *Economic Journal, 75,* December, 1965.

27.   P. A. Samuelson, "Principles of Efficiency—Discussion," *American Economic Review, 54,* Papers and Proceedings, May, 1964.

28.   L. J. Savage, *The Foundations of Statistics,* New York: Wiley, 1965.

29.   W. F. Sharpe, "Capital Asset Prices: A Theory of Market Equilibrium Under Conditions of Risk," *Journal of Finance, 19,* September, 1964.

30.   A. Smith, *The Wealth of Nations* (Modern Library reprint of Cannau edition).

31.   E. B. Staats, Statement of Honorable Elmer B. Staats, Comptroller General of the United States, Joint Economic Committee, Subcommittee on Economy in Government, *Interest Rate Guidelines for Federal Decisionmaking,* 90th Congress, 2nd Session (1968).

32.   W. Vickrey, "Principles of Efficiency—Discussion," *American Economic Review, 54,* Papers and Proceedings, May, 1964.

33.   U. S. Congress, Joint Economic Committee, Subcommittee on Economy in Government, *Interest Rate Guidelines for Federal Decisionmaking,* 90th Congress, 2nd Session (1968).

34.   J. A. Stockfisch, Prepared Statement of Jacob A. Stockfisch before Subcommittee on Economy in Government, Joint Economic Committee, *The Planning-Programing-Budgeting System: Progress and Potentials,* 90th Congress, 1st Session.

35.   U. S. Congress, Subcommittee on Benefits and Costs of the Federal Inter-Agency River Basin Committee, *Proposed Practices for Economic Analysis of River Basin Projects:* Report to the Federal Inter-Agency River Basin Committee, Washington, D.C.: Government Printing Office, May, 1950.

36.   U. S. Senate Document No. 97, *Policies, Standards Evaluation and Review of Plans for Use and Development of Water and Related Land Resources,* 87th Congress, 2nd Session.

Shadow Prices for Incorrect or Nonexistent Market Values

Julius Margolis

Market prices exist for the vast majority of transactions accounted for by the normal profit seeking enterprise. Accountants, of course, have traditionally shown an extreme aversion at transaction dates, even when other more current objective market prices exist. They have shown an even greater reluctance to adopt other "valuation" schemes.

A major difficulty in evaluating the benefits and costs of a public undertaking is the absence of market values for most outputs and many inputs. Indeed, one of the reasons why the government undertakes certain activities is because there is no market to enable private sector production and distribution to take place. One of the most pervasive aspects of social accounting is the necessity to develop values for outputs and inputs which coincide with those a market would have generated. It requires little imagination to suggest that this process may be one of the major problem areas in social accounting, not only due to the technical difficulties suggested here by Margolis, but in addition, because of the long accounting tradition of avoiding such analysis. Of course, accountants perform "valuations," under engagements other than conventional financial reporting and auditing.

Presumably social accountants will be required to develop some logical methodology for the determination of shodow prices, as Margolis suggests. It is interesting to note that Margolis' approach, like that of Baumol, is also consistent with the social contract conception of the relationship between the people and the government.

INTRODUCTION

The State of Israel retaliated for the machine gunning of one plane and the death of a passenger by sending troops across a border and destroying thirteen planes. The United Nations judged that the exchange was not appropriate and condemned—was there an implied judgment that the "price was fair?" Many persons would object in principle to retaliation, a forced exchange of losses, and though most of us would be prepared to state whether a specific retaliatory exchange was reasonable or not we would be very hard-pressed to offer a "scientific" defense of our opinion. The oratory at the Security Council may seem far removed from the more prosaic questions of public expenditures

---

Julius Margolis is Director of the Fels Center of Government at the University of Pennsylvania.

SOURCE: From *The Analysis and Evaluation of Public Expenditures: The PPB System*. A Compendium of Papers submitted to the Subcommittee on Economy in Government of the Joint Economic Committee, Congress of the United States (1969) Vol. 1, pp. 533-546.

analysis, but agreement about shadow prices is the essence of both problems, that is, the evaluation of exchanges which are not carried out under optimal market conditions. The problem of estimation of shadow prices exists wherever the market is imperfect or nonexistent and of course government services and regulation are instances *par excellence.*

In economic analysis the problem of evaluation of goods or activities is solved for the bulk of cases by market exchanges, where money enters on one side of the exchange. Whenever money is used, we can form a ratio of the amount of the good to the amount of money; the ratio is the price and this can be quoted for all goods and activities. However there are many cases where exchanges occur without money passing hands; where exchanges occur but where they are not freely entered into; where exchanges are so constrained by institutional rules that it would be dubious to infer that the terms were satisfactory; and where imperfections in the conditions of the exchange would lead us to conclude that the price ratios do not reflect appropriate social judgments about values. Each of these cases gives rise to deficiencies in the use of existing price data as the basis of evaluation of inputs or outputs. The enumeration and refined analysis of market imperfections has reached a high level; unfortunately the analysis of how to replace market numbers is still primitive.

Previous papers have gone into detail concerning the imperfections of the competitive market which both justify public intervention, and at the same time, make prices inappropriate as measures of social value. I shall focus on the analysis of how governments grope towards assigning price-like values, or shadow prices to their inputs and outputs. But before dealing directly with this issue there are several general background points about the market which should be discussed. The basic question asked by the analyst when he searches for shadow price is: what would the users of the public output be willing to pay. The The analyst tries to simulate a perfect and competitive market for the public output, estimate the price which would have resulted, and accept this as the shadow price. Unfortunately, even if the analyst succeeds in finding this price it is not clear that the Government would accept it as sufficient to establish a value. Markets and quasi-markets are one form of social interaction; it is not obvious that other forms of social interaction should be interpreted so as to be consistent with the logic of market exchanges.

I. MARKET LIMITATIONS

A simulated market is a useful approach so long as the market is the process by which all, or at least the overwhelming number of goods are exchanged. Economics has been subject to attack for its attempts to subject all social activity to the measuring rod of money; though there is much merit to this criticism, fortunately, the economist has persisted in extending his calculus. An aggregate index of the state of social welfare is still beyond our ingenuity but the national income figures which were created to estimate the level of welfare have proven invaluable for a wide variety of purposes and efforts to extend the concepts to social accounts are likely to bear fruit. But more important for our analysis is the huge area of valued social activity contained in the market sector of the economy and which is *not* directly priced. The costs of goods produced do not necessarily measure the value of resources which could have produced other benefits and the prices paid for goods need not be an appropriate measure of final products received.

Consider the case of production of a marketable commodity. Productivity indices are highly variable among nations; within nations, the range of variation among industries or plants is very great. Certainly, some of this variation can be attributed to variable amounts of consumption which occur in the sphere of production. In some cases, Government controls are exercised to encourage this consumption, but in other instances more mysterious processes are at work. It would not be surprising if the Government rejected the market price as not properly reflecting these other consumption aspects.

One of the most dramatic expansions of consumption in our society has been the reduction in the workday, workyear, and worklife. If leisure could be considered a commodity, it is likely that its volume has increased more than any other commodity. "As a rough measure of past growth in free time, the employed worker has about 1,200 hours per year more nonworking time than his 1890 counterpart. In addition to a shortened workyear, nonworking years have grown by about nine for a male at birth, with present life and worklife expectations."[1] Over the last half-century, about one-third of the gains from productivity have been taken by increased leisure—a non-marketed consumption good. The point of interest to us is that our society has chosen to take a very large percentage of its potential income in the form of reduced work and thereby reduced money income but increased leisure. It should be pointed out that this reduction has taken place by market choices and through Government actions. Numerous legislative actions have limited work at every stage in the production process. It would not be surprising to find comparable losses in productivity elsewhere, which might also be judged as consumption.

I would hazard that a very large part of "inefficiency" in production is attributable to consumption. We know too little about inefficiency but certainly the range of difference in productivity among firms, industries and nations is huge, even in identical facilities. Productivity gains in applying well-known techniques are often in the range of fifty per cent and great efforts are often necessary to initiate them.[2]

Why is there a willingness to accept lower productivity? Is it too unreasonable to say that a large part of inefficiency are potential losses which are really acts of consumption, and the resistance to reduce inefficiency is the unwillingness to to surrender consumption.

A willingness to accept lower productivity can be viewed in another perspective—a reluctance to change. It should not be surprising that men resist change in work patterns, especially as they grow older. New methods involve learning, an investment. What had been previously the consumption of potential income now becomes an actual investment and with advanced age, the expected value of increased income falls, so that investment becomes less desirable. The adaptation to a new process involves not only setup costs in new equipment and losses of production but also sacrifices in search for information and learning new habits at the expense of old comfortable routines. The organizational changes are often the most difficult to make.

I do not want to belabor the social role of "inefficient" production processes. Not only could it be interpreted as extra-market consumption, but I believe it casts some understanding about the production of public goods. For instance risk aversion is often stated as a common characteristic of individual decision-makers and sometimes it is argued that it is sufficient to explain why governments must act in some circumstance. The adoption of this position may mean that the government does not accept the individual's evaluations as expressed in market prices as binding; the rejection of this price has led to a lengthy and inconclusive debate. The sorting out of utility payoffs in production and investment has proven to be extremely difficult.

A second source of "inefficiency" which has plagued the analyst of the public sector is the immobility of resources. Inputs do move in response to income differentials, but it is clear that there are strong resistances to move, and these resistances grow with age of residents. Individuals have poor information about alternatives and the full range of social activities in the site of a new residence. A move means a necessity of building up their private social capital in a new place instead of consuming the private social capital already accumulated for the old place. Under these conditions, individual resistance to movement is not surprising.

It is equally not surprising that governments in their provision of public services accept this immobility. Many governments assume regional objectives as significant in shaping the public services. Governments are often not persuaded to abandon a depressed district by demonstrations that the costs of moving a population from a declining region may be less than the extra costs of providing services for depressed and less dense regions. On the contrary, the government may supplement the public services with efforts to encourage the expansion of economic activity to support the inefficiently located public services. The government may be responding to extra-market income and consumption.

There is nothing novel about the preceding remarks; the existence of nonpecuniary advantages and disadvantages is well-known. Unfortunately knowledge of their existence has not led to an appraisal of its importance. I hazard that it may be very important especially in the sectors where the government operates.

In the preceding illustrations we have stressed private evaluations of market activity which are not readily captured in the market. For these reasons, governments may not respect the market process and values. It is also true that there may be social valuations of the market process which vary drastically from the economists interpretation of prices. These social evaluations may lead to a rejection of market guides. For instance the economist's interpretation of market activity leads him to distinguish carefully between efficiency and distribution effects. If an entrepreneur discovers a better way to produce a commodity, it may lead to a price reduction. His profits may increase; the profits of his rivals may fall; the consumers will gain. Where we evaluate the desirability of the innovation we just look at the gain of the innovator; the losses of other firms and the gains to the consumer are considered to be offsetting and merely transfers. A well-organized competitive economy is constantly generating these transfers. Governments do not share the indifference of the economist toward these distributional effects.

Compensation is granted in many cases where the losses or damages would be considered transfers. If these were paid by the government as part of a project the benefit-cost calculus would include them in the costs. And yet it may be true that the project might never be authorized unless compensation were paid. It could be said that these payments are necessary to have the project be adopted though they do not reflect the value of any resources used for the project. Those who receive losses may have more political influence than the gainers and thereby be able to affect the political decision, or there may be a social judgment that the losses were incurred because of the government's decision, and it would be improper to allow any sector to have undue losses.

Government policies or programs are often massive in nature. Their effects are dispersed throughout the economy but they have major impacts in very restricted areas. A new bridge may create extreme losses along old traffic arteries; a zoning shift may create millionaires and shatter dreams. "Inequities," are charged; lengthy delays result; designs are altered; the distributional effects are relevant for policy but they will also affect the resource cost of getting the public service supplied. Further the certainty or uncertainty of compensation as a consequence of a public act will affect how the private sector behaves.

The thrust of these remarks is to cast some doubt on the standard interpretation of the price data available in the market. There are many situations, often characterized as transfers, where government has accepted transfers as costs and thereby has been criticized by economists, but where it may be that the government has been responding to distributional effects. Possibly, a more explicit accounting of these distributional effects might lead to a more effectively designed public program. Shifts in prices always have distributional consequences and we may err in too readily refusing to consider these "non-efficiency" aspects.

Finally, the market and the data it generates is limited in that it relies on a model of individuals as consumers, whereas in reality the purchasing decision-makers or the job choosing decisionmakers are one or both parents. Children ride in the car bought by the parent. If the parent chooses to balance his journey to work against garden space, the child does not face the same tradeoffs, he can only enjoy or suffer the consequence of the parental decision. In principle the parent considers the family welfare in making his decision. However, we need only look at the divorce rates to make it apparent that harmony in the family is far from universal. Many public services are directed toward the special problems of those who are disenfranchised in the private market. However, market prices reflect the values of the private decisionmakers in the families, not the social units for whom they act. Would mass transportation or neighborhood play grounds be more numerous if children could spend their "equitable" share?

My assignment is not the limitations of the market and therefore I will not extend these remarks. I believe it necessary to introduce the points about these limitations because my subsequent comments about shadow prices accept much of the economists views about the value content of market processes and prices. From here on, I will in large measure presume that if the market were not beset by technical imperfections as externalities, indivisibilities and information costs, relative prices would equal relative costs and therefore relative prices would reasonably reflect relative social values.

II. SHADOW PRICES: WHOSE SHADOW?

Shadow prices are computed to reflect social values; the estimation procedures assume that social welfare is derived by aggregating individual valuations. In practise, economists have accepted the task of generating support for this view of social welfare. Consistent with this position has been the rejection of the legitimacy of an active role of the political process or administrative structure as formulators of the public interest. The result which could be anticipated, is a tension between the economic analyst, with his view of the public interest, and the political and administrative decisionmakers who do not share the economists' view of the public interest. Those who accept the authority of administrative officials or political leaders have quite different views of appropriate objective functions and what numbers should be used to evaluate outputs and inputs.

The conflict between the two approaches can be crudely phrased by asking: Who is the client, who is the employer of the economist? The typical answer of the economist is that he is true to the principles of serving the public interest as defined by the profession in their scientific journals i.e. the aggregation of individual preferences. He selects his models and criteria so as to maximize the professional view of the public interest; the economist has selected a client who is neither an employer or decisionmaker. This is a noble perspective, unfortunately the purchasers of the economist's information and advice (the administrative officials or political leaders) are neither persuaded by the economist's insight nor do their incentives impel them to accept the perspective of the national interest as formulated by the economist. For instance, a municipal official, concerned with urban renewal, may assign a benefit to a project if there are net gains to his city while offsetting losses in adjoining cities are of "purely academic" interest. Or, a national transportation agency may assign benefits based upon improved traffic flows, but the agency is not expected to consider the losses elsewhere, for instance, the increase in noise or air pollution. Payoffs to decisionmakers, administrative or political, are not based upon what happens to an index of national welfare, even if it could be constructed, and therefore it is not surprising that evaluatory measures developed in response to an agency's needs are partial and sometimes inconsistent with social welfare.

It may be presumptuous for the economist to insist on the primacy of his imputed prices against the views of the legitimately constituted authorities who employ him. However disrespect for authority was not introduced by our rebellious students; professional bodies have long lobbied to influence policy on the basis of their special competency. In the next section we shall assume the economist's vision of the public interest, despite our reservation that there is an alternative scheme by which to evaluate public outputs and inputs. There are social processes by which public decisions are guided. We have alluded to some, e.g. political bargaining, bureaucratic myopia, professional self-interest; it is likely that outcomes of each process considered independently would be far from socially optimal, but this does not mean that the total set of processes are not optimal. For instance, when we analyze the market system we recognize that a unit may not be at its best position though the economy may be operating optimally. We realize that a firm tries to maximize its profits and that its behavior is socially optimal if the economic system is so organized that it behaves competitively. Is it possible that a similar structure exists among different decisionmaking systems? Are there conditions of social equilibrium which are related to economic or political equilibrium just as general economic equilibrium is related to the equilibrium of the firm? I am far from convinced that a concept of social equilibrium analogous to economic equilibrium is useful but certainly economic criteria are partial and it would be wise to keep an open mind about more general formulations. Meanwhile we see efforts to extend economic equilibrium concepts to political behavior, but as I said, hereafter I will accept the economist's limited view.

III. SHADOW PRICES AND INPUT COSTS

The correction of market prices, or the imputation of prices, is done for both inputs and outputs. Most of the controversies deal with outputs though the same conceptual difficulties apply to both cases. In principle inputs are valued in terms of what they could have produced elsewhere and, therefore, we are immediately driven to the valuation of outputs. In practice, it is usually assumed that the market price of the inputs reflects their alternative values and therefore they could be used to measure the value of the inputs. Unfortunately there are a few dramatic cases where this is incorrect and others where the correctness is disputed.

The most commonly advocated adjustment of an input price is for unemployed labor. Clearly, if labor had no alternative use then it would be incorrect to assign a price to it. This adjustment would make a project less costly and it would affect the design of the project. Of course, it would not be appropriate to assume the labor flow of a project over time would have been unemployed, but the problem of timing often holds for even the fairly shortrun. The time lag between analysis and the initiation of a program may extend for years and therefore current unemployment may not be an appropriate assumption. If one could not assume unemployment for the period of actual use of the resource then the full thrust of this adjustment, the substitution of unemployed labor for other inputs, would be lost.

A second input which may often be incorrectly priced, and too often does not bear an adjustment, is land. A program on public land is usually assessed the cost of the land to the agency rather than the opportunity costs of the land. Therefore a project on public land is "less costly" and would receive preference. The value of public land is often misstated because of the nature of the constraints imposed on government, that is, private alterative uses are rarely considered. Private land is also incorrectly valued, though for a different reason— a consequence of using a shadow price adjustment to value benefits overtime for the benefits from the publicly held land but not applying a similar adjustment to the benefits derivable from the same land, if privately held.

If the Government does not accept the market interest rate as a basis of valuing its benefits and costs over time, it adopts a "social rate of discount," typically well below the market rate.* In applying this rate the Government is in all likelihood grossly underestimating its land costs. For instance, the Government might purchase an agricultural area and convert it to recreational use if the recreational benefits exceeded the costs of the land which presumably should equal the agricultural benefits. However, the value of the land would be the sum of the returns to agricultural use capitalized at the market rate of

---

*Further discussion of this issue is found in the preceding article by Baumol.

interest, possibly twice the assumed social rate. Therefore it is possible that a project may show a favorable benefit-cost ratio solely due to applying a shadow price—the social rate of discount—in the public sector and not extending the adjustment to the private sector.

The preceding error: the setting of shadow prices for a public discount rate but not adjustment for the private market rate is a general problem. This criticism can be extended to all of the capital inputs used by the public sector. Since their foregone use is market values lost, valued at the market interest rate, they will be underestimated relative to public benefits solely because the use of too low an interest rate.

IV. SHADOW PRICES AND CONSTRAINTS

We mentioned in the preceding section that public land is often incorrectly priced since private alternative use is not considered. This difficulty can be generalized to many parts of the Government. Institutional rules are established and then prices are estimated within the confines of the rules. For instance, the value of a water supply to an area may be based upon the cost of supply to that area, but there may be a very low cost supply which is ruled out because of a Government policy of dedicating the water to another use. Therefore the assigned value of the water may be grossly overstated from the perspective of the Nation. Or, an agency may value its inputs in program A in terms of loss of benefits in program B for which the inputs are substitutes. However there may be a much more productive use in another agency, but the possibilities of transfer of funds may be very meager. For this reason, the evaluation of the worth of inputs may be understated.

A classic example of a set of constraints which may run counter to estimated shadow prices arises from budget allocations in conjunction with some discretionary authority residing with agencies. Funds for an agency are raised through taxes or bonds; they are not a concern of the decisionmakers of an agency. The agency has no knowledge of the social costs of these funds, but they are very sensitive to the fact that their actions are very limited by the funds assigned to them. They are told that if there exists unemployment or arbitrarily fixed exchange rates, payments made for labor or imported goods inputs will not reflect their approximate social costs. The central authority might calculate a shadow price and instruct the agencies to use, say, a very low price reflecting that it is in surplus. If the agency were to use this price in its calculations it would use relatively more labor than otherwise, in sensible agreement with the social evaluation of its labor inputs. But if the agency is subject to a budget limitation, which is usually the case, it would find that it would have spent relatively more on the process using labor, that is, from its perspective a dollar spent on labor is worth a dollar spent on machines and though it may cost society less for them to use labor they make the same budgetary sacrifice whether labor had been over or underpriced. They will be highly resistant to adopting these shadow prices as operational tools in their choices of design of programs.

V. ESTIMATION PROCEDURES

The estimation procedures used to assign values to public outputs can be described as efforts to simulate market outcomes. It is assumed that for a variety of technical reasons—externalities, public goods, and so on—the private market must be supplemented by public production and distribution. The essential character of the objective function according to this view requires the assignment of prices which would have resulted from market behavior, if there had been some way to overcome the technical limitations which gave rise to public supply and a perfectly competitive market were able to operate. This individualistic view is usually supplemented by a judgment in regard to the distribution of income, a far from trivial departure from consumers sovereignty. The measurement rule used to determine the value of a government output is: estimate what the users of the public product would be willing to pay. Since the products are distributed at zero or low, conventional prices there are no direct measures by which the price can be discovered and therefore several indirect procedures are used to reveal the price.

1. The most common technique used to evaluate public output is to consider the product as an intermediate good and then to estimate the value of the marginal product of the good in further production, that is, assume the user is a producer and then ask: by how much does the public output increase his income? Illustrations are found in natural and human resources development. Some goods are easily and naturally treated in this fashion. For example, water supply is used for home consumption, but the great bulk of it is consumed in agriculture, power generation and industrial processing. Let us consider agricultural water. Productivity studies of irrigated farms are used to estimate the value of the product of an incremental acre-foot of water; this is the agricultural value of the water. It is assumed that the farmer would pay this amount as a price for the water and therefore the marginal product is identified as the "imputed market price," or "shadow price" of water. The computation of this figure is not a simple task, but beyond these problems there are frequent errors in the application of this approach, even when the product is easily treated as an intermediate good.

In practice we find that the farmer is rarely asked to pay as a price to the Government the increment in income attributable to the water—an amount which is interpreted as the price he would be willing to pay. It is usually asserted that the unwillingness to charge this indicates a subsidy to agriculture.

While this may be true, it also may be true that the computed shadow price may be far greater than a simulated market price for several reasons.

a. There may be alternative sources of supply and the cost of this supply would put a ceiling on the price that the farmer would pay for the water, for example, ground water pumping costs may be greater than the charged price but below the imputed value. The failure to consider this alternative is a shortcoming of this analysis.

b. The budget studies usually computed an expected value over several years. If the farmer is a risk averter he will assign a lower value to this anticipated income. It might be correct for the government to plan its operations on the basis of average expected values, but then it would have to absorb the risk and sell the water below the price. This problem of individual risk and government preference for expected values has not been studied in reference to the design and management of programs.

c. The computation of incremental productivity usually refers to averages rather than marginals. If the water is supplied at a low or zero price then we know that the user will purchase it to the point where the value of the marginal product would equal price. Since the average value will be greater than the marginal, multiplying the total amount which will be purchased by the average value will greatly overstate the total revenue from selling the product at a market price.

The divergency between average and marginal suggests another ambiguity in the concept of the price the users would be willing to pay. A simulated market price equates demand and supply, it balances off marginal gains and costs. But the price users may be willing to pay for the quantity rather than do without it may be much greater. In principle, the users would be willing to pay a sum equal to the area under the demand curve in order to receive the quantity rather than do without the project. If there are reasonably good alternatives to the public output the demand curve will be highly elastic and the difference between the area under the demand curve and the product of the market-clearing price and quantity would be small. As we shall see the limiting factor of alternative supply is considered in the estimation of benefits in some cases, but not others.

The above difficulties of estimating the productivity values of public services are small compared to those which arise when we consider services like education and health which have been valued as intermediate goods. For educational output, statistical studies have found a correlation between years of schooling and income. Therefore, it is argued that the earning capacity of an individual has been increased by the additional years of schooling. Further, it is said that the individual should be willing to pay that increment of expected income, less his foregone earnings while he is in school, for the educational services provided him. In practice, of course, an individual would not be expected to make such a payment, but this is attributed to the immature judgment of a student and his lack of capital. But does this relationship between education and income, even if it could be convincingly established, exhaust the reasons for public education or is it even the dominant factor? Clearly, the government is interested in many consequences beyond the income of the person. For instance, will he be a better and more responsible participant in the political process; Will he be a better neighbor? Will he have developed values and insights which will make him a more effective parent? Many more goals for education have been asserted, but all we want to establish here is that governments will find unsatisfactory a rule for the design of educational programs, or for the determination of its scale, which is based only upon the enhancement of an individual's expected income.

In the case of health services, a different set of problems develop. Health is much more of a consumer good than education. Health, as an intermediate product, is valued by the additional working time and increased productivity associated with a reduction in disability. A saved life is valued at the present value of the expected income stream it would have earned. (Some would say that it should be net of the consumption of the saved life and therefore it should be the value of his savings.(Certainly individuals are concerned about the loss of working time but pain, discomfort and the fear of incapacity and death may be even more of a basis of willingness to pay to avoid illness. If the health program were designed to maximize benefits measured by income growth, then the diseases of the aged would be ignored and diseases of women would receive relatively little support. Neither individuals nor governments are prepared to accept the enhanced income as the sole basis for determining the private or social benefits of health.

2. A second indirect technique commonly used to estimate what individuals are willing to pay is based upon the cost savings of the public service, that is, the reduction in the costs that individuals would have incurred if the public service were not supplied. This approach is most commonly adopted in the fields of transportation and power. Generally, it is assumed that there is an inelastic demand for the output and, therefore, the public somehow would have managed to transport the goods or to develop energy though the costs would have been much higher. The major sources of savings are private carrier costs in the case of transportation and private generation of energy in the case of power.

The cost-savings approach to benefit measurement faces two problems: the identification of the real alternatives which were saved and the constraints imposed upon policy if the user savings are the basis of evaluation. In the case of transportation, the costs savings are realized by shippers and travelers. An improved highway would reduce the travel time and operating costs of traveling between any two points. Presumably the users of the highways would be willing to pay that difference.

The savings for many public services should be the alternative facilities or programs which would have been provided by the government. Unfortunately, public agencies are notoriously poor in considering alternatives. For instance, an apprenticeship training program may be an alternative to vocational training in a school, but the educational agency is unlikely to consider an inservice program as an interesting or feasible alternative. Importing goods may be an alternative to agricultural expansion, but this is not likely to be considered. Organizations are not active searchers for information about alternatives they are not likely to pursue. It is also true that many of the most feasible alternatives may be those ruled out by legal or administrative constraints and never even considered. For instance, a change in the tax structure may provide a very different set of incentives for private consumption but it might never be considered by an operating agency. As a consequence, estimates of the real costs of alternatives which are saved are notoriously bad, except for the calculation of user savings in some cases.

The assumption of inelastic demand leads to greatly inflated multiplier of overstated benefits. The increased traffic generated by a public project would not have existed at the old cost structure and therefore it would be an error to assume a benefit equal to the unit cost savings of the old traffic multiplied by the augmented new traffic, including the increased flow. This problem becomes very acute when activity shifts among cities or ports in response to slight improvement of facilities. There may be large movements responding to very slight gains in private transportation costs, possibly far below the amount necessary to pay for the capital costs of the facilities.

The limitations of the use of costs of alternative programs as a measure of benefits is reflected in the analytical studies of the PPBS groups. These studies are appropriately labeled as cost-effective rather than cost-benefit analyses. The objectives of the program are usually specified in physical terms and the alternatives where trade-offs are considered as restricted to those under the control of the agency. The narrow view is typified by the label given the function of the military system analysts: the most bang for the money rather than the most national security or social welfare.

The evaluation of public output in terms of costs or savings by users is based upon an assumption that we are to be guided by the efficiency calculation of the individual beneficiaries of the project. Political and administrative leaders resist the policy conclusions drawn from these studies since they see them as restrictive of their freedom to plan the development of the nation. For instance, the benefit-cost calculations might indicate the most efficient transportation network but efficiency has never been a sufficient criterion for governments in their locational policies. It is possible that governments have erred in trying to support their declining regions, to populate their empty places, or to stem the flow of population to their capitals, but the public support of these programs has been great. Though economic arguments of external economies and diseconomies have been used to defend these programs, it is clear that regional objectives have been pursued for their own sakes, with a willingness on the part of the government to sacrifice national income for these benefits.

Cost savings on the part of individuals or agencies need not be the only frame of reference in trying to discover shadow prices. There is an alternative formulation which views the legislature or administration as representatives of the aggregate of citizens. It is argued that unrestrained political bargaining is not optimal but that the addition of appropriate information to the decisionmaking process would lead to optimal outcomes. The first step of the analyst is to design a quantitative measure of the product of the public output. This is not difficult in the case of most commercial, marketable commodities like food, clothing, or machines, but for services like recreation, education, or national defense, an appropriate unit of output is not obvious. The most common measures refer to use of the service rather than their desired qualities; e.g., years of schooling rather than increased productivity, socialization, and so on. The second step is to estimate the real costs of resources necessary to produce the outputs. The above information is equivalent to the marginal rate of transformation between two public services. The decisionmaker is then asked to revise the expenditure levels among the public services—the revision, if the authorities are responsive to the public, would be in the direction of equating the marginal rate of substitution in utilities to the marginal rate of transformation in production. A decisionmaker who seeks to be most effective will welcome this information-structure, but there is a great gap between the decisionmaker's objective function and the social welfare, defined by aggregating individual preferences. In practice, this pattern of information of real costs and benefits for decisionmaking is appropriate to the view of a public interest, defined as a social ordering expressed by the government. The net result of applying this criterion, besides optimal allocation, is the derivation of an appropriate set of shadow prices. These are the relative costs of the different public services when the government has decided that the budget has been optimally allocated. The ratio of marginal costs of two public outputs will be the same as the ratio of their social values and therefore the marginal costs figures will have the same interpretation we give to competitive market prices.

3. The third major technique of shadow price estimation is to estimate directly the users prices by appeal to market information. This is the most difficult task, but it may prove to be the most fruitful. In many cases there are near substitutes for collective consumption. There is usually a private educational, health, or recreational market; the extensive study of this market may provide the needed price information. The difficulty facing the analyst is that the comparable private commodities are sometimes very different. The

characteristics of service of a private medical clinic may be sufficiently similar to a public clinic that the private data may be usable, but the differences between a public park and a private camp are huge and difficult to compare.

Another form of use of market data is more indirect, it relies on the responses of the private sector in gaining access to the free public services. Public services are free, but access to them may be costly. Parks are free, and since they are desirable men will pay higher rents for sites located close to them. There would be similar shifts in the demand for land because of differential quality of schools, medical facilities, highway systems, and so forth. Households will reveal their preferences by their locational decisions, and further, the revelation will be quantitative. An analysis of the household's costs may provide information about the value they assign to these public services. This form of analysis will require complicated econometric studies, since changes in behavior will be due to many factors and some shifts will be due to the initial changes of the users of the public services rather than to the public services themselves.

VI. SHADOW PRICES AND INCENTIVES

We have alluded to the problem of incentives to public officials, but that brief allusion greatly understates their importance. Shadow prices are useful pieces of information, but unless the decisionmakers benefit by acting on the basis of those prices little is gained. It is utopian to assume that disinterested scientists will compute the shadow prices and devoted public servants will accept them as binding. When I discussed the use of a low shadow price for unemployed labor I pointed out that since the agency is subject to a budget constraint they are not likely to be receptive to a rule which tells them to treat labor as though it were a free good when it is obvious to them labor inputs place a drain on their limited budget. A similar set of improper incentive is reflected in the continuous battling between highway authorities and conservationists. Public parks provide "free or cheap land" from the perspective of the construction agency and since their budget is limited—the use of public land maximizes the amount of traffic served per dollar of their budget.

The problems of incentives and shadow prices may be of even greater magnitude when we deal with the many decentralized programs initiated by the Federal government in the urban areas. The Federal government may identify targets and even assign values to outputs but if incentives to local governments are not consistent with these values the federal objectives are not likely to be achieved. For instance, fiscal profitability is of minor concern to the national interest but the payoffs of a project along this dimension often dominate the local design and execution of a program.

The thrust of the above remarks is that the problem of shadow price determination is not simply one of calculation. If the shadow prices are to guide behavior then those who must make and implement the decisions require incentives to provide the "correct" information needed for calculation and to use the prices. Therefore the study of shadow pricing rules opens up the even more difficult study of the optimal structure of government.

NOTES

1.   Juanita M. Kreps, *Lifetime Allocation of Work and Leisure,* Research Report No. 22, Office of Research and Statistics, Social Security Administration, U.S. Department of HEW, 1968, p. 36.

2.   For a survey and interpretation of the many studies, see Harvey Leibenstein, "Allocative Efficiency vs. X-Efficiency," *American Economic Review,* June, 1966.

Evaluating the Effectiveness of Social Services

Robert Elkin
and
Darrel J. Vorwaller

Most of the articles in this volume involve the development of measures expressed in terms of dollars, or at least the attribution of dollar values to social phenomena. Elliot argued in an earlier article that social accounting could also provide a useful contribution through the development of information and control systems for social projects.

The authors here describe the development and operation of an accounting control system for measuring the effectiveness of social services which operates without the assignment of dollar values. It is particularly interesting to note that the methodology selected is a socially-oriented modification of conventional accounting control techniques. It does not involve the development of radically new or different methologies or theories, and hence would appear to be almost immediately applicable.

Current developments, including changes in Federal laws, regulations, and guidelines, have imposed on public welfare departments new requirements for managing and reporting social services. At the same time, too, that their departments are attempting to meet demands for more and better services, public welfare administrators are on yet another firing line as they are called to account more and more frequently by taxpayers, lawmakers, clients and their professional peers. What populations are being served? What amount of what service is being provided? What changes in clients are brought about by social services? What programs are most powerful in bringing about desired changes? What programs are failing to achieve intended changes and must be weeded out? Such questions imply that a sound method should exist for evaluating the effectiveness of social services.

Many welfare programs are currently evaluated according to standards set by national or supervisory agencies, but these standards may not be suitable for evaluation purposes. Thus, the assumption is often made that a program is successful if its professional staff has attained a stated level of expertise, or if the staff-to-client ratio is at a recommended ratio. What is happening, however, is that the emphasis is on input into a program, while output is overlooked.

Robert Elkin and Darrel J. Vorwaller are associated with the accounting firm of Peat, Marwick, Mitchell & Co.

SOURCE: *Management Controls* (May, 1972), Vol. XIX, No. 5, Copyright © 1972, Peat, Marwick, Mitchell & Co., pp. 104-111.

Further, a case-by-case review of a sample of agency records may represent an attempt at program evaluation. But such a review usually reveals only limited program data—whether a staff has worked within defined limits, or if eligible clients have received program services. While case reviews do eventually contribute some information on welfare programs, they cannot provide the timely data a welfare administrator needs for ongoing planning, budgeting, or crisis-resolving. Hence, many welfare agencies resort to operational statistics to evaluate programs. Here, sheer numbers are presumed to imply success. If a great number of clients are interviewed, home visits made, days of care provided, etc., it is assumed that the program is successful.

The approach to evaluation of social services described in this article is based on systems concepts. Essentially, this approach requires clear definitions of the goals and objectives against which to assess the outcome of programs. The

---

Exhibit 1 — Profile of a Service Program

Service category

Family planning

Program

Training and counseling to enable families to plan the births of children and to enable unmarried persons to avoid pregnancies out-of-wedlock.

Problem description

Lack of knowledge and skills in family planning impairs family life and impedes the growth and development of children. This problem is reflected in unplanned births of children.

Goal

Assurance that the addition of children to families is by parental choice; and prevention of births out-of-wedlock.

Objectives

(1)   To reduce the rate of unmarried females 14 to 44 years of age who become pregnant.

(2)   To reduce the rate of pregnancies occurring in families who have requested family planning services.

Measures

(1)   The ratio of unmarried females 14 to 44 years of age who become pregnant, to all unmarried females 14 to 44 years of age registered with the Project.

(2)   The ratio of pregnancies occurring in families who have requested family planning services, to all families registered with the Project who have requested family planning services.

following basic steps are involved in establishing a systems-based evaluation of social services:

Identification and description of the social problems that are within the scope of the organization's interest.

Development of goals for resolving these problems.

Statement of the objectives of each service in quantifiable terms.

Establishment of measures of effectiveness for all objectives.

Formulation of evaluation standards for each service.

Implementation of the system begins with the development of profiles for each of the services.

SERVICE PROFILES

A service profile is a convenient format for organizing and displaying the elements required in an effectiveness evaluation system. The profile, illustrated in Exhibit 1, includes the service category, program description, problem description, goal statement, objectives statement, and measures of effectiveness.

A service definition represents the boundaries of a specific area to be evaluated. In an on-going social service program, the development of an evaluation system starts with the service to be evaluated. The service should be clearly stated in the definition, the specification of problem goals and objectives can be controlled by relating them to the limits of the service boundaries. Thus, in Exhibit 1, the service is described as all activities provided to enable families to plan the timing of births of children and to enable unmarried persons to avoid pregnancies out-of-wedlock. Several programs of activities may be related to the service, such as individual training and counseling, group counseling, group courses in sex education, and medical examination and prescription. All of these programs relate to achieving the stated goal.

After the services or programs have been clearly and concisely described in profiles, they are grouped into related categories. Services may be classified as either operational or program goal-oriented. The organization of services on an operational basis is generally well established and documented in written directives. Basically, individual organizational units are normally assigned responsibility for the delivery of services in certain functional areas, such as protective services to children. A study of the organizational structure of a welfare department should provide knowledge of how services are delivered under the current operational structure. The operational classification of services does not always parallel the goal-oriented structure. To meet social needs as they develop, responsibility for providing service is frequently assigned solely on the basis of available resources. The most appropriate organizational unit is often not used for new assignments due to a lack of resources or of operational flexibility, so that services classified along operational lines are frequently not classified into a consistent goal structure.

In classifying services along goal-oriented lines, it is necessary to determine relationships in results being achieved. If progress toward the goal of one service is a component of goal accomplishment for another service, the two services should be related under a goal structure orientation. Some restructuring and classification changes of on-going services and programs may prove necessary as the development of an evaluation system progresses.

Let us now turn to the basic steps entering into the development of an evaluation system, starting with the first—identification and description of the social problem.

PROBLEM DESCRIPTION

A problem is a situation or condition that adversely affects identified client populations. Examples of problems in the social welfare field are: children living in hazardous and substandard housing; lack of knowledge and skill in money management.

The basis of future measurement will be a determination of the amount of change that has occurred in the problem. Hence, a problem definition should be precisely drawn. In an on-going service, the process of definition starts with an analysis of current programs, but in the case of new services, the process is inductive and more complex inasmuch as the service components have not yet been spelled out.

In some cases, the service title (for example, "Services to Unwed Parents") suggests the nature of a particular problem or target group. When the problem is not immediately suggested by the service title (for example, "Housing and Homemaking"), a careful analysis must be made to determine the scope of the problem toward which the service is directed.

A review of Federal and state regulations and guidelines will provide clues concerning the particular problem toward which a service is being directed. Guidelines often include statements of conditions which can be used as a basis for problem descriptions. A review of these guidelines increases the validity of the evaluation system and insures that appropriate problems are addressed by the services mandated under regulations.

Where the evaluations relate to new social problems not yet augmented by specific social services, an analysis of social indicators, specific client situations, and validated research data is necessary for developing problem statements. A careful analysis of social indicators and other data will yield the problem statement needed both for the development of appropriate services and the specification of the elements of the evaluation.

A close examination of welfare problem situations will reveal at least two identifiable types of factors—symptomatic and causal. Symptomatic factors are the unfavorable social conditions that are observable in the problem situation. As a general rule they are readily discernible because they rise to the surface. For example, in the welfare field there are ample cases to illustrate the existence of children living in hazardous and substandard housing, and families requesting

---

Exhibit 2 — Cause-Symptom Linkage in Problem Definition

Level A

Symptomatic:	Members of a welfare family unit experiencing a high incidence of illness and disease.
Causal:	Lack of adequate living space, heat, and sanitary facilities in family residence.

Linking effect

Level B

Symptomatic:	Lack of adequate living space, heat, and sanitary facilities in family residence.
Causal:	Income level of family insufficient to allow family to move to more suitable quarters.

Linking effect

Level C

Symptomatic:	Income level of family insufficient to allow family to move to more suitable quarters.
Causal:	Lack of education and training prevents head of family from obtaining and holding job capable of providing adequate family income.

emergency financial grants to pay rent. Both conditions are symptoms of problems facing clients. Causal factors are more difficult to identify in problem situations than are the symptomatic factors. Causal factors are those elements that generate observable unfavorable social conditions. In the case of children living in hazardous and substandard housing, inadequate family income might be a cause. In the case of requests for emergency financial assistance where adequate resources appear to exist, a causative factor might be the lack of knowledge or skill in money management.

One aspect of the causal-symptomatic relationship in social problem situations which is essential in developing problem descriptions is that of cause-symptom linkage. Cause-symptom linkage describes the relationship that exists between a symptom at one level of a problem situation and a causal factor at the next level. This linkage can be explained through a simplified illustration in Exhibit 2 of the relationship drawn from a particular social problem context.

This illustration does not attempt to define fully the multiple characteristics of the relationships involved in the problem situation. Comprehensive identification of the interrelationship between causes and symptoms requires extensive in-depth research. To determine the course of action to be taken, the linkage effect should be traced to a point where the agency is capable of addressing its resources to the problem in an effective manner. For example, it is possible that a decision could be made to treat the problem at level A of the situation. Treatment of the problem at this level could involve making arrangements to move the family to more adequate quarters. Indeed, such action could provide a short-range remedy for the immediate physical needs of the family indicated as the "symptom" at level A. However, the family would still lack the capacity and resources to be economically self-sufficient and to maintain the higher standard of housing. The move to better housing would not necessarily increase the family's opportunities for becoming economically self-sufficient, and might actually impair the family's chances for financial improvement by increasing the family's financial burden to an intolerable level. In this illustration, dealing with problem needs at "causal" level C would indicate the need for a program designed to train the head of the household in a skill that would lead to future employment, and an adequate income, and eventual economic self-support. By attacking the problem at the proper level, the probability of achieving long-term success through service intervention is greatly enhanced.

Following analysis, a detailed description of the problem can be written. (See Exhibit 3 for examples of key words and phrases used in problem descriptions.) A problem description should include both symptomatic and causal factors appropriate to the level of the services being provided.

GOAL STATEMENTS

Goal statements should relate directly to specific problem situations or barriers requiring remedial social services. A service goal is a frame of reference for management decision-making and for program planning and evaluation. For example, the goal in providing assistance to past, potential, and expectant parents out-of-wedlock could be the prevention of births out-of-wedlock and elimination of the social, emotional, and legal problems associated with them. Such a goal is admittedly idealistic since the problem of unwed parenthood is a continuing one. However, the goal is still valid when viewed as an ideal outcome and a desirable state or condition toward which to direct service activities.

Exhibit 3 — Key Words and Phrases Used in Problem Descriptions

A problem description consists of an antecedent (causal) event or state; a subsequent action; the recipient (target) of the action; and the consequent (symptomatic) conditions.

Example

Antecedent state:	living in substandard housing; practicing unhealthy housekeeping
Action:	endanger and impede
Recipients of action:	family and children
Consequent condition:	unrealized potential for growth and development

Words describing antecedent states

absence	inadequate
default	incompetency
deficiency	interruption
deterioration	lack
disturbed	loss
disfunctional	maladjustment
failure	omission
inability	unmet

Action words transmitting the cause to the object

abuse	impair
damage	impede
endanger	injure
exploit	neglect
hamper	obstruct
hinder	prevent

Exhibit 4 provides some examples of key words and phrases used in goal statements.

A service effectiveness goal reflects the desired end state, and not the quantity or quality of activities and services to be applied to achieve the end state. For example, the goal for a family which is financially dependent could be the achievement of economic self-sufficiency. The statement of the goal does not specify the activities that will be employed to develop the economic self-sufficiency.

The very existence of goals can help to redirect program emphasis from its tendency toward process orientation (what was applied), to a stress on progress (what was the effect). An orientation directed towards achievement provides the foundation on which a system of social services evaluation of effectiveness can be established. In addition, goals for services indicate a commitment of the organization to purposeful action to bring about meaningful and significant improvements in conditions or problem situations that are adversely affecting the lives of client populations. The development of goals thus becomes an important step toward the initiation of effective services by social welfare organizations.

Goal statements should reflect the realistic constraints upon the organization offering the service, including availability of resources, authorization to provide a service, and geographic limitations. For example, it is not realistic for a social service agency to set as its goal the prevention of all unwed pregnancies when it has a legal mandate and finances for serving only a specified portion of a community.

Broad participation of staff personnel in goal development assists in insuring the accuracy and completeness of goal content. In addition, broad participation aids in developing a more willing acceptance and a deeper commitment by those who will ultimately play a significant role in goal attainment. The participation process of goal setting many times brings to the surface different orientations of different levels of staff. Thus, administrators tend to emphasize legal and financial constraints of the organization. Caseworkers tend to emphasize

---

Exhibit 4 – Key Words Used in Goal Statements

Used to describe end states:

assured	maintained
attained	preserved
eliminated	rehabilitated
improved	restored
insured	retained

professional autonomy in decision-making in determining specific programs for their clients. Supervisors and program directors tend to emphasize unmet needs and additional staff required to meet these needs. Concern is expressed in the field for the appropriate way to involve clients in the goal setting and evaluation process; but while consensus has emerged on the inadequacy of token client membership on advisory committees, other more effective measures have not as yet been identified.

OBJECTIVES

Objectives are specific targets for achievement which represent interim steps or progress toward a goal within a specified time span. Objectives should be comprehensive in nature and cover all activities leading to the achievement of a particular goal. Objectives describe the desired impact on a problem situation which should be produced by the services provided.

While goals provide the basic guidance for all activities in a service, they are, by definition, general and timeless and do not provide the explicitness required for measuring results. Objectives provide the detail necessary to enable decisions to be made, actions to be taken, plans to be implemented, and results to be evaluated. Objectives of a service should be determined after problems and goals have been identified and described.

Objectives should be stated in terms that permit quantitative measurement of achievement, wherever possible. When problems have not been clearly analyzed and defined, objectives are frequently described in terms that do not lend themselves to such measurement.

Both quantifiable and nonquantifiable objectives should indicate the direct relationship between the objectives and the goals of the service being provided. Thus, the aggregate of objectives established for a service indicates the results expected from the application of the service to a specific social problem. The function of quantifiable and nonquantifiable objectives may be illustrated using the example of a social service program that has as its goal, "To increase the number of AFDC families who are economically self-sufficient." Since economic self-sufficiency depends on a steady and adequate family income, and job training normally aids in achieving an adequate income, a quantifiable objective which would serve as an indicator of measurable progress toward achieving the service goal could be, "To increase the rate of AFDC family members completing a work training program." The percentage of AFDC family members completing such programs can be determined quantitatively, and thus the objective is measurable in numeric terms.

A nonquantifiable objective for the same goal could be, "To develop in AFDC family members the sense of self-esteem necessary to be functioning members of the community." Though it is difficult with present measurement devices to know precisely when a desired level of self-esteem is acquired or the precise level of self-esteem attained, it is possible to determine whether or not there has been a change in the self-esteem level. An increase in the self-esteem level would indicate progress toward the goal. Such nonquantifiable objectives should be used sparingly and avoided, if at all possible, in developing an objectively based evaluation system.

The detailed development of objectives requires an analysis of the service description, a study of legislation, and an understanding of the problem. A review of existing service descriptions is the first step in attempting to determine objectives for an on-going service. Frequently, objectives are suggested in the service descriptions in the organization's social service handbook or manual. However, objectives shown in manuals are not always developed in a parallel or consistent manner; objectives, goals, and benefits are often used interchangeably. As a consequence, objectives as described in such manuals may require refinement before being acceptable in an evaluation system. Federal and State legislatures have enacted statutes stating objectives for certain social services, and all such mandated objectives should be considered in service profiles.

By definition, achievement of an objective advances the service toward its identified goal. Accordingly, care must be taken in the development of objectives to insure that objectives reflect and support achievement of all established goals. The objectives must be precisely defined, however, and not become a new description of the goal. The requirement for developing quantitative measures is an effective restraint which assists in preventing the use of qualitative words such as "better," "acceptable," "appropriate," etc. in objective statements. Objectives must be measurable in a given time period and qualitative words such as the preceding are normally difficult to measure. Illustrations of key words and phrases used in objectives statements are shown in Exhibit 5.

MEASURES OF EFFECTIVENESS

One requirement of a system of evaluation is a method for determining whether or not objectives, and consequently goals, are being achieved. Measures of effectiveness provide this essential function in a social services evaluation system designed to appraise service impact. By clear and accurate identification of the extent to which objectives are being met, the effectiveness measure indicates the level of tangible impact of the service on the problem. Typically, effectiveness is measured by determining the amount of change that has occurred in specified conditions of the client group.

Measures of effectiveness for social service objectives should be capable of providing data that can be used in the following activities:

Exhibit 5 — Key Words Used in Objectives

Words indicating direction of impact

Negative direction	*Positive direction*
decrease	increase
reduce	expand
diminish	enlarge
minimize	maximize
lower	raise

Measuring the extent to which objectives are met.

Recording the tangible impact of program services in the stated problem situation.

Evaluating the adequacy of service efforts to accomplish an objective or produce an intended or expected result.

In complying with these conditions and establishing criteria for determining the degree of success or impact of social services, recognition and awareness of current community opinion should be included as a basis for measuring change. Measurement of change in social situations is usually expressed in such terms as trends, ratios, and comparisons. To be viable, the measurement should possess the following characteristics: be observable; be quantifiable; and have social consequences. Measures having these characteristics will permit the evaluation of social programs in quantifiable terms.

In determining the impact of social services on client groups, it is often necessary to measure changes in social behavioral patterns. Such measurable social behavior may be evidenced by an event (an occurrence involving one or more persons) or a state (a mode or condition of being). Social behavior is also evidenced in the material things which man creates and uses or the factors which reflect the substance and quality of human social existence.

Technically speaking, all events and states are ultimately observable and therefore measurable. However, phenomena that are observable only on a limited basis require elaborate and costly observation devices suited only for use by the sophisticated investigator, and thus are not applicable to the routine, on-going evaluation system. Such measurement techniques are required for indepth special evaluations and are elements of evaluative research techniques. Accordingly, for purposes of the on-going evaluation of social services, events and states which are highly susceptible to observation and measurement are used. Generally speaking, events are more easily observed than states, and therefore are more often used for measurement. Examples

Exhibit 6 — Examples of Observable Phenomena

Social Behavior

Event (occurrence)	Observation of act
Child abuse	Parent beating child
Job application	Potential employee making application
Physician appointment	Individual keeps appointment
Change of residence	Family moves to different quarters
Enrollment of child in day care	Parent enrolls child in day care
Adoption of child	Child moved to adoptive family
Run-away child	Child leaves home

Human Conditions

State of being	Observation of state
Injured child	Bodily injuries
Unemployed	Person without job
Illness	Symptoms of illness
Unsupervised child	Child left alone
Homeless child	Child without parents

Material factors

Factors	Observation	State or condition based on criteria	
Housing	Presence	Standard	—Substandard
Income	or	Adequate	—Inadequate
Food	Absence	Nutritious	—Non-nutritious
Toilet	of a	Usable	—Nonusable
Clothing	Specific	Sufficient	—Insufficient
Transportation	Factor	Satisfactory	—Unsatisfactory

of observable behavior, human conditions, and material factors are listed in Exhibit 6.

The following considerations should be incorporated in the development of effectiveness measures to insure that the evaluation system is useful.

Measures should relate directly to a specific objective.

Measures should be clearly stated.

Measures should provide the basis for defining statistical data to be collected.

Measures should not create a data collection burden out of proportion to the utility of the data.

Exhibit 7 — Key Words Used in Measures

Describing numerator and denominator components of ratios

Key word	Use	Definition	Example
Total population	Denominator	All individuals falling within the scope of the social service agency's accountability.	All families residing in a geographically bounded area; all persons registered with an agency.
Risk group	Denominator	A subunit of a population in jeopardy of being affected by a specific problem.	All unmarried female youths age 13 to 18; all married females age 19 to 45; all children age 1 to 17.
Target group	Denominator	A subunit of a population affected by a problem to which social services are directed.	All married females age 19 to 45 registered for family planning counseling; all children age 1 to 17 placed in foster care.
Impact group	Numerator	All members of a risk or target group affected in a specified way, either positively or negatively.	All unmarried females age 13 to 18 in risk group who become pregnant out-of-wedlock; all children age 1 to 17 in foster care who are reunited with their parents.

Appropriate program directors and supervisory personnel should be consulted in the process of developing measures of effectiveness. Their participation is beneficial for the following reasons:

The measures of effectiveness should relate directly to the actual objectives of those individuals delivering the service.

In most instances, the data needed for measurement must be collected by field operations personnel, who are probably most aware of potential problems involved in interpreting and collecting specific types of information.

Field operations staff will be more willing to make the additional effort required for the data collection if they participate in determining the data to be collected.

Participation contributes to the development of more knowledgeable and more effective staff members at the field operations level.

The process of developing measures is iterative in nature. It can be expected that progressively higher staff competence and skill levels in the technique of measures development will be attained as the process is repeated. Examples of effectiveness measures are given in Exhibit 7. Several important characteristics consistently presented in these examples should be noted.

All measures relate directly to objectives, which in turn are related to the service goals.

In each measure, the scope is carefully defined.

Each objective and corresponding measure related to a specific goal appraises different aspects of service impact that would indicate progress toward goal achievement.

In certain service programs, it may be difficult to establish quantitative measures of effectiveness. In such cases, efficiency measures are sometimes used as an alternative. Efficiency refers to the manner in which agency resources are applied for the purpose of providing services. An efficiency objective is process-oriented. Objectives relating to efficiency may stipulate minimum levels below which service activities should not fall, such as to provide a minimum number of interviews per client. Efficiency objectives may also set as a target the reduction of manpower required to complete a service activity. Or, an efficiency objective may call for an increase in the frequency or intensity of a service activity, reflected in the number of contacts per week. Essentially, efficiency measures are directed to *output* (numbers of interviews or days of care) while effectiveness measures are directed to *outcome* (impact on client). Certain service programs have traditionally been regarded as acceptable professional practice, but there has been no quantifiable measurement of the effectiveness of these programs. Attempts to define such service programs in the context of this evaluation system have often been unsuccessful because the objectives are frequently ill-defined.

Exhibit 8 — Some Standards Used in Measures

Mathematical Term Used in Measure	Range of Scale	Hypothetical Documented Performance at Time 1	Hypothetical Objective for Performance at Time 2	Example of Objective Based on Standard
Ratio	1/100 to 100 or 0.01 to 1.00	25/100 0.25	20/100 0.20	Reduce pregnancies out-of-wedlock in target group from 25/100 to 20/100.
Per cent	1% to 100%	25%	20%	Reduce pregnancies out-of-wedlock in target group from 25% to 20%.
Average	1 to 9 (theoretically from 1 to ∞)	7	6	Lower from the 7th to the 6th the average month of pregnancy at which time the first contact with the maternal child care clinic is made.

It is important, wherever possible, to avoid the traditional practice of activity counting (process orientation) as a substitute for measuring social service impact (results orientation). If program administrators overwork the use of efficiency measures, rather than devote the effort required to develop effectiveness measures, an evaluation system will be seriously impaired and have limited utility.

QUANTITATIVE STANDARDS FOR EVALUATION

Quantitative standards for evaluating effectiveness may be defined as specified levels of attainment expressed in discrete units of measurement. Evaluation standards specify quantitative results to be expected from a particular service within a predetermined period of time. Examples of quantitative standards are presented in Exhibit 8.

Although evaluation standards perform a valuable function in establishing expected levels of attainment for welfare services, two significant problems occur. The first involves a misinterpretation of quantitative standards by operational personnel. Effectiveness standards may mistakenly be viewed as maximum objectives for attainment rather than as benchmarks. Operational personnel may thus tend to strive for achievement of only the level of attainment indicated by the standard rather than for maximum achievement. Administrators may avoid the problem by communication of the purpose of standards to all personnel involved.

A second problem is the tendency for a standard to be accepted as permanent, never requiring revision. As a standard is approached or reached, it becomes increasingly difficult to change the standard, especially if the change would represent a higher level of desired accomplishment than is currently expected. When such a condition develops, effectiveness standards become retardants rather than motivators to achievement, thereby weakening the evaluation process. Administrators similarly should be aware of and remain alert to these and other potential problems which may develop in using standards of evaluation. All standards should be periodically reviewed to insure that they are recognized as benchmarks for measurement and not as ceilings for accomplishment.

CONCLUSION

Effectiveness measures concentrate on the *results* of a program, rather than on the operation of a program, and can alter the traditional focus of welfare managers from emphasis on process and input into services, to concern with the product turned out by these investments. This new welfare orientation can establish a new framework in which goals and objectives buttress a program's intent. On a day-to-day basis, therefore, welfare administrators may well begin to manage by objective. Management by objective is a powerful tool with considerable potential in welfare work. As it is increasingly accepted in the welfare field, it can help welfare administrators in three primary management functions—program planning, personnel administration, and internal and external communication. Effectiveness measures can pinpoint program areas where objectives are not achieved, and can cast a spotlight on those where additional study is needed. The end product will provide an improved basis for decisions as to which welfare programs should be maintained, which should be modified, and which eliminated so that a greater impact may be made on defined problems.

The concept of effectiveness measures for welfare programs has already been demonstrated as feasible and promising for improving welfare management. Of course, no management method, however enlightened, offers a ready resolution on how this nation's manpower and money can best be deployed to help millions of Americans improve the quality of their lives. Measures of effectiveness do, however, provide welfare administrators with a promising new tool for charting a new course among uncertain currents of social problems.

VIII
CASES IN SOCIAL ACCOUNTING

Financial Impact of
Legalized Abortion in New York City

Elizabeth Arfania

In this paper, Ms. Arfania, a student at New York University, examined the impact of legalized abortion on the cost of welfare and related services in the City of New York.

The paper is as interesting for its demonstration of the types of information that are available on the subject, as it is for its methodology. Utilizing a wide variety of statistics available from the City and State, Ms. Arfania estimated both the cost per welfare child born and the decrease in the birth rate due to the availability of abortions.

The results, which demonstrate a considerable saving to the City, were computed in an almost ultra-conservative way. Consideration was given only to the absolute decrease in births, although the more reasonable assumption of a decline from the upward growth curve of welfare births would have produced a significantly greater apparent saving to the City. In addition, as noted in the paper, Ms. Arfania calculated only the first year's effect. Obviously, the cumulative impacts are substantially greater.

Introduction

The purposes of this paper are: (1) to study 'abortion' as a problem and see why it is of social concern; (2) to discuss the economic effects of legalized abortion; and (3) to quantify the benefits resulting from the savings made on resources and services which otherwise would be demanded by children, if not

Elizabeth Arfania is a student at New York University Graduate School of Business Administration.

SOURCE: Unpublished term paper prepared in connection with a course in socio-economic accounting.

426

aborted. Families with dependent children in public assistance [programs] in New York City in 1971 formed the basis of the study.

To demonstrate my point effectively, I found it appropriate to describe the various outcomes of abortion prior to quantification of the social costs and benefits associated with prevention of children in Aid to Families of Dependent Children (AFDC) situations. I selected AFDC families as an example in order to limit the subject to an area in which there was more available data.

PART I

Abortion has been the subject of considerable controversy in recent years. Public attention was focused on the problem of abortion at the time of the German measles epidemic in the United States, and of the thalidomide tragedy in Europe in 1962. However, the actual movement toward abortion reform started in the late 1950s when The American Law Institute proposed a model abortion statute. The model law permitted therapeutic abortions only when necessary to preserve the life of the woman. At the present time thirty-eight states follow this law.

So far eleven states have adopted liberalized laws or have reformed the laws to a great extent. In New York, abortion was legalized in March 1970 "to permit physicians to perform abortions on any consenting woman no more than twenty-four weeks pregnant" [5, p. 5]. The position was that when a woman wants to abort her baby, any restraint carries consequences detrimental to her, her unwanted child, and to society.

Socioeconomics of Liberalized Abortion:

The socioeconomic effects of access to abortion are numerous. For example, one can argue that access to abortion reduces the number of unwanted children, it decreases the frequency of illegal abortions, it lowers the cost, it diminishes the number of out-of-wedlock births, and it controls population growth. One could analyze each of these and use different assumptions to conclude various relevant social benefits and finally quantify these social benefits in terms of dollar values. It is outside the scope of this paper to quantify every outcome of abortion. However, the various social economics of abortion are briefly discussed to clarify the issues.

Abortion and Population Control:

"Abortion is not the method of choice for population control despite the knowledgeable assertion of distinguished demographers that worldwide induced abortion was and remains the major means of birth control" [4, p. 1]. The most effective way of preventing population growth is through knowledge of contraception methods. However, until better means of contraception are found, abortion should be an accepted method of fertility control and should operate as a back up measure when contraception fails. The present population growth in the United States would be reduced to one-half its present rate if only wanted pregnancies occurred, which implies that abortion can prevent the present number of unwanted births—about 750,000 a year [3, p. 16].

In countries where abortions have been liberalized, the birth rate sometimes has fallen below the death rate and presented a negative rate of growth. For example, "in Hungary where abortions cost $1, the number of abortions exceeds the number of live births" [2, p. 160].

One interesting impact of liberalized abortion laws in New York City has been the reduction of the number of births and the birth rate. The number of births from January 1 to June 11, 1971 was 60,695, a 17.0 birth rate. These total births and birth rate can be compared to 64,667 (18.1) respectively for the same period in 1970 [5, p. 11]. So far in 1972, the birth rate has declined at a higher rate. We should bear in mind that the expansion of family planning services is an important factor deterring child bearing. Family planning services are present in almost all states, but the reduction of birth rates was the highest in New York State. So we can assume that the liberalized abortion law had an important effect.

Legalized Abortion and Unwanted Births:

Access to abortion helps couples to maintain a fertility level according to their income and their set of preferences for children, in terms of education, leisure, and material goods. Restriction on legal abortion increases the number of unwanted births.

The 1965 National Fertility Study showed that only twenty-six per cent of American women, who were interviewed about each of their children, were completely successful in exercising control over the growth of their families and in planning both the number of children desired and their timing. The births were classified as unwanted, as "timing failures" (wanted, but not then), "timing successes" (wanted and wanted then), or "non-failures" (contraception not used because pregnancy was desired). From 1960 to 1965 in the U.S. the number of unwanted births is estimated to be 4.7 million (Table 1) [2, p. 293].

Group Differences and Unwantedness:

In 1965, the National Fertility Study estimated that the number of unwanted children produced by the poor or "near poor" from 1960 to 1965 were 2.2 million—thirty-six per cent of all births of these couples. Excluding the near poor, forty-two per cent of all births in the poor class were unwanted. Among black, poor and near poor, about fifty-one per cent of all births were

Table 1
Estimated Number and Percentage of Unwanted Births in The United States, by Race and Economic Status: 1960–1965

Race	All income levels	Poor and near poor	Non-poor
	Number (million)		
All couples	4.685	1.976	2.709
White	3.282	0.950	2.332
Black	1.267	0.951	0.316
	Percentage		
All couples	19	32	15
White	17	25	15
Black	36	46	22

Table 2
Average Number of Children Expected and Wanted by Married Women, Based on Wife's Education and Family Income: 1965

Characteristic	Expected	Wanted	Difference (E–W)
All wives in study	3.4	2.7	0.7
Wife's Education			
College 4	3.0	2.7	0.3
College 1–3	2.9	2.6	0.3
High School 4	3.1	2.6	0.5
High School 1–3	3.6	2.8	0.8
Less	4.5	3.2	1.3
Family Income			
$15,000 or more	3.0	2.6	0.4
$10,000–$14,999	3.0	2.6	0.4
$8,000–$9,999	3.3	2.8	0.5
$7,000–$7,999	3.3	2.7	0.6
$6,000–$6,999	3.4	2.7	0.7
$5,000–$5,999	3.5	2.8	0.7
$4,000–$4,999	3.7	2.8	0.9
$3,000–$3,999	4.1	2.8	1.3
Under $3,000	4.6	2.9	1.7

unwanted. Low income families seek the same family size as higher income couples [1, pp. 910-923] but, they have greater failures in the use of contraceptive devices. Non-poor couples tend to have greater access to family planning services and accordingly use effective devices: pills, condoms or diaphragms. However, the poor woman who lacks proper education about contraception relies on less effective methods such as the douche [2, pp. 301-304].

The 1965 National Fertility Study also showed that success in controlling the size of the family depends to a great extent on the woman's education and economic status (Table 2) [2, p. 231]. The difference between number of children expected and number wanted is the number of unwanted children. The number of unwanted children varies with the level of education from 0.3 among college women to 1.3 for women who never attended high school.

The same inverse relation exists between socioeconomic status and the number of unwanted children. "People of all incomes want a similar number of children but poorer people expect more" [2, p. 223] (Table 2) [2, p. 231]. It is estimated that there are 5.5 million low-income women in the U.S. who need family planning assistance. Unfortunately, only 700,000 of those women receive help from planned parenthood, public health clinics, hospitals and

Table 3
The Percentage of Unwanted Births, 1960–1965,
Reported by Black and White Couples,
Based on Education of Wife, Family Income, and Poverty Status

Characteristic	Black	White
All Couples in Study	36	17
Education of Wife		
0–8 years	48	23
9–11 years	39	20
12 years	28	14
College	25	11
Family Income		
Less than $3,000	42	27
$3,000–$4,999	39	18
$5,000–$6,999	30	14
$7,000–$9,999	28	16
$10,000 and over	16	15
Poverty Status		
Poor	47	31
Near-poor	40	16
Non-poor	22	15

other services. Hospitals and local health departments have been pitifully inadequate means for helping the poor [2, p. 300]. One can infer from the above studies that low-income groups can hardly control their family size. Unless they can have free access to abortion, unwanted births prevail.

The unwanted child often has a negative effect on the family economic and personal life-style. For example, an unplanned child in premarital pregnancies often forces the couple to marry. The young father may be forced to leave school and take low-skilled jobs. The failure of timing of pregnancy for couples who marry at early ages may well be catastrophic. The impact of the unwanted child in terms of the economic life of a teen-age father is the reduction of his life time personal income, because he fails to complete a higher level of education.

Poverty and Social Costs

Another economic problem associated with uncontrolled family size is poverty. In 1966, the median incomes of a poor family of four, five, or six or more were $3,308, $3,590 and $3,440 respectively. These incomes were much below the budget standard of the Bureau of Labor Statistics—a median income of $5,916 for a four-person urban family in 1967.

Another important socioeconomic effect of unwanted children is their burden and cost to society. There have been many studies to prove that unwanted children cost more than wanted ones in terms of welfare, health, and education. The fact of unwantedness affects in the long-run, the life style of these children.

Research was performed by professors Han Farssman and Inga Thuwe in Sweden. They studied the lives of 120 children born by mothers who were not allowed to abort their babies legally. They observed the children from birth to age 21. About two-thirds of these children grew up in undesirable circumstances; either the child was out-of-wedlock, parents were divorced, or the child was raised by foster parents or in governmental care centers. The lives of these children were compared with a control group of the first, same-sexed children born in the same hospital. Twenty-eight per cent of the unwanted children had psychiatric treatment compared to fifteen per cent in the control group, eighteen per cent recorded delinquency compared with eight per cent for the control group. Most of the unwanted children had received public assistance, fewer attended university, and most had married and started raising children by the age of 21 [7, p. 71]. The above study implied that when a woman wants an abortion and she is denied it, her unwanted child runs a greater risk of having social and emotional handicaps. There have been further studies to link the child's psychological and mental handicaps to 'unwantedness.' Some researchers even attempted to relate unwantedness to schizophrenia. Shakow, in discussing psychophysiological aspects of schizophrenia observes that "Patient appears to . . . . attain in his illness the satisfaction of early fundamental needs which in contrast with normal persons, have never been adequately satisfied in the ordinary course of events, particularly in the familial setting. This ordinary course of events includes the thousands, nay millions of appropriate effective reinforcements of behavior which over the years lay the ground for what we call normal development" [8, p. 6]. The United States Children's Bureau and the Child Welfare League of America reported in 1968:

> More than 300,000 children are either wards of public and private agencies . . . . upward of 100,000 are probably "trapped" in foster care—have little or no hope of rejoining their parents—and are suffering severe personality damage as a result. Social workers call them the orphans of the living. Nearly half—46.5 per cent—of the children who are in foster care are placed because of parental neglect, abuse or exploitation. The rest? The reasons vary: broken homes, economic troubles, sickness, psychiatric problems. For one reason or another, the parents are unable or unwilling to care for their children. Mainly, foster children are rejected youngsters. And most show it [9, p. 203].

The above studies imply that the "unwanted" child has higher demands for health and welfare services than the average child. Statistics show that local authorities have greater expenditures for these children in: (1) child care services; (2) sickness benefits; (3) supplementary benefits; and (4) accomodation for the homeless [10, p. 3]. "A wanted child" has a much lower possibility of becoming socially and psychologically handicapped. Analyzing the extra costs involved to the government or foster parents in bringing up a child to a productive age (16-18), one realizes how much money can be saved if this child had been prevented by contraception or abortion. And, because of the low effectiveness of contraception among the poor, near poor, and teenagers, abortion becomes the number one solution to the problem of unwanted pregnancies. Abortion saves a very young female, who by virtue of youth alone, is in danger of pregnancy complications and premature delivery. And, if we add to her misery, the out-of-wedlock pregnancy, and membership in a poor minority group, then the abortion is a 'must' for her welfare, her infant, and her society. It is gratifying, according to the available data, that for the first time the trend of out-of-wedlock births has been reversed in New York City. A decline of 11.8 per cent is noted which is a greater decline than in-wedlock births (11.5 per cent) (Table 4) [11, p. 16]. As Table 4 shows, from 1960 through 1970 the number of out-of-wedlock births increased every year by approximately 2000. However, in 1971 this constant increase was reversed and a decrease of about 3000 was observed. It is a fair

Table 4
Total Live Births, Out-of-Wedlock
and In-Wedlock Births
New York City, 1960-1971

Year	Total live births	Out-of-wedlock births	In-wedlock births
1960	166,300	13,901	152,399
1961	168,383	15,723	152,660
1962	165,244	16,412	148,832
1963	167,848	18,436	149,412
1964	165,695	20,223	145,472
1965	158,815	20,980	137,835
1966	153,334	22,714	130,620
1967	145,802	24,336	121,466
1968	141,920	26,262	115,658
1969	146,221	29,325	116,896
1970	149,192	31,903	117,289
1971	131,920	28,126	103,794

conclusion that this reversal is due to the legality of abortion in New York.

Another economic implication of legalized abortion is the reduction of its cost. As predicted by two clinic directors in New York City, abortion cost dropped to $100 within a year. Eventually it will level off to $50 [12, p. 1]. At present, the cost of abortion in New York City varies. An abortion may cost a woman $500 if it is performed by a private doctor. Women referred by Planned Parenthood pay $150-$250 for first trimester abortions, $350-$450 for saline. The fee of $50-$200, (with some abortions performed free for low-income patients) are charged by the three of the larger free standing clinics. An all-inclusive fee of $150-$160 is charged by municipal hospitals [5, p. 7].

Social Welfare—Under Public Programs:

States receive grants from Federal funds for payments to various groups: the aged, the blind, the permanently and totally disabled, and families with dependent children; persons unable to take care of their medical bills.

The Federal government makes contributions to states for programs providing health and welfare services. These programs consist of child welfare services, vocational rehabilitation, aging activities, maternal and child health services, services for crippled children, maternity and infant care projects, comprehensive health services and various public health activities, such as community mental health centers, medical facilities construction, regional medical programs and control of specific diseases.

Public assistance programs provide other general aides such as food for the needy, food stamps, Job Corps, Neighborhood Youth Corps, and work-experience programs under the Economic Opportunity Act and related laws [13, p. 280].

In 1971, total social welfare expenditures in the U.S. were $170,322,000,000 or $813 per capita. Of this, public assistance expenditures alone resulted in a per capita cost of $104. In 1971, 16.9 per cent of the GNP was related to social welfare expenditures of which 51.2 per cent were financed by Federal funds and the rest were paid by States and Localities [13, p. 278].

Since this paper is confined to the study of AFDC families in New York State, I will now limit my discussion on social welfare under public program to AFDC families.

AFDC Families—Characteristics:

Families with dependent children account for about seventy-four per cent of total welfare recipients in the U.S. In New York State these groups represent about seventy-eight per cent of total individuals on welfare. During 1971, from total money payments of $9,381,000,000 to old-age, families with dependent children, blind and permanently, totalled disabled, $6,203,000,000 was paid to families with dependent children, about sixty-six per cent of total payments.

Table 5
Types of AFDC Families
New York State, 1969 and 1971

	1969	1971
Total Families Assisted	258,000	332,600
Families—		
Number of persons in the assistance group		
1	3,365	4,655
2	59,524	78,493
3	64,441	87,140
4	48,136	64,856
5	35,196	41,907
6	19,152	21,951
7	12,422	13,304
8	9,058	9,312
9	3,882	5,321
10	3,624	5,321

Table 6
AFDC Families, by Number of Child Recipients
New York State, 1969-1971

	1969	1971
Total Families—	258,800	332,600
Number of Children		
1	67,288	88,804
2	69,100	92,463
3	47,102	59,535
4	32,609	41,242
5	17,857	18,958
6	11,646	14,302
7	7,246	8,648
8	3,623	5,322
9	1,035	1,663
10 or more	1,294	1,663

Table 7
Number of Child Recipients in AFDC Families
in New York and the U.S., 1969-1972

	1969	1970	1971	1972
Number of children—total in U.S.	5,413,000	7,033,000	7,571,700	7,650,000
Number of Children—New York State	750,520	981,000	931,280	1,073,469

Sources: U.S. Department of Health, Education, and Welfare, findings of the 1969 and 1971 AFDC Studies.

In 1971, twenty-six per cent of the families consisted of three persons, twenty-three per cent of two persons and nineteen per cent of four persons. Of total families, twenty-eight per cent had two children, twenty-seven per cent had one child and eighteen per cent had three children (Tables 5, 6, 7).

The majority of families have one adult recipient, the father or the mother. Since the AFDC Study shows that about eighty-four per cent of fathers left the family for one reason or another, the one adult recipient is probably the mother (Tables 8, 9). Many of the children on assistance come from broken homes, receive little parental love, live in a battlefield atmosphere, are the scapegoats of their mother's aggravations and probably were unwanted at conception.

Table 8
Status of the Father in AFDC Families
New York State, 1969 and 1971

	1969	1971
Total Families	258,800	332,600
Status of Father		
Divorced	12,422	20,954
Legally separated	8,799	15,300
Separated without court decree	23,292	44,568
Deserted	74,534	94,126
Not married to mother	72,205	92,130
In prison	5,693	6,319
Other reason	7,505	5,322
Step-father case	518	665
Children deprived of support or care of mother	1,811	2,993
Unknown	52,021	50,223

Table 9
Status of Parents in AFDC Families
New York State, 1969 and 1971

	1969	1971
Child Recipients—Total	750,520	931,280
Status of Parents		
Divorced	34,682	58,671
Legally separated	24,637	42,840
Separated without court decree	65,218	124,790
Deserted	208,695	263,552
Not married to mother	202,174	257,964
In prison	15,940	17,693
Other reason	21,014	14,901
Step-father case	1,450	1,862
Children deprived of support or care of mother	5,070	8,380
Unknown	145,658	140,624

Source: U.S. Department of Health, Education, and Welfare, findings of 1969 and 1971 AFDC Studies.

Exhibit I
Food Program
New York State
1971

	1971
Food Stamp Program:	
Participants in U.S., June 30, 1971	10,567,000
Federal Costs for Food Stamp Program	$1,522,000,000
Federal Aid to New York Food Stamp Program	$ 112,000,000
Participants in Food Stamp Program — New York	1,270,000
AFDC Families — total recipients — New York	1,275,400
Number AFDC Participants in Food Stamp plan — New York	1,049,654
Percentage of AFDC recipients in Food Stamp plan	80.83%
Total Cost of Food Stamp Program 1971, AFDC Families:	$ 92,558,489
$\frac{(112,000,000 \times 1,049,654)}{1,270,000}$	
Average Cost Per Participant, 1971	$ 88.18
Average monthly cost Per Participant, 1971	$ 7.35
Food Distribution Program:	
Federal Donated Food Plan —Cost Per Participant, 1971	$ 80.83
Number of AFDC Participants in Donated Food Plan — New York	1,275,400
Total Cost of Donated Food Plan —AFDC Families, 1971	$ 10,203,200
Average monthly cost per Participant, 1971	$ 6.74
Average monthly cost of food program per participant	$ 14.09

Source: U.S. Department of Health, Education, and Welfare, Findings, of the 1971 AFDC
Study.
U.S. Department of Commerce, Statistical Abstract of the United States, 1972,
pp. 85-88.

AFDC Family Income:

Most AFDC families have little or no potential for earning and in most cases
their income is confined to their public assistance payments. These families
receive checks semi-monthly, based on two items: (1) basic grant and (2) rent.

The monthly average payments per recipient of $75.10 and $75.82 for 1971
and 1972 are based on total expenditures made by the state of New York for
AFDC Families for 1971 and 1972 respectively. These dollar figures are the
average of two items (a) basic grant and (b) rent. They exclude the cost of other
benefits granted to these families, such as Medicaid, food stamps, and other
social welfare.

Exhibit II
National Health Expenditures, 1971

National Health Expenditures	$75,011
Private expenditures	46,548
Public expenditures	28,463

National Health Expenditures Under Public Programs, 1971

Public expenditures	$28,463
Health and medical services	25,605
Medical research	1,819
Medical-facilities construction	1,039

Social Welfare-Medical Expenditures, Public Programs, 1971

Public Aid—Vendor Medical Payments	$ 6,494
Health and Medical Programs:	
Hospital and Medical Care	3,832
Maternal & Child health programs	448
Medical Research	1,722
School Health	258
Other Public Health Activities	1,618
Medical Facilities Construction	897
Total Medical & Health Expenditures	$15,269
Public Assistance—Number of Recipients in U.S.	14,389,600*
Medical expenditures per person ($15,269,000/14389600)	$ 1,061
Average monthly medical and health expenditures, 1971	$ 88.42

*In millions of dollars except *

Source: U.S. Department of Commerce, Statistical Abstract of The United States, 1972, pp. 65, 277–279, 299–304.

Food Program and AFDC Families:

The Federal Food program consists of commodity distribution, indemnity plan, special milk program, and food stamp program.

In arriving at the applicable cost of food program per AFDC participant in New York, I have considered the cost of commodities distributed among needy families and the cost of the food stamp plan. I disregarded the cost of school lunch programs, and the special milk program. These two programs are provided to many public institutions and specifically to welfare cases, and not necessarily only to poor children.

In order to 'estimate' the cost of food commodities donated and cost of food stamp plan per participant in AFDC Families the following facts and assumptions were used.

In 1971, out of 332,600 AFDC Families in New York State 82.3 per cent participated in the food stamp plan and 0.1 per cent participated in commodities donated. For 1971, the average monthly cost of commodities donated per participant in Federal Food Program for Needy families was $80.83. The $80.83 consists of commodity cost, warehousing, processing, repackaging, miscellaneous handling charges and transportation costs.

In 1971, the total cost of the Food Stamp Program to the Federal government was $1,522,000,000 of which $112,000,000 was allocated to state of New York. Further, in New York, the average monthly participants in food stamps were $1,270,000 of which 1,049,654 persons belonged to AFDC families. The cost of the Food Stamp Program in New York for families with dependent children is calculated as shown in Exhibit I.

The total cost of Donated Food plan in AFDC families is calculated by multiplying the average monthly number of participants by total costs and food distribution per person. The average monthly number of participants is the result of multiplication of the total number of New York AFDC's recipients by the percentage of participants in Food Donated Plan (1,275,400 x 0.1). (Exhibit I)

Benefits Under Health Programs

AFDC families, like other individuals in social welfare, benefit from various aspects of national health programs. National Health expenditures are financed by the federal government, states and localities. The health expenditures under public programs are subdivided to three categories: (1) health and medical programs; (2) medical research; and (3) medical-facilities construction. Health and medical services are provided both to civilians and the Defense Department. Medical facilities construction expenditures are related to Defense Department, Veteran Administration and social welfare.

I derived the average monthly medical and health expenditures per person, under public programs, by taking into account only costs involved in civilian programs. The total medical and health expenditure of individuals in public aid for 1971 is divided by total number of recipients in this program to arrive at annual medical expenditures per person. In doing this I treated equally all individuals in public aid, i.e., old age, families with dependent children, blind, permanently and totally disabled, and general assistance, in terms of medical expenses. For example, maternal and child health programs presumably are more relevant to AFDC families than to old age or permanently and totally disabled groups. Hospital and medical care are provided mostly to old age and permanently and totally disabled individuals. However, I think overall these discrepancies even up. Another point that might raise a question is the way the average monthly costs of medical, health, and other social welfare per person is calculated. I assumed that 100 per cent of the people in welfare use at least one type of service. In reality this might not be true but, because the majority use more than one type of service as a whole the calculated costs are good approximations.

There is no available data that shows how much of total medical expenditures were actually spent by families with dependent children. One can roughly estimate the related medical costs by multiplying the percentage of families who needed one or more types of services by the total number of families, and then taking the ratio of this result to total number of participants in medical and health programs and multiplying that ratio by total medical and health expenditures (Exhibit III). Table 10 shows the various medical services provided to AFDC families in the U.S. and New York State.

Table 10
Medical Services Provided to AFDC Families During 1971

	U.S.	N.Y.
Total number of families	2,523,900	332,600
Services relating to marital problems	278,800	58,538
Services relating to parent-child relationship or other child adjustment problems	442,900	77,496
Services for delinquent children	87,200	14,967
Services to the physically or mentally handicapped	234,800	34,258
Family planning information & counseling without medical referral	460,400	110,091
Services to obtain or use medical care or dental care	981,200	158,650
Family planning, information & counseling, with medical referral	190,500	31,930
Services not specified	84,000	7,317
Unknown	98,900	5,322

Health, Education and Welfare Services

The U.S. Department of Health, Education and Welfare provides various services to AFDC families. These services are administered by the Office of Economic Opportunity, Department of Welfare and Education. Table 11 shows the various services rendered to these families during 1971. The average monthly expenditures per person in other social welfare programs are calculated in the same way as the average monthly medical and health expenditure mentioned before (Exhibit IV). Other social welfare expenditures amounted to $424,400,000 (Exhibit V).

PART II: BENEFIT-COST ANALYSIS OF LEGAL ABORTIONS

In a previous section I discussed and analyzed the various government aids to families with dependent children and calculated the average monthly expenditures per person in every assistance category (Exhibit VI). In this section I have tried to obtain the marginal costs and benefits associated with the number of births prevented by abortion during 1971 among families with dependent children in New York City.

The portions of births prevented due to abortion is the difference between total reductions in births between years 1970 and 1971 and the number of

Exhibit III
Medical and Health Expenditures by AFDC Families
in New York in 1971

Public Aid—medical & health expenditures	$15,269,000,000
Public Aid—number of recipients in U.S.	14,389,600
AFDC Families—number of recipients in N.Y.	1,275,400
Percentage of families provided one or more services—N.Y.	70.5
AFDC families—number of persons provided one or more services—N.Y.	899,157
Medical & health expenditures—AFDC families—N.Y., 1971	
$\dfrac{899,157}{14,389,600} \cdot \$15,269,000,000 =$	$ 954,005,570

Source: U.S. Department of Health, Education & Welfare, "Findings of the 1971 AFDC Study," No, (SRS) 72-03756.

Exhibit IV
Other Social Welfare—Expenditure Under Public Program in 1971

Other Social Welfare	$5,305*
Vocational rehabilitation	790
Institutional care	170
Child nutrition programs	1,759
Child welfare	505
Special OEO programs	786
Others	250
Public assistance—number of recipients in U.S.	14,389,600
Other social welfare—average cost per person, 1971	$ 368.67
Other social welfare—average monthly cost per person	$ 30.72

*In millions of dollars.

births prevented through the use of contraception by those families who received family planning services in 1971. The contraceptive effectiveness is adjusted to the extent of possible failure rates among various methods (Exhibit VII).

The effects of legal abortion children, in AFDC families, to New York City for 1971 are substantial: an estimated saving of $2,814,367. Savings are the difference between total benefits realized by New York City, to the extent of average annual expenditures of $2,993,170 which otherwise would have been demanded by 1191 children, and total resource costs of 1191 abortion payments by New York City (Exhibit VIII).

Note that $2,814,367 is only the first year saving on 1191 cases. If one were interested in obtaining the present value of total savings to New York City for 16-18 years of dependency of these children, he could add to the first year savings 15 or 17 times $2,993,170, the annual expenditures, and discount

Exhibit V
Other Social Welfare Expenditures by AFDC Families
New York, 1971

Public aid—other social welfare	$5,305,000,000
Public aid—number of recipients in New York	14,389,600
AFDC families—number of recipients in New York	1,275,400
Percentage of families provided one or more services	92.1
AFDC families—number of persons provided one or more services in New York	1,174,643
Other social welfare expenditures—AFDC families, New York, 1971	
$\dfrac{1,174,643}{14,389,600} \cdot \$5,305,000,000 =$	$ 424,400,000

Source: U.S. Department of Commerce, Statistical Abstract of The United States, 1972, pp. 277–279, 299–304.

Exhibit VI
Monthly Average Expenditures Per Person by AFDC Families
New York City, 1971

Money payments	$ 76.20
Food stamps	7.35
Food distribution	6.74
Health and medical care	88.42
Other social welfare	30.72
Total monthly expenditures per person	$209.43

each back to present at some appropriate discount rate. However, the purpose of this paper was not to do this. The task was to show the economic benefits of legality of abortion and its effectiveness in prevention of the unwanted births. Exhibit VIII serves, however, to illustrate how rewarding government investments in this area can be.

Exhibit VIII gives an 'estimate' of realized savings and it might be subject to further quantitative adjustments. However, no matter what the absolute dollar values are, the essence of the matter still remains the same, i.e., the legality of abortion has been sharply beneficial to New York City.

Table 11
Services Used by AFDC Families During 1971

	U.S.	N.Y.
Total number of families	2,523,900	332,600
Services Used		
Legal services	321,200	67,185
Emergency services	435,900	92,795
Unmarried mother services	260,600	52,883
Services to establish paternity of children	299,600	78,494
Services to secure support of children	716,200	138,694
Homemaker services	113,200	19,291
Aftercare services following institutional or foster home care	50,200	13,304
Assist children to participate in recreation, group activities, or camping	195,700	58,538
Day care services	176,400	29,269
Adoption services	24,100	4,656
Foster care services	47,700	7,317
Protective services for neglected or abused children	107,400	19,956
Counseling, guidance, or other diagnostic services related to employment	1,030,100	169,626
Vocational rehabilitation services	201,300	34,923
Referral for employment or work training	597,800	79,824
Summer or part-time employment for children during school year	127,200	25,278
Pre-school education	176,500	33,925
Assist children to continue their education	440,600	81,487
Adult basic education or high school equivalency	213,800	42,240
Vocational education	193,900	35,921
Improve home & financial management	937,100	202,886
Secure better housing or improve housing conditions	685,600	144,681

Source: U.S. Department of Health, Education & Welfare, "Findings of the 1971 AFDC Study," No, (SRS) 72-03756.

Exhibit VII
Estimated Number of Aborted Births in AFDC Families
New York, 1971

Number of births, 1970	25,481
Number of births, 1971	23,643
Decremental number of births	1,838
Percentage of AFDC families received family planning information, with & without medical referral—1971	42.7%
Less: The average probability of failure rates in contraceptions*	7.5%
Total estimated percentage of births controlled by contraceptions	35.2%
Deduct: Decremental number of births due to contraceptive applications: (1,838 X 35.2% = 646.98)	647
Decremental number of births due to abortion—estimated	1,191

Source: New York State Department of Social Services, Office of Research

*Average contraceptive failure rates =

$$\frac{\text{Total failure rates in methods}^2}{\text{Number of methods}}$$

Average contraception failure rates =

$$\frac{\text{Pill, 4 per cent} + \text{IUD, 7 per cent} + \text{Condom, 16 per cent} + \text{Diaphragm, 18 per cent} + \text{Withdrawal, 21 per cent} + \text{Rhythm, 28 per cent} + \text{Foam, 29 per cent}}{7} =$$

0.175 = Average contraceptive failure rate in total population (100)

The average contraceptive failure rate in sample of 42.7 of AFDC families used contraceptions =

$$\frac{(0.175 \text{ X } 0.427)}{1.000} = 0.075.$$

Exhibit VIII
Distributional Effects of Abortion in AFDC Families
New York City, 1971

Resource Benefits:	
Money payment, [(76.20 · 1191) · 12]	$1,089,048
Food stamp, [(7.35 · 1191) · 12]	105,046
Food distribution, [(6.74 · 1191) · 12]	1,263,698
Health & medical care, [(88.42 · 1191) · 12]	439,050
Total benefits to New York City due to abortion of 1191 births in AFDC families in 1971	$2,993,170
Resource Costs:	
Average abortion cost, all inclusive fee of $150/case, (1191· $150)	178,803
Savings to New York City for 1971	$2,815,367

REFERENCES

1.   Jaffe, R. S., and Guttmacher, A. F., "Family Planning Programs in the United States." *Demography, 5,* 910-923, 1969.

2.   Westoff, L. A., and Westoff, C. F., 'From Now to Zero,' 1971.

3.   Guttmacher, A. F., M.D., and Pilpel, H. F., "Abortion & The Unwanted Child," An interview, Reprinted from *Family Planning Perspectives, 2,* March, 1970.

4.   Beck, M. B., "Abortion: The Mental Health Consequences of Unwantedness," Seminar in Psychiatry, *2,* 3, August, 1970.

5.   Pakter, J., and Nelson, F., "Abortion in New York City: The First Nine Months," *Family Planning Perspectives, 3,* 3, July, 1971.

6.   Orshansky, M.,"The Shape of Poverty in 1966," Social Security Bulletin, March, 1968.

7.   Farssman, H., and Thuwe, I., "One Hundred and Twenty Children Born After Application for Therapeutic Abortion Refused," *Acta Psychiat.,* 1966.

8.   Shakow, D., "Some Psychophysiological aspects of schizophrenia," in Mildred B. Beck, ed., "Abortion: The Mental Health Consequences of Unwantedness," Seminar in Psychiatry, *2,* 3, August, 1970.

9.   Haitch, R., "Orphans of the Living: The Foster Care Crisis," Public Affairs Pamphlet No. 418, published in cooperation with The Child Welfare League of America, 1968.

10.   Laing, W. A., "The Costs and Benefits of Family Planning," *Political and Economic Planning, 28,* Broadsheet 534, February, 1972.

11.   Pakter, J., M.D., "An 18 Month Experience in New York City with The Liberalized Abortion Law," *New York Medicine,* September, 1972.

12.   Johnston, L., "Abortion Clinics in City Face Rising Competition," *New York Times,* March 19, 1973.

13.   U. S. Department of Commerce, Social and Economic Statistics Administration, Statistical Abstract of The United States, 1972.

14.   U. S. Department of Health, Education, and Welfare, 'Findings of the 1971 AFDC Study,' DHEW Publication No. (SRS) 72-03756.

Environmental and Social Costs Impacts of Northeast Corridor Transportation System Strategies

Paul F. Dienemann

and

Armando M. Lago

The Northeast Corridor Transportation Project (NECTP) represents the most extensive, formal attempt to provide an integrated study of the problems and possibilities of providing a modern transportation system for a major portion of the United States. The Northeast Corridor (NEC) covers the area roughly from Boston through New York to Washington. The 44 million (1969 figures) inhabitants of the NEC make more than 130 million one-way trips between these major cities in NEC. NECTP, sponsored by the Office of High Speed Ground Transportation of the U.S. Department of Transportation has made a number of studies of various aspects of the transportation. A group of seventeen reports, providing detailed information on NEC, project methodology, descriptions of alternative systems and cost analysis techniques are referred to in this article. In the light of the preoccupation of this volume, it is interesting to note that a significant part of the work was performed by the consulting group of a major firm of public accountants, Peat, Marwick, Mitchell & Co.

This article utilizes some of the data developed in NECTP to make estimates of the dollar values of certain social impacts of the system. The conclusion that NECTP would have negligible impact on air pollution in the NEC is counter to the general impression, and has received little publicity.

The evaluation of transportation technologies has traditionally been conducted in terms of the user benefits they generate. Lately, new awareness has risen about the substantial external costs and benefits that accrue to third parties, i.e., people other than the operators and users of the transportation system, and the concern that these important impacts are rarely taken into account formally in the evaluation of transportation investments. Externalities or spillover effects occur whenever the outputs of a transportation alternative affect outputs, costs, utilities, location, and resource allocation decisions of

Paul F. Dienemann is with the Resources Management Corporation and Armando M. Lago is a professor at The Catholic University of America.

SOURCE: From *Transportation Science*, Vol. 5, No. 3 (August, 1971) pp. 256-282. Copyright by Operations Research Society of America.

other firms and households. Externalities can be pecuniary or real depending on whether there is a true change in the productivity or technology associated with the external effects. While pecuniary externalities have important distributional considerations, they are not reflected in social cost computations of project impacts, although they are certainly reflected in project feasibility analyses, in the form of constraints on the project selection decision process.

The literature[17] is well stocked with references to the inefficiencies in resource allocation that occur in the presence of externalities, and because of these reasons they must be thoroughly investigated since they will affect transport mode selections, facilities location, outputs, and costs throughout the Northeast Corridor region. This paper deals with the quantification of the major nonpecuniary external effects of transportation system alternatives in the Northeast Corridor region of the United States, quantification both in incommensurable and in money terms, and represents a first approximation to a very difficult and controversial topic. The social benefit and cost impacts figures presented in this paper, however crude the range estimates, provide an indication of the magnitude of impacts that transportation planners must take into account in decisions affecting both system design choices and location of facilities.

Nine alternative transportation systems have been defined as part of the Northeast Corridor Transportation Project (NECTP). The base case (or null case) includes all existing transportation modes—conventional air transport (CTOL), intercity bus, and automobile—projected to 1975 levels, plus the demonstration (DEMO) rail, which is assumed to be an extension of the current Penn Central Metroliner service.

New technologies examined include two high-speed rail modes (HSRA and HSRC), a tracked air-cushion vehicle (TACV), as well as Short Take Off and Landing (STOL) and Vertical Take Off and Landing (VTOL) systems. The HSRA is defined as the existing Penn Central route from Washington to Boston upgraded to permit runs at 150 mph, while HSRC and TACV utilize a completely new route that will permit travel at 200 mph and 300 mph respectively. For analyses purposes these transportation technologies have been combined into the transportation system simulation runs shown in Table [1].

The approach followed in this research is the quantification of only the incremental cost impacts of each transportation system alternative over and above the effects of the 1975 base (null) case. The assumption thus made is that external costs and benefits of the base case system can be considered as 'sunk' effects of systems that will certainly be in existence by 1975. Because the analysis is restricted only to incremental costs and benefits, the external effects associated with the null system need not be isolated for the analyses. All costs are expressed in constant 1970 dollars.

Table 1
Northeast Corridor Transportation System Alternative

Transportation system (NECTP run no.)	1975 CTOL bus auto	Transportation Mix						
		HSGT modes				New air modes	
		DEMO	HSRA	HSRC	TACV	STOL	VTOL
R101[a]	x	x						
R102	x	x					x	
R103	x		x				x	
R104	x			x			x	
R105	x				x		x	
R106	x	x					x	x
R107	x		x				x	x
R108	x			x			x	x
R109	x					x	x	x

[a]Base case.

The scope of the analyses has been restricted to the major environmental and social cost impact categories that would arise from the operation of the Northeast Corridor Transportation System, and thus some aspects regarding disruptions during the construction system and diffusion of innovations arising from the project have not been considered. An exception is the estimation of employment construction benefits from the project, by employing otherwise unemployed resources, mainly in the twenty-mile tunneling construction activity. However, according to an earlier research of ours,[5] these employment benefits are very small amounting to $0.73 annual millions of 1970 dollars during the 1972 to 1975 construction period.

Another important external effect excluded from the analyses concerns the dislocation of households and businesses through construction of the transportation systems. These dislocation effects include a mix of real and distributional effects.[12] The real effects including (a) the direct property losses of the affected parties along the right of way; (b) the moving costs of relocatees, both households and businesses; (c) the grief of relocatees; (d) utility losses caused by the loss of preferred locations of relocated households, and (e) increased transaction costs of relocatees. Distributional dislocation effects include higher housing prices in the affected neighborhoods and loss of markets to businesses, and of wages to the residents who remain in the affected neighborhoods.

Since this analysis is concerned only with nonpecuniary externalities and since the major real dislocation effects—such as direct property losses and moving costs—are to be included in the direct systems costs of the alternative transport systems, no major exceptions from the results of the following analyses are expected.

NOISE IMPACTS

Alternative modes of transportation can be sources of disturbing noise. The quantification of the noise effects of alternative transportation system technologies in this section is limited to incremental costs of new transportation modes. As stated previously, the effects of all base case transportation are assumed to be sunk.

Although it is possible to measure in physical terms the impact of noise on the surrounding environment, determining dollar measures of noise impacts is more difficult. Most analyses of dollar impacts of environmental effects focus on the relation between environmental effects and their capitalization into land values. It is assumed that the market mechanism will operate through land and property values to capitalize the external disbenefits of noise, since noise, pollution, and aesthetics affect the amenities of residential land uses, and amenities are the major components of residential land values.[7] A difficulty in developing dollar measures of noise impacts in this way arises because of the changes in accessibility and land use that accompany construction of transportation facilities such as airports, etc.

In general, there are two types of effects of transportation facilities on property and land values:

> an accessibility effect, which makes the area surrounding the transportation facility more productive, and is sometimes reflected in changes in land uses in the affected areas; and

> a neighborhood disturbance effect, which is characterized by increases in noise, air pollution, and aesthetic and safety effects on the adjacent area.

The net effect on property and land values depends, of course, on the mix of these two effects. With airports, for example, the increases in accessibility are typically claimed to outweigh neighborhood disturbance effects, while with railroad construction, where accessibility increases are restricted only to areas near stations, the neighborhood disturbance effects predominate.

Noise Effects of High-Speed Ground Modes

This section analyzes the noise impacts of alternative surface modes—HSRA, HSRC, TACV—by measuring the physical noise effects of each mode and the impact on land values of the affected area. The external costs of DEMO rail are assumed to be sunk.

One of the peculiarities of the noise impact analysis of alternative rail modes is that no major changes in accessibility of the affected areas occur, so that there is no problem in separating noise effects from accessibility impacts on land values. The area near or around stations is an exception, of course, since such areas experience changes in their accessibility potentials.

An earlier study of urban expressways' environmental effects on land values in the city of Chicago[12] found the land value differential between similar lots in the first and fifth block from a major expressway to be one per cent for surface and depressed highways and a four per cent differential for elevated highways. Assuming 400 ft per block in the city of Chicago, the outdoor perceived noise level in PNdB falls from eighty-two db in the first block to sixty-eight db in the fifth block; that is a decrease in noise levels of approximately seventeen per cent. Thus, the one per cent and four per cent land value differentials for surface/depressed and for elevated highways, respectively, are equivalent to noise elasticities of −0.06 and −0.24.

In another investigation of the impact of railroad noise for the Northeast Corridor Transportation Project, Resource Management Corporation[11] developed an estimating procedure that allows dollar measurement of the environmental noise impacts. Using regression analysis techniques on property along existing railroad rights-of-way, RMC found that the elasticity impact of increases in perceived noise levels (PNdb) on residential property values ranges from −0.10 to −0.20; that is, a 100 per cent increase in noise level diminishes long-term residential property values by ten to twenty per cent. These noise elasticity parameters are in general agreement with the conclusions of the research on the effects of air pollution on land values discussed later.[14] Thus, the costs of noise are capitalized in residential property values, and the dollar impact of increased noise from the HSRA, HSRC, and TACV can be ascertained. It is worthwhile noting that we assume no major noise impact on farm, commercial, and industrial property values along the right-of-way, since these land uses are not altogether incompatible with the noise created by the three alternative surface modes under consideration. The effects of noise on commercial and industrial land are much more diverse than the effects of residential land, and require separate studies.

High-Speed Rail A

The high-speed rail system using the present right-of-way (improved) is assumed to have perceived noise levels of approximately ten PNdB below the noise level of diesel freight trains that currently use the right-of-way, as shown in Fig. 1. Even if these levels are corrected for the number of hourly occurrences of the intermittent noise—by assuming two to seven HSRA passenger trains per hour and less than 0.2 freight trains per hour, HSRA will not contribute

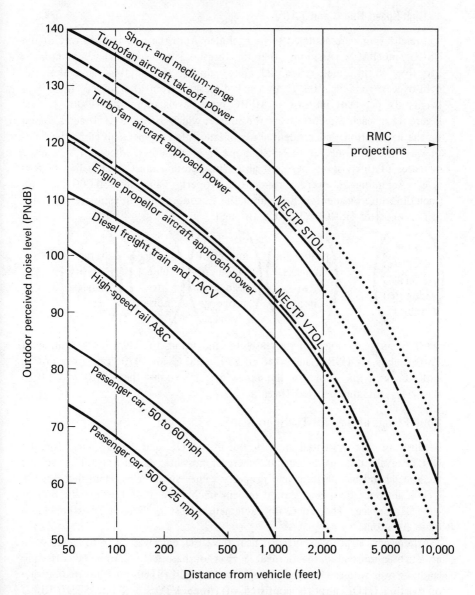

Figure 1. Typical PNdB values for vehicle noises heard at a distance.

significantly to an increase in noise along the existing right-of-way. Thus, HSRA will have no effect on noise levels along the improved right-of-way.

High-Speed Rail C and TACV

Freight trains are assumed to be excluded from the new right-of-way of the HSRC and TACV. Assuming that the threshold background level of noise is fifty-five db in quiet residential areas[2] during the daytime, and that the right-of-way extends 100 ft in each direction from the source, there is a twenty-six per cent increase in HSRC noise levels more than 2,000 ft (see Figure 1) in each direction from the source, which affects 31,150 acres. Based on the assumption that residential use of land is twenty per cent along the right-of way, the area subject to HSRC noise is 24,000 acres, whereas TACV noise increases of thirty-seven per cent above background noise levels affect 66,820 acres. Assuming an average residential property value of $60,000 per acre (including improvements) throughout the Corridor, one can estimate the range of noise cost of HSRC and TACV through:

$$
\begin{pmatrix} \text{total} \\ \text{decrease} \\ \text{in} \\ \text{residential} \\ \text{values} \end{pmatrix} = \begin{pmatrix} \text{proportion} \\ \text{increase} \\ \text{in} \\ \text{noise} \end{pmatrix} \begin{pmatrix} \text{elasticity} \\ \text{impact of} \\ \text{noise on} \\ \text{residential} \\ \text{property} \\ \text{values} \end{pmatrix} \begin{pmatrix} \text{acreage} \\ \text{subject} \\ \text{to} \\ \text{noise} \end{pmatrix} \begin{pmatrix} \text{average} \\ \text{property} \\ \text{values/} \\ \text{acre} \end{pmatrix}, \quad (1)
$$

which results in ranges of decreases in land values of $39 to $78 million of 1970 dollars for HSRC, and $148 to $297 millions of 1970 dollars for TACV, with the extreme values of the range determined by the -0.10 and -0.20 elasticity estimates referred to earlier.

Noise Effects of New Air Transport Modes

Because of the potential noise problem, VTOL and STOL ports for the NECTP evaluation were located, wherever possible, at existing CTOL airport facilities. Land use patterns and property values are already established for the CTOL air operations and should remain unchanged after the introduction of V/STOL service. Therefore, no incremental cost or benefit is estimated at these locations.

Where new airports are needed near the CBD, care was taken to locate them at existing railroad yards or near a river or harbor to permit takeoffs and landings over water. The resulting number of VTOL/STOL ports located outside of existing CTOL airports consisted of: three VTOL and one STOL River/ Harbor Ports near the CBD, and four VTOL and one STOL New Suburban Ports.

Residential property values per acre of $50,000 were assumed for suburban areas, and $100,000 near the CBD, plus residential acreage proportion of the impacted noise areas as twenty-five per cent in the impacted area near the

CBD, and 6.5 per cent in the impacted suburban area. Using the noise contours shown in Figure 1 for VTOL and STOL and assuming fifteen-acre VTOL ports with twenty-five-degree take-off angle, and twenty-five-acre CBD and 100-acre Suburban STOL ports both with ten-degree take-offs, the sizes of the impacted areas were computed for each type of port.[4] It was further assumed that all CBD ports would be surrounded by one hundred acres of commercial and industrial properties as a buffer to residential land uses. Conversion of the noise impacts on lands outlying the buffer areas into the physical and dollar cost of noise estimates shown in Table [2] was performed through equation (1). Resulting decreases in land value per STOL port range from $5.65 to $11.30 millions of 1970 dollars in suburban ports to $3.45 to $6.90 per CBD STOL port. Comparable figures for VTOL ports range from $0.35 to $0.70 millions of 1970 dollars per suburban VTOL port, to $0.45 to $0.90 for river or harbor sites near the CBD, to $3.0 to $6.0 millions of 1970 dollars for CBD inland VTOL ports. All the noise impact results are summarized in Table [2].

AIR POLLUTION IMPACTS

Methodologies for Imputing Social Cost Impacts

The estimation of dollar value impacts of air pollution has generally followed two main approaches. One approach to the estimation of air pollution externalities relies on the comparison of the direct, out-of-pocket costs of living among areas with different air pollution levels, focusing on expenditures such as house painting costs, car wash outlays, curtain cleaning, and general house cleaning expenditures among others.[15] This approach, however, does not take into account the impacts of air pollution on health and on the quality of life in the affected neighborhood, and their inclusion along with property value effects would lead to double counting.

An alternate approach concerns the impact of air pollution on residential land values by assuming that the additional costs associated with living in an area with high levels of air pollution would be reflected in its property values. A study of Ridker and Henning[14] on the effect of sulfates on land values conducted in St. Louis, estimated that for single-family units, a decrease in SO_2 exposure of 0.25 mg per 100 cm^2 per day would result in an increase in property value of $245. These figures result in elasticity ranges from -0.05 to -0.10; that is, a one hundred per cent increase in air pollution level will decrease property values by five to ten per cent. It should be noted that the approach we have followed considers only the incremental effects on the environment above the effects already occasioned by the null case of transport systems.

Table 2
Summary of Noise Effects of NEC Transportation System Alternatives

Effects on noise levels	R102	R103	R104	R105	R106	R107	R108	R109
Physical increase in Noise Level (per cent)								
• HSRA		0				0		
• HSRC (31,150 acres)			26				26	
• TACV (66,820 acres)				37				37
• STOL								
(1) CBD Port (5,000 acres)	28	28	28	28	28	28	28	28
(1) Suburb Port (63,000 acres)	28	28	28	28	28	28	28	28
• VTOL								
(2) CBD land ports (11,000 acres)					22	22	22	22
(3) CBD water ports (4,050 acres)					20	20	20	20
(4) Suburban port (22,000 acres)					22	22	22	22
Cost of Increased Noise[a] (millions of 1970 dollars)								
• low-estimate range	10	10	50–60	100–200	20	20	60–70	170–210
• high-estimate range	20	20	100–120	320–390	40	40	120–140	340–410

[a]Effect on residential property values only.

Effects of Ground Surface Technologies

The air pollution effects of HSRA, HSRC, and TACV are composed of two offsetting impacts, namely: (1) reductions in CO and hydrocarbon emission to the diversion of automobile and bus traffic to the alternative surface systems, and (2) increases in air pollution caused by the increases in SO_2 emission from the power plants that supply the alternative surface modes.

The effects of reducing air pollution through the diversion of automobile and bus traffic was found to be nil. For example, in NECTP Run 105, the best HSGT case, 1.4 million passenger miles per day are diverted away from highways to the TACV. Using 2.5 passengers per vehicle and 1,000 miles of interstate highway, 0.5 million vehicle miles per day or 500 vehicles will be diverted. The emission rate for gasoline-powered passenger cars is greater than that for diesel buses with respect to hydrocarbons and CO so the assumption will be made that all 500 vehicles are all automobiles to provide a worse case estimate. Using 500 vehicles per day and average emission rates of 0.0070 lb per vehicle miles of hydrocarbons and 0.076 lb per vehicle mile of carbon monoxide,[21] the following emission rates per mile emerge:

hydrocarbons: 3.5 lb per mile per day, and
carbon monoxide: 38.0 lb per mile per day.

Both of these rates would be very small compared with any urban and suburban concentrations along the corridor. According to the US Public Health Service, projected 1975 carbon monoxide mean emission density over the entire Washington SMSA will average 23,000 pounds of CO per day per square mile, with emission densities in the suburbs as high as 10,000 pounds of CO per day per square mile.[20] Therefore, substantial automobile traffic must be diverted before a dent is made on the air pollution levels of our urban and suburban areas. Turning to increases in pollution due to emissions from power plants serving alternative high-speed surface modes, the following power requirements emerge:

System alternatives	Daily power requirements
High-Speed Rail A	300,000 kwh per day
High-Speed Rail C	410,000 kwh per day
TACV	1,780,000 kwh per day

The assumptions of heat rates of 9,000 btu per kwh[18] and conversion factors of 26×10^6 btu released per ton of coal burned, coupled with emissions of 78 lb of SO_2 per ton of coal burned (corresponding to two per cent sulphur content in coal,[21] result in the following emission rates at each of five power stations assumed to serve the system's requirements:

System alternatives	Emission rates in tons of SO_2 per day at each of five stations	Increase in SO_2 emissions at power plants
HSRA	0.7	$\leq$ + 1 per cent
HSRC	1.0	$\leq$ + 1 per cent
TACV	2.7	1 per cent

Compared with SO_2 emissions of 98,000 tons per year for typical plants in the major Northeast Corridor urban areas,[18] the resultant increase in air pollution is negligible for the three alternative surface systems.

Air Pollution Effects of Air Transport Modes

The same methodology used to compute pollution reduction along interstate highways resulting from diversion of traffic to VTOL and STOL modes was used for the HSGT modes. In Run 106, both the VTOL and STOL alternatives are introduced to the 1975 base case and divert 5.2 million passenger-miles away from auto traffic. Using the same 2.5 passenger occupancy figure and 1,000 miles of interstate highway, the reduction in the average emission rates is estimated to be:

> hydrocarbons: 14.6 lb per mile per day, and
> carbon monoxide: 158 lb per mile per day

While these decreased pollution levels (less than or equal to two per cent for CO in the suburbs) are higher than those occurring for the HSGT modes, they are still too small to have any effect on the value of real estate along the interstate highway networks.

The major air pollution effects of VTOL and STOL aircraft occur through their carbon monoxide emissions. According to the Public Health Services,[21] a jet aircraft below 3,500 ft emits 20.6 lb of CO per flight. If these high jet-aircraft CO emission rates are applied to the thirty-eight flights per day from twenty-nine VTOL ports and thirty-two flights from thirteen STOL ports, the carbon monoxide emission rates that emerge are 782 lb per day for VTOL and 660 lb for STOL port. The increases in air pollution levels at each port are calculated from

$$\text{increase in CO levels} = \frac{20.6 \times \text{number of flights}}{(\text{air pollution levels at nearby area to station})}$$

Project carbon monoxide emission densities in Washington, D.C., for 1975 in pounds of CO per day range from 10,000 in the suburbs to more than 100,000 in the areas surrounding the CBD.[20] These figures suggest increases in carbon monoxide emission densities of less than one per cent at the CBD ports, and of less than eight per cent in the area immediate to VTOL suburban ports and seven per cent at STOL suburban ports. Thus, the air pollution impacts of VTOL and STOL, while slightly greater than the other surface systems, are so small as to be considered negligible.

A summary of the relative air pollution effects of alternative transportation systems appears in Table [3]. Again, it should be emphasized that reducing automobile and diesel bus traffic will reduce CO and hydrocarbon pollution by very small amounts, and replacing it with any of the electric-powered systems will increase the sulfur oxide pollution by very small amounts; the net impact on pollution is extremely small.

SAFETY IMPACTS

The quantification of dollar safety impacts of transportation system technologies has generally followed the estimation of the present value of earnings losses due to accidents,[13] plus injuries costs and property damage costs.

Ground Surface Technologies

The two high-speed rail technologies differ apart from their technologically induced safety characteristics in that grade-crossing elimination benefits will arise from the improvements implied in High-Speed Rail A. In addition to

Table 3

Summary of Increases in Air Pollution Levels of Transportation System Alternatives 1975 (in per cent)

Effects on air pollution levels	R102	R103	R104	R105	R106	R107	R108	R109
Effects on Carbon Monoxide Levels								
• Diversion of Conventional Surface Traffic from Highway Arteries (reduction in pollution)	Negligible	Negligible	Negligible	Negligible	≤2	≤2	≤2	≤2
• Increases in STOL Pollution								
• CBD Stations	≤1≥7	≤1≥7	≤1≥7	≤1≥7	≤1≥7	≤1≥7	≤1≥7	≤1≥7
• Suburban Stations					≤1≥7	≤1≥7	≤1≥7	≤1≥7
• Increases in VTOL Pollution								
• CBD Stations					≤1≥8	≤1≥8	≤1≥8	≤1≥8
• Suburban Stations								
• Effects on Sulfite Emissions from Power Plants HSGT modes)	—	≤1≥	≤1≥	1	—	≤1≥	≤1≥	1
• Effects on Decreases in Land and Property Values	Negligible	Negligible	Negligible	Negligible	Negligible	Negligible	Negligible	Negligible

reducing the accident rate of HSRA relative to the existing DEMO rail, the freight trains that use the improved right-of-way no longer will experience the dangerous grade crossings. Thus, seventy-six grade crossings, that is, thirty private cross-buck crossings and forty-seven crossings protected with flashing lights and automatic gates will be eliminated in the HSRA mode.

The benefits from grade-crossing elimination amount to annual rates of $189,000 of 1970 dollars assuming both annual train accident rates of $0.0417 for private crossing and 0.2580 for the flashing lights and automatic gate crossings, while rates for accidents not involving trains were put at 0.0942 for private cross signs and 0.5830 for the flashing lights and automatic gate crossings.[25]

In making the projections for high-speed ground surface modes, shown, in Table [4], it was assumed that fixed train lengths and raised passenger platforms would reduce the accident rate on all new high-speed ground modes compared with existing rates. Also, the elimination of grade crossings and use of chain-link fencing along the right-of-way will further reduce HSRA, HSRC, and TACV accidents. A low accident rate of switching accidents was projected for TACV because of the limited number of switches along the routeway. Despite the increases in speed, present derailment rates were projected for the DEMO, HSRA, and HSRC modes. It is assumed that improved track and vehicle design will offset the effects of higher speed. A much lower derailment rate was assumed for TACV in comparison with the other high-speed ground modes, since the guideway is more stable, self-contained, and less susceptible to derailments. The vehicle is also physically larger than the rail vehicle and has a lower center of gravity.

For the same reasons that accident rates for new HSGT modes are projected below existing rail operations, mortality and injury rates should likewise be

Table 4
Summary Table of Accident Costs of Alternative Transportation Modes (1970 dollars)

Mode	Rates per million vehicle miles			Cost/accident	Cost/million vehicle miles	Cost/million passenger miles
	Accident	Mortality	Injury			
Auto	7.00	0.027	0.97	$ 810	$ 5,600	$2,270
Bus	7.53	0.154	4.23	2,900	21,900	702
CTOL	0.03	0.186	1.51	2,190,000	65,700	976
STOL	0.06	0.412	3.36	2,290,000	137,000	1,840
VTOL	0.20	0.908	7.41	1,700,000	341,000	6,030
DEMO Rail	16.12	4.020	14.76	26,200	420,000	2,590
HSRA	11.92	1.100	12.01	12,900	155,000	758
HSRC	11.84	1.080	11.69	13,500	160,000	784
TACV	10.78	0.790	10.72	13,200	141,000	523
Air (C/STOL)	—	—	—	—	—	1,650

lower. Improvements in station platform design, higher use of standard length trains, improved vehicle design, elimination of grade crossings, and the use of fences along rights-of-way, all should lead to a safer, more reliable operation with fewer accidents and deaths.

The accident, mortality, and injury rates of the conventional auto and bus modes shown in Table [4], correspond to intercity, turnpike, auto, and bus travel.[5] Average lifetime earnings losses in ground surface accidents were assumed as $92,600 in 1970 dollars in accordance with HEW projections.[10] Injury costs of $356 per person injured were assumed representative of auto and bus injuries.[17] Property damage costs per accident were projected at $400 for auto, $800 for bus, $2,945 for DEMO Rail, $3,870 for High-Speed Rail A, $4,440 for High-Speed Rail C, and $4,850 for TACV respectively.[5]

Air Transport Technologies

In projecting the safety considerations of air transport modes, we must analyze the specific safety characteristics of the 110 passenger DC-9 representing conventional take-off and land technology (CTOL), the 122-passenger STOL craft, and the eighty-six-passenger VTOL craft. It was further assumed that load factors of sixty per cent would be representative of all the air modes by 1975.

In projecting the safety record of CTOL aircraft, an assumption was made that the accident rate per aircraft mile would remain close to current levels, but that relative passenger loadings of CTOL aircraft would increase. That is, current mortality and injury rates would be multiplied by 1.24, the ratio of average CTOL loadings (sixty-six passengers) to current Class I Intercity Carrier loadings (53.3 passengers).

Problems arise in projecting accident rates for VTOL and STOL aircraft because both are basically new systems. VTOL aircraft can be compared with domestic carrier helicopter service. Accident rates for helicopters have dropped from 0.92 per million miles in 1961 and 0.51 and 0.60 in 1964 and 1967 to a current level of 0.50.[24] For this analysis, the accident rate for VTOL service in 1975 is estimated at one half the projected helicopter rate, or 0.20 accidents per million aircraft miles. For STOL service in 1975, the accident rate was assumed to be twice that of present CTOL aircraft.

To project STOL and VTOL mortality and injury rates, the CTOL mortality per accident and injury per accident rates were adjusted by the passenger loadings of VTOL and STOL relative to CTOL. Thus, the CTOL mortality and injury per accident figures were multiplied by 0.782 for VTOL and 1.11 for STOL to arrive at comparable rates for the new air systems.

The present value of lifetime earnings losses per air passenger mortality was projected at $241,000 of 1970 dollars, while average injury costs per person were projected at $541 by weighting the proportions of serious (two per cent) and minor injuries (ninety-eight per cent) in air transportation by their respective values.[1] Property damage costs of air accidents were estimated by assuming average aircraft ages of three years at time of accident, annual depreciation rates of twelve per cent, and that only fourteen per cent of the aircrafts would be destroyed, fifty-seven per cent would be subject to substantial damage, while the rest sustained minor damages.[24] The cost of accidents of all technologies is summarized in Table [4] showing VTOL as the most expensive system from a safety viewpoint (on a passenger mile basis) followed by DEMO rail and private auto.

To cost the safety implications of alternative modal mixes in the Northeast Corridor Project, the NECTP model runs were evaluated in terms of their safety impacts in Table [5]. Where the air (CTOL or STOL) mode is used, it was assumed that the mix is seventy-eight per cent STOL and twenty-two per cent CTOL. From the table of results we see that introducing new modes of transportation diverts some traffic away from existing carriers but also generates additional travel volumes. For the most part, total annual accident cost increases with the traffic growth. However, in Runs 103 and 105 the relative safety of HSRA and TACV modes is enough to offset not only increased traffic but also the more costly STOL air mode. The total annual system costs are lower for these two alternatives than the 1975 base case.

In the last rows of Table [5], the accident costs appear as a cost per passenger mile. Runs 103, 104, and 105 all show a net savings over the base case value of cost per passenger mile. The cost referred to here has been weighted by the passenger miles of all transportation modes used in the individual run. In effect, the cost data has been normalized to a per passenger mile basis across all modes of travel. In this analysis, the TACV (Run 105) gave the best cost per passenger mile value of all transportation alternatives considered in these test runs.

AIR TRAFFIC CONGESTION

One of the major benefits anticipated with the development and introduction of new transportation modes into the NEC is the diversion of passenger travel away from conventional air and the attendant reduction in air traffic congestion at the existing CTOL airports. This analysis provides estimation of benefits to aircraft operators and users as a function of reduction in CTOL traffic in the Northeast Corridor (NEC). It is assumed that the VTOL and STOL modes will not contribute to air traffic congestion at CTOL airports. This assumption is predicated on the use of separate runways and control systems for these modes.

An existing FAA Airport Delay Model[6] was used for this analysis to relate the annual delay at an airport to the annual number of operations for a fixed

Table 5
Annual Accident Costs of Alternative NECTP Transportation Systems

Mode	R101 (base)	R102	R103	R104	R105	R106	R107	R108	R109
Annual Passenger Miles (billions)									
Auto	14.08	13.87	13.76	13.64	13.57	12.21	12.13	12.10	12.10
Bus	1.81	1.77	1.75	1.73	1.71	1.83	1.46	1.45	1.45
Air (CTOL & STOL)	1.83	3.06	3.05	2.99	2.88	3.00	2.29	2.28	2.30
DEMO	1.68	1.64				1.67			
HSRA			2.49						
HSRC				3.37			2.05	2.80	
TACV					4.10				3.42
VTOL						3.39	2.86	2.85	2.85
System Total	19.40	20.34	21.05	21.73	22.26	22.10	20.79	21.48	22.12
Annual Accident Costs (millions of 1970 dollars)									
Auto	31.92	31.40	31.15	30.90	30.75	27.65	27.50	27.40	27.40
Bus	1.27	1.24	1.23	1.21	1.20	1.29	1.03	1.02	1.02
Air (CTOL & STOL)	1.79[a]	5.05	5.03	4.93	4.75	4.95	3.78	3.76	3.80
DEMO[b]	4.28	4.25				4.32			
HSRA[b]			1.70						
HSRC				2.64			1.46	2.20	
TACV					2.14				1.79
VTOL						20.45	17.25	17.19	17.19
System Total Cost	39.26	41.94	39.11	39.68	38.84	58.66	51.02	51.57	51.20
Net Savings (cost) over base	0	(2.68)	0.15	(0.40)	0.42	(19.40)	(11.76)	(12.31)	(11.94)
Cost per Million Passenger Miles (1970 dollars)									
• System Average	2,024	2,062	1,858	1,826	1,745	2,654	2,454	2,401	2,315
• Net Benefit (cost) over base	0	(38)	166	198	279	(630)	(430)	(377)	(291)

[a]CTOL only. [b]Less grade-crossing benefits.

Practical Annual Capacity (PANCAP). An operation can be either a takeoff or landing. To estimate the benefits of reducing NEC traffic, the following four steps are necessary.

1. estimate the Practical Annual Capacity (PANCAP) of each airport,
2. estimate total number of aircraft operations at each airport,
3. estimate the amount of NEC traffic that can be diverted to other modes of transportation, and
4. estimate the benefits that accrue with these diversions to both the NEC and the non-NEC conventional take-off and landing (CTOL) air traffic.

It should be noted that the analysis considers only aircraft congestion and specifically excludes congestion at the terminal and taxiing to and from the terminal.

Airport Capacities

The NEC airports that are expected to have excessive congestion delays in 1975 are Washington National (DCA), Philadelphia International (PHL), Newark (EWR), Laguardia (LGA), John F. Kennedy (JFK), and Logan International (BOS). The subsequent analysis is limited to these six airports, and as such, it underestimates the total benefits by ignoring such air carrier airports as Friendship, Hartford, and Providence. Approximate PANCAPs for each of the critical airports have been derived by the FAA as follows:

Airport	DCA	PHL[a]	EWR[a]	LGA	JFK	BOS
PANCAP	295,000	365,000	315,000	260,000	260,000	290,000

[a]These values of PANCAP include the effects of runway improvements already under construction.

Forecasting CTOL Operations

In estimating the amount of NEC CTOL traffic, two approaches were used. One of these involved the examination of CAB operational aircraft data.[3,5] and schedules, and completely ignores the outputs of the NECTP computer simulation. The other uses the NECTP runs. The results of the separate approaches are comparable.

The total number of CTOL operations at each of the critical NEC airports has been forecast for 1975 by the FAA and includes both traffic into and within the NEC.[6,9] One estimate of the NEC portion of this figure is obtained by tallying the number of scheduled arrivals at each of the six listed airports that departed from each of the other NEC airports taking sure to avoid

Table 6
1975 Estimates for Number of NEC Flights (thousands of operations)

	DCA	PHL	EWR	LGA	JFK	BOS
Upper estimate	83	100	54	89	54	144
Lower estimate	47	20	32	56	24	90
NECTP base case (Run 101)	65	76	43	73	36	43

double-counting caused by flights that had stopovers in two or more NEC cities. The number of operations computed in this way include those operations resulting from short legs of longer multi-legged flights; this projection of CTOL traffic, therefore, provides an upper bound for operation at each of the NEC airports.

A lower estimate for these operations was obtained from a ten-per cent sample survey of passengers traveling via the scheduled airlines, which gives the number of passengers, outbound and inbound, between each city pair. These figures are a conservative estimate of NEC traffic insofar as only scheduled airlines are considered.

To forecast the NEC CTOL flights for 1975, the assumption is made that both the upper and lower bounds are proportional to the ratio of 1975 to 1968 total operations forecast by the FAA. The result of applying these ratios is given in Table [6] and compared with the CTOL demand forecasts in Run 101 of the NECTP analysis. Agreement between the two sets is seen to be reasonable with the exception of Boston, for which the NECTP model run estimate is considerably lower than the independent forecast.

Impacts on CTOL Air Traffic Delays

Having established values for Practical Annual Capacities at the major NEC CTOL ports and using the NEC CTOL traffic forecasts, the amount of total delay (both NEC and non-NEC CTOL delays) at each airport was computed for each of the NEC alternative transportation system (NECTP Runs 102 through 109) using the FAA Airport Delay Model.[6] The results are summarized in Table [7].

Costs of Delay

Costs of CTOL air traffic delays are computed for both the added cost to airline operators and to the traveler. The cost to the operators for aircraft delays is computed separately for each NEC airport using the following extrapolations of FAA figures of direct and indirect costs. Passenger delay times

Table 7
Summary Effects of Alternative NEC Transportation Systems on Total NEC and Non-NEC CTOL Air Traffic Congestion

	R101 (Base)	R102	R103	R104	R105	R106	R107	R108	R109
Annual CTOL Delay									
Times (thousands of minutes)									
DCA	560	375	365	363	360	340	330	328	325
PHL	585	300	295	293	290	283	285	283	280
EWK	755	560	555	554	553	528	530	529	528
LGA	1,770	1,050	1,020	990	960	960	960	960	960
JFK	3,120	2,485	2,465	2,460	2,455	2,420	2,420	2,415	2,410
BOS	1,370	1,135	1,115	1,088	1,060	1,060	1,055	1,055	1,055
Annual Delay Costs									
(millions of dollars)									
Aircraft Delay									
DCA	3.05	2.05	2.00	1.98	1.97	1.87	1.81	1.80	1.78
PHL	4.45	2.27	2.23	2.23	2.22	2.19	2.21	2.20	2.20
EWK	7.35	5.45	5.40	5.38	5.37	5.12	5.15	5.14	5.12
LGA	11.04	6.87	6.73	6.47	6.20	6.20	6.20	6.20	6.20
JFK	44.60	35.40	35.07	35.01	34.94	34.44	34.44	34.38	34.31
BOS	11.45	9.46	9.29	9.06	8.83	8.83	8.71	8.71	8.71
Passenger Delay									
DCA	5.38	3.59	3.49	3.48	3.45	3.26	3.16	3.15	3.12
PHL	6.32	3.25	3.19	3.16	3.13	3.12	3.15	3.12	3.09
EWK	8.12	6.02	5.96	5.95	5.94	5.65	5.68	5.67	5.65
LGA	19.10	11.34	11.05	10.62	10.34	10.34	10.34	10.34	10.34
JFK	64.70	50.90	50.60	50.50	50.03	49.60	49.60	49.50	49.40
BOS	14.78	12.60	12.05	11.78	11.49	11.49	11.32	11.32	11.32
Total Delay Cost	200.35	149.20	147.06	145.62	143.91	142.11	141.77	141.53	141.24
Saving over Base Case	0	51.15	53.29	54.73	56.44	58.24	58.58	58.82	59.11

were translated to dollar costs using the \$13.50 per hour imputed value of time derived from the NECTP demand analyses exercises[23] and separate occupancy factors for each airport.

	DCA	PHL	EWR	LGA	JFK	BOS
Cost per minute operation 1975	5.46	7.60	9.75	6.46	14.20	8.35

Table [7] summarizes the total costs of CTOL air traffic congestion and shows the annual savings over the 1975 base case. As one would expect, the greatest impact occurs with the introduction of STOL service (R102) and VTOL service (R106) since the largest diversion of traffic away from CTOL occurs with these modes.

EFFECTS OF INTERSTATE HIGHWAY CONGESTION

Automobile traffic now represents more than three-quarters of all intercity travel within the Northeast Corridor; and this percentage is projected to increase by 1975 to 1980 as the interstate highway system is completed, unless significant improvements are made in the common carrier modes. Attendant with this growth will be inevitable increases in auto traffic congestion, especially during peak periods, degrading travel times not only for intercity passenger but also for urban commuters who use the interstate highway system in metropolitan areas. Therefore, any diversion of traffic away from the interstate highway system by a proposed alternative transportation system is a benefit accruable to the alternative. Benefits to the urban commuters are clearly external effects, while savings to the intercity traveler are direct user benefits that eventually must be evaluated through the demand analysis. In this study we investigate the highway congestion levels for each of the NEC transportation alternatives and quantify the benefits of shifting traffic away from intercity highways. Benefits are measured in time savings and then translated to dollar values.

The analysis is limited to congestion problems along the intercity and intracity expressways. No attention is given to impacts on urban streets and highways arising from shifts in NEC intercity auto traffic volumes or from introducing new transportation terminals into metropolitan centers. Also, this study does not trace the impact of reduced highway congestion to the problem of safety; nor is the effect on truck freight movement quantified. Presumably, both conditions would improve. However, from the initial findings of this analysis, it seems that benefits to passenger safety and truck delays would be slight.

Model for Expressway Travel

For purposes of this analysis, the impact on highway congestion resulting from traffic volume decreases is measured by changes in average trip times for both intercity users and urban commuters under four highway conditions:

> Category 1: Intercity Expressway—off-peak conditions
> Category 2: Intercity Expressway—peak conditions
> Category 3: Intracity Expressway—off-peak conditions
> Category 4: Intracity Expressway—peak conditions

Average operating speeds for each highway category were computed using an empirical model for traffic flow on freeways and expressways under uninterrupted flow conditions developed by the Highway Research Board Committee on Highway Capacity.[8] The model gives the relation between operating speed and the ratio of demand volume to capacity. For purposes of this study, all intercity portions of the NEC highway network are assumed to be four-lane, seventy-mph expressways; the intracity expressways (interstate highways within urban centers) are assumed to be six-lane, sixty-mph highways. However, the assumption of lane numbers is not critical.

For each of the four highway categories described above, the Highway Research Board (HRB) model can be approximated with the following linear relation:

$$S = S_b + \epsilon (r - r_b), \qquad (2)$$

where

S = speed of alternative transportation system,
S_b = base case average speed,
ϵ = speed coefficient,
r = new volume/capacity ratio, and
r_b = base case ratio.

Two substitutions are needed to make the model dependent upon shifts in NEC traffic volumes:

$$r - r_b = \frac{N + V}{C} - \frac{N_b + V}{C} = \frac{N - N_b}{C}, \qquad (3)$$

$$C = \frac{N_b + V}{r_b} = \frac{N_b}{kr_b}, \qquad (4)$$

where

N = NEC intercity traffic—new,
N_b = base case traffic,
V = urban commuter traffic,
C = design capacity, and
k = intercity portion of total traffic.

Substituting these into equation (2) the model for computing average trip speeds for the various transportation alternatives reduces to

$$S = S_b + \epsilon \left(\frac{N - N_b}{N_b}\right) kr_b. \qquad (5)$$

NEC intercity traffic is estimated to range between ten to twenty per cent (k = 0.1 to 0.2) of the total in metropolitan areas based on an unpublished study by Peat, Marwick, Mitchell, and Company, and a report by Wilbur Smith and Associates for the NECTP.[16] For the intercity portion of the NEC network, all traffic is assumed by definition to be intercity travelers (i.e., k = 1.0).

The speed coefficient defines the slope of the line for relevant ranges of r, using the operating speed ranges and values for r for each highway category; nominal speed coefficients are computed from the HRB curves:

$$
\begin{aligned}
\text{Intercity—off-peak,} \quad & \epsilon = -28 \\
\text{peak,} \quad & \epsilon = -37 \\
\text{Intracity—off-peak,} \quad & \epsilon = -25 \\
\text{peak,} \quad & \epsilon = -50
\end{aligned}
$$

To establish nominal base case values for S_b and r_b for the four highway categories the level of service criteria defined by the Highway Research Board was used.[8] Level of service B is in the higher speed range of stable flow. For freeways and expressways, it is defined as having operating speeds at or greater than fifty-five mph (fifty-five to sixty mph range used for this study) and that traffic volume not exceed fifty per cent of capacity. We shall assume that all traffic on the intercity expressways at off-peak conditions (category 1) meet the requirement for level B. The volume/capacity ratio for this category ranges from 0.35 to 0.50.

Level of service C occurs when further increases in demand volume are accompanied by a resultant decrease in operating speeds and a service flow rate not exceeding seventy-five per cent of capacity. Level of service C is assumed in this analysis to characterize average off-peak conditions on the expressway through metropolitan areas (category 3) with speeds from fifty to fifty-five mph and volume/capacity ratios ranging from 0.25 to 0.45.

For level of service D traffic operation approaches instability and becomes very susceptible to changing operating conditions. Operating speeds range from forty to fifty miles per hour and flow rates do not exceed ninety per cent of capacity. We assumed that level of service D is an adequate representation for intercity traffic operating at peak conditions and is used to characterize this. Volume/capacity ratios range from 0.75 to 0.97 for this category.

Level of service E is the area of unstable flow, involving overall operating speeds of about thirty to forty mph, and involving volumes approaching and at capacity. Although level E operation is unstable, it is found on many freeways under peak-period conditions where demand increases gradually. This level is used as the model for the NEC intracity/peak-period category of operation with volume/capacity ratios varying from 0.82 to 1.00 according to the overall operating speeds.

Substituting the parameters and coefficients computed above into equation (5) along with projected NEC traffic volumes, average speed increases for the four highway categories were computed. As one would expect, the most noticeable shift occurs during peak traffic conditions. However, the effect is less on urban expressways because of the predominance of non-NEC traffic, considered fixed for this analysis.

Trip Time Estimates

Changes in average trip times for both the intercity and urban commuter resulting from the estimated increased speeds are computed using the following model:

$$T = \frac{(1 - \alpha)D}{\beta_1 S_1 + (1 - \beta_1)S_2} + \frac{\alpha D}{\beta_2 S_3 + (1 - \beta_3)S_3} , \tag{6}$$

where

T = total trip time, hours;

D = average trip distance, miles;

α = per cent of trip on urban expressway;

β_1 = per cent of intercity travel at off-peak conditions;

β_2 = per cent of intracity travel at off-peak conditions;

S_1 = average speed on intercity expressway, off-peak;

S_2 = average speed on intercity expressway, peak;

S_3 = average speed on intracity expressway, off-peak; and

S_4 = average speed on intracity expressway, peak.

The average trip distance for intercity passengers is estimated to be eighty miles using NECTP model outputs. Of the total distance, fifty per cent is estimated to be through urban areas. The average trip distance for urban commuters is estimated to be ten miles. Since this is totally within the metropolitan area, no commuter travel is assigned to the intercity portion of the NEC network. For lack of actual data, it is assumed that for ninety per cent of the time intercity expressways will operate at off-peak conditions; seventy-five per cent for urban expressways.

Substituting values for all these parameters into equation (6), a range of average trip times was computed for the two user classes. Differences from the base case were then determined. Results for each of the transportation alternatives are given in Table [8].

Benefits of Congestion Time Savings

Dollar benefits of the estimated time savings are computed for each transportation alternative as follows:

$$B = T_n(N)(C_n) + T_u(U)(C_u), \tag{7}$$

where

B = annual benefit, dollars;

ΔT_n = time saved per intercity trip;

ΔT_u = time saved per urban trip;

Table 8
Summary of Impacts on Interstate Highway Congestion Resulting from Reduced NEC Intercity Automobile Traffic

	Base case R101	R102	R103	R104	R105	R106	R107	R108	R109
NEC Automobile Traffic									
· Annual Passengers, millions	173.8	172.3	171.4	170.6	170.1	159.1	158.4	158.1	157.9
· Percent Change	—	-0.0086	-0.0138	-0.0184	-0.213	-0.0846	-0.0887	-0.0903	-0.0915
Average Speed Change mph									
· Intercity—off peak (low)	—	0.072	0.116	0.155	0.179	0.711	0.745	0.759	0.769
(high)	—	0.120	0.193	0.258	0.298	1.184	1.242	1.254	1.281
· Intercity—peak (low)	—	1.238	0.383	0.511	0.591	2.348	2.461	2.506	2.539
(high)	—	0.309	0.495	0.660	0.764	3.036	3.183	3.241	3.284
· Intracity—off peak (low)	—	0.005	0.009	0.012	0.013	0.053	0.055	0.056	0.057
(high)	—	0.019	0.031	0.041	0.048	0.191	0.199	0.203	0.206
· Intracity—peak (low)	—	0.039	0.063	0.084	0.098	0.388	0.407	0.415	0.420
(high)	—	0.096	0.155	0.206	0.248	0.940	0.995	1.011	1.024
Average time Saved, minutes									
· Intercity Passenger (low)	—	0.03	0.11	0.18	0.21	0.77	0.84	0.86	0.87
Trips (high)	—	0.15	0.24	0.32	0.36	1.46	1.48	1.51	1.53
· Intracity Passenger (low)	—	0.01	0.01	0.02	0.01	0.04	0.04	0.04	0.04
Trips (high)	—	0.01	0.02	0.02	0.03	0.10	0.10	0.11	0.11
Annual Value of Time Savings, millions of dollars									
· Intracity Passenger (low)	—	0.69	0.75	1.54	1.79	6.13	6.65	6.80	6.87
(high)	—	1.29	2.06	2.73	3.06	11.30	11.72	11.94	12.08
· Intercity Passenger (low)	—	0.25	0.25	0.25	0.25	0.98	0.98	0.98	0.98
(high)	—	0.25	0.49	0.49	0.74	2.46	2.46	2.71	2.71
· Total Passengers (low)	—	0.94	1.00	1.79	2.04	7.11	7.63	7.78	7.85
(high)	—	1.54	2.55	3.22	3.80	13.76	14.18	14.65	14.70

Table 9

Summary of Costs and Benefits of Alternative NECTP Transportation Systems in 1975[a]

Effect	R102	R103	R104	R105	R106	R107	R108	R109
Safety Impacts (1975)	-2.2	0.15	-0.40	0.42	-19.40	-11.76	-16.31	-11.94
Noise Costs (1975-1980)	-2.3	-3.0	-22.0	-72.0	-6.0	-6.0	-23.0	-76.0
Air Pollution (1975-1980)	negl.	negl.	negl.	negl.	negl.	negl.	negl.	negl.
Air Traffic Congestion (1975)	51.05	53.29	54.73	56.44	58.24	58.58	58.82	59.11
Interstate Highway Congestion (1975)	1.57	1.75	2.50	3.00	10.50	11.00	11.21	11.32
Net External Benefits	46.7	52.2	34.8	-12.0	43.3	51.8	27.7	-17.5
Increased Annual Net Revenue of Common Carriers	-5.6	-117.5	-155.8	196.3	-27.2	-149.2	-197.8	-241.6
Annual Value of Travel Time Service	126.3	273.4	330.8	354.6	401.1	465.8	494.8	579.5
Totals	240.1	208.1	209.8	146.3	417.2	368.4	324.7	320.4

[a]Net effects over, 1975. Base case in millions of 1970 dollars.

N = annual NEC intercity trips;
U = annual urban commuter trips;
C_n = average value of time for NEC passengers; and
C_u = average value of time for urban commuters.

The number of annual urban commuter trips is estimated by factoring NEC traffic volumes using an average value for the intercity traffic ratio

$$U = \frac{N}{k} - N, \tag{8}$$

where $k = 0.15$.

The value of time for intercity passengers is estimated at $3.00 per hour based on a survey of fourteen studies reported by J. R. Nelson.[9] This is the upper end of a range of values reported for average automobile passengers. The value of time for the urban commuter is estimated at the lower part of the range at $1.50 per hour. It is assumed that these values are constant on all ranges of time saved.

Benefit calculations for each of the NEC alternatives are summarized in the first section of Table [8]. The range of values reflects the variance in two output parameters. Based on the results shown, one may conclude that the benefits to urban commuters arising from decreases in NEC intercity traffic are small. This does not mean that travelers on certain portions of the NEC highway system will not see significant improvements in travel time. Unfortunately, evaluations of individual links would involve a much more comprehensive analysis than was performed here.

SUMMARY OF EXTERNAL EFFECTS

The external costs and benefits emerging from each transportation system alternative are summarized in Table [9]. All impacts are expressed as annual rates, while the nonrecurring social cost effects (e.g., noise, pollution, aesthetics) are amortized over the periods shown in the summary Table [9]. To contrast the magnitude of external effects with the direct benefit impacts, Table [9] presents also the effects on the net revenues of common carriers taken from the results of the NECTP runs,[19] as well as annual values of travel time savings accruing to normal diverted and generated traffic during 1975. These figures were adjusted to avoid double counting of the interstate and air congestion reduction benefits.

In the calculation of travel time savings benefits values per passenger hour of $4.50 and $3.00 imputed from the NEC demand analyses were ascribed to rail and bus respectively as well as the earlier imputed figures for air and auto passengers. In computing benefits from mode diversion the time savings were valued at midpoint between the imputed value of time in each mode, whereas

Table 9

Summary of Costs and Benefits of Alternative NECTP Transportation Systems in 1975[a]

Effect	R102	R103	R104	R105	R106	R107	R108	R109
Safety Impacts (1975)	-2.2	0.15	-0.40	0.42	-19.40	-11.76	-16.31	-11.94
Noise Costs (1975-1980)	-2.3	-3.0	-22.0	-72.0	-6.0	-6.0	-23.0	-76.0
Air Pollution (1975-1980)	negl.	negl.	negl.	negl.	negl.	negl.	negl.	negl.
Air Traffic Congestion (1975)	51.05	53.29	54.73	56.44	58.24	58.58	58.82	59.11
Interstate Highway Congestion (1975)	1.57	1.75	2.50	3.00	10.50	11.00	11.21	11.32
Net External Benefits	46.7	52.2	34.8	-12.0	43.3	51.8	27.7	-17.5
Increased Annual Net Revenue of Common Carriers	-5.6	-117.5	-155.8	196.3	-27.2	-149.2	-197.8	-241.6
Annual Value of Travel Time Service	126.3	173.4	330.8	354.6	401.1	465.8	494.8	579.5
Totals	240.1	208.1	209.8	146.3	417.2	368.4	324.7	320.4

[a]Net effects over, 1975. Base case in millions of 1970 dollars.

in estimating generated time savings benefits the demand curve was assumed to be linear over the generated traffic ranges.

Significant benefits are achieved in the relief of NEC traffic congestion on both the interstate highway network and CTOL air corridor. The VTOL mode (see Run 106) has the largest impact on the highway traffic and STOL (R102) accrues the most benefit in relieving CTOL delay at the major NEC airports. Noise presents a most serious environmental cost, particularly for HSGT modes where rights-of-way pass existing residential neighborhoods. STOL and VTOL modes add less to the noise pollution because of their smaller impact areas.

The net external benefits from the NECTP transportation system combinations are dominated by the tradeoffs between environmental effects—particularly noise—and air and interstate traffic congestion. Based on the assumptions and methodologies used throughout this report, runs involving STOL and High-Speed Rail A (R103), and the combination of these two modes with VTOL (R107) dominate all other system combinations on the basis of external social costs and benefits. Tracked air cushion vehicles exhibit negative net external benefits during the 1975-1980 period—in whatever system combination this technology appears—because of the effect of noise.

The summary of direct and external benefit impacts presented in Table [9] shows how the environmental and other external effects are dominated by the more significant direct impact categories. Unfortunately the lack of time-phased projections on all the transportation system alternatives prevented the calculation of present values of the net benefits generated by each alternative system. If the ground surface rail travelers' time is valued at the low values mentioned earlier the combination of VTOL and DEMO Rail (Run 106) ranks first in 1975 net benefits. However, the order is significantly altered if higher values of time are imputed to the high-speed rail travelers, with the TACV and VTOL alternative (Run 109) outperforming all others at hourly time values of $7.70 or higher for high-speed rail travelers.

REFERENCES

1.   E. Bollay, and Associates, *Economic Impact of Weather Information on Aviation Operation,* prepared for The Federal Aviation Agency, September, 1962.

2.   Bolt, Beranek, Newman, Inc., *Analysis of Community and Airport Relationships/Noise Abatement, Vol. II, Development of Airport Noise Compatibility Criteria for Varied Land Uses,* Report No. BBN-1093, 1964.

3.   Civil Aeronautics Board, *CAP Air Traffic Activity,* fiscal year 1968, Washington, D.C., 1968.

4.   John N. Cole and Robert D. England, *Evaluation of Noise Problems Anticipated with Future VTOL Aircraft,* Aerospace Medical Research Laboratories, Air Force Systems Command, Wright-Patterson Air Force Base, Ohio, 1967.

5. Paul F. Dienemann and Armando M. Lago, *External Costs and Benefits Analyses, NECTP,* Northeast Corridor Transportation Project Report No. NECTP-224. Prepared for the Office of High-Speed Ground Transportation, Department of Transportation, Resource Management Corporation, Bethesda, Maryland, December, 1969.

6. Federal Aviation Agency, *Airport Capacity Criteria Used in Preparing the National Airport Plan,* FAA Advisory Circular AC No. 150/5060-1, November, 1966.

7. R. N. S. Harris, G. S. Tolley, and C. Harrel, "The Residence Site Choice," *Rev. of Econ. and Stat.,* May, 1968.

8. Highway Research Report, *Highway Capacity Manual 1965,* Special Report 87, Washington, D.C., 1965.

9. L. N. Million, et al., *A Suggested Action Program for the Relief of Airfield Congestion at Selected Airports,* FAA Report, April, 1969.

10. J. R. Nelson, "Values of Travel Time," in *Problems in Public Expenditure Analysis,* Samuel B. Chase (ed.), Brookings Institution, Washington, 1968.

11. Resource Management Corporation, *Cost-Estimating Relationships for High-Speed Ground Transportation Systems, Appendix D, Third Party Costs,* RMC Report No. UR-023, May, 1969.

12. ————, *Highway Improvement as a Factor in Neighborhood Change,* RMC Report No. UR-128, March, 1971.

13. D. J. Reynolds, "The Cost of Road Accidents," *J. Roy. Stat. Soc. 119.,* Part 4 (1956).

14. R. G. Ridker and J. A. Henning, "The Determinants of Residential Property Values with Special Reference to Air Pollution," *Rev. of Econ. and Stat. 49,* No. 2 (1967).

15. ————, *Economic Costs of Air Pollution,* Praeger, New York, 1967.

16. Wilbur Smith and Associates, *Highway Travel in the Washington-New York-Boston Megalopolis,* New Haven, Connecticut, 1963.

17. R. Strotz, "Urban Transportation Parables," J. Margolis (ed.), in *The Public Economy of Urban Communities,* Resources for the Future, Washington, D.C., 1965.

18. U. S. Department of Health, Education, and Welfare, Office of Assistant Secretary for Planning and Evaluation, *An Economic Analysis of the Control of Sulfur Oxide Air Pollution,* Washington, D.C., 1967.

19. ————, Office of Program Coordination, *Motor Vehicle Injury Prevention Program,* Report No. 1966-1, Washington, D.C., 1966.

20. ————, Public Health Service, *Calculating Future Carbon Monoxide Emissions and Concentrations from Urban Traffic Data,* Publication No. 999-AP-41, Washington, D.C., 1967.

21. ————, ————, *Compilation of Air Pollutant Emission Factors,* Publication No. 999-AP-42, Washington, D.C., 1968.

22. U. S. Department of Transportation, Federal Railroad Administration, Office of High-Speed Ground Transportation, *Northeast Corridor Transportation Project Report,* Report No., NECTP-209, Washington, D.C., December, 1969.

23. ————, ————, *Passenger Demand and Modal Split Models,* Northeast Corridor Transportation Project Report No. NECTP-230, Washington, D.C., December, 1969.

24. ————, National Transportation Safety Board, *Annual Review of U. S. Carrier Accidents Occurring in Calendar Year 1967,* Washington, D.C., 1968.

25. Alan M. Vorhees, and Associates, *Factors Influencing Safety as Highway-Rail Grade Crossings,* National Cooperative Research Program Report No. 50, Washington, D.C. 1968.

The Economic Benefits of a Methadone Clinic

Joseph F. Dzaluk

This paper, while suffering slightly by comparison with the work of professional researchers, is probably the best illustration in this volume of the complexities of social accounting.

The basic problem is clear, and apparently simple; to ascertain the net economic value of a methadone treatment center. The value of this study itself—if the result is valid—would be substantial. Drug addiction had reached epidemic proportions in the New York metropolitan area by 1970. Addict related crime—and its prevention—was a critical political issue. There was, however, considerable and often vehement disagreement on the counter approaches that should be taken.

Methadone maintenance clinics—a pragmatic system that essentially institutionalized addiction, but to a less harmful drug—were seen by many as an effective, albeit slightly morally stained, solution to a disastrous problem. However, the clinics required appropriations of public monies for the rather dubious purpose of maintaining drug addiction. Funds, particularly outside of New York City, were often difficult to obtain. Dzaluk's purpose was to examine the effectiveness of the clinics, on a purely monetary basis. It should be noted that a simple, instinctive view of the economics of such an operation suggested a very favorable benefit-cost ratio.

The actual application was far from simple. In contrast to the abortion issue explored in Arfania's paper, there were no statistics available. The researcher had to develop basic data through some form of interrogation of a group of subjects who were less than totally amenable to questioning.

Beyond the data difficulties were the moral and philosophical problems raised by several of the writers in this volume. It was evident to members of Dzaluk's social accounting class that he became emotionally involved in the project. This involvement is clearly shown in the single case interview reproduced here. Thus, there is a clear problem of keeping the researcher's bias out of the results. In addition, there were problems of defining "crime." It is not clear, for example, that a reduction in prostitution should be considered in the same light as a reduction in check forgery. (The popularity of the latter crime with addicts had not been perceived prior to the study, except by merchants in the New York area, who have become highly reluctant to cash checks.)

INTRODUCTION

This paper is an attempt to quantify the socioeconomic value of a Methadone Maintenance Clinic to a community.

The clinic selected for the study was the Methadone Maintenance Clinic established by St. Vincent's Hospital and Medical Center of New York—

Joseph F. Dzaluk is a student at New York University Graduate School of Business Administration.

SOURCE: Unpublished term paper prepared in connection with a course in socioeconomic accounting.

Westchester Branch (Harrison, New York). The Clinic is located at 350 North Main Street in Port Chester, New York.

Port Chester is a socially, economically, and racially heterogeneous community of 28,000 people. It is in the county of Westchester, situated on the boundary line between New York State and Greenwich, Connecticut on Long Island Sound, twenty-six miles east of New York City.

Three general theories were explored in the quantification of the economic value of the Clinic to the community. First of all, heroin addicts, once they are on a methadone maintenance program tend to secure legitimate employment, or if they are working, to increase their earnings. Secondly, heroin addicts were engaged in illegal activities before entering the program but that their behavioral pattern changed substantially once they were in the methadone program. Finally, the program provides a net economic gain to the local society.

The methodology of the study is as follows:

1. Of all the people in the program, determine how many people were working and how much they were making before they came into the program. Section I and Section III indicate the techniques which were designed to measure the weekly income of the individuals.

2. How were the individuals' earnings (from legitimate work) affected after entering the program? Section I and Section III contain summary data describing this change.

3. What were the total operating costs of the Clinic? Section II addresses this question.

4. What illegal activities were the individuals engaged in before they entered the program and what are they doing now in terms of illegal activities? Survey Form A was designed and techniques developed to determine quantitatively this form of activity. Section III and Appendix II* document this study.

5. If the illegal activity level of the addicts was reduced, how do the savings from such reduction compare with the costs of the Clinic? In a similar comparison, how does the total (out-of-pocket) cost to society (welfare and illegal activities) compare with the savings to society from the addiction program (in terms of welfare saved, less illegal activity, higher legal earnings, etc.)

The final conclusion of the paper is that the *clearly measureable savings to society* (those that can be objectively described in dollar terms) far outweigh the costs of the Clinic.

---

*Appendices are not included in this reprint of the paper.

SECTION I.   INCOME EARNED (FROM LEGAL ACTIVITIES) BEFORE ENTERING PROGRAM COMPARED WITH EARNINGS AT DATE OF STUDY

Some individuals were working before they entered the program. The amount of money they were earning before they entered the program and what they are earning now was examined from two independent studies. Section I addresses one study and Section III another.

In talking with staff members at the clinic, I was informed that every person coming into the program was interviewed and certain data gathered. One of the pieces of information which the staff secured was the weekly amount of income which the individual was making. In late 1972, the individuals were again interviewed to ask how much they were making. This data was recorded in their files. The personnel files were and are strictly confidential. However, the staff agreed to the following procedure which would provide the data, yet still maintain the confidentiality of the individual's file.

I designed a Data Sheet onto which the staff would transcribe certain statistical data, among which was salary earned by the individual before entering the program and the amount of money the individual was earning now. The first person entered the program on December 29, 1970, and is listed as Case 1. A summary of Case 1, the approximate weekly income of that individual before entering the program and now, along with his current status is listed, together with all 204 individuals who ever entered St. Vincent's Methadone Maintenance Program, in Exhibit 1.

The total weekly amount that all persons earned before they entered the program, when summarized from the 204 Data Sheets, is $4,700. On an annual basis this becomes approximately $244,000.

The total weekly amount that the persons earned once they had been on the program or before they left the program according to the 204 Data Sheets is $9,793. On an annual basis this is approximately $509,000.

Of the 204 persons who had entered St. Vincent's program since it was established, the following is a summary status report as compiled from the Data Sheets:

> 116 Currently in the program
> 51 Left the program
> 17 Transferred to other methadone maintenance programs
> 16 In jail
>   2 In college
>   1 In U.S. Navy
> ___1 In U.S. Army
> 204 Total

Exhibit 1

Case Number	Approximate Weekly Income (dollars)		Status
	Before	Now	
1	$ 0	$ 0	In jail
2	0	125	*
3	0	100	*
4	0	77	In Navy, parental support
5	0	125	Parental support
6	0	125	*
7	0	150	*
8	100	150	*
9	100	135	*
10	0	100	*
11	0	100	*
12	125	125	*
13	0	0	Full time student
14	0	120	*
15	0	150	*
16	0	0	*
17	125	175	*
18	0	0	Left program
19	0	0	Left program
20	0	0	Left program
181	0	0	Transferred to Providence, R.I.
182	0	0	*
183	125	0	*
184	0	60	*
185	90	115	*
186	90	0	*
187	0	0	*
188	0	0	Left program
189	0	0	Left program
190	0	0	*
191	100	113	*
192	110	110	*
193	0	0	Left program
194	0	0	In jail
195	0	0	Left program
196	0	0	Transferred to Peekskill
197	0	0	Left program
198	125	125	*
199	150	150	*
200	0	0	Left program
201	0	95	*
202	0	0	In jail
203	105	105	*
204	85	0	Transferred to Yonkers
Total	$4700	$9793	

* In Program.

Note: Cases 21–80 have been omitted.

Exhibit 2
St. Vincent's Hospital and Medical Center of New York—Westchester Branch

Name of Agency
Methadone Clinic

STATEMENT OF EXPENDITURES AND RECEIPTS

FOR THE PERIOD ___Jan. 1___ , 19 _72_ THROUGH ___Dec. 31___ , 19 _72___

UNDER TERMS OF A CONTRACT WITH THE _____Westchester_____

COUNTY MENTAL HEALTH BOARD

Complete five (5) copies for each contract, forward four (4) executed copies to the Mental Health Board. Follow instructions for proper completion of this form.

Average Number of Clients or Patients on Rolls during 19 ___72_ : ___113___

Description	Amount Budgeted for Year 19 72	Actual Amount Expended for Year 19 72	Amount Claimed for Year 19 72
PERSONAL SERVICES (Itemized on page 3)			
Professional T –4682	$ 86,602 T	$ 80,068.30	$ 80,068.30
Non-Professional	25,032 T	24,343.43	24,343.43
T + 982			
TOTAL—PERSONAL SERVICES	$111,634	/ $104,411.73	$104,411.73
FRINGE BENEFITS			
F.I.C.A. Tax T +200	$ 4,500 T	$ 4,422.71	$ 4,422.71
Health Insurance	1,700	936.49	936.49
Retirement	1,700	1,631.76	1,631.76
N.Y.S. Unemployment	1,000	47.50	47.50
TOTAL—FRINGE BENEFITS	$ 8,900	$ 7,038.46	$ 7,038.46
EQUIPMENT*	$ 200	112.00	112.00
OTHER EXPENSES			
Office Supplies and Expenses (Includes Janitorial Services) T +200	$ 1,950 T	$ 1,751.80	$ 1,751.80
Therapeutic and Diagnostic Drugs	6,000	5,677.02	5,677.02
Insurance*	1,400	632.40	632.40
Communications Expense (Telephone, Telegraph, and Postage) T +300	2,000	1,704.76	1,704.76
Utilities (Gas, Oil, Electric, Sewer and Water			
Travel	500	418.59	418.59
SUB TOTAL—OTHER EXPENSES	$ 11,850	$ 10,184.57	$ 10,184.57

*SCHEDULE MUST BE ATTACHED
LS-153 (1/73)

Exhibit 2 (Continued)

Description	Amount Budgeted for Year 19 72	Actual Amount Expended for Year 19 72	Amount Claimed for Year 19 72
OTHER EXPENSES (Continued)	$ 11,850	$ 10,184.57	$ 10,184.57
Rent	7,000	7,000.00	7,000.00
OVERHEAD			
Maintenance in Lieu of Rent*	12,788	12,788.00	12,788.00
Other Expenses* Lab & Med. T +3,000	7,970 T	7,671.50	7,671.50
TOTAL OTHER EXPENSES	$ 39,608	$ 37,644.07	$ 37,644.07
1. TOTAL EXPENDITURES	$160,342	$149,206.26	$149,206.26

LESS REPORTABLE INCOME:

Patient Fees	$ 5,660.76
Medicaid	132,595.00
Medicare	
Third Party Payments	
Sales: Direct	
Contract	
State and Federal Contracts and Grants (Specify)	
Other (Specify)	

2. TOTAL INCOME $ 138,255.76

3. NET AGENCY EXPENDITURES (Total Expenditures less Total Income—
   Item 1 minus Item 2) $ 10,950.50

4. LESS: Gross Payment Received from County (Do not deduct agency's
   contribution to County) $ 10,950.00

   NET AGENCY EXPENDITURES IN EXCESS OF PAYMENT FROM
   COUNTY (Item 3 minus Item 4) $ -0-

*SCHEDULE MUST BE ATTACHED

LS-153 (1/73)

SECTION II.   FINANCIAL STATEMENT OF EXPENDITURES AND BUDGET

Exhibit 2 is a Statement of Expenditures and Receipts for the period January 1, 1972 to December 31, 1972 for the Methadone Clinic operated by St. Vincent's Hospital and Medical Center of New York—Westchester Branch.

The statement was prepared by the Controller's office. Mr. Arnold Jorgenson, Controller of St. Vincent's Hospital provided the report which is Exhibit 2.

SECTION III.   ILLEGAL PATTERNS OF INCOME BY CATEGORY BEFORE ENTERING THE PROGRAM AND NOW

An important part of the research on the socioeconomic value of St. Vincent's methadone maintenance program was the attempt to determine what were the categories and dollar volume of illegal activity of the individual before he entered the program compared with the activities and weekly dollar amounts engaged in by the individuals once they were on the program.

In talking with the staff and with selected individuals on the program whom I knew, it was determined that an attempt could be mounted to secure hard data on this subject. The physical facilities also at 350 North Main Street where the Clinic is located, proved conducive to private, individual, and confidential interviewing.

With respect to the Bernstein Clinic, Medical M Group in New York City at 255 Third Ave., it was practically impossible to conduct any meaningful total survey of the individuals primarily because of the complete lack of physical facilities. There is only one room which the individuals walk into as they receive their medication. There are no conference rooms. The staff has but one separate room. All the interviews with individuals at Medical M were conducted by me off site.

I designed a survey form which became the basis for the collection of data from the individuals at St. Vincent's Clinic in Port Chester. This form was reviewed and refined in meetings with the staff and individuals at the Clinic. This survey form became Survey Form A and was reproduced for use by the individuals in Port Chester.

From March 26, 1973 to April 4, 1973 every individual enrolled in the St. Vincent's program and who came for medication was privately interviewed and briefed on the survey. A sealed cardboard "Tang" orange juice box with a "smile flower" placed on it by an individual was established for the survey participants to deposit their responses.

During this period, 106 interviews were conducted, and the responses placed in the box. Upon opening the box on April 5, 1973, there were eight who had refused to comment since they felt that their anonymity would probably not be protected. The number in the right hand corner of the form following the alpha designation A is simply a numerical designation I assigned the form upon removing them from the "Tang" box.

I summarized the data from the Survey Form A sheets into Exhibits.

Exhibit 3 is a summary of the results of the ninety-eight responses. The exhibit contains the category of activity, the weekly dollar amount illegally engaged in before entering the program, a percentage distribution of that amount, the weekly dollar amount now engaged in and a percentage distribution of that amount. It excludes the categories Working and Welfare.

Exhibit 3

	Weekly			
	Before		Now	
Category	Dollars	Per cent	Dollars	Per cent
Shoplifting	1,475	3.7	200	9.5
Burglary	8,125	20.5	210	9.9
Pickpocketing	715	1.8	15	0.7
Stealing from trucks	1,810	4.6	180	8.5
Stealing at work	1,540	3.9	100	4.6
Stealing, other	1,680	4.2		
Mugging	555	1.4		
Forgery	4,595	11.6		
Running numbers	500	1.2		
Gambling	627	1.6	300	14.3
Selling drugs	12,140	30.6		
Pimping	645	1.6		
Prostitution	2,710	6.8	1,050	49.7
Assault with a weapon	1,580	4.0	60	2.8
Borrowing	1,000	2.5		
Total	39,697	100.0	2,115	100.0

Exhibit 4 is the same as Exhibit 3 except it contains the two categories Working and Welfare which were excluded from Exhibit 3. The reason for doing this is to show in Exhibit 3 a distribution of all the illegal activities.

Exhibits 5 through 20 are details of Exhibit 4 by each category: Shoplifting, Burglary, Pickpocketing, etc. showing the case number from which it was derived, the amount the individual indicated he was involved in that particular activity before he entered the program and his involvement now.

SECTION IV. PERSONAL INTERVIEWS WITH INDIVIDUALS ON THE PROGRAM

During March and April, 1973 extensive and private interviews were conducted with individuals on the Methadone Program.

The range of previous usage of heroin ran from one year to eight years.

The results of the personal interviews substantiate the quantitative results of Survey Form A which was summarized in Exhibit 4 in Section III.

Note: Only selected exhibits are included here.

Exhibit 4

| Category | Weekly | | | |
| | Before | | Now | |
	Dollars	Per cent	Dollars	Per cent
Shoplifting	1,475	3.1	200	1.8
Burglary	8,125	17.2	210	1.9
Pickpocketing	715	1.5	15	0.1
Stealing from Trucks	1,810	3.8	180	1.6
Stealing at work	1,540	3.3	100	0.9
Stealing, other	1,680	3.6		
Mugging	555	1.2		
Forgery	4,595	9.7		
Running numbers	500	1.1		
Gambling	627	1.3	300	2.7
Selling drugs	12,140	25.7		
Pimping	645	1.4		
Prostitution	2,710	5.7	1,050	9.5
Assault with a weapon	1,580	3.3	60	0.6
Borrowing	1,000	2.1		
Welfare	3,187	6.7	2,611	23.7
Working	4,414	9.3	6,313	57.2
Total	47,298	100.0	11,039	100.0

Exhibit 9
Stealing at Work

| Case Number | Weekly Dollar Amount | |
	Before Entered Program	Now
A4	400	0
A13	50	0
A15	100	0
A27	50	0
A38	100	0
A66	120	0
A68	20	0
A69	100	0
A79	50	0
A88	50	0
A100	500	100
	1,540	100

Exhibit 10
Working

	Weekly Dollar Amount	
Case Number	Before Entered Program	Now
A83	Yes	Yes
A84	120	137
A85	0	50
A86	140	136
A87	150	150
A88	100	100
A89	75	154
A91	0	116
A94	104	0
A93	0	180
A95	0	75
A96	0	Yes
A98	Yes	Yes
A99	0	115
A100	200	300
A101	90	90
A102	Yes	Yes
	4,414*	6,313*

*Totals do not add because forty seven responses were deleted in this reprinting.

Exhibit 11
Mugging

	Weekly Dollar Amount	
Case Number	Before Entered Program	Now
A18	50	0
A28	250	0
A31	25	0
A45	25	0
A52	5	0
A91	175	0
A95	25	0
	555	0

Exhibit 12
Forgery

Case Number	Weekly Dollar Amount	
	Before Entered Program	Now
A10	2,000	0
A15	100	0
A18	700	0
A22	200	0
A28	100	0
A33	400	0
A39	300	0
A45	15	0
A104	75	0
A61	50	0
A65	200	0
A68	150	0
A73	Yes	0
A75	Yes	0
A86	200	0
A91	5	0
A93	100	0
	4,595	0

*Respondent answered question relating to commission of a specific crime with "yes" instead of the dollar amount requested. This explains the use of "yes" in this and the following tables.

Exhibit 15
Selling Drugs

Case Number	Weekly Dollar Amount	
	Before Entered Program	Now
A1	1,500	0
A8	200	0
A10	500	0
A13	50	0
A18	300	0
A20	105	0
A24	100	0
A25	300	0
A27	300	0
A28	175	0
A31	200	0
A32	100	0
A33	500	0
A36	250	0
A38	100	0
A40	700	0
A42	80	0
A45	250	0
A46	1,000	0
A47	50	0
A49	100	0
A50	1,200	0
A57	200	0
A54	200	0
A58	190	0
A66	200	0
A67	Undetermined	0
A68	90	0
A70	500	0
A73	Yes	0
A75	Yes	0
A78	Yes	0
A81	Yes	0
A85	250	0
A91	150	0
A92	150	0
A93	50	0
A95	300	0
A97	200	0
A99	500	0
A100	1,000	0
A102	Yes	Yes
A104	200	0
	12,140	0

Exhibit 16
Welfare

Case Number	Weekly Dollar Amount	
	Before Entered Program	Now
A57	185	0
A64	Yes	Yes
A65	250	0
A68	70	0
A70	70	0
A71	90	100
A73	Yes	Yes
A81	Yes	0
A85	0	50
A86	215	0
A92	0	75
A95	347	166
A97	242	242
A98	Yes	Yes
A101	55	0
	3,187*	2,611*

*Totals do not add because twenty three responses were omitted in this reprinting.

Exhibit 17
Pimping

Case Number	Weekly Dollar Amount	
	Before Entered Program	Now
A12	Yes	0
A27	Yes	0
A43	20	0
A54	500	0
A55	Yes	Yes
A104	125	0
	645	0

Exhibit 18
Prostitution

| Case Number | Weekly Dollar Amount | |
	Before Entered Program	Now
A22	1,050	1,050
A27	Yes	
A34	1,000	0
A45	10	
A46	400	
A90	250	0
	2,710	1,050

Exhibit 19
Assault with a Weapon

| Case Number | Weekly Dollar Amount | |
	Before Entered Program	Now
A18	100	0
A27	Yes	
A35	1,000	
A43	Yes, with a gun	
A44	400	0
A54	50	60
A91	30	0
	1,580	60

I would like to relate just one response in some detail.

The case involves a woman, age twenty-four. Let us call her Miss S. Miss S. began using heroin eight years ago. She is Jewish. Her father was disappointed at her birth since he desired, very strongly, a son. Miss S. indicated that she did not know her name until she went to school at the age of five. Her father called her "stupid" and that was the only name she responded to. Her father committed suicide while she was in grammar school. Miss S. dropped out of high school. She was a poor student and had no desire to learn. At age sixteen, Miss S. gave birth to a baby girl. The child is currently being taken care of in a full time nursery. She married. Miss S. then underwent a major

Exhibit 20
Other

| | Weekly Dollar Amount | |
Case Number	Before Entered Program	Now
A10 Borrowing	1,000	0
A18 Stealing	100	0
A23 Stealing	100	0
A25 Stealing	100	0
A35 Stick up pushers	Yes	
A39 Stealing from cars	150	0
A45 Ripping off pocketbooks	30	0
A49 Stealing from cars	200	0
A51 Borrowing	Yes	
A63 Borrowing	Yes	
A69 Stealing from cars	50	0
A70 Stealing from cars	Yes	
A89 Stole from parents	Yes	—
	1,680	0

operation, hysterectomy. She discovered that her husband was an addict upon returning from the hospital. She started taking heroin and within two years became a heavy user, taking approximately ten to fifteen bags of heroin a day. Miss S.'s total activity was in finding drugs. She contracted hepatitis, nearly died, then subsequently lost a kidney. During the past year Miss S. supported an addict who provided her with drugs. Miss S. has the following expenses: $50 a week to support her child, Tracy, in a nursery; $17 a day for her hotel room; before she entered the methadone program in October of 1972 she was paying a minimum of $50-60 a day for drugs; her support of the male addict runs $90 a week for his room at another hotel; she also gives him currently on the average of a minimum of $20 a day; Miss S. is in fear of the male addict. She has only one kidney, he is mean and knows that he can hospitalize her by a blow to the remaining kidney. Miss S. in desperation joined the methadone program. She could not continue to raise the $25,000 plus per year, for drugs and the other expenses. Miss S. is now a lesbian and has been taken care of and mutually cares for her companion. Miss S. is now completely turned off by men. She has shut down all social contact and lives on welfare and other women with minimum prostitution.

The results of almost all the interviews are essentially the same. The behavioral patterns of individuals change dramatically, in about one year after they are on heroin. It is then that the increased tolerance levels produce such high requirements that significant changes may be observed. The individual requires more heroin just to combat withdrawal effects.

He will generally not engage in any activities which bring attention to him. This was repeatedly proven in all the interviews. The now anti-social individual withdraws, hides, desires self-destruction and anonymity.

The 98 responses also indicate that an addict's criminal activities are principally in nonviolent crimes such as selling drugs, burglary, forgery and prostitution. He avoids those situations that expose him physically such as mugging or assault. Prostitution offers the safest form of income since the "victim" is one who is willing to cooperate in the "crime." Also, the drug user receives cash which can readily buy drugs.

In all the individual interviews, none of the respondents admitted to or indicated the commission of violent acts while on heroin (before entering the program) in order to secure money for drugs.

The twenty in-depth interviews also indicated that although the addicts all recognize the benefit of methadone in blocking their heroin urge, they still do not want to be on methadone. They cite some reasons as: "It is just as habit forming;" "I can't travel or go anywhere on a vacation unless I get methadone;" "It completely restricts me;" "It is harder to detox from methadone than from heroin." From heroin they stop getting violently ill after one week of detox from heroin, but with methadone they get sicker and the detox period runs over one month.

The advantages of methadone are that they can lead a half-way normal life; that they can take a few bags of heroin, stop and by staying on methadone not suffer the withdrawal effects from heroin. Also, they get a good high from heroin *and* methadone which does not cost as much; they do not have to hustle as much to attain the same result.

Another remarkable response from all the individuals interviewed was their conviction that they could control heroin and that heroin itself was not destructive to them. "Heroin does not kill anyone but the addict who doesn't know how to handle it." They all claim that it is the additive to the heroin that causes the problems, that is, the flour or quinine that is mixed in. They contend that it is the shooting ten to fifteen bags of flour or other "junk" directly into the blood stream that kills. One respondent indicated that he knew of a dealer who suspected that a user had been talking about where he was purchasing the dope and that the police were going to ask him about the dealer. The next bag contained white acid that was mixed with the heroin. The user died instantly of an "overdose."

Section Summary: The Socioeconomic Value of St. Vincent's Methadone Maintenance Clinic

The following is a compilation of the data gathered and exhibited in Sections I, II, and III.

Schedule I

Income Earned Now	$ 6,313*
Income Earned Before Entering	4,414*
Net Increase in Weekly Earnings	$ 1,899

*Cf. Exhibit 10, Section III.

Schedule II

Welfare Before	$ 3,187*
Welfare Now	2,611
Net Decrease in Welfare	$ 576

*Cf. Exhibit 16, Section III.

Schedule III

Illegal Activities Before	$39,697*
Illegal Activities Now	2,115*
Net Decrease in Illegal Activities	$37,582

*Cf. Exhibit 3, Section III.

Schedule IV

Schedule I	$ 1,899
Schedule II	576
Schedule III	37,582
Total	$40,057

Schedule V

Exhibit 2.0 Total Annual Cost Divided by 52 to Produce Weekly Cost	=	$ 2,869

Schedule VI

Gross Value of Program	$40,057
Cost of Program	2,869
Net Value of Program	$37,188

On an annual basis, the net value of St. Vincent's Hospital Methadone Maintenance Clinic at 350 North Main Street in Port Chester, New York is $1,933,770 to the community.

This analysis does not attempt to evaluate methadone maintenance as a treatment of heroin addicts from a medical, social, ethical, religious, or individual viewpoint.

However, from a socioeconomic point of view the evidence is overwhelming that the clinic is of substantial economic value to society.

According to the survey data, for every addict that the clinic treats annually, the community is saved approximately $20,000. This estimate is extremely conservative, for the following reasons: The amount in Schedule III under illegal activities engaged in by the individuals before entering the program is $39,697. Shoplifting, burglary, stealing from trucks, at work and other which comprise $15,345 out of the $39,697 was counted as the value made by the individual. In order for him to "make" or take home this amount, he had to steal at least three to four times that amount. For example, he may have taken a T.V. set that you paid $100 for. The addict receives at most $25 to $35 for the set when he fences it. A more reasonable approach from an accounting point of view would be to multiply the $15,345 by three at a minimum. If this approach is taken, then the weekly amount stolen from society is $46,000. This is the value lost by the citizen. On an annual basis, this valuation would raise the value of the clinic by about $1.6 million.

A second aspect not quantified is the economic effect of heroin contamination "saved" in society by having one-hundred addicts on methadone. In an interview it was determined that a brother got his own sister hooked. When I asked, "Why?", the response was "so my mother would get mad at her too."

CLASS DISCUSSION COMMENTS ON DZALUK'S PAPER

Some questions were raised about the possibility of dishonest replies to the questionnaires. Dzaluk had given consideration to that problem. The method of submitting responses allowed complete anonymity and the staff of the clinic confirmed that the patients apparently trusted the system. In addition, the results had a certain logical consistency. For example, the amounts of weekly income derived from illegal activities were usually given in round figures, e.g. $50 or $100; salary figures were stated (apparently gross) with somewhat more precision, e.g., $85 per week; while welfare amounts were usually given on an exact basis, e.g., $167 every two weeks. This would seem to coincide with the actual level of information that the patients possessed.

A review of the actual questionnaires indicated that in a number of cases, the addicts had answered "yes," to the commission of a given crime, rather than provide an estimate of the income earned. Dzaluk had assigned no dollar value to these answers. He might have assigned the average amount given by the other respondents. This procedure results in an understatement of the amounts of illegal income earned by the addicts. Since there were substantially more "yes" answers in the "before" category than in the "during" group, the treatment understates the apparent social gains of the program.

Some considerable discussion was given to the nature of "illegal" activities, particularly prostitution and selling of drugs. In the case of prostitution, several students argued that since it was essentially a consensual activity between both parties, it was not clear that a social gain would occur from reducing its incidence. It does seem clear that prostitution should not be considered as "anti-social" as robbery, pickpocketing, etc. It is interesting to note too, that prostitution was reduced less than most of the other "crimes" by the addiction control program.

Different points were raised in relation to including the amount of income earned from "selling drugs," as criminal activity. Again, the idea that it is an illegal activity that involves mutual consent places it in a somewhat different category than violent crime. However, the general reprehensiveness of drug selling, a feeling which was apparently shared not only by the class, but by many of the addicts was strong enough that most agreed it was "a crime." A methodological question was also raised. Drug sales are made to addicts. (Reflecting the attitude toward drug selling; some respondents indicated that only sold to established addicts, never to non-users). The incomes received from robbery, burglary, etc. of the other addicts are used to pay for the drugs sold. The question, then, was whether the inclusion of amounts received from drug selling as a measure of criminal activity was not, in fact, double counting.

An Analysis of the Costs of Public and Private Elementary School Education in New York City

Robert E. Kempenich
and
Arthur J. Blum

One of the most publicized "remedies" for the supposed ills of public school systems has been the introduction of a voucher system. Advocated by Milton Friedman, among others, the proposal would give parents a "voucher," redeemable for educational services at the school of their choice. Supposedly, the chosen school could be either public or private, although the use of the system itself would undoubtedly blur that distinction.

The proponents of a voucher system argue that many of the difficulties in the present public school systems are caused by the virtual monopoly on the supply of educational services (especially at the elementary level) held by the local public school system. The voucher system would produce a diversity of supply, competition for students, and presumably better education.

One barrier to the introduction of a voucher system is the apparent difference in the present costs of private and public education. The "value" of the voucher should not exceed the cost of public education, and should constitute full payment for the education. If parents were allowed to make additional payments beyond the voucher amount, it is argued that the voucher system would simply act as a subsidy to the existing private schools.

Most figures seem to indicate that the cost of private school education is considerably in excess of the amounts expended in public schools. The authors of this article, two students at the Graduate School of Business Administration of New York University, questioned this assumption. They hypothesized that a large part of the apparent difference in public and private school costs was due to the inadequacies of municipal budgeting systems. Private school tuition is essentially "full cost," while the published budget of the public system fails to reflect all the operational costs.

INTRODUCTION

Milton Friedman, the noted economist, once observed that many of the problems of our public elementary education system are symptomatic of any monopoly. To introduce an element of healthy competition, and hopefully

Robert E. Kempenich and Arthur J. Blum are students at the Graduate School of Business Administration of New York University.

SOURCE: Unpublished term paper prepared in connection with a course in socioeconomic accounting.

494

thereby improve the whole system, he suggested giving each parent a "voucher," equal to the cost of public education, that could be redeemed yearly at any school. At first, most parents would have little choice but to continue sending their children to regular public school. In time, however, it can be assumed that groups of concerned parents would form, pool their vouchers, and start new schools to compete with the existing system. These new schools, and any private schools that wanted to join the system, would have to meet minimum curriculum standards and agree to accept the voucher as full payment.

The goal of this report is first to calculate the real per student per year costs of elementary public and private school education, and then compare them, with a view toward possible adoption of the voucher system.

Summary of the 1970–1971 New York City, Board of Education Budget

Direct instructional expenses	
High schools	$ 488.8 million
Junior high and elementary schools	903.7
Indirect expenses	
Interest on and repayment of debt	151.0
Central administration	94.9
Directed subsidies	
Federal Title I	117.7
New York State incentive programs	58.5
Total	$1,814.6 million

Besides the unweildiness of dealing with any $1.8 billion budget, several impediments to a direct calculation of the cost of public elementary school education were found.

First, major portions of the budget, specifically those labeled "indirect expenses" above, are school-wide, only a part of which should be charged to elementary schools. In general, these expenses were allocated among high school, junior high school, and elementary school on a per student basis.

Second, all direct educational expenses are accounted for through 31 independent community school districts, each of which contains different numbers of elementary and junior high schools. Allocation of these costs on the same per student basis could be only partly used, as it is generally agreed that it costs more to instruct an older student.

Third, the distribution of state and federal grants cuts across grades, and is dispensed according to need. The elementary school share of these funds had to be computed from a given breakdown of needy students.

A fourth impediment to any calculation of the cost of public elementary education is that a major expense—depreciation of school buildings—is not recognized in the operating budget. To adjust for this required the adoption of several assumptions relating to construction costs, useful lives, and salvage values. Those assumptions, as outlined in Schedule G, should be the only controversial portions of this report. Previous studies have not recognized depreciation as an expense, wherein, it is hoped, lies the uniqueness of this report.

The outline below develops a per student per year cost of elementary public school education of $1,363, comprised of $1,231 as the elementary school fair share of expenses recognized in the budget, plus a $132 per pupil depreciation charge.

Ingredients of the Cost of Public Elementary Education

	Total	Per Student
Recognized in budget		
Federal grants (Schedule A)	$ 66.3 million	
State grants (Schedule B)	27.6	
Interest expense (Schedule C)	17.5	
Central Administration (Schedule D)	51.8	
District costs (Schedule E)	240.5	
Instruction (Schedule F)	370.5	
	$774.2 million	$1,231
Not recognized in budget		
Depreciation (Schedule G)	$ 83.0 million	$ 132
Total	$857.2 million	$1,363

PRIVATE SCHOOLS

The calculation of the per student per year cost of private elementary school education is considerably more difficult because New York City private schools are so many and so varied. Some have independent accounting systems, but many, especially those affiliated with religious orders or private high schools, do not. Basic tuitions vary markedly from school to school. And, most have a sliding scale that increases according to grade level. Many schools, typically those affiliated with religious groups, operate at a loss, which is made up by charitable contributions and/or subsidies. Most schools grant full or partial scholarships.

Many of the sectarian schools provide room and board for their cadre, but often obtain their services at well below market rates. In addition to tuition, parents at some schools are required to purchase low interest or interest-free bonds. At some a charitable contribution of a specified amount is mandatory.

To overcome these obstacles the authors decided to select for analysis and comparison one private school fairly representative of private schools in general. The school selected had to have an independent accounting system, not be affiliated with a religious organization, and not run at a significant loss.

The Village Community School, which was organized in 1970 by a diverse group of concerned parents, was chosen because it purchased its school building, and hired its staff, at close to current market rates.

Because the organizers set tuitions so as to breakeven, the average tuition for grades kindergarten through six was accepted as the true cost of private elementary education in New York City, with adjustments for five exceptions:

1. "Breakeven" assumed charitable contributions of $15,000 per year.

2. Scholarships totaling $34,000 were granted.

3. A $500 interest-free bond had to be purchased for each student.

4. Depreciation on the building is not considered.

5. The mortgage was obtained at a rate well below fair market.

The outline below develops an average per student per year cost of private elementary education for grades K through 6 of $1,543.

Ingredients of the Cost of Private Elementary Education

Average tuition (Schedule H)	$1,471
Contributions (Schedule I)	72
Depreciation (Schedule J)	86
Scholarship aid (Schedule K)	(162)
Interest-free bond (Schedule L)	31
Mortgage rate adjustment (Schedule M)	45
Total	$1,543

COMPARISON (WITH A VIEW TOWARD ADOPTION OF THE VOUCHER SYSTEM

The real per student per year costs of elementary school education were calculated to be—

Private	$1543
Public	1363
Difference	$ 180

Several adjustments are needed before a comparison for the voucher system can be made.

First, the City may be underdepreciating. The seventy-three year average age of the buildings being replaced hints at this. Higher expenses for proper maintenance should equalize the lower depreciation charges, but it is also quite possible that the City is undermaintaining. If the average cost of new schools were written-off over forty years, instead of the present seventy-three years, the added per student per year charge would be $108.

The City's marginal interest rate, assumed to be about 6½ per cent, not its 4.2 per cent average interest rate, will apply to borrowings for any new schools. If this is considered, the added per student per year charge would be $16.

For a fair comparison, the cost of the hot lunch program should be backed-out of the public sector because voucher school pupils would also be eligible. This is a $43 adjustment.

The per student per year cost of public school summer activities ($19) should also be adjusted for, because voucher schools, like most private schools now, could and would charge separately for summer school.

Lastly, as can public schools now, voucher schools would be able to issue debt with tax-free status, which would save $34 per student per year.

The outline below reconciles these adjustments:

Private school excess cost (as calculated)	$180
Public school depreciation adjustment	(108)
Marginal interest rate adjustment	(16)
Public school hot lunch program	43
Public school summer activities	19
Voucher school tax-free debt	(34)
Pro forma difference between private and public elementary school	$ 84

CONCLUSION

The true cost of public elementary school education was calculated as $1,363.

The true cost of private elementary school education was calculated as $1,543.

The costs differed from each other by very little, on the order of twelve-thirteen per cent. Small changes in any of the major assumptions could significantly narrow or reverse the answers.

Pro forma adjustments reduced the cost differential to less than one-hundred dollars. With a little belt tightening, perhaps raising slightly the student/teacher ratio, a voucher equal to the true cost of public school would probably be adequate to run voucher schools.

SCHEDULE A

Federal funds under Title I of the Elementary and Secondary Education Act. These funds are used for programs to assist disadvantaged students (eg: free lunch program).

Appendix C-24 of the 1970-1971 Board of Education Budget lists grants to the thirty-one community districts. Total: $89.0 million.

Appendix B-1 shows:

	Elementary	Junior
Total student enrollment	629,090	237,212
Number of Title I eligible	359,863	123,265
Per cent of total eligible	74.5	25.5

Computation: 74.5 per cent of $89.0 million = $66.3 million elementary
school share of federal grant under Title I

SCHEDULE B

State funds under the Urban Education Act. These funds are distributed in relation to the number of reading retarded students per district.

Appendix C-24 lists grants to the thirty-one community districts. Total: $37.5 million.

Appendix B-1 shows:

	Elementary	Junior
Total student enrollment	629,090	237,212
Number of reading retarded	322,293	116,356
Per cent of total retarded	73.5	26.5

Computation: 73.5 per cent of $37.5 million = $27.6 million elementary
school share of the state grant under the Urban Education Act

SCHEDULE C

"Debt service on facilities and equipment" in the education budget. The total represents funds expended by the City Comptroller to pay interest on and redeem bonds issued to finance school construction and equipment purchases.

Exhibit I of the 1970-1971 Board of Education Budget reports a total of $151.0 million for elementary, junior, and high school debt service.

The Office of the Comptroller of the City of New York (Mr. Lewis) breaks the total down as $32 million interest on debt and $119 million as repayment of debt. The total outstanding debt is $761 million.

Appendix B-1 shows a pupil enrollment of 629,090 in elementary school and 237,212 in junior high. The Board of Education Research Department (Miss Adler) reports a high school enrollment of 285,171.

Calculated, by per cent of total enrollment:

Elementary	54.6%
Junior High	20.6%
High School	24.8%
Total	100.0%

Computation: 54.6 per cent of $32 million = $17.5 million pro rata share (based on student population) of the system's total yearly interest expense

NOTE: The City's present average interest rate on school debt is $32 million/$761 million = 4.2 per cent. Given current capital market conditions the City could not replace its debt at comparable rates. The rate now for long term money would be about 6½ per cent.

SCHEDULE D

Funds expended for light and heat for all schools, for central administration, personnel, curriculum development, and support services such as procurement and data processing.

Exhibit I shows a total of $94.9 million for all schools.

The student population in per cent as calculated in Schedule C was:

Elementary	54.6%
Junior	20.6%
High School	24.8%
	100.0%

Computation: 54.6 per cent of $94.9 million = $51.8 million pro rata share (based on student population) of the total yearly central administration expense.

SCHEDULE E

Exhibit II of the 1970-1971 Board of Education Budget shows:

Non-instructional district activities:

Supervision	$ 13.6 million
Summer activities	16.6
Fringe benefits	123.6
Custodial	47.4
School lunch	37.5
Transportation	27.0
Maintenance	23.7
Miscellaneous	4.0
Training	1.0
Unassigned	36.7
Total	$331.1 million for all junior and elementary schools

Assumption: These costs can be fairly allocated on a per student basis.
Appendix B-1 shows:

	Number	Per cent
Elementary students	629,090	72.6
Junior high students	237,212	27.4
Total district students	866,302	100.0

Computation: 72.6 per cent of $331.7 million = $240.5 million pro rata share (based on student population) of total noninstructional district activities

SCHEDULE F

Exhibit III of the 1970-1971 Board of Education Budget shows:

Instructional support (supplies and equipment, guidance counselors, school aides)	$ 41.2 million
School administration (salaries of principals, assistant principals, and secretaries)	$ 73.3
Teachers' salaries	$458.1
Total instructional costs	$572.6 million

Exhibit VII of the budget gives this breakdown:

Elementary school	$370.5 million
Junior high school	202.1
Total	$572.6 million

SCHEDULE G

Board of Education *Proposed 1972–1973 School Building Program and 1973-1978 Capital Improvement Plan (September 1971)* lists sixty-six elementary schools either currently under construction, planned, or proposed through 1978, to replace seventy-seven existing buildings.

The projected cost of the sixty-six new elementary school buildings is $533.6 million.

Assumption: There will be a twenty per cent cost over-run on construction.

Computation: 120 per cent x $533.6 million = $640.3 million total cost

Computation: $640.3 million/sixty-six new schools = $9.7 million average cost per new school

The average age in 1975 of the seventy-seven buildings being replaced will be seventy-three years.

Assumption: Each new building will also be used for seventy-three years and should be depreciated over that period on a straight line basis with no salvage value.

Assumption: "Kids are kids," and will wear out facilities equally everywhere. Note: This is probably not a fair assumption, but must be made nonetheless.

Computation: $9.7 million cost per school divided by a seventy-three year life = $133,000 straight line depreciation charge per elementary school per year

Appendix B-3 of the 1970-1971 Budget shows a present total of 624 elementary schools.

Computation: $133,000 per year per school x 624 schools = $83 million yearly depreciation expense

Appendix B-1 shows 629,090 elementary school pupils.

Assumption: Average student enrollment per new school will be unchanged from the present average enrollment per school.

Computation: 629,090 students divided by 624 schools = an average of 1,008 students per school

Computation: $133,000 average depreciation per year per school divided by 1,008 pupils per average school = an average annual per capita depreciation charge of $132

SCHEDULE H

Authorities at the Village Community School supplied the following tuition data:

Grade	1970-1971 Tuition
Kindergarten	$1200
1	1300
2	1400
3	1500
4	1600
5	1600
6	1700
7	(not taught)
8	(not taught)

Computation: Average tuition = (1200 + 1300 + 1400 + 1500 + 1700 + 1600 + 1600) divided by 7 = 10,300/7 = $1471 rounded

Note: Tuitions were raised by $100 per grade for 1971-1972.

SCHEDULE I

Mr. William Esty, Treasurer of the Village Community School, quoted the sum of $15,000 as being needed from contributions to make the budget breakeven. He also indicated a present student enrollment of 210.

Assumption: Operating losses should be allocated on a per student basis.

Assumption: Charitable contributions should be allocated on a per student basis.

Computation: $15,000 divided by 210 students = $72 operating loss per student.

SCHEDULE J

Given by school authority (Mr. Esty), cost of land and building: $332,000.

Assumption: The land is worth $250,000, therefore the building's depreciable base is $82,000. Note: The building was constructed in 1895.

Assumption: The building's remaining economic life is 20 years.

Computation: $82,000/20 years = $4,100 depreciation per year on building

Given by school authority, cost of interior renovations to building: $150,000; cost of furniture and fixtures: $25,000.

Assumption: The furniture, fixtures, and interior renovations will have an average life of ten years.

Computation: ($150,000 + $25,000) divided by ten years = $175,000/ten years = $17,500 depreciation per year on improvements to the building

   Given by school authority, capacity of school: 250 students.

Assumption: Depreciation should be calculated on capacity, not on present enrollment. The school is adding a seventh grade in 1971-1972, and an eigth grade in 1972-1973, and will soon be at capacity.

Computation: ($4,100 depreciation per year on building + $17,500 depreciation per year on improvements) divided by 250 pupils = $21,600/250 = $86 depreciation per student per year

SCHEDULE K

School authorities (Mr. Esty) quoted total scholarship aid of approximately $34,000.

Assumption: This cost should be allocated on a per student basis.

Computation: $34,000/210 = $162 scholarship contribution per student.

NOTE: Tuition may be viewed as composed of two elements:

Cost	$1,309
Gift	162
	$1,471

SCHEDULE L

School authorities advise that the parents of each pupil must purchase a $500 interest-free bond.

Assumption: The same money left in a savings bank could earn 6.18 per cent per year, and this lost interest must be recognized as an expense.

Computation: $500 x 0.0618 = $31 lost interest

NOTE: Beginning with 1971-1972 the purchase price of the bond is $600.

SCHEDULE M

School authorities advise that the school building was financed by a $280,000 Purchase Money mortgage at 5½ per cent interest, with 2 per cent per year amortization after a two year grace period. The holder of the mortgage is the seller, the Catholic Church.

Assumption: The fair market rate of interest for mortgages in comparable transactions in April, 1970, would be at least 9½ per cent.

Assumption: The Church was motivated by non-economic considerations, which must be adjusted for to calculate true cost.

Computation: (9½ per cent - 5½ per cent) ($280,000) divided by 250 pupils = $45 per student per year adjustment to fair market interest rates

REFERENCES

1.   City of New York. Board of Education. *Allocating Educational Funds to the Community School Districts.* November, 1970.

2.   City of New York. Board of Education. School Planning and Research Division. *Proposed 1972-1973 School Building Program and 1973-1978 Capital Improvement Plan.* September, 1971.

3.   City of New York. City Planning Commission. *1972-1973 Draft Capital Budget and Capital Improvement Plan for Ensuing Five Fiscal Years.* December 10, 1971.

4.   Garms, Walter I., and Smith, Mark C., "Development of a Measure of Educational Need and its Use in a State School Support Formula," *Study of the State of New York School Support Formula, Staff Study No. 4.* June, 1969.

5.   James, Thomas H., et al., *Determinants of Educational Expenditures in Large Cities of the United States.* Stanford, California: School of Education, Stanford University, 1966.

6.   Kelley, James A., *Resource Allocation and Educational Need in New York City's Public Schools.* New York: Teachers College, Columbia University, November, 1969.

7.   Leacock, E., *Teaching and Learning in City Schools.* New York: Basic Books, 1969.

8.   University of the State of New York. State Education Department. Bureau of Educational Finances Research. *Analysis of School Finances. New York State District.* 1967-1968.

Factors Associated with the Increasing Cost of Hospital Care

Ronald Andersen
and
J. Joel May

One of the key elements of modern managerial accounting is variance analysis—the breaking down of a gross change into its component causes. In this paper, two non-accountants utilize similar, if relatively unsophisticated, techniques in an attempt to determine the factors that have caused the great increase in hospital care. It would be of particular interest to apply a similar analysis to the operations of a single unit, and to determine which, if any of the causes might then be amenable to a greater degree of control.

The rise in hospital costs is a major reason for the growing public concern about a "health care crisis" in the United States. There are at least two basic causes for this concern: (1) hospital costs, as we shall document, are rising rapidly—much more rapidly than costs for more other goods and services; and (2) the visibility of this cost rise is becoming greater. Large insurers and other volume purchasers of hospital care such as Blue Cross, government, labor unions, and industrial firms are becoming increasingly aware of and critical toward the product they are buying. As a result, such groups are directly concerned with the question of rising hospital costs. In addition, national programs such as Medicare and Medicaid, not to mention the various proposals for a national health insurance scheme, include provisions for increasingly close scrutiny of hospital operations.

A great deal of the current literature, both in professional journals and in popular magazines, as well as much of the discussion on a national policy level, uses the basic premise that hospitals are not as productive as they might be, that they are "inefficient," and that therefore hospital costs are higher than they "ought" to be. The purpose of this paper is neither to support nor to refute

Ronald Andersen is a Research Associate in the Center for Health Administration Studies and Assistant Professor in the Department of Sociology, University of Chicago.

J. Joel May is Director of the Graduate Program in Hospital Administration and Assistant Director of the Center for Health Administration Studies, University of Chicago.

SOURCE: From *The Annals,* Vol. 399 (January, 1972), pp. 63-72, Copyright © 1972 by The American Academy of Political and Social Science.

Table 1
Changes in Annual Expenditures for All Hospitals,
Selected Years, 1950-1970

Year	Total Expenditures[a] (in $ millions)	Per Capita Expenditures[b]	Average Annual Increase[c] (in percentages)
1950	$ 3,651	$ 24.04	
1955	5,594	33.89	6.9
1960	8,421	46.79	6.5
1965	12,948	66.81	7.1
1970	25,556	125.35	12.6

[a]*Hospitals, Journal of the American Hospital Association*, Guide Issue, 1971, p. 460.

[b]Calculated by dividing total expenditure by civilian resident population as of July 1. Population taken from U.S. Bureau of the Census, *Current Population Records*, Series P-25, No. 458 (April 21, 1971).

[c]Calculated by the natural logarithm methods described in George W. Barclay, *Techniques of Population Analysis*, (New York: John Wiley, 1958), pp. 31-33.

these value judgments. Rather, it is to provide some factual information about the dimensions of the cost increase and the factors associated with it.

HOSPITAL COST INCREASES

Table 1 documents cost increases for all types of hospital care in the United States over the past twenty years. It shows that from 1950 to 1970, total expenditures increased from about $3.5 billion to over $25 billion per year. Further, expenditures increased during each five-year interval of this period. In 1950, annual expenditures for hospital care were $24 for each person in the country. By 1970, this amount had increased to $125, or more than five times as much. While expenditures increased during each time period, the annual rate of increase was about twice as great during the last five years (thirteen per cent) as it was during the previous fifteen years (between six and seven per cent). This recent acceleration is one of the main reasons for the mounting concern about medical care costs and the discussions about the "crisis" in the health care system.

The analysis to follow deals primarily with the 3,386 nongovernmental, not-for-profit, short-term general and other special hospitals in the United States, which we will subsequently refer to as *voluntary* hospitals. Voluntary hospitals were chosen for this analysis because they are the most prevalent type of hospital in the United States system, comprising forty-seven per cent of all hospitals and sixty-five per cent of all admissions in 1970. In the public mind,

Table 2
Changes in Total Expenditures, Per Diem Costs, and Per Admission Costs in Voluntary Hospitals, Selected Years, 1950-1970

Year	Total expenditures[a] (in $ millions)	Per diem costs[a]	Per admission costs[b]	Average annual increases (in percentages)
1950	$ 1,523	$16.89	$130.05	
1955	2,508	24.15	181.13	6.7
1960	4,139	33.23	245.90	6.1
1965	6,643	45.40	349.58	7.0
1970	14,163	81.86	671.25	13.1

[a]*Hospitals,* Guide Issue, 1971, p. 460.
[b]Calculated from reference[a] by dividing total expenses by annual admissions.

the term *hospital* is usually understood to refer to this group rather than to the myriad assortment of mental hospitals, tuberculosis hospitals, long-term chronic hospitals, and hospitals which, while short-term and providing general hospital care, are run by the various levels of government. There are very few hospitals operated for profit, and these have also been excluded. Analysis of the entire universe of hospitals would not prove very useful because of the vast differences in organization, financing, cost structure, and probably most important of all, what constitutes a "typical" hospital day.

Expenditures on the basis of costs per day of patient care (*patient care*) and per admission for voluntary hospitals are shown in Table 2. There has been a precipitous rise in per diem costs in these hospitals over the last two decades, reaching $82 a day in 1970. A similar rate of increase is noted in costs per admission, culminating in a cost per stay in the hospital for the average patient of over $650 in 1970. As was true for per capita expenditures, the average annual increase in cost per admission shows the rate of increase from 1965 to 1970 to be about twice that of the earlier periods.

The special concern about increasing hospital costs is generated largely because these increases seem to be out of step with cost increases in the rest of the economy. Table 3 shows the proportion of the Gross National Product (GNP) devoted to medical care in general and to all hospital care in particular. Thus, total expenditures for medical care amounted to 4.5 per cent of the GNP in 1950 but had increased to seven per cent in 1970. The hospital component is increasing faster than the total medical care component. It jumped from 1.3 per cent to 2.7 per cent during this same period. Of special note is the increase of 0.7 per cent in the last five-year period alone.

Changes in the GNP reflect changes both in the use of a service and in the cost per unit of that service. To get a better idea of the cost increase alone,

Table 3
Medical Care and All Hospital Expenditures as a Proportion of Gross National Product, Selected Years, 1950-1970

Year	Expenditures as a proportion of gross national product (in percentages)	
	All medical care[a]	Hospital care[b]
1950	4.5	1.3
1955	4.5	1.5
1960	5.4	1.8
1965	5.9	2.0
1970[c]	7.0	2.7

[a]Dorothy P. Rice and Barbara S. Cooper, "National Health Expenditures," *Social Security Bulletin* 34 (January, 1971), p. 5
[b]Ibid, p. 6; and Barbara S. Cooper and Mary McGee, *Research and Statistics, note 25* (December 14, 1970), Table 10.
[c]Fiscal year.

Table 4
Changes in the Consumer Price Index: All Items, Medical Care, and All Hospital Care, Selected Years, 1950-1970

Year	All Items		Medical Care		Hospital Care	
	Index	Average Annual Increase (per cent)	Index	Average Annual Increase (per cent)	Index	Average Annual Increase (per cent)
1950	83.8		73.4		51.8	
		2.1		3.8		6.3
1955	93.3		88.6		79.2	
		2.0		4.0		7.1
1960	103.1		108.1		112.7	
		1.3		2.7		6.2
1965	109.9		122.3		153.3	
		4.2		6.0		12.6
1970	135.3		164.9		287.9	

Sources: *Statistical Abstract: 1970*, p. 62, and Bureau of Labor Statistics, *Monthly Labor Review*. The 1970 indices have been adjusted from a 1967 base to a 1957-1959 base to be comparable with earlier periods.

Table 4 provides data from the Consumer Price Index. Annual rates of increase in each of the five-year periods suggest that the hospital component tends to reflect the increases in the economy as a whole, since the rate of increase of hospital charges and medical care fees is greatest in the same period in which it is greatest for the economy as a whole. However, the hospital component is unique with respect to the magnitude of increase in that the annual rate of increase is over three times that of the total CPI in each time period and roughly twice that of the total medical care component.

"Use" and "Price" as Components of Hospital Cost Increases

Having shown the magnitude of hospital cost increases we turn to the factors responsible for the rapid increases we have observed and, more specifically, to the relative contributions of increase in use and increase in per unit cost or unit price to the over-all increase.

The distinction between price and use is generally made to isolate the separate effects of quantity changes from changes in the costs of the care itself. It should be noted that the change in the price of hospital care as we will be able to measure it includes changes in: (1) over-all economic factors influencing the hospital; (2) the nature of the care itself; and (3) how efficiently or inefficiently it is given.

We will be primarily concerned with the time intervals 1960 through 1965 and 1965 through 1970. We will compare these periods because, as mentioned, price increases for all goods and services as well as prices for hospital services rose much more rapidly during the latter period. Further, this structure gives us the opportunity to examine the situation before and after Medicare and Medicaid, as both programs began in 1966.

The general approach will be to calculate total expenditure increase for the voluntary hospitals in each time period and then attempt to assess the relative importance of the use and price factors which determine these increases.

The data we are using come primarily from the American Hospital Association's annual "Guide Issue" of their semi-monthly journal, *Hospitals, Journal of the American Hospital Association.* The data were reported by individual hospitals on a mail questionnaire.

Cost Increases Attributable to Changes in Use

The factors we will consider for their impact on hospital costs associated with changes in use are shown in Table 5. The rationale is that some of the increase in the total cost of hospital care comes about simply because the hospitals are providing more service.

One reason for this is that they have increasing numbers of people to serve. The population increased from 178 million in 1960 to 202 million in 1970.

**Table 5
Factors Used to Measure "Use"
Increases for Voluntary Hospitals**

	1960	1965	1970
Civilian resident population (in millions of persons)[a]	178.1	191.5	201.6
Admissions per 100,000 population[b]	942	992	1,039
Outpatient visits per 100,000 population[c]	23,600	30,900	45,100

[a]*Current Population Reports,* Series P-25, No. 458 (April 21, 1971).
[b]*Hospitals,* Guide Issue, 1971, p. 462.
[c]Calculated from Part 2, *Hospitals,* Guide Issue, 1955, p. 57; ibid, 1971, p. 462.
NOTE: Since number of outpatient visits was not computed for 1960, the number was estimated using a linear extrapolation from visit totals reported for the years 1954 and 1962.

Total costs also increase because each individual person, on the average, is using more hospital services. Two measures of this increased use per person are the number of admissions and number of visits to hospital outpatient departments and emergency rooms per 100,000 of the population. Table 5 shows that admissions adjusted for population increased moderately in both time periods while outpatient visits increased at a more rapid rate.

It is necessary to use units which have the same meaning from one time period to another to measure use increase precisely. Even then, the meaning of both of our measures changes somewhat with changing medical technique and technology. Such changes will be highlighted by the following discussion of increase in prices.

The task is to see to what extent these use increases during the two time periods can account for the increases in total hospital costs. In Table 2 we saw that total costs in voluntary hospitals increased from $4.1 billion in 1960 to $6.6 billion in 1965 and $14.2 billion in 1970. Thus, we will be attempting to explain a $2.5 billion increase during the 1960–1965 period and a $7.5 billion increase during the 1966–1970 period.

Table 6 shows that an increase in the use of services provided by voluntary hospitals accounted for a relatively small proportion of the total increase in both the pre-Medicare (fourteen per cent) and the post-Medicare (twelve per cent) eras. Among the components of the use increase, population growth

Table 6
Increase in Voluntary-Hospital Costs Due to Changes in "Use"

Factors measuring use change	1960–1965		1965–1970	
	Increase in $ millions	Percentage of total increase	Increase in $ millions	Percentage of total increase
Total increase in expenditures	2,504.0	100.0	7,520.0	100.0
Change in population	188.4	7.5[a]	396.8	5.3[a]
Admissions/1000 population	132.9	5.3[b]	356.2	4.7[b]
Outpatient visits	29.8	1.2[c]	165.0	2.2[c]
All use factors	351.1	14.0	918.0	12.2

[a]
$$\frac{\text{Population: Period 2}}{\text{Population: Period 1}} - 1 \quad \text{(Total Expenditure Increase)}$$

[b]
$$\frac{\text{Admissions: Period 2}}{\text{Admissions: Period 1}} - 1 \quad \text{(Total Expenditure Increase)}$$

[c]To adjust for changes in outpatient visits, these were first converted to "outpatient-day equivalents" using an equation developed by the American Hospital Association. See *Hospitals,* Guide Issue, 1971, p. 446. The adjustment used was 1 day - 5.74 visits.

Table 7
Factors Used to Measure "Price" Increases in Voluntary Hospitals, 1960–1970

	1960	1965	1970
Average annual consumer price index (inflation factor)[a]	103.1	109.9	135.3
Payroll expense in current dollars per full-time equivalent hospital employee (wage level factor)[b]	$ 3,234	$ 4,043	$ 6,013
Number of hospital employee working days per admission/1,000 population (staff increase factor)[b]	12.27	13.83	17.22
Value of hospital physical assets per admission/1,000 population in current dollars (asset factor)[b]	$ 6,557	$ 9,151	$13,265

[a]*Statistical Abstract of the United States, 1970,* p. 344.
[b]*Hospitals,* Guide Issues, Part 2, 1961, pp. 394–395; ibid. 1965, pp. 439, 441; ibid. 1971, p. 462.

accounted for the largest percentage increase, with admissions accounting for somewhat less and increased use of outpatient services accounting for least. The relative contributions of the various use factors were similar in the two periods despite the fact that the rate of cost increase was much greater between 1966 and 1970 than it had been between 1960 and 1965. For both periods we must now turn to the price components in order to shed more light on the forces which were primarily responsible for expenditure increases in hospitals over the last decade.

Cost Increases Attributable to Changes in Price

Table 7 shows the factors we have chosen as measures of the increase in hospital costs associated with price changes. We have used the over-all Consumer Price Index as a measure of inflation in the economy generally, and have made the assumption that voluntary hospitals have experienced an inflation rate with respect to what they must pay for the goods and services they purchase which is the same as that experienced elsewhere in the economy.

Both the average wages paid hospital employees and the number of employee days required per admission have increased over the period in question. The net effect of both these factors taken together is measured by payroll costs incurred by hospitals. It nevertheless is useful to separate them so as to examine the individual effect of wage levels (which measure both the state of the market for such employees and their skill levels or quality) and staffing levels (which measure the intensiveness of care and reflect changes in the way in which the care of a patient is given).

Finally, the number of physical assets associated with a hospital admission provides a measure of the technology and equipment involved in hospital care.

Since all of these—the purchasing power of the hospital's dollar, the cost of obtaining labor services, the hours of labor involved in the daily functioning of a hospital, and the number of buildings and pieces of equipment necessary to to do the job—directly affect hospital costs, and since variations in these are typically associated not only with questions concerning the nature of the care given but with the efficiency with which the procedures are conducted, they will result in changes in the prices of hospital care.

Table 8 documents the extent of their importance in accounting for increases in hospital costs over the two periods in question. General economic inflation, while relatively unimportant in the first five-year period, assumed major importance in the latter five years. Wages were a major factor in both periods, the relative importance of this factor remaining essentially the same in the 1965–1970 period as it had been earlier. This observation would seem to contradict the arguments of hospital administrators and others that it is the personnel component which is most rapidly driving up hospital costs. The

Table 8
Increases in Voluntary-hospital Costs Due to Changes in Price

Factors Measuring Price Change	1960–1965		1965–1970	
	Increase in $ millions	Percentage of Total Increase	Increase in $ millions	Percentage of Total Increase
Total increase in costs	$2,504.0	100.00	$7,520,0	100.00
Inflation	165.1	6.59[a]	1,739.9	23.14[a]
Wage levels	432.8	17.28[b]	1,564.2	20.80[b]
Increase in staff personnel	318.3	12.71[c]	1,843.2	24.51[c]
Plant assets	777.4	31.04[d]	1,334.8	17.75[d]
All "price" factors	1,693.6	67.62	6,482.1	86.20

[a]
$$\frac{\text{Consumer Price Index: Period 1}}{\text{Consumer Price Index: Period 2}} - 1 \quad \text{(Total Cost Increase)}$$

[b] To avoid double-counting of the factors, a successive deflation process was followed. Thus, payroll expenditures as reported were first deflated by the associated value of the Consumer Price Index and the result divided by numbers of full-time equivalent hospital employes. Then the following formula was used:

$$\frac{\text{Real wages per employe: Period 1}}{\text{Real wages per employe: Period 2}} - 1 \quad \text{(Total Cost Increase)}$$

[c] Since admissions per 100,000 population had already been used to explain a portion of cost increase due to use, employe days (assuming a five-day week) were divided by our measure of admissions first. Then the following formula was used:

$$\frac{\text{Employe days per admission: Period 1}}{\text{Employe days per admission: Period 2}} - 1 \quad \text{(Total Cost Increase)}$$

[d] Following the argument of b. above, we computed "real" value of plant assets and divided by admissions per 100,000 population. Then the following formula was used:

$$\frac{\text{Real plant assets per admission: Period 1}}{\text{Real plant assets per admission: Period 2}} - 1 \quad \text{(Total Cost Increase)}$$

apparent contradiction led us to examine staffing levels separately. This factor accounts for twice as large a fraction of the increase in the latter period as it did in the earlier. Apparently it is the number of hospital employees rather than the wages they are individually paid which is the more important influence on hospital cost increases.

Finally, physical or plant assets, while exercising an important upward influence on hospital costs, assumed a less important role in the 1965–1970 period than during the first five years of the decade.

Since we assume that the total observed increase in hospital costs is due to either "use" or "price" changes, it is now necessary to deal with that fraction of the total increase over the period in question which has not been attributed to any of the factors we have discussed.

Of the total increase of $2.5 billion between 1960 and 1965, the "use" factors we have identified account for slightly more than fourteen per cent and the "price" factors for about 67.5 per cent, leaving 18.5 per cent of the total unaccounted for. In the 1965–1970 period, the total increase was $7.5 billion, with the "use" factors accounting for a little more than twelve per cent and the "price" factors for more than eighty-six per cent. Only about 1.5 per cent is unaccounted for.

Among the phenomena which probably create upward pressure upon hospital costs but which have not been dealt with in our analysis are such new developments as home care programs, "meals-on-wheels" (a program for providing hot meals to bed-ridden persons in their homes), school health outreach centers, and other similar programs which are part of the operations of certain hospitals and contribute to hospital costs. Similarly, certain aspects of internal hospital operation such as the decision to lease rather than buy certain equipment or to purchase disposable products rather than re-usable ones, and so on, while certainly exercising an upward pressure on costs, cannot be isolated and dealt with explicitly, given the data available.

Although it is interesting that the portion of the total cost increase not accounted for by the factors we have considered is quite a bit smaller in the later period than in the earlier, we do not view this as an important finding in and of itself. The causes associated with and the interrelationships between the factors we have considered which are discussed in the concluding section of this paper are so complex as to quite possibly obscure their true total effect. While we are confident that the orders of magnitude we report accurately reflect the actual contribution of the factor in accounting for hospital cost increases, we stop short of asserting the accuracy of the absolute magnitudes involved.

An example of the difficulty of drawing inferences concerning the absolute magnitudes involved is provided by a look at the effect of hospital size on the factors we have used to account for increases in charges. In Table 7 we showed the levels in 1960, 1965, and 1970 for all voluntary hospitals. We have subsequently proceeded in our analysis as if the indices constructed from these averages were relevant for the entire population. Although this is technically correct, it can be potentially misleading if certain important classes of hospitals deviate significantly from the mean.

Table 9 shows that this is, indeed the case. For example, in terms of payroll expense per employee, the largest hospital was paying, in 1970, an average amount forty per cent higher than the smallest. Furthermore, the largest hospital was employing more than twice as many people and investing more than twice as much physical capital per admission as was the smallest. Hence, our caveat as to the precision of our findings. Certainly the size distribution of hospitals and the effect of hospital size on the factors in question are worthy of much further study.

Table 9

Influence of Voluntary-Hospital Size on Factors Used to Explain Price Increases, 1970

Hospital size category	Number of hospitals	Percentage of total	Average cost per day	Average length of stay in days	Payroll expense per full-time equivalent employe	Employe working days per admission	Value of physical assets per admission
Fewer than 25 beds	114	3.5	$54.53	6.7	$4,665.99	13.58	$368.44
25–49 beds	519	16.0	58.85	6.8	5,253.35	12.25	405.22
50–99 beds	714	22.0	62.43	7.5	5,210.64	13.82	493.45
100–199 beds	808	24.9	71.12	7.6	5,577.60	14.92	558.48
200–299 beds	470	14.5	80.94	8.0	6,110.48	16.58	637.64
300–399 beds	296	9.1	82.78	8.3	6,105.68	17.29	659.27
400–499 beds	156	4.8	86.23	8.5	6,180.34	18.30	732.83
500 or more beds	166	5.2	95.21	9.6	6,478.30	21.86	832.71

SOURCE: *Hospitals*, Guide Issue, 1971, p. 464.

Possible Reasons for Hospital Cost Increases

So far, we have documented cost increases for hospital services over the last twenty years and have noted that the rate of expenditure increase was considerably higher in the most recent five-year period. We then looked in detail at the relative importance of various "use" and "price" factors which have contributed to these increases over the last decade. From this analysis it is apparent that increases in the amount of hospital care have accounted for a relatively small proportion of the total cost increase.

In this final section we will briefly consider some possible reasons as to why the price factors have been such major contributors to hospital cost increases. We will be particularly concerned with unique characteristics of the last five years which represent an acceleration of the rate of increase.

Reviewing Table 8 highlights the greater inflation in the economy over the last five years and suggests a reemphasis of the point that hospital service is an integral part of the economy and major trends in the latter must be expected to be reflected in the former. However, independent of general inflation, we have seen that wage rises, increases in staff personnel, and plant assets of hospitals have all had considerable impact on cost increases. A commonly held position in studies of hospitals is that the increase in third-party payers, who are thus providing hospitals with cost reimbursement for insured patients, may be an important reason for spiraling hospital costs.[1] Major insurers, including Blue Cross and the federal government under the Medicare program, generally pay the hospital the actual costs incurred in providing services to their subscribers. It is argued that this reimbursement method gives hospitals no incentive to hold down either their personnel or capital costs, since they are essentially guaranteed payment no matter what the total costs may be. Alternative reimbursement schemes which either "reward" the hospital for holding costs down or somehow penalize the hospital for cost increases have been proposed as cost containment mechanisms. Some experimentation with such schemes has begun.

Other ideas about the reasons for the increase are more directly related to one or another of the price components, such as wage levels. One reason for the observed impact of wages upon costs over the past ten years is that hospital employees have in the past been paid less than employees of similar skill levels in other fields. According to this argument, what we are observing in the past ten years is a "catch up" phenomenon, wage rates in hospitals simply coming up to levels comparable to those found elsewhere.[2] A related reason given for the wage effect is the growing proportion of hospital employees that is becoming unionized and the potential threat of unionization in non-unionized hospitals.[3] Of course, the assumption here is that unionization or the threat thereof increases the real wages of employees in the affected industry.

Another postulate having to do with wages deals with the growing technical skills needed to staff a hospital. In response to expanding medical technology, more people with new, specialized skills are being employed. Examples are medical technologists, radiologic technologists, and occupation therapists.[4] This growing component of more highly skilled persons in the hospital, demanding higher salaries, increases the over-all wage level. Still another reason for the wage effect is the longer preparation and the movement toward professionalization of various groups of hospital employees. For example, a regular four-year baccalaureate degree is rapidly becoming a common achievement for nurses as compared to the situation only a few years ago, when almost all graduates came from a three-year diploma school of nursing.[5] Increased professionalization is accompanied by increased demands for higher wages.

Staffing levels are another price component in Table 8 which have resulted in a considerable increase in hospital costs, particularly in the 1965–1970 period. It is suggested that hospitals are providing varieties of care which require greater numbers of personnel to serve a given number of patients. An example is found in intensive and coronary care units, which are characterized by continuous monitoring and surveillance procedures and thus require heavy staffing. It might also be argued that the staffing increases result in part from the continuing trend for the hospital to provide the patient with more amenities during his stay. Services such as television, air-conditioning, and meal choices require additional staffing and thus add to hospital costs. Increased staffing ratios may also reflect the growing risks of lawsuits based on the charge of negligence. Courts today are increasingly assigning joint responsibility for the patient's welfare to attending physicians and the hospital.[6] One possible response on the part of the hospital to this threat is to increase personnel, thus providing closer supervision of the patient (and of lower-level employees) with a view to reducing errors in medication and other unusual incidents from which such lawsuits may arise.

It should also be noted that what economists refer to as a *substitution effect* may be taking place. Staffing ratios may increase as the hospital's response to upward pressures on wage levels. As wages increase, one thing the administrator can do to keep total cost increases as small as possible is to hire more lower-priced personnel to perform tasks formerly done by higher-paid personnel. Thus, we would expect to see practical nurses and aides doing jobs formerly done by registered nurses, such as giving baths, straightening and making up beds, and even distributing medications.[7]

The major contribution of plant assets to increases in cost we believe has resulted from many of the same influences discussed under wage and staffing levels. Given rapid wage increases, hospital administrators may respond—and appear to have done so, particularly in the last five-year period—by substituting machines for human labor where possible. Examples of these possibilities for substitution include "auto-analyzers" in the laboratory, which will simultaneously perform up to a dozen test procedures; pneumatic tubes and other mechanical devices used to transport messages, forms, drugs, meals, and even specimens of tissue, blood, and the like, from one area of the hospital to another; and physiological monitoring devices, which are used to observe patients in intensive and coronary care units.

These expensive technological innovations, of course, add to the asset component of the price increase. Of special import to the asset component are rising construction costs, which have accelerated at a much faster rate than costs in most other segments of the economy.[8] Thus, the increasing costs of building new hospitals or expanding the facilities of existing ones most certainly contribute significantly to total cost increases.

The reasons provided above for recent increases in hospital costs are not exhaustive, but they do help to illustrate the changing nature of the task that hospitals are undertaking and how these dynamics might be related to cost increases.

Price increases result from the complex interaction of decision-makers, including patients, patients' families, physicians, and the larger society, as well as hospital management and staff. Together they determine the quality and quantity of hospital services delivered and the efficiency of the process designed to deliver them. While it is not the purpose of this paper to determine the "rights" and "wrongs" of what is taking place, nor to propose a solution to the hospital "cost crisis," our analysis does suggest that there is no single factor responsible for the current cost of hospital care. This indicates that any "solution" will be extremely complex and that hopes for any painless panacea are bound to remain unrealized.

NOTES

1.   See, for example, Herbert E. Klarman, "The Increased Cost of Hospital Care," in University of Michigan, *The Economics of Health and Medical Care,* 1964, pp. 243-245; Social Security Administration, *Reimbursement Incentives for Medical Care,* 1968; Mark V. Pauly and David F. Drake, "Effect of Third Party Methods of Reimbursement on Hospital Performance," in Herbert Klarman, ed., *Empirical Studies in Health Economics* (Baltimore: Johns Hopkins Press, 1970), pp. 297-314.

2.   Klarman, op. cit., pp. 230-232. In 1960, the average hourly wage of hospital employes was 68 per cent of that of production workers in manufacturing industries. By 1965, this percentage had increased to 74 per cent, and by 1969 it stood at 81 per cent. Computed from *Hospitals, Journal of the American Hospital Association,* Guide Issue, 1970, and *Statistical Abstract of the United States: 1970* (Washington, D.C.: U.S. Bureau of the Census, 1970), p. 231.

3.   Anne R. Somers, *Hospital Regulation: The Dilemma of Public Policy* (Princeton, N.J., 1969), pp. 61-65.

4.   *Health Resource Statistics, 1969* (Rockville, Md.: National Center for Health Statistics, 1970), Public Health Service Publication No. 1507, pp. 55-59, 197-199, 229-232.

5.   In 1960, 4,136 registered nurse graduates received bachelor's degrees. By 1969 the number was 7,145. Ibid., p. 150.

6.   Somers, op. cit., pp. 28-37.

7.   Between 1958 and 1970, the ratio of full-time practical nurses to full-time registered nurses in community hospitals increased from .32 to .55. Calculated from *Hospitals,* Guide Issues, 1971, p. 452, and 1959, pp. 424, 430.

8.   Between 1960 and 1969, the Composite Construction Price Index increased by 38 per cent while the Consumer Price Index increased by 24 per cent. Calculated from *Statistical Abstract,* op. cit., pp. 344, 675.

IX
QUESTIONING THE VALIDITY OF SOCIAL ACCOUNTING

Accounting and the Evaluation of Social Programs: A Critical Comment

M. E. Francis

Lest the readers of this volume and other tracts exhorting the accounting profession to action be too easily swayed, Mr. Francis' article is included to introduce a contrary note. Francis states that accountants are ill equipped to deal with the complexities or specialized knowledge required to carry out the functions that have been denoted as "social accounting." That Mr. Francis' view of accounting practices and the education of accountants has been heavily influenced by Dickens' description of Bob Cratchit is clear and somewhat irritating. However, one can only mutter a reluctant "touche," as he neatly uses the current deific status of generally accepted accounting principles to "demonstrate" that accounting and rational scientific inquiry are virtually antithetical.

Francis has ignored perhaps the strongest argument against accountants in social accounting; that is, their past disregard of the subject. The perceptive reader will note that few of the articles in this volume have been written by those openly admitting to being accountants. The excellent three volume report of the Joint Economic Committee, from which we have taken several papers, includes the works of fifty-seven different authors: not one is an accountant. This raises the obvious question: If the accountants have abstained from participation in social accounting for so long, why enter the arena now?

In recent years there has been increasing interest displayed by scholars in various fields, government agencies, and a few congressmen in the idea of "social

---

M. E. Francis is a statistical consultant for the World Health Organization Regional Office for South-East Asia.

SOURCE: From *The Accounting Review*, No. 2, April, 1973, pp. 245-257, Copyright by the American Accounting Association, 1973.

reporting," or "social accounting." The terms appear to be synonymous. Articles and papers on the subject have been devoted to: (1) suggestions regarding what quantitative information or statistics may be useful in assessing the conditions of society and the collection of statistical information for that purpose or (2) ways in which statistics may be used in assessing social programs.

The expressed need for social reporting or accounting and the increasing interest in the idea seem to be based on a belief that we must begin to think in terms of providing people who make policy with more complete and meaningful indicators or statistics so that their actions will be more effective or efficient. Others go further and argue that better statistics alone cannot insure more effective actions. Given the fact that resources will always be limited, policy makers must be provided with a kit of tools, a methodology, which takes financial constraints into consideration. It is hoped that this methodology will enable the policy maker to arrive at rational choices between competing goals and/or programs.

The accounting literature[1] indicates that at least some members of the profession believe that the accountant can and should contribute to the existing efforts directed toward (1) improving the methods of assessing the state of society and social programs and (2) the application of evaluative procedures in the allocation of resources to our efforts to improve social well-being. However, a number of the statements made to justify these beliefs would seem to suggest that the accountant is ill-equipped to contribute in a constructive way to either (1) or (2). An analysis of some of these suggestions seems in order.

To avoid confusion later, a "social program" is defined as a plan of action, a procedure, an *experiment*[2] introduced into society for the purpose of producing a change in society or the status of some of its members. Some social programs are designed to effect a change in the financial status of some individuals in society (e.g., aid to the blind and social security), while others provide goods and/or services to society with the purpose of producing a change (e.g., Head Start, school lunch programs, and educational institutions). It may be that the intent of many social programs is to produce a "beneficial" change. But the adjective has been purposefully left out since the kind of change is irrelevant to this discussion.

Most social programs are in reality nothing other than social experiments since they are based upon a set of assumptions or principles which are not beyond dispute. Thus, social programs ought to be planned so that the underlying assumptions can be tested. It may be debatable whether or not a program such as financial aid to the blind, for example, ought to be considered an experiment. However, few social programs fall into this gray area. "Assessing a social program" means scientifically evaluating the program to decide whether it has produced the intended result.

Specifically, it has been suggested that the accountant might expand his traditional attestation function into the social arena; that accountants ought to design detection and recording systems for social programs; and that accountants can help to improve the accuracy of economic data. These recommendations will be discussed in this article, followed by a discussion on the nature of the problems management has faced in its efforts to improve management rationale.

ATTESTATION FUNCTION

Various organizations and units of society have been charged with the responsibility of assessing the state of society and designing, implementing, and assessing social programs. It has been proposed by some that there is a need to insure the integrity of the reporting and measurement activities of these organizations; that someone or some group must be or should be society's watch dog. Since auditing is one of the functions the accountant has traditionally performed for business and industry, it seems to many that the accountant would be the most likely professional to assume this role of "public watch dog." A variety of types of information and activities has been suggested as areas where the accountant can perform the function of attestation. Before considering these suggestions it is necessary to come to grips with the meaning of "attest."

The dictionary defines the word "attest" as: "to bear witness to; certify, declare to be true or genuine." On the other hand, the American Institute of Certified Public Accountants defines the attestation *objective* by stating that "the primary purpose of an examination of financial statements by an independent auditor is to enable him to express an opinion as to the fairness of the statement, their compliance with generally accepted accounting principles, and the consistency of those principles with the prior period."[4]

With regard to the suggested sets of data, if the accountant is expected to attest in the strict (dictionary) meaning of the word, his only function seemingly would be to declare that certain figures were accurate. There is no evidence to indicate to this writer that this function is required. The use of an independent auditor to attest, in the strict meaning of the word, would be superfluous. This comment applies equally as well to suggestions[5] that the auditor might attest to:

1. The economic power of business entities.
2. The utilization of public resources.
3. The lost social welfare through unemployment.
4. The state of the national health.
5. The level and rate of change in occurrence of crime.
6. National business activity.

7.   Level of achievement and anticipated achievement data of national goals.

8.   Evaluation of the state and utilization of national goals.

9.   Demographic information.

All of these statistics are presently collected by the government (with the exception of the first, although the government does rank businesses in terms of monetary wealth). If one does see a need for attesting to the accuracy of the figures one must feel that arithmetic mistakes may be present. In this writer's opinion, the existing hierarchical structure in our government agencies significantly reduces compilation inaccuracies. In this sense, the structure audits itself.

However, the fact remains that most of the figures collected by the government and used in national planning are not accurate in the usual or layman's sense of the word and can never be,[6] because of the frame of reference of the data. Thus, the meaning attached to the attestation function must be more closely akin to that defined by the professional body. What is being suggested is that the accountant might be the person to attest to the reliability of data, to the fairness of the interpretation of data, and to the appropriateness of methods used to collect data. Since practically all the information presently being collected that pertains to the condition of society or some of its units is based on samples, attesting to the reliability or interpretation or method of collection necessarily means attesting to or auditing sampling methods.

It would not be unfair to say that the sampling theory knowledge the typical accountant possesses at the present time is no more extensive than that possessed by members of other professions (e.g., sociology, economics, education, statistics). In fact, the accountant's present knowledge is undoubtedly less extensive than that of the statistician and probably less than that of the economist. Sampling theory is that branch of statistics concerned with the development of sample selection procedures and of estimators that provide, at the lowest possible cost, estimates precise enough for the intended purpose. An *introductory* text in sampling theory suggests: "The minimum mathematical requirements for an easy understanding of the proofs is a knowledge of differential calculus as far as the determination of maxima and minima, plus a familiarity with elementary algebra, and especially with the handling of relatively complicated algebraic summations. Knowledge of the laws of probability for finite sample spaces, including conditional probabilities, the properties of expected values and conditional probability is extremely helpful. On the statistical side, the book presupposes an introductory course which covers such topics as means and standard deviations, the normal, binominal and multinomial distributions, confidence limits, student's t-test, linear regression and simple types of analysis of variance."[7] Moreover, the information contained in this text is only a prerequisite to understanding the newer developments in sampling theory which may be found in any one of the many regularly published journals of statistics.

In his formal training the accountant is generally presented with certain basic and elementary concepts of sampling theory.[8] It is certainly clear that this type of training in sampling theory is insufficient to enable an accountant to judge a sampling method since assessment depends upon the purpose of the survey and the statistical properties of the estimator or estimators. For example, the GNP index is a ratio estimate of a variable whose numerator and denominator are also variables. Examining the content of a textbook on sampling methods for accountants[9] one finds only three pages devoted to the topic of "estimating a ratio" and two of these pages are concerned entirely with how to compute a ratio estimate; the introductory text in sampling theory referred to earlier devotes an entire chapter to ratio estimators and their properties (thirty-four pages) in addition to scattered pages throughout other chapters. More importantly, this points out one of the basic differences between the training of a statistician and that of a nonstatistician. Sampling theory is concerned with the development of *estimators* and ascertaining which estimators are best. Estimates are derived from estimators and have no properties independent of these estimators. Yet, most statistical texts used in teaching nonmathematicians or nonstatisticians barely distinguish between an estimator and an estimate and are practically devoid of even the slightest reference to properties of estimators and how mathematically to derive such properties. The texts written for accountants are no exception.

This basic lack of knowledge—which is only part of the minimum statistical and mathematical knowledge necessary to understand sampling theory—indicates that suggestions that accountants attest to sampling methods and to the integrity of statistical series derived from samples are totally unrealistic. Undoubtedly, there are today some government agencies and private organizations whose published statistics are incomplete, unreliable, and misleading. The author believes that, in most cases, this is the result of lack of staff and/or lack of trained and qualified personnel. On the other hand, there is enough evidence to indicate that in the publication of some statistical series the primary purpose is to mislead. Still other published series lack integrity as a result of a combination of both factors.

For those series which are unreliable because of lack of knowledge on the part of the collectors, what is needed is better trained personnel—people who have been trained in the science of statistics and people who have been trained in the particular area of concern. The establishment of an independent body to audit statistical series would most probably serve as an impetus to better staffing of the organizations and agencies responsible for their collection.

Judging by the quality and quantity of the literature in the social science area there are people who are infinitely more qualified than the accountant to speak to the subject of the fairness of the statistical series which are collected, what data ought to be collected, and how they should be collected. Statisticians are certainly more qualified than accountants in this area and have long been interested in improving the quality, integrity, and interpretation of statistics. In 1952, A. J. Wickens suggested that the American Statistical Association or the statistical profession consider setting up examinations for "Certified Public Statisticians" and further that a U.S. Statistical Commission be established with the "responsibility for audit of statistical series, similar to accounting audit, empowered to put a certified label on a statistical product. It should also be charged with the investigation of methods, scope and suitability of statistics and make recommendations for future improvement and development work."[10] His suggestions were never followed through in this form. However, the Association has established upon its own initiative, and by request, the following permanent committees: committee on social insurance statistics and training; committee on statistics in accounting; advisory committee on agricultural statistics; advisory committee on statistical policy to the Bureau of the Budget; Census advisory committee; advisory committee for statistical research to the Civil Aeronautics Board; and the committee on computers in statistics. Further, since statisticians either are trained or develop interests in a particular area of the sciences and the problems of statistical inference in that area, the association membership has seen the need to establish the following special sections: Biometrics Section, Biopharmaceutical Section, Business and Economic Statistics Section, Social Science Section, Section on Physical and Engineering Sciences, and Section on Training Statisticians.

Statistical journals are replete with articles devoted to the collection, analysis, interpretation, and the general problems of government and nongovernment statistics.[11] The literature of other disciplines indicates that many are concerned about the inadequacies of our present socioeconomic statistical series and indicators.[12] Considering the already existing and very extensive efforts of statisticians alone to improve the collection and interpretation of government data, there simply is no evidence to indicate that the accountant of today has some unique experience or training which makes him more qualified or even equally qualified to attest to the integrity of most important statistical series.

It is certainly possible that a need exists to audit the sampling methods and statistical series collected by governmental and nongovernmental agencies. But the responsibility must be in the hands of those who are qualified to do this. There is no dearth of qualified people. Supporters of the thesis that the accountant is also qualified to perform this function in the social arena point only to the fact that traditionally he has been responsible for independent audits in the business world. This kind of experience is irrelevant when one examines what is involved in auditing social reports and statistical series. What is or is not a useful statistic, what is or is not the best statistic, what statistics are necessary for assessing certain conditions of society, these are questions that can be answered only by statisticians and the experts in the field of application working together. Maybe the time has come for society to consider establishing an independent body to put its stamp of approval on statistics and statistical series of public importance. But nothing can be gained by delegating this responsibility to inexperienced people—people who are not familiar with statistical theory and its problems, the data needs, and the data collection problems in the functional area of concern.

If the suggestion is that the accountant of the future ought to expand his attestation function into the social arena, it will be necessary to restructure, revise, and add to the present accounting programs to prepare future accountants for this role. It seems clear that the changes in the accounting curriculum necessary to produce an individual who is qualified to audit, for example, the certification of a new drug must be so extensive that the new curriculum would be almost identical to the existing programs that grant degrees in biostatistics; that the changes necessary to produce an individual qualified to audit economic series and projections must be so extensive that the new curriculum would be almost identical to the already existing programs which grant degrees in econometrics; and so on. Qualified people to audit in the social arena are being trained now in the various disciplines and there is no reason to believe these programs will cease. However, if the accountant of the future is to be expected to attest in the areas suggested, what he will be auditing will be the work of biostatisticians, econometricians, demographers, social statisticians, operation researchers, public health administrators, etc., and, at the very least, he must receive the same training or better than they have received. The question is not whether there should be an independent audit of all or some statistics and statistical series. The question is, given that independent auditing bodies should be established, does the accountant possess the training or experience to qualify him over others to audit in the social arena? The evidence seems to indicate that the answer to this question is negative.

DESIGN OF DETECTION AND RECORDING SYSTEMS

The development of a systematic body of knowledge may proceed in two principal ways: deduction and induction. In some sciences the body of knowledge has been developed through a mixture of deduction and induction. Deduction is, in a sense, evolutionary. The development of the body of knowledge called "accounting" has been evolutionary.[13] The method has been the method of deduction, not induction. Accounting has developed by first defining a set of axioms. They are:

1. Assets are anything of value owned by the business.

2. Equities are the rights or claims against the assets of the business.

In addition, the yardstick for determining value was defined as its monetary worth. This may be thought of as an axiom or as a definition. There may be some argument as to whether, Assets = Equities, should be considered an axiom or definition. However, there should be no disagreement that traditionally and perhaps today it is still viewed as an unquestioned truth.

Within this axiomatic framework one of the accountant's traditional functions has been to give order to what would otherwise be a hopeless jumble of disconnected facts. That is, the accountant has been responsible for the design of a system of classification—some categories not of his own doing, while others indeed were. In any field of scholarly endeavor, classification is of first importance, and so it has been with accounting. "Accounting" thus consists of

1. A set of axioms or facts.

2. A classification system to give order to these facts.

3. A system of operating with the facts to verify the integrity of those having access to company monies.

4. A system of operating with the facts to aid decisions by management.

Because the accountant has been responsible for or has participated in the development of (2), (3), and (4), some seem to proclaim this to be prima-facie evidence that the accountant can and should design and develop detection and recording systems for our social endeavors; that because he has provided the right information to management in the business community, this experience and acquired knowledge are necessary and will significantly contribute to the resolution of some of the problems faced by policy makers and managers of our social endeavors.[14]

It is undeniably true that the accountant has had experience in designing detection and recording systems. But one must not lose sight of two points: (1) since the starting point in the development of accounting theory was a set of axioms or postulates, the systems he developed were classification systems which rearranged the facts already contained in the axioms; and (2) whatever system of checks and balances he developed to validate these rearrangements had, as its rationale for existence, the protection of monies against fraudulent use. All would have to agree that the accountant is only one of many professionals with experience in designing classification systems. It is also true that in any classification scheme the reasons behind the scheme are very important. The resultant groupings and the validation procedures must reflect the underlying reasons. For example, in the field of medicine if the main matter at hand is the provision of wheelchairs, it is obviously useful to know whether muscular dystrophy affects the arms or the legs. However, there is no particular reason to believe that such a classification will help to elucidate the causes of the disorder and hence lead to its rational treatment. Similarly, one cannot simply handle or process data in a vacuum. What arithmetic manipulations, summarization, or compilations one does must reflect the underlying reasons for collecting the data in the first place.

The accounting literature often cites the work of the firm Touche, Ross, Bailey and Smart as exemplifying the accountant's capability to design systems in the social area. The firm undertook to structure for the city of Detroit "a modern information and management system" that would provide the information needed for effective management of the city's "war on poverty" programs.[15]

Briefly, a set of characteristics that have contributed to poverty was identified (e.g., health, education, and family income). For each of these characteristics a classification scheme was developed and a score assigned to each of the categories of the characteristic. In this way, an individual who avails himself of the services of any program (designated as a client) is given a score for each characteristic. These scores are the foundation of the information system. The report of this effort outlines the general nature of the characteristics (and their respective categories) that contribute to poverty, and the general nature of the method of assigning a score to a client but gives few details. It suggests that the information system will make available an answer to the question: To what degree is a program succeeding in the fulfillment of client needs? And yet there is nothing in the report to indicate that the system can provide an answer. The underlying premise or working hypothesis upon which the entire system is based is that a client's lot improves as his scores decrease. How was this hypothesis tested? A decrease in this measurement could be due to many factors and is, therefore, in no way necessarily indicative of the success of the program. One such factor is the measuring instrument itself. Just considering all the possible diseases that affect man and their varying stages of severity, it is difficult to believe that a kit of tools, rules, or decision tables could ever be constructed that could eliminate the subjective part of assigning a score that would reflect the financial impairment that a person's health imposes upon him. Procedures were designed so that the responsibility for insuring the accuracy of ratings would be in the hands of one person, but no mention is made of what procedures were incorporated into the system to examine the consistency of this person's rating behavior (was the individual's rating behavior changing with the passage of time?). Neither does the report describe or mention what techniques were used and incorporated into the system to examine the reliability of the rating procedure. If scores are to be treated like measurements (as they were in this system) and are to have any meaning, one attribute which the rating procedure must have is that, when used by two individuals of equal competence, the resulting ratings should agree (or be in close agreement).

To discuss further what appear to be major errors of omission in this effort would serve little purpose. Mr. Beyer admits that the information system developed is not perfect and has flaws. But the flaws are neither unimportant nor necessary. Some are present because the designers of the system failed to understand that the checks and controls of the type used in modern corporate accounting systems are almost meaningless outside of that realm. Many result from a conditioned way of thinking regarding the reasons for observing, recording, and analyzing data. Use of the data from this kind of information system to make decisions regarding social program planning and effectiveness seems ill-advised.

The thesis that the accountant should become more actively involved in designing detection and recording systems for our social endeavors is also open to question because of its seeming disregard for the differences in thought processes which must exist between an individual trained primarily in the deductive method and an individual trained in the inductive method. The first person starts with truths which are not open to question and argues forward. The second individual recognizes that there are no facts to begin with. His goal is to observe, in the most efficient and effective way he knows, in order to discover or uncover what unquestionable truths there may be or to test certain basic premises or theories. To say that the accountant's experience qualifies him to design detection and recording systems for measuring the effectiveness of social programs is to contend either (1) that the design of a system to detect and record events is, on the whole, independent of the reasons for observing and measuring those events; or (2) that the ability to design a system to detect the logical consequences of the available initial facts implies an ability to design a system that can uncover the basic truths that give rise to the observations.

Both propositions are totally without foundation. First, no one, including accountants who propose expansion of the design function in the social arena, believes that the rationale for measuring and observing does not play a major role in deciding what is to be measured or detected. The literature abounds with examples of data almost totally useless in helping us solve the very serious social problems of concern to the nation because the data were collected for particular and special reasons. With regard to the second possible contention, there simply is no evidence to indicate that it is true; in fact, even individuals quite experienced in the use of induction find it difficult to collect the right data.

If we ever hope to solve the problems that face this nation, the first step would be to recognize and accept the fact that social programs are social experiments. In their design, the beginning point is not a set of axioms. There are no facts or unquestionable truths. To design a detection and recording system in the social arena thinking otherwise is sheer folly. At the most there is only a set of possibly defensible assumptions. It is these premises which have a direct bearing upon the decisions as to what observations are to be recorded, how they are to be analyzed, and how the results may be interpreted. Demarcation lines just cannot be drawn between observing, recording, analyzing, and interpreting data. And yet the prevailing philosophy among accountants seems to be: "It is the accountant's job to handle the data, not to decide what data to handle." Who is to decide how the data are to be handled? Unless the accountant is to be merely a technician, it seems to be the opinion of many that the accountant has much to contribute toward the decisions as to how the data ought to be analyzed. What is this knowledge that he supposedly has? Clearly, the expertise unique to the accountant is his vast experience in processing data to uncover or discover errors in recording or observing events of a very specific nature. But in our social endeavors the important input to rational management action is statistical data. These data should be and need to be recorded, collected, and analyzed with the express purpose of leading to the prognosis, diagnosis, and prescription for cure of society's ills. That the accountant does have expertise in using computers efficiently for processing data is beyond question. However, administrators of large-scale social programs desperately need assistance in determining what statistical information should be collected and how this statistical data may be recorded, collected, and analyzed to throw light on to the important questions. The accountant of today simply has no expertise in these areas.

IMPROVING ACCURACY OF ECONOMIC DATA

An enormous amount of effort has been and continues to be directed toward improving the accuracy of data of social import. Accountants have focused their attention on what contributions they may make in improving economic data. In an often-cited paper, Linowes speaks of the credibility of basic economic data and the concern of economists who must use data to make forecasts.

> CPA's are uniquely qualified for the collection, classification, and validation of quantitative information. It would seem clear that they should be more involved in econometric projections.[16]

The question here is not whether the CPA is uniquely qualified in the collection, classification, and validation of statistical information. These points have already been briefly discussed. The important question is whether any supereminent collector, classifier, or validator will be able to solve the problems that the economist perceives as the real problems in his efforts to improve the accuracy of economic data and thus econometric projections.

The inaccuracies in economic data which economists are concerned with are better called "response errors" and "nonsampling errors." Oskar Morganstern, an economist, has written extensively on the subject of the inaccuracies of economic data and clearly explains what these errors are.[17] He speaks of inaccuracies in data due to deliberate lies or deliberate attempts to hide information of various types, of evasive answers at the source of the information, and of statistics that are often gathered and prepared sloppily by the business giving out the information. The most serious kind of mass error, he thinks, occurs because it is a physical impossibility to use "technically trained economists or statisticians" to collect the masses of data that are needed. Thus in field work we must use personnel who are collected "ad hoc," knowing at the same time that responses differ depending upon the type of observer even though the observer may be trained. Other problems are the inaccuracies due to the use of questionnaires, the length of the questionnaire, whether the questions are formulated so that unique answers are possible, whether the person being questioned has enough information to provide the correct answer, etc.

How can the accountant aid in eliminating, minimizing, or even estimating the types of errors mentioned: the "nonsampling and response errors"? Inaccurate data due to nonsampling errors is not a phenomenon of economics alone. The problem exists even within the traditional discipline of accounting— in the business world.[18] Yet there is little indication that accountants are aware that these types of errors are a problem for them also. The philosophy seems to be that accurate figures—figures free from any error—are not only possible for the here and now, but exist for the past as well (or at least someone knows how to make the past figures as accurate as desired). The economist at least has no such illusions.[19]

A major reason for the seeming fallibility of information available in the social arena is the fact that too often data collected for entirely different reasons are used in attempts to assess social well-being. This is a problem which is well recognized. On this problem Mr. Morganstern comments:

> But in general, economic statistics are merely byproducts or results of business and government activities and have to be taken as these determine. Therefore they often measure, describe or simply record something that is not exactly the phenomena in which the economist would be interested. They are often dependent on legal rather than economic definitions of processes.[20]

Yet, the available accounting literature on the proposed expanded role of the accountant indicates a lack of appreciation for the reasons why economists consider certain types of economic data inadequate or weak. For example:

> The lack of participation by CPA's [in the hierarchy responsible for the development of economic data] has resulted in some unnecessary weaknesses in national income accounting. One of them

is the use by the compiler of the data of terms not commonly used by accountants and businessmen.[21]

Economists follow two approaches in trying to make predictions and in establishing the science of economics. One approach is that of looking to see what has actually happened when circumstances have changed (inductive method), and then arguing backwards to some basic ideas about the working of the economic system. The other approach starts by making assumptions about the ways in which individuals or organizations (such as business firms) react to change. This method builds on simple and plausible assumptions, and by logical analysis works out the full implications of these assumptions (deductive method). The approach provides hypotheses about relationships which the economist is necessarily interested in putting to a test. In order to do this he must obtain appropriate information.

The problem compounds itself in economics because, as a rule, much of the data needed must cover long periods of time in order to be useful. Businesses may change their accounting policies, categorizations may become more extensive—in years past, one type of event may have been grouped in a category with several others and later, as a result of internal management needs, the event is reclassified. Inaccuracies in economic data resulting from these types of practices are all in the class of errors due to the lack of designed experiments in economics.

There are errors in our socioeconomic statistics. We simply have to learn how to live with errors. This means trying to understand their nature, origin, extent, and persistence. It is true that economists and the makers and users of all socioeconomic data must recognize the existence of errors and begin to deal with them. But dealing with them necessarily means avoiding those that can be avoided, using what knowledge we have now for estimating the effects of those that cannot be avoided, and continuing to develop new theories for estimating unavoidable errors in our data. It is very unlikely that the accountant can make any significant contributions to efforts in these areas.

IMPROVING MANAGERIAL RATIONAL

Without a doubt there has been a great deal of stumbling about in our efforts to find solutions to societal problems. For the most part these efforts have been unsuccessful. The programs which have been initiated in the past decade have not flourished; there have been few discernible improvements in the conditions which they were designed to affect. However, since the planners of these programs lacked basic knowledge about the interrelations of contingencies in the socioeconomic life-cycle, it should not have been unexpected that there were few discernible changes in the status of society and its members which could be attributed to these new social endeavors.

Although society may have thought that it delegated the responsibility for the amelioration of societal problems to certain people (i.e., the social scientists), the fact is that they have not traditionally perceived their function in this light.[22] For the most part they had been content to describe social phenomena and, where possible, to explain the underlying causes. The explanations have been primarily speculative and subjective, with the possible exception of the field of economics. More importantly, although there were many social scientists who were responsible for or contributed to the development of programs of social import, most of those programs were not perceived of as experiments. Consequently, the data that could have been recorded and analyzed and may have filled in some of the gaps in our knowledge failed to be even collected.

Consider, for example, the high school dropout problem. Some of the premises of a widely accepted theory—the "learner shortcomings" theory—as to why people drop out of school are:

1. Imperfect knowledge or foresight regarding future employment and income opportunities.

2. A lack of appreciation of the new quality of life further education will bring.

3. A financial situation which dictates no more than the required schooling.

4. Lack of ability to complete schooling.

The general theory in this case consists of many subtheories of which only four are listed. If one operates under the basic premise of "learner shortcomings" any program to reduce student dropout rate must direct itself to eliminating the effect of one or several of the causes. However, at the time Weisbrod[23] did his study on the prevention of high school dropouts (1961), of all the programs which had been initiated and which had as their basis of design "learner short-comings," none had been designed or evaluated in a way which would have enabled him to determine whether the program *itself* was responsible for any observed decrease in student dropout rate. Further, Weisbrod was unable to find any credible evidence as to the relative importance of any of the sub-theories. For example, it would have been extremely useful to have had an answer to the question: Is imperfect knowledge regarding future employment more important than lack of ability in a student's decision to drop out of school? Further, how much more important is it?

Upon careful examination of most of the areas of social concern one finds not only unsubstantiated theories, but conflicting theories as to the cause and, therefore, cures for society's ills. Thus, lacking certain basic knowledge about the functioning of society, finding even short-range partial solutions is not so simple.

Some have suggested that the proper use of cost-effectiveness and cost-benefit analysis procedures will be the major factor in reducing the number of social programs which fail in the sense that the program produces little change in the condition it was designed to ameliorate. But failures have usually not been the result of an absence of the use of these procedures in social program planning or to a lack of expertise in their use. Our failures are the direct result of the fact that most programs to alleviate social problems were planned and implemented lacking good knowledge as to the reasons for the existence of the problem. Having few theories which were both testable and tested, it follows that there was also lack of knowledge as to what effect a program might have if it were implemented.

If it is true that effective management decisions in our social endeavors can be achieved only if management has the facts or the right information to begin with, then the first order of business is to improve our estimates of effects of proposed programs. The major question remains: can the accountant contribute to improving these kinds of estimates? In the present scheme of things it is actually unimportant whether accountants can help the managers of our social endeavors in the use of the weaponry of modern management. The most sophisticated data processing procedures of modern management, or the most complex decision making models will not result in improved management rational if there are no facts to begin with, which is indeed the case in most of our social endeavors. Thus, every social program we now embark upon must be viewed as an unique opportunity to fill in gaps in our knowledge to discover what, if any, unquestionable truths are applicable.

Modern information systems used in business and industry are designed to provide whatever facts there may be about the effectiveness of the operation and administration of a program. However, the information needs of society and, therefore, the managers of our social endeavors are of a different nature. Of primary importance to them is information which will at least allow some answers to the crucial questions: Have the conditions which the program was designed to effect been ameliorated? Can any changes which have occurred be attributed to the program? Are the hypotheses of social functioning which have been assumed true actually valid? Experience indicates that rarely has the right information been collected for the wrong reasons. Therefore, it seems that accountants by expanding into the social arena, by designing systems which purportedly supply management with the information required to answer these kinds of questions about program effectiveness, may actually be doing a disservice.

SUMMARY

The papers in the accounting literature on the subject of the accountant's role in social accounting or social reporting contain statements and recommendations of far-reaching importance to professional accountants, to other professional specialists, and to society in general. Some of these recommendations have been examined in this paper and in this writer's opinion are unjustified.

A major reason for this difference in viewpoint is the different interpretation of the nature of the instrument of "social accounting," or "social reporting." In this paper the assumption is that the functions of "social accounting" are to[24]

1.   assess the state of society,

2.   assess the performance of a social program,

3.   anticipate the future,

4.   indicate control mechanisms, and

5.   guide social knowledge.

Accurate, reliable, and relevant information is important if social accounting is to serve as the basis for effective social planning. Accounting knowledge may enable one to be helpful in improving the accuracy (as narrowly defined) of data; however, it is of little use in improving the relevance and reliability of the data necessary for social planning.

Furthermore, since (a) practically all data needed for decision making in the social arena are statistics and result from statistical sampling, and (b) the interpretation of statistical data, the analysis of that data, and the method of its collection cannot be separated from one another, a knowledge of statistics is essential for "social reporting." Statistics is the science and art of dealing with variation in such a way as to obtain reliable results. To apprehend the rationale of a piece of statistical arithmetic is not synonymous with understanding statistics. Accountants lack that understanding.

NOTES

1.   Robert Beyer, "The Modern Management Approach to a Program of Social Improvement," *The Journal of Accountancy* (March, 1969), p. 37; Report of the Committee on Non-Financial Measures of Effectiveness, *The Accounting Review* (January, 1971), p. 165; David F. Linowes, "Socio-Economic Accounting," *The Journal of Accountancy* (November 1968), p. 38; and "Social Responsibility of the Profession," *The Journal of Accountancy* (January, 1971), p. 66.

2.   The Random House Dictionary of the English Language, unabridged edition, 1966.

3.   *Idem.*

4.   Herbert Arkin, *Handbook of Sampling for Auditing and Accounting,* Vol. I (McGraw-Hill, 1963).

5.   Report of the Committee on Non-Financial Measures of Effectiveness, op. cit., pp. 47-49.

6.   Most of the rates, indices and statistics which measure aspects of the conditions of society are estimates based on samples from the population.

7.   William G. Cochran, *Sampling Techniques* (Wiley, 1963).

8.   See, for example, footnote (4) and Edwin B. Cox, "The Teaching of Statistics in Business Schools—a Summary," *American Statistician* (February, 1965), p. 2; John Neter, *Some Applications of Statistics for Auditing*, in *Elementary Statistics for Economics and Business*, Edwin Mansfield (editor) (Norton, 1970), p. 130.

9.   See footnote (4).

10.   Aryness Wickens, "Statistics and Public Interest," *Journal of American Statistical Association* (1953), p. 1.

11.   Literally in every volume of the *Journal of the American Statistical Association* and the *American Statistician,* one finds several articles discussing errors or possible errors in published government statistical series. Also, well-known statistical reports, (e.g. government report on smoking and health) have been critically analyzed by statisticians and appear in these journals. Many government agencies themselves do a great deal of work in this area. See Family Income Distribution Statistics published by Federal Agencies. *American Statistician,* Vol. 20 (February, 1966), p. 18, and the bibliography attached to the paper "Comments," by R. T. Bowman, *American Statistician* (June, 1964), p. 10.

12.   See, for example, Vol. 371 (May, 1967); Vol. 373 (September, 1967); and Vol. 388 (March, 1970) of *Annals of the American Academy of Political and Social Science.*

13.   James Edwards, *History of Public Accounting in the United States* (Michigan State University Press, 1960).

14.   See Linowes (1968) and Beyer (1969).

15.   Beyer (1969), op. cit., p. 37.

16.   Linowes (1968), op. cit., p. 38.

17.   Oskar Morganstern, "Fide Sed Anti Vidi—Remarks to Mr. R. T. Bowmen's 'Comments,' " *American Statistician* (October, 1964), p. 15; also "Sources and Errors of Economic Statistics" in *Elementary Statistics for Economics and Business.* Edwin Mansfield (editor) (Norton, 1970), p. 13.

18.   Wilensky, Harold L., "Intelligence in Industry: The Uses and Abuses of Experts," *Ann. Amer. Acad. Pol. Sci.* (March, 1970), p. 47.

19.   See Morganstern (1964) op. cit., p. 15 and Moore, Geoffrey H., "Some Needed Improvements in Economic Statistics," *American Statistician* (December, 1967), p. 27.

20.   Morganstern (1970) op. cit., p. 40.

21.   Linowes (1968) op. cit., p. 38. The phrase in brackets was added by the writer for clarity.

22.   William B. Dickenson, Jr. (editor). *Editorial Research Reports on Challenges of the 1970's* (Congressional Quarterly, December, 1969). Muzafer Sherif and Carolyn W. Sherif (editors) *Interdisciplinary Relationships in the Social Sciences* (Aldine Publishing Co., 1969). William P. McEwein, *The Problem of Social Scientific Knowledge* (The Bedminster Press, 1963).

23.   Burton A. Weisbrod, "Preventing High School Dropouts" in *Measuring the Benefits of Government Investment,* Robert Dorfman (editor) (The Brookings Institution, 1965), p. 117.

24.   Michael Springer, "Social Indicators, Reports and Accounts: Toward the Management of Society," *Ann. American Acad. Pol. Soc. Sci.* (1970), p. 1

The Vitality of Mythical Numbers

Max Singer

This "little" article might initially be interpreted as a tirade against social accounting. To the contrary, Singer's principal point constitutes a strong argument for the entry of accountants into the area of social calculation. He suggests the ease with which "astounding" figures are concocted, published, and ultimately achieve the status of dogma. The answer is not to eliminate the outlandish numbers, but to evaluate them in the light of cold logic and scepticism. It is difficult to conclude other than that a skilled auditor, applying the identical overall tests used on any audit, would answer Singer's problem.

It is generally assumed that heroin addicts in New York City steal some two to five billion dollars worth of property a year, and commit approximately half of all the property crimes. Such estimates of addict crime are used by an organization like RAND, by a political figure like Howard Samuels, and even by the Attorney General of the United States.[1] The estimate that half the property crimes are committed by addicts was originally attributed to a police official and has been used so often that it is now part of the common wisdom.

The amount of property stolen by addicts is usually estimated in something like the following manner:

There are 100,000 addicts with an average habit of $30.00 per day. This means addicts must have some $1.1 billion a year to pay for their heroin (100,000 x 365 x $30.00). Because the addict must sell the property he steals to a fence for only about a quarter of its value, or less, addicts must steal some $4 to $5 billion a year to pay for their heroin.

These calculations can be made with more or less sophistication. One can allow for the fact that the kind of addicts who make their living illegally typically spend upwards of a quarter of their time in jail, which would reduce the amount of crime by a quarter. (*The New York Times* recently reported on the death of William "Donkey" Reilly. A seventy-four year old ex-addict who had been addicted for fifty-four years, he had spent thirty of those years in prison.) Some of what the addict steals is cash, none of which has to go to a fence. A large part of the cost of heroin is paid for by dealing in the heroin business, rather than stealing from society, and another large part by prostitution,

Max Singer is President of Hudson Institute.

SOURCE: From *The Public Interest*, No. 23, Spring, 1971, pp. 3-9, Copyright © by National Affairs Inc., 1971.

including male addicts living off prostitutes. But no matter how carefully you slice it, if one tries to estimate the value of property stolen by addicts by assuming that there are 100,000 addicts and estimating what is the minimum amount they would have to steal to support themselves and their habits (after making generous estimates for legal income), one comes up with a number in the neighborhood of $1 billion a year for New York City.

But what happens if you approach the question from the other side? Suppose we ask, "How much property is stolen—by addicts or anyone else?" Addict theft must be less than total theft. What is the value of property stolen in New York City in any year? Somewhat surprisingly to me when I first asked, this turned out to be a difficult question to answer, even approximately. No one had any estimates that they had even the faintest confidence in, and the question doesn't seem to have been much asked. The amount of officially reported theft in New York City is approximately $300 million a year, of which about $100 million is the value of automobile theft (a crime that is rarely committed by addicts). But it is clear that there is a very large volume of crime that is not reported; for example, shoplifting is not normally reported to the police. (Much property loss to thieves is not reported to insurance companies either, and the insurance industry had no good estimate for total theft.)

It turns out, however, that if one is only asking a question like, "Is it possible that addicts stole $1 billion worth of property in New York City last year?" it is relatively simple to estimate the amount of property stolen. It is clear that the two biggest components of addict theft are shoplifting and burglary. What *could* the value of property shoplifted by addicts be? All retail sales in New York City are on the order of $15 billion a year. This includes automobiles, carpets, diamond rings, and other items not usually available to shoplifters. A reasonable number for inventory loss to retail establishments is two per cent. This number includes management embezzlements, stealing by clerks, shipping departments, truckers, etc. (Department stores, particularly, have reported a large increase in shoplifting in recent years, but they are among the most vulnerable of retail establishments and not important enough to bring the overall rate much above two per cent.) It is generally agreed that substantially more than half of the property missing from retail establishments is taken by employees, the remainder being lost to outside shoplifters. But let us credit shoplifters with stealing one per cent of all the property sold at retail in New York City—this would be about $150 million a year.

What about burglary? There are something like two and one-half million households in New York City. Suppose that on the average one out of five of them is robbed or burglarized every year. This takes into account that in some areas burglary is even more commonplace, and that some households are burglarized more than once a year. This would mean 500,000 burglaries a year.

The average value of property taken in a burglary might be on the order of $200. In some burglaries, of course, much larger amounts of property are taken, but these higher value burglaries are much rarer, and often are committed by non-addict professional thieves. If we use the number of $200 x 500,000 burglaries, we get $100 million of property stolen from people's homes in a year in New York City.

Obviously, none of these estimated values is either sacred or substantiated. You can make your own estimate. The estimates here have the character that it would be very surprising if they were wrong by a factor of ten, and not very important for the conclusion if they were wrong by a factor of two. (This is a good position for an estimator to be in.)

Obviously not all addict theft is property taken from stores or from people's home. One of the most feared types of addict crime is property taken from the persons of New Yorkers in muggings, and other forms of robbery. We can estimate this, too. Suppose that on the average, one person in ten has property taken from his person by muggers or robbers each year. That would be 800,000 such robberies, and if the average one produced $100 (which it is very unlikely to do), $8 million a year would be taken in this form of theft.

So we can see that if we credit addicts with *all* of the shoplifting, *all* of the theft from homes, and *all* of the theft from persons, total property stolen by addicts in a year in New York City amounts to some $330 million. You can throw in all the "fudge factors" you want, add all the other miscellaneous crimes that addicts commit, but no matter what you do, it is difficult to find a basis for estimating that addicts steal over a half billion dollars a year, and a quarter billion looks like a better estimate, although perhaps on the high side. After all, there must be some thieves who are not addicts.

Thus, I believe we have shown that whereas it is widely assumed that addicts steal from $2-$5 billion a year in New York City, the actual number is *ten* times smaller, and that this can be demonstrated by five minutes of thought.[2] So what? A quarter billion dollars' worth of property is still a lot of property. It exceeds the amount of money spent annually on addict rehabilitation and other programs to prevent and control addiction. Furthermore, the value of the property stolen by addicts is a small part of the total cost to society of addict theft. A much larger cost is paid in fear, changed neighborhood atmosphere, the cost of precautions, and other echoing and re-echoing reactions to theft and its danger.

One point in this exercise in estimating the value of property stolen by addicts is to shed some light on people's attitudes toward numbers. People feel that there is a lot of addict crime, and that $2 billion is a large number, so they are inclined to believe that there is $2 billion worth of addict theft. But $250 million is a large number, too, and if our sense of perspective were not distorted by daily consciousness of federal expenditures, most people would be quite content to accept $250 million a year as a lot of theft.

Along the same lines, this exercise is another reminder that even responsible officials, responsible newspapers, and responsible research groups pick up and pass on as gospel numbers that have no real basis in fact. We are reminded by this experience that because an estimate has been used widely by a variety of people who should know what they are talking about, one cannot assume that the estimate is even approximately correct.

But there is a much more important implication of the fact that there cannot be nearly so much addict theft as people believe. This implication is that there probably cannot be as many addicts as many people believe. Most of the money paid for heroin bought at retail comes from stealing, and most addicts buy at retail. Therefore, the number of addicts is basically—although imprecisely—limited by the amount of theft. (The estimate developed in a Hudson Institute study was that close to half of the volume of heroin consumed is used by people in the heroin distribution system who do not buy at retail, and do not pay with stolen property but with their "services" in the distribution system.[3]) But while the people in the business (at lower levels) consume close to half the heroin, they are only some one-sixth or one-seventh of the total number of addicts. They are the ones who can afford big habits.

The most popular, informal estimate of addicts in New York City is 100,000-plus (usually with an emphasis on the "plus"). The federal register in Washington lists some 30,000 addicts in New York City, and the New York City Department of Health's register of addicts' names lists some 70,000. While all the people on those lists are not still active addicts—many of them are dead or in prison—most people believe that there are many addicts who are not on any list. It is common to regard the estimate of 100,000 addicts in New York City as a very conservative one. Dr. Judianne Densen-Gerber was widely quoted early in 1970 for her estimate that there would be over 100,000 teenage addicts by the end of the summer. And there are obviously many addicts of twenty years of age and more.[4]

In discussing the number of addicts in this article, we will be talking about the kind of person one thinks of when the term "addict" is used.[5] A better term might be "street addict." This is a person who normally uses heroin every day. He is the kind of person who looks and acts like the normal picture of an addict. We exclude here the people in the medical profession who are frequent users of heroin or other opiates, or are addicted to them, students who use heroin occasionally, wealthy people who are addicted but do not need to steal and do not frequent the normal addict hangouts, etc. When we are addressing the "addict problem," it is much less important that we include these cases; while they are undoubtedly problems in varying degrees, they are a very different type of problem than that posed by the typical street addict.

The amount of property stolen by addicts suggests that the number of New York City street addicts may be more like 70,000 than 100,000, and almost certainly cannot be anything like the 200,000 number that is sometimes used. Several other simple ways of estimating the number of street addicts lead to a similar conclusion.

Experience with the addict population has led observers to estimate that the average street addict spends a quarter to a third of his time in prison. (Some students of the subject, such as Edward Preble and John J. Casey, Jr., believe the average to be over forty per cent.) This would imply that at any one time, one-quarter to one-third of the addict population is in prison, and that the total addict population can be estimated by multiplying the number of addicts who are in prison by three or four. Of course the number of addicts who are in prison is not a known quantity (and, in fact, as we have indicated above, not even a very precise concept). However, one can make reasonable estimates of the number of addicts in prison (and for this purpose we can include the addicts in various involuntary treatment centers). This number is approximately 14,000-17,000 which is quite compatible with an estimate of 70,000 total New York City street addicts.

Another way of estimating the total number of street addicts in New York City is to use the demographic information that is available about the addict population. For example, we can be reasonably certain that some twenty-five per cent of the street addict population in New York City is Puerto Rican, and some fifty per cent are Negroes. We know that approximately five out of six street addicts are male, and that fifty per cent of the street addicts are between the ages of sixteen and twenty-five. This would mean that twenty per cent of the total number of addicts are male Negroes between the age of sixteen and twenty-five. If there were 70,000 addicts, this would mean that 14,000 Negro boys between the ages of sixteen and twenty-five are addicts. But altogether there are only about 140,000 Negro boys between the ages of sixteen and twenty-five in the city—perhaps half of them living in poverty areas. This means that if there are 70,000 addicts in the city, one in ten Negro youths are addicts, and if there are 100,000 addicts, nearly one in six are, and if there are 200,000 addicts, one in three. You can decide for yourself which of these degrees of penetration of the young Negro male group is most believable, but it is rather clear that the number of 200,000 addicts is implausible. Similarly, the total of 70,000 street addicts would imply 7,000 young Puerto Rican males are addicted, and the total number of Puerto Rican boys between the ages of sixteen and twenty-five in New York City is about 70,000.

None of the above calculations are meant in any way to downplay the importance of the problem of heroin addiction. Heroin is a terrible curse.

When you think of the individual tragedy involved, 70,000 is an awfully large number of addicts. And if you have to work for a living, $250 million is an awful lot of money to have stolen from the citizens of the city to be transferred through the hands of addicts and fences into the pockets of those who import and distribute heroin, and those who take bribes or perform other services for the heroin industry.

The main point of this article may well be to illustrate how far one can go in bounding a problem by taking numbers seriously, seeing what they imply, checking various implications against each other and against general knowledge (such as the number of persons or households in the city). Small efforts in this direction can go a long way to help ordinary people and responsible officials to cope with experts of various kinds.

NOTES

1.   New York RAND Issue Paper on Drug Addiction Control in New York, 1968; Howard Samuels, Position Paper on Narcotics, 1970; Speech by Attorney General Mitchell, October 6, 1969.

2.   Mythical numbers may be more mythical and have more vitality in the area of crime than in most areas. In the early 1950s the Kefauver Committee published a $20 billion estimate for the annual "take" of gambling in the United States. The figure actually was "picked from a hat." One staff member said: "We had no real idea of the money spent. The California Crime Commission said $12 billion. Virgil Petersen of Chicago said $30 billion. We picked $20 billion as the balance of the two."

An unusual example of a mythical number that had a vigorous life—the assertion that twenty eight Black Panthers had been murdered by police—is given a careful biography by Edward Jay Epstein in the February 13, 1971, *New Yorker.* (It turned out that there were nineteen Panthers killed, ten of them by the police, and eight of these in situations where it seems likely that the Panthers took the initiative.)

3.   A parallel datum was developed in a later study by St. Luke's Hospital of 81 addicts— average age 34. More than one-half of the heroin consumed by these addicts, over a year, had been paid for by the sale of heroin. Incidentally, these 81 addicts had stolen an average of $9,000 worth of property in the previous year.

4.   Among other recent estimators we may note a Marxist, Sol Yurick, who gives us "500,000 junkies" (*Monthly Review,* December, 1970), and William R. Corson, who contends, in the December, 1970 *Penthouse,* that "today at least 2,500,000 black Americans are hooked on heroin."

5.   There is an interesting anomaly about the word "addict." Most people, if pressed for a definition of an "addict," would say he is a person who regularly takes heroin (or some such drug) and who, if he fails to get his regular dose of heroin, will have unpleasant or painful withdrawal symptoms. But this definition would not apply to a large part of what is generally recognized as the "addict population." In fact, it would not apply to most certified addicts. An addict who has been detoxified or who has been imprisoned and kept away from drugs for a week or so would not fit the normal definition of "addict." He no longer has any physical symptoms resulting from not taking heroin. "Donkey" Reilly would certainly fulfill most people's ideas of an addict, but for thirty of the fifty four years he was an "addict" he was in prison, and he was certainly not actively addicted to heroin during most of the time he spent in prison, which was more than half of his "addict" career (although a certain amount of drugs are available in prison).

Index

Italicized numbers refer to major readings on the subject.

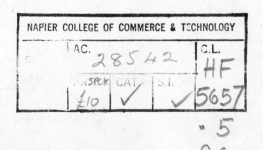